Lorenz

see #119 (page 76)
page 420

SONGS OF PRAISE DISCUSSED

Songs of Praise Discussed

A HANDBOOK TO THE
BEST-KNOWN HYMNS AND TO
OTHERS RECENTLY INTRODUCED

COMPILED BY

PERCY DEARMER

WITH
NOTES ON THE MUSIC BY
ARCHIBALD JACOB

GEOFFREY CUMBERLEGE
OXFORD UNIVERSITY PRESS
LONDON NEW YORK TORONTO

Oxford University Press, Amen House, London, E.C.4

GLASGOW NEW YORK TORONTO MELBOURNE WELLINGTON
BOMBAY CALCUTTA MADRAS CAPE TOWN

Geoffrey Cumberlege, Publisher to the University

First published 1933
Second impression 1952

PRINTED IN GREAT BRITAIN

CONTENTS

CONTENTS

CONTENTS

BOOK II

ACKNOWLEDGEMENT

We wish to express our gratitude to the Editors of THE HANDBOOK TO THE CHURCH HYMNARY *for their very great kindness in allowing us to make use of their notes on tunes and to draw freely from their biographical notes, and thus to avail ourselves of the researches of the scholars who contributed to the Handbook.*

P.D.
A.J.

INTRODUCTION

Modern Hymnody

THE beginnings of our English hymnody are associated with those of our Bible; for Dr. Miles Coverdale, whose complete translation of the Scriptures was brought to England in 1535, published about two years later his undated *Goostly Psalmes and Spiritualle Songes*, a unique copy of which exists at Queen's College, Oxford. This book, which, according to Foxe's *Book of Martyrs*, was prohibited in 1539, but was restored in 1546, contains several hymns—in the restricted use of the word—as well as 15 metrical psalms and some paraphrases of the Canticles, Creed, and other prose originals, 41 pieces in all. There were thus from the beginning of the modern period some real hymns in English. Of these none survive in our hymnals; but one, 'Now blessed be thou, Christ Jesu', will be found as no. 131 in the *Oxford Book of Carols*, 1928. About the same time some hymns were translated for the new English Primers, which were books for private use, and began to appear in 1534, as will be found in fuller mention under 33 below.

Cranmer's Policy

There is a well-known letter from Cranmer to Henry VIII in 1544 (soon after the publication of the English Litany) with which he enclosed a draft translation of *Salve festa dies*, to be sung to the plainsong melody. He says:

'I have travailed to make the verses in English . . . I made them only for a proof to see how English would do in song. But by cause my English verses want the grace and facility that I would wish they had, your majesty may cause some other to make them again, that can do the same in more pleasant English and phrase.'

This has been taken as a proof of Cranmer's inability to write verse; but, apart from the improbability that so supreme a master of language, and so learned a scholar, would be unable to translate Latin elegiacs into English, there are strong reasons for thinking that the Archbishop was merely excusing himself, in the hope of getting the whole question of the Latin hymns deferred until he had made up his mind about the advisability of using them at all: (1) English versions of some of the Latin hymns had already been competently done for the *King's Primer*, then in hand (the work was begun in 1539, and the *King's Primer* itself was issued in 1545). (2) Not only did more translations fail to appear, but those already in existence disappeared from the *Primer* of 1553.

Why then did Cranmer omit all metrical hymns from the Prayer Book when it appeared in the second year of Edward VI? Not, surely, because no one could write English verse: the beginnings of Coverdale and the Wedderburns had been successfully followed by the translations in the *King's Primer*. But because Cranmer was hesitating between the Lutheran and the Calvinist view—and in those days of rapid transition hesitation was often the wisest course. Moreover, he followed Cardinal Quiñonez in his plan for a reformed Breviary (his preface, 'Concerning the Service', in the Prayer Book is mainly a translation of Quiñonez); and the Cardinal favoured a great reduction of hymns: Cranmer, in his second draft for a Prayer Book, had reduced their proposed number to 26. Now Luther was strongly in favour of hymns: he loved those in the Breviary, *which were human compositions*; he loved German folk-song, and was himself a composer as well as a writer of hymns; also he was far-seeing enough to realize the enormous importance of hymn-singing if the Reformation was to win the people. But Calvin was made of stiffer and sterner stuff, besides being set against music by the frivolity of the current French songs. He disliked the ritual of the Church as a mere human contrivance; true, its Psalter was of divine origin; but *the hymns were not taken from the Word of God*. Thus, in the Calvinist churches only metrical versions of the Psalms were used.

Here then was the significance of Cranmer's letter. Eventually he came down on the side of Calvin, and on his side also was the bulk of popular feeling in the reign of Elizabeth. Thus, although there were hymns in the *Primer* of that year, there were no hymns in the actual Prayer Book of 1559; though the 49th Injunction of the same year left the matter open by allowing 'an hymn, or such like song', as we shall see.

The Calvinistic feeling increased as time went on. Hardly anything was sung that did not take the form of metrical translations of the Psalms; for the Psalms were regarded as virtually dictated by God. It was not till Isaac Watts attacked the stronghold, that the tyranny of the metrical psalm began to give way. And the reader may observe (e.g. in the notes to 332, 333, 336) how many books, even in the first half of the 19th century, were still called '*Psalms and Hymns*'.

The Old Version

Sternhold's first collection of metrical *Psalms* was published, undated, *c.* 1548, with a dedication to King Edward VI; his 2nd edition is dated 1549. The Metrical Psalter is thus slightly earlier than the First Prayer Book (1549). The 3rd edition (1551) included seven psalms by John Hopkins, and thus 'Sternhold and Hopkins' was begun. A few indifferent hymns were included in this (the *Old Version*) during the 17th century; but the monopoly of the Stationers' Company, and the fact that it was the official book, kept the poets out of it. The *Supplement* to the *New Version* (see under 82) kept a few hymns in use during the 18th century. From 'Sternhold and Hopkins' there survives the 'Old Hundredth' (443), and, from the hymns there included, 'The Lamentation' by Marckant (116), in an altered form. A few others remain from the *New Version* ('Tate and Brady'), as is mentioned on p. xviii.

The *Scottish Psalter* was begun by the General Assembly in 1562, and the first complete *Scottish Psalter* came out in 1564; the edition of 1575 contained five hymns proper—'Spiritual Songs': all hymns were dropped in Rous's version of 1650. The measures to replace them did not take effect; and it was not till 1781 that five hymns were again added to the Scottish *Paraphrases*.

Authorization of Hymnody

The idea has not yet disappeared that hymns are an unlawful, or, at best, an unauthorized, addition to the services of the Church of England; but the idea is without foundation. At the beginning of the Elizabethan settlement it was laid down in the *Injunctions* of 1559:

'In the beginning, or in the end of the common prayers, either at morning or evening, there may be sung an hymn, or such like song to the praise of Almighty God, in the best sort of melody and music that may be conveniently devised, having respect that the sentence of hymn may be understanded and perceived.'

This was begun immediately, and with much popular enthusiasm; Bishop Jewel speaks of 5,000 people singing at Paul's Cross; and Strype relates how at St. Antholin's in the City before 'the new Morning Prayer':

'A Psalm was sung after the Geneva Fashion, all the congregation, ... men, women, and boys, singing together . . . which custom was about this time brought also into St. Paul's.' *Strype's Grindal*, p. 27.

Archbishop Parker not only upheld hymn singing, but was himself a hymnist. An appeal was brought before him from Exeter Cathedral, where some people had disturbed the congregation by singing; the Dean and Chapter prohibited them, but Bishop Jewel, as Visitor, with others, reprimanded the Dean and Chapter; and the Archbishop upheld the Visitors. After Elizabeth's accession a new edition of 'Sternhold and Hopkins' was published, in 1561, by one of the earliest of music-printers, '*John Daye*, dwelling over Aldersgate'; and the author of this scholarly book was none other than the great Archbishop Parker himself. No wonder that the publisher could announce from 'over Aldersgate' that this collection was 'Newly set forth and allowed'. Such authorization continued time after time in the 17th century; and there were some hymns, as we have said, as well as metrical psalms like the Old Hundredth, in this *Old Version* as well as later in the *Supplement* to the *New Version*. With this may be compared the singing of Donne's hymn (123) at St. Paul's in the time of James II.

Moreover, in addition to the singing of a hymn both before and after Mattins and Evensong, a custom grew up of singing one after the Third Collect; and this was duly regularized in the well-known rubric of 1662, in the present English Prayer Book: 'In Quires and Places where they sing, here followeth the Anthem.'

'By this rubric', wrote an eminent Lord Chancellor, Selborne (*Hymns: Their History and Development*, 1892, p. 151), 'synodical and parliamentary authority was given for the interruption, at that point, of the prescribed order in the service by singing an anthem; the choice of which was left to the discretion of the minister. Those actually used, under this authority, were, from the first, hymns in verse, as well as unmetrical passages of Scripture.... There are such hymns in the earliest anthem-book of Charles the Second's Chapel Royal. . . . The word "anthem" had no technical signification which could be an obstacle to the use under this rubric of metrical hymns.'

Exclusion of the Great Poets

Yet it is curious that a nation so supreme in poetry should have waited so long for an adequate amount of poetry in public worship. The causes were almost fortuitous. At first Calvin's view, that only the divinely inspired Psalms should be sung, prevailed over the more intelligent and humane ideas of Luther, as we have explained. Thus the work of providing metrical versions of the Psalms was all-important; and this was given by the authorities, not, as it happened, to poets like Sir Philip Sidney and his sister, Lady Pembroke (605), but to men who were not poets, like Sternhold, a Groom of the Robes under Henry VIII and Edward VI, Hopkins, of whom Anthony à Wood could only say in the next century (*Athenae Oxonienses*, 1691) that he was 'poetarum sui temporis non infimum', Whittingham, a refugee divine in Geneva who married Calvin's sister, or Thomas Norton, a barrister who did indeed write sonnets, but owes his modest niche in literature to his translation of Calvin's *Institutions* and his collaboration in the earliest English blank-verse tragedy *Gorboduc*, with Thomas Sackville, Lord Dorset. Even Richard Cox, another contributor to the *Old Version*, who was Dean of Westminster in 1549, and one of the compilers of the English Prayer Book of that year, won no other distinction.

Sternhold's ambition was to make the Psalms the ballads of the court and people; and this consideration determined the metres and treatment. If they are judged by contemporary ballads, or even by the hymns in Henry VIII's *Primers*, or the religious poetry of the age, they will be found, in Fuller's words, 'to go abreast' with them. Indeed, the work of Sternhold, Hopkins, Whittingham, Pullain, Wisedome, and the other psalmodizers was far ahead of much of the other paraphrasing; Christopher Tye did the Acts of the Apostles into metre—'*The Actes of the Apostles, translated into Englyshe Metre and dedicated to the Kynges most excellent Majestye by Christofer Tye Doctor in Musike and one of the Gentylmen of hys Graces most honourable Chappell wyth notes to eche Chapter to synge and also to play upon the Lute.*' The music was excellent—we have some of it in 82; but of the verse this may serve as a specimen:

> A certayne man who was named
> Ananias trulye,
> With Saphira hys wife framed
> Unto the Lord a lye.

Such were the origins of the famous *Old Version*, which, as time went on, came to accumulate the abuse of the literary world. Yet it was regarded even by the cultivated with something like affection. Thomas Warton himself, in the 17th century, tempers his scorn by confessing that 'had they been more poetically translated, they would not have been acceptable to the common people'; and probably style was a minor consideration compared with faithfulness to what was regarded as the almost divinely dictated original.

The abuse lavished on Sternhold and Hopkins steadily increased in the prefaces to new translations of the Psalms. 'Their piety was better than their poetry'; 'they had drunk more of Jordan than of Helicon'; 'sometimes they make the Maker of the tongue speak little better than barbarism, and have in many verses such poor rhyme that two hammers on a smith's anvil would make better music', says Fuller. Rochester's epigram, on passing with Charles II while a parish clerk was singing, is well known:

> Sternhold and Hopkins had great qualms,
> When they translated David's psalms,
> To make the heart right glad:
> But had it been King David's fate
> To hear thee sing and them translate,
> By God 'twould set him mad.

Which is a precursor of Voltaire's epigram on Lefranc:

Savez-vous pourquoi Jérémie
A tant pleuré pendant sa vie?
C'est qu'en prophète il prévoyait
Qu'un jour Lefranc le traduirait.

Yet for us there is a certain attraction in the quaint old verses, which have a kind of hammering vitality and are quite free from the sloppiness of more recent times:

He hath to thee showed wonders great,
O Egypt void of vaunts:
On Pharaoh thy cursed king,
And his severe servants.

Or, with Pharaoh still as the theme, though he is differently spelt:

But there he whelmed then
The proud king Pharao,
With his huge hoast of men,
And Charets eke also.

There was no misunderstanding this sort of thing, though Wesley did call it 'scandalous doggrell'. And many simple folk thought it was the original: one parson, who asked a villager why he no longer joined in the singing, was answered, 'Well, Sir, David speaks so plain that us cannot mistake 'un; but as for Mr. Tate and Mr. Brady, they have taken the Lord away.' We can see why the *New Version* failed to replace the *Old* in the countryside. Indeed, some folk believed in a higher authorship than David's. Tate himself relates that at family prayers in the home of Dr. Patrick's brother, one of the maids explained her silence by saying, 'If you must know the plain truth, Sir: as long as you sung Jesus Christ's psalms, I sung along with ye; but now that you sing psalms of your own invention, ye may sing by yourselves.'

This *New Version* of Tate and Brady was indeed rather modernist in tone; and it follows the taste of 1696 in forsaking the faithful simplicity of the *Old Version* for an ornate style which was then thought more poetical. Occasionally it touches on politics: the exiled James II, for instance, appears on the scene, when Ps. 107: 40 ('Though he suffer them to be evil intreated through tyrants: and let them wander out of the way in the wilderness') becomes:

The prince who slights what God commands,
Expos'd to scorn, must quit his throne;
And over wild and desert lands,
Where no path offers, stray alone.

But even such embellishments did not win affection for 'Tate's poor page'. People used the *New Version* in fashionable centres like London, but without enthusiasm; and when a certain bishop was once asked what a drysalter was, he replied, 'Oh, Tate and Brady, of course.'

So it was. No one had asked a play-actor like Shakespeare to help in such high official work. The poets were none of them drawn in; and it never seems to have occurred to them that they might contribute. When, in the 17th century, some of them did write hymns, the ground was occupied by the *Old Version.* Men like George Herbert wrote their poems to please themselves; Milton may have had a new Puritan psalter in view when he made his metrical versions; Major-General George Wither (for so he became in the Civil War) had actually in 1623 succeeded in getting letters patent under James I for his *Hymnes and Songs* to be bound up with every copy of the authorized Psalter (the *Old Version*, which was then called *The Psalms of David in Meeter*); but the Stationers' Company, who enjoyed the monopoly of the Psalter, managed to make the patent a dead letter, until they secured its revocation by the Council in 1634. The Stationers were not scrupulous in their arguments: they charged Wither with making money out of the praises of God, adding that, in any case, such writing should be left to the clergy, and that those of Wither were 'Popish, superstitious, obscene, and unfit to keep company with David's Psalms'. He was more than their match in dialectic; but he fought in vain against vested interests when he published, in 1624, *The Schollers Purgatory*. Neither he nor really inspired hymnists like John Mason found their way into our church services till the 20th century. Mason's hymns may, indeed, have been sung in a few Church of England centres, but no notice was taken of them when the *New Version* was issued in 1696 and the *Supplement* in 1700. Bishop Ken was more fortunate; but Crossman's 'Jerusalem on high' only came into common use with the S.P.C.K. *Church Hymns*, of 1871, and his 'My song is love unknown', which we include (127), is still new to church-goers.

There was more opportunity for the Nonconformists: Mason's *Hymns* circulated widely among them, and they must have been sung; the 8th edition appeared in the year of Isaac Watts's first hymn-book. Richard Baxter himself was a pioneer in writing hymns and getting them sung: he was a friend of Mason, whose work also had a great influence upon Watts.

Efforts within the Church of England had indeed failed. John Playford, musician and publisher, whose *Dancing Master* (1650) is such a treasure-house of old tunes, was also parish clerk at the Temple Church, and had issued his *Psalms and Hymns* in 1671, which provides for the first time a collection of hymns and metrical psalms mingling together on a common footing. But the book was not kindly received, and none of its hymns were received into church use: so he fell back upon a new music edition, in 1677, of the *Old Version*; and his success in this only gave a fresh lease of life to the old metrical psalms. His son, however, Henry Playford, began the next century by publishing in 1701 *The Divine Companion; or David's Harp new tun'd*, which included hymns by Austin, Herbert, Crashaw, Drummond, and others, and, running into several editions, must have at least kept the idea of hymns alive.

The Struggle for Freedom

Thus by 1706 the atmosphere was ready for the magnificent youthful aggression of Isaac Watts. He was perhaps the first to say outright that some parts of the Psalter 'are almost opposite to the spirit of the Gospel', and to suggest that, after all, 'David' was not a Christian: he was certainly the first successful pioneer of the modern hymn-book, though his triumph did not come speedily.

When he produced his first book, *Hymns and Spiritual Songs*, July 1707, he was 'young Mr. Watts'—not the venerable Dr. Watts of so many title-pages; and he must have written 'When I survey' before he was thirty-three. There had been great hymns in the 17th century, but there had been no hymnals in common use. Metrical Psalms, with almost negligible appendixes (such as we have described under 82), had been all there was; though a slight movement had already begun when, in 1700, 'While shepherds watched' was included in the *Supplement* to the *New Version*. Watts, with enormous courage, pushed forward out of his age, and criticized the Psalms (which even Dr. Julian, just two centuries later, sometimes speaks of as alone 'inspired'). In his Preface, Watts speaks of religious indifference and says:

> I have been long convinc'd that one great Occasion of this Evil arises from the Matter and Words to which we confine all our Songs. Some of 'em are almost opposite to the Spirit of the Gospel: Many of them foreign to the State of the New-Testament, and widely different from the present Circumstances of Christians. . . . Thus by keeping too close to *David* in the House of God, the vail of *Moses* is thrown over our Hearts.

Watts, as Dr. Louis F. Benson notes (Princeton Lectures on *The English Hymn*, 1907, 1910), wrote and acted with a studied aggressiveness that meant to conquer. An evil so deeply rooted was not to be destroyed by conciliation. Passages, he said, and whole Psalms must be omitted because they were 'improper for any person but the Royal Author', and David must be always made to speak as if he were a fully instructed Christian, living in the age of Watts himself. So a new standard of church song was set up; it was to be (1) Evangelical; (2) Freely composed, as against the Reformation principle of keeping as close as possible to the letter of Scripture; (3) Expressing the thoughts of the singers, and not merely 'those of David or Asaph'. Ultimately 'Watts's Whims', as enemies called them, triumphed; the 18th century became the first age of hymn-books and popular hymns, though even in 1810, as Walter Wilson tells us in his *History of Dissenting Churches*, there were many in these, as well as in the more conservative Church of England, 'who prefer the rhyming of Brady and Tate, or the bald version of the Scotch'. In 1707, Dr. Dale says, in his *History of English Congregationalism*, the Independent congregations only numbered between 350 and 400, and were much reduced both in size and zeal. What Watts's reform did for their astonishing revival we can imagine. They were free; and one copy in the precentor's hands could serve for the whole congregation. Indeed, Watts would write a special hymn for the subject of his sermon. The Nonconformists, computed at about 5 per cent. of the population in the time of Queen Anne, grew enormously in numbers during the 18th century, at the expense of the Church of England, where the official *Old* and *New Versions* continued in use.

Yet we must not exaggerate the very great importance of Isaac Watts. He was not always inspired, and he wrote too much to be always infallible. For instance, many hymnals (e.g. the Canadian *Book of Common Praise*) include his 'Come, Holy Spirit, heavenly Dove'; but they all have to omit the lines:

Dear Lord, and shall we ever lie
At this poor dying rate?

He invented no hymn-measures and sought no musical development of congregational song; but, rather, accommodated himself to the musical decadence that had begun with the fashion for French tunes under Charles II. When he wrote, great stores of Psalm versions had been accumulating for a century and a half; Sternhold and Kethe in the 16th century were pioneers, and many excellent hymns had been written by Campian, Austin, Herbert, Cosin, Herrick, Mason, Crossman, Ken, Baxter, and others—and even Tate, as we have said, had already added in the *Supplement* of the *New Version*, six years before, 'While shepherds watched'. With his sagacity and discernment, as Dr. Louis Benson says, Watts 'could have compiled an English hymn-book out of existing materials, whose excellence would not be questioned to-day'.

We shall mention the work of the Wesleys many times in this book. The 18th century was a great age of hymnody, though the more exquisite poetic qualities of the 17th century had been left behind. But it must be remembered that the Wesleys wrote for their own people; and that the Church as a whole was still heavily conservative: for in most places the congregation had not even screwed themselves up to the point of adopting 'Tate and Brady': the *New Version* was almost confined to London and a few other centres; the village churches went on using 'Sternhold and Hopkins', as if they were still in the age of Queen Elizabeth. Most Prayer Books, indeed, of the 18th century will be found to be bound up with the *Old* and not with the *New Version*.

But there was some movement: Madan, was a rich young barrister who had intended to amuse some friends by taking off John Wesley—went out to hear him preach, and returned to say, 'Well, Gentlemen. He has taken me off.' He left the Bar for the Church; and in 1760 produced his *Psalms and Hymns*—170 in number and excellent in quality. By the close of the century about a dozen more had appeared outside Methodism, some merely local, but one was the *Olney Hymns* of Newton and Cowper in 1779.

Newton contributed 280 hymns to the *Olney Hymns*, and Cowper, far the greater poet, only 68; but three of Newton's seem to have reached immortality—473, 'Come, my soul'; 500, 'Glorious things'; and 527, 'How sweet the name'; and we have tried to bring back into use his once forgotten 'Kindly spring'. This matter of survival is an interesting one. As we have already noted on p. ix, the pioneer Coverdale only survives at the present moment in a carol; of Sternhold and of Hopkins nothing remains; but by Kethe, in the *Old Version*, one, the 'Old Hundredth' (443); and one from the few hymns printed with the *Old Version*, Marckant's Lamentation (116). All else of that collection, which to our forefathers had something of the sanctity of Holy Writ, has disappeared. The *New Version* survives in our book only in two centos from Tate or Brady, 'As pants the hart' (449) and 'Through all the changing scenes' (677); while from the 16 hymns of the first *Supplement* of 1700 we retain only 'While shepherds watched' (82); from the five additions in 1782 we have now two, 'Hark! the herald' (74) and 'Awake, my soul' (25); but the two added *c.* 1807, 'Jesus Christ is risen to-day' (145) and 'Glory to thee, my God' (45), are both with us.

Meanwhile, a large company of poets, neglected in the 17th and 18th centuries, have come to their own, and now have their revenge. The fact is that, with hymns as with other works of art, a process of sifting is always going on. Every book omits some hymns; and every book that is worth bringing out adds some. This is not only because new poets are born and new hymns appear, but also because we now endeavour to bring all the great hymn-tunes of the world into use, and are no longer content to say, when a tune is found, that it cannot be used because there are no words to fit it.

The sifting process is essential, but it is gradual and imperfect; and in the case of hymns it is always hampered by human psychology; people like what they are used to; and the most necessary omissions are certain to bring some objectors. Indeed, it has been said, not without truth, that even the wisest of men always have one bad hymn that they like. Such is the force of very early associations. The improvement of hymnody is thus always a matter of co-operation, involving a little sacrifice all round. Denominational books are at a disadvantage in this regard; they have indeed become an anachronism which is an increasing hindrance to the improvement of public worship, in much the same way that denominational galleries of religious art would be a hindrance. But the process of sifting never stops, for every user of a hymnal makes his own selection.

The Spate of Hymn-Books

During the 19th century the field of selection became immense; and, before the end of the Victorian era, Dr. Julian had to go through 400,000 hymns in various languages when he compiled the first edition of his *Dictionary of Hymnology* in 1891. Yet he did not include the books of the more eccentric sects, Southcottians, Shakers, Mormons, and such like; and during the forty years that followed the number must have enormously increased. This meant, of course, that an overwhelming mass of commonplace material was obscuring the light, and holding back from common use many hymns of high beauty and religious value.

The flood began with the century, when, largely owing to the Evangelical movement, there issued a spate of hymn-books quite unprecedented in the history of Christendom.

In the Church of England alone, between 1800 and 1820 forty-two new hymnals are known to have appeared, and the list will probably never be entirely complete. During the next ten years there were at least 14 new collections. Between 1831 and 1840, no less than 40 were published (ten came out in the twelve months of 1833); and there were 20 in the next decade. Forty-two more Church of England hymnals appeared between 1850 and 1861, while the number of Nonconformist books may have been even larger; but among these last 42 new Anglican collections were some that shaped the future of hymnody down to the present time: Dr. Neale's *Hymnal Noted* (1852–4), with free permission to every one to include in their collections as much as they chose of his 94 new translations from the Latin; *Murray's Hymnal*, and the *Church Hymnal* of Cooke and Denton (both also in 1852), and Mercer's *Church Psalter and Hymn Book* (1854). Then came the outstanding success of *Hymns Ancient and Modern* in 1861, helped by the withdrawal and co-operation of F. H. Murray and other hymnal owners.

After this there followed the *Hymnal Companion* in 1870, and *Church Hymns* in 1871, with 64 more by 1880.

But the promise of the 17th century was never fulfilled. Famous and beautiful things survive from the 600 hymns of Watts, and the 6,500 of Charles Wesley; but the object in this century was to enforce a particular body of doctrine, rather than to express the essence of religion, as poetry alone can do. The overwhelming effect of this tendency is shown by the enormous number of bad hymns produced during the output of the 19th century; book after book appeared which made no contribution whatever; and, if there was progress at all, it was extraordinarily slow, in contrast with the unparalleled production of high poetry outside the Church between 1800 and 1900. In the same way, the era was mighty in great music; but that music was also outside the Church.

Heber, writing the Preface for his *Hymns* in 1811, stands like a monument between the two centuries, protesting an ideal which the one had neglected and the other was destined to ignore. 'No fulsome or indecorous language', he writes, 'has been knowingly adopted; no erotic addresses to him whom no unclean lips can approach; no allegories, ill understood and worse applied.' The unworthy standard, which he thus reprobated, resisted all efforts to destroy it throughout the 19th century. And in one serious direction that century was an age of decadence: the 17th century was sometimes quaint, the 18th often crude; but neither was unmanly.

Because, after the 17th century, the principle of poetry was lost sight of, it was forgotten that the object of a hymn is to *express* and not define—to be, in fact, like the Gospels. This, with the inevitable loss of the principle of beauty, was probably the cause of the decline. As Lord Selborne said in *The Book of Praise*, 1867, p. ii:

> 'Nor are the principles, on which popular collections of hymns for congregational use are formed, favourable to that kind of selection, which is here attempted. In such collections, as a general rule, the taste

of the compilers is regulated by their theology: they seem to be very easily satisfied with all that they think orthodox and edifying, or liturgically appropriate; they do not submit hymns, derived from sources which they respect, to any free or independent criticism; and, on the other hand, they reject, with morbid fastidiousness, every sentiment and expression in which they think they detect the traces of opinions which they dislike. It is also their frequent habit to cut down the compositions which they approve, with little discrimination or judgment, to such arbitrary dimensions, as suit their ideas of the time which ought to be occupied, during Divine service, by congregational singing.'

Thus it was that hymnody came to be almost monopolized by the religious sects and parties. In the 17th century the normal Englishman could only express himself by kind permission of the Stationers' Company; in the 18th he was still in the deadening confines of officialism, with the *Supplement* to the *New Version* (1700) for the utmost limit of his excursion. Watts and the Wesleys had, indeed, won freedom for their own people; but it was a very peculiar religion that they expressed—how peculiar we do not realize now, because by general consent those verses which expressly proclaim their theology have been dropped out of our ordinary hymnals. In the 19th century, as Lord Selborne noted, hymnody was again in the hands of party managers, and the normal Englishman had little chance of being represented. So, while the religion of England was magnificently and truly expressed in the Bible and the Prayer Book, hymnody, tossed between officialism and sectionalism, was never able to take its rightful place by their side. As a learned writer in the *Quarterly Review* for July 1892 said:

'It is matter for serious reflection that there is still large room for improvement in the quality of the hymns that are offered as vehicles for the devotions of the congregation. As we turn over the pages of even the best of our popular manuals, with a critical eye to the merits of the compositions gathered into them from far and wide, what a distressing number we meet with to which their lack of spontaneity and fervour, their prosiness, flatness, and literary baldness . . . give the look of being mere rhymed commonplaces and platitudes, written to order, and certainly without any impulse of that "divine afflatus" which is the life of sacred as of all other poetry! Could any competent and impartial critic, we ask, exempt any one of our three great collections from the judgment, that it would gain rather than lose by the excision of half its contents?'

If this was all that could be said of the hymnody, not only in parish churches, but in great cathedrals and the chapels of scholarly colleges, and such-like centres of refinement, what of the rest? In less ambitious communities the standard was, indeed, much simpler, as in this from *Salvation Solos*, *c.* 1890:

Good Elijah went to heaven
  In a chariot of fire;
Bright and warm to glory driven,
  Fiery horses drew him higher.

Up God's deathless way to glory,
  Where God's holy seraphs burn,
Enoch travelled by translation,
  With no ticket to return.

There is an apophthegm somewhere to the effect that the deadest of all dead things is a hymn that has sprung from a dead theology; and perhaps nothing is so deadly to religion as the practice of singing such hymns. We are too near the last century for a final judgement to be yet possible: to some it is an age of recovery and revival, and all can see the many gains that have accrued to our generation; but others are more impressed by the loss of the old secure influence of religion on the nation, and of the decrease in that habit of church-going which was almost universal among decent people of all classes a century ago. Even as late as the period pictured in Anthony Trollope's novels, the Churches were enormously powerful. Is it true that during the last eighty years the Churches have been gently singing themselves downhill?

We may leave the question to the reader's consideration. But three things, we think, are certain: (1) Hymns survive by virtue of what in them is universally true; the dross is constantly being shed from the gold, and in many cases those very verses have disappeared which their writers thought of special religious importance. By tacit consent the dead theology has disappeared increasingly with each new compilation, while that which was truly seen, as well as intensely felt, remains. (2) It is true that the amount of distorted religion which has encumbered so many collections has produced profoundly bad effects and has implanted many strange ideas which are entirely foreign to the Gospels. Church-goers are sometimes rather naïve in their surprise at the number of people who dislike 'Christianity'; but if they will consider what has passed for Christianity in many hymns and in much preaching, they may find some explanation. (3) The bad hymns can be replaced by the better; and the profound improvement in hymnody which has been proceeding during this century, and is now being widely spread by modern hymnals, will prove the most valuable of allies in the new religious initiative that has already begun.

The extraordinarily educative effect of hymns cannot indeed be exaggerated. Much Christian thought is still distorted, and much Christian work hampered or paralysed, by the strange notions that have filtered in from the hymns of last century. But new principles are now spreading wide and deep. Let us take one example, noted while this book was being made: there was a sentence by Mr. Winston Churchill in the popular *Sunday Graphic* for Dec. 28, 1932, 'Without an equal growth of Mercy, Pity, Peace, and Love, science herself may destroy all that makes life majestic and tolerable.' It was in 1906 that we brought Blake's poem (682)—so incisive for the very centre of Christianity—into common and familiar use: nothing could illustrate better than a casual sentence like this how it is already sinking into the national consciousness.

Freedom and Development

But, although liberty was at first misused by sects and parties, and the national spirit, which expressed itself so abundantly in other forms of poetry, had little opportunity in the hymn-books that were provided, complete freedom had to be won. It is being won at last because liberty is the natural way with Englishmen. The stifling official hand, however, was only slipped off by slow degrees. We have shown under 652 how even the American colonists, who were free of the Stationers' Company and beyond the reach of the Privy Council, actually prosecuted John Wesley for introducing new hymns into public worship. When, in the 19th century, the official power of the *Old Version* and the *New* was being forgotten, some bishops were consulted on the subject of authorizing hymnals. Heber, in 1821, tried to obtain from Archbishop Manners Sutton and the Bishop of London authorization for his collection of *Hymns*, then in manuscript, because hymns were a 'powerful engine' outside the Church, and on the interesting ground that they were already being used inside in an irregular manner; but application was refused. This was probably a wise refusal; for it prevented the danger of a new official book. Yet Heber had been working with famous poets; and the idea of drawing in the poets did not occur to the compilers of hymnals again till nearly another century had elapsed.

The Archbishop of Canterbury, however, had not refused permission to a hymn-book; he had only refused to authorize a particular one. Two years before, the Archbishop of York had been forced into legal action through the Diocesan Court. And in this the great hymnist, James Montgomery, was involved, for the originality of Cotterill's famous 8th edition (1819) of the *Selection* of 1810 was due to him. There was a storm of conservative opposition at St. Paul's, Sheffield, when this 8th edition came out; the dispute was taken into court and brought before Archbishop Vernon Harcourt. He, also, avoided official action, and suggested that the matter should be settled out of court by the withdrawal of the 8th edition and the publication of a 9th, approved by and dedicated to him. This was done; and the wise British method of compromise succeeded. In more recent years various bishops did attempt to prevent the use of various different hymnals, but without success; though neither common sense nor the courts would be likely to deny the right of a bishop to forbid the use of any hymn that was objectionable, since—not to mention other considerations—the rights of the parishioners are for him to safeguard and maintain.

In this most important respect the Church of England is now more free than the Free Churches. Since the *New Version* and the *Supplement* were overwhelmed by the torrent of hymnals which began with the 19th century, it has been able to lead the van by a generation or more; and as, one after another, other Churches, some of them Anglican, fell under official control, the Church of England became almost the only body left to do pioneer work. Neither poetry, prose, nor music can ever be successfully handled by committees, which always contain some elderly representatives whose minds linger in the memories of the past, and which also cannot meet continuously and must necessarily handle their business as business has to be handled, besides being held back in other ways that will be obvious to those who know a little of the inevitable character of ecclesiastical machinery. There was a movement in the Church of England for an official book in the eighteen-eighties, as a result of which a joint Committee of the Upper and Lower Houses of the Convocation of Canterbury was formed. This body issued a Report in 1894, signed by Bishop Frederick Temple. They had collected statistics, and found that at that time 10,340 churches used *Hymns Ancient and Modern*, 1,478 used the *Hymnal Companion*, and 1,462 *Church Hymns*; 379 churches used other hymnals. The report (1894, Mo. 271) stated that such 'approximation towards a general use' might pass away and not occur again; and that no moment more favourable to an official book was likely to occur. They considered that the matter demanded 'the most careful consideration of Convocation'; but did not make any proposal; and the idea fell through. The Church was left free to go forward.

Songs of Praise is for all the Churches—not, indeed, for Lot's wife, but for the forward-looking people of every communion.

There were thus two methods of arrangement before its promoters —to classify the hymns under their subject-matter, or to follow the traditional seasons of the Christian Church as a whole. The latter method is certainly the most convenient for practical use, and it is used by the greatest number of Christians; it also sets free many hymns from Procrustean classification, and we have found it a gain to have as many hymns as possible under the General section. The old names, like 'Good Friday', are simpler also and less pretentious than the subject titles sometimes used under other systems.

In Puritan times there was a strong feeling against the observance even of such days as Christmas: the effects of this remained to a large extent in the 18th century, even in the Church of England; but now the convenience of having some commemorations is generally recognized; and members of those Churches which do not observe, for instance, the Sunday after Ascension Day may still find it convenient to look for hymns under the heading of the festival when they desire to find hymns on the subject.

We are reaching the time when denominational hymn-books will be recognized as an anachronism and a hindrance to the unity of the Spirit. Why should we thus emphasize and perpetuate our peculiarities? The hymns themselves show how catholic we have already become in spite of ourselves. They represent the whole of Christendom, without sectarian limitations; and the ideal for all the Churches is to use the same books, so that the distinction will not be between one denomination and another, but merely the still natural as inevitable one between those who are lingering behind and those who go forward.

THE PROSODY OF HYMNS

Songs of Praise is unusually rich in varied metres. It forms, indeed, a good basis for the study of prosody. For the benefit of our readers we give here a little elementary information, adopting, with Professor Saintsbury, the classical quantity-feet to our English accented verse.

Iambic

The Iambic foot is the most common in English, | ∪ – |: therefore its simpler forms are known to musicians by names instead of by the number of syllables.

SHORT MEASURE (or Short Metre) (S.M.) consists of the following syllables in each of the four lines of the stanza: 6 6. 8 6.

It is split up from a favourite early Tudor metre, called 'Poulter's Measure', because, it is said, poulterers were in the habit of giving twelve to the dozen on some occasions, and thirteen or fourteen at others. Poulter's Measure is a combination of lines of twelve and fourteen syllables, which are called respectively Alexandrines and fourteeners. Thus, the first couplet in S.M. has twelve; the second, fourteen syllables; and the split up of this is 6 6. 8 6. If we write Short Measure out in two lines, it comes out as Poulter's, 12 syllables in the first line, and 14 in the second: split these, and we have 6 6. 8 6. Thus, in Metrical feet:

∪ – | ∪ – | ∪ – | (6)
∪ – | ∪ – | ∪ – | (6)
∪ – | ∪ – | ∪ – | ∪ – | (8)
∪ – | ∪ – | ∪ – | (6)

e.g. 702.

Ye servants of the Lord,
Each in his office wait,
Observant of his heavenly word,
And watchful at his gate.

DOUBLE SHORT MEASURE (D.S.M.) is used for a tune in which the quatrain is repeated twice, e.g. the 'Old 25th' (i.e. the tune for the 25th Psalm in the *Old Version* of the Metrical Psalter, in this case from Day's or Daye's Psalter of 1563), as in 195, 'For ever with the Lord!' or Bach's 'Ich halte treulich still' to 480, 'Crown him upon the throne'.

COMMON MEASURE (C.M.), the ordinary ballad metre, consists of a quatrain of 8 6. 8 6 syllables, or 4 3. 4 3 feet, thus:

∪ – | ∪ – | ∪ – | ∪ – | (8)
∪ – | ∪ – | ∪ – | (6)
∪ – | ∪ – | ∪ – | ∪ – | (8)
∪ – | ∪ – | ∪ – | (6)

e.g. 598 O God, our help in ages past,
Our hope for years to come,
Our shelter from the stormy blast,
And our eternal home.

The rhymes are alternate, as in S.M., and are in the printing shown by indenting certain lines so that the beginnings of the rhymed lines coincide in position, a practice generally observed, but with a modification as above in S.M.

In the old ballads there are often tripping extra syllables, as in the second line of:

There lived a wife at Usher's well,
And a wealthy wife was she;
She had three stout and stalwart sons,
And sent them o'er the sea.

DOUBLE COMMON MEASURE (D.C.M.) is used when the Common Measure quatrain is repeated twice to form one stanza, which is embraced by the tune, e.g. *Forest Green*, to 79, 'O little town of Bethlehem'. This metre also is common in the Metrical Psalters, thus the glorious tune to the *Old 137th Psalm*, which is used for 526, 'How shall I sing that majesty'.

LONG MEASURE (L.M.) consists of a quatrain in which each line is of eight syllables, or four Iambic feet—in other words, an octosyllabic quatrain. It is the metre most common in the Latin hymns (which are never in C.M.):

◡ – | ◡ – | ◡ – | ◡ – | (8)
◡ – | ◡ – | ◡ – | ◡ – | (8)
◡ – | ◡ – | ◡ – | ◡ – | (8)
◡ – | ◡ – | ◡ – | ◡ – | (8)

e.g. 443, commonly called 'The Old Hundredth', because it is the old version, from Daye's Psalter (1560–1), of the 100th Psalm:

All people that on earth do dwell,
Sing to the Lord with cheerful voice;
Him serve with mirth, his praise forth tell,
Come ye before him, and rejoice.

Here the rhymes are alternate; but in the Latin hymns, and often in the English, the rhymes are coupled, as in Ken's Morning and Evening Hymns, 25, 45; though the earlier Latin hymns are unrhymed, e.g. 33, almost certainly by St. Ambrose:

Splendor paternae gloriae,
De luce lucem proferens,
Lux lucis, et fons luminis,
Dies dierum inluminans.

translated into rhymed English by Robert Bridges:

O splendour of God's glory bright,
O thou that bringest light from light.
O Light of light, light's living spring.
O Day, all days illumining.

In DOUBLE LONG MEASURE (D.L.M.) the stanza is of eight lines. This is not so common; but it is the metre for the tune called *Tallis's Lamentation*, 235, 'O Master, it is good to be'; and the metre is used, though with an added phrase in the music, for the famous *Addison's* or *London* tune to 659, Addison's 'The spacious firmament on high'. His 'The Lord my pasture shall prepare' (656) is intermediate between the two forms, since it consists of six octosyllabic lines—8 8. 8 8. 8 8.

The old Metrical Psalters were not adventurous in metrical forms in England, being content with Common Measure for most of their paraphrases; but the attraction of some stirring tunes, derived from the Genevan Psalter, led in the 16th century to versions being provided in 'P.M.', that is 'PECULIAR MEASURE', as they called it, though it still employs the national Iambic foot. Examples of this in the *Old Version* of Sternhold and Hopkins's, Kethe's 104, and the 136th by 'T. C.' (a misprint for 'J. C.', i.e. John Craig), whence our tunes, the *Old 104th* ('Disposer Supreme', 211) and the *Old 136th* ('Jerusalem on high', 197). The metre of these is 6 6. 6 6. 8 8 and 10. 10. 11. 11; and Kethe's original Old 104th is not yet forgotten:

My soule prayse the Lord, speak good of his name,
  O Lord our great God how dost thou appeare?
So passing in glory, that great is thy fame,
  Honour and maiesty in thee shine most cleare.

After the traditional metres, the metrical index begins on p. 872 with the shortest lines. One hymn happens to open with a line of two syllables only (505, 'Good cheer'), though the remainder of its stanzas is taken up with longer lines. The shortest line for a whole hymn throughout is 380, 'Winter creeps'; for, though this is enumerated in the music as in double lines of six syllables, it is really 3 3 3 3. 3 3 3 3. The index then proceeds step by step to the longest first lines, the fourteeners, ending with those hymns classified for musical purposes as 'irregular', though, of course, they have a rhythmical character of their own.

The DECASYLLABLE does not occur in the metrical psalters, and, largely because Watts was not interested in developing new musical forms, it was slow in coming into common English hymnody. Yet it had long been the staple of English poetry: of blank verse (which is not suitable for hymns or other songs), e.g.

Why art thou yet so fair? shall I believe
That unsubstantial death is amorous

(from *Romeo and Juliet*).

And of the sonnet, e.g., also from Shakespeare:

622. Poor soul, the centre of my sinful earth.

And of the heroic couplet (i.e. ten syllables with coupled rhymes), e.g. from Pope:

Know then thyself, presume not God to scan:
The proper study of mankind is Man.

This does occur in eight instances (53, 268, 279, 293, 437, 498, 560, 574), e.g.

437. Abide with me; fast falls the eventide:
The darkness deepens; Lord, with me abide.

Rather less frequently in our collection—and only in modern hymns—the decasyllabic line has alternative rhymes (102, 103, 208, 266, 270, 290, 299), e.g.

270. Here, O my Lord, I see thee face to face;
Here faith would touch and handle things unseen;
Here grasp with firmer hand the eternal grace,
And all my weariness upon thee lean.

Trochaic

Among the hymns are very many which consist of trochaic feet | – ᴗ |: they are always distinguished in the Metrical Index of the *Music Edition*, to save the choir-master from falling into a trap. A common trochaic form is 7 7. 7 7, which is like Long Measure with the first syllable omitted, having seven syllables instead of eight.

This happens to be the metre of our first two hymns:

1. For thy mercy and thy grace,

2. Kindly spring again is here.

Trochaic lines of an even number of syllables must end in a full trochee, and this involves double rhymes, as is the case with the next:

3. Lift your hidden faces,

where line 3 ends with the trochaic 'places'. Or with the next:

4. Spring has now unwrapped the flowers,
Day is fast reviving,
Life with all her glowing powers
Towards the light is striving.

Many Latin hymns are in the Trochaic metre, 8 7. 8 7. 8 7, which carries some famous tunes, such as *Pange lingua.*

129. Sing, my tongue, the glorious battle.

But these belong to the Dark and Middle Ages, and are not classical forms.

RHYMES are commonly noted by letters. Thus the alternate rhymes of 1, 3, and 4, are *ab ab*, the coupled rhymes of 2, *aa bb*. Occasionally such rhymes are more intricate, as in the case of Spenser's sonnet:

22. Most glorious Lord of life, that on this day
Didst make thy triumph over death and sin.

This is a 'Shakespearian' sonnet; and the rhymes are, *ab ab*, *bc bc*, *cd cd*, *ee*. ASSONANCE is a form of rhyme which counts only the vowel sound or other similarity of the chief rhyming syllable, as in the German of *Wachet auf* (687), 'Stimme', 'Zinne'. In Latin hymns it marked the transition from unrhymed classical verse to medieval rhymed verse, as in *Victimae Paschali*, where corresponding assonance is used in the translation in *E.H.* 130. In Spanish poetry it is much used, but is rare in English. It is employed very effectively in 692, 'We thank you, Lord of heaven'.

Other Metres

The classical *dactyl* | – ∪ ∪ | is more generally supplanted in English verse by the *anapaest* | ∪ ∪ – |, but the foot is nearly always shortened in some part or parts of the line, e.g.

| ∪ – | ∪ ∪ – | ∪ ∪ – | ∪ ∪ – |
535. Immortal, invisible, God only wise.

There are three classical metres which do fit very beautifully to music, the Sapphic (called after the Greek poetess, Sappho, who used this metre), the Elegiac, and, in one instance only, the Alcaic. *Sapphic* tunes abound both in old plainsong and in the modernized plainsong of the French service books of the 17th century, and in German hymnody also, the greatest example of the last class being Cruger's 'Herzliebster Jesu' as adapted by Bach, 99. Another example is 'Die Nacht ist kommen':

48. Now God be with us, for the night is falling,
Soon sleep will take us, restfully enthralling;
Then may the Father, while our dreams possess us,
Shelter and bless us.

The *Elegiac* metre was used by Bishop Venantius Fortunatus in the 6th century for his processional hymns, the *Salves*, and thus form five hymns in *Songs of Praise*, under 389, and one in the next number where the metre is described:

389. Hail thee, Festival Day! blest day, that art hallowed for ever;
Day whereon Christ arose, breaking the kingdom of death.

390. Welcome, Day of the Lord, the first and the best of the seven,
Day whereon Christ arose, brought us the promise of life.

For these five alternatives, both the plainsong and Vaughan Williams's modern tune are given.

The *Alcaic* metre has seldom been attempted in English, though Tennyson included an example among his 'Experiments', in his poem on Milton:

O mighty-mouth'd inventor of harmonies,
O skill'd to sing of Time or Eternity,
God-gifted organ-voice of England,
Milton, a name to resound for ages.

As there is a fine, lilting German tune in this rhythm, a very lovely hymn with triple rhymes has been written for *Songs of Praise* to carry it:

236. O saint of summer, what can we sing for you?
How can we praise you, what can we bring for you?

One other special form needs mention, the *Sonnet*, in its English or Shakespearian form. By a happy inspiration, this closely wrought shape of fourteen decasyllabic lines was fitted in the *English Hymnal* to tunes of 10 10. 10 10, and three sonnets thus set to music, without alteration of the words, are included in *Songs of Praise*: one by Spenser, 22; one by Robert Bridges, 484; and one by Shakespeare, 622.

Often there are deliberate irregularities. We have already pointed out that in the traditional ballad the normal C.M. is often lightened by tripping anapaests, as in 229:

And the green comes after the grey.

Sometimes iambs, trochees, and anapaests are combined in a very musical rhythm, as in 700, 'Who within that stable'. Other less common feet do also very definitely appear in hymns and songs with great musical value, the amphibrach | ⏑ – ⏑ | in e.g.

396. O Father | above us, | our father | in might.

The amphimacer or Cretic | – ⏑ – | is also found here and there, e.g.

502. God is love: | his the care,

with strong musical effect; and also in the refrain of 386, V ('He is love'), and elsewhere, as is pointed out under certain hymns, such as 'Winter creeps' (380), which is Cretic throughout.

In 325 ('O England, my country') amphibrachs and amphimacers,
| – ◡ ◡ – |
combining with a distinct choriamb ('Mother of mine'), have inspired Mr. Holst with a beautiful melody.

The special classical foot, the spondee, | – – |, can also be found once isolated in

505. Good cheer!

But C.M. always begins with spondaic rhythm in the psalm-tunes, with their long initial note:

– –
All people that on earth do dwell.

The best hymns have, indeed, far more craft bestowed on them than their singers imagine; and they are far richer in poetic qualities, as is pointed out in many parts of this book, such as under 82, 443, 598, 639, and 648. A knowledge of the elements of prosody is essential to the appreciation of all poetry; and we have written these introductory notes in the hope of helping some readers to appreciate a little more those of our hymns which are real poetry: they are in truth the only hymns that are worth preserving; and they will endure.

EXPLANATORY NOTES

The sign † after an author's name means that an alteration has been made in one line only; the sign ‡ denotes alterations in two or three lines. When more than one writer has materially altered the original (as in the case, for instance, of 'Hark! the herald angels sing'), the words *and others* may be added. The letter *V* (version) denotes that a hymn has been recast: thus *S.P.V.* means that it is a version made for *Songs of Praise*. Where there is no sign, the verses are as the author wrote them, unless the word *cento* is added to show that a selection of lines has been made in order to make a poem possible for congregational singing. When verses are omitted (as with many well-known hymns) is only stated in the notes. Doxologies are not included in this system: they are generally not frequent in this book; but when they occur, they are not necessarily by the author of the hymn to which they are affixed. The letters *Tr.* are prefixed to the names of all translators; but when the rendering is so free as to amount to a paraphrase the letters *Pr.* are used.

To avoid frequent repetition, in the Metrical notes the phrase 'Unique in this book' is abbreviated to 'Unique'. The meaning of the familiar metrical initials has been elaborated in the Note on Prosody.

Again, to avoid repetition, a number, without 'p.' for 'page', stands for the number of a hymn: thus, 'cf. 22' means 'compare hymn no. 22'.

BOOK I

Part I

TIMES AND SEASONS

By a convenient development the words *psalm*, *canticle*, *anthem*, *hymn*, and *carol* have acquired distinctive meanings. Anciently psalm, hymn, and canticle were interchangeable terms, because the metrical hymn in our sense of the word did not exist, Hebrew technique resting on the device of parallelism, which is marked by a spaced colon in the Prayer Book Psalter, as in the glorious verse, 'In his hand are all the corners of the earth: and the strength of the hills is his also.' Thus our Lord and his Apostles sang a 'hymn' before they went to Gethsemane (Mk. 14: 26), which was probably a psalm, as were also the songs which Paul and Silas 'hymned' in Acts 16 : 25. On the other hand, the original word for 'I will sing' in 1 Cor. 14 : 15 is in the Greek, 'I will psalm'; and this, with every man's 'psalm' in the same chapter, clearly refers to the common worship of the Corinthian Christians. In James 5 : 13 the word for 'sing' again is from *psallein.* St. Paul, in Ephesians 6 : 19 and Colossians 3 : 16, speaks of 'psalms and hymns and spiritual "odes" '—all three being words applied in the Greek of the Septuagint to the Davidic Psalms. The Lukan Canticles are also 'hymns', following the forms of Hebrew poetry; and there are passages in the Epistles (Eph. 5 : 14; 1 Tim. 3 : 16; and 6 : 15–16; 2 Tim. 2 : 11–12) which also may be quotations from very early Christian hymns; two of them seem to be brought in as quotations, and the third has not only rhythm but some rhyme as well.

Hymns naturally came to leave the Hebrew method and to follow the laws of classical prosody. The earliest is probably *Phōs hilaron*, 50, below; and the Latin hymns can be seen in many parts of this book. An enormous amount of hymnody is to be found in the Greek service books, though for the most part they are not amenable to modern use; Dr. Neale computed that four-fifths of the Greek services are hymns—5,000 pages of the different books.

NEW YEAR

1 For thy mercy and thy grace. *Henry Downton,*† 1818–85.

Written in 1841, and first published in the *Church of England Magazine* in 1843, this hymn was altered in *Hymns Ancient and Modern* and other collections. It is printed in the author's form in the *English Hymnal* (286) with the omission of one verse, and here in *Songs of Praise* (as in the *Hymnary*) with the omission of two, with one line altered in ver. 2, l. 2 'Thee, our perfect Sacrifice'. Less weak and sentimental than other New

Year hymns, it seems to be the one of Downton's contributions that is destined to survive. There are many hymns of first-rate quality suitable to New Year's Day, as our list of cross references suggests.

Trochaic, 77. 77.

MUSIC. CULBACH is found in *Heilige Seelenlust, Oder Geistliche Hirtenlieder . . . von Johann Angelo Silesio und von Herren Georgio Josepho mit aussbundig Melodien geziert* (Breslau, 1657), where it is set to the hymn 'Ach wann kommt die Zeit heran'. The above work is in three books, and two others were published later. Of the 205 melodies contained in these five books, 185 are believed to be by Joseph; some, however, are adaptations of secular melodies, and a few, of which this is one, are marked 'To a well-known melody'. The tune itself is a good example of an easy melody, well adapted to congregational singing, since the limitation of its compass to an octave brings it well within the range of all voices. Its plan is of the simplest, in alternate lines of parallel structure, but in this simplicity lies its strength and adequacy (cf. 'Da Christus geboren war', 2).

Nature Hymns

While the classical influence survived, the earliest Latin hymns had many allusions to the beauty of Nature, as in the sparkling charm of *Nox et tenebrae* (37) of the 4th century Prudentius, so finely translated by Mr. Pope, 'Ye clouds and darkness' (37), or in the *Salve, festa dies* of the 6th century Venantius Fortunatus (389). Thenceforward the nature-influence faded out, except that it was retained in the Psalter in the Latin services, and in the English Psalms and Metrical Psalms after the Reformation.

The 18th century had a petrifying influence on this kind of poetry; and in religious verse the insistence was extreme on 'doctrine', which really meant the dominant theological ideas of the age. Bishop Heber, as will be seen in 21, was a pioneer of the revival of the nature hymn in the early 19th century. But, in spite of his work, and of a few original poets of earlier date like Christopher Smart (17), there remained even to the middle of the 19th century a strange Puritan dislike of nature hymns.

In 1855 the once famous 'Rivulet Controversy' gathered round T. T. Lynch (the author of 297, 506, and 699) because he had hymns sung from his book of poems, *The Rivulet*, which contained many references to nature: this was felt to be profane; and the scandal reached a climax when Lynch, being presented with a bunch of flowers one Sunday morning, took them into the pulpit and made them the theme of his sermon. The fact that a large number of Nonconformists, led by Dr. John Campbell, 'the Pope of Dissent', as Dr. W. F. Adeney calls him, could have violently objected to thus considering the lilies, throws a flood of light upon the religious ideas of eighty years ago, and supplies one reason for the 'ritualist' reaction then commencing. Cf. 389, 506.

Newman Hall, Binney, and Baldwin Brown stoutly defended Lynch, but Spurgeon condemned him for 'negative theology' and 'a non-doctrine scheme'. Lynch met the attack with admirable temper: 'The air will be all the clearer for this storm. We must conquer our foes by suffering them to crucify us, rather than by threatening them with crucifixion.' But the controversy undermined his already feeble constitution, and hastened his death.

SPRING

2 Kindly spring again is here. *John Newton,*† 1725–1807.

Olney was the village in Buckinghamshire where Newton was rector, and where Cowper lived, 1767–95, and acted as his lay-reader: this was contributed to the *Olney Hymns* in 1779, the first word being originally 'Pleasing'. Newton, like Bunyan, had probably never been so sunk in depravity as he imagined; at least he was never a drunkard, and he preserved his pure devotion to Mary Catlett, with whom he had fallen in love when she was 14 and he 17. But he certainly joined in the slave-trade. He had gone to sea when he was 11 and made six voyages with his father. As a midshipman in the Navy he deserted, was captured, and reduced to a common seaman. Next he became the servant of a slave-dealer in Africa. When he was 23 he began to change, after an awful night steering a water-logged ship in the face of death. He was converted; but went on for six years as the now pious skipper of a slave-ship. In 1750 he married Mary Catlett, and in 1755 settled down as customs officer in Liverpool, and an enthusiastic disciple of Wesley and Whitefield, with the acquaintance also of Grimshaw, Venn, Romaine, and other Evangelical leaders. His stupendous courage was not least shown in the way he struggled to learn Greek, Latin, Hebrew, and mathematics—with a smattering of Syriac! So he passed on to ordination, and to Olney.

Trochaic, 7 7. 7 7.

MUSIC. DA CHRISTUS GEBOREN WAR appears in the *Vierstimmiges Choralbuch* (Leipzig, 1785) of Johann Friedrich Doles. It is probably an old melody arranged by him. It is of the same type as 'Culbach' (hymn 1), which it closely resembles in the first two lines, and in its general range. It is, however, a less powerful tune, owing to a slight lack of balance; the formal analogy being not between alternate lines, as in 'Culbach', but between the last two lines only, which are, therefore, out of relation with the first two, in which a similar correspondence is not found. It is a good tune but less satisfying than the former.

3 Lift your hidden faces. *Rose Fyleman.*

Written for the *Oxford Book of Carols* (1928) to carry the tune of 'Une vaine crainte', these words are based upon the French original, the refrain being taken from the 147th Psalm.

Trochaic, 6 5. 6 5. D. with a refrain in freer rhythm. Unique.

MUSIC. GRACE SOIT is the traditional French tune to the carol on which the above words are based. It is given, headed 'Une vaine crainte', in J. L. Roques's *50 Noëls anciens* (1897), a collection of carol tunes arranged for the organ, with variations. It is also found to the words 'Grâce soit rendue', and there are many variants of the tune in Champagne, Burgundy, and Anjou. It appears thus in L. Eugene Grimault's *Noëls Angevins* (1878). The present arrangement, by Martin Shaw, appeared in the *Oxford Book of Carols*, 156.

The tune is very characteristic of many French carol melodies, in its narrow compass, in its insistence on a repeated phrase, and in its mood of childlike mirth which aptly expresses the spirit of a spring or summer festival, and it is an excellent specimen of its kind.

4 Spring has now unwrapped the flowers. *Piae Cantiones* (1582). *Tr. O.B.C.*

The original Latin words of the splendid spring hymn, *Tempus adest floridum*, in *Piae Cantiones* are here translated. Unfortunately, when that unique Swedish book was brought to England by the British Minister at Stockholm, *c.* 1852, and given by him to Dr. Neale, the latter wrote for it the words 'Good King Wenceslas', a poor ballad, difficult to understand, and unworthy of the writer of so many good carols. Habits are difficult to break, but we may hope that gradually the tune will become less associated with Christmas (for which there are so many glorious carols without it), and increasingly sung to its proper spring theme. The doxology, as is often the case with doxologies, is an addition. This translation was first published in the *Oxford Book of Carols* (1928).

Trochaic, 7 6. 7 6. D.

MUSIC. TEMPUS ADEST FLORIDUM is found in *Piae Cantiones* (1582) as the melody proper to this spring carol. The present harmonization is by Martin Shaw, and is to be found in the *Oxford Book of Carols*, 99, with a fa-burden for vv. 2 and 4 and a more elaborate arrangement for vv. 3 and 5. It is to be hoped that the original association will, in time, be generally restored.

5 Spring bursts to-day. *Christina Rossetti*, 1830–94.

The words of this vigorous Easter and spring song were published by Christina Rossetti in *A Pageant and other Poems* (1881).

Iambic, 4 10. Unique.

MUSIC. SPRING was composed by Martin Shaw especially for this hymn in the enlarged *Songs of Praise* (1931). The setting may appear, at first sight, more complicated than it actually is; the changes of key offer no difficulty since the whole tune is founded on one simple musical phrase, immediately apprehensible by any congregation, and the vigorous rhythm makes it easy and enjoyable to sing.

6 The year's at the spring. *Robert Browning*, 1812–89.

'From without is heard the voice of Pippa singing': the first of her songs that are overheard in *Pippa Passes* (1841).

Browning has often, during the depressed era of the post-War years, been accused of 'optimism'; and this little song has been generally adduced as an example of that vice. But the criticism is a little obtuse; for Pippa's words belong to a special dramatic setting and are put in the mouth of a maid who has every right to them. There are as a matter of fact many pessimistic lines in Browning's works, for those who prefer pessimism; though after all it is more Christian to be optimistic.

Anapaestic, 5 5. 4 5. D. Unique.

MUSIC. BAMBERG is an arrangement by R. Vaughan Williams, for *Songs of Praise*, of a 17th-century German melody of a characteristic popular type, which was obviously suited, by rhythm and general character, to dancing as well as singing. It is a satisfactory specimen of this large class of melodies.

SUMMER

7 Summer suns are glowing. *Bishop W. Walsham How*, 1823–97.

First published in the S.P.C.K. *Church Hymns* (1871), of which Dr. Walsham How was joint-editor. 'His broad sympathies and large and genial humanity, as well as his apostolic zeal,' says the *Handbook to the Church Hymnary*, 'attracted all classes.' It was these qualities which gave a special power to his hymns. (See also under 15.)

Trochaic, 6 5. 6 5. D.

MUSIC. GHENT (ADORO TE, No. 2) is the melody of the hymn 'Adoro te devote' as given by Canon P. J. Van Damme of Ghent, and appeared in the *English Hymnal* (1906), set to the hymn 'Father, see thy children bending at thy throne'. The tune is of a very simple pattern, being founded on a single musical shape, slightly varied in each line, but with a closer correspondence of the 1st to the 2nd, and the 3rd to the 4th line. Such a scheme certainly results in a well-balanced tune, but it also produces an effect of extreme simplicity, making it suitable only for equally unaffected words.

8 The summer days are come again. *Samuel Longfellow*,‡ 1819–92.

Samuel Longfellow, the younger brother of the more famous author of *Hiawatha*, wrote three verses, each beginning 'The sweet June days are come again', for use in the open air: the hymn has been altered in the *English Hymnal* and in *Songs of Praise*, as in other books, to make it suitable for use in church, the first verse being omitted altogether.

Dr. F. M. Bird justly remarks in the first (1891) edition of Julian's *Dictionary of Hymnology* (p. 59): 'The English use of American hymns has been, until recent years, very limited, and mainly confined to the older collections of the English Nonconformists. . . . In Great Britain the noblest forms of American hymnody are known to the few.' In fact, while English compilers and translators were ransacking the material of the Dark Ages, and adding translations from hymns of the Counter-Reformation to those of Medieval origin, the modern American school was hardly consulted—if at all—by Anglican compilers; and, as it happened, it was just in America that the best hymns, and those which are most in accord with the convictions of the present age, were then being written.

D.C.M.

MUSIC. SOLL'S SEIN is from the 1658 edition of D. G. Corner's *Geistliche Nachtigal der Catholischen Teutschen, das ist Auserlesene Catholische Gesänge, &c.* The collection was first published in 1631, and passed through several editions before 1700. The tune is curiously like some of the melodies of Henry Lawes; indeed, had it been found anonymously in England, it might well have been attributed to Lawes on internal evidence. This is to give the tune high praise, for Henry Lawes, though now a too neglected composer, was more worthy of Milton's high opinion of him than later critics have been willing to admit.

HARVEST

9 Come, ye thankful people, come. *Henry Alford*,‡ 1810–71.

The Dean made considerable changes in the original form of this, his most popular hymn, which was first published in his *Psalms and Hymns*

(1844), and in its revised form in his *Poetical Works* (1865). He repudiated the altered version in *Hymns Ancient and Modern*, which contains such lines as 'All upon the golden floor', and otherwise changes the original. But we have felt compelled to alter 'all is safely' to 'all be safely', in vv. 1 and 4, to be more in accordance with fact; and the following words are changed to others which seem nearer to the New Testament: ver. 2, 'We ourselves are' (All this world is), 'Grant, O harvest Lord' (Lord of harvest, grant), 'that day' (to-day), 'ears' (wheat), 'garner' (barn). It is, after all, the tares of evil that are burnt up.

Dr. Alford was a most distinguished scholar; but the verdict of James Davidson in Julian's *Dictionary of Hymnology* (p. 39) is perhaps true: 'As a hymn-writer he added little to his literary reputation. The rhythm of his hymns is musical, but the poetry is neither striking nor the thought original. . . . They are somewhat cold and conventional. They vary greatly in merit.'

Trochaic, 7 7. 7 7. D.

MUSIC. ST. GEORGE, composed by Sir George Elvey, appeared in *A Selection of Psalm and Hymn Tunes, edited and arranged by E. H. Thorne. . . . Adapted to Psalms and Hymns compiled by the Rev. T. B. Morrell and the Rev. W. W. How* (1858), where it was set to the hymn 'Hark! the song of Jubilee'. It is now, however, and has long been, associated with the present words, to which it is in every way excellently suited. The tune is too well known to need further comment.

10 Fair waved the golden corn. *John Hampden Gurney*, 1802–62.

This, like several others, a children's hymn that has become popular with adults, was first published in Gurney's Marylebone *Psalms and Hymns* (1851) when he was rector of St. Mary's, Bryanston Square. It applies to harvest festivals the idea of the offering of First Fruits, a custom of the Jews and many other nations (see Exod. 23 and 34, Deut. 18 and 26; and cf. Frazer, *The Golden Bough*, ii. 68–90, 373–84).

S.M.

MUSIC. SELMA is found in *Sacred Music . . . sung in St. George's Church, Edinburgh, edited by R. A. Smith* (1825). There it is set to Psalm 67, and described as an 'Ancient Scottish Melody. Noted in the Island of Arran, and harmonized by Mr. Smith.' It is possible that the tune is really Mr. Smith's own composition, or, at least, that the adaptation has been so considerable as to leave very little of the original. During the 18th and the beginning of the 19th century innumerable tunes were invented, more or less in the pentatonic scale, and attributed to a Scottish origin, and this particular tune may be one of this type.

11 Fields of corn, give up your ears. *Eleanor Farjeon.*

Another example of the overlapping of the hymn and the carol. Miss Farjeon's verses are based upon the main idea of the German song or hymn to which the tune belongs in M. Vehe's *Gesangbuechlin* (Strasburg), 1537, and in other old collections; and the German words of 'Der Tag der ist so freudenreich', are themselves a translation of the Latin *Dies est laetitiae*, a 15th-century precursor, as Julian notes, of the carol. Miss Farjeon's verses appeared first in the *Oxford Book of Carols* (158), 1928, with the name 'Thanksgiving Carol'.

Trochaic, 7 6. 7 6. 7 7 6. 7 7 6. Unique.

MUSIC. CORNFIELDS is an arrangement by Geoffrey Shaw of the melody found in M. Vehe's *Ein New Gesangbuechlin Geistliche Lieder* (1537), as above. This tune appears also in several later collections, and various versions of the German words are found to different tunes. The Latin words, 'Dies est laetitiae', are given, from a 15th-century manuscript, by F. J. Mone in his *Lateinische Hymnen des Mittelalters*, and Riemann considers that the present melody is, at latest, of the same century.

12 Let us, with a gladsome mind. *John Milton,*‡ 1608–74.

According to Milton's biographers, Warton and Mitford, this paraphrase of Psalm 136 was written in 1623, when he was fifteen years old, a boy at St. Paul's School. It was published in his *Poems in English and Latin* (1645), in 24 two-line stanzas and with the refrain as in our text. The original is not always regular enough for singing; but this version, now generally accepted, does not alter any essential words, such as the poetic phrases about the golden-tressed sun and the horned moon with her spangled sisters, which Sir H. W. Baker reduced to the libretto level of 'And the silver moon by night, Shining with her gentle light'. The words of the original altered are: 3 'Who by his' (He with), 'Did fill' (Filled), 4 'And caused' (He), 'All the day long' (Caused all day), 5 'Amongst' ('Mid), 6 'All living creatures' (All things living), 'And with full' (His full).

Trochaic, 7 7. 7 7.

MUSIC. MONKLAND appeared in *Hymn Tunes of the United Brethren* (edited by John Less, Manchester, 1824), where the composer's name is not given. When it appeared in *Hymns Ancient and Modern* (1861) it was 'arranged by J. Wilkes', who was organist at Monkland, where Sir Henry Baker was vicar; and this version is used here. The alternative version (descant) was written by C. Charlton Palmer especially for the enlarged *Songs of Praise* (1931).

13 To thee, O Lord, our hearts we raise.

William Chatterton Dix, 1837–98.

This example of Dix's rather facile style was printed in the St. Raphael's (Bristol) *Hymns for the Service of the Church* (1864). Its popularity has not been dimmed by the rhyming of 'accepted' and 'elected' in ver. 3.

Iambic, 8 7. 8 7. D.

MUSIC. ST. GALL is from *Katholisches Gesangbuch zum Gebrauch bei dem öffentlichen Gottesdienste* (1863), the revised edition of the old hymn-book of St. Gall. This Benedictine monastery, founded in 614 by the Irish monk, St. Gall, became one of the most famous centres of Church song in the Middle Ages, and was the original source of the type of hymn called Sequence, as we know it. The monastery, which began to decline in the 12th century, was suppressed in 1790, but its library, containing 2,258 *incunabula* and 1,725 manuscripts of great value, remains intact.

The present is a sturdy tune, with a candid, symmetrical melody, and with a good swinging rhythm when taken fairly fast.

14 We plough the fields, and scatter.

Matthias Claudius, 1740–1815. *Tr. Jane Montgomery Campbell*, 1817–78.

Wir pflügen und wir streuen
Den Samen auf das Land,
Doch Wachstum und Gedeihen
Steht nicht in unsrer Hand.
Alle gute Gabe
Kommt oben her, von Gott,
Vom schönen blauen Himmel herab.

Miss Campbell has admirably reproduced the folk quality of this song, clean, strong, vigorous, and simple. 'Wir pflügen und wir streuen' made its way to the top of harvest song through a happy marriage with a second tune. Claudius published in 1783 at Hamburg a description of a harvest thanksgiving in a north German farm-house, *Paul Erdmann's Fest*: the neighbours come to Erdmann's house singing a 'Peasant's Song' of 17 four-line stanzas with a refrain. 'The music they said was Italian' is Claudius' statement about the tune which he prints. In 1800 a tune-book for schools appeared in Hanover, and in it the now famous tune by Schulz was set to vv. 3–10 of the song, the refrain being altered to carry the new tune. The hymn at once leaped into popularity through the school hymn-books of Germany. Miss Campbell's translation was printed in C. S. Bere's *Garland of Songs* (1861).

Iambic, 7 6. 7 6. 7 6. 7 6; refrain 6 6. 8 4. Unique.

MUSIC. WIR PFLÜGEN, composed by J. A. P. Schulz, appeared in *Lieder für Volkschulen* (Hanover, 1800), where it is set to some stanzas of this hymn. Its earliest appearance in England seems to have been in the *Bible Class Magazine* (Nov. 1854), where it is set to another translation of the German hymn. The tune, in spite of its wide compass, has become one of the most famous and favoured of all hymn-tunes, and fully deserves its popularity.

AUTUMN

15 The year is swiftly waning. *Bishop W. Walsham How*, 1823–97.

Written for *Church Hymns* (1871), and brought into further use by the *English Hymnal* (1906). Dr. Julian, in his *Dictionary of Hymnology*, p. 540, sums up the Bishop's sincere and penetrating work in a true sentence: 'Without any claims to rank as a poet, in the sense in which Cowper and Montgomery were poets, he has sung us songs which will probably outlive all his other literary works.' (Cf. under 7.)

Iambic, 7 6. 7 6.

MUSIC. HAMBRIDGE is an arrangement by R. Vaughan Williams of a folk-tune sung in Somerset, and appeared in the *English Hymnal* (1906). It was one of the tunes collected in Hambridge by Cecil Sharp, and is remarkable even among the many beautiful melodies preserved by him and other collectors. It is completely satisfying in form and expression, and it is not too much to say that it would be conspicuous in any group of tunes in the world.

WINTER

16 'Tis winter now; the fallen snow. *Samuel Longfellow*, 1819–92.

Two Harvard students, Samuel Longfellow (whose brother was to become so famous) and Samuel Johnson, disgusted with the hymn-books in use, determined with the zeal of youth to produce a more modern collection; and in the year of their graduation in theology, 1846, they published *A Book of Hymns*. None of their own contributions to this daring venture survive, however, in *Songs of Praise*: this, like several others, is from their later collection, *Hymns of the Spirit* (1864). We owe much to the work of these two friends, and to those through whom they were, slowly enough, introduced into England—Dr. Martineau, in his *Hymns* (1873), Dr. Garrett Horder, in his *Congregational Hymns* (1884), and his *Worship Song* (1905). This delicately etched winter hymn appeared in the *English Hymnal* (1906), together with the folk-tune that fits it so beautifully.

L.M.

MUSIC. DANBY is an arrangement, by R. Vaughan Williams, of a traditional English ballad air, and appeared in *Songs of Praise* (1925). A different arrangement, set to the same hymn, is to be found in the *English Hymnal* (1906). The melody is typical, in rhythm and semi-modal character, of a large group of English ballad-tunes, particularly connected with narrative ballads, both legendary and historical.

SEASONS: GENERAL

17 All the scenes of nature quicken. *Christopher Smart*, 1722–71.

The appreciation of Christopher Smart, one of the most original poets of the 18th century, has increased in modern times. It was the first *Songs of Praise* that first included some of his work in a hymn-book. This from Hymn 13 for St. Philip and St. James, of 19 stanzas, first published in his *Translation of the Psalms of David* (with 'Hymns and Spiritual Songs for the Fasts and Festivals'), 1765. For more about the poet see 521 and 690.

Trochaic, 8 7. 8 7.

MUSIC. SHANGHAI is an adaptation of a Chinese melody; it first appeared in the original *Songs of Praise* (1925). The pentatonic character of Chinese tunes is well known owing to frequent western imitations of 'oriental' music; but this scale seems to have been always used rather in popular and folk music, which appears to have been despised by educated Chinese, whose conceptions of music are said to have been very different from those attributed to them by western ideas. The whole question of Chinese music is, however, a much vexed one; and totally opposed theories are to be found in their own writings, as well as in those of foreign commentators. The present tune, at least, corresponds, in its squareness, its rhythm, and its scale to what the occident has agreed to expect from Chinese melodies, and it is a good specimen of its type.

18 By the breadth of the blue that shines in silence o'er me.
Henry van Dyke, 1852–1933.

This stirring open-air hymn, by Dr. van Dyke, 'pastor, poet, and diplomat', who was Professor of English Literature at Princeton University as well as United States Minister to Holland, appeared first in New York, 1904, and was included in the enlarged *Songs of Praise* (1931).

Irregular; but anapaestic in character, the lines varying from 13 to 16 syllables. Unique.

MUSIC. HICKLING BROAD was composed by Geoffrey Shaw especially for the enlarged *Songs of Praise* (1931). It is a broad unison tune, of rather large compass, but, apart from this, easy to learn and to sing, and is conspicuous for its bold skips in the melody, symbolic of the expansive character of the words.

19 Hark, my soul, how everything. *John Austin*, 1613–69.

Published in Austin's *Devotions in the Antient Way of Offices* (1668), as the hymn for Monday at Lauds. George Whitefield included it in his *Collection* (1753), altered; and it is turned into Long Measure ('Hark, my dull soul, how everything') in John Wesley's *Psalms and Hymns* (Charlestown, S. Carolina, 1736–7), published during Wesley's American ministry.

Trochaic, 7 7. 7 7.

MUSIC. LYNE appeared in *Hymns . . . used at the Magdalen Chapel* (*c.* 1760), where it is set to the hymn 'Let us, with a gladsome mind'. It is a simple little tune, in triple time, typical, in rhythm and melodic line, of a large class of melodies, many of them traditional, found in song collections of the late 17th and early 18th centuries; the present melody has also a characteristic air of happy innocence.

20 Thou art, O God, the life and light. *Thomas Moore*, 1779–1852.

The author of *Irish Melodies* published in 1816 a little volume of 32 *Sacred Songs*, written to popular airs of various nations, from which this and 679 are taken. It was first given a wide circulation in the Church of England by the *English Hymnal*.

Iambic, 8 8. 8 8. 8 8.

MUSIC. NEW 113TH, by William Hayes, appears in *Sixteen Psalms . . . set to music for the use of Magdalen College Chapel in Oxford* (*c.* 1774), set to Merrick's version of Psalm 134.

21 When spring unlocks the flowers, to paint the laughing soil.
Bishop Reginald Heber, 1783–1826.

Appeared in the *Christian Observer* (1816) six years before Heber went to Calcutta as Bishop for the whole of India; revised by him, and reprinted in his posthumous *Hymns, &c.* (1827), from which the text here used is taken. He had died suddenly in Trichinopoly after three years in India; for the climate and the vastness of his work had been too much for him.

Iambic, 13 13. 14 14.

MUSIC. GOSTERWOOD is an arrangement by R. Vaughan Williams (in the *English Hymnal*, 1906) of a traditional air, which seems to have been known at one time in the Isle of Man as a carol-tune. The style of the melody also confirms this; for, though it is not possible to draw a hard-and-fast line between the various types of tune, the general character of this one is more that usually found associated with carols than with ballads or folk-songs.

SUNDAY

22 Most glorious Lord of life, that on this day.

Edmund Spenser, c. 1552–99.

The sonnet was first brought into use as a hymn in the *English Hymnal* by the device of repeating the last half of the melody for the concluding couplet. The author of the *Faerie Queene* included this as Sonnet lxviii in his *Amoretti and Epithalamion* (1595). It is now used sometimes as a marriage hymn, by beginning at 'This joyous day'.

A sonnet, and therefore in 14 decasyllabic lines; but musically enumerated as Iambic, 10. 10. 10. 10, in three quatrains and a half. This sonnet is in the Shakespearian form, ending with a rhymed couplet: the rhymes, which are variable in the sonnet, are here: *abab*, *bcbc*, *cdcd*, *ee*. See Note on Prosody, p. xxxi, and cf. 484.

MUSIC. FARLEY CASTLE appears in *A Paraphrase upon the Divine Poems*, by George Sandys (1638), set to Psalm 72. This, the 2nd edition of Sandys's metrical version of the Psalms, contains a number of tunes in two parts, treble and bass, which are here anonymous, but, in later editions, ascribed to Henry Lawes. This particular tune is not very characteristic of Lawes, as a composer; it is a good, direct melody, obviously imitative of the psalm tunes found in the earlier psalters.

23 This is the day the Lord hath made. *Isaac Watts*, 1674–1748.

This vigorous and simple hymn forms a good introduction to a Sunday service. Watts called it 'Hosanna: the Lord's Day; or, Christ's Resurrection and our Salvation', in his *Psalms of David* (1719). The first line is from Psalm 118 : 22. There is little of the rest of the Psalm in the five-stanza hymn which is here given as he wrote it; but Watts was busy weaning the English people from the idea that only the Psalms (being alone 'inspired') could rightly be sung in church, as we have noted on p. xvi. Watts, as we have said, was in this way almost the father of modern hymnody; and he fought a long battle for the right to sing hymns distinctively Christian in Christian churches. (Cf. also under 389.)

C.M.

MUSIC. BROMSGROVE is from *Psalmodia Evangelica, Part II* (1789), where it is anonymous. Variants of the tune are found in other collections; it is here given as in the above work, except for bars 7–9, which, in the original run as follows:

The present harmonization is by Martin Shaw. The tune itself is a representative example of the rather elaborate style which is found in numerous 18th-century collections, and was especially favoured and popularized by the new Wesleyan and Methodist sects. They are very distinctive in character, and were frequently derived from, or imitative of, contemporary secular melodies.

MORNING

24 At thy feet, O Christ, we lay. *William Bright*, 1824–1901.

Published first in the *Monthly Packet* (Oct. 1867) and in Dr. Bright's *Hymns and Poems* (2nd ed. 1874). The hymn is made less heavy by the omission of the 3rd verse, 'We in part our weakness know', which reduces it to four serviceable stanzas.

Trochaic, 7 7. 7 7. 7 7.

MUSIC. RATISBON (JESU, MEINE ZUVERSICHT) is found in C. Runge's *D.M. Luthers Und anderer vornehmen geistreichen und gelehrten Männer Geistliche Lieder und Psalmen, &c.* (1653), where it is set to the hymn 'Jesu, meine Zuversicht' as follows:

The following variant set to the same hymn appears in J. Crüger's *Praxis Pietatis Melica* (1653), but the tune is not attributed to Crüger until P. Sohren's edition of this work in 1668:

It seems probable that Crüger adapted his version from Runge's book, but the priority of neither can be absolutely established. The tune, with its characteristic lengthening of the 2nd line, is typical of many German chorales, both in its regular movement and the natural style of the melody.

25 Awake, my soul, and with the sun.

Bishop Thomas Ken, 1637–1711.

One of the hymns that got into official use in the Church of England because they were added to the *New Version* (Tate and Brady), though not an early addition (see 82); for it appears first in the *University Edition* of the *New Version* (1782). In 1674 Ken had issued a *Manual of Prayers* for use at Winchester College, in which the boys are told to 'be sure to sing the Morning and Evening Hymn in your chamber devoutly': in 1695 the Morning, Evening, and Midnight Hymns are printed in an appendix to the *Manual*; in 1705 the Morning and Evening hymns appeared in *A Conference* (2nd ed.), with two added stanzas; thereupon C. Brome, the owner of the copyright, published, in the same year, another edition of the *Manual* with a protest, and in 1709 another edition with the text revised by Ken—two years before his death. Ken used to sing these hymns to the viol or spinet, we know not to what tunes.

Since some have asserted that all hymns should be in the first person plural, Alford's remark apropos of this hymn is worth quoting: 'The very best experimental and spiritual hymns of all ages of the Church have been in the singular, from the fifty-first and twenty-third Psalms downwards.'

In the first chapter of *Adam Bede*, the hero sings ver. 3 as he walks home across the fields after his day's work. We omit two after the first six stanzas, and one stanza after our ver. 7, the original having fourteen.
L.M.

MUSIC. I. MORNING HYMN appeared in *The Hymns and Psalms used at the Asylum or House of Refuge for Female Orphans. Printed for W. Gawler, Organist to the Asylum* (178–?), where it is set to the present hymn, and headed 'New Tune. Published by permission of Mr. Barthélémon'. The book is undated, but must have been printed between 1783 and 1788, since Barthélémon's connexion with the asylum began in the former year, and a copy in the possession of Dr. W. H. Cummings has the autograph of a former owner and the date 1789. The tune attained popularity, probably because its undistinguished phrases, being musical common-places, were easy to catch and remember, but, on the score of quality, it does not deserve its fame. The alternative version (descant) by Geoffrey Shaw appeared in the *Descant Hymn-Tune Book* (Bk. I, 1925).

II. RICHARD, by Morfydd Owen, was discovered by Martin Shaw in 1916. While Miss Owen was a student at the R.A.M., Dr. Shaw heard her play this tune among various other compositions and hymn-tunes. This one was put into use at St. Mary's, Primrose Hill, and incorporated in *The Public School Hymn Book* (1919). Miss Owen, who became the wife of Dr. Ernest Jones, the well-known psycho-analyst, was a composer of great promise, but unfortunately died at the early age of 25.

III. WARRINGTON appeared in Ralph Harrison's *Sacred Harmony, or A Collection of Psalm Tunes, Ancient and Modern, &c.* (2 vols., 1784–91), with his name attached as composer. It is no. 73 of part I which is 'intended to contain the more easy tunes, and such as are suitable to congregations in general'. The present version of the melody is as in the original except that bar 6 there runs

and the penultimate bar

The tune is an excellent one, both in form and melody, combining strength and smoothness in a remarkable manner. Its effect is partly due to the satisfactory equipoise of movement by step and leap, the latter being in no case greater than a fourth, thus preserving the flow of the melody while infusing vigour into the whole.

26 Christ, whose glory fills the skies. *Charles Wesley*, 1707–88.

Of the many hymns that Charles Wesley wrote, James Montgomery, himself the author of what are perhaps the best hymns of the 19th century, marked this as 'one of C. Wesley's loveliest progeny'. John and Charles Wesley worked together; and we cannot say for certain of any piece that either was the author, except that the translations from the German, impressive but less graceful, were done by John; but the vast majority are certainly by Charles, and it is customary to attribute all except the translations to him. He, therefore, and Watts must be held the two greatest hymnists of the 18th century; and, comparing the two, it seems to the present writer that Charles Wesley excels as a teacher in brilliant verse, but that Watts is the finer poet; though of course of such an enormous output as we have described on p. 34, only a fraction reaches the highest standard.

As this hymn was printed in the Wesleys' *Hymns and Sacred Poems* (1740), the year in which Toplady was born, the once common attribution to Toplady is improbable; but he included it in his *Psalms and Hymns* (1776); and it was Montgomery who first pointed out that it was not his own composition.

Charles Wesley had a 'fair escape' from worldly greatness. Being the eighteenth child of his parents, a rich relation offered to adopt him. He refused; and the cousin who was adopted in his place, taking the name of Wesley or Wellesley (as it was sometimes spelt), became Lord Mornington, and was the grandfather of the great Duke of Wellington.

Trochaic, 7 7· 7 7· 7 7·

MUSIC. MINISTRES DE L'ÉTERNEL is set to Psalm 135 in the complete *Genevan Psalter* of 1562. The rhythm of the second line has been slightly simplified, the original being

The present form is easier for congregational singing. It is a very massive, forthright melody, with a markedly decisive rhythm, which gives added weight to the regularly balanced alternation of the movement of the individual phrases. Well sung, with due observance of accent, but without vigour, it produces a noble and inspiring impression.

27 Come, thou bright and morning star.

Christian Knorr, Baron von Rosenroth, 1636–89.
Tr. Richard Massie,‡ 1800–87.

Knorr, who became Kanzlei-direktor or prime minister to the Palgrave of Sulzbach in 1668, published seventy hymns in his *Neuer Helicon* (Nürnberg, 1684), of which this (originally of seven stanzas) is the only one much known in England. Fischer, in his *Kirchenlieder-Lexicon*, says that this is one of the freshest and most spirited of morning hymns, 'as if born from the dew of the sunrise'. The translation, here somewhat altered, was contributed by Massie to Mercer's *Church Psalter and Hymn Book* (1857), the most popular of the precursors of *Ancient and Modern*, and is familiar to old Marlborough and Rugby boys.

Trochaic, 7 8. 7 8. 7 3.

MUSIC. MORGENGLANZ DER EWIGKEIT is the tune set to the original hymn in Freylinghausen's *Geistreiches Gesangbuch* (Halle, 1704). This is a beautiful tune in melody and, especially, in rhythm, the lengthening of the 2nd (4th) line in a sense anticipating the long notes of the short last line, while the 5th line preserves the balance by its structural analogy with the 1st. Thus the sense of proportion is satisfied by the equilibrium felt, perhaps unconsciously, through the comparative freedom of rhythm of the whole tune, while weakness is avoided by the steady march of minims within the individual phrase.

28 Father, we praise thee, now the night is over.

Ascribed to St. Gregory the Great (540–604). *Tr. E.H.*

Nocte surgentes vigilemus omnes,
semper in psalmis meditemur, atque
viribus totis Domino canamus
dulciter hymnos.

The St. Gregory who saw the Angle youths in the slave-market at Rome, and sent Augustine to Kent in 597, was a great reformer of the church services, and won the title of *Magister Caeremoniarum*. His name is one of the landmarks of Latin hymnody both in words and in music, for he established the melodies, more severe than those used by St. Ambrose, which are called 'Gregorian'. The mendacity of the old monastic writers, which so often baffles the historian, makes it impossible to be sure which, if any, hymns Gregory wrote; but this unrhymed hymn is doubtless of his time and may well be his work.

The translation (from the *English Hymnal*, 1906), like the Latin, is in one of the classical metres, the Sapphic; and although English prosody is determined by accent instead of by quantity, the best prosodists keep to the classical terminology.

Sapphic, 11 11. 11 5. As this is the first of our Sapphic hymns (the others being 48, 99, 186, 231, 262, 281, 330 (and cf. 349)), the metre, as adapted to English accentuation, which carries some of the most beautiful tunes, both plainsong (authentic and late) and German, may be here set out:

```
— ∪ ∪ | — ∪ || — ∪ | — ∪ | — ∪
— ∪ ∪ | — ∪ || — ∪ | — ∪ | — ∪
— ∪ ∪ | — ∪ || — ∪ | — ∪ | — ∪
                     — ∪ ∪ | — ∪
```

MUSIC. PLAINSONG is the proper festal melody to 'Nocte surgentes' from the *Sarum Antiphonal*, arranged by Martin Shaw for the enlarged *Songs of Praise* (1931). All plainsong melodies depend much, for their true effect, on the speed at which they are sung, as well as upon the true rhythmic accordance with the words. With this melody, if the general tempo is too slow, the graceful outline of the whole, a curve rising and falling evenly and gently, will not receive its value. It must not be hurried, but sufficiently fast to present the quality of the contour as a whole.

UT QUEANT LAXIS is a Rouen Church melody. During the 16th and 17th centuries there came into use, throughout the churches and cathedrals of several dioceses in France, a number of tunes in measured form, taking the place of the older unmeasured plainsong melodies. These tunes were in many cases founded on the plainsong melody, and in others on favourite secular airs; but the original sources of the individual tunes have not been ascertained.

The present tune is clearly founded on a substructure of plainsong, and is one of the best of the 'church melodies' so formed. It is a noble tune, with a rich and ample sweep of phrase.

29 Forth in thy name, O Lord, I go.

Charles Wesley, 1707–88.

Published in *Hymns and Sacred Poems* (1749), 'For Believers before Work', in six stanzas; and included in five stanzas in the *Wesleyan Hymn Book* (1780). The *Handbook to the Church Hymnary* says of the omitted stanza, 'Curiously enough, this verse has been omitted from the Methodist collections, but is included in the *English Hymnal*.' The reason is interesting: this stanza, 'Preserve me from my calling's snare', strikes just the notes of social duty and avoidance of anxiety that are prominent in modern religion, but were apparently not thought of so much importance by the followers of the Wesleys in the Methodist revival. Indeed the 19th century, with its powerful and pious wealth-makers, is being rather fiercely attacked at the present day for not having avoided the 'calling's snare'.

On the other hand, one verse has always been difficult to sing because of the line, 'And prove thy acceptable will'; and this, rather than alter the text, *Songs of Praise* omits, five verses making a long enough hymn. Alteration is necessary sometimes, but when it can be avoided by omitting a recalcitrant verse, this is often the best course.

L.M.

MUSIC. ANGEL'S SONG (SONG 34) appeared in *The Hymnes and Songs of the Church, by George Wither* (1623). The poet obtained from the King a patent authorizing the issue of his book bound up with the Psalter, i.e. the Old Version of the Psalms; but, as we have noted on p. xv, the Company of Stationers offered strenuous and successful opposition, and in this form Wither's book never passed into circulation. It contained a number of tunes in two parts, treble and bass, by Orlando Gibbons, the present melody being set to the song beginning 'Thus angels sung and thus sing we':

It is also set to another song in six-line form by the addition of two lines as follows:

Other variants of the tune occur (e.g. in Playford's *Psalms and Hymns*, 1671), and in the early 18th century there came into use the form, in triple time throughout, which is usually found in English and Scottish collections down to a comparatively recent date.

The alternative version (descant) was written by Guy Warrack especially for the enlarged *Songs of Praise* (1931).

The four-line form, as here given, is much to be preferred to the lengthened version, which is clearly a makeshift, and altogether out of proportion. There is an attractive air of innocence about this tune.

30 Morning has broken. *Eleanor Farjeon.*

There being no known hymn in this short dactylic metre, and something being also wanted on the theme of Thanksgiving for each day as it comes, Miss Farjeon was asked to make a poem to fit the lovely Gaelic tune.

Dactylic, 5 5. 5 4. D.; i.e. a dactyl followed by a trochee for three lines, – ∪ ∪ | – ∪, giving a double rhyme, while the fourth line drops the last unaccented syllable. Unique.

MUSIC. BUNESSAN is an arrangement, by Martin Shaw, of an old Gaelic melody in L. Macbean's *Songs and Hymns of the Gael* (1900). There is a majestic sweep in the movement of this tune which prevents any sense of monotony being caused by the rhythmic reiteration; indeed, in this case, the nature of the metrical unit adds, by repetition, an element of starkness to its dignity. The only defect in the tune is the weakness of its close.

31 New every morning is the love. *John Keble, 1792–1866.*

Keble wrote 16 stanzas in Sept. 1822, and published them in the *Christian Year* (1827), beginning, 'Hues of the rich unfolding morn'. A few collections have included this opening stanza; many more have begun with stanza 5, 'O timely happy, timely wise'; but Keble did not get into the swing of direct unlaboured expression till stanza 6, with which the hymn opens in the most widely used form—'New every morning'. We follow this custom; and also, with the *English Hymnal*, we include its 'Old friends, old scenes', which is perhaps the best and most profound stanza, and which gives its intended meaning to the next, 'We need not bid'.

L.M.

MUSIC. MELCOMBE is found in *An Essay on the Church Plain Chant*, 1782 (cf. Hymn 78). The tune appears in the second part of the work, set to the words 'O Salutaris hostia', and is headed 'At Exposition, Elevation, or Benediction of the Blessed Sacrament'. No composer's name is attached, but in *A Collection of Motetts, &c.* (1792), it is one of the pieces to which Webbe's name is appended as composer. It appeared as a hymn-tune under its present name in vol. ii of R. Harrison's *Sacred Harmony* (1791), and here also Webbe is named as the composer.

This famous and very beautiful melody fully deserves its great popularity. The build of the tune is interesting; the structure of the first two lines is similar, and is again paralleled in the last line, the analogy here being strengthened by the occurrence of two downward impulses, while, as a counterpoise, the third line presents the movement upward, that is to say inverted. The result is an extremely well-balanced tune, of great dignity.

The alternative version (fa-burden) by Martin Shaw appeared in *An English Benediction Manual* edited by Francis Burgess.

32 Now the morn new light is pouring.

Heinrich Albert, or *Alberti*, 1604–51. *Tr. Henry James Buckoll*,‡ 1803–71.

Gott des Himmels und der Erden,
  Vater, Sohn, und heil'ger Geist,
Der es Tag und Nacht lässt werden,
  Sonn' und Mond uns scheinen heisst
Dessen starke Hand die Welt
Und was drinnen ist, erhält.

Albert the composer wrote also the words of 118 songs and 74 hymns and published them at Königsberg in parts, 1638–50, in his *Arien etliche*. Of 'Gott des Himmels' here freely translated by Buckoll, the Rugby master, originally consisting of seven stanzas, a Königsberg writer, Dr. Cosack, said, that few morning hymns could compare with it in popularity and value, because of its simplicity and devotion. The last stanza is often used 'by children, by brides, by old and young, as a morning prayer': it runs in the German:

Meinen Leib und meine Seele
  Sammt den Sinnen und Verstand,
Grosser Gott, ich dir befehle
  Unter deine starke Hand;
Herr, mein Schild, mein Ehr' und Ruhm,
Nimm mich auf, dein Eigenthum.

Trochaic, 8 7. 8 7. 7 7. This metre with its double rhymes is more easily used in German, because of the abundance of unaccented endings, than in English; and there is therefore an abundance of German tunes for it. Two are given here.

MUSIC. GOTT DES HIMMELS, by Heinrich Albert, is from his *Arien oder Melodeyen* (vol. v, 1642), where it is set to the hymn 'Gott des Himmels und der Erden'. It is also found in duple time and this form is adopted by Bach in his *Christmas Oratorio*. The present is the original form of the melody. In either form the tune is quite a pleasant one, but is not very distinctive in any respect.

ST. LEONARD, by J. C. Bach, appeared in the *Neu-vermerhtes . . . Meiningisches Gesangbuch, &c.* (Meiningen, 1693), where it was set to 'Ich begehr nicht mehr zu leben', and is found in many later collections to various words. According to Gerber (who is, however, not a very trustworthy authority), the tune was originally written for the hymn 'Jesus, Jesus nichts als Jesus'. The melody is uneven; it begins excellently in the first two (four) lines, but the fifth halts and, though partial recovery is made with the last line, the tune consequently gives an impression of disproportion. The defect is partly due to the repetition of the first two lines, which makes the beginning of the fifth seem pleonastic. In spite of this, however, the tune, as a whole, is most attractive.

33 O splendour of God's glory bright.

St. Ambrose, 340–97. *Tr. Y.H.* (*Robert Bridges*, 1844–1930).

Splendor paternae gloriae,
de luce lucem proferens,
lux lucis et fons luminis,
dies dierum inluminans.

This—the office hymn for Lauds in the earliest monastic cycles contemporary with St. Benedict himself in the 6th century, and the hymn also for Lauds on the Mondays from the Epiphany till Lent in the Sarum Breviary—is almost certainly by St. Ambrose, with whose thought it is in close accord; indeed in his *De Fide*, iv. 9, he uses the phrase 'Splendor paternae gloriae' of the Son. It is ascribed to him by Fulgentius, who died in 533: the earliest MS. is *c.* 890. The old Breviary hymns are dignified and reserved, the antithesis indeed to mawkish sentimentalism in hymnody: they are often preoccupied with the fear of incontinence, and are limited in range though their thought is expressed with a classical dignity. The fine translation was printed by the late Poet Laureate in his *Yattendon Hymnal* (1899). Several of the stanzas make a good opening verse on occasions when such may be wanted, and four such single stanzas can be associated each with its own tune.

L.M.

MUSIC. Part I. PLAINSONG is an arrangement by J. H. Arnold, for *Songs of Praise*, of a melody from the *Sarum Antiphonal*. It was not attached to any particular words, but was in general use, at Vespers of weekdays (except Saturdays), from the Octave of Epiphany until the first Sunday in Lent.

SOLEMNIS HAEC FESTIVITAS is an Angers Church Melody (see 28). The tune is probably founded on a popular melody, and is of a familiar type.

Part II. PLAINSONG is an arrangement by J. H. Arnold of the melody, from the *Sarum Antiphonal*, proper to the hymn 'Splendor paternae gloriae'. This is one of the great plainsong melodies. The mere curve of the notes on paper is beautiful and perfectly proportioned. When well sung, in exact accordance with the rhythm of the Latin words, it produces an impression of unsurpassed sublimity.

SPLENDOUR (PUER NOBIS NASCITUR) is from Michael Praetorius's *Musae Sioniae* (Part VI, 1609), where it is set to No. 61, 'Geborn ist Gottes Söhnelein'. It is evidently a variant of the tune associated with the 15th-century carol 'Puer nobis nascitur' (cf. 385), and, as the present form does not seem to be found earlier than the *Musae Sioniae*, the adaptation is probably by Praetorius himself. The earliest printed form seems to be in Spangenberg's *Christlichs Gesangbüchlein, &c.* (Eisleben, 1568), as follows:

and this form, but more regularly in triple time, is found in several other collections. The present version should be compared with the form given to 385 (q.v.).

The Reformed Primers

Although Cranmer later on gave up the idea of providing English translations of the old Latin hymns (see p. ix), they were provided in the Primers for private use. The first reformed one had been drawn up by Marshall, *c.* 1534. This contained English hymns, as also did that of Bishop Hilsey in 1539; and in 1545 the first of many editions of *The King's Primer*, which had a fresh selection of hymns taken with one exception from the Sarum Breviary, some in Long Measure and some in Trochaic sevens. The Bible in English had been ordered to be read twice on every Sunday and holy day in 1542, and the English Litany had been issued in 1544: so this was the third step. Here is an example of 'Splendor paternae gloriae' from this Primer, 'Felowe of thy fathers light', with the spelling modernized:

Fellow of thy Father's light,
Light of light and day most bright,
Christ that chaseth away night,
Aid us for to pray aright.

Drive out darkness from our minds,
Drive away the flock of fiends,
Drowsiness take from our eyes,
That from sloth we may arise.

Christ vouchsafe mercý to give
To us all that do believe;
Let it profit us that pray
All that we do sing or say.

The rhythm is not always very singable, and though the lines are vigorous, as translations they are so vague that in some verses one would not know what original they represent.

34 So here hath been dawning. *Thomas Carlyle*, 1795–1881.

The author of *Sartor Resartus* published this in his *Miscellaneous Essays*, where he dates it as 'between 1822 and 1833'. Introduced as a children's hymn in the original *Songs of Praise* (1925), it is now printed among hymns for adults (which include those for schoolboys and girls), only those for very young children being in a section by themselves.

6 5. 6 5. Irregular, but anapaestic in character: ∪ – | ∪ ∪ – | ∪ | | ∪ – | ∪ ∪ –. Unique.

MUSIC. HARDWICK is an arrangement, by R. Vaughan Williams, for *Songs of Praise* (1925), of an English traditional air.

It belongs to the large class of folk-tunes in rather strongly accented triple time, the stress of the rhythm being emphasized, in these melodies, by the quavers on the first beat of many bars, and by repeated notes, equally accented, on the first and second beats of others. It is a very distinctive but frequent rhythm, in tunes of this kind, and always has a rather 'rustic' effect. The present tune is an excellent specimen of its kind.

35 The splendours of thy glory, Lord.
Charles Coffin, 1676–1749. *Tr. Archbishop Benson*, 1829–96.

O Luce qui mortalibus
Lates inacessa, Deus,
Praesente quo sancti tremunt
Nubuntque vultus angeli.

Charles Coffin wrote 100 hymns in all, beginning with those for the *Paris Breviary* (1736), where most of them, including this, appeared. He wrote them, he tells us, 'not so much to gratify the poetic spirit as to achieve elegance and piety'; and in this perhaps he succeeded. Dr. Benson's translation first appeared in the *Wellington College Hymn Book* (1860) (when he was head master), and it passed to *Church Hymns* (1871). Chandler had translated the hymn in 1837, 'O thou whose throne is hid from men'; the version of *Hymns Ancient and Modern* (1861), 'Great God, who, hid from mortal sight', was adapted from this; it was omitted in the 1875 edition, but restored with alterations in 1889.

A C.M. version, the original being in the L.M. of the normal Latin office hymn.

MUSIC. CREDITON, by Thomas Clark, is found in *A Second Set of Psalm Tunes adapted to the use of Country Choirs* (1810?), where it is set to the new version of Psalm 8, 'O thou to whom all creatures bow'. It is an acceptable tune, with a very pleasing and vocal melody, and well-made in alternately parallel structure. With this tune, as with many others of its type, it is better to err on the side of slowness, for though this imposes on it a solemnity that it is not intended to bear, too fast a pace destroys its true character.

The Parisian Hymns

There were three revisions of the Parisian Breviary as a result of the New Learning. (1) That of 1527, which confined itself to emendations of the texts of hymns, e.g. for *Urbs beata Hierusalem* (190) was substituted *Urbs Jerusalem beata*. (2) That of 1680, under Péréfixe and Harlay, successively Archbishops of Paris, which added many new hymns by Claude and the more famous brother, Jean-Baptiste de Santeüil, but retained about 70 of earlier date than the 11th century. (3) That of 1736, under Archbishop Vintimille, who employed the Rector of the University of Paris, Charles Coffin. This was more drastic. Only 25 hymns of earlier date than 1527 were retained; the compositions by J.-B. de Santeüil rose to 89; there were 83 by Coffin, and 97 by other French contemporaries—269 in all. The example spread to other dioceses—for the Gallican Church had considerable independent existence in those days—and by the end of the 18th century the ancient Latin hymnody was all but banished from France.

These late Latin hymns by Coffin and others have had a curious history in England. In 1837, when there was much sentimental romance, largely induced by the novels of Sir Walter Scott, about what was somewhat vaguely called the Ancient Church, John Chandler published his *Hymns of the Primitive Church*. For his material, he wrote in his preface, 'I got a copy of the Parisian Breviary, and one or two other old books of Latin Hymns'. He was in happy ignorance of the fact that most of the hymns he admired were later than Dr. Watts (cf. 67). In 1861 *Hymns Ancient and Modern* appeared, with 17 of Chandler's translations, 29 of Neale's, and 17 of Caswall's. There were 273 hymns in the collection, of which 132 were from the Latin. The new element in the book was very small, 11 from the Latin, 1 from the German, and 12 original hymns. Dr. Julian in his *Dictionary* asks why such success attended a book with so little in it that was new; and concludes that the two main causes were the tunes of W. H. Monk and his school, and the magic at the time of the word 'Ancient', though, as he points out, about one half of the Latin hymns are not as old as Sternhold and Hopkins. Curiously enough, Monk, who was musical editor, also suggested the title, which won those who were longing for 'things old and primitive'.

36 When virgin morn doth call thee to arise.

Based on Robert Herrick, 1591–1674.

This was included at the desire of many schools where it had become very popular, although the original would not at first sight have promised success as a hymn. Some teacher seems to have begun its adaptation, and then it was taken up by many, doubtless under the impression that Herrick had written it as it stood. There are some other hymns of this nature, either 'adapted' or by the author 'and others': in the case of a poet's work they are legitimate if they are a satisfactory answer (as we think this one is) to the question, 'Would the author have adapted his original in some such way, if he had wished to turn it into a hymn?' Since 17th-century poets had no hope then of their work being used in church (little even, when, like Wither and Mason they wrote whole books of hymns), there is justification for such shaping, precarious though it must be (cf. under 74). Herrick's 'Mattens, or Morning Prayer' is as follows:

When with the Virgin morning thou do'st rise,
Crossing thy selfe; come thus to sacrifice:
First wash thy heart in innocence, then bring
Pure hands, pure habits, pure, pure every thing.
Next to the Altar humbly kneele, and thence,
Give up thy soule in clouds of frankinsence.
Thy golden Censors fill'd with odours sweet,
Shall make thy actions with their ends to meet.

Iambic. 10. 10. Occurs also in 125.

MUSIC. GARDEN is an adaptation by Martin Shaw of an English traditional melody slightly abbreviated, which appeared in *Songs of Praise for Boys and Girls* (1929). The original is a happy little tune, and much of its spirit of innocent gaiety is retained in this adaptation.

37 Ye clouds and darkness, hosts of night.

Prudentius, b. 348. *Tr. R. M. Pope.*

Nox et tenebrae et nubila
confusa mundi et turbida,
lux intrat, albescit polus,
Christus venit, discedite!

Caligo terrae scinditur
percussa solis spiculo,
rebusque jam color redit
vultu nitentis sideris.

This extract from the *Cathemerinon* of Aurelius Clemens Prudentius, admirably translated by R. M. Pope, has an interest akin to that of 'O gladsome light' (50), since, though not the earliest hymn, it is by the first Latin Christian poet. His hymns are obviously not meant for use in public worship; but this and other extracts from them were included in the old Latin Breviaries and Hymnaries, 'Nox et tenebra' being the hymn for Wednesday and Thursday in the Breviaries of Salisbury, York, Aberdeen, and Rome. The original poem consists of 72 lines. The translation is from *The Hymns of Prudentius*, translated by R. Martin Pope and R. F. Davis, 1905.

It may be noticed, in this as in other translations, that the apparent terseness of Latin is due to its inflective construction. When one comes to counting syllables in verse, less can be said in Latin than in English; and consequently English translations generally contain epithets and phrases which do not exist in the Latin. For instance, in these fine English verses, the original is enriched by 'hosts of', 'that breed', 'o'erhead', and 'flees', 'dispersed', 'piercing', and the beautiful touches in 'eyes rain influence' and 'glimmer to sight'.

L.M.

MUSIC. AETERNA CHRISTI MUNERA, from Guidetti's *Directorium Chori* (1582), is a late and rather debased form of the plainsong melody usually associated, on the Continent, with St. Ambrose's hymn, 'Aeterna Christi munera'. In the above work the complete melody is found in the section at the end of the book, headed 'Toni hymnorum ad horas in festo duplici, per omnes horas', and given with the words 'Jam lucis orto sidere'; in the due place, however, it is directed to be sung to St. Ambrose's hymn. It is noticeable that the plainsong has been forced into a semi-metrical form, an approach to the tunes coming then into use, and soon popularized by the *Andernach Gesangbuch* (1608).

LUCIS CREATOR is an Angers Church Melody (cf. 28). This tune seems to be an adaptation of a popular melody, of a frequent 16th-century type. It is of semi-modal character, and is a good example of its class.

38 You that have spent the silent night.

George Gascoigne, c. 1525–77.

Note the date of Gascoigne. He was one of the earliest of English dramatists, and is a generation older than Spenser, who was born about 1552, while Shakespeare was not born till 1564. Besides being a pioneer hymn-writer in the early part of Queen Elizabeth's reign, he was the first English satirist and the first English critic of poetry. These stanzas from 'Good Morrowe' came into some hymnals with the first line stupidly altered to 'We that have passed in slumber sweet'. In the original the birds of our ver. 3 are introduced by the following delightful stanza:

The carrion crow, that loathsome beast,
  Which cries against the rain,
Both for her hue and for the rest
  The Devil resembleth plain;
And as with guns we kill the crow
  For spoiling our relief,
The Devil so must we overthrow
  With gun-shot of belief.

C.M.

MUSIC. GRÄFENBERG (NUN DANKET ALL) is from the 5th edition of Crüger's *Praxis Pietatis Melica* (Berlin, 1653). The present is the original form of the melody. This is a stately tune, its poise being due largely to the inversion of analogous phrases. It must be sung at a very moderate speed for its true dignity to be apparent.

NOON

39 Behold us, Lord, a little space.

J. Ellerton, 1826–93.

A midday hymn for weekdays, written in 1870 for a service in a London City church, and published first in *Church Hymns* in 1871. It must be one of the earliest hymns in which science and art are mentioned and are recognized as part of God's work; and it is characteristic of Ellerton's work at its best. Free from the sentimentality of the period, it handles tersely and epigrammatically the modern world of business and labour, and after more than sixty years it is modern still.

C.M.

MUSIC. FERRY is found in James Green's *Psalmody* (1731), which was first published in 1724 under the name *A Book of Psalm Tunes with variety of Anthems in four parts*, and from the 8th edition (1734) onwards changed its name to *A Book of Psalmody containing Chanting Tunes . . . with Eighteen Anthems and Variety of Psalm Tunes in Four Parts*. The present tune is found set to Psalm 103, 'My soul, give laud unto the Lord', the form being as here given except that the last notes of lines 1, 2, and 3 are semibreves with minim rests before the following lines. The melody is of the psalm-tune type, of very simple structure, the first halves of lines 3 and 4 being inversions of the movement of lines 1 and 2, while the second halves are identical. This produces a slightly rigid, but at the same time a very solid and impressive tune.

40 Blest are the moments, doubly blest.

William Wordsworth, 1770–1850.

One is tempted to wonder how much higher the level of British hymnody would have been in the 19th century if our great poets had been asked to contribute to the collections which were already pouring forth when Wordsworth was Laureate. Heber was an early and a rare exception; for he did ask Walter Scott and Southey to contribute to his MS. Collection, which, however, was not published owing to Archbishop Manners Sutton's refusal to authorize it in 1820. Wordsworth wrote 'The Labourer's Noon-day Hymn' in 1834. Here is his introduction, together with the first three stanzas, omitted from our version in the necessary process of shortening:

The Labourer's Noon-day Hymn

Bishop Ken's Morning and Evening Hymns are, as they deserve to be, familiarly known. Many other hymns have also been written on the same subject; but, not being aware of any being designed for noon-day, I was induced to compose these verses. Often one has occasion to observe cottage children carrying, in their baskets, dinner to their fathers engaged with their daily labours in the fields and woods. How gratifying would it be to me could I be assured that any portion of these stanzas had been sung by such a domestic concert under such circumstances. A friend of mine has told me that she introduced this hymn into a village-school which she superintended, and the stanzas in succession furnished her with texts to comment upon in a way which without difficulty was made intelligible to the children, and in which they obviously took delight, and they were taught to sing it to the tune of the old 100th Psalm.

Up to the throne of God is borne
The voice of praise at early morn,
And he accepts the punctual hymn
Sung as the light of day grows dim:

Nor will he turn his ear aside
From holy offerings at noontide.
Then here reposing let us raise
A song of gratitude and praise.

What though our burthen be not light,
We need not toil from morn to night;
The respite of the mid-day hour
Is in the thankful Creature's power.

L.M.

MUSIC. HERR JESU CHRIST is found in *Pensum Sacrum, Metro-Rhythmicum, CCLXVII Odis . . . denuo expansum expensumque Opera et Studio Tobiae Hauschkonii* T.B. (Görlitz, 1648), a collection of 267 Latin odes with 80 melodies, the present being set to six of the odes as follows:

In the *Gothaer Cantional* (1651) it is set to the hymn 'Herr Jesu Christ, dich zu uns wend'. Many variants of the tune are found in later collections, the present arrangement being J. S. Bach's in his *Choralgesänge* (1765).

This later version compensates for some loss of flexibility by an increase of dignity, and, by the change at the end of the 2nd line, avoids the monotonous effect due to the identity of the modulation in lines 1 and 3 and of the close of lines 3 and 4; a solemn and impressive tune.

EVENING

41 And now the wants are told that brought.

W. Bright, 1824–1901.

An evening hymn, scholarly and devout, this was written in 1865, after Dr. Bright had returned to Oxford, and three years before he became Regius Professor of Ecclesiastical History there. It was first published in his *Hymns and Other Poems* in 1866.

C.M.

MUSIC. CORNHILL was composed by Harold Darke especially for the enlarged *Songs of Praise* (1931). This is an attractive flowing tune, built on the inversion of the movement of alternate lines, with an interesting change of key in the 3rd line.

42 At even when the sun was set.

H. Twells,‡ 1823–1900.

The author, Henry Twells, a canon of Peterborough, stated that this hymn was written under unusual circumstances. Sir Henry Baker in 1868 wrote to ask him to compose a new evening hymn for the 1868 Appendix to *Hymns Ancient and Modern:*

> 'Being at that time headmaster of a large grammar-school—the Godolphin School, Hammersmith—I wrote it one afternoon while the boys were under examination (paper work), and I was supposed to be seeing "all fair". I am afraid I could not have been very energetic or lynx-eyed in my duties that day, but I little anticipated the popularity the hymn would attain. . . . Copies have been kindly sent to me in Greek, Latin, German, French, Welsh, and Irish. I like to think it may have brought souls nearer Christ, and if so, I heartily thank God for it.'

Twells wrote 'At even, ere the sun was set'; but in later books this has been generally altered, because St. Mark says (1 : 32), 'At even, when the sun did set', and if the people had brought their sick before sunset, they would have broken the Sabbath.

It may be noticed as characteristic of the way in which Christ's work of healing the body by spiritual means was ignored until the present century, that the hymn in its usual form makes the lesson lead up to the pressure of sin, and thus changes the significance of the 'signs' of Jesus, which in such an overwhelming number of instances were the release of the body from disease. The balance of the hymn is considerably restored by the omission of two verses in common use—'And some have found the world is vain', and 'And none, O Lord, have perfect rest'. It is thus possible to use the hymn without entirely losing sight of Christ as the healer of sickness.

One verse, however, the fourth in the original, had already been rightly cut out in most books:

And some are pressed with worldly care,
And some are tried with sinful doubt;
And some such grievous passions tear,
That only thou canst cast them out.

L.M.

MUSIC. CALVISIUS (ACH BLEIB BEI UNS) appears in *Geistliche Lieder* (Leipzig, 1589), in S. Calvisius's *Hymni Sacri Latini et Germanici* (1594) (where it appears in the alto as a descant to another melody, set to the hymn 'Danket dem Herrn heut und allzeit', being no. 5 of the 'German hymns') and various other contemporary collections. The present version is from J. S. Bach's *Vierstimmige Choralgesänge* (1769). It is one of the most famous of German chorales.

ANGELUS (DU MEINER SEELEN) is founded on a melody by G. Joseph in *Heilige Seelenlust, oder geistliche Hirten-Lieder . . . von Johann Angelo Silesio, und von Herren Georgio Josepho . . . Breslau* (1657). But though this book has always been cited as the source of the present tune, only the 1st line and half of the 2nd are really to be found there. The earliest publication in which the entire tune, in its present form, has been found is *Cantica Spiritualia, oder Auswahl der schönsten geistlichen Lieder älterer Zeit*, &c. (vol. ii, Munich, 1847), where it is set to the hymn 'Du meiner Seelen güldne Zier'. As the source of hymn and tune the editor names *Heilige Seelenlust* and Braun's *Echo Hymnodiae Coelestis*, in both of which books the melody is as follows:

Dr. W. Bäumker is of opinion that this, the original melody, was arbitrarily altered by the editor of *Cantica Spiritualia*. In any case the result is a good tune, too well known to need comment.

43 Behold the sun, that seemed but now.

George Wither, 1588–1667.

From *Hallelujah, or Britain's Second Remembrancer*, which Wither addressed to the High Court of Parliament in 1641, directing to their notice 'the sweet perfume of pious praises compounded according to the art of the spiritual apothecary'. There were hymns, as we have noted under 176 and 657, for many, as well as for a Merchant or Chapman (with an eye to his special snares and temptations), and to each he prefixed a note, serious or jocular; for this one of ours, 'At Sunsetting', he wrote: 'The singing or meditating to such purposes as are intimated in this Hymn, when we see the sun declining may perhaps expel unprofitable musings, and arm against the terrors of approaching darkness.'

The hymn consists of these three verses only. Wither's great harvest of 'golden sheaves', unequal but full of beauty, has been wrongfully neglected in the hymnals of the English Church, of which, Puritan though he became, he was always a devoted son. This one was included in Lord Selborne's *Book of Praise* (1862), in Thring's excellent collection twenty years later, and in the *Westminster Abbey Hymn Book* of 1883.

D.C.M.

MUSIC. OLD 18TH appeared first in the *English Psalter* of 1561, set to Psalm 18, and was retained in subsequent editions. The present version of melody and harmony is from W. Cobbold's setting in *Este's Psalter* (1592). The tune is typical, in its step-wise movement and the steady, almost ruthless, march of the melody, of many of the old psalm-tunes. They are almost primitive, not in the sense of being uncouth, but as possessing the stubborn grandeur of a natural force.

44 Creator of the earth and sky.

St. Ambrose, 340–97. *Tr. Charles Bigg.*

Deus creator omnium
polique rector, vestiens
diem decoro lumine,
noctem soporis gratiâ.

Nearly a hundred hymns used to be attributed to St. Ambrose; critics first winnowed them to twelve, and now there are only four of which we can be certain. This one is unassailable because it is quoted by his disciple, Augustine, as having comforted him on the death of his mother, Monica. He says in his *Confessions* (Bk. ix):

> And this also I confess unto thy mercy, Father of the fatherless, that I bathed, and was the same as before I bathed; for the bitterness of sorrow could not pass out of my heart. Then I slept, and woke up again, and found my grief not a little softened; and, as I was alone in my bed, I remembered those true verses of thine Ambrose: for thou art *Deus creator omnium*. . . .

The hymn has been always in very frequent use, especially in the Sarum and other English breviaries where it is appointed for Saturday Evensong from the Epiphany till Lent.

This fine translation was made for the *English Hymnal* by Dr. Charles Bigg (1840–1908), Regius Professor of Ecclesiastical History at Oxford from 1901 and Bampton Lecturer in 1886.

L.M.

MUSIC. PLAINSONG is an arrangement by J. H. Arnold of the melody, in the *Sarum Antiphonal*, proper to the hymn 'Deus creator omnium', in use at Evensong of Saturdays from the Octave of Epiphany until Lent.

BEATA NOBIS GAUDIA is from *Psalterium Chorale cum suis Antiphonis: Collectis: Precibus: Et hymnis*. Thus the title-page. The first page is headed: *In nomine domini Incipit psalterium chorale secundum ritum insignis ecclesiae Constantienae*. There is no date, but the book was probably printed at Strasbourg *c.* 1500 by J. Pryss. The present melody is set to the hymn 'Beata nobis gaudia'. This is a beautifully smooth tune, with a gently undulating outline, rising to a peak and sinking back to a reminiscence of the opening phrase. It produces a remarkable impression of confident tranquillity.

45 Glory to thee, my God, this night. *Bishop T. Ken*, 1637–1711.

'Awake, my soul' (25) did not get into the *Supplement* to the *New Version* till 1782; and the entry of Ken's Evening Hymn was delayed till the nineteenth century—some time after 1807, but Julian and Mearns were not able to trace the precise year. Of the two hymns the Archbishop of Armagh (whose wife, Mrs. Alexander, was herself one of our famous hymn-writers) wrote: 'No other hymns are so suitable to the homely pathos and majesty of the English liturgy.' Our version gives the first four verses and the doxology, out of the original which has eleven verses before the doxology: the remaining verses begin: (5) 'When in the night I sleepless lie'; (6) 'Dull sleep of sense me to deprive'; (7) 'But tho' sleep o'er my frailty reigns'; (8) 'The faster sleep the senses binds'; (9) 'O when shall I in endless day'; (10) 'O may my guardian while I sleep' (1695, 'You my blest guardian, whilst I sleep'); (11) 'May he celestial joys rehearse' (1695, 'Thought to thought with my soul converse').

The 1695 edition begins 'Glory' as above; but the 1709 version begins 'All praise to thee my God this night': it also reads 'beneath' (as here) instead of 'under' in 1695. The last couplet of ver. 3 is a cento: 1695 reads:

Teach me to die, that so I may
Triumphing rise at the last day.

Ken's sense of rhythm, here as in other places, failed him: 1709 reads:

To dye, that this vile body may
Rise glorious at the awful day.

In other respects the two versions agree in these verses, except that the doxology of 1695 has:

Praise him above y'Angelick Host.

The resemblance to Sir Thomas Browne's hymn, 58, will be noticed. Ken does seem to owe something to the Norwich physician. On the other hand, both are probably indebted to the Latin evening hymns, 'Te lucis ante terminum' and 'Salvator mundi, Domine'. But, after all, no hymns possess so little originality as evening hymns, and they are in general all very much alike. It is hardly necessary to add that during the time—now approaching two and a half centuries—when Ken's hymn has been known in part and loved by many millions, it has been divided, subdivided, and rearranged in a great variety of ways.

L.M.

MUSIC. TALLIS' CANON is from *The whole Psalter translated into English Metre, which contayneth an hundreth and fifty Psalmes*. This version of the Psalms bears neither date nor author's name, but is known to be the work of Matthew Parker, Archbishop of Canterbury, and was probably printed about 1561. It contains, at the end, nine tunes in four parts by Thomas Tallis. Of the first eight one is in each of the ecclesiastical modes, the present tune being the eighth, and referred to Psalm 67. The melody in the original is the same as at present, except that each line is repeated before the next is introduced. The four-line form appears in Ravenscroft's *Whole Book of Psalms* (1621). The alternative version (fa-burden) is from Ravenscroft. This is a perfect canon, in that the necessities of the form nowhere obtrude themselves, the tune being as clear and 'natural' as if these necessities did not exist. It is too well known to require further comment.

46 God, that madest earth and heaven.

(1) *Bishop Heber* (1827), and (2) *Archbishop Whately*,‡ (1855).

The original consisted of the 1st verse only and was first published in Heber's posthumous *Hymns written and adapted to the Weekly Church Service of the Year* (Murray, 1827). This was the collection for which Heber had failed to secure authorization in his lifetime (see 40): it contained 57 hymns by Heber, 12 by Milman, and 29 by others.

The 2nd verse by Richard Whately (1787–1863), Archbishop of Dublin, author of *Historic Doubts relative to Napoleon Buonaparte* (which ridiculed the attacks on the historicity of the Gospels), was first added in Darling's *Hymns for the use of the Church of England* (1855). It is based upon the Compline antiphon, 'Salva nos, Domine, vigilantes, custodi nos dormientes, ut vigilemus in Christo et requiescamus in pace'. Whately was considered a Broad Churchman in his day; but his original words seem now antiquated enough in their picture of the departed lying in their graves, to be awakened at the last trump. Therefore the concluding lines are altered in *Songs of Praise* from

When the last dread call shall wake us,
Do not thou our God forsake us,
But to reign in glory take us
With thee on high.

Trochaic 8 4. 8 4. 8 8. 8 4. Unique.

MUSIC. AR HYD Y NOS is an arrangement by R. Vaughan Williams of the Welsh traditional melody usually known in England as 'All through the night'. It appeared in the *English Hymnal* (1906).

The fa-burden was written by Dr. Ernest Bullock especially for the enlarged *Songs of Praise* (1931).

47 Holy Father, cheer our way. *R. H. Robinson*, 1842–92.

One of the few remaining four-verse hymns which stretch the doctrine of the Trinity to the utmost (e.g. 'Father of heaven, whose love profound', *E.H.* 387) and are rather characteristic of the 19th century, this hymn was contributed to the S.P.C.K. *Church Hymns* in 1871, by the Rev. Richard Hayes Robinson, and owes much of its popularity to the shortened last line, which lends itself to a certain type of tune. A new tune has now been adapted to the metre with the consent of the composer.

Trochaic, 7 7 7. 5.

MUSIC. TON-MÂN was composed by David Evans in 1912 for a hymn written by the Rev. E. Rees (Dyfed), the Archdruid. It appeared in *Cân a Moliant* (1917). The present version is the second half only of the original form, but it is in itself a completely satisfactory tune.

48 Now God be with us, for the night is falling.

Petrus Herbert (1566). *Tr. A.G.*

Die Nacht ist kommen, drin wir ruhen sollen;
Gott walt's zu frommen nach sein'm Wohlgefallen,
Dass wir uns legen, in sein'm Gleit und Segen,
Der Ruh zu pflegen.

There are too many evening hymns; but there are not enough hymns of any sort in the Sapphic metre (see 28) to carry all the fine tunes that have come to us in this form from Germany, from the old plainsong, and from the late plainsong of France: therefore this translation was made of the distinguished Petrus Herbert's admirable evening hymn, which was, in Catherine Winkworth's version (with the same opening words), already in Thring's collection and other books. In Sapphic verse the caesura in the midst of the first three lines is all-important, and tunes in this metre have to be sung as if the stanza consisted of seven lines, thus:

Now God be with us,
For the night is falling.

For this among other reasons, Miss Winkworth's versions are unsuitable, e.g. in ver. 2 she has:

Let evil thoughts and
Spirits flee before us

(if we mark the caesura by using two lines instead of the one) and lines like 'All day serve thee, in all that we are doing', in ver. 3, miss the metre altogether.

Schein (see below) introduced a new verse which is generally included as ver. 5, but is omitted in *Songs of Praise*. It is inferior in quality (the second line is, 'Als zu dir, O Herr, in dem Himmel droben'): it begins in Miss Winkworth's *Chorale Book*,

We have no refuge; none on earth to aid us,
Save thee, O Father, who thine own hast made us.

Sapphic, 11 11. 11 5.

MUSIC. DIE NACHT IST KOMMEN is from J. H. Schein's *Cantional* (1627), being an adaptation of a melody by P. Nigidius (1550), set to the Sapphic ode 'Ipse cum solus varios retracto' as follows:

This original form follows more closely the Sapphic rhythm, but possibly the present version is more satisfactory for congregational singing. It is also found in virtually the above form in the Bohemian Brethren's *Kirchengeseng* (1566). In all the versions the tune still remains an unusual and attractive one.

CHRISTE SANCTORUM is from La Feillée's *Nouvelle Méthode . . . du Plain-Chant* (1782), the 5th issue (4th ed.) of the work first published in 1748; the present edition was augmented and 'revised by an ecclesiastic', and many others followed it. Though this tune appears in a manual of plainsong, it is itself a measured melody with few of the characteristics of plainsong. It is rather in the style of the 'church melodies' (see 28).

49 Now the day is over. *S. Baring-Gould*, 1834–1924.

Written in 1865, this was included in the 1868 Appendix to the original *Hymns Ancient and Modern*, and has since found its way into many books.

Trochaic, 6 5. 6 5.

MUSIC. EUDOXIA was written for this hymn by the Rev. S. Baring-Gould; it appeared in the Appendix (1868) to *Hymns Ancient and Modern*. Mr. Baring-Gould afterwards said that he wrote the hymn to a tune he wished to popularize for his Mission at Horbury Bridge in 1865. He fancied the melody EUDOXIA to be original, of his own, but afterwards discovered it was a reminiscence of a German air he had heard as a child. The German air in question remains unidentified.

50 O gladsome light, O grace. *3rd cent. or earlier. Tr. Y.H.*

Phōs hilaron hagias doxēs, 'The Candlelight Hymn', is probably the oldest in existence (excluding the Canticles and passages like the *Ter Sanctus*); and it is still in the service books of the Greek Church as an evening hymn. It is quoted by St. Basil, who died in 379, as of unknown authorship and date; and we know that in the second century hymns were sung at cock-crow and lamp-lighting. Its very simple words have proved a difficulty to many translators. The most familiar has been Keble's:

Hail, gladdening Light, of his pure glory poured,
Who is the immortal Father, heavenly, blest,
Holiest of Holies, Jesus Christ, our Lord!
Now we are come to the sun's hour of rest.

This is not only more an anthem than a hymn (and, with Stainer's tune, unsuitable at that), but, as H. C. Beeching says (doubtless expressing the view also of his parishioner, Robert Bridges): 'It misses the directness which is so great a charm of the Greek; and I am not sure that the cumbrous relative sentence in the second line, and the restless interpolation of "Holiest of Holies" in the third, does not obscure to the ordinary reader the fact, which should be absolutely luminous, that the hymn is addressed to Christ.' Keble's lines first appeared in 1834, and Beeching's criticism is from his introduction to Methuen's edition of *Lyra Apostolica*.

Doubtless such considerations as these, and the desire to provide worthy words for foreign tunes requiring the double rhymes that are less usual in English, led Robert Bridges to make the free translation which was first popularized by the *English Hymnal* (1906). Bridges had written 'O gladsome light' for the congregation at Yattendon, where he lived, superintending the music, with Beeching as Rector; and he published it in his *Yattendon Hymnal* (1895–9). At his own request, all Bridges' hymns are headed by the initials of the collection, Y.H.

Iambic, 6 6 7. 6 6 7.

MUSIC. NUNC DIMITTIS is from the *Genevan Psalter* of 1549, for which

L. Bourgeois composed the music, or adapted it from existing sources. It is there set to the version of the 'Nunc dimittis'—'Or laisses, Créateur, En paix ton serviteur'. The present harmonization is mainly from Goudimel's setting of the Psalter. These famous arrangements began with the *Premier livre contenant huite pseaumes de David, &c.* (Paris, 1551), which was followed by other similar volumes containing various psalms. The first complete editions appeared in 1565: *Les Pseaumes mis en rime françoise.... Mis en musique à quatre parties, &c.* (Lyons or Geneva, 1565) and *Les cent cinquante Pseaumes de David, &c.* (Le Roy and Ballard, Paris, 1565). The most important subsequent editions were Pierre de Saint-André's in 1580, the Delft edition of 1602, and a German edition at Zürich in 1641. A reprint of the 1580 edition was published in *Les Maîtres Musiciens* (Paris, 1895–7). The present tune is an excellent one, with a very agreeably varied rhythm.

51 O Trinity of blessèd light.

St. Ambrose, 340–97. *Tr. J. M. Neale.*

O lux beata Trinitas,
et principalis unitas;
jam sol recedit igneus:
infunde lumen cordibus.

These early Latin hymns possess many fine qualities, simplicity, terseness, directness, singableness; but one cannot claim them for poetry, which had already, in the decay of Graeco-Roman culture, frozen into rhetoric. It seems indeed as if poetry was purposely shunned in the encircling puritanism of the age that produced Ambrose and his successors. This hymn cannot be ascribed to him with the certainty of 44; nor, on the other hand, is it among the outlying examples included in the ninety-two given to him by Daniel (who included one about the saint himself); but it is among the twelve which the Benedictine editors accept, and is probably by him, though the earliest reference to it seems to be by Hincmar of Reims, A.D. 857. The almost universal use of *O lux beata* was at Evensong on Saturday, as in the Sarum, York, Paris, and older Roman breviaries: it was altered in the Roman Breviary of 1632, where it begins *Jam sol recedit igneus.*

The original, which consists of only two stanzas with a doxology, as here, was translated by Neale for the *Hymnal Noted* (1852), as we give it, and is a fine example of exact rendering.

L.M.

MUSIC. PLAINSONG is a melody from the *Sarum Antiphonal*, arranged for *Songs of Praise* by J. H. Arnold; it was proper to the hymn 'Conditor alme siderum' at Vespers of Sundays in Advent.

ADESTO SANCTA TRINITAS is a 'church melody' of Chartres (see 28). It is one of those clearly founded on some popular tune, but the actual melody has not been identified.

52 Round me falls the night.

W. Romanis, 1824–99.

A good hymn by an accomplished writer who produced little, it is specially welcome for musical reasons. First appearing in the *Public School Hymn Book* of 1903, it was further popularized by the *English Hymnal* in 1906.

Trochaic, 5 5. 8 8. 5 5. Unique.

MUSIC. ARNSTADT (SEELENBRÄUTIGAM) is from the Darmstadt *Geistreiches Gesangbuch* (1698), where it is set to A. Drese's hymn 'Seelenbräutigam, Jesu Gottes Lamm'. Zahn holds that Drese composed the tune as well. The melody is altered in later German books, and both melody and rhythm vary in English books. The present form of the air is almost exactly that of the original. It is a tune of a pleasingly ingenuous tinge, very simply constructed on a single rhythmic unit, but avoiding monotony by the 'doubling' of this unit in the two middle lines.

53 Saviour, again to thy dear name we raise.

J. Ellerton, 1826–93.

The most popular of Ellerton's hymns, this has been a good deal altered in various books, sometimes with the author's consent. Its original form, written for a Cheshire festival in 1866, seems the best. Most collections shorten the original five verses to four. It seems to have been based on the practice of using the Blessing from the Communion Service at every evening occasion. In reducing the hymn to the usual number of four verses, the *English Hymnal* therefore omitted the lines which so much emphasize the liturgical 'word of peace', in order to make room for those which deal with the wider aspects of peace in Church and Nation, and as the work of the Spirit in the individual.

Iambic, 10 10. 10 10.

MUSIC. MAGDA was composed by R. Vaughan Williams especially for the original edition of *Songs of Praise* (1925). This is a broad, fluent tune, built throughout on the contrasted movement of the two halves of the 1st line. Noticeable is the variety of rhythm, and the expressive urgency obtained by the telescoping of the end of the 3rd line into the beginning of the 4th, a trait found in many of this composer's tunes.

54 Saviour, shed an evening blessing. *J. Edmeston*,‡ 1791–1867.

Edmeston, an architect who numbered the unforgettable Gilbert Scott among his pupils, wrote over 2,000 hymns, of which this and 'Lead us, heavenly Father, lead us', survive. The originals of the altered lines, as they were written in 1820, are: 'Saviour, breathe an evening blessing', the four lines (9–12) 'Though the night be dark and dreary, Darkness cannot hide from thee; Thou art he who, never weary, Watchest where thy people be', also (14) 'And our couch become our tomb', and (16) 'Clad in light and deathless bloom'.

It appeared first in Edmeston's *Sacred Lyrics* (1820), with the note: 'At night their short evening hymn, "Jesu mahaxaroo", "Jesus forgive us", stole through the camp. *Salt's Travels in Abyssinia.*' Edward Bickersteth included it in his *Christian Psalmody* (1833); and Bishop E. H. Bickersteth in *The Hymnal Companion* (1870), adding in 1876 an additional verse, 'Father, to thy holy keeping'.

Trochaic, 8 7. 8 7. D.

MUSIC. GWALIA appeared in the book known as the *Lock Hospital Collection*, edited by Martin Madan, 1769 (see p. xviii). There it is entitled 'Love Divine' and is set to the hymn 'Love Divine, all love excelling'. In the Rev. H. Parr's *Church of England Psalmody* it is included under the same name, and the editor notes that it is from 'a Welsh melody'.

It is therefore uncertain whether it was an original tune in 1769, or an adaptation from an older melody known in Wales (cf. MORIAH, 573, i, which seems to be another adaptation, with some changes, from the same original).

The present form of the melody is, with very slight exceptions, the same as that in Madan's book, and is harmonized by David Evans. The characteristic principle, or germ of the tune, is the second bar; there are only three actual lines of melody in this six-line tune, and the proportions are preserved by the repetition of the 3rd between the recurring 1st and 2nd lines. In a long hymn such a scheme might result in a tiresome repetitiveness, but as there are here two verses only, this effect is not produced, and the tune obtains its full value.

Prolific Hymnists

Many poets have written too much, and, like Coleridge, have seemed incapable of self-criticism; but the swollen output of some hymnists suggests a lack of reverence for the art of divine singing. For a good hymn is a real poem. The worst offender seems to have been Mrs. Van Alstyne, 'Fanny Crosby', the brave blind lady who wrote the once popular 'Safe in the arms of Jesus', and who was salaried by a New York firm to produce three hymns a week all the year round; she went on at the business till her death at the age of 84, and is said to have produced for two firms alone 5,059 hymns; she used 216 pen-names as well as her maiden and married names, and her known *œuvre* is about 8,000 hymns, besides innumerable sentimental songs. Charles Wesley comes next with his 6,500 hymns, drawn from him by the exigencies of a vast evangelism; his masterpieces would have been more if he had had more of the craftsman's conscience, and Methodism would have been saved from a sea of hymnic monotony. Isaac Watts's more modest 600 was justified by the circumstances in which he lived, but he also necessarily wrote much that was without distinction: indeed 'it was discovered', as a real admirer acknowledges, 'that a considerable percentage of Watts' work was prosaic and mechanical, and sometimes in questionable taste'. In Germany, Count Zinzendorf, the Moravian leader, wrote over 2,000 hymns. James Edmeston wrote 2,000, of which survive the two mentioned above; two survive also of the 767 that Thomas Kelly wrote (132, 175); but most hymn-writers of distinction in the Victorian era produced much less and wrought more carefully at what they made—John Ellerton is perhaps a little over the average with 87.

A few more instances may be of interest. Richard Baxter published 167 hymns, of which 4 are in *Songs of Praise*; the tale of James Montgomery is given as 355, of which we have 8; Bishop Heber wrote 57, all of which were still in various books of common use when Dr. Julian's 1st edition of his *Dictionary of Hymnology* appeared in 1891; 8 are in our book. Addison wrote only 5 hymns, of which 4 are in our book. The author of *Tom Brown's Schooldays* wrote only one, 'O God of truth', 597.

With poems as with pictures, time pronounces the final verdict; but in hymnody it is often only one or two works—or one alone—that finally emerges in the struggle for existence. Charlotte Elliott's 150 or more provide only 2 in our collection; Bishop Christopher Wordsworth has a larger proportion with 4 out of 120; Monsell has 3 per cent., for he wrote nearly 300. Of the prolific Germans (to whom Luther had set the good example of an *œuvre* of 37) Benjamin Schmolk, the 17th-century pastor who comes next to Zinzendorf with 900, provides us with nothing; nor does the third, the poet-pastor, Johann Rist, who wrote 680. Of Paulus Gerhardt, who, like Rist, lived through the Thirty Years War (1618–48), on the other hand, we have 5 out of his more modest 120 or thereabouts—though some ran to 100 and even 120 lines each.

Germany is calculated to have produced even more hymns than Great Britain, though they are far more limited in their range. Dr. Philip Schaff of New York reckoned half a century ago that there must be 100,000. As far back as 1786 a catalogue of the first lines of 72,733, now in the library of Halberstadt, was made by Dean Georg Ludwig von Hardenberg. In early days Luther had said: 'He that gave to the people in their own tongue the Bible and the Catechism gave them also the hymn-book; as one has well said, so that God could speak directly to them in his word and they might in their songs directly answer him.' Their effect was immense: Luther relates how a beggar at his door told him that 'a shout of deliverance was sounding' far away on the Baltic; and the priests complained that the people were singing themselves into heresy.

There are some curiosities too: Beddome, an English Baptist, is perhaps completely forgotten in England, in spite of his 830 hymns, though he may be still remembered in America, where he was more popular; but the most remarkable is Joseph Proud, who made 300 original hymns in three months for the Swedenborgians in 1790, and who only appears in this Handbook (under 282) as a warning.

55 Sun of my soul, thou Saviour dear. *J. Keble*, 1792–1866.

The immense vogue of the *Christian Year*, which was published anonymously in 1827, and had reached its 43rd edition, with 108,000 copies sold, in 25 years, and continued thereafter with still further increase, led to nearly a hundred poems and centos being used as hymns in various books. The book had many faults. Wordsworth proposed to the author that they should 'go over the work together with a view to correcting the English'; but its simple sincerity won all hearts at the time, and its love of Nature made a new era in religion as well as hymnody. There are 11 in *Hymns Ancient and Modern*, 10 in the *English Hymnal*, 8 in the *Hymnary*, and 5 in *Songs of Praise*. Of these 'Sun of my soul' is the most widely loved. The poem describes a benighted traveller, pushing on after the sun has set; and before what has become the famous opening of the hymn, the two following stanzas occur:

> 'Tis gone, that bright and orbèd blaze,
> Fast fading from our wistful gaze;
> Yon mantling cloud has hid from sight
> The last faint pulse of quivering light.
>
> In darkness and in weariness
> The traveller on his way must press,
> No gleam to watch on tree or tower,
> Whiling away the lonesome hour.

L.M.

MUSIC. BIRLING was discovered by Geoffrey Shaw in an early 19th-century manuscript collection of hymn-tunes, which was made by the grandfather of Mr. Harris, Town Clerk of Nottingham. The tune has no composer's name attached, but may, from internal evidence, be ascribed to the late 18th or early 19th century. The melody is here given exactly as it appears in the manuscript, and is remarkable for the wide skips, in one case a tenth, which give it a strong individuality and beauty of its own. The present arrangement, by Geoffrey Shaw, appeared in the *Public School Hymn Book* (1919).

56 The day thou gavest, Lord, is ended. *J. Ellerton*, 1826–93.

Written in 1870 for *A Liturgy for Missionary Meetings* and revised for *Church Hymns* (1871), these lines of a writer who was, as Julian says, 'elevated in tone, devotional in spirit, and elegant in diction', must have been one of the causes which woke the popular insularity to the realization of the world. Many must have been set thinking about oversea missions, and many also about the imperial idea that became so great a force before the end of the century. Most appropriately it was chosen by Queen Victoria as one of the hymns for the Diamond Jubilee, and was sung on that day, with its constraining last verse, in tens of thousands of churches throughout the world.

Iambic, 9 8. 9 8.

MUSIC. LES COMMANDEMENS DE DIEU was composed or adapted by L. Bourgeois, and set in the *Genevan Psalter* (1543) to the metrical version of the Ten Commandments by Clément Marot. The present is the original form, and again shows the variation of rhythm characteristic of these tunes. The melody is balanced by the similarity of the 2nd and 4th lines, and the inversion in the 3rd line of the movement of the 1st. It is a good tune, but must not be sung too fast.

JOLDWYNDS was composed by Sir Charles Stanford for this hymn, and appeared in the revised edition of *Hymns Ancient and Modern* (1904). It is a well-knit tune with an individual rhythm and cadence.

57 The duteous day now closeth.

Y.H. (*Robert Bridges*), *based on* '*Nun ruhen alle Wälder*'.
P. Gerhardt, 1607–76.

Only the first two verses of this are free translations of Gerhardt's hymn, which (in nine stanzas) appeared in Crüger's *Praxis Pietatis Melica* (3rd ed., 1648); the last two travel beyond his range, and are a fine example of Robert Bridges's own work. 'Nun ruhen' was not appreciated in Germany till the 19th century: 'töricht und dummes Zeug', 'foolish and stupid stuff', was the opinion of Frederick the Great in the age of 'flat rationalism'. But it was a special favourite of Schiller, and has been a household word in Germany for a hundred years. Bridges wrote this version for the *Yattendon Hymnal* (1899), in order to bring in the tune.

Iambic, 7 7 6. 7 7 8. Unique.

MUSIC. INNSBRUCK has been commonly attributed to Heinrich Isaak. So far as is known it first appeared in print in *Ein ausszug guter alter ün newer Teutscher liedlein* (Nürnberg, 1539). It is there set to the song 'Innsbruck ich muss dich lassen' in the following form:

Later the melody was adapted to the hymn 'O Welt ich muss dich lassen', and later still to Gerhardt's hymn 'Nun ruhen alle Wälder'. The melody appears in a large variety of forms in German collections from the above date to the present day. The arrangement here is that adopted by Bach in his *St. Matthew Passion* and elsewhere. The original tune was possibly a folk melody, and only arranged by Isaak.

58 The night is come like to the day.

Sir Thomas Browne (*cento*),† 1605–82.

This poem is printed in the *Religio Medici*, edition of 1643; and Ken seems to owe much in his Evening Hymn to it. Browne is speaking (ii. 12) of sleep:

'We term sleep a death; and yet it is waking that kills us. . . . Sleep is that death by which we may be literally said to die daily; a death which Adam died before his mortality; a death whereby we live a middle and moderating point between life and death. In fine, so like death, I dare not trust it without my prayers, and an half adieu unto the world, and take my farewell in a colloquy with God: *The night is come. . . .*' He then continues: 'This is the dormative I take to bedward; I need no other *laudanum* than this to make me sleep; after which I close mine eyes in security, content to take my leave of the sun, and sleep unto the resurrection.'

The original is too irregular for singing; but by arranging iambic and trochaic lines in quatrains a new form is here provided which offers a fresh musical oportunity—an ordinary iambic quatrain in Long Measure, followed by a quatrain of trochaic metre. In the original after the first four come two regular lines which are here omitted:

> Keep still in my horizon; for to me
> The sun makes not the day, but thee.

After 'sentry keep' these lines are omitted:

> Guard me 'gainst those watchful foes
> Whose eyes are open while mine close.
> Let no dreams my head infest
> But such as Jacob's temples blest.

And after 'what it is to die', we omit eight more lines, beginning:

And as gently lay my head
On my grave as now my bed.

With the omission of these lines regularity can be obtained and the hymn is less like that of Ken, especially as it is in the shortened form of 45. The longer version (*English Hymnal*, 267) shows further imitation on Ken's part.

Iambic and Trochaic, 8 8. 8 8. 7 7. 7 7. Unique.

MUSIC. OAKLEY was composed by R. Vaughan Williams especially for the original edition of *Songs of Praise* (1925); it is a good strong tune in the folk-song manner.

PART II

THE CHURCH'S YEAR

WE have adopted this heading in *Songs of Praise*, because to some minds the phrase 'The Christian Year' suggests that the year cannot be otherwise observed in a Christian manner. 'One man', says St. Paul, 'esteemeth one day above another: another esteemeth every day alike. Let each man be fully assured in his own mind.' By the phrase 'the Church's Year' we recognize this complete freedom from all such obligations; yet in the blessed company of all faithful people', as the Church is so truly defined in the Prayer Book, there are vast multitudes who find help in observing the traditional anniversaries or commemorations, and few indeed who ignore the chief festivals altogether.

ADVENT

59 Ah! think not, 'The Lord delayeth'. *P. Dearmer.*

Written to carry the Norwegian tune which the musical editors were anxious to include in *Songs of Praise*. The reference in the first stanza is to Matthew 24:48, 18:20, and 15:17; in the second, to the 13th chapter both of St. Matthew and of St. Luke; in the third, to Acts 1:7.

Trochaic, 8 8 7. D.

MUSIC. ST. OLAF'S SEQUENCE is a Norwegian ecclesiastical melody from *Koralbok for den Norske Kirke* (1926), arranged by R. Vaughan Williams for *Songs of Praise* (1931). It is a fine Aeolian tune of great dignity and expressiveness, very characteristic of its nationality in the phrases of the 4th and 5th lines, and in the general contour of the long melodic line.

60 Christ is the world's true Light. *G. W. Briggs.*

Written for the Bach tune. Like other new Advent hymns, this substitutes for the crude eschatology of older collections thoughts more in accord both with the actual teaching of Christ and the most Christian aspirations of the present day.

Iambic, 6 7. 6 7. 6 6. 6 6.

MUSIC. RINKART (KOMMT SEELEN), by J. S. Bach, comes from G. C. Schemelli's *Musicalisches Gesangbuch* (1736), where it is set to the hymn 'Kommt, Seelen, dieser Tag muss heilig sein besungen'. This is a typical 'Bach' tune, fluent, natural, and beautifully proportioned; its structure will repay more elaborate analysis than can here be given. The compass is rather wide, but the expressive flow of the tune makes it most attractive to sing.

61 Hark! a herald voice is calling. *6th cent. S.P.V.*

Vox clara ecce intonat
obscura quaeque increpat;
pellantur eminus somnia,
ab aethere Christus promicat.

No longer ascribed to St. Ambrose, this hymn is based on Romans 13 : 11 (Epistle for Advent 1) and Luke 21 : 25 (Gospel for Advent 2). It was the Lauds hymn during Advent in the Sarum, York, Aberdeen, and other books; in the modern Roman use it has been altered to 'En clara vox redarguit'. It may be interesting to take this hymn as an example of the many different ways of translators: here are some first lines:

Vox clara

In music, lo, yon orb appears to rise (*Hymnarium Angl.*, 1844).
Lo! what a thrilling voice sounds forth (J. D. Chambers).
Hark, the clear voice, whose thrilling tone (W. J. Blew).
Hark! what a thrilling voice invades (Chambers, 1857).
Hark! a clear-toned voice, as thunder (J. W. Hewitt).
Give ear! the voice rings clear and true (J. Keble, 1869).
Hark to the voice whose thrilling tone (*Hymner*, 1882).
Clear rings a voice; it chides a world (Lord Braye).

En clara

Hark, a joyful voice is thrilling (J. H. Newman).
Hark, an awful voice is sounding (E. Caswall, 1849).
Hark, a gladsome voice is thrilling (W. J. Blew).
Hark to the voice that loudly cries (J. A. Johnston).
Hark, a thrilling voice is sounding (Murray's *Hymnal*, 1852).
Voice of mercy, voice of terror (B. H. Kennedy).
Hark, a trumpet voice of warning (R. C. Singleton).
Hark, the Baptist's voice is sounding (*Hymnary*, 1872).

Perhaps these are enough to give food for reflection; but Julian records twelve more, beginning with a Primer of 1706 ('A heavenly voice, an early Ray'), and including Bishop Mant's 'Hark, a voice of warning, hark' (1837), and a version of 1874 that rides cheerfully in with 'Hark, hark, the voice of chanticleer'. When one remembers that the most familiar version, that of Caswall, is altered more or less in nearly all books (including even the *English Hymnal*, which alters one line only, the first, to 'Hark! a herald voice is calling'), one gets an idea of the enormous number of variants in the translation of most Latin hymns. We have here recast the hymn once more, in the hope of bringing out that which is nearest the truth for thoughtful people in the present century.

Trochaic, 87.87, and therefore unlike the L.M. of the Latin in having trochaic (sometimes, though not correctly, called 'feminine') endings to the 1st and 3rd lines, and thus framing a different type of melody.

MUSIC. MERTON, by W. H. Monk, appeared first in the *Parish Choir* (1850), without name of composer. It is quite well built on the familiar analogy of alternate lines (with inversion of the movement in the 3rd), but its individual phrases are not markedly original.

62 Hark the glad sound! the Saviour comes.

P. Doddridge, 1702–51.

Lord Selborne justly wrote of this classic: 'A more sweet, vigorous, and perfect composition is not to be found even in the whole body of ancient hymns.' This was in 1866, when the qualities of ancient hymns were still perhaps over-estimated; and to us, weary with the sentimental weakness of Victorian hymns, it is the manly strength and hopefulness of Doddridge's poem that most appeals. Its look of finished perfection is partly due to the omission of three inferior verses. The original 4th verse was taken almost bodily from Pope's 'Messiah'; and the 6th is:

The silver trumpets publish loud
The Jub'lee of the Lord
Our debts are all remitted now
Our heritage restored.

This is from the original manuscript, which is dated 'Dec. 28, 1735'. It appeared first in Scotland, 1745, where it is called 'The 39th Paraphrase'; it was altered, and altered again, but not improved (by W. Cameron) when the *Tunes and Paraphrases* of 1781 was published. In England it did not appear in print till Job Orton's edition of the posthumous *Hymns, &c.* of Doddridge was published in 1755. It next appeared in Conyer's Hymnal of 1774, and gradually entered into universal use, so that it has been for long the best known of Doddridge's hymns, and no book would now be complete without it.

C.M.

MUSIC. BRISTOL is set in *Ravenscroft's Psalter* (1621) to Psalms 16 and 64; it is there called 'Bristol Tune', and classified among the English tunes. The alternative version (fa-burden) is by Ravenscroft himself in the above work. This is one of the simpler psalm-tunes, being composed of phrases of standard shape and character. It is a good tune and a capital foil to more imposing melodies.

63 High o'er the lonely hills. *Jan Struther.*

The music editors originally marked 'Hark! 'tis the watchman's cry' for the sake of Mr. Ingham's tune; but after consultation with the editors of the Scottish *Church Hymnary* it was agreed that the words were not worth preserving (they are anonymous, and appeared in a periodical, *The Revival*, in 1859, whence they were taken into the *Hymnal Companion*, 1876, and other books); and therefore Jan Struther was asked to write new Advent words. The result was this beautiful lyric, which gives a fresh charm to the tune by its use of triple rhymes.

Dactylic, 6 4. 6 4. 6 6 6. 4. Unique.

MUSIC. WATCHMAN, by T. H. Ingham, appeared in *Songs of Praise* (1931); its mood of serene beauty is perfectly expressed in the words.

64 Hills of the North, rejoice. *Charles E. Oakley*, 1832–65.

This one relic of a short and brilliant career of 33 years has gradually made its way by sheer merit. It appeared in Bishop T. Valpy French's long-forgotten *Hymns Adapted to the Christian Seasons*, and thence passed into the *Hymnal Companion* in 1870. From there it has found its way into an increasing number of collections. A stirring missionary hymn, it is equally suitable for Advent and the Epiphany, and for general use.

Iambic, 6 6. 6 6. 8 8.

MUSIC. LITTLE CORNARD was composed by Martin Shaw for this hymn; it appeared in *Additional Tunes and settings in use at St. Mary's, Primrose Hill* (1915). It is a fine, bold tune, the change of rhythm in the last two lines adding a vigorous impulse to the whole, in keeping with the spirit of the words.

65 Lo! he comes with clouds descending.

C. Wesley (1758), *and others.*

Few hymns are more universal in Anglo-Saxon use than this—mainly because it pictures (with a poetic force that makes it still possible to imaginative minds) the eschatology which had once so deep a hold on Christendom; but hardly less for the glorious tune, 'Helmsley'. Yet no hymn has been more altered and none is so intolerable in its original form. Here it is (without his 3rd verse), as it was written by John Cennick, sung in the Moravian Chapel at Dublin, 20 April 1750, and printed in the 5th edition of Cennick's *Collection of Sacred Hymns* (1752):

Lo! he cometh, countless trumpets
  Blow before his bloody sign!
'Midst ten thousand saints and angels,
  See the Crucified shine.
    Allelujah!
  Welcome, welcome bleeding Lamb!

Now his merits by the harpers,
  Thro' the eternal deeps resounds!
Now resplendent shine his nail-prints,
  Every eye shall see his wounds!
    They who pierced him,
  Shall at his appearing wail.

All who love him view his glory,
  Shining in his bruised Face:
His dear Person on the rainbow,
  Now his people's heads shall raise:
    Happy mourners!
  Now on clouds he comes! he comes!

Now redemption, long expected,
  See, in solemn pomp appear:
All his people, once despised,
  Now shall meet him in the air:
    Allelujah!
  Now the promised kingdom's come!

View him smiling, now determined
  Every evil to destroy!
All the nations now shall sing him
  Songs of everlasting joy!
    O come quickly!
  Allelujah! come Lord, come!

We can see from this why 19th-century intelligence revolted against 18th-century religion, and why we have not yet recovered from the resulting agnosticism. However, though the clamorous outburst attracted the notice of Charles Wesley, his literary sense obliged him to alter it into the form that is now, with various changes, familiar (in his tract, *Hymns of Intercession for All Mankind*, 1758). M. Madan, in his *Collection of Psalms and Hymns* (1760), made a cento of the two versions, which, with continual alterations, passed from one book to another, and was the form most generally known. Our version is that of Charles Wesley (passing over Madan), with the following words altered: ver. 2, '*dreadful* majesty';

'*the* true Messiah'. Ver. 3, '*The* dear tokens'; '*endless* exultation'; '*ransomed* worshippers'; '*gaze we on those glorious* scars'. Ver. 4,

JAH, JEHOVAH.
Everlasting God, come down.

Wesley's text, with Cennick's last stanza, was translated into Latin by C. B. Pearson, 'Nube vectus en descendit' in his *Latin Translations of English Hymns* (1862).

Trochaic, 8 7. 8 7. 4 7, giving alternate double rhymes. Wesley avoids Cennick's unrhymed last lines.

MUSIC. HELMSLEY is attributed to Thomas Olivers, who is said to have adapted it from a tune he had heard whistled in the street. In Wesley's *Select Hymns* (2nd ed., 1765) it appears in the following form:

In Martin Madan's *Collection* (1769) it is found in virtually the same form as the present. The descant has been written by R. Vaughan Williams especially for the enlarged *Songs of Praise* (1931).

On the whole the present version is certainly an improvement on the original, as given above, especially in the third bar and the second 'alleluya'. It is a splendid tune, too well known to need any comment.

66 O come, O come, Emmanuel! *18th cent. Tr. T. A. Lacey.*

Veni, veni, Emmanuel
captivum solve Israel,
qui gemit in exilio,
privatus Dei Filio.
  Gaude, gaude; Emmanuel
  nascetur pro te, Israel.

Because of the tune this is popular with many, including children, who have very little idea what it all means; and doubtless also the poetic suggestiveness of Dr. Lacey's noble translation conveys images to simple minds. It is full of references to Biblical and Medieval ideas; and more immediately it comes from the seven Greater Antiphons, which were sung at Evensong in Advent after 16 Dec.—a custom of which there is a relic in the Calendar of the Book of Common Prayer, which inserts opposite 16 Dec. the cryptic words 'O Sapientia'. At the Magnificat the seven antiphons (dating from before the 9th century) were then sung each day until Christmas Eve. Their opening words are:

O Sapientia, quae ex ore altissimi.
O Adonay et dux domus Israel.
O Radix Jesse qui stas in signum populorum.
O Clavis David et sceptrum domus Israel.
O Oriens, splendor lucis aeternae.
O Rex gentium et desideratus.
O Emanuel, rex et legifer.

Somewhere about the 13th century, an unknown author wove five of these 'Great Os' into a metrical hymn, changing their order and adding the refrain. Neale translated this and published it in his *Mediaeval Hymns* (1851), as 'Draw nigh, draw nigh, Emmanuel'. He altered his text two years later in the *Hymnal Noted*, and it soon reached many other books (with many variations), including the Wesleyan *Hymn Book* of 1875 and the Presbyterian *Church Hymnary* of to-day. Neale's text was never quite satisfactory as it stood; and therefore Lacey re-translated it for the *English Hymnal* (1906).

The reader can trace many of the references with a Bible concordance. 'Adonai' is the Hebrew for 'lord', and was substituted, in reading aloud, for 'Yahve' or 'Jahweh', which was too sacred to be pronounced: hence the vowels of 'Adonai' came to be added in Hebrew Bibles to the consonants of 'Jahweh'; then, at the time of the Reformation (1520), the consonants of 'Jahve' were conflated with the vowels of 'Adonai'; and the name 'Jahova' or 'Jehovah' was the result.

The first verse of the original antiphons is:

O Sapientia, quae ex ore altissimi prodisti attingens a fine usque ad finem, fortiter suaviterque disponens omnia: veni ad docendum nos viam prudentiae.

The original of our verse 1 is:

O Emmanuel, rex et legifer noster, expectatio gentium et desideratus earum, veni ad salvandum nos, Domine Deus noster.

The older way of keeping Advent, not in meditation upon death, judgement, hell, and heaven, but as a joyful looking forward, with an almost festive character will be noticed in these antiphons, which are probably non-Roman in origin, though they were adopted in Rome before the 9th century.

Iambic 8 8. 8 8. 8 8.

MUSIC. VENI EMMANUEL is found in the *Hymnal Noted* (Part II, 1856), where the melody is said to be 'From a French Missal in the National Library, Lisbon'. These Missals have all been examined by the Rev. W. Hilton of the English College, Lisbon, but this melody is not to be found in them. In all probability it is not a genuine medieval melody, but has been made up of a number of plainsong phrases, most of these being found in settings of the Kyrie. The tune in its present form cannot be traced to an earlier source than the *Hymnal Noted*, and the likelihood is therefore that the adaptation was made by Thomas Helmore for that book to suit Dr. Neale's translation. In any case it is an excellent tune, with a noble sweep of outline. It is too famous to require illustration, but it may be pointed out that, in spite of its length, it is formed of only three phrases.

67 On Jordan's bank the Baptist's cry.

C. Coffin, 1676–1749. *S.P.V.*

Jordanis oras praevia
Vox ecce Baptistae quatit:
Praeconis ad grandes sonos
Ignavus abscedat sopor.

Another example of cheerful songs of praise for Advent, this was first published by Charles Coffin in his *Hymni Sacri* of 1736, and in the

Paris Breviary of the same year, as the Lauds hymn for Sundays and festivals in Advent. It was therefore 40 years after Watts had written his first hymns, and 30 years after he had published his *Horae Syricae* (1706) and *Hymns and Spiritual Songs* (1707). John Chandler (cf. 35, 68), thinking it was ancient, translated it for his *Hymns of the Primitive Church*, in 1837. From thence it passed, with many alterations, into a large number of collections. The *Songs of Praise* version ('S.P.V.') retains the familiar phrases of Chandler (which will be found in full in *E.H.* 9); but gives a new translation of the 4th verse, which in Chandler (characteristically of the age) ignores the reference to beauty in the original, and hides up the thought of healing the sick, besides beginning with the unpleasant line—

Stretch forth thine hand, to heal our sore.

The Latin of this verse is:

Aegris salutarum manum
Extende; prostatos leva:
Ostende vultum, jam suus
Mundo reflorescit decor.

L.M.

MUSIC. AUCTORITATE SAECULI is a 'church melody' from Angers (cf. 28). This is probably founded on a popular tune; it is one of the finest of these church melodies.

68 The advent of our God. *C. Coffin*, 1676–1749. *Pr. S.P.*

Instantis adventum Dei
Poscamus ardenti prece,
Festisque munus inclitum
Praeoccupemus canticis.

Another of Coffin's hymns taken from the Paris Breviary of 1736 by Chandler, and translated in his *Hymns of the Primitive Church* (1837). Few compilers have found Chandler's version acceptable, and in all the best-known books it is much altered. As the hymn is popular in church circles (the more so since it was set in the *English Hymnal* to the delightful 'St. Thomas', which has come to have Advent associations for this reason with the younger generation) the editor of *Songs of Praise* has retained it; but as we are not bound to re-echo the theology of Paris in the reign of Louis XIV, he has modernized it rather freely, and we thus have here a paraphrase rather than a translation of Coffin.

S.M.

MUSIC. ST. THOMAS is found in Aaron Williams's *New Universal Psalmodist* (1770), under the name 'St. Thomas's', set to Psalm 48, 'Great is the Lord our God'. This was the 5th edition of his work, first published as *The Universal Psalmodist* in 1763. In the original the 2nd line begins

and the 3rd ends

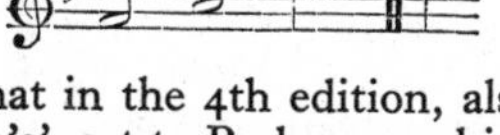

It should be noted that in the 4th edition, also dated 1770, there is a tune called 'St. Thomas's', set to Psalm 39, which bears no resemblance to the present one.

69 With Jesus for hero, for teacher and friend. *N.B.L.*

This was first provided by the editor for children, to be sung to 'Cradle Song' (353), with a note to the effect that 'pagans' includes those at home who have been led to misunderstand Christ. Like so many children's hymns, it came to be sung by adults; and the metre gives a fourth opportunity for a fine type of tune which has few occasions for use in hymnody.

Anapaestic, 11 11. 11 11.

MUSIC. MALDWYN is a Welsh hymn melody from David Evans's great collection of standard tunes *Moliant Cenedl Dinbych* (1920). It is an excellent, well-proportioned melody, though, in some respects, it seems to show traits of English rather than of Welsh folk-tunes.

CHRISTMAS DAY AND THE CHRISTMAS SEASON

70 A great and mighty wonder.

St. Germanus, 634–734. *Tr. J. M. Neale.*‡

This was first used in the *English Hymnal* to carry Praetorius's melody, by using the 3rd stanza as a refrain (omitting its first line, 'And we with them triumphant') . Neale published his translations in his *Hymns of the Eastern Church* (1862), mistakenly attributing the original to St. Anatolius. In the Greek service for Christmas Day in the *Menaea* it is rightly attributed to Germanus. Besides the omission of line 1 in ver. 3, alterations are made in *Songs of Praise* as follows: ver. 1, '*holy* cure', '*the Virgin bears the Infant With virgin honour pure*'; ver. 2, 'The Word *becomes Incarnate, And yet remains* on high', 'Cheru*bin*'; ver. 4, 'he comes to *ransom*'.

Iambic, 76. 76. 676. Also in 223.

MUSIC. ES IST EIN' ROS' ENTSPRUNGEN is a traditional carol-melody of the Rhineland, and is to be found in the *Alte Catholische Geistliche Kirchengesang* (Cologne, 1599). The present setting is from M. Praetorius's *Musae Sioniae* (1609). This is a most appealing tune, with a very interesting and attractive rhythm, which, though it may at first sight appear difficult, will be found quite easy and 'natural', once it has been understood. On analysis it will be found that much of the charm of the tune lies, inexplicably, in the curious little intercalary passage; it has rather the effect of an intimate 'aside'.

71 Angels, from the realms of glory. *J. Montgomery*, 1771–1854.

First appeared in the Sheffield *Iris* (of which Montgomery was the editor), 24 Dec. 1816; it was printed in the once famous 8th edition of Cotterill's *Selection*, 1819 (see p. xxiii). In the *Christian Psalmist* (1825) Montgomery altered 'flock' in ver. 2 and 'waiting' in ver. 4 to the present text. It was included among 'Three new carols' in the *Christmas Box* (1825), which was the first complete book of the Religious Tract Society. Later it appeared in the *Salisbury Hymn Book* (1857), *Church Hymns* (1871), Thring's Collection (1880), and now in many other books. In 1928 we used it in the *Oxford Book of Carols* for the French Carol tune

'Iris', with very similar words. This version (now in *Songs of Praise* also) omits Montgomery's last verse, which began:

> Sinners, wrung with true repentance,
> Doomed with guilt to endless pains,

and substitutes a 5th verse taken from one of the other carols in the *Christmas Box* of 1825.

Cotterill was incumbent of St. Paul's, Sheffield, and Montgomery was closely associated with him in the 8th edition of his *Selection*. There had been a growing opposition to the new custom in the Church of England of using hymn-books; and on the appearance of Cotterill's 8th edition, 1819, the storm burst in Sheffield. The Archbishop of York, Vernon Harcourt, prevented the case coming into court (the results of which might at that time have been disastrous) by suggesting before the trial a compromise: the book was withdrawn, and a new book, the 9th edition, was produced, dedicated to the Archbishop after each hymn had been submitted to him for approval. This won the battle for hymn-singing; but it was the withdrawn 8th edition that moulded hymn-books up to the middle of the century, and after: nearly nine-tenths of the hymns thus popularized by 1850 are still in common use in Britain and America. 'Christians, awake' (73) and 'Rock of ages' (636) are examples, and usually in whatever altered form was given them in the *Selection* of 1819. A comparison of this with the seven preceding editions shows that the honour is largely due to Montgomery, much the abler man, several of whose hymns are still famous, while Cotterill's are forgotten.

Montgomery was once asked by a Whitby solicitor, 'Which do you think of your poems will live?' and he answered, 'None, Sir, nothing, except perhaps a few of my hymns'. He was right: some of his hymns, among the hundred still found in various collections, will not die. John Ellerton, the author of 'The day thou gavest', who had every right to speak, described Montgomery as 'Our first hymnologist, the first Englishman who collected and criticized hymns, and who made people . . . understand something of what a hymn meant, and what it ought to be'.

Trochaic, 8 7. 8 7, with refrain in the same metre. Unique.

MUSIC. IRIS is the melody of an old French carol 'Les anges dans nos campagnes', harmonized by Martin Shaw. It appeared in the *Oxford Book of Carols* (1928), where it is set to 'Angels from the realms of glory'. Here, as in 'Grâce soit', appear the characteristic traits of French carols (*v.* hymn 3). The present tune is slightly more elaborate than the former, but the same spirit of innocent gaiety pervades it.

72 Behold the great Creator makes. *T. Pestel,‡ c.* 1584–*c.* 1659.

No poem of Thomas Pestel was used as a hymn until modern times, when Dr. Garrett Horder in 1894 included five stanzas of 'Come ravisht Souls with high delight' in his *Hymns Supplemental* (though they do not appear in *Worship Song*, 1905), and the *English Hymnal* printed the 5 stanzas of 72 from the Christmas hymn, 'Fairest of Morning Lights appear', omitting stanzas 1–4. Pestel's hymns are in *Sermons and Devotions old and new. Revived and publisht as an obligation of gratitude to all such of the nobility, gentry and clergy as retain the noble conscience of having ministered to the weak condition of the Author, now aged 73 . . . by Thomas*

Pestel, the meanest among his late Majesties Chaplains in Ordinary. The book was published in 1659. He had been turned out of his Rectory of Packington, Leicestershire, by the Westminster Assembly in 1646, and had evidently been helped to live by charitable sympathizers. His verses have a good 17th-century fragrance, and he deserves his niche in the *Dictionary of National Biography*.

C.M.

MUSIC. THIS ENDRIS NYGHT comes from a manuscript of the 15th century, where it is set to the old English carol beginning 'Thys endris nyght I saw a syght'. In the original manuscript (B.M. Royal Appendix 58) it is set for three voices, with melody in the tenor. The present arrangement, by R. Vaughan Williams, is from the *English Hymnal* (1906). In the *Oxford Book of Carols* (1928) may be found also a fa-burden by Martin Shaw. (Cf. 664.)

73 Christians, awake, salute the happy morn.

John Byrom,† 1692–1763.

We really owe this, with so many others, as has been said under 71, to Montgomery, through whom doubtless it was included in Cotterill's crucial 8th edition of his *Selection* (1819). Byrom's poem was published in his posthumous *Poems, &c.* (1773), and in his *Works* (1814). It consisted of 48 lines; but in Cotterill's *Selection* this was reduced to the form still retained in *Hymns Ancient and Modern*, 36 lines in 6 verses. The *English Hymnal* reduced this further to 5 verses or 30 lines, using some of those which had dropped out; but it was felt by many advisers for *Songs of Praise* that it was still too long, and thus it now stands at 4 verses of 24 lines. The original has in ver. 3 'rung' and 'sung', forms which still appear in Dickens but are now obsolete, and also 'Peace upon earth, and *mutual* goodwill', which is awkward to sing.

We owe the hymn to Byrom's daughter, Dolly. He asked her one day what she would like for a Christmas present, and she answered, 'Please write me a poem'. When she came down to breakfast on Christmas Day, 1749, she found on her plate a sheet, still preserved in Manchester, headed, 'Christmas Day. For Dolly'. Soon after, Wainwright wrote 'Yorkshire' for it, and the following Christmas the Byroms were awakened by the choir of Manchester Parish Church singing beneath their windows, 'Christians, awake'.

John Byrom was a remarkable man: extremely tall, he wore a peculiar slouched hat, under which peered a face at once benignant and inquisitive; he was the son of a linen-draper in Manchester, an M.A. of Trinity College, Cambridge, and the chief inventor of modern shorthand (his *Universal English Shorthand* was published in 1767). He was also the inventor of Tweedledum, in his lines:

Some say, compared to Bonancini,
That mynheer Handel's but a ninny;
Others aver that he to Handel
Is scarcely fit to hold a candle.
Strange all this difference should be
'Twixt Tweedledum and Tweedledee.

He taught shorthand to the Wesleys; and it was in shorthand that most of Charles Wesley's hymns were dashed down as they came into his mind.

When the Pretender marched into England in the '45, the Wesleys went quietly on, praying and preaching; but Byrom came out indiscreetly on the side of the Stuarts. He covered himself, however, by another famous epigram:

God bless the King—I mean the faith's defender;
God bless—no harm in blessing—the Pretender:
But who Pretender is, or who is King,
God bless us all! that's quite another thing.

He lived at first by his shorthand, was elected a Fellow of his College in 1714, an F.R.S. in 1724; and he succeeded to the family estates about the same time.

Iambic, 10 10. 10 10. 10 10.

MUSIC. YORKSHIRE (or STOCKPORT). In Byrom's note-book there is this entry: 'Christmas, 1750. The singing men and boys with Mr. Wainwright came here and sang "Christians, awake".' The tune is said to have been first sung in Stockport parish church on the day this entry was made, but it was not published till ten years later, in Ashworth's *Collection* (*c.* 1760). Subsequently it appeared in Wainwright's own *Collection of Psalm Tunes* (1766). This splendid tune deserves fully to have become, as it has, one of the most famous of English hymn-tunes. The prevalent movement of the melody is upward, expressing the festive spirit of the words, but there is sufficient downward motion, partially in the 4th and wholly in the 5th, to act as a counterpoise, and, by its position, to emphasize the joyous reascent of the final line. Thus both musically and emotionally the tune is completely satisfactory.

The alternative version (fa-burden), by Martin Shaw, appeared in *Two Christmas Carols, &c.* (1924).

74 Hark! the herald angels sing.

C. Wesley (1743), *G. Whitefield* (1753), *M. Madan* (1760), *and others.*

Perhaps the most popular English hymn in the world. Julian wrote in 1891 that four hymns stood at the head of all in the English language: 'Awake, my soul' (25), 'When I survey' (133), 'Rock of ages' (636), and this. It is interesting to note also that none of these have been commonly sung as they were first written. Of high literary merit, the 'Herald angels' disproves two common assertions—that hymns should of necessity be sung just as their authors left them, and that all composite efforts must result in mere 'patchwork'. Charles Wesley's fine original of 1743 will be found as 88 below: it may well be sung after Christmas, but woe to the church that sings it on Christmas Day! It is universalist in character, and Whitefield altered it in his *Collection* of 1753 partly doubtless because he was a Calvinist; but he gave it the familiar first line. So 'Hark! the herald angels sing' passed to Madan, who in his *Psalms and Hymns*, 1760, made further alterations, as did Conyers in 1774 and De Courcy in 1775. Then it was added in 1782 to *The Supplement* to 'Tate and Brady' and thus came to be bound up in many places with the Prayer Book. This version in *The Supplement* is that now everywhere used, but with one exception—for it had not even then quite emerged from revision—ver. 3 had ended with the line, 'Jesus our Immanuel here', and that line was improved by the omission of 'here': it appears in this final form in Kempthorne's

Select Portions (1810). The refrain which so much helped its popularity was not added till it appeared in *The Supplement*; but even then the tune, which seems to us an integral part of the Christmas Hymn, of course did not exist. The 1904 edition of *Hymns Ancient and Modern* altered the first line back to the original; but this is a conservative world, and the outcry in Church circles against the 'Welkin' was one of the causes of the failure of that book, its gallant attempt to improve the music of the familiar edition being another. The *English Hymnal* ended the dispute, which was still raging when that book was made, by including the 'Welkin' version as well, and exactly as Wesley wrote it. It is indeed too noble a thing to be lost.

Trochaic, 7777·7777, with refrain. The paean-like jubilant character of this and others, such as the Easter Hymn, owes much to their trochaic metre. Unique.

MUSIC. MENDELSSOHN is from Mendelssohn's *Festgesang for Male Chorus and Orchestra*, composed for and first performed at the festival held at Leipzig in June 1840 to celebrate the invention of printing. The tune is adapted from the chorus No. 2 of that work. When Dr. W. H. Cummings was organist at Waltham Abbey it struck him that this chorus would be a suitable setting for the hymn 'Hark! the herald angels sing'. He copied out the parts, and had the tune sung by the choir at Waltham Abbey. Finding that it was received with favour, he published the adaptation in 1856, and it soon found its way into many hymn-books, the first of these being R. R. Chope's *Congregational Hymn and Tune Book* (1857), where the tune is called ST. VINCENT. In some collections it is known also as BETHLEHEM.

It is curious that some years previous to the publication of Dr. Cumming's adaptation, Mendelssohn in writing to his English publishers on the subject of an English translation of the *Festgesang*, said: 'I must repeat the wish I already expressed in my letter to Mr. Bartholomew. I think there ought to be other words to No. 2. If the right ones are hit at, I am sure that piece will be liked very much by the singers and hearers, but it will *never* do to sacred words. There must be a national and merry subject found out, something to which the soldier-like and buxom motion of the piece has some relation, and the words must express something gay and popular as the music tries to do it.'

Improvement or Mutilation

Much has been said about the alteration of hymns, and we have already commented on it under 35. Wesley is the victim here in 74, as in 172. In the Preface to one of his books he said that many had done him and his brother the honour to reprint some of their hymns:

> Now they are perfectly welcome to do so, provided they print them just as they are. But I desire they would not attempt to mend them; for they really are not able. Therefore I must beg of them one of these two favours: either to let them stand just as they are, to take them for better or worse; or to add the true reading in the margin, or at the bottom of the page, that we may no longer be accountable either for the nonsense or for the doggrel of other men.

Yet Wesley himself had mended Herbert and Watts (e.g. 652, 598); and Toplady and Madan hashed Charles Wesley; others recooked Toplady; Heber made free with Jeremy Taylor; James Montgomery altered—and suffered alteration; Milman and Alford twisted the hymns of others in their turn; and Keble was a particularly bad offender.

The fact is that we cannot include some hymns at all unless they are altered; many a good hymn would have to be rejected because of an unsingable line, or some word that had changed its meaning or syllabic value, or some really impossible *gaffe*. The crime is to print an altered hymn without notifying honestly that it is not as the author wrote it; and Wesley was right there—though he did not practise what he preached. In *Songs of Praise* we carry on the method inaugurated by the *English Hymnal*, of printing the author's name in small italic at the top, so that, once the hymn is begun, he may be forgotten; and we make the condition of the text quite clear.

But we have always to remember that some of our most successful hymns are, like this one, the result of considerable alteration. Other famous examples are 65, 172, 207, 455, 557, 619.

It is the bad emendations that do harm. Compilers have sometimes shied at every bit of poetry in a hymn, and levelled it all down to the commonplace, as, e.g., in the case of Milton's 'golden-tressèd sun' (12), or Milman's 'wingèd squadrons' (137), or Charles Wesley's 'nearer waters' (542); though sometimes even a great hymn has to be pruned, as with Toplady's breaking eye-strings (636). But poetic emendation needs a sure instinct, and some caution also, to avoid such a slip as that of the Rev. William Burkitt in 1693, who misliking the worldly associations of

Thy gardens and thy gallant walks

in 395, and forgetting the context, produced the startling statement about the heavenly Jerusalem,

Thy gardens and thy pleasant fruits
Continually are green.

It is worth remembering also that in all composite hymns it is the last editor who matters; and, if there is anything amiss with the result it is he who is responsible.

75 In the bleak mid-winter. *Christina Rossetti*, 1830–94.

First used as a hymn by the *English Hymnal* (1906), whence it has been taken by the *Church Hymnary* and other recent books, it sprang at once into popularity, its intrinsic beauty helped by Mr. Holst's tune. The poem is stated in Christina Rossetti's *Poetical Works* (1904) to be 'Before 1872'.

'Irregular' from the musical point of view; but really the *plan* is a definite one—Trochaic trimeter with some lines shortened and some lengthened (as, very effectively, 'Snow had fallen, snow on snow'), and the last line always shortened, as 'Long ago'. The syllables in the first stanza are: 6 5. 6 5. 7 3. 6 3. In ver. 2, 'Our' is redundant, and the obvious 'Nor can earth sustain' is very deliberately docked of a syllable by the omission of 'can'; and so the verses surge and tumble, carried along for singing by the swing of the tune.

MUSIC. CRANHAM was composed by Gustav Holst for this hymn, and appeared in the *English Hymnal* (1906). The music is simple and unpretentious, and thus in accordance with the spirit and the expression of the poem.

76 It came upon the midnight clear. *E. H. Sears*, 1810–76.

A strangely significant thing is that most Victorian hymn-books offered little or no application of the social message of Christmas—'Peace on earth, goodwill towards men'. Much current theology was content to say 'Lord, Lord', with intricate doctrinal emphasis; and the influence of Maurice and Kingsley did not spread fast enough to reform the hymnals. The hymns that began to express the teaching of Christ came at that time from New England, and at first established themselves in America only; and it is notable that this one was written by a Unitarian minister, one supposed not to say 'Lord, Lord', in the orthodox way, though indeed Sears wrote in a letter to Bishop Bickersteth that 'I believe and preach the Divinity of Christ'. This hymn, which was one of the first to be popularized among Anglican congregations by the *Hymnal Companion* (1870) and *Church Hymns* (1871), was first published in the American *Christian Register* (1850). By a tragic irony the Civil War followed in ten years.

D.C.M.

MUSIC. NOEL appeared in *Church Hymns with Tunes* (1874). Sir Arthur Sullivan, the editor, received from a friend the melody of the first four lines; he altered it slightly, harmonized it, and composed the second half of the tune, setting it to the present hymn. These first four lines seem to have been a traditional air, as internal evidence also suggests, and as only the 5th and 6th lines are new, the original character has been preserved, though the alterations in the melody are considerable (cf. 393).

77 It was the calm and silent night! *A. Domett*, 1811–87.

Domett is remembered as the hero of Browning's 'Waring' in the *Dramatic Romances* (1845):

> What's become of Waring,
> Since he gave us all the slip . . .?

In the poem he is described as a genius who could do anything, and might blaze out as a painter, musician, poet, leader; but who was almost unknown and unappreciated, and therefore had disappeared and hidden himself no one knew where. Browning imagines him as last seen, the skipper of a smuggling ship off Trieste. As a matter of fact, he had gone to New Zealand in 1842, and after being secretary for the Colony, became Prime Minister in 1862, returned to England in 1871, and died a respectable C.M.G. His last volume of verse, *Flotsam and Jetsam* (1871), is dedicated to Browning.

This fine poem has not been used as a hymn before. It is included in Quiller-Couch's *Oxford Book of Victorian Verse* (1912), where two more stanzas are given; and it is dated 1837.

The verse is of unusual form, unique in our book: Iambic, 8 8 8 8. 8 8 8 8. 6 5.

MUSIC. FREYLINGHAUSEN (MACHT HOCH DIE THÜR) is from J. A. Freylinghausen's *Geistreiches Gesangbuch* (1704), where it is set to 'Macht hoch die Thür, die Thor macht weit'. In the original the first strain is not repeated, and the last lines run:

The accidentals in the penultimate bars of lines 5 and 6 are not found till the edition of 1713. The tune occurs, with some variations of rhythm, in many later collections. It is in the style of popular traditional melodies, and may perhaps be founded on an actual song; it is an excellent specimen of its kind.

78 O come, all ye faithful. *18th cent. Tr. F. Oakeley, and others.*

Adeste, fideles,
laeti triumphantes;
venite, venite in Bethlehem:
natum videte
regem angelorum:
Venite adoremus Dominum.

Deum de Deo,
lumen de lumine,
gestant puellae viscera;
Deum verum,
genitum non factum:
Venite adoremus Dominum.

This is probably of French or German origin, of the 17th or 18th century; but no manuscript copies are earlier than the middle of the 18th. It was sung a good deal in France, and it may have been composed there about 1700. There were three forms of it, one in eight verses; Julian gives references to 38 English translations. Frederick Oakeley, incumbent of Margaret Street Chapel, London, made the version beginning, 'Ye faithful, approach ye', 1841: it was sung in his church, but not published until it appeared as 'O come, all ye faithful' in Murray's *Hymnal* (1852). It is a pity that Murray did not alter it more than he did; for Oakeley in the 2nd verse really repeats the unsatisfactory English of the Te Deum, when he gives 'God of God, Light of Light' and the ugly 'Abhors not the Virgin's womb', instead of translating the original. We should have preferred to alter these lines; but our advisers agreed with us that they were too universally familiar. Until the *English Hymnal* was published, the only verses in common use were 1, 2, 6, and 7. The other verses not only make a longer hymn possible, but also continue the hymn into the Epiphany season.

Irregular in the extreme, to the extent of being stressed prose: e.g. line 1 of ver. 1 may be scanned, ◡ – ◡ ◡ – ◡, while the corresponding line of ver. 2 is, – ◡ –.

MUSIC. ADESTE FIDELES has been stated to have been composed either by John Reading, who was organist of Winchester College, and died in 1692, or by another English musician of the same name, who was a pupil of Dr. John Blow, and died in 1764. This assertion seems to rest solely on the authority of Vincent Novello. In a collection published by him in 1843, entitled *Home Music, the Congregational and Chorister's Psalm and Hymn Book, &c.*, the music appears arranged as a psalm tune, set to Psalm 106. It is headed 'Air by Reading, 1680', and the following note is appended: 'This piece obtained its name from the accidental circumstance of the Duke of Leeds, who was a director of the Concert of Ancient Music, many years since (about the year 1785), having heard the hymn first performed at the Portuguese Chapel, and who, supposing it to be peculiar to the service in Portugal, introduced the melody at the Ancient Concerts, giving it the title of the "Portuguese Hymn", by which appellation this very favourite and popular tune has ever since been distinguished; but it is by no means confined to the choir of the Portuguese Chapel, being the regular Christmas hymn "Adeste Fideles", that is sung in every Catholic chapel throughout England.'

As Novello was for many years organist of the Portuguese Chapel, this note may be taken as giving a correct account of how the tune received the name of "The Portuguese Hymn". Novello's statement as to the composer of the music is, however, a different matter. Nothing in the least resembling the music of 'Adeste Fideles' has been found either in any of the second John Reading's published works, or in two manuscript volumes in his autograph long in the possession of Dr. W. H. Cummings. For the ascription of the tune to the older John Reading, the organist of Winchester, no evidence whatever has been produced.

So far as has yet been ascertained, the earliest book in which the music appears in print is a small volume entitled *An Essay on the Church Plain Chant* (London: Printed and published by J. P. Coghlan, in Duke Street, Grosvenor Square. MDCCLXXXII). The book is in three parts, and the 'Adeste Fideles', with its music, is in the second of these, which is headed 'Part Second, containing several Anthems, Litanies, Proses and Hymns, as they are sung in the Public Chapels at London'. In his 'Advertisement' to the public, Coghlan, the publisher, says, 'It is necessary to observe that the Third Part, or Supplement to this work, was not compiled by the Gentleman who did the other Two Parts.' It seems highly probable that the 'Gentleman' so referred to was Samuel Webbe, senior, for nearly all the pieces in the second part of the volume (including the 'Adeste Fideles' and the tune now known as 'Melcombe') appear again in Webbe's *Collection of Motetts or Antiphons* (1792), and several of them have his name appended to them there as composer.

Although the *Essay on the Church Plain Chant* is at present the earliest book known to contain the 'Adeste Fideles', it is found in manuscripts of earlier date. One of the earliest of these yet discovered is a volume preserved at Stonyhurst College, Lancashire, dated 1751. It is the work of John Francis Wade, who seems to have employed himself in writing out music for use in Roman Catholic families and institutions. The 'Adeste Fideles' is given in four stanzas, with the music repeated to each, and is headed 'In Nativitate Domini Hymnus'.

The conclusion seems to be that the hymn and tune came into use together, in the services of the Roman Church, during the first part of the 18th century; that they were in circulation in manuscript for some time before they appeared in print, but that nothing definite can as yet be stated as to the author of words or music.

The tune has some affinity with 'Helmsley' (65), and may, like that tune, be originally an adaptation of a secular melody, though this is only conjecture; internal evidence, at least, would not assign the tune to an earlier date than the 18th century.

The alternative version (fa-burden), by Martin Shaw, appeared in *Two Christmas Carols, &c.* (1924).

79 O little town of Bethlehem. *Bishop Phillips Brooks*, 1835–93.

Another New England hymn which gives the Christmas message. This was written in 1868, for his Sunday School, by Phillips Brooks, who became Bishop of Massachusetts in 1891. The greatest Anglican preacher since F. W. Robertson, noble and broad-minded, his influence in Boston was immense. That the children also loved him is shown by a story of a girl of five, who, when her mother told her with tears that the Bishop had just died, exclaimed, 'O Mother, how happy the angels will be!' The hymn was hardly known in England till it appeared in the *English Hymnal* (1906); but now (like its author) is as popular with adults as with children, for whom originally it was written.

D.C.M., with some irregularities.

MUSIC. FOREST GREEN appeared in the *English Hymnal* (1906), and is an arrangement by R. Vaughan Williams of a traditional English melody. It is a bold tune of a type commonly associated with narrative ballads.

CHRISTMAS CAROL, from *Worship Song* (1905), was composed for this hymn by Sir Walford Davies. This is a pleasant tune which, rather refreshingly, makes no attempt to imitate the style of traditional carol melodies.

80 The holy Son of God most high. *Henry More*, 1614–87.

Another hymn introduced as a needed short piece of fine literary character. It is by Henry More, one of that little band of Cambridge Platonists, with John Smith, Whichcote, Culverwell, and Cudworth, who almost alone of 17th-century theologians are still of interest to-day. More was typical of these quiet unambitious men (he twice refused to be a bishop) who in a turbulent age set themselves to work out a Christian philosophy and to destroy the divisions between Protestant Christians. John Wesley took More's *Divine Dialogues, with Divine Hymns* (1668) with him when he embarked for Georgia in 1735, and in 1780 moulded one of its contents into two hymns, now little known. Ours is the first of the *Divine Hymns*, the 1st, 2nd, 4th, and 5th out of 10 stanzas.

L.M.

MUSIC. VON HIMMEL HOCH appeared first in V. Schumann's *Geistliche Lieder* (Leipzig, 1539), set to Luther's carol 'Vom Himmel hoch da komm ich her', which was written for his little son Hans, and first published in Klug's *Gesangbuch* (Wittemberg, 1535); in this earlier book the carol was set to a popular tune, but the present melody, sometimes attributed to Luther himself, supplanted it and became one of the best-known chorales. J. S. Bach made several settings of the tune; the present version being from his *Christmas Oratorio*.

JENA (DAS NEUGEBORNE KINDELEIN) is from Melchior Vulpius's *Ein schön geistlich Gesangbuch, &c., durch M.V. Cantorem zu Weymar* (Jena, 1609). This was Vulpius's second collection, the former being published in 1604. J. S. Bach wrote one of his cantatas on this chorale, and the dignified character of the tune merited this honour.

81 Thou whose birth on earth. *A. C. Swinburne*, 1837–1909.

Swinburne also gives the Christmas message. He was always a mouthpiece rather than a thinker, though a mouthpiece of rare quality, 'a tube through which all things blow into music', Tennyson said of him. His opinions varied; but he ought not to be held responsible for 'Thou hast conquered, O pale Galilean', words which he puts into the mouth of a conservative Roman in the last days of the Empire, who is lamenting the decline of the old gods. From *Songs before Sunrise* (1871).

Trochaic, 5 5 5 5 5: an uncommon short metre of which this is our only example; highly wrought, with internal rhymes.

MUSIC. DANBURY was composed by Armstrong Gibbs especially for the original edition of *Songs of Praise* (1925). The tune skilfully solves the problem set by the rather unusual metre of the poem, without pretentiousness or intricacy. A simple, but original little melody.

82 While shepherds watched their flocks by night.

Nahum Tate, 1652–1715.

This famous carol or hymn is from *The Supplement* (1700).

The Supplement

The *New Version* of the metrical Psalms by Tate and Brady was first published in 1696. *The Supplement* which was bound up with it, and which is important because it provides a few authorized hymns (as had the *Old Version*—see 116), is now known to be as early as 1700, because there is a copy in Julian's library at the Church House bearing that date. This edition of *The Supplement* contains the following:

1. O God, we praise thee, and confess. (*Te Deum.*)
2. Come, Holy Ghost, Creator, come. (*Veni Creator*, L.M.)
3. Come, Holy Ghost, Creator, come. (*Veni Creator*, D.C.M.)
4. Now blest be Israel's Lord and God. (*Benedictus.*)
5. My soul and spirit filled with joy. (*Magnificat.*)
6. Lord, let thy servant now depart. (*Nunc Dimittis.*)
7. I steadfastly believe in God. (*Creed.*)

8 and 9. Our Father who in heaven art. (*Lord's Prayer.*)

10. God spake these words. (*Decalogue.*)
11. While shepherds watched their flocks. (*Christmas.*)
12. Since Christ, our Passover, is slain. (*Easter.*)
13. Christ from the dead is raised and made. (*Easter.*)
14. Thou God, all Glory, Honour, Power. (*Communion.*)
15. All ye who faithful servants are. (*Communion.*)
16. To God be glory, peace on earth. (*Communion.*)

It will be noticed that in spite of the official sanction and the huge circulation of *The Supplement*, 15 of these are completely forgotten. Bad hymns may, like Charles II, be unconscionably long in dying; but they do die in the end. No. 11, 'While shepherds watched', is the only one of these that has survived. Cosin's *Veni Creator* was already in the Ordinal (see 178), and the 'Lamentation' (116) was not taken over from the *Old Version* till the 6th edition of *The Supplement* (1708); but after these, 'While shepherds watched' is the earliest original hymn (as distinguished from metrical psalms) in *Songs of Praise*.

Tate was one of the editors of the *New Version*, Poet Laureate, and 'a butt of Swift and Pope'. This example of his work (with 449 and 677, where he is not extricated from Brady) remains as his monument wherever English is spoken; but it was altered in the Paraphrases of the Church of Scotland, where it begins, 'While humble shepherds watched their flocks'.

C.M.

MUSIC. WINCHESTER OLD is from *The Whole Booke of Psalmes with their wonted Tunes, as they are song in churches, composed into foure parts . . . Compiled by sondry authors* (London, Thomas Est, 1592). There it is set to Psalm 84, the name of G. Kirby being attached to it, meaning that the arrangement is by him. In the editions of this book issued in 1584, 1604, and 1611 the tune does not appear, Psalm 84 being set to the tune known as 'Old Common Tune'; but in Ravenscroft (1621) and Playford (1671 and 1677) that Psalm is again set to WINCHESTER. The name of the tune appears first in Ravenscroft, from whose book is taken also the fa-burden which is to be found in the alternative version given in the *Songs of Praise.*

The tune seems to be partly adapted from the second half of the melody set to chap. viii in C. Tye's *Actes of the Apostles* (cf. p. xiii), which is as follows:

The second last note is shown by the harmony to be a misprint for E. The tune is now indissolubly united to the present words, and is, perhaps, the best known of all 'Christmas' melodies.

NORTHROP, by A. Northrop (?), appeared in the *English Hymnal* (1906). It is a very popular tune in Cornwall.

Hymns as Poetry

Much harm has been done by the unfounded notion that real poetry is not acceptable by the people, that words which are not commonplace cannot be understood, and that therefore hymns must be either doggerel or libretto. The truth really is that 'common people' often have more poetry in them than professors, and that an unaccustomed word loses that disadvantage when it comes into use. Such words will be found, mingled with poetic imagery, in all our popular classics. Even here, in a specially simple hymn, we have a blaze of imagery; and, are all the words so very simple? We fancy there are many educated men who would be floored by, 'Explain the meaning of "swathing", "seraph", "addressed".' Or, 'How do you distinguish between a seraph and a cherub? Give the plural forms.' It would indeed tax the most learned doctors to describe what one of them has called 'the ambiguous cherub', who seems to be a personification of the thunder-cloud, as the seraph is of the lightning; while Dr. Cheyne, who must have known, wrote, 'The popular notion of the seraphim as angels is, of course, to be rejected. They are, indeed, more like Titans than placid Gabriels or Raphaels.' (See also under 443, 598.)

83 As with gladness men of old. *W. Chatterton Dix*, 1837–98.

Dix was ill in bed on the Epiphany, *c.* 1858, and, after reading the Gospel of the day, he wrote this hymn and finished it by the evening. It was in the trial copy of *Hymns Ancient and Modern* (1859), and therefore the author's note, 'about 1860', can be put back a year or two. Dix's epithets are always the obvious ones; but the verses are straightforward, sincere, and popular, though they do not quite deserve the singular praise given them by Lord Selborne at a Church Congress in 1866, a tribute which secured their admission into most subsequent books.

Trochaic 7 7. 7 7. 7 7. Dix was unfortunate in the tune with which it is always associated. He wrote, 'I dislike it, but now nothing will displace it.'

MUSIC. DIX is an abridgement of a melody by Conrad Kocher, which originally appeared in *Stimmen aus dem Reiche Gottes . . . herausgegeben von Conrad Kocher* (Stuttgart, 1838), set to the hymn 'Trever Heiland, wir sind hier'. The complete tune was as follows:

In a case such as this, where the adaptation is so familiar and the original comparatively unknown, the force of association makes it extremely difficult to judge fairly between them; but it may at least be said that the change has not been for the worse.

84 Bethlehem, of noblest cities. *Prudentius, b.* 348. *Tr. E. Caswall.*

O sola magnarum urbium
major Bethlem, qui, contigit
ducem salutis caelitus
incorporatum gignere.

From the *Cathemerinon* of Prudentius (see 37), translated from the cento in the Roman Breviary of 1570. Many people have regretted that 'Earth has many a noble city' is not in *Songs of Praise* or the *English Hymnal*, the answer being of course that it is, but in the form in which Caswall wrote it. As in many other instances, the alterations made by various editors have been for the worse. The translation first appeared in his *Lyra Catholica* (1849), and (with the great improvement of 'Solemn things', for 'Offerings') in his *Hymns and Poems* (1873).

Trochaic, 8 7. 8 7.

MUSIC. STUTTGART is adapted from a melody by C. F. Witt in *Psalmodia sacra, oder, Andächtige und schöne Gesänge* (Gotha, 1715), where it is set to the hymn, 'Sollt es gleich bisweilen scheinen', as follows:

The alternative version (descant) was written by W. H. Harris especially for the enlarged *Songs of Praise* (1931).

Here it can be definitely stated, without hesitation, that the revised version is an improvement; the analogous structure (by inversion) of the alternate lines is preserved, closely enough, in the new 3rd line, which is certainly more melodious than the original. In this form it has become closely associated with the present hymn.

85 Brightest and best of the sons of the morning.

Bishop R. Heber, 1783–1826.

Dunderheaded critics held this back from use on the ground that it involved the worshipping of a star. Most people used to treat the Bible in a similar way. Others objected that the metre (so fashionable in the age of Tom Moore) was Terpsichorean, being averse to praising God with cymbals and dances. One of the best of Heber's pioneer hymns, it was first published in the *Christian Observer* (then edited by Zachary Macaulay of Clapham, the historian's father), Nov. 1811, and reprinted in his posthumous *Hymns, &c.* (1827). Cotterill included it in the famous 8th edition of his *Selections* (see 71), but dropped it (apparently the Archbishop was the cause) from the 9th. Elliott's *Psalms and Hymns* (1835) did the same, first including it, and then in the 2nd edition dropping it. Many other books included it. *Hymns Ancient and Modern*, by rejecting it in 1861, caused large sections of Victorian church-goers to be ignorant of it, together with 'The Lord my pasture' and 'The spacious firmament' and other classics which their fathers had loved: it is now included in the *Supplementary Hymns* of that collection.

Dactylic, 11 10. 11 10.

MUSIC. LIEBSTER IMMANUEL is from *Himmels-Lust und Welt-Unlust, &c.* (Jena, 1679), where it is set to the hymn 'Liebster Immanuel, Herzog der frommen' as follows:

At * the printed note is G, but the bass shows that this is a misprint for F. The above is the earliest form of the tune. Later collections show a very large number of variants, the present version being based on J. S. Bach's arrangements in his Church Cantata on this chorale. Both the original and the later version are sterling tunes; the motive of some of the alterations, however, is not apparent, especially in the 1st and the 9th and 10th bars.

LIME STREET, by Geoffrey Shaw, appeared in the *Public School Hymn Book* (1919). This tune must be sung at a good round pace for its vigorous nature to be duly apparent. With some rhythms, of which this is one, any considerable change of speed will seriously alter the character of the melody, and the present tune, if taken too slowly, will lose some of its due trenchancy.

86 By weary stages. *John Masefield.*

Written for the mystery play, *The Coming of Christ*, performed in Canterbury Cathedral, 1928, and published that same year.

Iambic, 5 5. 5 4. D.

MUSIC. HILL CREST was written for these words, being taken from Gustav Holst's music to Masefield's mystery play mentioned above. This fine tune perhaps owes some of its impressiveness to the mixolydian mode, but it is, apart from this, a stately and excellently proportioned melody, while the setting is equally dignified and imposing.

87 Hail to the Lord's Anointed! *J. Montgomery*, 1771–1854.

Generally esteemed the finest of Montgomery's hymns, this is known to have been sung in a Moravian settlement at Christmas, 1821, to have been sent in manuscript next month to a missionary in the South Seas, and to have been printed in the *Evangelical Magazine* in the following April, and at the end of 1822 in the author's *Songs of Zion*. Still in this year Dr. Adam Clarke, who had been chairman at a missionary meeting where Montgomery recited it, gave it great publicity by printing it with a special note in his famous Bible Commentary; and to-day there are few hymnals without it. The original has eight stanzas. The *English Hymnal* restored the social message of Christmas, ver. 2, and the missionary ver. 4. *Church Hymns* had at that time reduced it to 3 verses, retaining our 1, 2, and 5 only.

Montgomery was indeed not only a keen worker in the missionary cause but one of the foremost social reformers of his age, and was sent to jail in York Castle for nine months because of an article in his *Sheffield Register*. He was an ardent advocate of the abolition of slavery; and he formed an association for the rescue of the miserable little boys employed to climb up chimneys as sweeps: as readers of Kingsley's *Water Babies* will remember, it took a long time before Lord Shaftesbury secured an Act which made that cruelty illegal.

Iambic, 7 6. 7 6. D.

MUSIC. CRÜGER is from J. Crüger's *Newes vollkömliches Gesangbuch, &c.* (1640), where it appears as follows:

In *Psalmodia Sacra* (1657) and late editions of *Praxis Pietatis Melica* the 2nd line (*) runs:

and many other variants are found in different collections.

The present adaptation was made by W. H. Monk, apparently from the version in J. C. Kuhnau's *Vierstimmige alte und neue Choralgesänge, &c.* (1786), where the 7th line is a repeat of the 6th, and the 5th line is Monk's 6th, the present 5th line being Monk's own composition. This adaptation first appeared in *Hymns Ancient and Modern* (1861), and is undoubtedly an improvement on all previous variants, Monk's new line being an imitation of the 1st, and therefore preserving the character and balance of the whole tune, while avoiding the triteness of the repetition.

88 Hark, how all the welkin rings. *C. Wesley*, 1707–88.

As we have said under 74, this is Charles Wesley's own text, as revised by himself in *Hymns and Sacred Poems* (1743), the original having been in the earlier edition of 1739. Eight stanzas are given here, out of the ten, and we gain the two fine concluding verses. In this form the hymn is more than the song of praise that 'Hark! the herald angels' is: it is a prayer for all; and its universalist tendency is shown also in 'Universal nature say, "Christ the Lord is born to-day",' as indeed it is perhaps implied in 'all the welkin'. Whitefield, the leader of the Calvinist section opposed to the Wesleys, doubtless saw this when he altered the lines. The other changes in 74 are, 4 'to dwell' for 'to appear', and the omission of 'here' (*c.* 1810); 5, 'heaven-born' for 'heavenly'; and the repetition of Whitefield's opening couplet as a refrain, first in *The Supplement* of 1782.

Trochaic, 7 7. 7 7.

MUSIC. DENT DALE, from the *English Hymnal* (1906), is an arrangement by R. Vaughan Williams of an English traditional melody.

89 Hearts at Christmas time were jolly.

A. G., based on Fröhlich soll, *P. Gerhardt* (1653).

Paulus Gerhardt's hymn of 15 stanzas was included in the Frankfort edition of Crüger's *Praxis* (1656), but Crüger's tune came to be dropped in favour of 'Bonn'. It was thus brought into use with us, in Miss Winkworth's version (from her *Lyra Germanica*, 1858) by *Church Hymns* (1871), and by some American books; in 1880 a cento was added to the Baptist *Psalms and Hymns*. There was little of Gerhardt left in the various centos of Miss Winkworth's very free version; and for *Songs of Praise* the editor prepared a hymn for the present day, based on the general plan of the original.

Trochaic, 8 3 3 6. D.; an intricate but very musical arrangement of rhymes. There is no other example in the book.

MUSIC. BONN is from *Geistliche Andacht-Lieder Herrn Paul Gerhardt . . . gesetzt von J. G. Ebeling* (Berlin, 1666, 1667), where it is set to Gerhardt's hymn 'Warum sollt ich mich denn grämen'. This is a very attractive tune, with an unusual but most happy lilt, very simply constructed with two lines of inverted movement, each followed by the refrain, slightly varied the second time. The unforced gaiety of the whole effect is irresistible.

90 How brightly beams the morning star!

P. Nicolai (1599) *and J. A. Schlegel* (1768), *O.B.C.V.*

Wie schön leuchtet der Morgenstern
Voll Gnad und Wahrheit von dem Herrn!
  Du süsse Wurzel Jesse,
Du Davids Sohn aus Jacobs Stamm,
Mein König und mein Braütigam,
  Hast mir mein Herz besessen:

Lieblich, freundlich, schön und herrlich,
Gross und ehrlich,
Reich von Gaben
Über alles hoch erhaben.

Nicolai, the author and composer of 'Wachet auf' (687), during the same pestilence that inspired that great production, sat one morning in great distress, thinking of the misery around him, when his heart suddenly rose up to God, and he wrote this hymn, forgetting his noon-day meal, and working on till he had finished it in the late afternoon. It was first published in his *Frewden Spiegel* (1599), as founded on the 45th Psalm; it also has reminiscences of Ephesians 5, and of the Canticles. It soon came to be reckoned indispensable for weddings, and was often sung round death-beds. Much of its popularity was due to the famous chorale with which it is associated. Schlegel's version (in Zollikofer's *Gesangbuch*, 1766, &c.) alters the original so much as to be almost a new composition on the theme. Our translation began with Miss Winkworth's version, which in the end was considerably altered; it first appeared in the *Oxford Book of Carols* (1928) (hence the initials above), as no. 104; but it was further altered for *Songs of Praise*, in order to provide the internal rhymes which the music needs in the 7th line of each verse, e.g. 'Newly, truly'.

Mixed iambic and trochaic, 8 8 7. 8 8 7. 8 4 4 8. Unique.

MUSIC. WIE SCHÖN LEUCHTET DER MORGENSTERN appeared with the words in Nicolai's above-mentioned book, and may therefore be by him. The famous tune, which was soon set on many city chimes in Germany, may have been in part suggested by earlier melodies, especially by 'Resonet in Laudibus' (see 700). The first version here given is Bach's harmonization, the second that of Mendelssohn in *Christus*. This magnificent tune needs no comment.

91 In Asia born, from Asia hailed. *P. Dearmer.*

When the first *Songs of Praise* was in preparation for 1925, it was felt that Chandler's translation (cf. 35) of Coffin's *Quae stella* ('What star is this') added nothing to what was much better said in a multitude of hymns and carols; but that the tune in the *English Hymnal* must not be lost to Epiphany. At the same time a request came from Dr. Dwelly, now Dean of Liverpool, for a hymn expressing what the Epiphany means to us to-day. So 'Ein Kind gebor'n' was saved.

L.M.

MUSIC. EIN KIND GEBOR'N is derived from a German carol tune found in Klug's *Geistliche Lieder zu Wittemberg &c.* (1543), where it appears as follows:

A later form appeared in Lossius's *Psalmodia, hoc est Cantica sacra veteris ecclesiae selecta, &c.* (1553), and may be found in the *Oxford Book of Carols* (1928). This later tune was originally a descant to the older one, but gradually ousted the parent melody. The 1st line of the present version is that of the newer tune, the rest being nearer to the earlier.

92 Love came down at Christmas. *Christina Rossetti*, 1830–94.

At the time of the publication of Dr. Julian's 'Supplement' to his great *Dictionary of Hymnology* (1907), this gem, where so much is said in so little space, had not been used as a hymn and therefore was not included. The large numbers of people who were consulted for *Songs of Praise* were all agreed as to the need of more very short hymns; and thus the inclusion of Christina Rossetti's poem was the more welcome. It was first printed in *Time Flies: a Reading Diary* (1885). In this edition the last line was 'Love the universal sign'; it was greatly improved in the last edition—'Love for plea and gift and sign'.

Trochaic, 6 7. 6 7.

MUSIC. HERMITAGE was written by R. O. Morris especially for the original edition of *Songs of Praise* (1925). It is a fine tune in the folk-song tradition, but without any 'Wardour Street' archaism.

93 O worship the Lord in the beauty of holiness!

J. S. B. Monsell, 1811–75.

Dr. Monsell raised a protest against the gloom of Victorian hymnody, desiring it to be 'more fervent and joyous'. 'We are too distant and reserved in our praises', he said, 'we sing not as we should sing to him and of him, who is chief among ten thousand, the altogether lovely.' Perhaps also the fact that he was a compatriot of Tom Moore led him to the tripping metre, which makes this a companion to 'Brightest and best' (85). He practised what he preached: of his home at Guildford Rectory a witness wrote that it was an 'ideal household, full of the beauty of holiness, with genial brightness and gaiety playing like sunshine over all the troubles of life'. This hymn was first published in his *Hymns of Love and Praise* (1863). It got into many collections in America and Great Britain, but not into those most used in the Church of England.

Dactylic, 13 10. 13 10. With the omission of 'O' and 'With' in the first and last verses, this would consist of four complete dactyls, alternating with three feet of dactyls and a fourth from which the last two syllables are dropped. The perfect dactyls in the 1st and 3rd lines result in triple rhymes. This metre also, adding another musical opportunity, is unique in our book.

MUSIC. CRASSELIUS, by J. S. Bach, is from Schemelli's *Musicalisches Gesangbuch, &c.* (1736), where it is set to the hymn 'Dir, dir, Jehova'. The rhythm has been slightly adapted, in the present version, at the end of the 1st and 3rd lines, and in the original tune the first two lines are repeated. A good tune with some characteristic touches, especially in the latter half with its vigorous and enterprising outline.

DYMCHURCH is by Geoffrey Shaw and originally appeared in *Additional Tunes and settings in use at St. Mary's, Primrose Hill* (1915). Noticeable here are the rather large compass and the wide skips in the melody, traits which are found in many of this composer's vital tunes.

94 The greatness of God in his love has been shown. *T.S.N.*

There are several good folk-tunes to the carol 'A virgin unspotted'; but the words written by Bramley to replace the rough texts of the carols were not felt to be desirable; and therefore the editor wrote new words, in order, among other things, that the supreme teaching of the parable of the Prodigal Son should not be unmentioned in hymnody.

Anapaestic, 11 11. 11 11, and refrain.

MUSIC. BRAMLEY (A VIRGIN UNSPOTTED) is the English traditional carol melody here harmonized by Martin Shaw. It is one of the many tunes traditionally sung to the carol 'A virgin most pure', of which, also, several versions are extant. The present arrangement is from the *Oxford Book of Carols* (1928), where other 'Virgin unspotted' tunes may also be found. These tunes vary in complexity, but there is a strong family likeness between them, though it is not, perhaps, sufficient to justify their attribution to a common original. The present tune is a particularly good example, since it combines features both of the more complex and the simpler members of the family.

95 The Lord is come, on Syrian soil.

Arthur Penrhyn Stanley, 1815–81.

First published in *Macmillan's Magazine* (1872). Like his other hymns, this was included in the *Westminster Abbey Hymn Book* (1883), but did not get into many collections. Originally in six stanzas, this is another of the hymns that bring out the duty of our neighbour in connexion with the Incarnation; and it is useful for the Sundays after Epiphany, of which there are many in some years.

D.L.M.

MUSIC. CANTATE DOMINO was composed by Sir Joseph Barnby for the hymn 'Sing to the Lord a joyful song', and appeared in *The Hymnary* (1872). This is one of the best of this composer's hymn-tunes. It is not marred by the excessive chromaticism which disfigures many of his compositions, and thereby it gains an unwonted breadth.

96 The race that long in darkness pined.

J. Morison, 1750–98 (*Scottish Paraphrases*).

No. 19 of the Paraphrases brought into use (together with five hymns) in the Church of Scotland in 1781, this is as it appeared in the Scottish *Translations and Paraphrases* of that year (a version of Isaiah 9 : 2–8), and as it is still used in Scotland, but with the omission of one verse, the 3rd, of the original:

For thou our burden hast remov'd,
and quell'd th' oppressor's sway;
Quick as the slaughter'd squadrons fell
in Midian's evil day.

In America it appeared in the Episcopal *Hymn Book* (1826) and in the Baptist *Psalmist* (1843). It came to be a good deal altered in some English books, so that the fine diction of the proper version is still not universally known.

C.M.

MUSIC. ST. JAMES, by Raphael Courteville, appeared in *Select Psalms and Hymns for the Use of the Parish Church and Tabernacle of St. James's, Westminster* (1697). The descant in the alternative version was written by Henry G. Ley especially for the enlarged *Songs of Praise* (1931).

In the original the last line runs thus:

The tune is in the tradition of the earlier psalm-tunes, and is a not unworthy addition to their number.

LENT

97 Forty days and forty nights. *G. H. Smyttan* (1856), *and others.*

First published in the *Penny Post* (1856) as 'Poetry for Lent', in 9 stanzas, Smyttan's hymn was altered by F. Pott and included, as a piece of 6 verses, in his *Hymns* (1861). *Hymns Ancient and Modern* (1861) and *Church Hymns* (1871) made this composite form well known and popular. We have here omitted Pott's alterations, and recast it ourselves. The references to the Temptation are mainly from Mark 1 : 13.

Trochaic, 7 7. 7 7.

MUSIC. HEINLEIN (AUS DER TIEFE) in the *Nürnbergisches Gesangbuch* (1676? 1677) is set to the hymn 'Aus der Tiefe rufe ich'. There the melody has the initials M. H. attached to it, and Zahn conjectures that these may stand for Martin Herbst. But the tune was occasionally attributed to Paul Heinlein; hence its present name. The alternative version (descant) is by Alan Gray and appeared in his *A Book of Descants* (1920).

Variants of the 2nd line are sometimes found, but the present original form is to be preferred. This superbly solemn tune merits in every way the celebrity it has attained.

98 Now quit your care. *P. Dearmer.*

First printed in the *Oxford Book of Carols* (1928), this was written to carry the fine tune which is outside ordinary metres. The references are to the Sermon on the Mount, Matt. 6 : 16–34, and to Isa. 58, the First Lesson for Ash Wednesday at Mattins, which emphasizes the social duty of the season.

Iambic (some lines being spondaic in character), 4 7. 4 6. 4 7. 6 4 8; of course unique.

MUSIC. QUITTEZ, PASTEURS is found in L. Roques's *Noëls Anciens* (19th century, undated); there is a slightly different version in L. Eugène Grimault, *Noëls Angevins* (1878). The present harmonization is by Martin Shaw; and a more varied arrangement is to be found in the *Oxford Book of Carols* (1928). This tune, though of rather larger compass than many, otherwise shows the characteristics previously mentioned (cf. 3).

LENTEN HYMNS

99 Ah, holy Jesus, how hast thou offended?

J. Heermann, 1585–1647. *Pr. Y.H.* (*Robert Bridges*).

Herzliebster Jesu, was hast du verbrochen,
Dass man ein solch scharf Urtheil hat gesprochen?
Was ist die Schuld? in was für Missethaten
Bist du gerathen?

Robert Bridges evidently chose this (which had been translated by Miss Cox, but was not in the hymn-books) because of the glorious Sapphic tune, when he included it in the *Yattendon Hymnal* (1899): he himself noted that it was partly based on St. Augustine (and in another place, by a slip, on St. Anselm); and indeed it forms a very free paraphrase of Heermann's 15 stanzas, most of it consisting of the recurrent ideas of hymns of this type, expressed with great nobility of phrase. It was made known to a wider public by the *English Hymnal* (1906). Heermann wrote during the miseries of the Thirty Years War, and was himself the victim of continued ill health patiently borne. He published this in his *Devoti Musica Cordis* (Breslau, 1630) as 'From Augustine', i.e. from the 7th of the *Meditations*. Bridges's first stanza is a free translation of ver. 1; 2, of Heermann's 3; 3, of his 4; while 5 and 6 contain suggestions only of his 6 and 7 and of the rest of his verses.

Sapphic (see 28), i.e. 11 11. 11 5.

MUSIC. HERZLIEBSTER JESU is from Johann Crüger's *Gesangbuch* (Berlin, 1640). In Crüger's original the opening phrase is

It is so given in the *Oxford Hymn Book*, but the present form is in most later German books, and is that adopted by J. S. Bach. The alternative version is Bach's harmonization in *The Passion according to St. Matthew*.

The grandly impressive tune owes some of its intensely solemn character to the prevalence of the downward movement (nearly five-sevenths of the whole melody); there is enough of the contrary motion to maintain the poise of the contour, but this is due more to position than to quantity. The tune will repay an elaborate analysis which cannot be given here.

100 Be thou my guardian and my guide. *I. Williams*, 1802–65.

It is significant that many hymns now included in the Lenten section were set down for general use in the older books. We have already noticed how the thought of love and peace has been brought back into our Christmas and Epiphany hymns: the increase of the element of joy completes St. Paul's first three fruits of the Spirit. Isaac Williams first published this in his *Hymns on the Catechism* (1842), as illustrating 'Lead us not into temptation'. The 1875 edition of *Hymns Ancient and Modern* popularized it, with the alteration to 'Be thou our guardian and our guide', and the plural throughout; but Williams had the Psalter—and how much else!—on his side in preferring the singular.

C.M.

MUSIC. ABRIDGE is from *A Collection of Psalm Tunes in Three Parts . . . by Isaac Smith* (*c.* 1770). In *Sacred Harmony for the Use of St. George's Church, Edinburgh* (1820), it appears under the name 'St. Stephen's', and with the following form of the last line:

This was adopted in some later books published in Scotland, but the present form is in accordance with the original.

The original form is undoubtedly the better. This is a beautifully fluent and graceful melody, built on the inverted analogy of alternate lines. It is in the best 18th-century style of this class of tune.

The alternative version (fa-burden) by Geoffrey Shaw appeared in the *Tenor Tune Book* (1917).

101 Jesus, name all names above. *Theoctistus, c.* 890. *S.P.V.*

Neale, in his endeavour to bring the old Greek hymns into English use, published a cento translation, in his *Hymns of the Eastern Church* (1862), of this 'Suppliant canon to Jesus' from the *Paracletice* or 'Great Octoechus', a volume containing the ferial service for eight weeks. Theoctistus, a monk of the Studium at Constantinople, lived *c.* 890; and this is his only known work. We call ours 'Songs of Praise Version' because Neale's translation has been much altered—but not the two fine lines in ver. 3, beginning 'Who, in that most lost estate'. Four verses of Neale's original six stanzas, unaltered, are in the *English Hymnal.*

Trochaic, 7 6. 7 6. 8 8. 7 7. Unique.

MUSIC. WERDE MUNTER is from *Johann Risten Himlischer Lieder mit sehr anmuhtigen mehren theils von Herrn Johann Schopen gesetzten Melodeien* (Lüneberg, 1641–2). This was issued in five sets of ten, the first in 1641, the rest during 1642. The present tune is no. 8 of the third set, 'Werde munter mein Gemüte', and runs as follows:

Several variants are found in later collections, particularly of the opening phrase and of the last two lines.

The original form of the tune here is the more varied in rhythm and balance; the present version, however, has become established, being more in accordance with the usual style of German chorales. As it stands, the melody is quite satisfactory and retains its individuality.

102 Lead us, O Father, in the paths of peace.

W. H. Burleigh, 1812–71.

William Henry Burleigh, Unitarian, printer, editor, and for 15 years Harbour Master at New York, had a true vein of poetry, though a melancholy one. His poems were more used as hymns in Great Britain than in his native country; and, because of the prejudice against Unitarians, the use was mainly among the freer books, the *New Congregational Hymn Book* (1859), the *Baptist Hymnal* (1879, Thring's *Church of England Hymn Book* (1880), the *Congregational Hymns* (1884), and *Worship Song* (1905) of Garrett Horder (to whom compilers of the present century are always deeply indebted), and the *English Hymnal* (1906), which included 'Still will we trust, though earth seem dark and dreary', the other of Burleigh's more popular hymns. Julian notes that all the dates of first publication are most difficult to determine. This was included in *Lyra Sacra Americana*

(1868), but that was later than the *New Congregational* book; and the first date of printing is unknown.

Iambic (but with a long opening syllable to each stanza), 10 10. 10 10, a solemn measure.

MUSIC. PETRIE is an adaptation by Martin Shaw of a traditional Irish melody from the *Petrie Collection of the Ancient Music of Ireland*, and was made especially for the enlarged *Songs of Praise* (1931). It is a pleasant flexible tune, not very characteristically Irish (since the ending is not, as is often believed, typical), but with a tranquil charm of expression.

103 Lighten the darkness of our life's long night.

Mrs. Frances M. Owen, 1842–83.

Another fine but sad poem, in the same solemn metre, this was written by Mrs. Owen, the wife of a master at Cheltenham College, who herself was fated to a short life. It was first published anonymously in *Trefoil, Verses by Three* (1868).

Iambic, 10 10. 10 10.

MUSIC. SONG 24, by Orlando Gibbons, was set to a paraphrase of Lamentations 1 in the *Hymnes and Songs of the Church* (1623) [see 29]. It is a grave melody, with the solidity which seems inherent in the Dorian mode.

104 Long did I toil, and knew no earthly rest.

J. Quarles, 1624–65, *and H. F. Lyte*, 1793–1847.

In his *Poems chiefly Religious* (1833), Henry Francis Lyte notes that it is 'Imitated from Quarles' (John, son of Francis Quarles, for whom see 670). Two stanzas of the original six are omitted from most hymnals.

Iambic, 10 10. 10 10. 10 10.

MUSIC. OXENBRIDGE was composed by Martin Shaw especially for the enlarged *Songs of Praise* (1931). This is a bold tune, to which the regular rhythm and the metrical change at the cadences gives an air of strenuous determination.

105 Lord, it belongs not to my care. *Richard Baxter*,† 1615–91.

'This Covenant my dear wife, in her former sickness, subscribed with a cheerful will', is the note of the author of *The Saint's Rest* to a later edition of his *Poetical Fragments*, the date of its first appearance having been stated as 'London, at the Door of Eternity; Richard Baxter, Aug. 7, 1681', with for title the conceit, 'The Concordant Discord of a Broken-hearted Heart'. The 1st line was 'My whole though broken heart, O Lord', and the poem was in 8 stanzas of 8 lines: here it is reduced to 5 stanzas of 4 lines. The line altered is ver. 2, l. 4, 'That shall have the same pay', where the accent is too forced. We have here kept the meaning: the *English Hymnal* alters to 'To end my little day' and the *Church Hymnary* to 'To welcome endless day'. A favourite hymn of the discoverer of the electro-magnetic character of light, Clerk-Maxwell.

C.M.

MUSIC. CHESHIRE is set to Psalm 146 in *The Whole Booke of Psalmes with their wonted Tunes, as they are song in Churches, composed into foure parts . . . Compiled by sondry authors* (London, Thomas Est, 1592). It is one of several tunes 'newly added in this booke', and named 'Chesshire Tune'. The alternative version (fa-burden) was composed by C. Hylton Stewart especially for the enlarged *Songs of Praise* (1931).

The melody is a good example of the psalm-tunes of the middle period; a sober, serious tune but with a curious effect of sudden light in the 2nd line.

106 Lord Jesus, think on me.

Bishop Synesius, 375–430. *Tr. A. W. Chatfield*.

This hardly suggests the spirit of the genial squire-bishop of Kingsley's *Hypatia*; but Chatfield, when he published the translation in his *Songs and Hymns of the Earliest Greek Christian Poets* (1876), admitted that in 'this Ode I have given my spirit more liberty', and that it is really a paraphrase. A soldier and statesman, Synesius was Bishop of Ptolemais, and Gibbon says that 'the philosophic bishop supported with dignity the character which he had assumed with reluctance' (*Decline and Fall*, cap. xx).

The Greek lines are not so concentrated on dark misery and the sin-obsession as the translator was fifty years ago. Here is the literal prose translation, kindly provided by Dr. Costley White, the Head Master of Westminster School:

Be mindful, Christ Son of God
Who rules on high, of thy servant,
Sinful of heart, who wrote these words.
And grant to me release from passions breeding death,
Which are inborn in my unclean soul.
But give me to behold, Saviour Jesus,
Thy divine brightness, wherein appearing
I shall sing a song
To the healer of souls,
To the healer of limbs,
With the great Father
and the Holy Spirit.

S.M.

MUSIC. SOUTHWELL is set to Psalm 45 in Damon's *Psalmes of David* (1579), and is called by this name in Ravenscroft's book (1621). Originally the melody was in the Dorian mode, and had C♯ in line 3.

The alternative version (fa-burden) by Martin Shaw appeared in *Additional Tunes and settings in use at St. Mary's, Primrose Hill* (1915).

This is a characteristic psalm-tune; its nature has been much changed, but not deteriorated by the C♮.

107 Lord, thou hast told us that there be.

Thomas Washbourne, 1606–87.

From Washbourne's *Divine Poems* written during the Commonwealth (1654); he was reinstated at the Restoration as a canon of Gloucester.

Iambic, 8 8. 7 5. Irregular. Unique.

MUSIC. WONDER was composed by Arnold Bax especially for the enlarged *Songs of Praise* (1931). It is clearly founded on the style of the early psalm-tunes, but has some individual touches in rhythm and expression.

108 Lord, when we bend before thy throne.

J. D. Carlyle, 1759–1804.

This has become too widely known in the Church of England to be omitted. It appeared in six verses, as 'A Hymn Before Public Worship', in Fawcett's *Collection of Psalms and Hymns by Various Authors* (1802), when Professor Carlyle was Fawcett's neighbour as Chancellor of Carlisle, and attended the church of which Fawcett was vicar, St. Cuthbert's.

C.M.

MUSIC. HUNNYS is from *Seven Sobs of a Sorrowfull Soule for Sinne comprehending those seven Psalmes of the Princelie Prophet David commonlie called Pœnitential . . . by William Hunnis one of the Gentlemen of hir Majesties honourable Chapell, and maister to the children of the same, &c.* (1583). The present tune is from the second part of the little volume, which bears a separate title-page *A Handfull of Honisuckles. Gathered by William Hunnis, &c.*, where it is set to 'Certeine short & pithie praiers unto Iesus Christ our Saviour', the first of which begins 'O Iesu meeke, o Iesu sweet'. It is a sincere, innocent little tune, well suited to the childlike simplicity of the original words.

109 Lord, who hast made me free.

G. W. Briggs.

Written, in order to carry the tune, by one who has done much for the new movement in hymnody.

Iambic, 6 6. 7 7. 7 7. Unique.

MUSIC. REGNART (AUF MEINEN LIEBEN GOTT) was originally set by Jacob Regnart, in 1574, to a song beginning 'Venus du und dein kind', as follows:

In J. Schein's *Cantional* (1627) it is found, set to the hymn 'Auf meinen lieben Gott', in virtually the same form as the present version, which appeared in the *Chorale Book for England* (1863).

The original tune has here undergone a complete transformation, both in form and feeling. In its new dress, however, it still shows an agreeable freedom of rhythm, and, apart from this, a certain ease and independence, which distinguishes it from the severity of many chorales.

110 My God, I love thee; not because.

17th cent. S.P.V.

Not by Francis Xavier after all; and if this had been then known, Caswall would probably not have translated it, since it is not a good Latin poem, though his rendering is perhaps the best verse he made. References to the latest researches into the source are given in Dr. Moffat's *Handbook to the Church Hymnary* (1927). The original is printed in *Coeleste Palmetum* (Köln, 1669), and is a version of a Spanish sonnet of unknown origin. Caswall's translation appeared in his *Lyra Catholica* (1849). He ended the first stanza with '*Must burn eternally*', which is literal enough. We have endeavoured to make the version a little more Christian by reducing its egoism; but otherwise Caswall remains. He wrote: ver. 2, l. 1, '*Thou, O my Jesus, thou didst me*', and '*me*' in l. 3; ver. 3, l. 3, 'and all for *me*'; ver. 4, l. 4, '*Or of escaping* Hell'. The Spanish sonnet begins: 'No me mueve, mi Dios, para quererte'. The Latin:

O Deus ego amo te,
nec amo te ut salves me,
aut quia non amantes te
aeterno punes igne.

and farther on:

Cur igitur non amem te,
O Jesu amantissime,
non ut in caelo salves me,
aut ne aeternum damnes me.

and so on, in schoolboy fashion.

C.M.

MUSIC. SOLOMON is an adaptation of the air 'What though I trace each herb and flower' from Handel's *Solomon* (1748). It has assumed, in this metamorphosis, a guise indistinguishable from that of the formal psalm-tunes.

111 My spirit longs for thee. *John Byrom,*‡ 1692–1763.

By the author of 'Christians, awake', this was published in his posthumous *Miscellaneous Poems* (1773). He called it 'The desponding Soul's wish', and added an 'Answer', also in four chain verses, beginning 'Cheer up, desponding soul'. In the original the 1st line has 'longeth'; and the 3rd line is 'Although I be unworthy'. For John Byrom see under 73, as well as among the biographies.

Iambic, 6 6. 6 6, in the form called *chain verse* because of the repetition carrying one verse into another.

MUSIC. MAINZ (MARIA JUNG UND ZART) appeared first in *Ausserlesene Catholische, Geistliche Kirchengesänge von Pfingsten, biss zum Advent &c.* (Cologne, 1623). It is found in many later collections, with some variation in the last two lines, the present version of melody and harmony being from *Psalteriolum Harmonicum Sacrarum Cantilenarum, &c.* (1642).

112 O for a closer walk with God. *W. Cowper,* 1731–1800.

In Dec. 1769, Mrs. Unwin, 'the chief of blessing I have met with in my journey', was seriously ill; and Cowper, in his 'sharp trial', nerving himself for the surrender that he dreaded, wrote these lines, and sent them to another friend explaining his distress—'O for no will but the will of my heavenly Father!' and continuing: 'I began to compose the verses yesterday morning before daybreak but fell asleep at the end of the first two lines: when I awaked again, the third and fourth were whispered to my heart in a way which I have often experienced.' Dr. John Ker, in his *Letters* (p. 320), says that on a visit to Olney in 1880, he heard from the owner of the garden and summer-house, where Cowper used to write, a tradition that 'The windows of an old shoemaker's cottage, now in ruins, looked into it, and the old man at his work used to hum the tune of "Ludlow". Cowper was taken with it, and wrote the hymn . . . to suit it, and walked up and down often to hear it sung.' It was first published in Conyer's *Collection of Psalms and Hymns* (1772), reprinted in Toplady's *Psalms and Hymns* (1776), and in the *Olney Hymns* (1779), where it had for title, 'Walking with God'. It is based on Gen. 5 : 24, 'And Enoch walked with God'.

C.M.

MUSIC. CAITHNESS, from *The Psalmes of David, &c.* (Edinburgh, Hart's heirs, 1635), is one of the 31 Common Tunes appearing in this edition of the Scottish Psalter. A smooth tune, with an elegant contour; it is noticeable that the stepwise movement is only twice interrupted throughout its length, and then in parallel positions. It is very regularly built in alternate lines of analogous construction, the 2nd and 4th by inversion. A very satisfying tune is the result.

113 O for a heart to praise my God. *C. Wesley*, 1707–88.

From the *Hymns and Sacred Poems* (1742), in eight stanzas, this is one of the most widely used of Charles Wesley's hymns. It is based on the Prayer Book version of Psalm 51 : 10.

C.M.

MUSIC. STOCKTON, by T. Wright, organist of Stockton Church, 1797–1818, was first printed in the original edition of *Hymns Ancient and Modern* (1861), with the melody of the last line altered. It is here given in its original form. It may be profitably compared with the last tune; its angularity (eight movements by leap) gives it an air of determined energy, while its build, less regular than that of 'Caithness', adds to this effect.

114 O help us, Lord! Each hour of need.

H. H. Milman, 1791–1868.

First published in Heber's posthumous *Hymns* (1827), in six stanzas, Milman reduced it to four in his *Selection of Psalms and Hymns* (1837), so that each verse begins with the same words; and in this form it became very popular. It was set down in Heber's book for the Second Sunday in Lent as based on the Gospel for that day, the story of the Syro-Phoenician woman, with which, however, it has little in common. All the hymns in Heber's collection were intended to be sung after the Nicene Creed and before the Sermon.

C.M.

MUSIC. BEDFORD is found in several undated books of the early 18th century. Probably the earliest of these is *The Divine Musick Scholar's Guide, wth the Famous Mr. Tho. Ravenscroft's Psalm Tunes in four parts . . . Collected and Printed by Francis Timbrell.* In this volume the tune is printed twice, first to Psalm 27 and second to Psalm 84. The latter is headed 'Bedford tune. By Wm. Wheal'. It is in three parts, Cantus, Medius, and Bassus, the melody being as in the present edition.

As set to Psalm 27, it is headed 'Bedford Tune', without name of composer, the melody of the third line being as follows:

The British Museum catalogue gives '1715?' as the date of Timbrell's book. This is probably too early, but a copy formerly in the possession of Sir John Stainer contains the inscription 'Thomas Bradford ejus liber, 1723'.

In *A Choice Collection of Psalm Tunes, Hymns and Anthems . . . Collected and Printed by Michael Broom, Singing Master, Isleworth, Middlesex*, the tune appears again set to Psalm 84. It is headed 'Bedford Tune, by W. Wale, organist of Bedford, B. of M.' and the melody is the same as in the setting to Psalm 27 in Timbrell's book. Broom's book is also undated, but a copy in the Ewing Library, Glasgow, has the autograph of a former owner and the date 1731. In Matthew Wilkins's *Book of Psalmody* (undated, but probably about 1730) the tune is set to Psalm 84, the melody being the same as in the setting to that psalm in Timbrell. Mr. Havergal says in his *Old Church Psalmody* that he had found the tune in the *Psalm-Singer's Magazine* (1729). This has not been verified, as no copy of this book can now be discovered. In all the older psalmodies and in most modern books the tune is in triple time (sometimes without the syncopation at the end of the 1st and 3rd lines). Probably its first appearance in common time is in William Gardiner's *Sacred Melodies* (1812). Here it is set to the hymn 'Our God, our help in ages past', the melody being as follows:

In his *Music and Friends* (1838) Gardiner gives information as to the sources of some of his Sacred Melodies, and says, regarding the above: 'This fine old tune was written by Wm. Wheal, organist of Bedford. Originally printed in the key of F and in triple time, I have changed the key to D and written it in common time, a measure that is more stately and better accords with that solemn grandeur in which it is disposed to move.' This opinion, however, is completely mistaken.

For over a hundred years the bells of St. Paul's Church, Bedford, where Weale (or Wheal, or Wale) was organist from about 1715, rang out this famous tune.

The alternative version (fa-burden) was written by E. C. Bairstow especially for the enlarged *Songs of Praise* (1931).

115 O let him whose sorrow.

H. S. Oswald, 1751–1834. *Tr. F. E. Cox.*‡

Wem in Leidenstagen
  Alle Trost steht fern,
Der vertrau' sein Klagen
  Seinem Gott und Herrn.

Three or four of Oswald's hundred hymns have found their way into German books, and one was introduced into English collections by Miss Cox, whose work has been generally altered, though her ver. 5, with its threadbare rhyme of 'languish' and 'anguish' survived. Our ver. 4, l. 4 is altered from 'Heart and courage fail' (with 'Should' for 'When' in l. 2); those other tired rhymes, 'sadness' and 'gladness', have been given a rest in our ver. 5, which ran before: 'All our woe and sadness, In this world below, Balance not the gladness We in heaven shall know.' Our last stanza began in Miss Cox's version, '*When thy* gracious'; and had '*Crowns thee*', and '*Fills thee*' in ll. 3 and 4. The hymn was sung at the funeral, 11 May 1882, of Lord Frederick Cavendish, Chief Secretary for Ireland, after his murder in Phoenix Park, Dublin. For such an occasion it was well fitted; but for ordinary congregations it is perhaps hardly in place even among the lachrymose little group that we are now annotating. It appeared first as 14 verses in Oswald's *Letzte Mittheilungen* (1826), and was noted as 'For the suffering'.

Trochaic, 6 5. 6 5. D.

MUSIC. SUTTON VALENCE was written by S. L. Russell especially for the enlarged *Songs of Praise* (1931). This is a rather unusual, and very attractive tune, well meriting inclusion among the hymns in frequent use.

DUN ALUINN is a setting of an Irish folk-song melody in 6/4 time, noted in Co. Clare, and adapted by 'The Irish Guild of the Church'. The change, though somewhat altering its character to a greater severity, has not destroyed its individuality. It is marked 'rather slow', but this must not be exaggerated.

116 O Lord, turn not away thy face.

J. Marckant (*Old Version*, 1560).

The oldest English hymn (apart from the metrical Psalms) in our book, this owes its use to the fact that it has been sung in church ever since 1560, when it appeared among the 'Songs' appended to the *Old Version* of Sternhold and Hopkins (see 433, and cf. 123) first in Daye's edition, often called *Day's Psalter*. All the other supplementary matter of the *Old Version* is now forgotten. In the present writer's copy, London, 1607, there are 23 such pieces nearly all with their special tunes, the *Veni Creator* in C.M., metrical versions of the Prayer Book Canticles—including the Athanasian Creed!—our hymn, which was then called 'The Lamentation of a Sinner' (in 1561, it was called 'The Humble suit of a Sinner') as no. 9, followed by another Lamentation (the wickedness of the Elizabethans and Jacobeans was their constant preoccupation, at least in church, and the religious verse of the period overflows with lamentation). Next are paraphrases of the Lord's Prayer, Decalogue, and Creed; a hymn before the Sermon, a hymn for Peace, headed '*Da pacem Domine*' ('Give peace', by Archbishop Grindal, from the German '*Gieb Fried zuu nser Zeit, O Herr*'), another 'Complaint of a sinner', and a 'Lamentation', a very long 'Thanksgiving after the receiving of the Lord's Supper'; then the hymn (based on Luther) beginning:

> Preserve us Lord by thy dear word,
> From Turk and Pope defend us Lord,
> Which both would thrust out of his throne.
> Our Lord Jesus Christ thy dear son.

and two short hymns to be sung before Morning and Evening Prayer.

This should be compared with the contents of *The Supplement* to the *New Version*, which is described under 82. The importance of the subject is great; for it shows that hymns were authorized and sung, not only before and after service (and as 'the Anthem' after the Third Collect) but also before the sermon and at Communion, in fact very much as they are sung to-day. But it must be confessed that the standard of these pieces is not high. Marckant (or Market or Maquaunt) seems to have survived because of his merit; for this hymn was included, in an altered form, in *The Supplement* of the *New Version*; though it must be remembered that the *New Version* made way slowly, at first only in London, and the *Old* was still used in the villages throughout the 18th century.

Marckant was appointed incumbent of Great Clacton, in 1559, the year following Queen Elizabeth's accession. In the edition of the Psalter of 1565, the Lamentation (then in 11 verses) is attributed to him, together with 4 psalms. The version in the 6th edition of *The Supplement* (1708) begins:

O Lord, turn not thy face from me,
  Who lie in woful state,
Lamenting all my sinful life
  Before thy mercy gate.

As so often, the new version is not any better than the old. The change to the first person singular is distinctly for the worse: we often evade amendment by exaggerating our offences.

C.M.

MUSIC. ST. MARY is set to the second psalm in *Llyfr y Psalmau, wedi eu cyfansoddi ar fesur cerdd, yn Gymraeg* (1621), the Welsh Metrical Translation of the Psalms by Archdeacon Prys. There the 2nd line reads thus:

There is no B flat in the signature, so that the tune is apparently in the Dorian mode, the B in the 1st line remaining natural. As, however, the music printing in the volume is very faulty the omission of the flat may be accidental. The tune is found in its present form in Playford's *Book of Psalms* (1677).

The alternative version (fa-burden) by Geoffrey Shaw appeared in the *Tenor Tune Book* (1917).

It is a forcibly angular tune with a mien of importunate urgency which gives it a marked personality.

117 O thou from whom all goodness flows.

T. Haweis, 1734–1820, *and others.*

A twopenny tract of 1791 on the death of a certain Mr. Browne of Bristol is the earliest source of this, which had probably appeared already in some magazine. Haweis, who was a prominent Evangelical, assistant preacher to Martin Madan at the Lock Hospital, London, and chaplain to Lady Huntingdon, himself published the hymn in his *Carmina Christo* (1792). After appearing in several collections, it was included in (Montgomery and) Cotterill's famous *Selection* of 1819 (see 71); and, as Montgomery included it in the same form, with the two last verses added, in his *Christian Psalmist* (1825), it is probable that these verses, 5 and 6, were by him. Haweis' original had varied each verse-ending (e.g. ver. 2: 'In love remember me'), Montgomery has made each the same, 'Good Lord, remember me'; and in this perhaps inferior form, it became familiar. The 'others' are therefore Montgomery and ourselves. We have recast the last verse; but otherwise only a few words are altered, vv. 1–4 being from Haweis, and 5–6 by Montgomery.

Henry Martyn, in his *Diary* for 23 Aug. 1811, wrote that the Mullah Aga Muhammad Hussan was a 'very sensible candid man', who 'has nothing to find fault with in Christianity except the divinity of Christ'. It is this doctrine, he says, that exposes him to their sneers which—

are more difficult to bear than the brickbats which the boys sometimes throw at me: however both are an honour of which I am not worthy. How many times in the day have I occasion to repeat the words,

> If on my face for thy dear name
> Shame and reproaches be,
> All hail reproach, and welcome shame,
> If thou remember me.

On 12 June, next year, the year of his death in Persia, he tells how one of the Viziers told him to say 'God is good, and Muhammad is the prophet of God'; but he replied 'God is good, and Jesus is the Son of God'. They were fiercely enraged and cried, 'What will you say when your tongue is cut out for this blasphemy?' Martyn went out to spend the rest of the day in the heat and dirt, comforting himself with the same hymn.

C.M.

MUSIC. OLIVER, by Oliver A. King, was composed for *The Hymnary* (1872), where it was unnamed, the present name 'Oliver', being attached to it for *Songs of Praise*. The structural correspondence is between the two pairs of lines (the 1st line being parallel to the 2nd, and the 3rd to the 4th), the sum of movement of the 1st pair being inverted in the 2nd, forming a solid tune of a very regular shape.

118 Shepherd divine, our wants relieve. *C. Wesley*, 1707–88.

Appeared first in the second selection of John and Charles Wesley's hymns, *Hymns and Sacred Poems* (1740), the assumption being that it is by Charles. See 191.

C.M.

MUSIC. ATTERCLIFFE is from William Mather's *Sacred Music consisting of Twenty Six Psalm & Hymn Tunes . . . composed in an Easy Style for the Children of Charity Schools by William Mather, Organist of St. Paul's & St. James's Churches, Sheffield, &c.* (no date. 1802?). It is there marked 'Lively' and set to Psalm 23, 'My Shepherd is the living Lord'. It is here harmonized by Martin Shaw and well sustains the original marking.

119 Take up thy cross, the Saviour said. *C. W. Everest*,‡ 1814–77.

Charles William Everest, afterwards rector of an Episcopal church in Connecticut, published this when he was 19 in his *Visions of Death, and other Poems* (1833). Brought into popularity by the original edition of *Hymns Ancient and Modern* (1861), which took it, already in an altered form, from an earlier collection, this is one of those hymns of poor quality which have to be always changed in order to make them possible for use—ver. 4, l. 2, for instance, was originally, 'And calmly sin's wild deluge brave'. Our version follows the original, with some of the common alterations, but rejects the change of 'Upon a cross on Calvary's hill' into 'To save thy soul from death and hell', for which the young author was not responsible.

L.M.

MUSIC. DAS LEIDEN DES HERRN has been long associated in Germany with the hymn 'Da Jesus in den Garten ging', but it is not known in what book it first appeared. According to Baümker the melody is an old one. It is given in Erk and Böhme's *Deutsche Liederhort* (1893–4), where it is stated that the melody was widespread, 'orally', in Germany in 1840, and the authors of that work conjecture that the tune is possibly of the 17th century.

120 Thou say'st, 'Take up thy cross'.

Francis Turner Palgrave, 1824–97.

Palgrave, who was Professor of Poetry in the University of Oxford from 1885 to 1895, published this first in *Macmillan's Magazine* (1861), and afterwards in his *Hymns* (1867). Palgrave's work was used in the more literary collections of the period, such as the *Marlborough College*, Thring's, Horder's, and the *Westminster Abbey* books.

S.M.

MUSIC. WIRKSWORTH appeared in *A Book of Psalmody containing Variety of Tunes for all the Common Metres of the Psalms in the Old and New Versions, and others for Particular Measures . . . all set in Four Parts, within such a compass as will most naturally suit the voices in Country Churches, yet may be sung in Three or Two without any Disallowances. By John Chetham* (1718). Here the tunes are not named, and no composers are given. The present tune is set to Psalm 50, as follows:

In the 3rd edition, 1724, of the same book, the last line is altered to

The present form of the tune is derived from *A Book of Psalm Tunes with variety of Anthems in Four Parts . . . By James Green* (5th ed., 1724) through the *Wesleyan Hymn Book* (1847). As it stands it is of exceedingly simple construction, being wholly built on the first four notes.

ST. EDMUND is found in *Parochial Harmony; consisting of a Collection of Psalm-Tunes . . . by William Riley, Principal Teacher of Psalmody to the Charity Schools in London, Westminster and Parts adjacent* (London, 1762). It is there marked 'St. Edmund's Tune by Mr. Edmd Gilding', and set to

Psalm 67, ver. 3 ('Let diff'ring nations join') as follows:

The present form is a slightly simplified version, the original being more characteristic of its century, and less sedate. Both versions have an agreeable air of unpretentiousness.

121 To my humble supplication. *Joseph Bryan* (*c.* 1620).

A cento from a poem by Bryan (wrongly attributed in Farr's *Select Poetry* (1845) to Francis Davison), made by the editor of the *English Hymnal* in order to carry a tune which otherwise Vaughan Williams could not have included in the book. It is from a manuscript, *c.* 1620, in the British Museum (*Harl.* 6930, f. 67). Nothing is known of Bryan, except that he made some metrical Psalms.

Trochaic, 8 8. 7 7. D. The first couplet in each stanza thus has double rhymes, and the tune covers two stanzas. Unique.

MUSIC. MON DIEU, PRÊTE-MOI L'OREILLE is from the *Genevan Psalter* (1543), being there composed, or adapted, by L. Bourgeois for the 86th Psalm. A fine tune, the first two lines being paralleled, by inversion, by the 5th and 6th, with the others as a kind of refrain. Sung at a very moderate pace it has a noble and stately sound.

122 When the unquiet hours depart.
George William Russell, ('*A.E.*').

First printed in *The Earth Breath, and other Poems*, 1897.

L.M.

MUSIC. PLAISTOW is from *Hymns, &c. used at the Magdalen Chapel* (*c.* 1760). It is a straightforward tune, serious, but not sombre, which, however, must be sung slowly for its full effect to be obtained.

123 Wilt thou forgive that sin, where I begun.
John Donne, 1573–1631.

Dr. Donne's greatness, both as a poet and as a maker of prose of unparalleled magnificence, has been increasingly recognized during the present century. He frequently had this fine hymn (one of two published in his *Poems*, 1633) sung by the choir of St. Paul's when he was Dean, which is another instance that hymns were not considered unlawful, even when they were not in the authorized collections. In the *English Hymnal*, which introduced this to ordinary use, a slight alteration was made; but now that it is known, there seems every reason to return to the archaic 'I begun', for 'began' of the 1st line. The hymn proved to be of particular value to the musical editor, who could not otherwise have included the tune. It is of course a play upon the Dean's name, and shows that he pronounced it 'Dunn'. John Wesley quoted 'I have a sin of fear' during the storm on his return from America, 1738.

Iambic, 10 10. 10 10. 8 4. Unique.

MUSIC. DRESDEN (SO GIEBST DU) is from *Geist und Lehr-reiches Kirchen- und Hauss-Buch, &c.* (Dresden, 1694). It is also found in Schemelli's *Musicalisches Gesangbuch* (1736), with J. S. Bach's figured bass. In both the 2nd line ends thus:

Apart from this, the present version is J. S. Bach's.

This noble tune, beautifully balanced and proportioned, maintains throughout its considerable length a curve of stately magnificence. Its grandeur needs no comment.

PASSIONTIDE

124 A voice upon the midnight air. *James Martineau*, 1805–1900.

Appeared first in *Hymns for the Christian Church and Home*, 1840.

Dr. Vernon Bartlet, in his *Commentary on St. Mark* (*Century Bible*, 1922), says that the spirit of Gethsemane is admirably caught in these verses by the philosopher and theologian Dr. Martineau.

L.M.

MUSIC. BABYLON'S STREAMS is first found as a psalm-tune in *Harmonia Perfecta* (1730), a collection edited by Nathaniel Gawthorn. But the melody comes from Campian's *First Booke of Ayres* (1613). It derives its name from the fact that it was set to a metrical version of Psalm 137, beginning,

> As by the streams of Babilon
> Farre from our native soyle we sat.

A fine, solemn tune, in rhythm and style reminiscent of some of the narrative ballad tunes (cf. 'Danby', 16). Noticeable is the metrical change in the last two lines, as if a sudden impulse drove the tune to its end.

125 Drop, drop, slow tears. *Phineas Fletcher*, 1582–1650.

It is not easy to say whether the beauty of this little lament, which may be called either a hymn or an anthem for Good Friday and Easter Even, is most due to the delicate phrases or to the tune with which it was so happily wedded in the *English Hymnal*, whence we have taken both. It is to be found in the poet's *Piscatorie Eclogs, and other Poeticall Miscellanies*, 1633.

The beautiful use to which the thought of tears is put in this poem may be contrasted with the crude insistence on blood that began in the 18th century to be out of all measure, and continued in the 19th. Just as the concrete imagination of the Hanoverian period caused the piercing metaphor, in the Apocalypse, of the Lamb to be used as if it were a mere name, even by Cowper (e.g. 112)—and the more so because it made convenient false rhymes with words like 'name' and 'frame'—so the theological metaphor of Blood, once mystically understood, came to be used with a familiar literalism that is repellent to a more sensitive age. Again it was the gentle Cowper who was among the worst offenders: all attempts to defend 'There is a fountain filled with blood' are deteated by the physical realism of the next line, 'Drawn from Emmanuel's veins'. There are but few traces left in our book of this fault (cf. 595), which may be partly due to atavism and partly to mistaken ideas of atonement. In recent years all schools of thought have quietly dropped from their hymnals much that was once prominent. But enough remains in some quarters to repel many people from public worship. The harm that is still being done should not be ignored. We therefore quote (from *Salvation Solos*) an extreme modern example:

> I'll plunge into the Saviour's blood,
> Another dip, another dip!
> Another dip will do me good,
> I'll have another dip.

We print this with some reluctance; and we refrain from other and worse examples from other sources. It is thus really unique in this book.

Iambic, 10 10. in the music, but as printed it is 4 6. 4 6; and the first four words are really spondees.

MUSIC. SONG 46 is the first half of the melody, by Orlando Gibbons, to a hymn for Christmas Day in *The Hymnes and Songs of the Church* (see 29), but it forms, perfectly satisfactorily, a complete tune in itself.

Although 'SONG 46' is accepted as the name of the tune in modern usage, the number is apparently due to a misprint, the tune being originally set to No. 45 in Wither's collection (1623).

126 Into the woods my master went. *Sidney Lanier*, 1842–81.

First published in the *Poems* (New York, 1901) of this short-lived musician and poet, this was reprinted in the *Methodist Hymnal* (New York, 1905) a generation after his death.

Irregular, 8 6. 8 6. 8 8 8. 7. Unique of course.

MUSIC. MANTEGNA, by R. Vaughan Williams, was written especially for this hymn in the enlarged *Songs of Praise* (1931). It is an unusual, but beautiful tune; its unfamiliar idiom, especially among hymn-tunes, is not difficult to grasp, once the inertia of novelty is overcome. Its very personal mood excludes it from those tunes which can be fitted to a variety of words, but to the present poem it is perfectly adapted.

127 My song is love unknown. *Samuel Crossman*, *c.* 1624–84.

Crossman, who died a few weeks after being made Dean of Bristol, had published a few sermons, two of which were for the 'Days of public Humiliation for the execrable Murder of King Charles I', 1681, and a small pamphlet, *The Young Man's Meditation, or some few Sacred Poems upon Select Subjects, and Scriptures. By Samuel Crossman, B.D.* (London, 1664—the year before the Plague.) From it are taken the well-known 'Jerusalem on high' (197), and this, which was reprinted in the *Anglican Hymn Book* (1868). The whole pamphlet had been reprinted by D. Sedgwick in 1863. Crossman's work has a strong and naïve directness and charm, which must have made his poetry sound a little old-world when it was published, and perhaps makes us appreciate it the more to-day.

This hymn of Crossman's illustrates the fact that 17th-century Britain was free from that unwholesome treatment of the Passion which is shown, for instance, in the Spanish sculpture of that age, and has appeared more than once in certain countries and periods. It was never worse than among Count Zinzendorf's Moravians, among whom a veritable spirit of sadism and something like that of the cannibal appears. We will not stain these pages by quoting examples: two are given in Dr. Louis F. Benson's learned lectures on the *English Hymn*, p. 267, others, too indecent for him to print, are described in Southey's *Life of Wesley*; they can all be seen in the Moravian *Collection* of 1754, and in two collections which John Wesley considered it 'his bounden Duty to publish to all the World', in 1749 and 1750, 'as a standing Proof that there is no folly too gross for those who are wise above that is written'. He had at first been attracted by the fervour of the Moravians; and, with his imperfect knowledge of German, had only partially apprehended their doctrine and imagery as it was then. Charles Wesley caught some of their style; but, says Dr. Benson, 'John Wesley maintained a close watch upon his brother's hymns for anything in the amatory way; and this presumably explains the omission of "Jesu, lover of my soul" from the Methodist Collection of 1780'.

Error on the other side was more common three centuries ago, when extreme flatness was sometimes achieved, as in this from a Palm Sunday hymn by George Wither:

Possession of his House he got,
    The Marchants thence expelled;
And though the Priests were madde thereat,
    His Lectures there he held.
Oh, how should any be so dull,
    To doubt who this might be?
When they did things so wonderfull
    And workes so mighty see.

Iambic, 6 6. 6 6. 4 4. 4 4. With the four last lines treated as two, this is one of the metres used, to carry new tunes, in Sternhold and Hopkins, from the editions of 1561–2 onwards (6 6. 6 6. 8 8, see the Old 136th, 197, i; Croft's 136th, 657; Darwall's 148th, 701). All the new metres were called P.M. (Peculiar Measure), to distinguish them from the ordinary C.M., and the few L.M. and S.M. of the Psalter. Here is an example of an alternative version of Ps. 148, with the last lines printed as four 4s, in the *Old Version:*

Give laud unto the Lord,
From heav'n that is so hie:
Praise him in deed and word,
Above the starry Skie.
    And also yee,
His Angels all,
Armies royall,
    Praise him with glee.

MUSIC. LOVE UNKNOWN was composed by John Ireland for this hymn, and appeared in *Songs of Praise* (1925). It is an attractive tune of an unusual type among hymn-tunes, in the irregular rhythm often found in this composer's melodies. The last two lines are especially admirable.

RHOSYMEDRE is from *Original Sacred Music, Composed and Arranged by The Rev[d] John Edwards, B.A. Jesus College, Oxford* (London?, 1840?), where it is named 'Lovely', and ends with an extended 'Hallelujah'. Edwards published a second volume with the same title at Carnarvon in 1844. This tune, as some of the others in his volumes, shows the influence of the 18th-century Methodist hymn-tunes. With its air of precipitancy towards the end, the melody, as a whole, has a distinct flavour of its own.

128 O sacred head, sore wounded. *P. Gerhardt*, 1607–76, *based on* Salve caput cruentatum (*possibly by Arnulf von Loewen*, 1200–51). *Pr. Robert Bridges.*

Salve caput cruentatum
totum spinis coronatum,
conquassatum, vulneratum,
harundine verberatum,
facie sputis illita.

O Haupt voll Blut und Wunden,
Voll Schmerz bedeckt mit Hohn,
O göttlich Haupt umwunden
Mit einer Dornenkron'!
O Haupt, das andrer Ehren
Und Kronen würdig ist,
Sei mir mit frommen Zähren,
Sei tausendmal gegrüsst!

By the 13th century the crucifix was established throughout the Latin part of the Church, and there begin to appear what we may call 'crucifix hymns' and other devotions ('Attolle paulum lumina', *E.H.* 103, and 'Labente jam solis rota', *E.H.* 265, are later examples) inspired by contemplation of the painted roods, and in complete contrast to the unrealistic thought and mystical exultation of the earlier hymns, such as the 'Pange lingua' and 'Vexilla Regis', which immediately follow here. 'Salve caput' is the last of seven poems addressed, in a manner characteristic of the new spirit, to the limbs and head of Christ, as he hangs upon the cross. It used to be attributed, like 'Jesu dulcis memoria', to St. Bernard; but this seems to be an unsupported invention emanating from the monastery at Clairvaux. Arnulf is said to be more likely; but it looks later than Arnulf, and the manuscripts (which vary much) are none dated earlier than the 14th century. The Lutherans retained the crucifix; and the nature of German pietistic hymnody made it fitting that Gerhardt, the greatest Lutheran hymn-writer after Luther himself, should be the author of the free translation (more fervent and more Scriptural than the original) which is associated with so great a musical tradition. It appeared first in Crüger's *Praxis* (1656), in ten stanzas. There have of course been many translations: ours is what may rather be called a paraphrase from the *Yattendon Hymnal* (1899).

Lauxmann thinks there is a reference to Luther's words on the death of his daughter, Magdalen, 'Who dies thus, dies well'; indeed the closing verse is associated with the death of many eminent Germans. When Schwartz the missionary lay dying in Tanjore, his pupils sang in Tamil the last verses, while he joined in, as long as his breath endured; and when the great theologian, Ritschl, was dying he asked for the last verse to be read to him, though in his *History of Pietism*, he had criticized the undue stress laid by the earlier verses on the physical sufferings of the Saviour.

7 6. 7 6. D., the Iambic metre used so much in German hymns.

MUSIC. PASSION CHORALE is an adaptation of a melody from *Lustgarten Neuer Teutscher Gesäng . . . Componirt durch Hanns Leo Hassler von Nürmberg* (1601), where it is set to a secular song beginning 'Mein Gmüt ist mir verwirret', as follows:

In *Harmoniae Sacrae* (Görlitz, 1613) it is set to the hymn 'Herzlich thut nich verlangen', and in later books it is generally associated with 'O Haupt voll Blut und Wunden', of which the present hymn is a free translation. Bach used the chorale five times in his *St. Matthew Passion*, and the two versions here given are both his.

This great and famous chorale perhaps owes some of its renown to Bach's use of it, as already mentioned, but it is worthy of the honour he conferred upon it.

129 Sing, my tongue, the glorious battle.

Bishop Venantius Fortunatus, 530–609. *Tr. A. F.*

Pange, lingua, gloriosi
praelium certaminis
et super crucis tropaeum
dic triumphum nobilem,
qualiter redemptor orbis
immolatus vicerit.

Many inventions came from the monasteries; and it may or may not be true that Fortunatus wrote this to celebrate the occasion when Queen Radegund, having secured a fragment of the True Cross, deposited it in the Convent at Poitiers, which she had founded, and which she ruled. The original was in 10 stanzas, and was used after a while in many service books: there is a Mozarabic MS. of the 10th and two English Hymnaries of the 11th century in the British Museum which contain it. In the pre-Reformation Breviaries it was appointed for Passiontide, in two parts, as it is given in *E.H.* 95, 96, where the beliefs of the age can be easily unravelled—the reference in the 2nd verse of the full text to the legend that the seed of the forbidden tree was handed on through successive new trees from Adam, through Solomon and the Queen of Sheba, till it was used for the cross, which was subsequently 'invented' (i.e. discovered) by St. Helena. Ver. 3 in the original is still in the early theology of the atonement that held the field until St. Anselm—the bait and hook theory—that the Devil, in swallowing the bait (the human Saviour) swallowed the hook (the Cross); and this is more refined than the comparison to a mouse-trap, which was accepted even by St. Augustine. Simple congregations of the present day do not think of Piero della Francesca's frescoes at Arezzo when they sing 'Then another tree was chosen', nor are they troubled by:

> Thus the scheme of our salvation
> Was of old in order laid,
> That the manifold deceiver's
> Art by art might be outweighed,
> And the lure the foe put forward
> Into means of healing made.

But the editor of our version here thought it better to drop the idea that God cheated the Devil, deeply interesting though it is as showing how early theologians understood Christianity, and classical as the full hymn is in its splendour, with its plainsong setting. We therefore have omitted the above vv. 2 and 3, with ver. 4 of *E.H.* 95, and vv. 2, 4, 5 of 96; but the reader may like to be reminded of that strange and moving 4th verse in Neale's translation, the clashing consonants of which are borne triumphantly along by the surging plainsong melody:

> Bend thy boughs, O Tree of glory!
> Thy relaxing sinews bend;
> For awhile the ancient rigour
> That thy birth bestowed suspend;
> And the King of heavenly beauty
> On thy bosom gently tend!

Nothing could better illustrate the contrast between the rough but virile religion which, sharing in part their own limitations, tamed the barbarian invaders, and the increasingly morbid decadence of the Later Middle Ages.

The unrhymed trochaic verse of the Latin is followed, but with the use of alternate rhyming lines, in the translation, which is 8 7. 8 7. 8 7.

MUSIC. PLAINSONG is the proper melody (Sarum Mode iii) of this hymn, here harmonized by Martin Shaw (cf. 280). It is one of the most famous and beautiful of all these melodies.

GRAFTON is a French Church Melody to be found in *Chants Ordinaires de l'Office Divin* (Paris, 1881). It shows a considerable affinity with traditional popular melodies. Sung at its due speed, which should be rather slow, it is a very moving and expressive tune.

130 The royal banners forward go.

Bishop Venantius Fortunatus, 530–609. *Tr.* 1689, *&c.*, *S.P.V.*

> Vexilla regis prodeunt;
> fulget crucis mysterium,
> quo carne carnis conditor
> suspensus est patibulo.

This also, like 129, is associated with Queen Radegund; Gregory of Tours, writing not long afterwards in the 6th century, describes the ceremony, though without mentioning the hymn: 'Eufronius, bishop of Tours, came with his clergy, with much singing and gleaming of tapers and fragrance of incense, and in the absence of the bishop of the city, brought the holy relics to the monastery.' The Abbé Briand brings in the hymn and Fortunatus in person; but he wrote in 1887. The hymn was originally of 8 verses. The doxology and the verse 'O Cross, our one reliance' (*E.H.* 94. 6) were added for liturgical use, vv. 2–7 being used on Holy Cross Day in the Breviaries, and the whole hymn at Evensong in Passiontide. It occurs in manuscripts of the 8th and 9th centuries, and in the Durham *Rituale* of the 10th. Our free version is partly based on Neale, his fine opening lines being retained, and partly on the 17th-century translation in Blount's *Office of the Holy Week*, Paris, 1670, which was used in *Church Hymns* (new ed., 1903), as by Dryden (with a query), beginning, 'Abroad the regal banners fly'. But a version must be very free, if it is to be faithful to the truth. The original of ver. 3, for instance, is accurately rendered by Neale:

Fulfilled is all that David told
In true prophetic song of old;
Amidst the nations, God, saith he,
Hath reigned and triumphed from the tree.

The reference is to Psalm 96: 10; but neither in the Hebrew, the authentic Septuagint, the present Vulgate, nor of course in the English Versions, is there anything answering to this; though the interpolation, ἀπὸ ξύλου got in as early as the 2nd century, and 'a ligno' has survived in the Roman Breviary at Vespers of Sept. 14. The verse in our Prayer Book version is:

'Tell it out among the heathen that the Lord is King: and that it is he who hath made the round world so fast that it cannot be moved; and how that he shall judge the people righteously.'

Neale's translation (*E.H.* 94) also brings out the same fundamental belief in the old legend, and the atonement as a trick to 'spoil the spoiler of his prey', which we noted under 129. There are medieval parodies of the 'Pange lingua'; one describing the death (1312) of Piers Gaveston, the favourite of Edward II, reprinted in T. Wright, *Political Songs of England* (1839).

L.M.

MUSIC. PLAINSONG is the proper melody (Mode i) to this hymn from the *Sarum Antiphonal*, harmonized by J. H. Arnold. Another great melody, a worthy companion to the 'Pange lingua'. It is sung at Evensong on Passion Sunday and daily until Wednesday in Holy Week.

ANDERNACH is the melody set to this hymn in *Catholische Geistliche Gesänge* (Andernach, 1608). This book represented a departure from the plainsong type of melody in favour of others of a more popular kind. It contained Latin hymns with German translations, and original German hymns, and was produced by the Guild of St. Cecilia at Andernach, in the district of Coblenz on the Rhine. The present tune, however, shows that both in rhythm and melody, some of the influence of plainsong still remained; though it was only a general influence, and did not involve any particular correspondence with individual melodies. It is a powerful tune, of considerable dignity.

131 There is a green hill far away. *Mrs. C. F. Alexander*, 1823–95.

Like some other popular hymns, this was written for children and appropriated by adults. Mrs. Alexander composed a series on the Church Catechism for her Sunday School, and this was to illustrate the clause 'Suffered under Pontius Pilate, was crucified, dead, and buried' (see 174). The opening line is of course untrue. There is no statement in the Gospels that our Lord was crucified on a hill—only that it was at 'a place' called 'the Skull' (Lk. 23 : 33), of which name the word 'Calvary' is merely a latinization. It may have been so called because there was a slight rounded eminence; but it seems more likely that there were relics of former executions. And in any case the sun-bitten hills of Judaea are not green. It is in fact an example of the sentimental fallacy: Mrs. Alexander, when she went shopping in Derry, had to drive by a little grassy hill near the road, and she tells us that she used to fancy this was like 'Calvary'. It is a curious innocent example of the way facts come to be overlaid by tradition in much more serious matters. First published in her *Hymns for Little Children* (1848, for which Keble wrote a preface), it is based on the old ideas of the atonement, which were, as we have seen, modernist views in the time of St. Anselm. Especially was this the case with ver. 4 of the original five. Some one said to Mrs. Alexander that children would misunderstand 'Without' in the 2nd line of ver. 1; she therefore consented to the alteration 'Outside', reluctantly no doubt, since it turns the line into a jingle.

C.M.

MUSIC. HORSLEY is the third tune in *Twenty-Four Psalm Tunes and Eight Chants, composed by William Horsley* (1844), where, however, it has no name.

The alternative version (fa-burden) was written by Patrick Harvey especially for the enlarged *Songs of Praise* (1931).

This well-known tune, now inseparably associated with Mrs. Alexander's words, needs no comment.

132 We sing the praise of him who died. *T. Kelly*, 1769–1854.

First appeared in *Hymns by Thomas Kelly* (Dublin, 1815), in five verses. This is therefore as he wrote it, the last couplet having been altered by himself in later editions from:

'Tis all that sinners want below;
'Tis all that angels want above.

Lord Selborne said in 1866 that it 'is distinguished by a calm subdued power, rising gradually from a rather low to a very high key', and he says it was worthy of Montgomery. Kelly wrote over 700 hymns.

L.M.

MUSIC. BRESLAU is from *As hymnodus sacer. Zwölff Geistliche anmuhtige und theils newe Gesänge* . . . (Leipzig, 1625), where it is set to the hymn 'Herr Jesu Christ, meins Lebens Licht', in the following form:

Later German books show variations in every line. The present form is that adopted by Mendelssohn in the oratorio *St. Paul.*

The alternative version (fa-burden) by H. V. Hughes appeared in the *Tenor Tune Book* (1917).

This is one of the greatest of the German chorales; its dignity equals that of 'Dresden', or the 'Passion Chorale', but it is pervaded, not with an emotion of exaltation or passionate grief, but with a spirit of noble serenity.

133 When I survey the wondrous cross. *I. Watts*, 1674–1748.

Watts wrote over 600 hymns, of which many are naturally not of high quality, 'prosaic and mechanical', as Dr. Louis F. Benson says; but in his moments of inspiration he belongs to the great line of English poets. Poetry endures; and that of Watts is more used now in the Church of England than 30 years ago (there are 14 to his name in *Songs of Praise*). Matthew Arnold thought 'When I survey' the finest hymn in the language. He heard it sung at Sefton Park Presbyterian Church, Liverpool, on the last Sunday of his life; and, shortly before his sudden death in 1888, he was overheard repeating the 3rd verse.

This poem belongs to the birth of the modern hymnal; it appeared in the first of 'young Mr. Watt's' books (i.e. the first of his major works: he had published *Horae Lyricae* in 1705) *Hymns and Spiritual Songs*, which we have discussed on p. xvi. Since 1892 three copies of this book of 1707 have been found, and the original 2nd line is discovered to have been:

Where the young Prince of Glory dy'd.

We can only suppose that, as with 131, some one who had no feeling for poetry persuaded the young author to change it; for he did so in the enlarged edition of 1709. We should have liked to restore the finer and more original line of the 1st edition; but, after all, the alteration was the author's own and has been sung for over two centuries. It was Whitefield, in his *Supplement* of 1757, who first popularized the 4-stanza version (omitting our starred verse). Then came an orgy of emendations; of one of the 'improved' versions Lord Selborne said in 1866: 'There is just enough of Watts left here to remind one of Horace's saying, that you may know the remains of a poet even when he is torn to pieces'; but Julian notes that the versions in the books of Cotterill, E. Bickersteth, Keble, and others were as bad. *Hymns Ancient and Modern* was more merciful; it added a rather trite doxology, and followed the common custom of omitting ver. 4; but otherwise it only made the following changes: ver. 2, l. 2, 'Cross' for 'death'; ver. 3, l. 2, 'mingled' for 'mingling'; ver. 5, l. 2, 'offering' for 'present'. 'Cross' was as old as Madan, 1760; the others were already in some 19th-century books, while 'tribute' had also been substituted for 'present'; for there is nothing more common with poor writers than the desire to change strong, simple words for those that sound more pretentious. The oddest example of a hymn, not only mutilated but turned upside down, is Basil Woodd's version, *c.* 1810, which begins this hymn with 'Arise, my soul, with wonder see'. Cf. 74 and 598.

In *Adam Bede*, Dinah Morris, dying at a great age, exclaims, 'How good the Lord is; praise his holy name!' then she repeats 'When I survey'. The description is said to be that of an actual occurrence.

L.M.

MUSIC. ROCKINGHAM is from *The Psalms of David for the Use of Parish Churches. The Music Selected, Adapted and Composed by Edward Miller, Mus. Doc.* (1790), where it occurs seven times. It is named 'Rockingham' and headed 'Part of the melody taken from a hymn tune'. Dr. Miller may have adapted the tune from one named 'Tunbridge', which is found in a *Supplement to Psalmody in Miniature* published by A. Williams about 1780. In Scotland it seems to have appeared first in the collections edited by R. A. Smith and John Wilson. It is there attached to Paraphrase xxxv, and called 'Communion', doubtless from the fact that this paraphrase is almost invariably sung on Communion occasions. In both these books the 3rd note in the 2nd line of the melody is flattened, but this reading has now been universally dropped in favour of the original. In *Harmonia Sacra* (1835?) the tune is attributed to 'Emanuel Bach', but the grounds for this ascription are obscure. This beautiful and famous tune is now always united with the present words.

The alternative version (fa-burden) by Geoffrey Shaw appeared in the *Tenor Tune Book* (1917).

134 When my love to God grows weak.

J. R. Wreford (1837), *S. Longfellow* (1848).

This is one of those hymns that, without any very special distinction, have survived and are now spreading because of their usefulness. The original by John Reynell Wreford appeared in Beard's Unitarian *Hymns* of 1837, but was not thought good enough for inclusion in the American Unitarian *Book of Hymns* (1848), till it had been re-written by Samuel Longfellow, the brother of the more famous Henry Wadsworth (see 8, 16, &c.): in this improved form it got into several of the better English books, notably Martineau's (1873), Thring's (1882), and Horder's (1884). Like other good hymns of the 19th century, its usefulness is largely due to its being nearer to the Gospel records, and therefore free from the theological presuppositions and emotional morbidity which disfigure so many Passion hymns, both Catholic and Protestant. Wreford, an Englishman, became a schoolmaster in Edgbaston, when his failing voice compelled him to give up his ministry at the New Meeting, Birmingham. That he had qualities which put him in advance of his age is shown by his other hymn, 'Lord, while for all mankind we pray', 320.

Trochaic, 7 7. 7 7.

MUSIC. SONG 13, by Orlando Gibbons, was set to a metrical paraphrase of part of the Song of Solomon (cf. 29). This simple but impressive tune begins with a lovely and tranquil phrase, of perfect shape, and the contour of the whole tune expresses the same deep sense of peace. Orlando Gibbons has here produced a small but faultless work of art.

135 All glory, laud, and honour.

St. Theodulph of Orleans, d. 821. *Tr. J. M. Neale.*‡

Gloria, laus, et honor tibi sit, rex Christe redemptor,
cui puerile decus prompsit Hosanna pium.

Israel tu rex, Davidis et inclyta proles,
nomine qui in Domini, rex benedicte, venis.

Telling the truth is an accomplishment of the modern era; but a few ascriptions have so far survived investigation, and this probably was really written by Theodulph, Bishop of Orleans, when in prison in the cloister at Angers. It cannot be true, however, that King Louis 'the Pious', taking part in the Palm Sunday procession, A.D. 821, and hearing the saint as he sang from the open window of his cell this hymn (just composed for the occasion), was so delighted that he set Theodulph free and restored him to his bishopric, ordering at the same time that the hymn to which they had listened should be henceforth sung on Palm Sunday—for a king could act as head of the Church in those days. It cannot be true; because

Theodulph was imprisoned (under suspicion over the plot of Bernard of Italy) in 818, and Louis was never in Angers after 818, and Theodulph was never restored to his see, but died in prison in 821. The hymn was soon used, however, in the Palm Sunday procession in the French and English rites, and is still used in the Roman, though the first 4 verses are no longer sung (as they were at Salisbury and York) by 7 boys at 'a high place' near the south door.

The original elegiacs consist of 39 couplets; but of these only the first 12 or 18 at the most appear in the various service books. Among the stanzas that were sung until the 17th century was this, as translated by Neale:

Be thou, O Lord, the rider,
  And we the little ass,
That to God's holy city
  Together we may pass.

When they sing this fine hymn, however, such a description of the congregation is undeserved. Neale's strong and simple version gives us 6 quatrains, the first of which is repeated as a chorus, instead of the 39 verses which a full translation would have provided; but this would have been none too long in old times, because the procession used to go out of doors; at Hereford, for instance, it went to the gates of the town, and when these were shut, 7 boys went to the top of the gate-house and there sang. The original is based on Pss. 24:7–10; 118:25–6; Mt. 21:1–17; and Lk. 19:37–8.

The Latin elegiacs (rendered in the same metre by W. J. Birkbeck, *E.H.* 621, based on Neale's elegiac translation in his *Medieval Hymns*, 1851) were translated by Neale into the familiar Iambic, 7 6. 7 6. D., in his *Hymnal Noted* (1854), and afterwards slightly revised.

MUSIC. ST. THEODULPH (VALET WILL ICH DIR GEBEN) comes from *Ein andächtiges Gebet . . . so wol ein tröstlicher Gesang, darinnen ein frommes Herz dieser Welt Valet gibet, &c.* (Leipzig, 1615), a small tract of six leaves containing the hymn by Herberger 'Valet will ich dir geben', and two melodies set to it by Melchior Teschner. Both are arranged for five voices. The present is the second of the two, and is as follows:

The substitution of C for A at the 11th note is found in the *Gothaer Cantional* (1648), and the melody appears in many later collections with slight variations in the outline. The present version of melody and harmony is J. S. Bach's. The well-known tune probably owes much of its popularity to the refrain, and also to the fact that the whole thing has a cheerful and festive air, in many ways reminiscent of some popular carols.

136 Come, faithful people, come away.

G. Moultrie (1867), *and others.*

There are two carols, 19th century both in words and music, which, to our mind, have the authentic character, and do not date. One of these is the American 'We three kings of Orient are' (*Oxford Book of Carols*, 195);

the other this English Palm Sunday carol. Gerard Moultrie's original appeared first in his *Hymns and Lyrics* (1867). We felt obliged to alter the statement, written when New Testament scholarship was in its infancy, that two beasts were used and that the Saviour rode upon a little foal. This involved changing the original (*E.H.* 619) ver. 3, 'An ass and foal tied shall ye see', and 'them'; then (omitting *E.H.* ver. 4) in our ver. 4 we alter 'found the ass' and 'on the colt their clothes'. In the last verse the last couplet of the original is: 'Arrayed in royalty of woe, Assumed for sinners here below.'

Iambic, 8 8 8. 7.

MUSIC. COME, FAITHFUL PEOPLE, melody by the Rev. C. Bicknell, appeared in the *English Hymnal* (1906), set to the present hymn. The tune is in the manner of many traditional melodies; it is itself a beautiful and very distinctive composition, with a most unusual ending out of the key, which gives it great individual significance.

137 Ride on! ride on in majesty! *Henry Hart Milman*, 1791–1868.

One of the very finest poems in our hymn-books, this was first published with Heber's posthumous *Hymns* (1827). Milman was among the great Deans of St. Paul's, well known as a poet, and even as a playwright (for his *Fazio* was a triumphant success at Covent Garden and was translated into Italian), before he published his *History of the Jews* in 1829 and his classic *History of Latin Christianity* in 1855. Being a real poem, 'Ride on' was too good for most of the 19th-century compilers: they altered ver. 1, l. 6, to 'O Saviour meek, pursue thy road', which is mere libretto verse, and even to 'With joyous throngs pursue thy road'; and in ver. 3 'the winged squadrons' were reduced to 'the angel armies'; others altered 'expects' in ver. 4; while some (even including *Church Hymns* in 1871) omitted the first stanza altogether.

When Heber received the manuscript of 'Ride on' for the collection in which he was trying to include the best living poets, he is said to have exclaimed, 'A few more hymns like this, and I need not wait for the help of Scott and Southey!'

L.M.

MUSIC. WINCHESTER NEW is from *Musicalisch Hand-Buch der Geistlichen Melodien a Cant. et Bass* (Hamburg, 1690), where the following form of the melody is set to the hymn 'Wer nur den lieben Gott lässt walten':

In Moore's *Psalm-Singer's Delightful Pocket Companion* (Glasgow, 1762) the tune appears in the following form, and is named 'Winchester':

this version being found also in earlier 18th-century collections under the names 'Swift German tune' and 'Frankfort'.

The present form is derived from Havergal's *Old Church Psalmody* (1847). The tune is now invariably connected with the present words.

The alternative version (descant) by Geoffrey Shaw appeared in the *Descant Hymn-Tune Book* (Bk. I, 1925).

138 In the place of sorrow, waiting. *A. F.*

In the Middle Ages a growing Mariolatry caused the tendency to concentrate on the sufferings of the Mother rather than of the Son. This was much helped in the 13th century by the new practice of displaying in the churches carved roods with Mary and John on either side. A still later iconology invented the Pietà, in which Christ is represented dead in his mother's lap; and this replaced the Entombment, in the Gospel account of which St. Mary does not occur. In the Synoptic Gospels indeed her presence at Jerusalem is not mentioned at all, a fact that weighs heavily with scholars at the present day. The 'Stabat mater' is the classical example of the Medieval tendency. The early date once assigned to it (it was even ascribed to Gregory the Great) has now given place to the 13th or 14th century. At first regarded with some wariness, it had crept into liturgical use at Breslau in 1414, and into a few other places later in the 15th century; but the Roman Missal or Breviary did not admit it till 1727, when it was inserted in the office of the Seven Dolours of the Virgin. It was never used in England. For these reasons it does not occur in our book. The best tunes have, however, been continued for Passiontide use by these new words; which endeavour to supply the need of a hymn about the actual scene of the crucifixion and the sufferings of Christ himself upon the Cross.

Trochaic, 8 8 7. D., and therefore with a preponderance of double rhymes.

MUSIC. STABAT MATER is the tune found in several printed and manuscript collections of the 18th century, set to 'Stabat mater dolorosa'. It goes back to the form in the *Mainz Gesangbuch* of 1661, which is as follows:

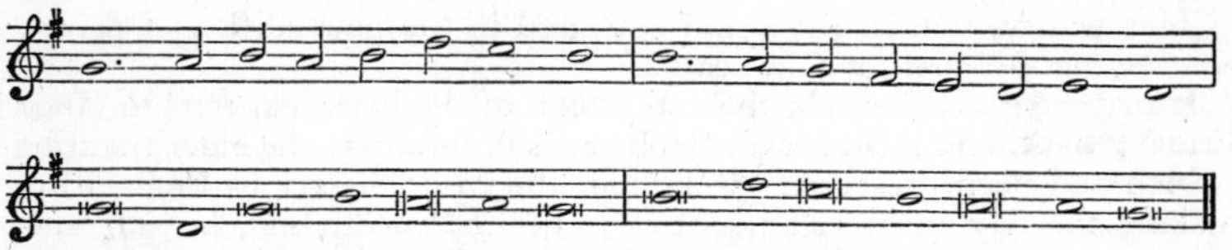

CORNER (CHRISTI MUTTER STUND VOR SCHMERZEN) is from G. Corner's *Gross Catolisch Gesangbuch, &c.* (1625), where it is set to the hymn 'Christi Mutter stund vor Schmerzen'.

Both these tunes have a 'feeling-tone' of pathos, difficult to define, but not due only to the association with the words; in the 1st tune it seems to lie mainly in the 2nd bar, in the 2nd tune chiefly in the last line, but it is here more diffused throughout the whole. The 2nd tune is perhaps the better; it must be taken very slowly, with also a clearly defined pulsation of the triple time.

139 It is finished! Christ hath known. *Gabriel Gillett.*

These lines, shapely and melodious, were written by Mr. Gillett for the *English Hymnal* (1906), in order to supply a worthy hymn on the saying, 'It is finished', and at the same time to carry Freylinghausen's great tune.

A rather intricate metre, unique in this book. Trochaic, 7 8. 8 7. 8 7. 8 7.

MUSIC. SEBASTIAN (JESU MEINES GLAUBENS ZIER) is the arrangement by J. S. Bach of a melody from Freylinghausen's *Neues Geistreiches Gesangbuch* (1714). It is found in Schemelli's *Musicalisches Gesangbuch* (1736).

140 O come and mourn with me awhile.

F. W. Faber,‡ 1814–63.

Faber's original, which first appeared in 12 verses in his *Jesus and Mary* (1849), owed more to the 'Stabat Mater', the realistic crucifix, and the Three Hours service than to the Gospels. It has for its second line, 'See, Mary calls us to her side', and one verse begins, 'His mother cannot reach his face'. Faber followed the Roman Catholic teaching (as against Mark 15 : 25, 33) that the crucifixion only lasted three hours, when he wrote, 'Seven times he spoke, seven words of love; And all three hours his silence cried.' A sentimentalist born, he did not resist the tendency of his age to accentuate sentiment in dealing with those scenes about which the Gospels show such noble reticence. One verse calls upon the people to weep, another cries, 'O break, O break, hard heart of mine', and asserts that its 'weak self-love and guilty pride His Pilate and his Judas were'. The original refrain is 'Jesus, our Love, is crucified'. Unfortunately the hymn, with its all too appropriate tune by Dykes, was brought into common use in the Church of England in 1861; and the only course at present seems to be to make the best of it by removing its more regrettable features.

L.M.

MUSIC. ST. CROSS, composed for this hymn by J. B. Dykes, appeared in *Hymns Ancient and Modern* (1861). This well-known tune, invariably associated with these words, needs no comment.

141 Throned upon the aweful tree.

J. Ellerton, 1826–93.

This was written in 1875, and appeared in the new edition of *Hymns Ancient and Modern* for that year.

It may be noted here, at the conclusion of the hymns special to Good Friday, that the English Prayer Book keeps faithfully to the older tradition (which had been preserved throughout the Middle Ages in England) of making the day an occasion, not of unhealthy meditation, but of quiet intercession for human needs, mingled with the reading of long extracts from the restrained records of the Gospels. The ancient note is struck by our three Good Friday collects, and maintained in the appointed services of the Litany, and the Ante-Communion service ending with the collects for the conclusion of that service. The references in *Songs of Praise* to other hymns are intended to maintain the same principle.

Trochaic, 7 7. 7 7. 7 7.

MUSIC. ARFON is arranged from a Welsh folk-song melody by the Rev. Hugh Davies, and appeared in the *English Hymnal* (1906), set to the present hymn. The tune, however, seems to be derived from a French original; it is found in R. Guilmant's *Noëls* (1885) as the traditional melody to the carol 'Joseph est bien marié'; and in G. Legeay's *Noëls Anciens* (1875) to 'Un nouveau présent des Cieux', in a slightly simplified form.

142 At eve, when now he breathed no more. *J. R. Darbyshire.*

Written by Dr. Darbyshire, now Bishop of Glasgow, for this book, in order to keep in use the tune 'Bohemia', as used in the *English Hymnal* (121). It was felt that the original words of Dr. Gregory Smith were difficult as a matter of theology and hardly adequate as verse. Therefore the new hymn was written.

Iambic, 8 8 8. Also occurs in 401. Cf. 143 below.

MUSIC. BOHEMIA (O MENSCH SIEH) is from the Bohemian Brethren's songbook *Kirchengeseng darinnen die Heubtartickel des Christlichen Glaubens kurtz gefasset und ausgelegt sind, &c.* (Prague? 1566). It is there set to the hymn 'O Mensch sieh, wie hie auf Erdreich' as follows:

The present arrangement appeared in the *English Hymnal* (1906).

EASTER DAY AND THE SUNDAY AFTER

143 Alleluya, alleluya, alleluya! Ye sons and daughters of the King. *16th and 17th cent. Tr. J. M. Neale.*‡

O filii et filiae,
rex caelestis, rex gloriae,
morte surrexit hodie:
Alleluya.

Neale's translation of this charming carol-hymn was deservedly popularized by *Hymns Ancient and Modern* in 1861; it is there altered, and it has been altered again by us. His text is in the *English Hymnal* (626); but there are some lines that are difficult to sing, such as, 'And said: "Peace be unto you here" '; and it needed a few verbal alterations to bring it into better line with the records. We have also arranged the verses so that Part II can be sung separately when the incident of St. Thomas is commemorated on the Sunday after Easter. Neale fancied that the hymn was of 13th-century origin; Julian dated it not earlier than the 17th; and the earliest known text is in the *Office de la Semaine Sainte* (Paris, 1674). But Dr. Grattan Flood in *Musical Opinion* (1916), pp. 445–6, says that some of the verses have been traced to a booklet published in France between 1518 and 1546, and he thinks they may be ascribed to Jean Tisserand, who had died 30 or 40 years before. But further evidence is needed.

Iambic, 8 8 8. and Alleluyas.

MUSIC. O FILII ET FILIAE is the proper melody to this hymn, and is to be found, in various forms, in books of the 17th and 18th centuries, the earliest apparently being *Airs sur les hymnes sacrez, odes et noëls* (Paris, 1623). In the Jesuit publication *Nordsterns Führers zur Seeligkeit* (1671) the following form of the melody is given to a German translation of the words:

Variants appear also in, among others, La Feillée's *Méthode . . . du Plain Chant, &c.* (1745), *A Pious Association* (London, 1748), *An Essay on the Church Plain Chant* (1782), and Webbe's *Collection of Motetts or Antiphons* (1792), the last named being the source of the alternative version here given.

The melody is of the second mode, and may be an adaptation of a French traditional melody, the internal evidence supporting this view.

144 Come, ye faithful, raise the strain.

St. John Damascene, c. 750. *Pr. J. M. Neale.*‡

A vigorous rendering by Neale (and the only hymn from the Greek that is in any sense a translation) of the Greek Canon for St. Thomas's Sunday (the Eastern name for the 1st Sunday after Easter, called also Little Easter and Low Sunday), written probably by St. John of Damascus, the last of the Greek Fathers and the best of the Greek hymnodists. A Greek church canon is a series of odes, normally eight: at the beginning is an acrostic, usually founded on a Bible canticle, and on this acrostic the odes are threaded (cf. 146). This ode is based upon the Canticle of Moses, Exod. 15. Neale first published his version in an article in the *Christian Remembrancer* (April 1859), in four verses, as in the *English Hymnal*, 131. Here the hymn is shortened to three verses by the omission of the second half of vv. 1 and 2, which reduces the references to the passage of the Red Sea, so common in ancient writers. As was the case with the really ancient Passiontide hymns, the early writers about Easter also were more concerned with symbolic and Old Testament ideas than with the actual historic events; and this, by the way, is why 'Ye sons and daughters' above, 143, is comparatively modern in its method. The changes here are: ver. 1, l. 3, 'his Israel'; ver. 2, l. 5, 'to glad Jerusalem'; ver. 3, l. 3, 'the watchers nor the seal'; l. 7, 'That thy peace'.

Trochaic (as so often with jubilant hymns), 7 6. 7 6. D.

MUSIC. AVE VIRGO VIRGINUM is a German traditional melody, to be found in collections from the 15th century onwards as a setting to various hymns but principally to 'Ave virgo virginum'. In *Ein Gesangbuch der Brüder in Behemen und Merherrn, &c.* (Nuremberg, 1544) it is set to the hymn 'Nun lasst uns in dieser Frist' and headed 'Gaudeamus pariter omnes'; the present version being from Leisentritt's *Catholicum Hymnologium Germanicum* (1584), where it is set to 'Lob sei Gott im höchsten

Thron' and headed 'Ave virgo virginum'. The rhythm of the 7th bar is here slightly simplified, the original being:

This is a cheerful, spirited tune with a resolute rhythm, easy and grateful to sing. It should be taken rather on the fast than the slow side.

145 Jesus Christ is risen to-day, Alleluya!

Lyra Davidica (1708), *and the Supplement* (1816).

The 'Easter Hymn' *par excellence*, became popular by its inclusion in a late *Supplement* to the *New Version* (Tate and Brady, see 82), *c.* 1816. It had originally appeared in a rare book called *Lyra Davidica, or a Collection of Divine Songs and Hymns, partly newly composed, partly translated from the High German and Latin Hymns, and set to easy and pleasant tunes* (London, J. Walsh, 1708). It is based upon some verses of an Easter carol, which appears first in three German and Bohemian manuscripts of the 14th century:

Surrexit Christus hodie
humano pro solamine:
  Alleluja.
Mortem qui passus corpore
miserrimo pro homine; etc.

The English original (in two verses with a curious doxology) had in ver. 1, l. 3, 'Who so lately on the cross'; and the 2nd verse ran:

Haste ye females from your fright;
Take to Galilee your flight;
To his sad disciples say,
Jesus Christ is risen to-day.

This is therefore yet another example (cf. e.g. 74, 'Hark, the herald') of a popular classic owing its existence to considerable alteration. The modern form of the hymn appeared first in Arnold's *Compleat Psalmodist* (1749), where the 2nd and 3rd verses are entirely new, without any reference to the Latin; this has come to us through the *Supplement*, where Arnold's ver. 2, l. 1 is altered from 'Hymns of praises let us sing'.

Trochaic, 7 4. 7 4. D., the refrain supplies the alternate lines of four syllables.

MUSIC. EASTER HYMN is a modified form of the melody set to this hymn in *Lyra Davidica* (1708). (The original form of the tune is given to hymn 172.) Several variants of the melody are found in different publications, the present form being, like the words, derived from Arnold's *Compleat Psalmodist* (1st ed., 1741), in the several editions of which both words and tune show a gradual alteration. The tune has been ascribed to various composers, but none of these attributions has been supported by convincing evidence.

The tune is now one of the most famous of all hymn-tunes; noticeable is the prevalent rising movement throughout. The melody fully bears out the remark in the preface to the above book, 'there is a desire for a little freer air than the grand movement of the psalm-tunes'. The melody was a precursor of the 'new style' of hymn-tune afterwards popularized by the Methodists, which has had so immense an influence on all subsequent compositions of this kind.

146 The day of resurrection!

St. John Damascene, c. 750. *Pr. J. M.-Neale.*‡

This, the first ode of the Golden Canon, is sung in the East at midnight, for the dawn of Easter Day, the people holding their yet unlighted tapers: at midnight in Greece a cannon is fired, all the tapers suddenly fill the whole church with a glow of light; drums and trumpets sound; and the news is carried far abroad with cries of 'Christos anesti'; in Russia the same greeting was used by all on Easter Day; the Emperor as he left his palace would kiss the sentry at the gate as he gave it.

John of Damascus (cf. 144) was a great defender of images during the Iconoclastic Controversy which raged in the 8th century. A certain Cosmas is said to have been exposed for sale as a slave in Damascus, where a citizen, struck by his appearance, bought him, and made him tutor to his son, who was our John of Damascus: years after, Cosmas retired with John to the monastery of St. Sabas in the savage wilderness by the Kedron valley, some ten miles from Jerusalem; and here many hymns were written. Neale's very free version first appeared in his *Hymns of the Eastern Church* (1862) as ''Tis the day of Resurrection', and appeared without the first word in the *Parish Hymn Book* (1863). His original has indeed been found to need alteration, even in the *English Hymnal* (137), where every effort was made throughout to alter his words as little as possible; this version we have used here. The hymn has the ancient characteristics to which we have already referred (144), and is little more than a shout of jubilation.

If the fault of much modern hymnody is that it is too subjective, the Greek hymns represent the opposite danger. As was pointed out by Leigh Bennett, its discouragement of human emotion narrows its range of subject and of reflection, 'and the repetition of the same types, metaphors, and epithets issues in sameness, conventional diction, and fossil thought'.

'Entirely absent is the deep spiritual analysis of St. Paul or the interpretation of the changing moods of the soul which is the glory of the Psalter.' They cannot be really translated into English. 'The sparkling Greek freezes in our metres, and the unity, proportion of parts, compactness, and selection of allied ideas, which we demand, have no correlative in the loose, wandering, disconnected strophes.' Therefore Neale's so-called translations are really centos of a few ideas to which he has given his own individuality in his own manner of verse (cf. 168).

Iambic, 7 6. 7 6. D.

MUSIC. GÖRLITZ (ACH GOTT VOM HIMMELREICHE) is from M. Praetorius's *Musae Sioniae* (7th part, 1609), where it is set to the hymn 'Ach Gott, vom Himmelreiche'. This collection, published in nine parts (1605–10), was mainly composed of well-known melodies, but contained also some original tunes, possibly by Praetorius himself, of which this is one. The tune, however, is in the popular traditional manner, and, though an excellent one, cannot be definitely ascribed to him.

147 The strife is o'er, the battle done.

Ascribed to 18th cent. Tr. F. Pott.

Finita jam sunt praelia,
est parta jam victoria:
gaudeamus et canamus,
Alleluya.

Of unknown authorship and late origin, this has not been traced earlier than *Hymnodia Sacra* (Münster, 1753). It was once thought to be 'ancient'; Neale, for instance attributed it to the 12th century. Francis Pott made this translation of its original 5 verses and published it in his *Hymns fitted to the Order of Common Prayer* (1861). 'In the same year,' says Julian, 'it was given with extensive alterations in *Hymns Ancient and Modern*, 114. This altered text has failed to commend itself to later compilers.'

Iambic, 8 8. 8 4.

MUSIC. VICTORY is an adaptation from the 'Gloria Patri' of the 'Magnificat Tertii Toni', contained in the work entitled 'Magnificat Octo Tonorum' published by Palestrina in 1591. The present arrangement (with Alleluya) was made by Dr. W. H. Monk for this hymn, and appeared in *Hymns Ancient and Modern* (1861), and, since then, has become one of the most celebrated of Easter hymns.

EASTER DAY TO ASCENSION DAY

148 A messenger within the grave.

4th or 5th cent. Tr. T. A. Lacey.

Sermone blando angelus
praedixit mulieribus:
'In Galilaea Dominus
videndus est quantocius.'

Of early date, 'Aurora lucis rutilat' used to be ascribed to St. Ambrose. It is in the Junius MS. of the 8th century, and found its way into most Breviaries. Being long, it was made into separate parts; the divisions used in the Salisbury books are given in the *English Hymnal*, 123, Parts I and II, and 124, Parts I and II. There have been many translations, that of Neale not being among his best efforts; and, as none were felt to be very good, Dr. Lacey made his version, which has a strength and amplitude not often reached in translations. This he did for the *English Hymnal* (1906), 'His cheering message from the grave'. He altered the first line for *Songs of Praise*, in order to bring it into line with the Marcan account, leaving open the identity of the 'young man' at the tomb.

L.M.

MUSIC. PLAINSONG is the melody from the *Sarum Antiphonal*, arranged by J. H. Arnold for *Songs of Praise* (1925), which was appropriated to 'Aurora lucis rutilat' at Mattins, and to 'Sermone blando angelus' at Lauds on Low Sunday and all Sundays after Easter, and daily until Ascension Day (when the Service is of the season).

MONT RICHARD, by Dr. Percy Buck, was originally composed for the hymn 'Ride on, ride on in majesty', for use in Harrow School chapel. It is a tune with a peculiar flavour of its own, of very economical construction, and with a curious quality of reserve, which gives it an unusual attractiveness.

149 All the toil and sorrow done, Alleluya!

A. P. Stanley (cento), 1815–81.

There are several fine tunes in this metre with its Alleluyas; and therefore a cento has been here made for *Songs of Praise* from 'He is gone—Beyond the skies' (which first appeared in *Macmillan's Magazine*, June 1862, in 7 verses), in order to bring one more of these tunes into use, and at the same time to provide a forward-looking hymn which could be used both in Eastertide and for the Ascension. This was the more suitable, because it made possible a selection of the best lines. It was said of Stanley, the famous 'broad-church' Dean of Westminster, and the reputed original of 'Arthur' in *Tom Brown's Schooldays*, that he wrote prose like poetry, and poetry like prose. It was certainly more as a scholar with a brilliant academic career and as one of the most widely influential men of his age, than as a verse-writer that he was known. But all he wrote was wise; and therefore this cento is alive and true for us at the present day.

Trochaic, 7 4. 7 4. D.

MUSIC. LLANFAIR, by Robert Williams, is named BETHEL in the composer's manuscript book, and dated 14 July 1817. It appeared in J. Parry's collection *Peroriaeth Hyfryd* (1837), harmonized by John Roberts, Henllan. The tune, in structure and style, shows many of the common characteristics of Welsh hymn-tunes.

150 Alleluya, alleluya! Hearts to heaven and voices raise.

Bishop Chr. Wordsworth, and others.

Bishop Christopher Wordsworth was a good scholar but an indifferent poet—'of unequal merit', as Dr. Julian said; and this hymn was felt by the compilers of the *English Hymnal* to be (in its original form as found in many books) rather beneath a satisfactory standard of hymnody. Since, however, it was widely asked for when *Songs of Praise* was compiled, we have made the attempt to remedy its deficiencies. In order to carry the unusual metre required by the tune, which we have called 'Cöthen', a new refrain was written by Jan Struther. The hymn can therefore now be sung in two forms.

Trochaic. For 'Cöthen', 8 7. 8 7. 12 12. 11 11, the refrain being anapaestic. Unique. For 'Würzburg', 8 7. 8 7. D., without refrain.

MUSIC. CÖTHEN (EINS IST NOT), melody and bass by J. S. Bach, is from Schemelli's *Musicalisches Gesangbuch, &c.* (1736), where it is set to the hymn 'Eins ist not!' This is a tune thoroughly typical of Bach in its steady, almost relentless rhythm, and in the natural yet individual flow of the melody; a most enjoyable tune to sing.

WÜRZBURG is from *Andächtige und auserlesene Gesänger* (Würzburg, 1705), where it is set to the hymn 'O du Brunn des wahren Lebens'. It is a broad, fluent tune, solidly built, the germ of the whole tune being in the first two bars, and with a good swinging rhythm. The pace should err, if at all, on the fast side.

151 Awake, arise! lift up thy voice. *Christopher Smart*, 1722–71.

Six stanzas from the poem 'Easter Day', first published in *A Translation of the Psalms of David, &c.* (1765), by the remarkable poet who is described under 521 and 690. He was one of Dr. Johnson's friends, and is the author also of 17.

C.M.

MUSIC. ST. FULBERT, by H. J. Gauntlett, is from the *Church Hymn and Tune Book* (1852), edited by W. J. Blew and H. J. Gauntlett, where it was set to the hymn 'Now Christ, our Passover, is slain'. The original name of the tune was 'St. Leofred'.

The alternative version (fa-burden) by Martin Shaw was written especially for the enlarged *Songs of Praise* (1931). The tune is in the tradition of the older psalm-tunes, but has no very distinctive qualities of its own.

152 Christ is risen! Christ is risen!

A. T. Gurney (1862), *and others.*

Like 150, this was omitted by the compilers of the *English Hymnal*, as being, in its original form (in Gurney's *A Book of Praise*, 1862), below the most indulgent standard, but in response to a wide demand we have endeavoured to improve it, remembering that some famous hymns have had an inauspicious beginning, and hoping that this might at least carry its chorus with success, in the jubilant metre to which it doubtless owed its popularity.

Trochaic, 8 7. 8 7. 7 5. 7 5. 8 7. 8 7. Unique.

MUSIC. MIDHURST was written by Nicholas Gatty especially for the enlarged *Songs of Praise* (1931). It is in the nature of a march-tune, somewhat rigid in rhythm, but with the solidity which goes with such precision.

153 Christ the Lord is risen again!

Michael Weisse, c. 1480–1534. *Tr. C. Winkworth.*

Christus ist erstanden
Von des Todes Banden,
Des freuet sich der Engel Schar,
Singend im Himmel immerdar,
    Halleluja.

When the Bohemian Brethren, the followers of John Hus, sent Michael Weisse to Luther in Wittenberg, with a copy of their confession of faith and of the hymns and tunes which they had taught their people, Luther took the hymn-book and said, 'It is the work of a good poet'. This example was first published in *Ein new Gesengbuchlen*, at Jungen Bunzel in Bohemia, 1531. Miss Winkworth's translation appeared in her *Lyra Germanica* (2nd series, 1858).

Trochaic, 7 7. 7 7. 4. Unique.

MUSIC. ORIENTIS PARTIBUS is derived from a medieval French melody. In some parts of France, notably at Beauvais, during the Middle Ages, there was celebrated on 14 Jan. a church festival known as the Feast of the Ass, commemorating the flight into Egypt. A young woman holding a child in her arms and seated upon an ass was led in procession through the streets of the town and, finally, into the principal church, where mass was celebrated while the ass with its burden stood beside the high altar. During the service a hymn (*conductus*), written in a mixture of medieval Latin and old French, was sung, of which the first lines were 'Orientis partibus adventavit asinus', to which a form of the present melody was sung.

The two chief sources of the tune are a manuscript in the library of Sens, *Office de la Circoncision à l'usage de la ville de Sens*, which was the work of Pierre de Corbeil, Archbishop of Sens, who died in 1222; and a similar manuscript in the British Museum (Egerton 2615), originally from Beauvais, in which the tune appears with the words on the first folio of the manuscript, the first verse, on the obverse, being much rubbed, but later verses, on the reverse, being excellently clear.

The Sens manuscript has been frequently described and annotated, and a full account, with bibliography, is to be found in Henri Villetard's monograph *L'Office de Pierre de Corbeil* (Bibliothèque Musicologique, no. 4, 1907); here the notes of the melody are the same as in the present tune, though the rhythm has been read in a variety of ways, and from this manuscript R. Redhead derived his version in common time, which appeared in his *Church Hymn Tunes* (1853), and has been followed in some later collections. There is little doubt, however, for reasons of notation, period, and the rhythm of the words, that the tune should be read in triple time.

In the Beauvais manuscript the form of the melody differs considerably, and (preserving a similar rhythm) runs as follows:

The refrain, 'hez hez', is repeated between each verse, and at the end there is a 'coda' thus:

It seems clear that those commentators who have regarded this 'Prose of the Ass' as a piece of burlesque have been mistaken, and that in the original festival the ass was taken as seriously as the other participators in the ceremony (see Félix Clément's *Notices sur les Chants de la Sainte Chapelle*, 1852).

The present arrangement appeared in the *English Hymnal* (1906).

154 Good Christian men rejoice and sing! *C. A. Alington.*

Written by the Dean of Durham, when he was Head Master of Eton, for our book, in order to carry the tune which we have called 'Vulpius'.

Iambic, 8 8 8. 4.

MUSIC. VULPIUS (GELOBT SEI GOTT) is from Melchior Vulpius's *Ein schön geistlich Gesangbuch* (Jena, 1609). The present arrangement, by

Dr. Henry G. Ley, appeared in *Songs of Praise* (1925). This is evidently a traditional melody, and is an excellent tune.

155 Jesus lives! thy terrors now.

C. F. Gellert, 1715–69. *Tr. F. E. Cox.*

Jesus lebt, mit ihm auch ich;
  Tod, wo sind nun deine Schrecken?
Er, er lebt, und wird auch mich
  Von den Toten auferwecken:
    Hallelujah.

This is the best-known hymn of Christian Fürchtegott Gellert, the saintly Professor of Philosophy and Poetry at Leipzig (where Goethe and Lessing were among his pupils), who was so generous that, when Prince Henry of Prussia sought him out, he was found to be living in one empty room without food or fire. Once indeed a peasant had walked in with a load of firewood, as a tribute of gratitude for Gellert's *Fables*. 'Jesus lebt' was first published in his *Geistliche Oden und Lieder* (1757), with the title 'Easter Hymn', based on John 14: 19. It soon passed into all German hymnals, and is now not less universal among English-speaking people. It has often been sung as a funeral hymn. Miss Cox herself agreed to the alteration of her original unfortunate first line, 'Jesus lives! no longer now'; her name is not therefore marked with an obelus in our book. The translation first appeared in her *Sacred Hymns from the German* (1841), and she revised it twice afterwards.

Death had no terrors indeed for Gellert. When he was told that he had about an hour more to live he lifted his hands—'Now God be praised, only an hour!'

Trochaic, 7 8. 7 8. 4. Unique.

MUSIC. CHRIST IST ERSTANDEN is a German melody of, at latest, the 12th century. The Easter hymn 'Christ ist erstanden', to which it was sung, is referred to in various manuscripts of the 13th century, which show it to have been well known and popular at that period. The tune is found in a 15th-century manuscript in Munich, where it appears in virtually its present form, but with an extended Alleluya. Its first appearance in print seems to be in P. Schöffer's *Liederbuch* (Mainz, 1513) as the canto fermo of a motet for four voices; as an independent melody it is first found in Weisse's *Ein New Gesengbuchlen* (1531). Numerous variants are found in later collections, both Catholic and Protestant, the refrain being in some books 'Hallelujah' and in others 'Kyrie Eleison'. It has been said that this melody occupies the same place in German music as 'Sumer is icumen in' does in English.

ST. ALBINUS is from the *Church Hymn and Tune Book* (1852), edited by W. J. Blew and H. J. Gauntlett. It was composed by Dr. Gauntlett for an Easter hymn, 'Angels to our jubilee', but has now become associated with the present words, and one of the most popular of Easter hymn-tunes.

156 Let all the multitudes of light. *F. B. Macnutt.*

Written to carry the tune for our book, and to provide a hymn suitable also for the Ascension, by F. B. Macnutt, Provost of Leicester Cathedral.

Iambic, 8 7. 8 7. 8 8 7.

MUSIC. WITTENBERG (ES IST DAS HEIL) appeared in *Etlich Cristliche Lyeder* (Wittenberg, 1524), set to Luther's 'Ach Gott, vom Himmel', though the melody is seemingly of earlier date. In later German books it is associated with other hymns, especially with the Easter hymn 'Freu dich, du werte Christenheit'. The present version, both of melody and harmony, is J. S. Bach's. In grandeur and dignity this splendid tune can bear comparison with the greatest chorales.

157 Let us rejoice, the fight is won. *T.S.N.*

The great tune, popularized by the *English Hymnal* to the words of 'Ye watchers' (519), is really just as much an Easter tune as 'Jesus Christ is risen to-day'. In ignorance of this, several new hymns appeared for the tune in various collections, when once the *English Hymnal* had made it known. The only way to save it in the end from multifarious and inappropriate use was to write an Easter hymn; and so 'Lasst uns erfreuen' now has its original opening, 'Let us rejoice'. The hymn was at the same time so written as to make it serviceable for general use at other times of the year; and a doxology (suggested by an occasion of community singing when a vast crowd sang several hymns and doxologies) was added as 415 in our book. The hymn can thus be lengthened by this addition when necessary, and the doxology can also be sung separately to its glorious tune, which we have now called 'Easter Alleluya'.

Iambic, 8 8. 4 4. 8 8, with Alleluyas; in other terms the metre is L.M. with refrains. Unique.

MUSIC. EASTER ALLELUYA (LASST UNS ERFREUEN) in the *Geistliche Kirchengesäng* (Cologne, 1623) is set to the Easter hymn 'Lasst uns erfreuen herzlich sehr'.

This now famous tune is built altogether on a single musical unit of four notes, by imitations and inversions. It is a remarkable example not only of economy of structure but of the accumulating force of repetition—when the repeated phrase, as here, is strong enough to bear it. It has a notable resemblance to 'Psalm 68' (246).

158 Life is good, for God contrives it. *P. Dearmer.*

Easter always used to suffer in comparison with Christmas from the small number of exceptionally stirring and beautiful tunes, as well as from the excess of references, derived from the old Latin hymnals, to the Paschal Lamb and the Red Sea. This was therefore written to carry the tune 'Trefaenan', among other efforts to improve the musical character of the long Easter season.

Trochaic, 8 7. 8 7. 8 8. 8 7.

MUSIC. TREFAENAN is an arrangement by Martin Shaw of the traditional Welsh melody, which is found in another version for 462. It appeared in *Songs of Praise* (1931).

159 Lo, when the day of rest was past. *A.F.*

This was written for our book in order to give expression to the New Testament accounts of the Resurrection and the successive appearances of our Lord; and at the same time to provide a long hymn with Alleluyas, such as is needed for processions and for other occasions.

Iambic, 8 8. 8 8. 4, in other words, L.M., in alternate rhymes, with the Alleluya refrain. Unique.

MUSIC. HERMANN (ERSCHIENEN IST DER HERRLICH TAG) is set to three hymns in Nicolaus Hermann's *Die Sontags Evangelia uber das gantze Jar in Gesenge verfasset* (Wittenberg, 1560), but became particularly associated with the third, 'Erschienen ist der herrlich Tag'. The present version of melody and harmony is J. S. Bach's.

The melody is claimed to have been based on a French folk-song, 'Quand Jean Renaud de guerre vint'. Its original form, in the above book, is as follows:

It is a fine Dorian tune, with a strange effect of sudden brightness in the little leaping figure of the 4th line, which makes it most attractive.

160 Love's redeeming work is done. *C. Wesley,*† 1707–88.

This fine hymn was lost sight of to a large extent, and but little sung, because its opening line caused it to be confused with other Easter hymns. The *English Hymnal* therefore began it with the above stirring and distinctive opening, and dropped the first verse, which runs:

'Christ the Lord is risen to-day',
Sons of men and angels say!
Raise your joys and triumphs high:
Sing, ye heavens; thou earth reply.

Six verses in all are omitted; for the original (*Hymns and Sacred Poems,* 1739) had 11, the *English Hymnal* selection, which we follow, being 2–5 and 10. Curiously enough, John Wesley omitted the hymn from the *Wesleyan Hymn Book* (1780); and it did not reappear till 50 years later, when it was, in 1830, included in a *Supplement.* Present-day biblical knowledge made it advisable to alter in the 2nd verse the reference to the seal, and incidentally to eliminate a rather harsh false rhyme. So there is now an obelus.

Trochaic, 7 7. 7 7.

MUSIC. SAVANNAH (or HERRNHUT) is from a manuscript *Choralbuch* (Herrnhut, *c.* 1740), and appears in the *Collection of Tunes as they are sung at the Foundery* (1742), which was compiled by John Wesley.

The alternative version (fa-burden) by Martin Shaw appeared in the *Tenor Tune Book* (1917).

This is a tune of extreme ingenuousness; from its repetitive form and general character it might almost be a traditional melody of the cradle-song type.

161 Rejoice and be glad! he lives who was slain. *T.S.N.*

Written for our book in order to carry another suitable tune for Eastertide, and to provide material appropriate also for Ascensiontide.

Anapaestic, 11 11. 11 11. As we have said above (p. xxx), English anapaestic or dactylic verse is generally abbreviated. Thus a complete anapaestic line would run—'So rejoice and be glad! for he lives who was slain.'

MUSIC. HARWICH is by B. Milgrove and appeared in his *Twelve Hymns and a favourite lyric poem written by Dr. Watts . . . dedicated to the Right Honourable the Countess of Huntingdon by Benjamin Milgrove. Book III* (Bath, 1781). It is there set to hymn VII, 'All ye that pass by', for four voices, the form of the melody being as at present except that there are four antiphonal bars between the sopranos and the other voices before the last line, and the last line itself is repeated. It is here without name, but is found later in the *Union Tune Book* (1812), in its present form. The tune is a typical specimen of the more 'popular' kind of hymn-tune favoured by the Methodists in the 18th century.

162 Round the earth a message runs. *Jan Struther.*

Written for our book to carry a beautiful proper Easter tune, this is one of those hymns that combine the Easter with the spring motive.

Iambic, 7 8. 8 8. 8 8, that is, six eights, but with the first syllable missing. Unique.

MUSIC. VICTOR KING (CHRISTUS IST ERSTANDEN) is an old German carol melody which appears as here in the *Gesang- und Gebetbuch für die Diocese Trier* (1871). The melody is said to be by Johann Paul Schiebel, Domkapellmeister in Rothenburg. It is found in several German collections from 1837 onwards. The tune is of a characteristic 'carol' type; it may be noted that the 2nd line is identical with the 1st line of a very well-known English folk-song.

163 Sing, all ye Christian people! *Jan Struther.*

Also written to carry (as it does with great felicity) a proper Easter tune of great beauty from a German source.

7 7. 7 7. 14 10. This delightful and unique metre begins with an iambic quatrain of '7 7', and then breaks into a couplet of '10', the first line being lengthened to 14 syllables by the reiteration (with variations) of a clause.

MUSIC. COLOGNE (CHRISTUS IST AUFERSTANDEN) appears in the *Auserlesene Catholische Geistliche Kirchengesäng* (Cologne, 1623) set to the Easter hymn 'Christus ist auferstanden'. It is obviously much older than this, however, and is of a type popular at the end of the 15th and beginning of the 16th centuries. It has a very considerable affinity with some of W. Cornysshe's melodies *c.* 1520.

164 Sing, brothers, sing and praise your King! *C. A. Alington.*

In this case the words were chosen first for our book, and the tune was composed to fit the very uncommon metre.

Iambic, 8 7. 8 7. 8 7. 8 7. 7 7, with internal rhymes. Unique.

MUSIC. CHELSEA was composed by John Ireland especially for the enlarged *Songs of Praise* (1931). It is a well-sustained, long tune with a Mixolydian flavour, and showing the composer's habitual dislike for 'square' regular rhythms (cf. 127 [i]).

165 Sing, men and angels, sing. *John Masefield.*

Our present Poet Laureate wrote this lyric as part of *Easter*, a play published in 1929.

Iambic, 6 6 6. 5. D. Unique.

MUSIC. LEMON'S FARM is from Martin Shaw's music to Masefield's play *Easter*.

It is a broad, flowing tune, knit together by references throughout to the rhythm or the melody of the second bar, and with an uninterrupted continuity due to the avoidance of any suggestion of the tonic (at the half-cadences) until the final chord.

166 Take heart, friends and neighbours. *O.B.C.*

This first appeared as 147 in the *Oxford Book of Carols* (1928), and was written by the editor to carry the tune. The text has been slightly changed by the author for this new issue, and the last verse omitted and left for carol use only.

Trochaic, 6 5. 6 5. D.

MUSIC. NOUS ALLONS is a French carol melody 'Nous allons ma mie', and is to be found in several collections including J. L. Roques's *50 Noëls anciens, &c.* (1897), and L. Eugène Grimault's *Noëls Angevins* (1878). A characteristic French carol-tune (cf. 3).

167 The whole bright world rejoices now.

Hilariter. *German*, 1623. *Tr. O.B.C.*

The statement about 166 applies to this also, except that it is 96 in the *Oxford Book of Carols* and has not been altered here. Hilarity was one of the chief virtues among the early Christians: it is personified among the 'strong maidens' who stand between the four corners of the Tower in *The Shepherd* of Hermas (*c.* A.D. 150)—Simplicity, Guilelessness, Holiness, Hilarity (*hilarotēs*), Truth, Understanding, Concord, Love.

L.M., or 8 8 with refrain, this being *Hilariter* ('Hilariously'), as in the original.

MUSIC. HILARITER (DIE GANZE WELT) is a German carol tune to the words 'Die ganze Welt', and appears in several collections of which the earliest is the *Auserlesene Catholische Geistliche Kirchengesäng* (Cologne, 1623); the words 'Hilariter, hilariter' occur as a refrain between the German lines of the carol. This is clearly a traditional tune, with a suggestion of the Dorian mode; as befits the words, it is a cheerful melody, which should be sung distinctly on the fast side.

168 Thou hallowed chosen dawn of praise.

St. John Damascene, c. 750. *Tr. J. M. Neale, and others.*

In *Songs of Praise* there are as few hymns as possible that have to be restricted to Easter Day and Little Easter, and as many as possible that can be used throughout the long season after Easter (and some of them even later). This text has therefore been altered in order to prevent its being confined to the octave of Easter. Like 144 and 146, the original is by John of Damascus, this being in fact the 8th 'Ode of the Golden Canon' (146), which is called also the 'Queen of Canons', though here a different metre is used. Julian considered that Neale's translations 'have not the exultant freedom of the original' (see also under 146); and we have omitted ver. 2 (which can be read in Neale's text, *E.H.* 138), 'Come, let us taste the Vine's new fruit', with 'To-day the branches with the Root', as well as the rather too metaphysical doxology, for which another verse is here substituted. In ver. 1 we have generalized by changing 'morn' in l. 1, and 'Lady and queen and day of days'; and in ll. 4–5, 'Of things divine, divinest! On thee our praises Christ adore'.

Iambic, 8 7. 8 7. 8 8.

MUSIC. SCHEIN (MACH'S MIT MIR GOTT), composed by J. H. Schein for the hymn 'Mach's mit mir, Gott, nach deiner Güt', was issued as a separate sheet the year after the publication of his great work *Cantional, oder Gesangbuch Augsburgischer Confession* (Leipzig, 1627), and was incorporated in the 2nd edition of that collection (1645). Schein's original tune was as follows:

The present is the later form adopted by J. S. Bach.

The adaptation of many of these tunes on the Procrustean bed of the usual chorale form is in some ways to be regretted; they do sometimes assume, in their new dress, a solemnity and stateliness which was not there before, but they also often lose part of their individuality by being thus all cut to one pattern. The present tune is built on the common plan of inversion, in the latter half, of the movement of the first part. It is not one of the 'grand' chorales, but retains, even in its later version, a suave, song-like character.

DIES IST DER TAG, by P. Sohren, is found in his edition of *Praxis Pietatis Melica* (1668), where it is set to the hymn 'Dies ist der Tag der Frölichkeit' as follows:

The rhythm of the present version is slightly adapted. The tune is in the characteristic style of the older German carol melodies.

EASTER DAY TO TRINITY SUNDAY

169 How great the harvest is. *O.B.C.*

Written for the *Oxford Book of Carols* (152), 1928, by the editor in order to carry the tune and to provide a hymn suitable for any of the Great

Festivals, from Christmas and the Epiphany through Easter to Trinity Sunday, especially for the period from Easter to Trinity.

Iambic, 6 7. 6 7. D., and refrain. Unique.

MUSIC. VRUECHTEN is a Dutch tune 'De Liefde Voortgebracht', a very popular song in the 17th century. It was set to 'Hoe groot de Vruechten zijn' in the Amsterdam Psalter of J. Oudaen. The present arrangement, by Geoffrey Shaw, appeared in the *Oxford Book of Carols* (1928). It is a vigorous, swinging melody with a very attractive rhythm and metre.

ROGATIONTIDE

170 God of mercy, God of grace. *H. F. Lyte*, 1793–1847.

First published in Lyte's *Spirit of the Psalms* (1834), as a second version of Psalm 67. It is, however, not so much a paraphrase of the psalm as a hymn based upon some of its ideas.

Trochaic, 7 7. 7 7. 7 7.

MUSIC. HEATHLANDS, by Henry Smart, was originally set to this hymn in *Psalms and Hymns for Divine Worship* (1867), and since then has been generally, though not invariably, associated with it.

CROYDON, by Hubert J. Foss, appeared first in *Songs of Praise* (1931), but was written much earlier when the composer was still in his 'teens, and much interested in church music. It is a bold, straightforward tune of a very regular but vigorous construction and outline.

171 Lord, in thy name thy servants plead. *J. Keble*,† 1792–1866.

Written at Malvern in 1856, and published anonymously in the *Salisbury Hymn Book* (1857). Ver. 3, l. 4 ran, 'All thine, are ours by prayer': at the request of those who pointed out that the statement was not true, this has been altered.

C.M.

MUSIC. LINCOLN is from Ravenscroft's *The Whole Booke of Psalmes* (1621), where it is set to Psalms 7 and 56, being named an 'English' tune. The alternative version (fa-burden) by W. Harrison is set, in the same book, to Psalm 142. It is a good melody of the 'common psalm-tune' type, but noticeable for the curious restlessness of its modulations.

ASCENSIONTIDE

172 Hail the day that sees him rise, Alleluya!

C. Wesley,‡ 1707–88.

Another famous hymn which, like 74, is a successful patchwork, the original appeared in the Wesleys' *Hymns and Sacred Poems* (1739), the first verse being:

> Hail the day that sees him rise,
> Ravish'd from our wishful eyes!
> Christ, awhile to mortals given,
> Re-ascends his native heaven.

The present form is mainly due to Cotterill's *Selection* (9th ed., 1820) (see 71). This gave, in ver. 1, 'Glorious to his native skies', and 'Enters now the highest heaven'; in ver. 2, 'glorious' (instead of 'pompous') before 'triumph', and other familiar lines which we have omitted, e.g. 'See, the heaven its Lord receives', and 'His prevailing death he pleads'. The Alleluya, now such a prominent feature, was not added till 1852, in White's *Introits and Hymns*. We have so far as possible used Wesley's own words; but we have altered in ver. 1 'wishful' to 'longing', and have followed Cotterill in changing 'pompous' in ver. 2, because the meaning of the word has degenerated since Wesley's day. Otherwise ver. 2 is as Wesley wrote it. Ver. 3 is unchanged. The first couplet of ver. 4 is from the original ver. 8, which runs:

> Grant, though parted from our sight,
> High above yon azure height,
> Grant our hearts may thither rise,
> Following thee beyond the skies.

To this couplet in ver. 4 we have added the couplet which concludes the tenth and last verse of the original, thus reducing the hymn, now so lengthened otherwise by the Alleluyas, to four verses.

Trochaic, 7 4. 7 4. D.

MUSIC. LYRA is the original version, *Lyra Davidica* (1708), of the tune EASTER HYMN (145).

173 See the Conqueror mounts in triumph.

Bishop Christopher Wordsworth,‡ 1807–85.

First published in his *Holy Year* (1862), in ten verses, of which six are printed unaltered in two parts, in the *English Hymnal* (1906). In our version the following lines are changed: ver. 1, l. 3, 'Riding on the clouds his chariot', l. 4, 'To his heavenly palace', l. 7, 'portals high'; in ver. 2, l. 3, 'Lord of battles, God of armies'; in ver. 3, l. 2, 'In the clouds to God's right hand'.

Trochaic, 8 7. 8 7. D.

MUSIC. IN BABILONE is a Dutch traditional melody ot which the present arrangement appeared in the *English Hymnal* (1906). It is much the same type as 'Vruechten' (169), and shows similar national characteristics.

REX GLORIAE, by Henry Smart, appeared in the Appendix to *Hymns Ancient and Modern* (1868). This is a confident and vigorous tune, but, like most of Smart's melodies, rather unoriginal both in phrase and rhythm. It is, however, soundlv constructed, and one of his best melodies.

174 The eternal gates lift up their heads.

Mrs. C. F. Alexander, 1823–95.

Contributed to the S.P.C.K. *Hymns* (1852), and reissued in Mrs. Alexander's *Hymns, Descriptive and Devotional* (1858), in five verses, as 'The golden gates are lifted up'. Both forms are in common use; but the earlier has remained the more popular.

C.M.

MUSIC. PRAETORIUS (FÜR DEIN EMPFANGEN SPEIS UND TRANK) is from *Harmoniae Hymnorum scholae Gorlicensis* (Görlitz, 1599). It appeared later in M. Praetorius's *Musae Sionae* (Part VI, 1609), set to 'In Bethlehem ein Kindelein', and was supposed therefore to have been written by him. It may be a traditional melody, but shows no very pronounced traits of this kind.

175 The head that once was crowned with thorns.

T. Kelly, 1769–1854.

Appeared in the 1820 edition of Kelly's *Hymns*. It is based on Hebrews 2:10, and borrows extensively from John Bunyan, who had written:

The head that once was crowned with thorns
  Shall now with glory shine;
The heart that broken was with scorns
  Shall flow with life divine.

Kelly was a magnificent if irresponsible preacher who set up chapels of his own in Ireland; but his broad-minded liberality made him beloved of the poor, especially during the Famine of 1847, when a poor man in Dublin is said to have comforted his wife by saying: 'Hold up, Bridget! Bedad, there's always Mister Kelly to pull us out of the bog, after we've sunk for the last time.'

C.M.

MUSIC. ST. MAGNUS (NOTTINGHAM) appeared in *The Divine Companion: or, David's Harp new tun'd. Being a Choice Collection of New and Easy Psalms, Hymns and Anthems . . . the second edition* (1709). There it is anonymous, but the three preceding tunes are said to be by 'Mr. Jer. Clark', and in W. Riley's *Parochial Harmony* (1762) the tune bears its present name and is assigned to Clark. In Gawthorn's *Harmonia Perfecta* (1730) it is called NOTTINGHAM. The alternative version (fa-burden), by Geoffrey Shaw, appeared in the *Tenor Tune Book* (1917).

This well-known tune has long been associated with the present words. It is a good solid melody, built on familiar lines.

176 To God, with heart and cheerful voice.

George Wither, 1588–1667.

The author ot these manly verses, was a pioneer of the modern hymn, though his own hymns were hardly every sung till quite recently, being excluded from most 19th-century books, apparently from sheer ignorance; for both Churchmen and Nonconformists could claim him. Imprisoned by James I for his satire, *Abuses Whipt and Stript*, he wrote some of his best poetry during his detention. He served Charles I as a captain of the horse; but, forced 'to prefer a kingdom to a king', he reluctantly became a Roundhead, sold his estates, and raised a troop of horse for Parliament, bearing for motto on his colours, '*Pro Rege, Lege, Grege*'. Taken prisoner by the Royalists, his life is said to have been saved by a good-humoured jest of Sir John Denham, 'His Majesty must really not hang George Wither, for so long as he lives no one will account me the worst poet in England'. Among the most famous of his poems is, 'Shall I, wasting in despair'. 'He suffered', says James Montgomery, the hymnodist, 'almost to martyrdom, both for his loyalty and his orthodoxy' (cf. 43, 657).

D.C.M.

MUSIC. OLD 22ND was set to Psalm 16 in the *Anglo-Genevan Psalter* of 1561, and in other 16th-century Psalters, but in Day's harmonized edition (1563), and in Este's and Allison's Psalters, it is set to Psalm 22, though it soon dropped out of use in England. Why this should have been so it is not easy to see, for it is an excellent tune, certainly superior to some which remained in constant use; but the caprices of popularity are always unintelligible.

WHITSUNTIDE

177 Come down, O Love divine.

Bianco da Siena, d. 1434. *Tr. R. F. Littledale.*

Discendi, amor santo,
Visita la mia mente
Del tuo amore ardente,
Sì che di te m'infiammi tutto quanto.

Bianco's hymns, edited by T. Bini, were published in Lucca, 1851. Littledale translated these four of the original eight stanzas for the *People's Hymnal* (1867).

Iambic, 6 6. 11. D. Unique.

MUSIC. DOWN AMPNEY, composed by R. Vaughan Williams for this hymn in the *English Hymnal* (1906), is named after his birthplace. This is a strong, dignified tune, with an interesting metrical scheme and a very characteristic ellipsis in the rhythm of the two long lines.

178 Come, Holy Ghost, our souls inspire.

Bishop J. Cosin, 1594–1672. *Based on* Veni, creator Spiritus.

Of unknown date and authorship, the *Veni Creator* was the only legacy of pre-Reformation hymns in the Book of Common Prayer, or rather in the Ordinal of 1552, where a poor version in common measure was printed in the Form of Ordering Priests. In 1662 this C.M. version was revised, and Cosin's L.M. version was added to the older. It had been first published in Cosin's *Collection of Private Devotions in the Practice of the Ancient Church* (1627), when he was still rector of Brancepeth. He had not intended it to be sung in church, but to be said privately every morning at nine in memory of the descent of the Holy Spirit upon the Church. Cosin was one of the revisers of the Prayer Book in 1661. This version is not very close to the original, and misses its almost martial note, which is more nearly approached in Robert Bridges's fine translation (179). The *Veni Creator* in one form or another has survived through a thousand varied years in England, and has associations with the most solemn functions of the Church, councils, coronations, consecrations, ordinations. In old times its singing was accompanied on great occasions by the ringing of bells and the use of lights and incense. Its use at Whitsuntide can be traced back to the 10th century, at ordinations to the 11th.

Joinville relates how, when the French sailed in 1248 with St. Louis for the Sixth Crusade, the captain of the King's ship called to his men in the prow, 'Are you ready?' and the clerks came forward. 'Sing, for God's sake!' cried the captain; and they chanted *Veni creator*. Then he cried,

'Unfurl the sails, for God's sake!' and soon they were out of sight of land. The disastrous Crusade had begun; the walls of Cairo were soon to be decorated with Christian heads, and King Louis a prisoner.

L.M.

MUSIC. VENI CREATOR (TALLIS) is generally attributed to Thomas Tallis, but the ascription is not certain. It is here given as in the *English Hymnal* (1906). The setting is clearly of the latter part of the 16th century, and, if not certainly by Tallis, may at least, without hesitation, be ascribed to his 'school'.

179 Come, O creator Spirit, come.

Before 10th cent. Tr. Y.H. (*Robert Bridges*).

Veni, creator Spiritus,
mentes tuorum visita,
imple superna gratia
quae tu creasti pectora.

This is a closer translation of the *Veni Creator* than the skilfully condensed paraphrase of Cosin. For a much looser paraphrase see Dryden's, 181. Since the hymn was written at the close of the Dark Ages, when the prayer for deliverance from foes was urgent and continually needed, the word 'comforter' has changed its meaning from 'strengthener' to 'one who brings comfort'; and 'comfortable' witnesses to its further degradation. Once *confortare* did not mean anything specially soothing: it is recorded of a schoolmaster in the Chronicles of the Monastery of St. Edmund that, *confortavit pueros baculo*, 'he fortified the boys with the stick'. Hooker uses the word in the earlier sense, 'doth not a little comfort and confirm the same'. The original Latin gives the real meaning of the word 'Comforter' as applied to the Holy Spirit; it is present in Bridges's translation. Yet nothing quite gives the force of the original:

Accende lumen sensibus,
infunde amorem cordibus,
infirma nostri corporis
virtute firmans perpeti.

Hostem repellas longius,
pacemque dones protinus;
ductore sic te praevio
vitemus omne noxium.

We asked Dr. Bridges if he would consent to the alteration of 'Comforter' in ver. 2 to the word used in the original, *qui Paraclitus diceris*; and he agreed to this, which also is a slight metrical improvement.

The main deficiency perhaps of Cosin's version, 179, is that it omits the idea of the *creative* Spirit, which both this and Dryden's version (181) preserve by retaining *creator* as an attributive noun.

L.M.

MUSIC. VENI CREATOR (MECHLIN), from the *Vesperale Romanum* (Mechlin), has been the plainsong melody proper to this hymn since its first use in the church services, but was previously associated with St. Ambrose's Easter hymn, 'Hic est dies verus Dei'. An impressive plainsong melody, it has here been adjusted to a more or less measured form, but the accents of the music must, nevertheless, follow those of the words and not those of the apparent triple time.

180 Come, thou holy Paraclete. *13th cent. Tr. J. M. Neale.*

Veni, sancte Spiritus,
et emitte caelitus
  lucis tuae radium:
veni, pater pauperum,
veni, dator munerum
  veni, lumen cordium.

The 'Golden Sequence', as it was often called in the Middle Ages, has been generally held to be one of the masterpieces of late Latin poetry—not for any originality, for it is as little original as most Latin hymns, but for 'a stately grace, a perfect rhythmic melody and a faculty for saying just the right thing in just the fitting words'. It has been ascribed to King Robert II of France and many others, including Stephen Langton; but the authorship is really quite unknown: it belongs to the second and not to the earlier Notkerian form of sequence (a sequence being a hymn introduced after the more primitive Gradual, which followed the singing of the Gospel), and the metre is unknown earlier than the 12th century. The earliest manuscripts are early 13th century. It did not displace the older Whitsuntide sequences; but when the many sequences which had accumulated during the Middle Ages, to the great enrichment of hymnody, were suppressed by the restriction to four in the Roman Missal of 1570, this was allowed to remain, together with *Victimae Paschali* (*E.H.* 130), *Lauda Sion* (*E.H.* 317), and *Dies irae* (*E.H.* 351).

Neale's translation, a fine effort at the difficult task of rendering the original in its proper metre, appeared in the *Hymnal Noted* (2nd ed., 1854), in 10 stanzas, 5 of which are here given, unaltered. The other well-known version gets over the double rhymes in the 3rd and 6th lines of each verse by omitting the last syllable, and thus involves a mutilation of the proper tune. Neale adopts the charming device of an assonance that preserves the final 'y' in each of these lines.

Trochaic, 7 7 7. D., the lines above mentioned being in reality dactylic. This metre may also be described as trochaic dimeter catalectic.

MUSIC. THE GOLDEN SEQUENCE is the proper melody to the sequence 'Veni, sancte Spiritus', and is found in two 13th-century manuscripts, the *Dublin Troper* and the *Chichester Troper*, in the *Hereford Missal* of the 14th century and the *York Missal* of the 15th century; the first being in the Cambridge University Library, and the other three in the Bodleian. It was long attributed to King Robert of France (10th cent.), and later was claimed by Prof. Peter Wagner for Pope Innocent III (1198–1216), but is now assigned, upon evidence considered conclusive by the Benedictines of Solesmes, to Archbishop Stephen Langton (d. 1228). The manuscripts cited prove that it came early into widespread use, and that its popularity was continuous. It is a most interesting and beautiful melody, very expressive, and with a lovely contour.

VENI SANCTE SPIRITUS is anonymous in *An Essay on the Church Plain Chant* (1782), but in the *Collection of Motetts or Antiphons* (1792) it is marked 'published by permission of Mr. Webbe', i.e. Samuel Webbe, the elder. He wrote much excellent church music, and the present tune has a simplicity and ease of expression which give it a beauty of its own.

181 Creator Spirit, by whose aid.

J. Dryden, 1631–1700. *Based on* Veni, creator Spiritus.

It is very interesting to compare this with the Latin of the *Veni Creator*, or with Robert Bridges's translation, 179. Life (the harsh dangers of the Dark Ages being so long past) has become more 'comfortable', and gentlemen in full-bottomed wigs can sing with graceful piety Dryden's excellent verse to the accompaniment of excellent music. So he can embellish the stern Latin verses, 'From sin and sorrow set us free, And make thy temples worthy thee'; 'Make us eternal truths receive And practise all that we believe'; what admirable sentiments! And indeed the hymn is a good one; but it has not the character of the original. It appeared first in Dryden's *Miscellaneous Poems* (1693), in seven stanzas of unequal length, 39 lines in all. One of the first to adapt it for congregational purposes was John Wesley in 1741, and he was shortly followed by Whitefield and Toplady; but it has always been used in an altered and abbreviated form. In our version the 39 lines are reduced to 24, but there are no alterations.

Iambic, 8 8. 8 8. 8 8, i.e. L.M. with an additional couplet.

MUSIC. VENI CREATOR (ATTWOOD) was published in separate form: 'Come Holy Ghost, a Hymn for Four Voices . . . composed by Thomas Attwood, organist of St. Paul's Cathedral' (1831). It was written as an anthem for an Ordination Service at St. Paul's Cathedral on Trinity Sunday, 1831, at the request of the Bishop of London, Dr. Blomfield. Attwood, who only received the Bishop's note on the Saturday, is said to have finished the composition while driving up from Norwood on the Sunday morning (Bumpus, *History of English Cathedral Music*, ii. 407). This always appears to be regarded as something of a feat, but, even in its original form, the anthem was not of great length, and Attwood, who had been for a time a pupil of Mozart's, was a competent craftsman capable of producing, if not an inspired, at least a respectable piece of music of twice the length in the time. The abysmal doctrine of 'art for art's sake' had not yet been invented. The tune is, in fact, a 'respectable' one, and though it halts rather in the middle, it has a grace and refinement of movement and a certain elegant charm which make it most attractive.

182 Our blest Redeemer, ere he breathed.

Harriet Auber, 1773–1862.

The story has been denied that Miss Auber (who lived a quiet life of 89 years, mostly at Hoddesdon in Hertfordshire) wrote this with her diamond ring on a window-pane, because she was sitting in her bedroom without writing materials; but it does seem true that it was so written in her house at some time. Duncan, in his *Popular Hymns and their Authors* (3rd ed., 1903), quotes a writer in *The Kingdom*, who says that the Rev. Dawson Campbell, who had occupied the house, told him that the pane was there seventeen years after her death; he also quotes Mr. C. W. Lock of Hoddesdon, who testified that the pane had been there but had since been removed by some unknown person. The hymn was first published in her *Spirit of the Psalms* (1829), in seven verses, and speedily attained great popularity, though in a shortened form. Our ver. 2 is often omitted, but it is one of the best. We omit:

He came in semblance of a dove,
With sheltering wings outspread,
The holy balm of peace and love,
On earth to shed.

which follows the common error of making the reference to a bird too specific. C. S. Calverley translated the hymn into Latin.

Iambic, 8 6. 8 4.

MUSIC. WICKLOW is an adaptation by R. Vaughan Williams, for *Songs of Praise*, of an Irish traditional tune from Joyce's *Old Irish Folk Music* (No. 296).

183 Our Lord, his Passion ended. *F. C. Burkitt.*

Written by Professor Burkitt, to carry the tune.

Iambic and Trochaic, 7 7. 7 7. D. The change to trochees in the second quatrain of each stanza makes the metre unique in this book.

MUSIC. FORTEM VIRILI PECTORE is found in the various editions of the Strasbourg *Catholisches Gesangbuch* from 1697 onwards, set to a German version of the hymn 'Fortem virili pectore'. The tune gives the impression of having been adapted from a popular song, and is of a type familiar in German folk-tunes.

184 Spirit of mercy, truth, and love.

Foundling Hospital Collection (1774).

Nothing is known about this excellent little hymn, typically 18th century in style, except that it has been traced to the *Collection* printed for the Foundling Hospital, London, 1774.

L.M.

MUSIC. O JESU MI DULCISSIME is found in the *Clausener Gesangbuch* (1653), set to the hymn of the title. It is a grave tune, with a strong Dorian flavour and a passionate emotional significance.

185 When Christ had shown God's dawning Reign. *B.R.*

Written for our book to provide a hymn without references to Sinai, and in accord with the description of Pentecost in Acts 2.

C.M.

MUSIC. STROUDWATER is from Matthew Wilkins's *A Book of Psalmody* (1st ed., 1725 (?); 2nd ed., 1735 (?)), where it is set to Psalm 146, 'My soul, praise ye the Lord always', and headed 'Stroudwater new tune'. There is also a different tune, headed 'Stroudwater old tune', set to Psalm 40. The present version, from the *Psalter in Metre* (1899), agrees with the original except that in the latter there are pauses between each line and that the melody of the 3rd bar of the 3rd line runs

The tune is of a familiar type, but noticeable for the rather unusual melodic progression at the beginning of the 1st line, and at the end of the 3rd. It is an excellent tune, and should rapidly become very popular.

TRINITY SUNDAY

186 Father most holy, merciful and tender. *c. 10th cent. Tr. E.H.*

O Pater sancte, mitis atque pie,
O Jesu Christe, Fili venerande,
paracliteque Spiritus O alme,
  Deus aeterne.

The Latin is in two manuscripts of the 11th century in the British Museum, and was a Trinity Sunday office hymn in the Sarum, York, Aberdeen, old Roman, and other breviaries. The translation was made for the *English Hymnal* (1906).

Sapphic Metre (11 11. 11 5). See 28, and the Note on Prosody, p. xxx.

MUSIC. PLAINSONG is an arrangement by J. H. Arnold, for *Songs of Praise*, of the melody, from the *Sarum Antiphonal*, proper to 'O Pater sancte' at Lauds on Trinity Sunday and daily to Corpus Christi; and also used for the Lauds hymn, 'O nimis felix', of the Nativity of St. John the Baptist, and the Mattins hymn, 'O sator rerum', of the Transfiguration.

HERR, DEINEN ZORN, by J. Crüger, is found in Runge's *Geistliche Lieder* (1653). It may have made a previous appearance in the 4th edition of Crüger's own *Praxis Pietatis Melica* (1st ed., 1644), but of that issue no copy is now known. The present harmonization is by Martin Shaw. It is a soundly built tune, the second half being, mainly, an inversion of the movement of the first half, but is not marked by any unusual features.

187 Holy, holy, holy! Lord God Almighty!

Bishop R. Heber, 1783–1826.

First printed in Heber's posthumous *Hymns, Written and Adapted to the Weekly Church Service of the Year* (London, J. Murray, 1827), this is the best known of his hymns. It was the more valuable because in the Victorian books there were so few hymns about God; and this, free from all subjectivity, filled a large gap, expressing the pure spirit of worship in stately language based upon Rev. 4 : 8–11. Heber perhaps inaugurated the more flowing measures of our later hymnody, with its increasing width of metrical range. Tennyson said of this: 'Of hymns I like Heber's "Holy, holy, holy" better than most; and it is in a fine metre too.'

11 12. 12 10. Trochaic in general character, but the last line of each stanza is really iambic. Unique.

MUSIC. NICAEA, by J. B. Dykes, composed for this hymn in *Hymns Ancient and Modern* (1861), was thus named because the hymn deals with the doctrine of the Trinity as expounded in the Nicene creed. The tune shows less weakness than is often found in Dykes's tunes; its celebrity places it beyond the reach of useful comment.

BROMLEY COMMON, by Martin Shaw, appeared in *Additional Tunes and settings in use at St. Mary's, Primrose Hill* (1915). It is a very satisfactory substitute for the older tune.

188 Most ancient of all mysteries. *F. W. Faber*, 1814–63.

Faber, an unequal writer, much given to sentimentality, once or twice produced first-class verse. But he did not rise to his best until he had got well under way, and his opening lines are often like those gestures that are familiar in a certain game. Another inept beginning, which we, in common with some other editors, have dropped, will be found in 666. He began our Trinity hymn, which appeared in *Jesus and Mary* (1849), with 11 verses (though it is now always abbreviated):

> Have mercy on us, God most high,
> Who lift our hearts to thee;
> Have mercy on us, worms of earth,
> Most holy Trinity.

But to Faber belongs the great distinction of being one of the few English hymn-writers of the 19th century who could compose a hymn about Almighty God.

C.M.

MUSIC. ST. FLAVIAN is the first half of the tune which first appeared in the *English Psalter* of 1562, set to Psalm 132, as follows:

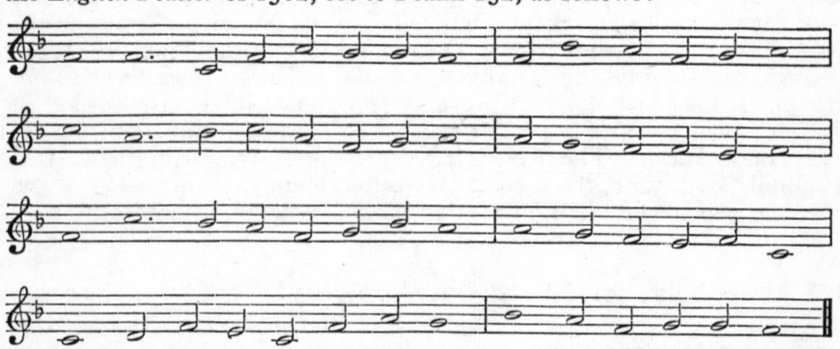

It was retained in the succeeding Psalters with some small changes of rhythm, the alteration of the 3rd and 15th notes occurring in the 17th century. The present form seems to be due to Redhead's *Ancient Hymn Melodies* (1853), being derived from Ravenscroft's *Psalter* (1621), from which the present alternative version (fa-burden) is also taken; the tune has not in any way suffered by its dichotomy.

The Hymnic Worm

A chapter might be written on the vermicular hymn, and the curious idea that the Creator must be pleased by the depreciation of his handiwork: as, for instance, in the line,

> He calls a worm his friend.

But, as it was with the word 'blood', so this word had lost its original meaning for hymnists, or they could not have written such a couplet as:

Earth from afar has heard thy fame,
And worms have learnt to lisp thy name.

Or such a verse as:

O may thy powerful word
  Inspire this feeble worm,
To rush into thy kingdom, Lord,
  And take it as by storm.

Nothing indeed is more significant than to study the 18th-century Methodist and other hymnals, and to notice how, in the elimination of this and hundreds of other ideas, the distinctive theological peculiarities of the age have been quietly dropped by editors of all schools of thought. There are not very many of the older hymns that could now be printed in full. In no book of to-day shall we find the line

Permit this humble worm to bow.

In that, as in many other turns of thought, the dross has disappeared with time, and the gold remains.

All these examples are from hymns once in common use (the first being from the original of 'The God of Abraham praise'); but the following reputed example cannot be verified:

Worms! strike your harps, your voices tune,
  And warble forth your lays;
Leap from the earth with pious mirth,
  To trumpet forth his praise.

DEDICATION FESTIVALS AND ANNIVERSARIES

189 All things are thine; no gift have we.

J. G. Whittier, 1807–92.

Written for the opening of Plymouth Church, Minnesota, and published in his *Complete Poetical Works* (1876). By contrast with the spendour of a great church, one may think of the Quaker farm of Whittier's boyhood, as Lady M'Dougall describes it in *Songs of the Church* (p. 295): 'The fire-place with its settles occupied one wall, whilst from the beams across the ceiling hung guns, fishing-rods, bunches of herbs, flitches of bacon, and strings of apples, onions, and pumpkins; the pewter plates shone from the old black oak dresser.'

L.M.

MUSIC. BUCKLEBURY is an arrangement by Alan Gray of a melody in *Harmonia Perfecta* (1730), and appeared in his *A Book of Descants* (1920). It is an energetic, well-sustained tune, with a swinging gait, characteristic of the new type of hymn-tune which was introduced about the beginning of the 18th century, and later popularized by the Methodists.

ALFRETON is found in the *Supplement to the New Version of the Psalms* (6th ed., 1708), where it is set for three voices, and headed 'An hymn on the divine use of music. A new tune', but without name of composer. It is in the tradition of the older psalm-tunes.

190 Blessèd city, heavenly Salem. *c. 7th cent. Tr. J. M. Neale.*‡

Urbs beata Hierusalem, dicta pacis visio
quae construitur in caelis vivis ex lapidibus,
et angelis coörnata ut sponsata comite.

This 'rugged but fine old hymn', as Archbishop Trench called it, is older than most of the kind, and may go back as far as the 6th century. It is based on 1 Pet. 2 : 5, Rev. 21, and Eph. 2 : 20. Trench says that 'the hymn coheres intimately in all its parts. . . . It is most truly a hymn "of degrees", ascending from things earthly to things heavenly, and making the first to be the interpreters of the last'; but Daniel and Neale both considered that ver. 7 is a later addition. Neale's translation appeared first in his *Mediaeval Hymns* (1851), and was revised in the *Hymnal Noted* (1852). The *Salisbury Hymn Book* (1857) gave us the couplet, 'Who, the two walls', &c., in ver. 5, a change which Neale thought 'true and happy'; he did not like the changes in *Hymns Ancient and Modern*; but 'Bridal glory round her shed' (ver. 2, l. 2) is surely a great improvement on his own 'Ready for the nuptial bed', though even that is a softening of the original, 'Nova veniens e caelo nuptiali thalamo, praeparata ut sponsata copuletur Domino'. Neale's lines have sometimes the ruggedness of the original; and even the *English Hymnal* had to alter more than one line. Our version is that of *E.H.* 169, 170, omitting 170, ver. 4.

Trochaic, 8 7. 8 7. 8 7.

MUSIC. PLAINSONG is an arrangement, by J. H. Arnold, of the Sarum melody to this hymn, for *Songs of Praise* (1925). It differs from the York version in the last two lines, which are, in the latter, merely a modified repetition of lines 3 and 4. The present version, from the *Sarum Antiphonal*, is probably the older and more authoritative form. There is a close connexion between this melody and that of 'Tibi, Christe, splendor Patris', the one being a derivative of the other. The present melody, as it stands, was also transferred to other hymns, such as 'Angulare fundamentum', 'Christi miles gloriosus', and others, and its superb quality makes its extended use understandable, especially the magnificently expressive phrase allotted to the last two lines.

ORIEL is from *Cantica Sacra in usum Studiosae juventutis. Collegit et edidit J. Michael Hauber . . . Cantui Chorali accommodavit vocem organi Casparus Ett, &c.* (Monachii, 1840). There it is set in four parts to the hymn 'Pange lingua'. It is not certain whether the tune was composed, or only arranged, by Ett, but it has not been traced to any earlier source. In *Easy Music for Church Choirs* (Part III, 1853), Ett is named as the composer. The tune is now very well known. It is of quite simple construction, consisting, in reality, of only two lines, the others being either repetitions, or direct imitations. There is an air of determination about it, which has, possibly, been the cause of its popularity. It is noticeable that, except in the 5th line, the movement is by step throughout.

191 Lo, God is here! Let us adore.

G. Tersteegen, 1697–1769. *Tr. J. Wesley.*‡

Gott ist gegenwärtig! lasset uns anbeten
Und in Ehrfurcht vor ihn treten!
Gott ist in der Mitten: alles in uns schweige
Und sich innig vor ihm beuge!

Wer ihn kennt,
Wer ihn nennt,
Schlagt die Augen nieder.
Kommt, ergebt euch wieder!

It is not known which of the Wesleys' hymns are by John and which by Charles. Since, however, only John knew German, it has been usual to assign the translations to him, together with such as are traceable to him through his *Journals* and other works, and to assign the remainder to Charles. Tersteegen was a mystic who went his own way, ministering individually to many people in Holland as well as in Germany, not identifying himself with any Church. This hymn has attained a wider use than any other of his; it first appeared in his *Geistliches Blumengärtlein* (1729).

Iambic, 8 8. 8 8. 8 8.

MUSIC. OLD 117TH appeared in the *Genevan Psalter* of 1551. The present form is from the *Psalmes of David, &c.* (Edinburgh, 1635), the most important musical edition of the 'Scottish Psalter'. The tune is mixolydian in character, but not strictly in this mode; it is remarkable for the extreme regularity of the alternate upward and downward movement. The melody may seem a little disconcerting at first, owing to its slightly unusual nature, but closer acquaintance will bring appreciation of its quality.

192 O Light, from age to age the same. *F. L. Hosmer*, 1840–1929.

Written in 1890 for the fiftieth anniversary of the Second Congregational Church, Quincy, Illinois, and included in his *The Thought of God in Hymns and Poems* (2nd series, 1894).

C.M.

MUSIC. EATINGTON, by W. Croft, is from Playford's *Divine Companion* (3rd ed., 1709), where it is set to Psalm 116, 'I love the Lord because he heard', in three parts. It may be noted that, in the same volume, there is a tune by Jer. Clarke, set to 'A Morning Hymn. Awake, my soul', of which the 1st line is identical with that of the present tune, except for the last note. This is the more interesting in that the present tune bears a strong family likeness to Clarke's tune 'St. Magnus'; though the actual identity extends only to the ends of the 1st and 3rd lines, the general shape and character are very similar (see 175).

193 Sing, all good people gathered. *Geoffrey Dearmer.*

Written for the *Oxford Book of Carols* (111) (1928) for the tune that carries the 22 verses of a carol commemorating the splendours and treasures of Angers Cathedral, which very likely originated with some humble fiddler singing for alms outside the great church.

Iambic, 7 6. 7 6. D.

MUSIC. CAERLEON is a Welsh hymn melody harmonized by David Evans. It appeared originally in the *Llyfr Tonau* (1859) of Ieuan Gwyllt. This is one of the finest of these Welsh tunes, with a stately, unusual rhythm, and a very strong melody.

ELLACOMBE is from *Vollständige Sammlung der gewohnlichen Melodien zum Mainzer Gesangbuche . . .* von *Xavier Ludwig Hartig* (Mainz, *c.* 1833), where it is set to the hymn 'Der du im heil'gsten Sakrament' as follows:

It is there dated 1700. Dr. Baümker states that Hartig is very incorrect as to the sources of tunes, and believes that the present melody is not older than the beginning of the 19th century, to which period a manuscript version of the tune, slightly varying from Hartig's, may be assigned. After 1833 the tune is found in several collections. It is a cheerful, unpretentious tune, now very well known, and frequently associated with the hymn 'Come sing with holy gladness'.

194 Our Father, by whose servants. *G. W. Briggs.*

Written in 1920 for Loughborough School (which was founded before 1496) by the Rector of Loughborough. In its original form it was suitable only for ancient foundations, but is here adapted to suit more modern ones also. The emphasis is still on the continuity of tradition, whether of School, College, or Church.

Iambic, 7 6. 7 6. D.

MUSIC. DANK SEI GOTT IN DER HÖHE is found in two publications by B. Gesius, both of 1605, viz. *Christliche Hauss und Tisch Musica, &c.*, where it is set to 'Jesus Christ, unser Herre', and *Ein ander new Opus Geistlicher Deutsche Lieder, &c.*, where it is set to 'Geduld die soll'n wir haben'. In both books the tune is as follows:

In the second work the B♮ marked * is a G.

The present form is J. S. Bach's in his *Vierstimmige Choralgesänge* (1769), many variants being found in different collections (see 168).

LOUGHBOROUGH, by G. W. Briggs, appeared originally in 1920, having been written for Loughborough School, for the composer's words.

Part III

THE COMMUNION OF SAINTS

THE CHURCH IN HEAVEN

It is, we think, worth while to continue the plan, common to many hymn-books, of providing a hymn for each red-letter day as well as the more general hymns about the saints; they are wanted in cathedrals and large churches especially; but other churches are often dedicated to a patron saint; again saints' days fall often on Sundays; also, such hymns are sometimes useful for sermons on a New Testament subject, apart altogether from commemoration. The task of providing a good hymn for every such day has never proved an easy one; there have been many failures. To pass over those that are familiar, there has been printed a hymn which begins:

Ever noble be our aims,
Like St. Philip and St. James;
Ever seeking to be good,
Like St. Simon and St. Jude.

There used to be others of like sort. In a hymnal, for instance, rather widely used fifty years ago, there is a saint's day hymn that begins:

Let our choir, with voice sonorous,
To the Maker sing in chorus.

Another begins:

Agnes, fair martyr,
  Steadfast and lowly,
Nothing can part her
  From the Most Holy.

But banality is a greater pitfall, especially in translations when the difficult coupled rhymes of the Latin are followed. To avoid the invidious task of quoting examples still in common use, let us instance the *Hymnal Noted*, admittedly the best of its kind. The first has not the usual excuse of most, since the rhymes are alternate:

Ye captains of a heavenly host
  Ye princes of a heavenly hall,
Stars of the world in darkness lost,
  And judges at its funeral.

Another begins with the incredibly flat remark:

Our festal strains to-day reveal
The joys that faithful spirits feel.

Another attempts the dramatic:

He met the wolf's impetuous shock,
  His cunning wiles defied;
And for his flock—his own dear flock—
  Was ready to have died.

Women suffer worst, because the writers can only think of one feminine virtue—or two, when martyrs are in question:

For chastity, as lily white,
For martyrdom, as ruby bright.

Otherwise the author seems at a loss to describe any endearing quality:

High let us all our voices raise,
In that heroic woman's praise,
Whose name, with saintly glory bright,
Shines in the starry realms of night.

Beyond this we are told nothing except that 'She spurned all love of things below', and 'With fasts her body she subdued'. Nor is all this banality really the fault of a rigid metrical form. Varied metres produce similar results, as with the hymn that begins:

To the Virgin He sends
  No inferior Angel.

Ineptitudes indeed abound in the books of half a century ago, which were once a good deal used by churches that were not satisfied with the amount of saints' hymns in *Hymns Ancient and Modern*, such as this for St. Augustine:

Soon the Pagan King he baptized
  Now no longer Satan's thrall,
And the people in their thousands
  Came obedient to his call.

Or this, for St. Anne:

Mother, from whose bosom's veil
  Fell the Star of Israel. . . .
Kings and queens of royal shoot,
  Sprung from Jesse's parent root:
Count no more! the swelling list. . . .

but it would lack reverence if we finished the verse. Sometimes ineptitude fades into obscurity, as in this:

And there find Paul the aged
  Who wrought the tents of old
Camps, in the time thereafter
  For liegemen of the fold.

But torments abound to supply the brighter side, and they are generally described with zest:

While the furnace flamed around him,
  Crimsoned with his gushing blood,
Yet he still endured intrepid,
  Faithful ever to his Lord.

Even in the best books good hymns were sometimes hindered by technical difficulties, as with the line which has to be sung, 'Thus, Lord, thy Barna, Bass in memory keeping'. But, as time went on, the number of adequate hymns increased; and each new hymnal had better opportunities than its predecessor. It has become less difficult to retain what was excellent in the older books, and to supply, so far as one can, new hymns where they seem to be most needed.

We have been quoting from the higher ranks of 19th-century hymnody. From humbler sources oddities emerge in much larger numbers, as, for instance, in this from *Hymns and Spiritual Songs for Camp Meetings and Revivals* (*c.* 1850), which is not saved even by its borrowings:

We'll sit on thrones of glory bright,
Where perfect day excludes the night,
  Above th' ethereal blue;
With glittering crowns upon our heads
With him we'll rest on heavenly beds,
  Our pleasures ever new.

If we go still farther afield, we might glance, for instance, at the Shakers, whose patron saint is, or was, their foundress, Mother Ann Lee. In their *Collection of Millenial Hymns* (1847, Canterbury, New Hampshire), hymns in her honour abound; but the first verse of one of the milder examples must suffice:

In sweetest love we'll raise the sound
  Of praise to blessed Mother Ann;
Our Mother who redemption found
  For fallen, lost, and sinful man.

It must, in fact, be admitted that there has been justification for the contempt into which hymnody fell some fifty years ago—from which, indeed, we have not yet recovered, so that even now in many circles people are shy about alluding to hymns. We can understand how the Master of the Rolls, half a century ago, a learned lawyer who retained certain traces of his vernacular, said of an eminent judge: ''Ere 'e comes, the 'oly 'umbug, 'umming 'is 'ymn! 'Ow I 'ate 'im!'

195 'For ever with the Lord!' *J. Montgomery*, 1771–1854.

This is one of those hymns which our generation has come to dislike unjustly, because of its association with a dreadful tune. Many musicians would have ironically assented to Dr. Farrar's statement, 'I can scarcely ever join in singing "For ever with the Lord" without tears'. Set to a manly old psalm-tune, the quality of the verses is not below Montgomery's level. He was anything but mawkish; he spent three months of 1795 in prison, and six months of 1796, for publishing outspoken articles in his newspaper, *The Sheffield Iris*. Eleven verses of this hymn were published in his *A Poet's Portfolio* (1835), or rather twenty-two, since it was in stanzas of four lines.

D.S.M.

MUSIC. OLD 25TH was first set to Psalm 25 in the *Anglo-Genevan Psalter* of 1558, and is invariably linked with that psalm throughout the later psalters. The rhythm has been slightly adapted in the present version, without detriment to the tune.

196 I would choose to be a doorkeeper.

Katharine Tynan Hinkson, 1859–1931.

This beautiful poem is from Mrs. Hinkson's *Collected Poems* (1930).

Irregular: a varying use of the iambic four and three foot quatrain, arranged in stanzas of eight lines.

MUSIC. DOORKEEPER was composed by Martin Shaw for this hymn in the enlarged *Songs of Praise* (1931). It is a clear, large-minded tune, with an effective modulation, which might be described as an extended 'fa fictum', in the 5th line. It is out of the rut of the usual 'hymn-tune' manner, with a slight folk-song flavour.

197 Jerusalem on high.

S. Crossman,‡ *c.* 1624–84.

Like 127, this is from his *Young Man's Meditation* (1664), and it is in the same metre. Leigh Bennett well says in Julian's *Dictionary*, 'The vision of the heavenly city and the delight and sadness which it inspires are portrayed with equal delicacy; and the crisp rhythm, the longing refrain, and a trace of Puritan feeling add to its charm'. The original is a long poem in two parts, and is shortened and altered in hymnals. Here the six verses of the *English Hymnal* version are reduced to five by the omission of two separate couplets ('The patriarchs' and 'The harpers', which involved two rhymes on 'behold'), and the first two lines of ver. 3 are recast.

'P.M.', i.e. Iambic, 6 6. 6 6. 4 4. 4 4. (or 8 8.), as in 127.

MUSIC. OLD 136TH is set to Psalm 136 in T. Este's *Whole Book of Psalmes* (1592). The tune has a distinct individuality, due to the regular alternation of B♮ and B♭ throughout, and to the metrical change in the last line.

CHRISTCHURCH, by C. Steggall, appeared in *Hymns for the Church of England* (1865). The alternative version (descant) by Alan Gray appeared in his *A Book of Descants* (1920). The tune has become closely associated with the present words; it is a good, bold melody, influenced by the older psalm-tunes. Steggall wrote much church music, and, as this tune shows, contrived as a rule to avoid many of the worst traits of his period, e.g. excessive chromaticism and its attendant sentimentality.

198 Jerusalem the golden.

Part of Hora novissima. *Bernard of Cluny, 12th cent. Tr. J. M. Neale.*

This miracle of verse, a poem of about 3,000 lines, styled *De Contemptu Mundi*, was written by a monk of Cluny, *c.* 1145, and begins:

> Hora novissima, tempora pessima sunt: vigilemus.
> ecce minaciter imminet arbiter ille supremus.
> imminet, imminet, ut mala terminet, aequa coronet,
> recta remuneret, anxia liberet, aethera donet.

The opening verses were translated as 'The world is very evil' (*H. A. & M.* 226, *E.H.* 495). It will at once be seen that such a 'rhythm of intense difficulty', carried through to such a length, cannot be rendered into tolerable English verse; Neale took refuge in one of the easiest metres in our language, and did not attempt the 'dactylic hexameters, with the leonine (sometimes a trisyllable or dactylic) and tailed rhyme, each line being broken up into three parts'. Another part of the poem will be found in 459, 'Brief life'. Here are the opening lines of 'Jerusalem the golden':

> Urbs Sion aurea, patria lactea, cive decora,
> omne cor obruis, omnibus obstruis et cor et ora.
> nescio, nescio, quae jubilatio, lux tibi qualis,
> quam sociala gaudia, gloria quam specialis.

And, of course, Neale was right in retaining the 'social joys', which some popular versions have altered. His 'conjubilant' is straight from the Latin; and we think he was justified in coining a word which also conveys the idea of fellowship, and sounds here like an organ-note.

Our congregations little realize, as they sing about the heavenly city, that these parts are but a few consolatory reflections upon what has been without exaggeration called 'a bitter satire on the fearful corruptions of the age'. All medieval writers, almost without exception, discourse on the incredible wickedness not only of the world, but of the Church, in their day; and Bernard only differs in doing so with such incredible skill. He himself attributed his success to special divine grace and inspiration.

Neale published his admirable translation—only, alas, of the first 218 lines out of 3,000—in *The Rhythm of Bernard de Morlaix, Monk of Cluny, on the Celestial Country* (1858). Bernard did not come, however, from Morlaix in Brittany, though there is just a possibility that he came from Morlas in the Basses-Pyrénées. His place of origin is, Mearns says, in the *Appendix* to Julian, quite uncertain. Translations have been attempted in the metre of the original; but the snag is that incongruous words creep in to make the rhymes, as in Duffield's, which is one of the best: 'These are the latter times, these are not better times: let us stand waiting.'

Iambic, 7 6. 7 6. D.

MUSIC. EWING was composed by A. Ewing for the hymn 'For thee, O dear, dear country', which is also translated from *De Contemptu Mundi*. It was published on a single sheet in 1853, and was in triple time as follows:

In this form it appeared, under the name 'St. Bede's', in *A Manual of Psalm and Hymn Tunes . . . edited by the Hon. and Rev. J. Grey* (1857).

The present form of the tune seems to have appeared first in *Hymns Ancient and Modern* (1861), where it was set to the present words. Colonel Ewing himself never liked it in common time; of this form of it he said, 'It now seems to me a good deal like a polka'. But, writing in 1861, Dr. Neale said: 'I have so often been asked to what tune the words of Bernard may be sung, that I may here mention that of Mr. Ewing, the earliest written, the best known, and with children the most popular; no small proof in my estimation of the goodness of church music.'

In spite of the composer's own opinion, the tune is preferable in its present form. The tune is certainly not above criticism, but there is a kind of struggling ecstasy in its phrases, especially in the 5th and 6th lines, which accords well with the spirit of Bernard of Cluny's poem.

PEARSALL is from the St. Gall *Catholisches Gesangbuch* (1863). The work contains five settings of hymns for the service of the mass. The present tune is that of the Sanctus in the first setting, the German words beginning 'Singt Heilig, heilig, heilig, ist unser Herr und Gott'. No composers' names are attached to the tunes, but the preface states that this tune was composed by Pearsall, who also harmonized about half of the tunes in the work.

199 Light's abode, celestial Salem.

Ascribed to Thomas à Kempis, 1380–1471. *Tr. J. M. Neale.*

Jerusalem luminosa
verae pacis visio,
felix nimis ac formosa,
summi regis mansio,
de te, O quam gloriosa
dicta sunt a saeculo!

There really seems to be much doubt whether Thomas of Kempen wrote this. The hymns ascribed to him are found in a Carlsruhe MS. of the 15th century; but they are neither in his *Opera* nor in the Zwolle MS. of *c.* 1480. 'Dreves', says Mearns, rather optimistically, 'is probably right in ascribing them to Thomas, but he does not give his reasons for doing so.' Neale's translation appeared first in the *Hymnal Noted* (1858).

Neale's extraordinary linguistic skill is illustrated in the story told by Gerard Moultrie of his visit to Hursley. Keble was called out of the room for a short time; and, when he returned, Neale said, 'Why, Keble, I thought you said the *Christian Year* was entirely original'. 'It certainly is,' said Keble. 'Then how', said Neale, 'is this?' and he handed Keble the Latin of one of his hymns. Keble was utterly confounded, and protested that never in his life had he seen that original before. After a few minutes of quiet enjoyment, Neale confessed that he had turned Keble's hymn into Latin while he was out of the room.

Trochaic, 8 7. 8 7. 8 7.

MUSIC. TANTUM ERGO (WEBBE) is from S. Webbe's *A Collection of Motetts or Antiphons* (1792). The alternative version (descant) by Alan Gray appeared in his *A Book of Descants* (1920). This famous tune is a worthy example of Webbe's musicianship; it still displays his inveterate habit of repetition of the same note, but the practice is here kept within reasonable bounds. In some of his tunes the whole of a phrase will consist almost entirely of such repetition, and it must be admitted that, competent musician as he was, his gift of melody was intermittent.

200 O what their joy and their glory must be.

Peter Abelard, 1079–1142. *Tr. J. M. Neale.*

O quanta qualia sunt illa sabbata
quae semper celebrat superna curia!
quae fessis requies, quae merces fortibus,
cum erit omnia Deus in omnibus!

The great Abelard, or Abailard, famous as a modern thinker before his time, and famous also for his association with Héloise and for the persecution he suffered, performed the extraordinary feat of writing a whole hymnal (the *Hymnus Paraclitensis*); and he did it for the convent of Héloise. This, for use on Saturday evening, was translated by Neale for the *Hymnal Noted* (1858), preserving the dactylic character of the Latin, and omitting two stanzas (*E.H.* 465). We have omitted three stanzas more.

Dactylic, 10 10. 10 10, the other example of this metre being 238.

MUSIC. REGNATOR ORBIS is an adaptation of a melody in La Feillée's *Méthode . . . du plain-chant, &c.* (1808), which is set to the hymn 'Regnator orbis summus et Arbiter'. The adaptation was made for the present hymn in Helmore's *The Hymnal Noted*, and has been linked with it ever since. The alternative version (descant) was written by Harold E. Darke especially for the enlarged *Songs of Praise* (1931).

The melody is not found in any other edition of La Feillée's work, but nevertheless is probably, at latest, of the early 18th century. The extreme regularity of the dactylic bars is here an integral constituent of the melody itself, in other words it is metrical; were a rhythmic pattern to be repeated thus, it would become excessively wearisome, and be a sign of weakness in the melody, whereas in the present case the metrical precision is a source of strength.

201 There is a land of pure delight. *I. Watts*, 1674–1748.

One of the most beautiful of Watts's poems, and doubly beautiful when sung to 'Mendip', this appeared in his *Hymns and Spiritual Songs* (1707 and 1709). T. Wright, in his *Life*, says that it was probably composed in 1706: 'According to tradition it came upon him one summer day, while he was gazing across the gulf-river, Southampton Water; and the pleasant meadows near Netley are said to have suggested the "sweet fields beyond the swelling flood".' From West Quay at Southampton it is only three-quarters of a mile across to the New Forest by the ferry. 'Few cities can boast a fairer landscape than that which greets the tourist when, standing on Southampton Pier, he looks out over the broad water of the estuary, and the swelling uplands, and ample meadows which stretch beyond, as far even as the waving masses of the New Forest.

C.M.

MUSIC. MENDIP was arranged for the *English Hymnal* (1906), from a ballad air collected by Cecil J. Sharp, which is familiar in Somerset and elsewhere. It is a good example of the straightforward type of folk-tune, both in melody and rhythm, the last line, especially, being characteristic of many Somerset tunes.

THE SAINTS

202 For all the saints who from their labours rest.

Bishop W. W. How, 1823–97.

This, which has the fine directness of a great popular song and has become one of our chief national hymns, was first published in Lord Nelson's *Hymns for Saints Days* (1864), as 'For all thy saints', with eleven verses. We print the version which the author preferred.

Iambic, 10 10. 10. 4.

MUSIC. SINE NOMINE was composed by R. Vaughan Williams for this hymn in the *English Hymnal* (1906). This splendid melody is certainly one of the finest hymn-tunes written during the present century. In the 'alleluya' is found the rhythmic ellipsis which has already been mentioned as characteristic of this composer.

203 For thy dear saint, O Lord.

Bishop R. Mant,† 1776–1848.

A new hymn included among Mant's translations in his *Ancient Hymns* (1837). He was one of the earliest translators; but only this and another original hymn from the same book have survived in our book (460), though there are two of his translations in the *English Hymnal*. In order to avoid confusion with 202, and to make the hymn available for any saint's day, we have, in common with some other books, altered the opening line from 'For all thy saints'.

S.M.

MUSIC. MOUNT EPHRAIM, by B. Milgrove, is from *Sixteen Hymns as they are sung at the Right Honourable the Countess of Huntingdon's Chapel in Bath* (1769). (See reference in Mrs. Gaskell's *Cousin Phillis*, Part I.) It is a tune of a similar type to 'Harwich' (see 161).

204 Give me the wings of faith to rise.

I. Watts, 1674–1748.

First published in his *Hymns and Spiritual Songs* (2nd ed., 1709).

C.M.

MUSIC. SONG 67, by Orlando Gibbons, was set to a hymn for St. Matthias's Day (see 29). It is therefore sometimes known as ST. MATTHIAS. It is not especially characteristic of the composer, but is in the normal psalm-tune tradition.

205 Hail, glorious spirits, heirs of light.

J. Austin,‡ 1613–69.

First published in his *Devotions in the Antient Way of Offices* (1668). It has been made more general here by altering the 1st line from 'Hail, glorious angels', and the 3rd, from 'burn chaste'; and in ver. 3, from 'Hail, great Apostles of the Lamb'.

C.M.

MUSIC. DORKING is an adaptation by the editors of an English traditional melody, and was made especially for *Songs of Praise* (1931).

206 Hark the sound of holy voices.

Bishop Christopher Wordsworth,† 1807–85.

From his *Holy Year* (1862), omitting the 'sawn asunder' verse (*E.H.* 198, ver. 3). The general idea, as the author pointed out, is the final triumph of the blessed, suggested by Rev. 2. We have altered the conclusion, which in the original is:

God the Father, God the Son, and
God the Holy Ghost adore.

Trochaic, 8 7. 8 7. D.

MUSIC. VISION, by S. Mason, a blind musician, was composed for *Songs of Praise* (1925). It is a clear, broad tune, rather in the style and design of some of the traditional Welsh hymn-tunes.

207 How bright these glorious spirits shine!

I. Watts and others, 18th cent.

Watts's original (in his *Hymns and Spiritual Songs*, 1707) is never used. This recast was first made in the draft of the Scottish *Translations and Paraphrases* (1745), keeping the original 1st line, 'These glorious minds how bright they shine'. Slight further alterations were made in the draft of 1751; and in the authorized issue of 1781 of the *Translations* considerable changes were made, this version being by W. Cameron, according to the claim made by his daughter. Thus the hymn, which is based on Rev. 7: 13–17, reached its present form, 'How bright these glorious spirits shine'. Another example of a successful patchwork. A further alteration here is that of ver. 2, l. 3, from 'And in the blood of Christ have washed'.

C.M.

MUSIC. BALLERMA is found in *A Selection of Original Sacred Music. . . . Intended to form the sixth Vol. of Steven's Selection of Sacred Music, edited by John Turnbull* (Glasgow, 1833). There it is attributed to R. Simpson, but it seems to be an adaptation from a melody published by F. H. Barthélémon, set to a poem entitled 'Belerma and Durandarte', which appeared in the once famous romance *The Monk*, by M. G. Lewis. It is an extremely simple tune, the second pair of lines being only a slightly varied repetition of the first pair, with a melodic line of a very candid character.

208 Rejoice, ye dead, where'er your spirits dwell.

Robert Bridges.

From *The Growth of Love*: sonnet 19.

Iambic, 10 10. 10 10.

MUSIC. PSALM 93 is from the *Genevan Psalter* (1562), where it is set to Psalm 93, 'Dieu est regnant de grandeur tout vestu'. The present arrangement is adapted from Goudimel's setting (*v.* 50). It is a stately tune, with a freely varied rhythm; one of the finest melodies in this psalter.

209 What are these that glow from afar.

Christina Rossetti, 1830–94.

First printed in *Lyra Mystica* (an anthology compiled by Orby Shipley) (1865), and reprinted in the *Prince's Progress* (1866).

Irregular.

MUSIC. MONK'S MARCH is an arrangement of the Welsh traditional melody, known as 'Ymdaith y Mwnge', which is supposed to have been sung by the monks of Bangor Isycoed during their march to Chester when this town was besieged by Ethelfrith, King of Northumbria. The latter here won a victory over Brochwel, Prince of Powys, and after putting the monks to the sword, proceeded to invade Wales, and lay it waste, destroying Bangor Isycoed and the monastery, with its library and other valuable possessions. The tune is, however, evidently of a far later date; it is a vigorous march, with a strongly marked rhythm, and first found in Playford's *Dancing Master* (1665) as 'The L. Monk's March', i.e. General Monk.

210 Who are these, like stars appearing.

H. T. Schenck, 1656–1727. *Tr. F. E. Cox.*‡

The only hymn by Heinrich Theobald Schenck (or Schenk); this is found in the *Neu-Vermehrtes Gesangbüchlein* (Frankfurt-am-Main, 1719), in 20 stanzas. Miss Cox's translation of 15 stanzas appeared in her *Sacred Hymns from the German* (1841); and from this Alford's *Psalms and Hymns* (1844) made the present well-known selection. Miss Cox published a revision of her work in her *Hymns from the German* (1864); and this admirable version we print unaltered. The hymn, like 207, is based on Rev. 7 : 13–17.

Trochaic, 8 7. 8 7. 7 7.

MUSIC. ALL SAINTS is from the *Geistreiches Gesangbuch* (Darmstadt, 1698), where it is set to the hymn 'Zeuch mich, zeuch mich, mit den Armen'. The present form differs slightly from the original in the 2nd bar and the antepenultimate and last bars. The alternative version (faburden), by Herbert W. Sumsion, was written for the enlarged *Songs of Praise* (1931). The tune, which is very simply built, and is a characteristic example of the plain, straightforward chorale without any outstanding emotional significance, is now closely associated with the present words.

PSALM 146 is from the *Genevan Psalter*, the harmony being by Goudimel in the Delft edition of 1602.

APOSTLES AND PROPHETS

211 Disposer supreme, and judge of the earth.

Based on Supreme quales, Arbiter, *J.-B. de Santeüil* (1686).

Supreme quales arbiter
tibi ministros eligis,
tues opes qui vilibus
vasis amas committere.

Santeüil was asked to help reform the Paris and the Cluniac Breviaries; and his work evoked the flattering objection that it showed more of the classical than of ecclesiastical manner. This was in the Cluniac Breviary (1686). Isaac Williams made a translation for the *British Magazine* (1836), as 'Disposer supreme', which became popular in many books, always altered, because the original is too uncouth for use. Even when considerably amended, as in *H. A. & M.* 431 or *E.H.* 178, Williams's words are crabbed and difficult to understand. We have made further alterations in vv. 2 and 4; ver. 3 is written afresh, and a word is changed in the doxology.

Anapaestic, 10 10. 11 11. Unique.

MUSIC. OLD 104TH is from Ravenscroft's *Whole Booke of Psalmes* (1621), where it is set to Psalm 104. In the earlier psalters this psalm is set to a tune from the *Anglo-Genevan Psalter* (1561). The accents and rhythm are exceedingly bad, and this may have induced Ravenscroft to discard it and substitute the present tune, which may be his own composition. The alternative version (descant) by Alan Gray is from his *A Book of Descants* (1920). This, one of the most famous of the psalm-tunes of the middle period, well merits the continuous popularity it has always enjoyed.

212 Prophets, teachers, true recorders. *P. Dearmer.*

Written for our book to include prophets, evangelists, and all inspired writers; and also because there were not enough hymns for the number of fine tunes in this metre.

Trochaic, 8 8 7. D.

MUSIC. AUCTOR OMNIUM BONORUM (ALLES IST AN GOTTES SEGEN) is from J. B. König's *Harmonischer Lieder-Schatz, oder Allgemeines Evangelisches Choral-Buch, &c.* (1738), where it is set to the hymn 'Alles ist an Gottes Segen' in the following forms:

It appears in many later collections and is found in virtually its present shape in J. C. Kühnau's *Vierstimmige alte und neue Choralgesänge, &c.* (vol. ii, 1790). It is here given as in the *Charterhouse Founder's Day Service Book.* The comparison of it with the above forms is interesting; it will be seen that the 4th bar of the first form has become an important *motif* in the present version, which otherwise is derived in almost equal proportions from both the previous varieties. Analysis of all three variants, which cannot be detailed here, will throw much light on the evolution of such tunes in general.

213 Servants of God, or sons. *Matthew Arnold (cento),* 1822–88.

A selection of lines made up into verses from Arnold's famous poem on *Rugby Chapel*, in which he pays a magnificent tribute to the great head master, his father, Dr. Arnold, who had died in 1842 at the age of 47. The poem was written in Nov. 1857, and not published till 1867 in *New Poems.*

7 7. 7 7. 7 7. Irregular. Dactylic in character.

MUSIC. CUMNOR was composed by R. Vaughan Williams for this hymn in *Songs of Praise* (1925). It is a broad, shapely tune, with a slightly modal flavour, in triple time; it is characteristic in many ways, e.g. the opening phrase and the 4th line, of this composer's less complex tunes.

EVANGELISTS

214 Virtue supreme, thy mighty stream. *P. Dearmer.*

Written for our book to provide another hymn for Evangelists and other inspired writers, and to carry a tune difficult for versification.

Iambic. 8 7. 8 7. 8 8 7; but unlike the other tunes with these syllables, this metre has an internal rhyme and caesura in four lines of each verse, so that it may rather be described as 4 4 7. 4 4 7. 4 4 4 4 7. Unique.

MUSIC. MIT FREUDEN ZART is from the Bohemian Brethren's songbook, *Kirchengeseng darinnen die Heubtartickel des Christlichen Glaubens gefasset und ausgeleget sind, &c.* (1566) where it appears as follows:

The present form is found in various later collections. The original rhythm is effective in some ways, especially in the 4th line, but the later version still preserves the attractive contrast between the long sustained first phrase, and the shorter rhythms of the following section. The tune is probably older than the above book, and has considerable affinity with the melody 'Psalm 138' (661, i), this being still more evident in the original form.

215 Let us now our voices raise.

St. Joseph the Hymnographer, d. 883. *Tr. J. M. Neale.*‡

Joseph, who had been for many years a slave in Crete, was a prolific hymn-writer; Neale, while protesting all the time against his 'tediousness, verbiage, and bombast', was so fond of antiquities that he 'translated' several of Joseph's hymns—or, rather, he made new hymns out of a few thoughts scattered up and down the Greek odes; and, indeed, his 'O happy band of pilgrims' and 'Safe home' are really original hymns and not by Joseph at all. Neale's words, 'Let our choir new anthems raise' (*Hymns of the Eastern Church* (1862), will be found unaltered in *E.H.* 187. It seemed better to discard the device of using 'anthem' as a two-syllabled synonym for 'hymn', and also to give the first verse a more general use (the original is a canon on the martyrdom of the deacon, St. Timothy, and his wife, St. Maura). There are a few changes also in the first half of ver. 2. The rest is unaltered.

Trochaic, 7 6. 7 6. D.

MUSIC. WEIMAR, by M. Vulpius, appeared in his *Ein schön Geistlich Gesangbuch, &c.* (1609), set to the hymn 'Jesu Kreuz, Leiden und Pein', as follows:

Variants occur in later collections, virtually the present form being found, set to the hymn 'Jesu Leiden, Pein und Tod', in Vopelius's *Neu Leipziger Gesangbuch* (1682).

In its present form the tune conforms to the regular type of chorale, both in phrase and rhythm. It is used thus by J. S. Bach in *The St. John Passion* (No. 20).

216 The Son of God goes forth to war.

Bishop Reginald Heber, 1783–1826.

From Heber's *Hymns* (1827), this famous hymn was written for St. Stephen's Day. We have therefore starred vv. 3, 4, so that these can be omitted if desired, and also the next two verses referring to the Apostles. The ascription of martyrdom to all the Apostles except John rests on no better historical basis than that of the Apocryphal Acts which bear the names of Thomas, Paul, &c. (cf. 234). We have arranged the hymn in three parts, so that two very short hymns are now available, as well as a longer hymn made up of Parts I and III, a hymn for St. Stephen (vv. 1–4, with Part III), while ver. 5 with Parts I and III provides a hymn for the Apostles, if sung to a C.M. tune such as 'St. Anne'.

In Mrs. Ewing's *Story of a Short Life*, the dying cripple boy asks the soldiers to sing 'The Son of God' outside his window, to the 'tug-of-war tune'; and as the men came to 'They climbed the steep ascent of heaven', 'the V.C. stopped as if he had been shot. For a man's hand had come to the Barrack Master's window, and pulled the white blind down.'

D.C.M., or C.M.

MUSIC. OLD 81ST (OLD 77TH) appeared first in Day's *Whole Booke of Psalmes* (1562), set to Psalms 81 and 77, this being also the first appearance of metrical versions of these two psalms. In subsequent Psalters the tune varies slightly, and is also found in duple as well as triple time. The present form is from *Este's Psalter* (1592). The alternative version (fa-burden), by Ernest Bullock, was written especially for the enlarged *Songs of Praise* (1931).

The tune, especially in its duple form, bears a strong likeness, in more than one line, to 'Tallis' Ordinal' (see 664), but it is probably a mere coincidence, since many of the older psalm-tunes have a number of phrases in common. It is a remarkable example of its kind.

SPECIAL DAYS AND OCCASIONS

ST. ANDREW

217 Jesus calls us! O'er the tumult.

Mrs. C. F. Alexander, 1823–95.

From the S.P.C.K. *Hymns* (1852). In 1871 a mutilated text in the S.P.C.K. *Church Hymns* led Mrs. Alexander to revise her work, but not for the better; she changed the refrain of vv. 1–3 to 'Softly, clearly—"Follow me"'.

Trochaic, 8 7. 8 7.

MUSIC. OMNI DIE is from D. G. Corner's *Gross Catolisch Gesangbuch* (Nuremberg, 1631), where it was set to the hymn 'Omni die dic Mariae'. The present arrangement, by W. S. Rockstro, appeared in the *English Hymnal* (1906), and presents the melody in its original form except at the end of line 2, where the rhythm was 𝅗𝅥. ♩ | 𝅝 ||, as in the 4th line. The tune is an agreeable one, with a metrical scheme which is simple, but always attractive.

GOLDSCHMIDT (O, DER ALLES) is found in Freylinghausen's *Geistreiches Gesangbuch* (2nd issue, 1705), as follows (the signature being as here, i.e. flat to E only):

It does not appear in the 1st issue, but in the 4th (1708) it is in common time, as at present, the only differences being that the 5th bar runs

and the last two bars

In the *Chorale Book for England* (1863), from which the present version is taken, the tune is attributed to *Geistreiches Gesangbuch* (Darmstadt, 1698), but this attribution is a doubtful one. There is a melody in that work, set to the hymn 'Gott, so machst du's mit den Deinen', as follows:

and this might possibly be regarded as an earlier variant of the present tune; the 1st line is the same, and there is a slight resemblance of shape and rhythm in the rest. But, on the other hand, the 1st phrase is almost a commonplace of the period, and begins many melodies, both secular and ecclesiastical, and greater similarity can be traced in many tunes which are certainly unconnected, especially when the earlier form in Freylinghausen's book is taken into consideration. It seems more probable, therefore, that Freylinghausen's 2nd version was perhaps influenced by a reminiscence of the Darmstadt tune in the minds of congregations acquainted with both, than that the one was definitely derived from the other.

ST. THOMAS

218 Who dreads, yet undismayed.

J. R. Darbyshire, Bishop of Glasgow.

Written for our book in order to carry a tune in a very unusual metre, and to provide a new hymn commemorating the courage and faith of the 'doubting Apostle'.

Iambic, 6 5. 6 5. 6 6 6. 5. Unique.

MUSIC. MOAB, by Ieuan Gwyllt (John Roberts), is to be found in his *Llyfr Tonau Cynulleidfaol* (*Ychwanegiad*, 1870), the recognized tune-book of the Calvinistic Methodists. Sir Henry Hadow has declared the present tune to be one of the greatest in the world; and, though this is perhaps rather too high praise, it is certainly an excellent tune.

ST. STEPHEN

219 When Stephen, full of power and grace. *Jan Struther.*

Written for our book, to provide a new hymn for St. Stephen.

D.C.M.

MUSIC. WELLINGTON SQUARE, by Guy Warrack, was written especially for the enlarged *Songs of Praise* (1931). Obviously influenced by some of the traditional English carol melodies, this is an energetic modal tune, of simple structure, the whole tune being founded on the first four notes and their inversion.

ST. JOHN THE EVANGELIST

220 On the moorland of life God's Shepherd is seen.

J. M. C. Crum.

Written for our book to provide a new hymn for the Evangelist, the author of the Fourth Gospel, and to carry a fine uncommon tune. Scholars now commonly distinguish three Johns: (1) John the Apostle, the son of Zebedee; (2) John the Elder, who may well be the same as the Evangelist and author of the three Epistles; and (3) John the Seer, who wrote the Apocalypse. In this hymn it is only the second who is referred to, the question of the son of Zebedee being left open. A reformed calendar might perhaps make 25 July (234) the day of St. James and St. John, i.e. James the Greater and John the Apostle, both sons of Zebedee.

Anapaestic, 11 12. 11 12. Unique.

MUSIC. MASON ('OLD GERMAN') is from *Harmonia Sacra or A Choice Collection of Psalm and Hymn Tunes . . . by Mr. Thos. Butts* (London, 1760 [?]), where it is set to 'All Glory and Praise To the Antient of Days', as follows:

The present adaptation appeared in J. Mason's *A Companion to the Wesleyan Hymnbook, &c.* (London, 1847), set to 'My God, I am thine'. The tune has been lengthened by the insertion of four bars before a repeat of the 2nd line.

INNOCENTS' DAY

221 When Christ was born in Bethlehem. *Laurence Housman.*

Appeared first in the *English Hymnal* (611) (1906). Like several others, it was originally classed among children's hymns.

C.M.

MUSIC. RODMELL, from the *English Hymnal* (1906), is an arrangement by R. Vaughan Williams of an English traditional melody.

It is a cheerful, resolute tune, with a quick-moving rhythm; the use of the phrase of the 2nd line to form the 3rd line, with an extended ending, is characteristic of a large number of English folk-tunes.

ST. PAUL

222 'To Damascus!' Paul had shouted. *Geoffrey Dearmer.*

Written for our book.

Trochaic, 8 7. 8 7. 8 7.

MUSIC. BLAENCEFN, by John Thomas, is from *Llyfr Tonau, Ail Attodiad* (1890). A gentle fluent tune of very simple build, being composed throughout of repetitions or direct imitations of the 1st line; it is easy and agreeable to sing.

THE PRESENTATION

223 When Mary brought her treasure. *Jan Struther.*

Written for our book, to provide a hymn for Candlemas Day, and to carry the tune.

Iambic, 7 6. 7 6. 6 7 6. The other example of this metre is 70, where the last triplet forms a refrain.

MUSIC. AVE MARIA KLARE is first found, according to W. Baümker, in Leisentritt's *Catholicum Hymnologium Germanicum* (1587), where the form of the melody is as follows:

It also appears in *Catholische Kirchen Gesäng* (Cologne, 1619), and in *Psalteriolum Harmonicum* (1642), from which latter book the present version of melody and harmony is taken. Töpler's *Alte Choral-Melodien* (1832) gives a form in common time, from which Havergal made a four-lined adaptation in his *Old Church Psalmody* (1847), with the name NARENZA; this form has been included in several subsequent collections, sometimes under the name COLOGNE.

Any appreciable curtailment, such as Havergal's adaptation, must here be destructive of almost all the attractiveness of the tune, which largely lies in the little interpolated 5th line, and the subsequent return to the previous rhythm (cf. 'Es ist ein Ros' entsprungen', 70).

ST. MATTHIAS

224 When Judas did his Lord reject. *Geoffrey Dearmer.*

Written for our book. Common Measure was chosen because there are still many good C.M. tunes waiting to be made use of.

C.M.

MUSIC. EPWORTH is from *The Psalmist: A Collection of Psalm and Hymn Tunes*, edited by Vincent Novello (Part III, 1838). There it is called 'Loughton', and headed 'Charles Wesley. Arr. by S. Wesley'. It is a tune with a rather unusual contour, owing to the frequency and width of the skips in the melody, which give it a very bold and determined individuality.

ST. DAVID

225 We praise thy name, all-holy Lord. *E. J. Newell*, 1853–1916.

First appeared in the *Northern Churchman and St. David's Weekly* (29 Feb. 1896), as a hymn for David and the Welsh Saints, in seven verses; first printed in three verses for St. David alone in the *English Hymnal* (1906).

D.C.M.

MUSIC. STETTIN (NUN SEHT) is from the Bohemian Brethren's songbook *Kirchengeseng darinnen die Heubtartickel des Christlichen Glaubens gefasset und ausgeleget sind, &c.* (1566), where it appears in the following form:

THE ANNUNCIATION

226 A message came to a maiden young. *O.B.C.*

From the *Oxford Book of Carols* (100) (1928), the 1st verse being a free translation of a traditional Dutch carol, *De boodschap van Maria* ('Er was een maagdetje'). The lovely carol music was printed in the *Nederlandsch Volksliederenboek* (1896). The remaining verses by the editor are, of course, modern.

Iambic and anapaestic, 9 7. 9 7. 7 7. 4 4 6. Unique.

MUSIC. DE BOODSCHAP, from the *Nederlandsch Volksliederenboek* (1896), is the traditional Dutch melody to the words of 'De Boodschap van Maria'. The present arrangement, by Martin Shaw, appeared in the *Oxford Book of Carols* (1928).

This Dutch carol-tune shows much of the same vigorous character as 'Vruechten' (169), but it also bears a considerable resemblance to some of the English popular tunes of the late 17th and early 18th centuries, especially in the 'refrain-like' 2nd and 4th lines. It is a good tune with a very attractive close.

ST. GEORGE

227 Lord God of Hosts, within whose hand. *Laurence Housman.*

Written for the *English Hymnal* (1906). It will be noticed that hymns for the national saints are provided, as well as for those in the Calendar.

Iambic, 8 8. 8 8. 8 8.

MUSIC. FALKLAND, by Henry Lawes, is from G. Sandys's *A Paraphrase upon the Divine Poems* (London, 1638), where it is set to Psalm 12, 'Helpe, Lord, for godly men decay'. This tune shows some distinctive touches of Lawes's personal manner. Being written in the traditional psalm-tune style, it cannot display his typical adaptation of musical to verbal rhythm, for which Milton, no mean judge, praised him; the melody of the 5th and 6th lines, however, is very characteristic, and, in a less degree, the manner of the introduction of the modulation in lines 3 and 4. Though formal in expression the tune has a decided individuality of its own.

ST. MARK

228 The saint who first found grace to pen. *Laurence Housman.*

Written for the *English Hymnal* (1906). The special debt we owe to St. Mark's Gospel in the light of New Testament criticism is here recognized.

L.M.

MUSIC. BROCKHAM, by Jeremiah Clark, appeared first in Playford's *The Divine Companion; or David's Harp new Tuned* (1709), where it was set to Psalm 121, 'Up to the hills I lift mine eyes'. Several tunes by Clark are found in this collection, and, though they are almost all written on a familiar model, he does succeed, quite often, in weaving an independent thread into the formal pattern; this may be seen here in the 2nd line, and in the interruption of the sequence, and the consequent transference of its accent, in the 3rd line.

ST. PHILIP AND ST. JAMES

229 The winter's sleep was long and deep. *E.H.*

Written by the editor for the *English Hymnal* (1906), to provide a hymn for May Day to the tune of the May Carol. There was much confusion in old times about the saints named James, as a consequence of which one of the Apostles, James the Less, is not really commemorated at all. The St. James of May Day is James the Just, the Lord's brother. For St. James the Greater see 234. The reference in v. 4 is to John 14 : 8–10, in v. 5, to James 1 and 2.

C.M., with a strong anapaestic element, as in many ballads.

MUSIC. KING'S LANGLEY appeared in the *English Hymnal* (1906), and is an arrangement of the traditional melody of a Hertfordshire May-Day Carol collected by Miss L. E. Broadwood. It is a delightfully gay tune, very characteristic of this class of folk-song.

ST. BARNABAS

230 True Son of Man, thou crown of human valour. *A. G.*

Written for this book to the metre associated with tunes on St. Barnabas's Day. The name 'Barnabas' means, not 'the Son of Consolation', but 'the Son of Inspiration', the man, that is, who inspires and encourages, or, as the Greek word suggests, the man who acted as a 'paraclete' to the Antioch missionaries, coming to their side to help them—for such he was found to be. Ver. 3 refers to Acts 4: 36–7, 11 : 22–6; ver. 4, to Acts 14: 12.

Iambic, 11. 10. 11 10. D.

MUSIC. LONDONDERRY is an arrangement, by Henry G. Ley, of the famous Irish traditional melody known as 'The Londonderry Air'. This very beautiful tune has unfortunately been so much 'arranged' for every combination, both vocal and instrumental, and so frequently imitated, that it is now within the danger line of the proverbial contempt. It remains, however, a most notable tune, with a lovely contour, and a remarkable emotional significance in the gradual rise to and quick descent from the climax, which is placed, with great, though perhaps unconscious, skill at exactly the most 'telling' point in the curve, roughly three-quarters of the way through the tune. The present arrangement appeared in *Songs of Praise* (1931).

ST. JOHN BAPTIST

231 Let thine example, holy John, remind us.

Paulus Diaconus, 8th cent. Tr. R. Ellis Roberts.

UT quaeant laxis REsonare fibris
MIra gestorum FAmuli tuorum,
SOLve polluti LAbii reatum,
Sancte Iohannes.

We print in capitals certain syllables of the Latin, because UT, RE, MI, SOL, LA, with SI (the initials of Sancte Iohannes) were taken from this hymn by Guido of Arezzo to indicate the notes of the scale; since, in the plainsong melody associated then with these words, they fell on the consecutive rising notes of the scale. Afterwards, as *ut* was found inconvenient, it was changed, and so we got the familiar *Do*, *Re*, *Mi*, *Fa*, *Sol*, *La*. Paul the Deacon is remembered only for this hymn, which occurs in most of the old breviaries. The translation was made by Mr. Ellis Roberts for the *English Hymnal*, 223 and 224, which supply respectively our ver. 1 and vv. 2–5.

Sapphic, 11 11. 11 5.

MUSIC. ISTE CONFESSOR (ANGERS) is an Angers church melody (see 28). Internal evidence suggests that this stately and impressive tune is one of those derived from plainsong.

ST. PETER

232 Look up, by failure daunted. *T. S. N.*

Written for this book to provide an historically true hymn about St. Peter, and to carry a tune recently discovered.

Iambic, 7 6. 7 6. 8 6. 8 6. Unique.

MUSIC. OSLO is an arrangement by R. Vaughan Williams, for *Songs of Praise* (1931), of a Norwegian traditional melody. It is an excellent tune with a very strong 'folk' flavour; the first two lines can be paralleled in some English carols, but the rest of the tune has a more definitely racial character, hard to define, but very clearly felt.

ST. MARY MAGDALEN

233 Unto Mary, demon-haunted. *Jan Struther.*

St. Mary Magdalen was identified in the Middle Ages with the sinner-woman of Luke 7: 37. She was really one of the women who 'ministered unto them [or him] of their substance', as she is described in Luke 8: 2–3. This hymn was written (for the tune 'Pisgah') so as not to go beyond what we know to be true of her.

Trochaic, 8 7. 8 7. D.

MUSIC. PISGAH, by David Evans, was written in 1922 and published separately for Psalmody Festivals; it first appeared in book form in *Songs of Praise* (1925). It is in the manner of the traditional Welsh hymn-tunes; the structural scheme is that of 'Gwalia' (see 54), with slight variation in the repetitions, but the melody is of a more solemn and grave character.

ST. JAMES THE GREATER

234 Lord, who shall sit beside thee. *W. Romanis*, 1824–99.

William Romanis, after being a master at Cheltenham College, was Vicar of Wigston Magna; he published this and 52 (with another hymn) in his *Wigston Magna School Hymns* (1878), whence they were transferred to the *Public School Hymn Book* of 1903 and the *English Hymnal* three years later. 'St. James the Greater' probably means just 'Big James', used to distinguish him from the other Apostle 'Little James', the man of shorter stature. 'James', or 'Jacob' ('Iakōbos' or 'Iacob' in the Greek Septuagint and New Testament), was, like 'John', a very common Jewish name. Thus we have three saints called in English 'James': (1) James the Just, the brother of the Lord to whom the Epistle General of James is attributed, but who was not an Apostle (May Day, 229); (2) James the Less, son of Alphaeus, an Apostle (not commemorated, owing to his having been confused with James the Just); (3) James the Greater (25 July), the other and more famous Apostle, son of Zebedee and brother of John. The references in the hymn are to Mark 10: 37. A martyr's hymn is also suggested, because James the Greater is the only Apostle whose death is recorded. See Acts 12: 2; and also under 216 and 229.

Iambic, 7 6. 7 6.

MUSIC. PADERBORN is first found in N. Beuttner's *Catholisches Gesangbuch, &c.* (Grätz, 1602), where it is set to 'Es wolt gut Jäger jagen' in the following form:

In the Cologne *Gesangbuch* (1610) it is found in a shape closely resembling the present version, which is from *Alte Catholische Geistliche Kirchengesäng, &c.* (Paderborn, 1616). Yet another variant is in D. G. Corner's *Gesangbuch* (1632). The tune is probably of the 15th century, and belonged to the secular song on which the above hymn was based.

THE TRANSFIGURATION

235 O Master, it is good to be. *Arthur Penrhyn Stanley*,‡ 1815–81.

Stanley published a poem of six stanzas in an article on the Transfiguration in *Macmillan's Magazine* (April 1870), 'Master, it is good to be'. This appeared in full in the *Westminster Abbey Hymn Book* (1883). We use the version as in the *Hymnary* (1872), which omits ver. 5, and parts of verses 1 and 2; adding 'O' to each verse, and reading 'Till' in our ver. 3 for 'Still'.

D.L.M.

MUSIC. TALLIS' LAMENTATION is found in Day's *The Whole Booke of*

Psalmes (1562), where it is headed 'A prayer. M. Talys', and set to 'O Lord, in thee is all my trust'. It is a long, serious tune which manifests a strangely importunate character owing to the insistence of the closes on D and A.

ST. BARTHOLOMEW

236 O saint of summer, what can we sing for you?

Jan Struther.

St. Bartholomew has been a difficulty to compilers of Hymnals, because of the uncertainty of his identity. It has even been said that there is a hymn beginning:

O blessèd Saint Bartholomew,
There's nothing that we know of you.

But this is doubtless quite untrue!—although the type of hymn is familiar that asks whether he really was the same as Nathaniel, and whether he ever sat beneath a fig-tree. The *English Hymnal* (239) met the difficulty with an acrostic in the manner of the Greek hymnodists. Jan Struther has written for this book a poem that takes the elusiveness of fame very simply as its theme, though in a lovely metre that is not simple.

Alcaic, 11 11. 9 10. For this metre, very rarely found in English, and unique in this book, cf. the Note on Prosody, p. xxxi. The Greek metre of Alcaeus was slightly modified by Horace; for the first couplet, – – ⏑ | – – | – ⏑ ⏑ | – ⏑ ⏑, in the 3rd line, – – ⏑ | – – | – ⏑ | – ⏑, and in the 4th line, – ⏑ ⏑ | – ⏑ ⏑ | – ⏑ | – ⏑.

Tennyson's ode to Milton is unrhymed and begins:

O mighty-mouth'd inventor of harmonies,
O skill'd to sing of Time or Eternity,
  God-gifted organ-voice of England,
    Milton, a name to resound for ages.

Our hymn (which carries so gracefully the added difficulty of rhyme) may be scanned, – ⏑ ⏑ | – ⏑ | – ⏑ ⏑ | – ⏑ ⏑; the 3rd line, – ⏑ ⏑ | – ⏑ | – ⏑ | – ⏑; and the 4th, – ⏑ ⏑ | – ⏑ ⏑ | – ⏑ | – ⏑.

MUSIC. ALCAIC ODE, by M. A. von Löwenstern, is from *Geistliche Kirchen- und Hauss-Musik, &c.* (Breslau, 1644), where it is no. 12 of his 'Symbola und Oden', a collection of some 30 hymns written in classical metres with melodies and basses by Löwenstern himself. The present tune, which is set to the words 'Nun preiset alle Gottes Barmherzigkeit', is one of his most successful compositions. It also appears in Löwenstern's *Früelings-Mayen, &c.*, which is undated, but probably previous to the above work. In some of Löwenstern's tunes the effort to adapt the musical metre and rhythm to the requirements of classical prosody is too evident, resulting in a feeling of artificiality and 'tightness' in the melody; in the present case, however, he has succeeded in combining most satisfactorily the musical and verbal demands, and in producing a free and excellent tune.

ST. MATTHEW

237 He sat to watch o'er customs paid.

W. Bright, 1824–1901.

Dr. Bright's hymn, which is one of the really good saint's day hymns, combining in lines of classical finish the historical facts with their practical application, was first published in the *Supplementary Hymns* to *Hymns Ancient and Modern* (1889).

L.M.

MUSIC. ALFRETON, see 189 (ii).

MICHAELMAS

238 Angels and ministers, spirits of grace. *P. Dearmer.*

The fine tune, 'Quedlinburg', became associated with Michaelmas through the *English Hymnal* (245); and these words were written for it because the advisory committee of *Songs of Praise* desired something for Michaelmas that was less mythological than the 'Stars of the morning' of Joseph the Hymnographer (cf. 215).

Dactylic, 10 10. 10 10, the other example being 200.

MUSIC. QUEDLINBURG is from J. C. Kittel's manuscript chorale book (1790), where it is set to 'Grosser Prophete, mein Herze begehret' as follows:

It is found, with slight variations of rhythm, in several subsequent collections.

239 Around the throne of God a band. *J. M. Neale*, 1818–66.

From Neale's *Hymns for Children* (2nd series, 1842), another example of a children's hymn taken over by adults. There is a pretty, and true, story of a little boy who witnessed a kill in the hunting field. He was so distressed that he could not go to sleep when bed-time came. At last his mother said, 'Shall I sing you something?' 'Yes, Mummy,' he said, 'Sing me "Around the throne", only put in foxes instead of angels.' So his mother sang the hymn with this alteration throughout; and he went gently to sleep.

L.M.

MUSIC. SOLOTHURN, from the *English Hymnal* (1906), is an arrangement of a Swiss traditional melody. The tune, both in rhythm and general form, has several counterparts among Swiss folk-songs, and, in particular, resembles strongly 'Dursli und Bäbeli', which may be found in *Sammlung von Schweizer Kühreihen und Volksliedern* (1826), a large collection of such songs, while others may be found in *Lieder aus der Schweiz, &c.* (1837), and *Recueil de Chants populaires suisses* (1920), &c. Apart from the *ranz-des-vaches*, which is of necessity formed on the harmonies of the Alpine horn, the Swiss folk-tunes are mostly of a very simple type, though often attractively gay and rhythmic; the present tune is a good specimen of a more staid kind.

240 Service and strength, God's angels and archangels.

Christina Rossetti, 1830–94.

From *Called to be Saints* (1881), and not, we believe, set as a hymn before.

This interesting and effective metre is Sapphic in character, but has five lines—11 10. 11 10. 5. Each line has the Sapphic feet – ◡ ◡ | – ◡ | – ◡ | – ◡ | – ◡, and line 5, – ◡ ◡ | – ◡, but the final short syllable is wanting in the 2nd lines of vv. 1, 3, 4; and the caesura is shifted one syllable back, e.g. 'Service and strength, God's angels and archangels'.

MUSIC. ENNISKERRY was composed by Miss Ina Boyle especially for this hymn in the enlarged *Songs of Praise* (1931). It is a sober, modal tune with a slight emanation of Ambrosian plainsong in its phrases.

ST. LUKE

241 Great is their joy who hide their own.

J. R. Darbyshire, Bishop of Glasgow.

Written for the tune in order to provide a hymn suitable to St. Luke. The reference in ver. 4 is Luke 15, St. Luke being the writer who recorded the parable which is the heart of Christ's message, the story of the Prodigal Son.

Iambic, 8 7. 8 7.

MUSIC. BRYNHYFRYD is a Welsh hymn melody (here harmonized by J. T. Rees) by John Williams of Dolgelly, which first appeared in John Parry's *Peroriaeth Hyfryd* (1837).

ST. SIMON AND ST. JUDE

242 Christ is the King! O friends rejoice.

G. K. A. Bell, Bishop of Chichester.

Written for our book, to carry the tune.

Iambic, 8 8 8. D. Occurs also in 338.

MUSIC. LLANGOEDMOR is a Welsh hymn melody from *Y Gwyliedydd* (1826), harmonized by David Evans. It is a tune with an effect of great directness, due to its being built largely on the tonic chord; the melody is of a type which might be described as 'campanological'.

ALL SAINTS

243 For the brave of every race. *G. W. Briggs.*

First appeared in 1920: written for Loughborough College, whose students come from all over the world. The medieval hymns for All Saints (e.g. *E.H.* 249) treated the occasion as a summary of the saints already in the Calendar, which may be the reason why All Saints has no octave in the Sarum and other medieval rites. The modern practice is to extend greatly the scope of this commemoration, and to praise especially (as in Lowell's poem) those who are not otherwise remembered. Some names got into the official lists because they were royal, like Edward, King of the West Saxons, some because besides being royalties they refused to get properly married, like Aetheldred or 'Etheldreda', others by sheer blunder like Amphibalus, who was St. Alban's great-coat, and was naturally with him when he was arrested (*amphibalus* is a synonym for *paenula*, the overcoat, which eventually became the chasuble); St. Alban himself is legendary, though his is the kind of legend that suggests an historical foundation; but there are many names of saints who never existed. Meanwhile, those who belonged to the thin stream of men and women who kept Christianity from being destroyed altogether from age to age are the 'all saints' whose names are nearly all forgotten; with these are often included the larger company of good men and matrons, heroes, worthies—'The salt of the earth', in fact—who are remembered in this hymn.

Trochaic, 7 7. 7 7. D.

MUSIC. LOUGHBOROUGH COLLEGE, by G. W. Briggs, was written in 1920 for his words, for use at Loughborough College. It is an attractively straightforward tune, without intricacy of melody or rhythm.

244 Unknown and unrewarded. *P. Dearmer.*

Written for the original *Songs of Praise* (1925) on the theme, 'By their fruits ye shall know them'.

Iambic, 7 6. 7 6. D.

MUSIC. AU FORT DE MA DÉTRESSE is from the *Genevan Psalter* (1542), where it was set to Psalm 130.

The rhythm of the present version is slightly simplified from the original, which is as follows:

It is a long, well-sustained melody, with a noble strength; undoubtedly one of the finest of the Genevan tunes.

THE CHURCH ON EARTH

245 Christ hath a garden walled around.
I. Watts (1707) *and Y.H.* (*Robert Bridges*).

Here we see a great poet doing what so many lesser men have done, taking an old hymn, and proceeding from one small improvement to another, until the thing has become his own. There is more than one hymn in which, by the end of the work, there was nothing left of the original except the metre. In this, however, some of Watts survives. Bridges took it from *Hymns and Spiritual Songs* (1707–9), and published the hymn thus, as he said, 'adapted for weddings', in the *Yattendon Hymnal* (1899).

L.M.

MUSIC. LEIGHTON is from Sir William Leighton's *The Teares or*

Lamentacions of a sorrowfull soule, composed with Musicall Ayres and Songs, both for Voyces and diuers instruments (1614), which contains 'Consort Songs' (for instruments as well as voices) and unaccompanied madrigals, &c., for four and five voices. In this collection Leighton had the assistance of most of the eminent musicians of his day, though he was himself responsible for a large part of the work. The present arrangement is harmonized by H. E. Wooldridge, and appeared in the *Yattendon Hymnal* (1896), the melody having also suffered extensive adaptation.

246 O Faith of England, taught of old. *T. A. Lacey.*

Dr. Lacey wrote this fine hymn in order that the tune might be included in the *English Hymnal* (1906), and to provide a hymn that should take the place of the somewhat hysterically sentimental 'Faith of our fathers', which threatened at one time to get into common use in the Church of England.

Iambic, 8 8 7. 8 8 7. D. Unique.

MUSIC. PSALM 68 was composed, or possibly adapted, by Matthäus Greiter. Set to words written by him, it appears in the *Strassburger Kirchenamt* (1525), and was adapted to Psalm 36 in *Aulcuns pseaulmes et cantiques mys en chant* (Strassburg, 1539), being retained for this psalm in the subsequent editions of the *Genevan Psalter*. In the complete psalter of 1562 it is also set to Beza's version of Psalm 68, 'Que dieu se monstre seulement', which became 'Le Psaume de Batailles', the battle-song of the Huguenots. In the *Anglo-Genevan Psalter* (1561) it is set to Kethe's version of Psalm 113, and psalm and tune were included in the complete English and Scottish Psalters of 1562 and 1564. It was known in England as 'Old 113th', and is frequently found in an abbreviated form. A striking instance of its use by the Huguenots, when they drove back the attack on La Rochelle in 1573, is cited by Lord Ernle in the *Psalms in Human Life*, chap. vii. It was also sometimes known as 'Patriarch's Tune', and was an especial favourite of John Wesley. It is a superb tune with a remarkable resemblance to 'Easter Alleluya' (see 157). In Germany it came into general use, at the end of the 16th century, to the hymn 'O Mensch, bewein dein Sünde gross', and was used by Bach as the basis of the loveliest of his choral preludes, and of the chorus (No. 35) of the *St. Matthew Passion*, with the original (Strassburg) version of line 4:

The common English version spoiled the tune by its cadence, thus: 𝅗𝅥 𝅗𝅥 𝅝; therefore, as is noted above, the new words were written to preserve the strength of the original form.

247 Sing alleluya forth in loyal praise.

Mozarabic (5th–8th cent.). S.P.V.

Alleluia piis edite laudibus,
cives aetherei, psallite naviter
Alleluia perenne.

The hymn for the first Sunday in Lent in the Mozarabic Breviary—

and a stable evidence against the idea (fostered by a hymn, 'Alleluya, song of sweetness') that 'Alleluya' may not be sung after Quinquagesima. J. Ellerton translated it in the *Churchman's Family Magazine* (1865), and it soon appeared in several hymnals, but always with alterations, the original not being of great merit. The verse is indeed so slight that every phrase needs to be carefully wrought. Dr. Buck's tune impelled us to make another and more free version, in order that his music might be in use, so far as we could assist it.

Iambic, 10 10. 7. Unique.

MUSIC. MARTINS, by P. C. Buck, was originally written for this hymn. It appeared in the composer's *Fourteen Hymn Tunes* (1913). It is a short tune, built of two lines of contrasted movement, the 3rd line being made out of the 1st by interchange of the members of the phrase; this gives a firm, satisfactory form to the whole outline.

248 The Church of God a kingdom is.

L. B. C. L. Muirhead, 1845–1925.

Dr. Bridges was a friend of Mr. Muirhead, and included this in his *Yattendon Hymnal* (1899). The hymn is obviously inspired by the picture of the Adoration of the Lamb, by Hubert van Eyck, at Ghent, the more noticeably if ver. 3 is sung.

C.M.

MUSIC. CAPEL is an arrangement, by R. Vaughan Williams, of a traditional English carol tune noted by Miss Lucy Broadwood from some gipsies of the name of Goby, in 1893. They sang it to words, beginning 'King Pharim (Pharaoh) sat a-musing', which describe two of the miracles performed by the infant Jesus in Egypt, and may go back to the apocryphal *Gospel of the Infancy*. The full text may be found in the *Oxford Book of Carols* (1928), p. 115, and further information in Miss Broadwood's *English Traditional Songs and Carols*, and *Journal of the Folk-Song Society* (1910), iv. 24. The melody is characteristic of a large class of English folk-tunes.

249 The Church's one foundation.

S. J. Stone, 1839–1900.

This was written as a counterblast to Bishop Colenso, 'out of admiration for the opposition shown by Bishop Gray of Capetown to Bishop Colenso's teaching', which is referred to in ver. 3. Colenso had to explain the Old Testament to Zulus; he did so as a scholar would, frankly and honestly; and subsequent history has shown that he was in the right. Mr. Stone's hymn was first published in the author's *Lyra Fidelium* (1866), in seven verses; the revised form of 1868 is that always used: a further form of ten verses was also made. It became enormously popular in Church circles during the period that has been called 'the Victorian sunset', and in 1888 it was sung at all the three great services of the Lambeth Conference. The late Archbishop Temple used to complain that he found it sung wherever he went, as other bishops have complained of 255. Duly vested in 'Aurelia', it is the typical representative of an era.

Iambic, 7 6. 7 6. D.

MUSIC. HERZLICH THUT MICH ERFREUEN is found in J. Walther's

Ein schöner Geistlicher und Christlicher newer Berckreyen, &c. (1552), where it is set to his hymn 'Herzlich thut mich erfreuen', as follows:

Walther's hymn was founded on a medieval secular song beginning with the same words, and the tune was the traditional melody of the original song, being a typical melody of its kind.

AURELIA was originally composed by S. S. Wesley for the hymn 'Jerusalem the golden' in *A Selection of Psalms and Hymns . . . edited by the Rev. Charles Kemble and S. S. Wesley* (1864). It seems to have been first set to the present words in the *Appendix to Hymns Ancient and Modern* (1868), and thus came to be too often associated with this hymn.

BAPTISM

Fortunately two special hymns for Christenings are found to be enough, with the addition of those of a general character, of which there are many charming suitable examples. There are, indeed, few good baptismal hymns in the old books: and there are many bad ones—verses such as this:

Christians, all is not comprised
In being solemnly baptized;
He who has done so much for you
Appoints much more for you to do.

In quoting queer examples like that, we need not stir susceptibilities by naming the book; nor need we particularize the community that used to sing:

Whoever after Baptism's bath
Again in mire wallowed hath,
Should as a swine and dog indeed
Without the door be thrust with speed.

250 In token that thou shalt not fear. *H. Alford,*† 1810–71.

These 'lines on the sign of the cross in Baptism' were suggested to Alford by a passage in Hooker's *Ecclesiastical Polity* (bk. 5, sec. 65), when he was staying with his uncle at Heale in 1832. They were sung four years afterwards at Wymeswold church when his first child was christened, were printed in the *British Magazine* (Dec. 1832), and afterwards included in his anonymous *Poems* (1833) and in his subsequent collections. The most used of baptismal hymns.

C.M.

MUSIC. ST. STEPHEN is from *Ten Church Pieces for the Organ, with four anthems in score composed for the use of the Church of Nayland in Suffolk, by William Jones* (1789). The tune appears at the end of this work set to Psalm 23, and called 'St. Stephen's Tune'. It is also found under the names 'Nayland' and 'Newington'. The alternative version (faburden) by Harvey Grace appeared in the *Tenor Tune Book* (1917).

251 O Lord, thy people gathered here. *Mrs. K. E. Roberts.*

Written for our book to provide a baptismal hymn of a very simple and intimate character, from the parent's point of view.

L.M.

MUSIC. PHILIPPINE was composed by R. E. Roberts for this hymn in *Songs of Praise* (1925). It is a simple tune, well suited to the innocence of the words.

CONFIRMATION, ADULT BAPTISM, AND SELF-DEDICATION

252 Father of all, to thee. *J. Julian*, 1839–1913.

Most hymnals include this nowadays as a token of gratitude to the editor of the great *Dictionary of Hymnology*. Dr. Julian wrote it in 1874, and contributed it to Thring's *Church of England Hymn Book* (1882).

Iambic, 6 6. 6 6. 8 8.

MUSIC. WARSAW, in Holdsworth's edition of *Chetham's Psalmody* (1832), appears with the composer's name given merely as 'Clark'. It may possibly be by Thomas Clark of Canterbury (1775–1859). The tune is here presented as in the *Church Hymnary* (1928).

253 Just as I am, without one plea. *Charlotte Elliott*, 1789–1871.

Some of the most popular hymns of the Victorian era were invalid hymns; such were 'Lead, kindly Light', 'Abide with me', and those of the patient and heroic Charlotte Elliott, who wrote this for her *Invalid's Hymn Book* (1841), with John 6 : 37 for text (see also 392). Her book was very successful; and she contributed no fewer than 112 hymns to it in various editions, the result of 'more than half a century of patient suffering'. When Dora, the daughter of William Wordsworth, was dying, a friend sent this hymn to her: she said, 'This is the very thing for me', and often repeated it until her death. Her husband wrote to Miss Elliott that it formed part of Mrs. Wordsworth's daily solitary prayers, adding about the poet Wordsworth, 'I do not think that Mr. Wordsworth could bear to have it repeated in his presence, but he is not the less sensible of the solace it gave his one and matchless daughter'. Miss Elliott with marvellous will-power worked diligently through almost overpowering pain and weakness, and lived to be 82. When she died, more than a thousand letters thanking her for this hymn were found.

Bishop Moule of Durham, a relative, told the story of its origin: about

1834, her brother was holding a bazaar in order to build a school at St. Mary's Hall, Brighton; Charlotte had lain awake all night, oppressed with the sense of uselessness, 'tossed about with many a doubt'. While every one at Westfield Lodge was out and busy over the bazaar, she lay in greater misery than ever, and determined to fight it out then and there; so she took a pen and wrote this hymn.

Iambic, 8 8. 8 6.

MUSIC. ISLEWORTH, by Samuel Howard, is from *Melodies of the Psalms of David according to the version by Christopher Smart* (1765), where it is set to the version of Psalm 6.

254 My God, accept my heart this day. *M. Bridges*, 1800–94.

From his *Hymns of the Heart* (1848), its usefulness for Confirmations has preserved it from disappearance.

C.M.

MUSIC. DIBDIN is a melody from the *Standard Psalm Tune-book* (1852), where it is attributed to Dr. Jackson, but considerable research has not revealed the identity of the composer, since there were several of this name.

255 O Jesus, I have promised. *J. E. Bode*, 1816–74.

Bishops have been known to implore their clergy that this should not be sung at all the Confirmations they attend; but it is really one of those hymns that have been engulfed under a sentimental tune, till its merits have been lost and forgotten. It is in fact the work of an Oxford don of considerable attainments, who wrote it on the occasion of the Confirmation of his daughter and two sons as 'O Jesus, we have promised'. Confirmation hymns have not been very good, probably because they were composed by people who had to imagine themselves in the position of neophytes. Probably general hymns of direct spiritual experience are more inspiring for such occasions. But this is better than most, and may well be preferred to 254 or 258. It was published in the S.P.C.K. *Appendix* to *Psalms and Hymns* (1869). The musical editors have in our book given the bishops a full possibility of relief.

Iambic, 7 6. 7 6. D., a metre that lends itself all too readily to facile writing and composing. Cf. 249.

MUSIC. KOMM, SEELE, by J. W. Franck, was originally set, in *Geistliche Lieder, &c.* (Hamburg, 1681), to the hymn 'Komm, Seele, Jesu Leiden', which appears in the second section devoted to hymns on the Passion. In the original the last quaver of bar 5 is D, and there are various slight differences of rhythm from the present version. It is a fluent melody, of a graceful song-like character, with a flexibility and a sense of rhythmic 'continuity', often found, later, in the melodies of J. S. Bach; a most attractive tune.

BREMEN is an adaptation of a melody from Störl's *Neu bezogenes Davidsches Harpfen- und Psalter-Spiel, Oder: Neu aufgesetztes Würtembergisch-vollständiges . . . Schlag-Gesang- und Noten-Buch, &c.* (Stuttgart, 1710). It is a tune with something of the same character as the last but rather more staid and normal.

THORNBURY was composed by Basil Harwood for the hymn 'Thy hand, O God, has guided', and is found in the second supplement (1916) to the old edition of *Hymns Ancient and Modern*. It was composed for the 25th Annual Festival of the London Church Choir Association (1898), and first appeared in the Association's Festival Book of 17 Nov. 1898; afterwards being printed in the composer's *Hymn Tunes original and selected, &c.* (1905).

256 O thou who camest from above. *C. Wesley,*† 1707–88.

From the Wesleys' *Short Hymns on Select Passages of Scriptures* (1762) this is based upon Lev. 6 : 13, 'The fire shall ever be burning upon the altar, it shall never go out'. John told Samuel Bradburn, when they were together in Yorkshire in 1781, that 'his experience might always be found in the first two verses of this hymn'. We have, however, omitted ver. 2 (see *E.H.* 343), because 'inextinguishable' cannot (as most choirmasters have found) be properly sung. In ver. 1 we have altered 'mean altar' to 'low altar', because the original epithet has acquired a different emphasis since Wesley's time.

L.M.

MUSIC. ST. BARTHOLOMEW is from Riley's *Parochial Harmony* (1762), where it is headed 'By Mr. Henry Duncalf, organist of St. Barth'.

257 Take my life, and let it be. *Frances R. Havergal,* 1836–79.

The author's own story of how this was written throws so vivid a light on the intense evangelical fervour which was still not uncommon in 1874, that we give it here:

> 'There were ten persons in the house, some unconverted and long prayed for, some converted but not rejoicing Christians. He gave me the prayer "Lord give me ALL in this house". And He just did. Before I left the house every one had got a blessing. The last night of my visit, after I had retired, the governess asked me to go to the two daughters. They were crying. Then and there both of them trusted and rejoiced. I was too happy to sleep, and passed most of the night in praise and renewal of my own consecration; and these little couplets formed themselves and chimed in my heart one after the other, till they finished with "Ever, ONLY, ALL for Thee!" '

First published in her *Loyal Responses*, in 11 couplets the hymn has been translated into many European languages, including Russian, and many of Africa and Asia.

Trochaic, 7 7. 7 7. D.

MUSIC. BENEVENTO is from S. Webbe's *A Collection of Motetts or Antiphons, &c.* (1792), being taken from a motet on the words 'Tibi omnes angeli'. The present form is a much patched adaptation of various parts of the original composition.

258 Thine for ever! God of love. *Mrs. M. F. Maude,* 1819–1913.

Mrs. Maude recorded that this was 'written in 1847 for my class in the Girls' Sunday School of St. Thomas' Church, Isle of Wight, and published in 1848 at the beginning of a little book called *Twelve Letters on*

Confirmation, by a Sunday School Teacher'. The letters had been written week by week during Mrs. Maude's absence, and the original verses occurred almost impromptu at the end of one of them. They were included in *Church Hymns* (1871).

Trochaic, 7 7. 7 7.

MUSIC. HORSHAM is an arrangement, from the *English Hymnal* (1906), of an English traditional melody, collected by Miss L. E. Broadwood.

COMMUNION

The practice of singing a hymn during the communion of the people, illustrated by the long communion hymns in the *Old Version*, must have been well established in the reign of Elizabeth. George Wither, writing in 1623 (*The Hymnes and Songs of the Church*), says:

> 'We have a custom among us, that, during the time of administering the blessed Sacrament of the Lord's Supper, there is some Psalme or hymne sung, the better to keepe the thoughts of the Communicants from wandering after vaine objects.'

259 According to thy gracious word.

James Montgomery, 1771–1854.

From his *Christian Psalmist* (1825). In many books the excellent Scriptural line in ver. 2, 'Thy testamental cup', has been altered to 'The cup, Thy precious Blood I take'.

C.M.

MUSIC. BANGOR is from *A Compleat Melody: or, The Harmony of Zion . . . by William Tans'ur* (Preface dated 29 Sept. 1734). There it is set to Psalm 12, and headed 'Bangor Tune. Composed in Three Parts. W.T.' It is doubtful whether the tune is an original composition by Tans'ur, or was merely harmonized by him. In some books the tune has appeared in the Dorian mode with no flat in the signature; but in the original it is in D minor (here transposed to C minor). Its popularity as a psalm-tune was very great in Scotland in the 18th and early 19th centuries. In Burns's *The Ordination* its fame is implied in the following verse:

> Mak' haste an' turn King David owre,
> An' lilt wi' holy clangor;
> O' double verse come gie us four,
> An' skirl up the 'Bangor'.

260 Alleluya, sing to Jesus. *W. Chatterton Dix*, 1837–98.

From his *Altar Songs* (1867), in five verses, with special reference to the Ascension. It makes up in heartiness what it lacks in beauty and intellectual power.

8 7. 8 7. D.

MUSIC. HYFRYDOL, by R. H. Prichard, is from *Haleliwiah Drachefn* (Griffith Harris, Carmarthen, 1855). A long tune of a smooth and very simple nature, which moves throughout, except for one note, within the compass of a fifth. This compactness gives it a certain strength and weight which are particularly noticeable when it is sung to the present words.

261 And now, O Father, mindful of the love.

William Bright, 1824–1901.

This hymn, which appeared in six verses in the *Monthly Packet* (1873), has been greatly liked by some, and disliked by others, on theological grounds, objection having been specially made to the concluding lines of ver. 2. The division into two Parts may be of use in some cases. 'And then' is indeed not an unexceptionable beginning, but 'And now' is only a little better. In what is perhaps the best essay on hymnody in the last century (*The Quarterly Review*, July, 1892) the writer notes a cluster of 43 hymns in Julian that begin with 'And', pointing out that 'the number of hymns disfigured by this unmeaning commencement' reach altogether to 'some 120 instances in which the writer, finding himself in want of an additional syllable for the first line, has absurdly prefixed to it the copulative particle'. Dr. Bright did so again in 41 ('And now the wants are told'); Blake's 'Jerusalem' begins in the same way, but that poem occurs after two paragraphs as part of the Preface to his *Milton*.

Iambic, 10 10. 10 10. 10 10.

MUSIC. SONG 4, by Orlando Gibbons, is set to the Song of Hannah, 'Now in the Lord my heart doth pleasure take', in *Hymns and Songs of the Church* (1623) (see 29). It is a tune with a definite individuality due partly to the last two bars of lines 2 and 4, and to the leap between the 2nd and 3rd line, as well as to a peculiar quality of suppleness in the melody.

262 As the disciples, when thy Son had left them. *P. Dearmer*.

An attempt to express the religion of the Eucharist in its historical setting; and also to provide a new musical form for a Communion hymn.

The metre may be called 'Double Sapphic': two Sapphic stanzas are combined into one hymn-verse of eight lines.

MUSIC. COELITES PLAUDANT and DIVA SERVATRIX are 'church melodies' from Rouen and Bayeux respectively (see 28). The effect of the association of these two tunes, which are sung consecutively to each verse, is excellent. The contrast between the rather more flexible first and more massive second is not too great, but enhances the essential fine qualities of both.

263 Author of life divine. *J. and C. Wesley* (1745).

From John and Charles Wesley's *Hymns on the Lord's Supper* (1745) in two stanzas, as here. There is no evidence to show which of the brothers made this fine short hymn.

Iambic, 6 6. 6 6. 8 8.

MUSIC. DOLGELLY first appeared in Griffith Harris's *Haleliwiah Drachefn* (Carmarthen, 1855).

264 Bread of heaven, on thee we feed. *J. Conder*,‡ 1789–1855.

Josiah Conder was one of the most eminent hymn-writers and editors of the first half of the 19th century. Another hymn by him, remarkably modern in feeling, is 454, 'Beyond, beyond that boundless sea'. He edited the *Congregational Hymn Book, a Supplement to Dr. Watts' Psalms and Hymns* (1836). This hymn appeared in his *Star of the East* (1821) as 'Bread of heaven, on thee I feed': it has been much changed in some books, but here the text is as he printed it, except that the first person singular has been altered to the plural throughout.

Trochaic, 7 7. 7 7. 7 7.

MUSIC. NICHT SO TRAURIG is from J. S. Bach's *Vierstimmige Choralgesänge* (1769), where it is set to the hymn, 'Nicht so traurig, nicht so sehr'.

265 Bread of the world in mercy broken.
Bishop R. Heber, 1783–1826.

From his posthumous *Hymns* (1827). This little cry of adoration is admirably suited for musical expression.

Iambic, 9 8. 9 8. D. Occurs also in 616.

MUSIC. RENDEZ À DIEU was composed or adapted by L. Bourgeois for Psalm 118 in the *Genevan Psalter* (1543). In the *Scottish Psalter* of 1564 it was set to John Craig's version of the same psalm. This lovely and impressive tune is, in some ways, the finest of all the early psalm-tunes; it is perfectly proportioned; it begins with a phrase of remarkable expressiveness, and continues with others as significant as they are logically consistent, while the beauty of the change of rhythm in the downward scale of the 5th line is extraordinary. This is a tune which gives the true 'spinal thrill'; of its kind it is unsurpassed.

266 Come, risen Lord, and deign to be our guest. *G. W. Briggs*.

Based on the supper at Emmaus (Lk. 24: 28–31): itself a parallel to the supper in the Upper Room. It lays stress on the idea (not generally expressed in Communion hymns) that Christ himself may be regarded as the celebrant.

Iambic, 10 10. 10 10.

MUSIC. BIRMINGHAM is from the Rev. F. Cunningham's *A Selection of Psalm Tunes* (2nd ed., 1834), where it is set to the hymn 'Come, gracious Spirit, heavenly dove'. The tune does not appear in the 1st edition of 1826. In the original the first two notes of bar 3 are thus: 𝅗𝅥. ♩, and the last bar of the 3rd line is

267 Deck thyself, my soul, with gladness.
J. Franck, 1618–77. *Tr. C. Winkworth*.

Schmücke dich, O liebe Seele,
  Lass die dunkle Sündenhöhle,
Komm ans helle Licht gegangen,
  Fange herrlich an zu prangen,

Denn der Herr voll Heil und Gnaden
Will dich jetzt zu Gaste laden,
Der den Himmel kann verwalten,
Will jetzt Herberg in dir halten.

This, both in words and music, is the most classical and famous hymn of Burgomaster Johann Franck. The first stanza appeared in Crüger's *Geistliche Kirchen-Melodien* (1649), with the tune. Nine stanzas were subsequently published in the Crüger-Runge book of 1653. Miss Winkworth translated six verses first in her *Lyra Germanica* (2nd series, 1858), and re-wrote them in the proper metre to the tune (as here), publishing it with the music in her *Chorale Book for England* (1863).

Trochaic, 8 8. 8 8. D. Occurs also in 528 (II).

MUSIC. SCHMÜCKE DICH, by J. Crüger, from his *Geistliche Kirchen-Melodien* (Berlin, 1649), has always been associated with this hymn in Germany. It is found in *Praxis Pietatis Melica* from 1653 onwards, the earlier editions giving the 5th bar thus

while the Darmstadt *Gesangbuch* (1687) has the rhythm

throughout the tune, which, in the original version, occurs only in lines 5 and 6. The melody appears, with very slight variation, in many other collections. It is a beautifully expressive tune, especially with the original rhythm of lines 5 and 6.

268 Draw nigh and take the body of the Lord. *7th cent. S.P.V.*

Sancti, venite, Christi corpus sumite,
sanctum bibentes, quo redempti sanguine,

salvati Christi corpore et sanguine,
a quo refecti laudes dicamus Deo.

Neale found 'a certain pious simplicity' in the halting Latin, prosaic and tautological, of a Communion hymn from an obscure antiphonary, *Antiphonarium Benchorense*, written, 680–91, at the monastery of Bangor, co. Down, Ireland. It is certainly an interesting relic of a phase in the brave struggles of the Dark Ages. He made it known by a translation in his *Mediaeval Hymns* (1851) in ten verses. The makers of anthologies are sometimes accused of searching previous anthologies for their material. Hymnal compilers of half a century ago were impelled by more than one motive to a similar course. Thus between 1867 (*People's Hymnal*) and 1870 (*Hymnal Companion*), Neale's lines, more or less altered, had got into all the books in general use. We ourselves, retaining three verses, have ventured on a very free paraphrase in which the English Prayer Book has its place as well as the old Irish Antiphonary.

Iambic, 10 10. 10 10.

MUSIC. ST. SECHNALL is an arrangement, by L. L. Dix, of an Irish traditional melody, found in W. H. Grattan Flood's collection, in a slightly different form: the present version was originally made for use in St. Ann's

Church, Dublin, and was subsequently published in the *Irish Hymnal* (1919). It is a splendid tune, with a most attractive five-bar rhythm, and a characteristic fluent melody in the Mixolydian mode, very dignified and with great emotional significance.

269 Father, we greet thee, God of Love, whose glory.

J. G. Adderley.

First printed in *The People's Hymn Book*, 1924, this hymn may be said to express much eucharistic doctrine of the early Church, so far as recent historical knowledge has recovered it for us, as well as much aspiration of to-day.

Iambic, 11 10. 11 10.

MUSIC. PSALM 80 has not been traced earlier than the complete *Scottish Psalter* of 1564, where it is set to Robert Pont's version of that psalm. It may therefore be of Scottish origin. The present version is from the edition of 1635, in which the tunes are, for the first time, given in harmony, by Edward Millar. It is a tune in the grand style, with an attractive freedom of rhythm.

270 Here, O my Lord, I see thee face to face.

H. Bonar, 1808–89.

Dr. J. J. Bonar used to print a leaflet after each Communion at St. Andrew's Free Church, Greenock; and on the first Sunday in Oct. 1855, he asked his brother, Horatius, to furnish a hymn for this purpose. The hymn was reprinted in *Hymns of Faith and Hope* (1857) in ten verses. It is inevitably shortened in all books; but we have endeavoured here to keep enough verses to preserve the character of a famous hymn.

Iambic, 10 10. 10 10.

MUSIC. ERFYNIAD is a Welsh hymn melody which is found in Ieuan Gwyllt's *Llyfr Tonau* (1859), and is here harmonized by David Evans. It differs somewhat in manner from the majority of the Welsh tunes, and seems to show some influence of the traditional psalm-tunes; noticeable is the extension of rhythm in the close of lines 2 and 4.

271 Holy God, we show forth here. *E.H.*

Written, to bring in the music of the Meistersinger Chorale, for the *English Hymnal* (1906), and slightly revised for our book. St. Paul's own words, 'we show forth', now stand in the 1st line, in order that different points of view may be reconciled.

Trochaic, 7 7. 7 7. 7 7. 4 4. 5 5. Unique.

MUSIC. MEISTERSINGER CHORALE (DA ZU DIR DER HEILAND KAM) is from Richard Wagner's *Die Meistersinger*, where it is sung at the opening of Act I. It is founded, to a certain extent, on the traditional chorale style, but it is by no means a close copy of the pattern.

272 I hunger and I thirst. *J. S. B. Monsell*, 1811–75.

From his *Parish Hymnal* (1873). Monsell wrote nearly 300 hymns, of which about a quarter were once in use, according to Julian, who says that they 'are as a whole bright, joyous, and musical; but they lack massiveness, concentration of thought, and strong emotion. A few only are of enduring excellence.' The others in our books are 93, 'O worship the Lord in the beauty of holiness', and 491, 'Fight the good fight', both of which seem likely to endure.

Iambic, 6 6. 6 6, which for the music is treated as 6 6. 6 6. D.

MUSIC. O MENTES PERFIDAS is from Petri's *Piae Cantiones* (1582) (see 4). This is a fine Dorian melody, noticeable for the well-sustained continuity of its long individual phrases and for the exact equilibrium of its proportions.

273 Let all mortal flesh keep silence, and with awe and welcome stand.

Liturgy of St. James. S.P.V.

The 'Prayer of the Cherubic Hymn' from the Liturgy of St. James was rendered into prose in Neale and Littledale, *Translations of the Primitive Liturgies* (1868–9), and into metre by G. Moultrie, as 'Let all mortal flesh keep silence', in his *Lyra Eucharistica* (1864), in four verses which have become well known (*E.H.* 318). Our advisory committee felt that a free paraphrase of the original, on the lines of Moultrie's version, was now needed; and this 'Songs of Praise Version' was therefore made, the metre being kept, for the sake of the tune.

Trochaic, 8 7. 8 7. 8 7.

MUSIC. PICARDY is found in Tiersot's *Mélodies* (Paris, 1887), entitled 'Romancero' . It is a French carol, probably of the 17th century. The present form appeared in the *English Hymnal* (1906). This tune is not of the type to which the previous French carol tunes in this book have conformed; there is no childlike mirth or gaiety here whether the tune be sung fast or slow. In the present instance it must be sung very slowly, when its character appears rather sombre, but at the same time dignified and ceremonious; if, however, it is sung fast the sombreness changes to fierceness, and though it may suggest a dance, it is a dance of no amenable kind. All tunes change their character, to a certain degree, with a considerable change of speed, but the cleavage here is of a very remarkable nature, and denotes an unusual tune.

274 Lord, enthroned in heavenly splendour.

G. H. Bourne, 1840–1925.
Pt. II. *B.R.*

In his *Post-Communion Hymns* (privately printed, 1874). Of the six verses, five are in *E.H.* 319. Here we give two; and, for the sake of the tunes which are more in number than suitable words, we have added, with the permission of Dr. Bourne's representatives, a new hymn as Part II, with a second tune, which can be used with either part.

Trochaic, 8 7. 8 7. 4 7. Set for the Second Tune as 8 7. 8 7. 8 7.

MUSIC. BRYN CALFARIA is a melody by W. Owen, the present arrangement being found in the *English Hymnal* (1906). The trochaic metrical scheme always gives a determined, not to say vehement character to the tunes which employ it, owing to the very strong accent which is thrown on the first minim of each bar; in the present melody this effect is enhanced by the twelfth bar, where there is a kind of simultaneous diminution and contraction of the metre. The tune has a very strong individuality of its own.

AD PERENNIS VITAE FONTEM is said to be from the *Tours Breviary*, but its actual source is unknown. The present form is from the *English Hymnal* (1906).

275 O God, in whom we live and move. *G. W. Briggs.*

A Communion hymn—emphasizing the immanence of God. Written for this book.

C.M.

MUSIC. FARRANT is adapted from the anthem 'Lord, for thy tender mercies' sake', usually attributed to Richard Farrant, but by some writers to John Hilton, by others to William Mundy. The alternative version (fa-burden), by Martin Shaw, was written especially for the enlarged *Songs of Praise* (1931).

276 O most merciful! *Bishop R. Heber*, 1783–1826.

From his posthumous *Hymns* (1827), this, like 265, is of great musical as well as devotional value. It was written for use as an Introit.

Dactyllic; as printed, 5 5 7· 5 5 7, but as set down for the music, 10 7. 10 7.

MUSIC. SCHÖNSTER HERR JESU is from *Melodeyen über die Gesänge und Psalmen dess Münsterischen Gesang-Buchs, &c.* (1677), where it is set to the hymn 'Schönster Herr Jesu, Herrscher aller Herren'. The tune has a slightly sentimental air, unusual for its period, owing mainly to the 3rd line; it must, however, be admitted that this impression is largely due to later abuses of the phrase; the melody, as a whole, has great charm.

277 O Saviour victim, opening wide.

St. Thomas Aquinas, 1227–74. *Tr. cento.*

O salutaris hostia
quae caeli pandis ostium,
bella premunt hostilia,
da robur, fer auxilium.

Indispensable because of its classical musical settings, this hymn of Aquinas, like 279 and 280, reflects the more sober theology of the 13th century rather than the later developments with which it is commonly associated. It is part of a longer hymn, of which a translation by Neale and others is in *E.H.* 330, 'Verbum supernum prodiens, nec Patris linquens dexteram', written about 1263 for Corpus Christi, on the model of the Advent hymn, 'Verbum supernum prodiens, a Patre olim exiens' (*E.H.* 2, 'High Word of God')—an early example of the confusion of first lines by forming a new hymn out of an old one. Like 280, this is part of the service for Corpus Christi, which Pope Urban IV commissioned Aquinas to draw up when, in 1262, he made the Liége festival of Corpus Christi obligatory over Western Europe. Urban had been Archdeacon of Liége. The hymn became associated later with the new service of

Benediction. Immense pains were taken by Neale and others to provide an exact translation; but none has been satisfactory, to judge by the use of centos from different versions in most hymn-books. We use here the *English Hymnal* version, changing in l. 1 'saving', and in l. 2 'gate of heaven'.

St. Thomas of Aquino in Castile belonged to the family of the Counts of that place; he became a Dominican at the age of 17, and rose to be the great scholastic of the 13th century, the 'Angelical Doctor'; his *Summa* is a stupendous attempt to bring what was then known of Aristotle—for Plato was unknown altogether—into a universal theology. The honour paid to him two centuries later may be studied in the famous Spanish Chapel in the Dominican church of Santa Maria Novella in Florence, where his apotheosis is represented among the triumphs of medieval learning. His figure is familiar in all the picture galleries of Italy, Spaniard though he was; but not as in life; for he was not only one of the most erudite but also one of the fattest men who ever lived, and it is recorded that a special altar had to be made for his ministrations, concave in the middle. In the pictures of his apotheosis he is represented as enthroned with the Evangelists and St. Paul clustered about him, as in the Spanish Chapel at Florence; or, as in Zuberan's picture at Seville, in ecstasy, surrounded by St. Paul, St. Dominic, and the Four Doctors of the Church, Augustine, Gregory, Jerome, and Ambrose.

L.M.

MUSIC. VERBUM SUPERNUM is a melody from the Mechlin *Antiphonarium Romanum*. It is one of the 'church melodies' referred to in the note on 28. The present version is from the *English Hymnal* (1906). Internal evidence would suggest that it is an adaptation of a popular melody.

ERHALT' UNS, HERR, in Klug's *Geistliche Lieder zu Wittemberg* (1543), was set to Luther's hymn 'Erhalt' uns, Herr, bei deinem Wort'. It seems probable that it was originally a plainsong melody which was thus adapted to this hymn. In later German books, and in English psalters after 1561, it is found in various settings, the melody being, as a rule, in equal notes throughout, without the passing notes which appear in the 1st and 3rd lines of the present version, which is from Bach's *Vierstimmige Choralgesänge* (1769). In its present form it has assumed the habitual pattern of the German chorale.

278 Strengthen for service, Lord, the hands.

Liturgy of Malabar. Tr. E.H.

The Syriac text of the Malabar Liturgy (printed in the *Uniat Missal*, 1844) is really from the old Nestorian Rite, belonging to the much neglected but numerous Asian group of Liturgies in Persia and elsewhere; for there are in reality, not two groups, Eastern and Western, but three, Byzantine, Latin, and Asian: the latter was considered heretical by the two former—but then so were the two former by the latter; it was really a matter of where one happened to live. The ancient Christian church of St. Thomas in Malabar, South India, uses one of the Asian Group, the so-called Nestorian Rite. This hymn is a metrical rendering of the prayer in the Liturgy of Malabar, said by the deacon while the people are communicating. The prayer is in Brightman's *Liturgies Eastern and Western* (1896, p. 300); but Mr. C. W. Humphreys used the translation in Neale's

Liturgies of St. Mark, &c. (1859). Mr. Humphreys' lines had to be modified in order to fit the tune which Vaughan Williams wished to use for the *English Hymnal* (329); and, as the author was living in South America, he asked the editor to make the needed modifications in his verses.

Iambic, 8 7. 8 7.

MUSIC. ACH GOTT UND HERR seems to be ultimately derived from the tune set to the hymn 'Ach Gott und Herr', in *As Hymnodus Sacer* (Leipzig, 1625), which is as follows:

Its development can be traced through J. Crüger's *Newes vollkömmliches Gesangbuch* (1640), where the second section runs:

and a form in the major scale in C. Peters's *Andachts Zymbeln* (Freiburg, 1655) thus:

to the *Neu-Leipziger Gesangbuch* (1682) and the present version, which is from J. S. Bach's *Vierstimmige Choralgesänge* (1769). The tune is also found, with slight variation, in many other collections.

279 Thee we adore, O hidden Saviour, thee.

St. Thomas Aquinas, 1227–74. *Tr. Bishop J. R. Woodford.*

Adoro te devote, latens deitas,
quae sub his figuris vere latitas;
tibi se cor meum totum subicit,
quia te contemplans totum deficit.

This hymn of Aquinas was never incorporated in the public services, but was added at an early date to various missals for private devotion. The line which addresses Christ as a pious pelican (*Pie pelicane, Jesu Domine*) was too much for the editors of the Paris Breviary of the 18th century, who altered it to *O fons puritatis, Jesu Domine.* Of many translations, Bishop Woodford's, from his *Hymns Arranged for the Sundays, &c., of the Church of England* (2nd ed., 1855), has become the best known, owing to its use in *Hymns Ancient and Modern* (1861), and in other collections. There have been many alterations in his text, sometimes by himself or with his permission, sometimes not. We keep the word 'Supper' as Woodford wrote it; some editors altered it to 'Sacrament', in accordance with a once current prejudice against St. Paul's word.

Iambic, 10 10. 10 10.

MUSIC. ADORO TE is the proper plainsong melody to this hymn, from the Solesmes version. It will be noticed that the melody differs somewhat, in manner and feeling, from the great plainsong melodies such as, for example, 'Deus creator omnium' (see 44), and that it approximates to a later and different type of tune, in which a harmonic consciousness begins to make itself felt.

280 Therefore we, before him bending.

St. Thomas Aquinas, 1227–74. *Tr. cento.*

Tantum ergo sacramentum
  veneremur cernui,
et antiquum documentum
  novo cedat ritui;
praestet fides supplementum
  sensuum defectui.

Here again, as with the original of 277, St. Thomas Aquinas uses one of the more ancient office-hymns as a basis for a hymn on the later sacramental theory. 'Tantum ergo' is a part of 'Pange lingua gloriosi corporis mysterium', which is based on the much finer 6th-century Passiontide hymn, 'Pange lingua gloriosi praelium certaminis', careful theological distinctions taking the place of the rugged emotion and primitive theology of the original model. The remarks on 277 apply to this companion Corpus Christi hymn, which was used at Vespers in the Roman and at Mattins in the Sarum rite, and also as a processional and in other ways. We print the last two of the six verses; these have many musical associations, being used in the service of Benediction. Neale pronounced the remarkable opinion that this hymn contested the second place among Latin hymns with the *Stabat Mater*; but, as Duncan Campbell remarks in *Hymns and Hymn Makers*, the grounds of this judgement are 'not so much literary as dogmatic'. Neale's translation (as with 277) is not very successful, and centos have generally taken the place of his originals in the *Hymnal Noted*. Ours is that of *E.H.* 326.

Part I we omit, as we have done also with 277. The attempts to elucidate the eucharistic accretions by over-subtle attempts at explanation come out badly in English. Neale in the *Hymnal Noted* tried:

Word made Flesh—true bread He taketh:
  This He makes true Flesh to be.

This obviously would not do; and later hymnals tried various adjustments. But, as a learned critic said in the *Quarterly Review* (July, 1892):

'Of the fault of ingenious obscurity instances may be found in the painfully laboured versions of ancient dogmatic hymns; as in the verbal puzzle of the following lines, taken from the translation in *Hymns Ancient and Modern* [also in *Church Hymns*, 1903], of the *Pange lingua* of St. Thomas Aquinas:

Word-made-Flesh true bread He maketh
  By His Word His Flesh to be.'

Trochaic, 8 7. 8 7. 8 7.

MUSIC. PANGE LINGUA is the form, from the *Mechlin Gradual* (1848), of the plainsong melody which is given, in its Sarum version, at 129, to its proper words. The present is a later version of the melody; a comparison of the two forms will show that the Sarum version is in a 'purer' style of plainsong.

TANTUM ERGO (NO. 2) is traditionally associated with this hymn, and is probably by G. P. da Palestrina. Its use is widespread in Europe, and various forms are found, slightly differing in rhythm and melody, though in general the versions show a close correspondence. The following form, which is a common one, will show to what degree the variants usually differ:

281 Wherefore, O Father, we thy humble servants. *S.P.*

Written for our book to provide a short hymn, doctrinally in accord with the Prayer Book, in the metre for which there are so many beautiful tunes. The lines are a paraphrase of the Prayers of Oblation and Thanksgiving.

Sapphic metre, 11 11. 11 5. See 28.

MUSIC. CHRISTE FONS JUGIS is a Rouen 'church melody' (see 28). This majestic melody lies wholly within the compass of a sixth and gains great solidity from its compact construction; it gives the impression of having been founded on plainsong.

MARRIAGE

Not many successful wedding hymns have been written; and Keble's 'The voice that breathed o'er Eden' can only have been included in hymnals because of his name, and—*faute de mieux*: on many occasions the line, 'Be present, awful Father, to give away the bride', has suggested incongruous ideas. That phrase, by the way, was again misapplied in lines which Sir J. C. Squire once quoted as the worst in his long experience of minor poetry:

> O, never, never she'll forget the happy, happy day,
> On which she stood at altar step, and gave herself away.

But perhaps the most remarkable actual wedding hymn is one by Joseph Proud, who helped to found the Swedenborgian 'New Church', and as his biographer, W. T. Brooke, said, 'at once broke into song', to the extent of writing 300 hymns in three months: he published in 1790, with a 3rd edition in 1798, *Hymns and Spiritual Songs for the Use of the Lord's New Church, signified by the New Jerusalem*; among them a marriage hymn containing this stanza:

Where then is the rapturous pair
  Who conjugal pleasures possess?
'Tis found with the man and the fair
  Whose only delight is to bless;
Whose love is so ardent a flame
  That nothing can equal its fire;
Whose will is in all things the same,
  The same is their every desire.

282 God, whose eternal mind. *Jan Struther.*

Written for our book, to provide a hymn of thankfulness for marriage, to be used at commemorations of marriage as well as at weddings themselves, and to carry a beautiful tune of unusual metre.

Iambic and trochaic, 6 6. 6 6. 7 7. 6 6 6, the 1st, 3rd, and 7th lines being iambic. Unique.

MUSIC. FAITHFUL is a Scottish traditional melody, first adapted by John Goss in the *Daily Express Community Song Book* (1927), and arranged by Martin Shaw especially for this hymn in the enlarged *Songs of Praise* (1931). The tune is built on the plan found in many Welsh hymn-tunes (see 'Gwalia', 54); it is a quiet, serene melody, which must not be sung too slowly.

283 O perfect Love, all human thought transcending.

Mrs. Dorothy F. Gurney.

Written by Miss Blomfield, afterwards Mrs. Gurney, for her sister's wedding in 1883, to the tune, 'O Strength and Stay'. It rapidly became the most popular of wedding hymns, and has gradually freed the choral wedding from 'The voice that breathed o'er Eden'.

Iambic, 11 10. 11 10.

MUSIC. CHARTERHOUSE was composed by David Evans for the hymn 'O Son of Man, our Hero strong and tender', and appeared in the *Church Hymnary* (1927). It is a straightforward unison melody, with a broad well-proportioned outline.

284 O thou who gavest power to love.

Bishop Mandell Creighton, 1843–1901.

This, the only hymn that Dr. Creighton wrote, was sung at the wedding of Miss Sarah Lyttelton to Mr. J. C. Bailey, 26 Apr. 1900, at St. Margaret's, Westminster, and was first printed in the Bishop's *Life* by Mrs. Creighton, whence it came to the *English Hymnal* (1906).

L.M.

MUSIC. AFFECTION is from John Greenwood's *Psalmody harmonised in score, with accompaniment for organ and pianoforte* (Halifax, 1838).

THE SICK: HOSPITAL SUNDAY

285 From thee all skill and science flow.

Charles Kingsley, 1819–75.

It is significant that Kingsley had been so little drawn upon for hymnody that his name did not appear in the original Julian's *Dictionary of Hymnology* (1891), although Julian, Mearns, and their collaborators showed that the total number of Christian hymns (in 200 or more languages and dialects) was then not less than 400,000, and 30,000 were annotated in the *Dictionary* by 1891. In the last decade of the 19th century, however, some American collections and Garrett Horder in England began to include one or two of Kingsley's poems that are suitable as hymns, and so his name appears in Julian's *New Supplement* of 1907. This hymn was written in 1871 for the laying of the foundation-stone of the working-men's block of the Queen's Hospital at Birmingham, in six verses, beginning 'Accept this building, gracious Lord', and was sung by a choir of a thousand voices.

C.M.

MUSIC. FARNHAM is an arrangement, by R. Vaughan Williams, for the *English Hymnal* (1906), of an English traditional melody.

286 Life and health are in the name.

J. R. Darbyshire, Bishop of Glasgow.

Written for our book, to include the modern aspects of health and healing, and to bring a fine tune into use.

Trochaic and iambic, 7 6. 7 6. 7 8. 7 6, a unique and very peculiar metre, the trochaic lines (1, 3, 5, 7) alternating with the iambic, while the 6th line has an extra foot.

MUSIC. AMSTERDAM is found in Wesley's *Sacred Harmony, A Set of Tunes Collected by the late Revd. John Wesley, M.A. &c.* (London, 1822), where it is set to 'God of unexampled grace, Redeemer of mankind', as follows:

In the previous edition of *Sacred Harmony* (1789), the first part of the tune is simply repeated without the variation at the first cadence; otherwise it is as above. The present version of the melody is very slightly simplified. It is a representative example of the 'robust' tunes introduced by Wesley, many of them, like the present tune, adaptations from the chorales used by the Moravian Brethren, whom he visited in 1738. These vigorous tunes soon became popular, and considerably influenced all later types of hymn melodies.

287 Thine arm, O Lord, in days of old.

E. H. Plumptre, 1821–91.

Written in 1864 for King's College Hospital, London (Plumptre was Professor of Exegesis at King's College), and first printed as a leaflet; in 1865 he included it in the 2nd edition of his *Lazarus, and Other Poems*, whence it got into many hymnals.

D.C.M.

MUSIC. ST. MATTHEW appeared in *A Supplement to the New Version of Psalms by Dr. Brady and Mr. Tate . . . The Sixth Edition* . . . (1708), under its present name, and marked in the Index as a new tune. It was set to Psalm 33, in two parts, treble and bass, the melody being as follows:

The above publication contains no composers' names, but it is generally believed that Dr. Croft was concerned in its production, and that 'St. Matthew' is his composition. From the middle of the 18th century his name is invariably attached to it in all the collections in which composers' names are found. In its later form it has become one of the most famous hymn-tunes, and deserves its popularity.

THE LIFE BEYOND

FUNERALS AND COMMEMORATIONS

288 Christ who knows all his sheep. *Richard Baxter*,‡ 1615–91.

This stirring and beautiful hymn is from the *Additions to the Poetical Fragments of Richard Baxter* (1689). These are the last 3 of 31 stanzas of *The Exit*, which he dates 19 Dec. 1682.

Unfortunately some words had to be changed: in order to make the hymn suitable for the purpose it here fulfils. For the last 4 lines of our 1st verse Baxter has:

He will not lose his Blood,
  Nor Intercession:
Nor we the Purchas'd Good
  Of his dear Passion.

Ver. 2, last line, for 'here I' Baxter has, less suitably for singing, 'I here'. In ver. 3, l. 1, 'my spirit'; l. 2, 'I trust'; l. 3, 'this wandering sheep'.

Iambic, 6 6. 6 5. 6 5. Unique.

MUSIC. CAMBRIDGE was composed by Charles Wood for this hymn in *Songs of Praise* (1925). It is a broad, stately tune, with a striking sense of continuity in the rhythm, and a very firm outline; there is a strong underlying feeling of simple sincerity in the melody, and it is certainly one of the finest modern hymn-tunes.

289 For those we love within the veil. *W. Charter Piggott.*

Written for a commemoration service in the earlier part of the War, 1915.

Iambic, 8 8. 8 4.

MUSIC. MEYER (ES IST KEIN TAG) is from *Geistliche Seelenfreud* (Ulm, 1692); the editor of this work was J. D. Mejer (or Meyer), and this melody is marked as his own composition.

290 How can I cease to pray for thee? Somewhere.

Mrs. J. R. C. Dorr, 1825–1913.

This tender, thoughtful poem is from *Friar Anselm and other Poems* (1879).

Iambic, 10 10. 10 10.

MUSIC. BATTLE, by H. Lawes, appeared in G. Sandys's *A Paraphrase upon the Divine Poems* (1638), where it is set to Psalm 31, 'Who trusts in thee, O let not shame deject'. In the original the last bar of line 2 runs

and the 4th and 5th notes of the last line are semibreves. It is written in the familiar psalm-tune style, but the melody has some features characteristic of the composer, especially in the 3rd and 4th lines (cf. 'Falkland', 227).

291 Joy and triumph everlasting.

Adam of St. Victor, *c.* 1170. *Tr. Y.H.* (*Robert Bridges*).

Supernae matris gaudia
repraesentat ecclesia,
dum festa colit annua,
suspirat ad perpetua.

This, one of Adam of St. Victor's finest sequences, exists in more than one gradual of the 13th century. The translation is in the *Yattendon Hymnal* (1899), marked 'adapted R.B.'; he selected his metre, as always, for the sake of the tune he wanted. The five stanzas (*Y.H.* 27, *E.H.* 200) are here reduced to four.

Trochaic, 8 7. 8 7. 7 7. 8 8. Unique.

MUSIC. PSALM 42 was composed or adapted by L. Bourgeois for this psalm in the *Genevan Psalter* (1551). In the *Anglo-Genevan Psalter* (1561) the tune is set to Kethe's version of Psalm 27, and this was taken over into the complete *Scottish Psalter* (1564). As the scansion and rhythm of Kethe's psalm are quite different from those of the French version by Beza, that adaptation was exceedingly bad. Modern books give the tune in a variety of forms. It has an unusual rhythm, which gives fresh life and character to the melodic line.

292 Now thy earthly work is done. *P. Dearmer.*

Written for the original *Songs of Praise* (1925), to carry the tune.

Trochaic, 7 7. 7 7. 7 7.

MUSIC. PRESSBURG (NICHT SO TRAURIG) is from Freylinghausen's *Neues Geistreiches Gesangbuch* (1714), where it is set to Gerhardt's hymn 'Nicht so traurig, nicht so sehr', in the following form:

The same form is found in Schemelli's *Musicalisches Gesangbuch, &c.* (1736) and other collections.

293 O valiant hearts, who to your glory came. *J. S. Arkwright.*

Published in *The Supreme Sacrifice, and other Poems in Time of War* (1919).

Iambic, 10 10. 10 10—the metre of 'Abide with me'.

MUSIC. VALIANT HEARTS, by Gustav Holst, was written especially for this hymn in *Songs of Praise*. It is a good bold tune, in triple time, with a suggestion of bell-chimes in the repeated first phrase, an effect which is enhanced by the nature of the accompaniment to the alternative unison version.

VALOR is an arrangement, by R. Vaughan Williams, of a traditional melody, and appeared in *Songs of Praise* (1925).

294 They are all gone into the world of light.

Henry Vaughan the Silurist, 1622–95.

George Herbert was Vaughan's model; but the younger poet was led more than the elder to the mysterious themes of eternity, communion with nature and childhood, and with the departed. The death of a younger brother caused a sequence of poems in which the poignant sense of loss is exceeded in prominence by a wistful brooding over man's relations with the unseen and eternal. Our hymn is another example, and is said to have been inspired by the loss of his Cavalier friends who fell in the Civil War. He published it in *Silex Scintillans*, Part II, 1665.

Henry Vaughan called himself 'Silurist' because Brecknockshire, the County of his birth, was anciently inhabited by the Silures. His studies at Jesus College, Oxford, where he matriculated in 1638, were interrupted by the Civil War; he left Oxford, and subsequently became a physician. His great book, *Silex Scintillans*, was written after a deep period of conversion. Though he had largely modelled himself upon 'the blessed man, Mr. George Herbert', he was a notably original poet; and, in his intimate love of nature, linked with a sense of the timelessness of things, he is the precursor of Wordsworth. He knew that he was 'cross to fashion': only one of his books reached a 2nd edition.

Iambic, 10 8. 10 6. Unique.

MUSIC. FANAD HEAD is an arrangement, by C. H. Kitson, of an Irish traditional melody from the *Petrie Collection of Irish Airs*, and first appeared in the *Irish Hymnal* (Dublin, 1919), of which Professor Kitson was co-editor. It was there set to 'Fierce raged the tempest', and is here slightly modified to suit the present words. It is a very individual tune, the continual recurrence of the initial phrase and its inversion in the last lines giving a noteworthy emotional quality to a very moving and beautiful melody.

295 They whose course on earth is o'er.

J. M. Neale, 1818–66, *and others.*

Originally published in his *Hymns for the Young* (1844), and subsequently revised by him, this version is that of *E.H.* 500, with four lines omitted. One of the most prolific and talented of hymnists, the devout and gentle-minded Neale suffered much opposition in his comparatively short life; that his only reward was £27 a year as Warden of Sackville College is well known; but he had been offered a living which his health prevented his accepting, and he refused the Provostship of St. Ninian's Cathedral, Perth.

MUSIC. NUN KOMM, DER HEIDEN HEILAND is set to this German version of 'Veni, Redemptor Gentium' in the Wittenberg *Geystliche gesangk Buchlein* (1524), edited by Johann Walther, and in *Enchiridion, Oder eyn Handbuchlein, &c.* (Erfurt, 1524), and several other song-books of about that date. Its early form is as follows:

It is a simplified form of the plainsong melody associated with the original Latin hymn, and many variants are found. The present version is that adopted by J. S. Bach in his cantata on this hymn.

296 Where is death's sting? We were not born to die.

G. F. Bradby.

From his *Hymns without Tunes* (Rugby, 1929, 2nd impression).

Iambic, 10 10. 10 10. 10 10.

MUSIC. SONG 1, by Orlando Gibbons, was set to a paraphrase of the Song in Exodus 15 (see 29). The tune is given an individual character by the rather unusual nature of the phrase in line 3, very characteristic of the composer.

MINISTERIAL SERVICE

297 Dismiss me not thy service, Lord. *T. T. Lynch*, 1818–71.

From the 1st edition of the once famous *Rivulet* (1855). For the Rivulet Controversy see p. 2.

Iambic, 8 6. 8 6. 8 6.

MUSIC. BRUNSWICK is an adaptation, probably dating from the middle of the 18th century, of Handel's aria in *Saul*, 'Sin not, O King, against the youth'; in Edward Miller's *Psalms of David* (1790) it is headed 'never before printed', but this is apparently incorrect, since it is stated that it appeared in its present form in the *Christian's Magazine* of 1760, though research has failed to discover a copy of this magazine. The adaptation makes an excellent hymn-tune.

298 Pour out thy Spirit from on high. *J. Montgomery*, ‡1771–1854.

Much confusion is caused when the first word of a hymn is altered. It has been frequently said that this hymn is absent from the *English Hymnal* and *Songs of Praise*, because they use the author's own first line, and many are familiar with 'Lord, pour thy Spirit', an unnecessary change that only made the line less euphonious. There are some inevitable alterations, however, even in the conservative *English Hymnal*, whose version we use here. The original was written in 1833 for J. Birchell's *Selection of Hymns* and repeated in Edward Bickersteth's *Christian Psalmody* in the same year.

L.M.

MUSIC. DUKE STREET appears first in *A Select Collection of Psalm and Hymn Tunes . . . By the late Henry Boyd, Teacher of Psalmody* (Glasgow, 1793). It is there headed 'Addison's 19th Psalm', no composer's name being given. In *Euphonia*, a collection of tunes, edited by W. Dixon, and published in Liverpool about 1805, it is found under its present name, and attributed to John Hatton. It belongs to the type of tune popularized by Wesley and his followers, and is an example of the later development of the type.

SERVICE OVERSEA

299 Far round the world thy children sing their song.
Basil Mathews.

Originally written in 1909 for a Sunday School Anniversary at Bowes Park, London; 'but', the author states, 'the verses dealing with the peoples of Asia, Africa, and the Islands were added about three years later'.

Iambic, 10 10. 10 10.

MUSIC. WOODLANDS, by W. Greatorex, first appeared in the *Public School Hymn Book* (1919); it is named after one of the school houses at Gresham's School, Norfolk, where the composer is Director of Music. It is a bold, unison tune, with a resolute, four-square rhythm, and a character of cheerful animation.

300 God is working his purpose out as year succeeds to year.

A. C. Ainger, 1841–1919.

'One of the most distinguished of Eton masters, a man of clear head, wide accomplishments, a fine scholar with a remarkable memory, an incisive critic, a good speaker, a good critic, fertile in suggestion, complete in execution', Ainger set no punishments, and his justice, courtesy, and unruffled good humour won the respect and admiration of the boys. He wrote this at the school in 1894, dedicating it to Archbishop Benson, and publishing it in leaflet form. It was included in the *Church Missionary Hymn Book* (1899). The burden of each verse is from Habakkuk 2 : 14, 'For the earth shall be filled with the knowledge of the glory of the Lord, as the waters cover the sea'. See also the similar passage in Isaiah 11 : 9.

Anapaestic quatrains, irregular in character.

MUSIC. PURPOSE was composed by Martin Shaw especially for this hymn in the enlarged *Songs of Praise* (1931). It is a broad solid tune, with a suggestion of the style of some of the English folk-tunes. The freedom and natural flow of the melody is admirable, its skilful construction to admit of a canon throughout in the bass being nowhere obtrusive.

301 Lift up your heads, ye gates of brass.

James Montgomery, 1771–1854.

An early missionary hymn, from the *Evangelical Magazine* (1843), and also in Montgomery's *Original Hymns* (1853). It will be remembered that his 'Hail to the Lord's Anointed' (87) is also a hymn of early date for oversea missions.

L.M.

MUSIC. ST. DAVID is from *Ravenscroft's Psalter* (1621), where it is set to Psalms 43 and 95, the arrangement of the tune being by Ravenscroft himself. In the Index it is under the heading 'Welsh Tunes'. The melody is as follows:

In John Playford's *Psalms and Hymns* (1671) the melody appears exactly in the above form, but in his *Whole Book of Psalms* (1677) it is found in its *present* form.

The alternative version (descant), by Cyril B. Rootham. was written especially for the enlarged *Songs of Praise* (1931).

The tune is a remarkably angular one, still more so in the original form than in the later; this quality gives it a robust and rugged character which differentiates it from the general pattern of its class, and is not without its attraction.

302 Servants of the great adventure. *P. Dearmer.*

Written at the request of the Church Missionary Society, and sung first at the World Call services in York Minster, 1929, from a leaflet.

Trochaic, 8 7. 8 7. D.

MUSIC. MARATHON was contributed by R. Vaughan Williams to *Songs of Praise for Boys and Girls* (1930), but it is an arrangement of a march tune from his music to *The Wasps* of Aristophanes, written for the production at Cambridge in 1910; it is a vigorous, broad melody with a folk-song flavour, and very characteristic of that period of the composer's development. The trenchant vitality of its rhythm and contour make it a most enjoyable tune to sing.

303 Thou whose almighty Word. *J. Marriott,*‡ 1780–1825.

John Marriott (to whom Walter Scott dedicated the second canto of *Marmion*) was too modest to publish his hymns, or even to allow them to be quoted. This one he wrote about 1813. Six weeks after his death, it was read at a meeting of the London Missionary Society, 12 May 1825; and, the audience being greatly impressed, was printed next month in *The Evangelical Magazine*, and shortly after in *The Friendly Visitor.*

Iambic, 6 6 4. 6 6 6. 4.

MUSIC. MOSCOW, by F. Giardini, comes from *A Collection of Psalm and Hymn Tunes, never published before* (1769, edited by the Rev. M. Madan), which is known as the 'Lock Collection'. It was composed for the hymn 'Come, thou almighty King', and headed 'Hymn to the Trinity, set by F. G.'. Its original form was as follows:

The alternative version (descant), by Alan Gray, appeared in his *A Book of Descants* (1920). The later form is an improvement, since the alterations in the first two lines add considerably to the robustness of the rhythm and melody. It is now one of the most famous hymn-tunes, and merits its renown.

PART IV

SOCIAL SERVICE

GENERAL

Songs of Praise is intended for use not only in church, but also at public meetings and in the home. Otherwise there would be no chance of all the tunes in the book being sung; for in this collection there is no padding with a mass of hymns that are never used. But, since service at home is now recognized, as a part of the Christian 'Duty to my Neighbour' as well as service oversea, and the moral obligations of the Christian religion better understood, many of the hymns in this section are increasingly sung in church. Some also are being used with other application: the first, for instance, *Pioneers*, is sung at Ordinations.

The present writer was first impressed by the deficiencies in the 19th-century hymnals when, as Hon. Secretary of the Christian Social Union in London, he was responsible in 1894 for the first midday sermons delivered in the City, which were at the church of St. Edmund, King and Martyr, Lombard Street. We could find in the book used in the church no hymns that were concerned with man's duty to his neighbour; and we grew weary of the doleful tune and depressing words of 'Thy Kingdom come, O Lord'. We wanted hymns that expressed faith and hope. Next year, as a result of this experience, we printed a four-page leaflet of *Hymns for Social Services*, which a little later developed into a small red paper-covered book; and we were helped, I remember, by Percy Alden's similar work at the Mansfield House Settlement in East London. Thus a small beginning was made in the work of supplying that deficiency which was noticed in the new *Hymns Ancient and Modern* of 1904. 'The defect', said the Preface, 'lies with the composers of our hymns, and not with the compilers of the collections . . . few apparently have been inspired by the social and national aspects of Christianity which appeal so largely to our time.'

304 All the past we leave behind. *Walt Whitman* (*cento*), 1819–92.

A cento from 'Pioneers, O Pioneers', those lines being selected which are of such equality of length as to permit of their being sung. Whitman first published *Leaves of Grass* in 1855, the 8th revised edition in 1882, from which last our text is taken.

Trochaic, 7. 8 8. 8 8. 7. in these selected lines. Unique.

MUSIC. PIONEERS was written by Martin Shaw for this hymn in *Songs of Praise* (1925). The tune is notable for the unbroken continuity of its line, due to the avoidance of any suggestion of a cadence in the tonic key until the last bars; the whole tune is, indeed, one long phrase.

305 Little things that run and quail. *James Stephens.*

From his *Collected Poems* (1926).

7 8. 7 8. irregular; iambic in character.

MUSIC. TRES MAGI DE GENTIBUS is a melody from the Andernach *Catholische Geistliche Gesänge* (1608) [see 130]. The rhythm is here very slightly adapted, as is also the melody in one or two places, to fit the varying rhythm of the words. It is a very simple little tune of the cradle-song or 'nursery' type.

306 Men, whose boast it is that ye. *J. R. Lowell*, 1819–91.

From his *Poems* (1844), written during the struggle in America for the emancipation of the slaves.

Songs of Praise having such special sections as 'Social Service: General' and 'National', it is possible to include, as well as hymns in the usual sense, such songs of moral import, or cansons, as they have been called, as are more likely to be sung at meetings than at ordinary church services. Ethical causes of vast importance for the future of the world are indeed essentially religious, and the problems that confront mankind can only be solved by the Spirit of Christ.

7 7. 7 7. D.

MUSIC. IVES is a melody from the *Plymouth Collection of Hymns and Tunes* (New York, 1855), which was edited by Henry Ward Beecher, the musical editors being John Zundel and the Rev. Charles Beecher. The tune itself bears a considerable likeness to the Irish traditional melody generally known by Moore's poem 'The Minstrel Boy'.

307 O brother man, fold to thy heart thy brother.
J. G. Whittier, 1807–92.

Written in 1848, and published in his *Poems* (1850). From his poem 'Worship', in 15 stanzas, beginning:

> The Pagan's myths through marble lips are spoken,
> And ghosts of old beliefs still flit and moan
> Round fane and altar overthrown and broken,
> O'er tree-grown barrow and grey ring of stone.

These are the last 3 stanzas of the poem, to which is affixed the reference to 'pure religion and undefiled', James 1 : 27.

Whittier's family were Quakers who had lived for nearly 200 years in the house they had built in Massachusetts: in the old days attacks by Indians had been frequent, but the Whittiers always refused to use the garrison house of the village, relying instead upon their faith and the kindness of the Indians. When John was a lad, his sister sent one of his poems to William Lloyd Garrison for his *Free Press*. Garrison rode over to see the young poet, and pressed old Mr. Whittier to give him a good education, so that he could be a writer. 'Sir,' he replied, 'poetry will not give him bread.' But John learned shoe-making in his spare hours on the farm, and paid for himself a term at Haverhill Academy. Later, he joined Garrison in the fight against slavery, and gave up his chances of political preferment. But he became the poet of the struggle; and the soldiers used to recite 'The Slave Mother's Lament' and 'The Hunters of Men' by their camp-fires.

Iambic, 11 10. 11 10.

MUSIC. INTERCESSOR was written by Sir Hubert Parry for the hymn 'O word of pity, for our pardon pleading' in *Hymns Ancient and Modern* (1904). It is a grave Aeolian tune, of a broad, solid type, very characteristic of this composer.

308 O God of earth and altar. *G. K. Chesterton.*

Originally printed in Scott Holland's monthly magazine, *The Commonwealth*, this was given to the editor of the *English Hymnal*, who included it in that book (1906). The author once told the present writer that, not knowing one tune from another, he had written this with the idea that 'Aurelia' (generally associated with 249) was the typical tune for hymns, and therefore had used that metre.

Iambic, 7 6. 7 6. D.

MUSIC. KING'S LYNN is an arrangement by R. Vaughan Williams of an English traditional melody. It appeared in the *English Hymnal* (1906). The tune is a broad, Aeolian melody, very characteristic of a large number of the folk-songs which have been collected in the last 40 odd years. The first phrase has a fine, individual sweep of outline, and the whole tune is splendidly dignified and impressive.

309 Once to every man and nation. *J. R. Lowell,*‡ 1819–91.

From his *Poems* (vol. i, 1849). The original begins, 'When a deed is done for freedom', and is called *The Present Crisis* (with the date, 1845): the crisis was the war with Mexico, which he held was unjust and would only enlarge the area of slavery. Garrett Horder made a hymn of it in England by including the selected stanzas in his *Hymns Supplemental* (1896), and then in his *Worship Song*. The *English Hymnal* next included it. From a poem of 90 long lines, or 180 if each line is divided into two, Dr. Horder made a hymn of 32 short lines, by selection, rearrangement, and substitution (i.e. the first half of stanza 4 is his own, corresponding to Lowell's

> Careless seems the great Avenger . . .
> Truth for ever on the scaffold, Wrong for ever on the throne).

For the first two lines of our ver. 3, Lowell had, as one line:

> By the light of burning heretics Christ's bleeding feet I track.

To make a cento, indeed, from the long poem, regular enough to be sung, much alteration was inevitable.

Trochaic, 8 7. 8 7. D.

MUSIC. EBENEZER (TON-Y-BOTEL), by T. J. Williams, is a tune from *Llawlyfr Moliant* (1890).

This tune is known by the alternative name of 'Ton-y-Botel', and the picturesque legend is widely credited that it was so named because it was found in a bottle washed ashore in a storm on the Welsh coast. The story, however, is entirely without foundation. It is a solemn tune, of very simple structure, being formed, throughout, of imitations of the first bar. The melodic sequence in the middle section is characteristic of many Welsh tunes (cf. 'Hyfrydol', 260), and of 'revivalist' imitations of them.

310 The day of the Lord is at hand, at hand.

C. Kingsley, 1819–75.

Full of apocalyptic fervour and of the fighting, hopeful spirit of the men who gathered round F. D. Maurice in 1848, under the name of Christian Socialists, this is from *Andromeda and other Poems*, 1858, in the group of 'poems connected with 1848–9'.

Irregular, anapaestic in character.

MUSIC. REMEMBER THE POOR is an adaptation, from the *Irish Hymnal* (Dublin, 1919), of an Irish traditional melody, in the *Petrie Collection of Irish Melodies*, which was originally sung to words beginning 'Remember the poor'. It is a very fine, dignified tune, and extremely characteristic of a large class of Irish folk-tunes, both in rhythm and in the general lay-out of the melody; particularly noteworthy is the varied emotional significance of the G♭ in the 2nd (4th) line, and the octave drop at the end of the 6th line; it is, altogether, a remarkable tune, and one of the most beautiful of its kind.

311 The world's great age begins anew.

P. B. Shelley, 1792–1822.

Three stanzas from the chorus of seven stanzas at the end of *Hellas*, which was written at Pisa in 1821. In the Preface Shelley says: 'Our laws, our literature, our religion, our arts, have their root in Greece. But for Greece . . . we might still have been savages and idolaters.'

Shelley goes on to foretell the freeing of Italy: 'The Spanish Peninsula', he says, 'is already free'—for so it then seemed. He looks forward to the liberation of Greece: 'The English permit', he says, 'their oppressors to act according to their natural sympathy with the Turkish tyrant, and to brand upon their name the indelible blot of an alliance with the enemies of domestic happiness, of Christianity and civilization.' Greece was to obtain her final independence in 1833; but Shelley's words about the English abetting the Turkish tyrant retained some bitter truth during most of the 19th century. The still common idea that so religious a man was an atheist is due to a silly tract on the subject which he wrote as an undergraduate. He apparently meant it as a joke to annoy the Oxford authorities—who sent him down for it; but Shelley's gifts did not include either an ear for music or a sense of humour.

We have included these verses because the debt of Christianity to Hellenism, as well as to Hebraism, has been unrecognized in hymnals, and few outside the circle of philosophic theologians have understood that there is a mystical New Athens as well as a mystical New Jerusalem for 'our green and pleasant land'. Charles Wesley came nearest to the thought: indeed, in a hymn on the Crucifixion (552 in the old Methodist *Hymns*, 1840, &c.) he goes so far as to say:

Dies the glorious cause of all!
The true, eternal Pan
Falls, to raise us from our fall
To rescue sinful man!

The recognition of the legacy of Greece in Christianity goes back to Clement of Alexandria, to Origen, and to Justin Martyr himself: in the Middle Ages the authority of Aristotle (the works of Plato being then lost) was enormous; but Protestantism has suffered through its almost exclusive Hebraism.

The chorus ends:

O cease! must hate and death return?
Cease! must men kill and die?
Cease! drain not to its dregs the urn
Of bitter prophecy.
The world is weary of the past,
O might it die or rest at last!

Iambic, 8 6. 8 6. 8 8. Occurs also in 532 and 663.

MUSIC. PEMBROKE was written by Patrick Hadley for this hymn in *Songs of Praise* (1925). It is a solemn unison melody, in the Aeolian mode (though by no means harmonized as such) with a smooth largeness of outline, and the peculiar emotional significance inherent in the Ambrosian fourth, here used at the cadences of ll. 2 and 6.

312 These things shall be! A loftier race.

J. A. Symonds, 1840–93.

From his *New and Old* (1880), a poem called *A Vista*, 'Sad heart, what will the future bring?' This hymn, beginning at stanza 4 of the original, first appeared in the *Methodist Hymn Book* (1904), and next in the *Fellowship Hymn Book* (1909); it came into general use during the War, being included in the S.P.C.K. collection, *In hoc Signo*, and since then the League of Nations Union has reprinted and circulated it in a fly-sheet; it is also in the *League of Nations Song Book* (Stainer & Bell). We have omitted ver. 5 in the original *Songs of Praise* (1925) ('Women shall be man's mate and peer') at the request of those who considered that this had now ceased in the English-speaking countries to be a dream of the future. The poem begins:

Sad heart, what will the future bring
To happier men when we are gone?
What golden days shall dawn for them
Transcending all we gaze upon?

Will our long strife be laid to rest?
The warfare of our blind desires
Be merged in a perpetual peace,
And love illume but harmless fires?

Shall faith released from forms that chain
  And freeze the spirit while we pray,
Expect with calm and ardent eyes
  The morning of death's brighter day?

These things shall be, &c.

There are fifteen stanzas in all.
D.L.M.

MUSIC. MERTHYR TYDVIL (DIES IRAE), by Joseph Parry, appeared in Ieuan Gwyllt's *Llyfr Tonau* (1870). Both melodically and structurally it is written in the manner of the traditional Welsh hymn-tunes (see 54).

313 Through all the long dark night of years.

Gerald Massey, 1828–1907.

From his *Cries of '48* (1848), reprinted in H. S. Salt's *Songs of Freedom*, and other collections, and to be found as part of the poem 'To-day and To-morrow' in his book *My Lyrical Life* (vol. ii, p. 282). By the end of the 19th century there was a feeling that the strenuous aspirations for freedom, which had been voiced by poets since the days of Shelley and his friends in the early part of the century, had been fulfilled, and were now obsolete—and a little violent. Since the War—and indeed since 1914—we have learnt that man cannot rest in that easy assumption; and old-fashioned poets, like Gerald Massey, have still their message. He had been a Chartist and became a member of the Christian Socialist Party of Kingsley and Maurice in 1850. 'George Eliot' afterwards based on Massey's career some features of her *Felix Holt, the Radical* (1866).
Iambic, 8 7. 8 7. D.

MUSIC. NACHTIGALL (ACH! WAN DOCH JESU, LIEBSTER MEIN) is from F. Spee's *Trutz Nachtigal, oder geistlichs-poetisch Lust-Wäldlein, &c.* (Cöllen, 1649), where it is set to the hymn 'Ach, wann doch Jesu, liebster mein'. It is found in many later collections set to various hymns. The present is the original form of the melody.

314 When wilt thou save the people?

Ebenezer Elliott,† 1781–1849.

Published posthumously in Elliott's *More Verse and Prose*, 1850. His contemporaries would have been surprised to know that it would ever appear in a hymn-book, as it did in the *Congregational Church Hymnal* (1887). It was also included in the *English Hymnal* (1906). The 3rd line is altered from 'Not kings and lords, but nations', the corresponding line of ver. 3 being substituted.
Iambic, 7 6. 7 6. 8 8 8. 5. Unique.

MUSIC. KENDAL, by Sir Arthur Somervell, appeared in the *English Hymnal* (1906), set to the present hymn. It is a straightforward unison tune, which presents no difficulties of rhythm or melodic contour.

315 With wonderful deathless ditties.

Arthur O'Shaughnessy, 1844–81.

This song, which proclaims the creative function of poetry and the prophetic inspiration of the poet, is from *Moon and Moonlight* (1874), by the shy and gentle O'Shaughnessy.

Irregular, anapaestic in character.

MUSIC. MARYLEBONE is an arrangement, for *Songs of Praise*, of an Irish traditional melody collected by Cecil Sharp in Marylebone Workhouse.

MUSIC-MAKERS, by Sydney H. Nicholson, appeared, set to these words, in the *Motherland Song Book* (1919). It is a strong modal tune, with a certain dignified austerity, which expresses well the claim of the words.

NATIONAL

316 England, arise! the long, long night is over.

Edward Carpenter, 1844–1929.

From *Chants of Labour* (1888). Two stanzas are omitted, which the author always preferred to have included; but, although they are still, alas, not without truth, recent reforms have already done so much, and so much more improvement is being accomplished, that even now they begin to appear forced and unreal, which they certainly were not when they were written. The omitted stanzas (the 2nd and 4th) are:

By your young children's eyes so red with weeping,
By their white faces aged with want and fear,
By the dark cities where your babes are creeping,
Naked of joy and all that makes life dear;
From each wretched slum
Let the loud cry come;
Arise, O England, for the day is here!

Over your face a web of lies is woven,
Laws that are falsehoods pin you to the ground,
Labour is mocked, its just reward is stolen,
On its bent back sits Idleness encrowned.
How long, while you sleep,
Your harvest shall It reap?
Arise, O England, for the day is here!

Iambic, 11 10. 11 10. 5 5. 10, the 5th and 6th lines being trochaic. Unique.

MUSIC. GUILDFORD was written by R. Vaughan Williams for this hymn in *Songs of Praise* (1925). It is an animated unison melody with a swinging march rhythm, strongly accented by the characteristic triplets in the alternate lines. It is an excellent tune, well-balanced, with a fine climax, and, when taken at a good pace, most invigorating to sing.

317 God of our fathers, known of old. *Rudyard Kipling.*

Written in 1897 for Queen Victoria's Diamond Jubilee; contributed to *The Times*, 17 July 1897, and included in the *Five Nations* (1903).

Inspired by the Diamond Jubilee of Queen Victoria, 1897, and specially alluding to the Procession and the Naval Review, this solemn warning against the perils of that imperialism, which was then sweeping over the country, was the more weighty because the writings of Mr. Kipling had done so much towards the rise of imperialistic consciousness.

The fourth stanza is sometimes criticized; but after all the 'lesser breed without the Law' does not mean, as a recent writer has stated, 'foreigners'. There are certainly races and tribes in existence who without arrogance may be considered to be as yet 'lesser' in relation even to our still very imperfect civilization. Although it is not indeed true that Christianity has failed, it is true that we have failed to absorb enough Christianity. But we are not 'without the Law'.

Iambic, 8 8. 8 8. 8 8.

MUSIC. FOLKINGHAM is from *A Supplement to the New Version of the Psalms* (6th ed. much enlarged, 1708), where it is described as a new tune, and set to a metrical version of the Lord's Prayer. It is a long dignified tune in the style of the older psalm-tunes.

318 God save our gracious King. *Official Peace Version,*† 1919.

'The words to which the tune is sung are no part of the National Anthem,' said the Chancellor of the Exchequer, then Mr. Snowden, in the House of Commons, on 25 Feb. 1931. 'It is only the tune itself which is the National Anthem.'

The origin of the words is obscure. Ver. 1 is in *Harmonia Anglicana*, about the year 1745, the first line being

God save our lord the King,

which had to be altered when Victoria became Queen.

Ver. 2 was the familiar

O Lord our God, arise,
Scatter his enemies
And make them fall!
Confound their politics,
Frustrate their knavish tricks,
On him our hopes we fix,
O, save us all!

In the *Gentleman's Magazine* (1745) appears the earliest copy with an exact date. This gives the 3rd verse:

Thy choicest gifts in store
On George be pleased to pour;
Long may he reign!
May he defend our laws,
And ever give us cause
To say with heart and voice
God save the King!

The whole thing may have grown up and developed from unknown sources; till, when it became familiar, it was too well established—or too carelessly regarded—to be altered. After the War the *Peace Version* which we give here was drawn up and duly authorized by the Privy Council. It was almost as good an improvement as the cramped metre allowed; but it forgot India. Ver. 3 began:

Kinsfolk in love and birth.

After printing the official version in the original *Songs of Praise* (1925) we thought we might venture in our new edition to change this line into:

Of many a race and birth.

And so it now stands.
Iambic, 6 6 4. 6 6 6 4.

MUSIC. NATIONAL ANTHEM. The origin of the air is as obscure as that of the words. Resemblances of rhythm or phrase have been found in melodies by various composers, from Dr. John Bull downwards, but none of these is sufficiently convincing to justify the attribution of the tune to any of them. Henry Carey was for some time credited with both words and music, but his claim is equally inadequate. He is said to have sung the anthem about 1740, but neither in *Thesaurus Musicus* nor in the *Gentleman's Magazine* (1745) is any acknowledgement made of his authorship. These are the earliest copies, yet known, of the anthem, and the attribution to Henry Carey seems to depend on a statement of his son, George S. Carey, made in 1795. According to Dr. Arne, who arranged the anthem for performance in 1745, 'it was a received opinion that it was written for the Catholic Chapel of James II', and this 'opinion' may have some foundation. The actual source of the melody remains undiscovered.

319 I vow to thee, my country, all earthly things above.

Sir Cecil Spring-Rice, 1859–1918.

Sir Valentine Chirol's *Memoir* of the author of this hymn, after quoting it, opens thus:

'Written on 12 Jan. 1918, by Sir Cecil Arthur Spring-Rice, His Majesty's Ambassador to the United States, on the eve of his final departure from Washington. The vow recorded in them had been kept long before he put it into words, for he had served his country for a quarter of a century with the "love that never falters"; and, though he knew it not, he was already a dying man.'

He died on the night of 13/14 Jan.

Irregular, but straightforward iambic 7 6 7 6. 7 6 7 6. 7 6 7 6. in character.

MUSIC. THAXTED, by Gustav Holst, is an arrangement of a melody from the composer's orchestral suite *The Planets* (1921), where it forms the principal section of *Jupiter*. It is a tune of what is popularly regarded as an 'Irish' type, and makes, as here, an excellent unison melody.

ABINGER was written by R. Vaughan Williams especially for the enlarged *Songs of Praise* (1931). It is a flowing unison melody, very flexible and expressive, yet of simple and economical construction; a most attractive and moving tune.

320 Lord, while for all mankind we pray. *J. R. Wreford*, 1800–81.

Contributed in 1837, the year of Queen Victoria's accession, to Beard's *Collection of Hymns for Public and Private Worship.*

C.M.

MUSIC. ABERDEEN seems to have first appeared in a collection printed by James Chalmers in Aberdeen in 1749. The only known copy lacks the title-page, but the date is ascertained from the names of the provost and bailies of Aberdeen, to whom the work is dedicated. The tune is in two parts, tenor and bass, and is named 'St. Paul'. The title-page of the 3rd edition (1753) states that the tunes are 'collected by Andrew Tait, Organist'. As Tait was organist of St. Paul's Episcopal Church it is possible that he was the composer of the tune. It is included in Bremner's collection issued in Edinburgh in 1756, under the name 'Aberdeen or St. Paul'.

321 Men of England, who inherit. *Thomas Campbell*, 1777–1844.

From *The New Monthly Magazine*, 1822.

Campbell had preceded Walter Scott, who was his friend, in the revival of the ballad; and it is in certain of his ballads that his once vast popularity survives (his monument in Westminster Abbey is almost as prominent as that of Shakespeare, and more so than that of Wordsworth); such are *Mariners of England* (1901), *Hohenlinden* (1803), *The Battle of the Baltic* (1809), and others which children still learn at school.

Trochaic, 8 7. 8 7.

MUSIC. SUSSEX appeared in the *English Hymnal* (1906). It is an arrangement by R. Vaughan Williams of an English traditional melody.

322 O beautiful, my country! *F. L. Hosmer*, 1840–1929.

Written in 1884, and published in the *Chicago Unity Festivals* that year, and again in *The Thought of God* (1885). In ver. 1 the word 'cherish' was substituted by permission for 'Lift up'.

Iambic, 7 6. 7 6. D.

MUSIC. FREEDOM was written by Geoffrey Shaw for this hymn in the *Motherland Song Book* (1919). It is characteristic of many of this composer's tunes, in the wide melodic skips, and in the rather austere nature of the general outline.

HELDER (WOHLAUF THUT NICHT VERZAGEN), by B. Helder, appeared in the *Gothaer Cantional* (1648), set to the hymn 'Wohlauf thut nicht verzagen'; the present form of the melody is virtually that of the original. It is in the normal tradition of German chorales; the tune has a considerable likeness to 'Winchester Old' (82).

323 O Lord almighty, thou whose hands. *Sir Henry Newbolt.*

From *Poems: New and Old*, 1919.

C.M.

MUSIC. WORCESTER is found in Ravenscroft's *Whole Booke of Psalms*

(1621); it does not appear in Este's or previous psalters, but is one of the English tunes introduced by Ravenscroft, and named after places, and appears also later in Playford's *Whole booke of Psalms* (1677). The present arrangement, by Sir Ivor Atkins, appeared in *Songs of Praise* (1931). The alternative version (fa-burden), by Thomas Tomkins, is from Ravenscroft's book above.

324 The King, O God, his heart to thee upraiseth.

Y.H. (*Robert Bridges*).

We have divided this into parts, so as to facilitate its use on many occasions. Dr. Bridges printed it in the *Yattendon Hymnal* (1899) with a note, 'Jubilee Hymn, 1897. R.B.'. The former heading of this hymn was 'Y.H., based on F. R. Tailour', but the *Yattendon Hymnal* does not borrow a single line from Tailour's version in the book of 1615 (*Sacred Hymns, Consisting of Fifty Select Psalms*), and does not even keep the metre. We have therefore deleted Tailour's name. The 1st verse of Tailour's version of the 21st Psalm (in 7 verses) is:

The King, (Lord,) toward thy glorious face
Victorious eys dooth ioyful rear:
His strength, thy spirit; his health, thy grace;
With doubled triumphs his soule dooth chear.
What hart could wish, what lips did crave;
Thy bounteous hand him strangely gave.

As was usual with him, Dr. Bridges made the hymn specially to fit the tune he wished to have sung at Yattendon.

Iambic, 11 10. 11 10.

MUSIC. DONNE SECOURS was composed or adapted by L. Bourgeois for Psalm 12 in the *Genevan Psalter* (1551). It is a nobly impressive melody, one of the finest of the Genevan tunes.

325 What heroes thou hast bred.

G. K. Menzies.

This was written for the Stepney Children's Pageant, produced at the Whitechapel Art Gallery in May 1909, when Holst wrote the music for Rosabel Watson, who was conducting her women's orchestra for the Pageant. It was next published, with Holst's setting, by the League of Arts in the *Motherland Song Book* (1919). An example of a 'canson', intermediate between a popular song and a hymn, not for use in an ordinary service, but valuable as it is beautiful on some occasions.

6 6 6 3. 6 6 6 4. A unique and interesting metre. Lines 1 and 3 are iambic; l. 2 consists of two amphibrachs; l. 4 ('Pass in line') is a complete amphimacer (cf. 502); the following triplet (ll. 5, 6, 7) is dactylic in character. The last line is a choriamb | – ◡ ◡ – |, a compound foot, less uncommon in English verse than might be supposed.

MUSIC. STEPNEY was composed by Gustav Holst for the Stepney Pageant (1909), as noted above. It was included in *Songs of Praise* (1925). It is a robust, stirring tune, with a strong march rhythm, in complete emotional accord with the spirit of the words.

326 Father eternal, ruler of creation. *Laurence Housman.*

Mr. Housman wrote this at the request of Dr. H. R. L. Sheppard in 1919, when he was Rector of St. Martin's-in-the-Fields, for the Life and Liberty Movement, and it was subsequently reprinted in the original *Songs of Praise* (1925).

Iambic, 11 10. 11 10. 10. Unique.

MUSIC. LANGHAM was originally composed by Geoffrey Shaw for the present words on the occasion of a meeting of the Life and Liberty Movement in Queen's Hall. It is a broad, forcible melody, with a good sense of climax in the refrain of the last line.

327 Sound over all waters, reach out from all lands.
J. G. Whittier, 1807–92.

From his *Complete Poetical Works* (Boston, 1876), where it is dated 1873; reprinted by Garrett Horder (who did more than any one else for the raising of our hymnody from its poverty-stricken condition at the end of the last century) in his *Worship Song* (1905). The word 'gratulations' in ver. 2 is perfectly good English; and the only wonder is that the longer word should have taken its place in common usage.

Anapaestic, 11 11. 11 11. 12. 11 11 11. Unique.

MUSIC. ALL WATERS was written for this hymn by Martin Shaw especially for the enlarged *Songs of Praise* (1931). This vigorous unison tune, though unlike it in rhythm and melody, is constructed on much the same lines as the same composer's 'Spring' (see 5).

328 The night is ended and the morning nears.
Frederick Tennyson, 1807–98.

Frederick, the elder brother of Alfred Tennyson, and a contributor to the famous *Poems by Two Brothers* (Alfred and Charles) in 1827, published these exalted stanzas in *Poems of the Day and Year*, 1895.

Iambic, 10. 10 10. 10 6. Unique.

MUSIC. DOWNSHIRE HILL was written by Martin Shaw for this hymn in *Songs of Praise* (1925).

TENBURY, by Heathcote Statham, also appeared first in *Songs of Praise* (1925).

Of these two tunes the first is slightly the easier for congregational singing, but both are excellently suited to the words, and the second is by no means difficult.

329 Turn back, O Man, forswear thy foolish ways. *Clifford Bax.*

Written by Mr. Bax for Mr. Holst, who composed a motet on the tune; and published with the music in the League of Arts' *Motherland Song Book* (1919). Mr. Bax's admirable words took the place of the previous texts written for the great melody in *E.H.* 114 and 352, and have become widely known through the wireless. He published it in his *Farewell my Muse* (1932), where he dates it 1916, and says, 'The regular structure of these verses and the large number of long monosyllables were necessitated by the form of the music.'

Iambic, 10 10. 10 10. 10, the metre of 'Abide with me' (437)—i.e. heroic couplets—with one additional line. Unique.

MUSIC. OLD 124TH is from the *Genevan Psalter* (1551), where it is set to Psalm 124. The present form of the melody is that found in the English psalters, while the harmony has been adapted by Martin Shaw from W. Parson's version in Day's *Whole Book of Psalmes* (1563). The English differs from the French form of the tune in lines 2 and 3, which in the latter are as follows:

The tune, in its present form, has always been popular in England among the Nonconformist bodies, and has remained one of the best known of the Genevan tunes. It was sung as a hymn of triumph and thanksgiving by the Genevans on the repulse of the Duke of Savoy, in December 1602, an event which has been familiarized to English readers by Stanley Weyman's novel *The Long Night*.

Part V

SPECIAL OCCASIONS

The provision of hymns for special occasions has been sometimes overdone: there are hundreds of 'General' hymns that are suitable for Bible classes or for colleges, while to provide one or two for 'working men', as if the other hymns were for the *bourgeoisie*, is very odd indeed. We found that many hymns, such as nearly all those for occasions of thanksgiving, were more usefully placed in other parts of the book; and we have endeavoured to avoid the lure that caused George Wither to publish hymns (not, however, without prefatory notes spiced with sly humour) for 'a House-warming', 'A Hymn whilst we are washing', and 'when slandered'; and special ones 'For Members of Parliament', 'For Artists', 'For Lovers', 'For a Physician', 'For a Shepherd', 'For a Musician who is more out of Order than his Instrument', and 'For a Widow delivered from a troublesome Yoke-Fellow'. Yet there do seem to remain a few classes and a few occasions for which hymns can be used that are not otherwise appropriate.

ABSENT FRIENDS

330 Father all-seeing, friend of all creation. *Maud Bell.*

Written by Miss Bell for our book to carry another Sapphic tune, the problem always being to find enough texts for the number of the finest tunes that exist in this metre. Also to provide a new hymn for Absent Friends. It was felt that the phrase 'anxious prayer' in the old hymn was difficult to defend, and the representatives of the author of that hymn were not willing to consent to an alteration.

Sapphic, 11 11. 11 5.

MUSIC. DIVA SERVATRIX is a Bayeux 'church melody' (see 28 and 262 (ii)).

ALMSGIVING

331 Thine are all the gifts, O God. *J. G. Whittier*, 1807–92.

Written for the anniversary of the Children's Mission, Boston, 1878, and included in Horder's *Congregational Hymns* (1884). Whittier had been fired as a child by poetry when a Quaker preacher stayed at the farm and read aloud some of Burns's lyrics. He borrowed the book, and saw what poetry was; so he learnt the art which he devoted, all his life, to God's service.

Trochaic, 7 5. 7 5. This simple metre occurs nowhere else in the book.

MUSIC. ST. AIDAN was written by Herbert Popple for this hymn in *Songs of Praise* (1931): an ingenuous tune with an affective cadence.

332 We give thee but thine own. *Bishop W. W. How*, 1823–97.

The hymns of 'The Poor Man's Bishop' are true to the character of that most lovable, trustful, and robust Christian: they are practical, and they fulfil his own ideal when he said, 'A good hymn should be like a good prayer—simple, real, earnest, and reverent'. This was written in 1858, and published in *Psalms and Hymns* (by Morrell and How, 1864). It had no doxology: such an end really spoils the fine conclusion. Next to 'For all the saints', it is the most widely used of his hymns. 'We give thee but thine own', wrote Dr. George Matheson, 'sounds the real humanitarian note to the fatherless and widows. Hymnology is feeble and ineffective when it ignores the humanitarian side of religion.'

But for this the humanitarian side would have been ignored in the older hymnals, where almsgiving is recommended either as a tribute, for instance,

Debt we may not choose but pay,

in Mrs. Alderson's hymn 'Lord of glory' (1864), or an act of homage and reparation, as in Monsell's very curious 80 lines (under the heading 'Offertory') in *Church Hymns* (1871), beginning 'Holy off'rings, rich and rare' (1867), or frankly as an investment, as in Bishop Wordsworth's 'O Lord of heaven' (1863):

(*mf*) Whatever, Lord, we lend to Thee
(*crescendo*) Repaid a thousandfold will be;
(*fortissimo*) Then gladly will we lend to Thee,
Who givest all.

Our much abused capitalist system is normally content with repayment at par.

S.M.

MUSIC. WINDERMERE, by Sir Arthur Somervell, appeared, set to this hymn, in the *English Hymnal* (1906), being composed especially for that book.

ASSEMBLY AND DISMISSAL

333 Lord, behold us with thy blessing. *H. J. Buckoll*, 1803–71.

Julian describes four hymns beginning 'Lord, dismiss us with thy blessing', dated *c.* 1773, 1807, 1850, and this by Buckoll, which is also 1850, having been included at that date in the *Psalms and Hymns* for Rugby School, where he was a master. He added the first part, 'Lord, behold us with thy blessing', for the beginning of term; and these two parts passed into most school hymnals. We follow the *English Hymnal* in selecting from each part two verses, omitting, e.g. in Part II, those beginning 'Bless thou all our days of leisure', and 'By thy kindly influence cherish'.

Trochaic, 8 7. 8 7. 8 7.

MUSIC. CALVARY, by S. Stanley, was originally set to the hymn, 'Hark the voice of love and mercy', in his *Twenty-four Tunes* (*c.* 1800). It is a typical example of the kind of tune popularized by the Methodists during the 18th century; it is rather weakened by the similarity of the modulation at the end of ll. 2 and 4, but the last two lines are very characteristic.

DISMISSAL, by W. L. Viner, appeared in Flood's *Harmonist* (1845), set to the present hymn, with which it has ever since been associated. It is in much the same idiom as the previous tune.

FAREWELL

334 God be with you till we meet again. *J. E. Rankin*, 1828–1904.

Dr. Rankin stated that this was not written for any special occasion, but to provide a Christian Good-bye on the etymology of 'God be wi' ye'. First sung at his own First Congregational Church, Washington, in 1882, it was popularized in *Sacred Songs and Solos* ('Moody and Sankey'), which by 1888 consisted of 750 hymns (in 1873 there were only 24 pages; by 1903 there were 1,200 hymns). Dr. Rankin, who was President of Howell University, Washington, stated, 'I wrote the first stanza, and sent it to two gentlemen for music. After receiving the music [by T. G. Tomer], which was revised by Dr. J. W. Bischoff . . . I wrote the other stanzas.' It had the refrain:

Till we meet, till we meet, till we meet
At Jesu's feet, till we meet, till we meet, till we meet,
Till we meet again.

This adscititious chorus was omitted in Horder's *Worship Song* (1905), as also in the *English Hymnal* and in the Presbyterian *Church Hymnary*.

Trochaic, 9 8. 8 9. Unique.

MUSIC. RANDOLPH, by R. Vaughan Williams, was composed for this hymn in the *English Hymnal* (1906). It is, as befits the words, an unsophisticated tune, very simple in rhythm and structure, being formed of two middle lines of inverted movement, with the 4th line a repeat of the 1st, thus following the form of the poem. In sentiment, as in build, the melody accords perfectly with the poem.

GREETING

335 O welcome in our midst. *S.P.B.G.*

Written in collaboration with the composer for a welcome to Dr. Maude Royden, and published a few months after in *Songs of Praise for Boys and Girls* (1 Jan. 1930).

Iambic, 6 6. 4 4 6; with refrain, dactylic, 5 5. trochaic, 7. Unique.

MUSIC. ROYDEN was composed by Martin Shaw for this hymn in *Songs of Praise for Boys and Girls* (1930). It is an appropriately cheerful and animated tune, with a straightforward melody and rhythm, easily learned by children, and enjoyable to sing.

FOR THOSE AT SEA

336 Eternal Father, strong to save. *W. Whiting*, 1825–78.

Written in 1860, the original text is to be found in the *Anglican Hymn Book* (1868); it began, 'O thou who bidd'st the ocean deep'. As various compilers felt rightly that it needed improvement, two more versions came into use, that of *Hymns Ancient and Modern* (1861), and that, revised by the author, in the Appendix to the S.P.C.K. *Psalms and Hymns* (1869). This last was repeated in the S.P.C.K. *Church Hymns* (1871), and, being the official version, is used by us. The hymn filled a conspicuous gap; for, curiously enough, seafarers were forgotten in the old books. 'It is much used', wrote Sir Evelyn Wood, 'by those at sea, and, when the wind blows hard, by those on land.' Sometimes the choir used to ask for it when the wind provided no justification. But our music editors have removed that temptation.

Iambic, 8 8. 8 8. 8 8.

MUSIC. LODSWORTH is an arrangement by R. Vaughan Williams of an English traditional melody noted by W. Percy Merrick, in 1900, from the singing of Henry Hills of Lodsworth in Sussex. The present arrangement appeared in the *English Hymnal* (1906), the original air being first printed in the *Folk-Song Society Journal* (vol. i, 1901).

337 Lord, in the hollow of thy hand. *G. W. Briggs.*

The author is an old navy chaplain, and contributed this to the original *Songs of Praise* (1925).

L.M.

MUSIC. CANNONS, by G. F. Handel, was originally set to Charles Wesley's hymn, 'Sinners, obey the Gospel word'. It is one of the three tunes which Handel composed for hymns by Wesley. The manuscript of these is in the Fitzwilliam Museum, Cambridge, and they remained unpublished until their discovery by Samuel Wesley in 1826 (cf. 632). It is a good solid tune, but not otherwise very characteristic of the composer.

TRURO was set to the hymn 'Now to the Lord a noble song' in *Psalmodia Evangelica: A Collection of Psalms and Hymns in Three Parts for Public Worship, by Thos. Williams* (2 vols., 1789). It has been attributed to Dr. Burney, but is anonymous in the above and in subsequent collections, and there appear to be no good grounds for the attribution, while the tune itself, in a familiar 18th-century idiom, has no definite traits which would justify any ascription on internal evidence. It is, itself, a fine springing tune, and an excellent specimen of its type.

SOCIETIES, ETC.

338 Father of men, in whom are one.

H. C. Shuttleworth, 1850–1900.

Shuttleworth, who was a follower of Maurice and Kingsley and a leader of the Christian Socialist movement in the days of the Guild of St. Matthew, had been a minor canon of St. Paul's; and, a keen musician, he wrote many carols and hymns. This appeared in the St. Nicholas Cole Abbey *Hymnal Appendix*, 1897, and, with music by the author, in the *Church Monthly* (1898). It was written for Friendly Societies, but is a useful and appropriate hymn for many occasions of a more general character.

Iambic, 8 8 8. D. Occurs also in 242.

MUSIC. EXETER, by William Jackson (of Exeter), appeared in Boyd's *Select Collection of Psalm and Hymn Tunes, &c.* (1793). In Rippon's *Selection of Tunes, &c.* (1791) there is another tune by Jackson, also called 'Exeter', but it is in triple time, and a totally different melody in every way. The present is a cheerfully robust tune, with an animated rhythm, in the 'new style' favoured by the Methodists and Wesleyans during the 18th century, which Lampe, Milgrove, and others did much to foster.

339 Son of God, eternal Saviour. *S. C. Lowry*, 1855–1932.

Written in 1893, and included in the magazine, *Goodwill* (Feb. 1894). At our request, Mr. Lowry altered 'birth incarnate' in vv. 1 and 5 to 'birth among us', and in ver. 4, 'Ah! the past is dark behind us' to 'Hush the storm of strife and passion'.

Trochaic, 8 7. 8 7. D.

MUSIC. YN Y GLYN, by David Evans, was first published in *Cymru* (1921), as a memorial tune to Mr. John Thomas, a prominent Welsh amateur musician, set to words, 'Cilio mae fy hen gyfeillion', by Dyfed the Archdruid. It is a dignified, resolute melody with something of the style and spirit of the traditional Welsh hymn-tunes, as befits its original purpose.

FRIENDLY AND TEMPERANCE SOCIETIES

340 Father, who on man dost shower. *E.H.*

Written for the *English Hymnal* (1906) by the editor, reprinted in the *Church Hymnary* (1924), and here slightly altered. The tune 'Quem pastores', for which it was originally composed, being felt to be too pastoral for this subject, that tune is now left to 540 alone.

Trochaic, 8 8. 8 7. Occurs also in 540.

MUSIC. CHARING, by S. L. Russell, was written for this hymn in the enlarged *Songs of Praise* (1931). It is a straightforward tune which derives a robust directness from the largely pentatonic nature of its melodic line.

MEDICAL GATHERINGS AND HEALTH SOCIETIES

341 Quick sympathy, hands that brought health. *A. G.*

Written for a beautiful and unusual tune, and to the theme of physicians and nurses as the helpers of the divine *vis medicatrix naturae*.

Anapaestic, 8 9. 8 8. D., the rhymes interlace thus—*abacdbdc*. Unique.

MUSIC. SION is an arrangement by Martin Shaw of a melody from Mason's *A Companion to the Wesleyan Hymnbook, &c.* (London, 1847), where it is set to the hymn 'All glory to God in the sky'. It is in the tradition of the Wesleyan and Methodist tunes introduced during the 18th century; in triple time, with a strongly marked pulse, it owes something also to contemporary popular songs.

MOTHERS

342 Lord of life, who once wast cradled. *W. Charter Piggott.*

Mr. Charter Piggott, a member of our committee, was asked by his colleagues to write a good wholesome modern hymn for Mothers, a task which, as we hope the reader will agree, he has admirably fulfilled.

Trochaic, 8 7. 8 7. 8 7.

MUSIC. ST. THOMAS seems to have come into use in Roman Catholic churches in England about the same period as 'Adeste Fideles', but nothing definite has yet been discovered as to its composer or source. It is found in *An Essay on the Church Plain Chant* (1782), in Webbe's *Collection of Motetts, &c.* (1792), and in the Wade manuscript at Stonyhurst College (1751) (see 78). In all of these the melody is virtually the same as the present one, and is set to the Hymn at Benediction 'Tantum ergo sacramentum'. A slightly different form appeared in Gardiner's *Sacred Melodies* (vol. ii, 1815), where it is headed 'Subject from the Missal Book', and set to the hymn 'Lord, dismiss us with thy blessing', and this version is to be found in later collections under the names 'Dismission' and 'Augustine'.

The present form is also known by the name 'Holywood', and is now one of the best known of all hymn-tunes.

SONGS FOR CAMPS AND MEETINGS OF BOYS AND GIRLS

343 Lord God, from whom all life.

E. A. Burroughs, Bishop of Ripon.

Written by Dr. Burroughs in 1906 for schoolboy camps. Linc 7 of ver. 2 is adapted from Tennyson's song, 'Blow, bugle, blow!' in *The Princess*.

D.S.M.

MUSIC. MILITES is an adaptation of a tune in Wesley's *A Collection of Tunes Set to music as they are commonly sung at the Foundery* (1742). This famous collection was the first of the Methodist hymn-books, and took its name from the meeting-house which John Wesley had founded on the ruins of a cannon-foundry in Moorfields; it introduced many German chorales to English worship, and also contained several of the newer psalm-tunes, such as 'Burford' and 'Hanover', but not many of the more popular tunes which later became specifically connected with the movement, though the present melody may be regarded as one of the precursors of these, in its animated march-like rhythm, and its general lack of austerity.

344 Lord, who didst send, by two and two before thee.

Steuart Wilson.

Written for our book, to provide a hymn suitable for Girl Guides, but suitable also for all of either sex to whom any work of guidance is committed.

Trochaic, 11 10. 11 10.

MUSIC. SCHOOL HOUSE was written by Thomas Wood especially for 'O Son of Man' (611) on the occasion of a visit by the author, Frank Fletcher, to the school at which Dr. Thomas Wood was music master. It is a spirited tune, with an easy four-square rhythm, and a straightforward, 'natural' melody.

345 Working together. *S.P*

Written, in collaboration with the composer, for our book, to provide a hymn for Boy Scouts, the members of Boys' Brigades, and others.

Dactylic and anapaestic, 5 4. 5 4. 3 7. 5 7 5. and refrain. Unique.

MUSIC. WORKING, by Martin Shaw, appeared first in sheet form as a unison song *Working together* (1930), to the present words. It is a stirring march tune, with a vivacious, inspiriting rhythm, very easy and enjoyable to sing.

TEACHERS

346 Lord, from whose hand we take our charge.

W. Charter Piggott.

Like 342, this was written for us; and it is a worthy companion to the hymn for Mothers, for whom indeed it is suitable, as well as for Teachers.

Iambic, 8 8. 8 8. 8 8.

MUSIC. LAMBETH, by S. Akeroyde, appeared in Henry Playford's *The Divine Companion, or David's Harp New Tun'd, &c.* (1701), where it is headed 'A Hymn for Good Friday set by Mr Akeroyde'. The melody is as at present except that the opening bar runs:

TIMES OF STRESS OR TROUBLE

347 Father, to thee we look in all our sorrow.

F. L. Hosmer, 1840–1929.

Written by him in 1881, on the death of a member of his congregation, and published in his *Thought of God* (1st Series, 1885).

Iambic, 11 10. 11 10.

MUSIC. L'OMNIPOTENT was composed or adapted by L. Bourgeois for Psalm 110 in the *Genevan Psalter* of 1551, replacing the melody formerly used for it. In the Scottish Psalter of 1564 it was set, with some alterations, to a version of the psalm by John Craig. It is a firm, satisfactory melody, a good average example of the Genevan tunes.

348 In this world, the Isle of Dreams. *Robert Herrick*, 1591–1674.

From *Noble Numbers* (1647), and, so far as we know, not used before as a hymn.

Herrick, a country parson in Devonshire, was thus cut off from the Cavalier poets with whom he had so much in common. His sacred poems have never taken hold as have those by Herbert and Crashaw, his love poems are exquisite creations that do not go very deep; but he was a devout lover of nature, and a new and consummate artist; and, as Palgrave says, the bulk and sustained quality of his work, with the variety of his artistic achievement, entitle him to the foremost place among English lyrical poets before the great roll of modern names begins with Robert Burns.

Trochaic, 7 7. 7 3. Occurs also, rather unexpectedly, in 467, 'Christian, seek not yet repose'.

MUSIC. BROOKEND was composed by Gustav Holst especially for *Songs of Praise*. It is a compact little tune, which gains a certain individual colouring from the rising fourths in the 1st and 3rd lines.

349 Lord of our life, and God of our salvation.

P. Pusey,‡ 1799–1855. *Based on* Christe du Beistand,
M. von Löwenstern, 1594–1648.

Christe, du Beistand deiner Kreuzgemeine,
Eile, mit Hülf und Rettung uns erscheine,
Steure den Feinden, ihre Blutgerichte
Mache zu nichte, mache zu nichte!

Matthäus Apelles von Löwenstern wrote a 'Sapphic ode. For spiritual and temporal peace', in 1644. On this Philip Pusey based the hymn (in 1834) which he contributed to Reinagle's *Psalms and Hymn Tunes* in 1840. It has only a general resemblance to the original, and has the caesura in the wrong place for a Sapphic ('Lord of our life, | and God of our salvation'). Philip Pusey wrote in a letter to his famous brother: 'It refers to the state of the Church, that is to say, of the Church of England, in 1834—assailed from without, enfeebled and distracted within, but on the eve of a great awakening.' His friends were soon to show what being 'distracted within' could be like. For the rest, there has seldom been a period which the voice of the Jeremiahs has not pronounced to be one of abnormal weakness and peril. It is certain that in 1834 the Church had a deeper hold on the people of England than now; and church-going was wellnigh universal, except in some places where a new proletariat had grown up. Great efforts had been made to meet this population problem as early as 1818, when the Speech from the Throne preluded a grant of a million pounds; by the year of Pusey's complaint, over six million had been raised. The 'enfeebled Church' was a myth, the 'hungry billows' were not curling. And the extraordinary fact is that in the very year before, the greatest religious triumph in this Empire—the greatest moral event surely in all Christian history—had happened: slavery was abolished by the Great Emancipation Act. Strangely enough, that year had also been the year of the chief Factory Act, another Christian victory, which rescued children and women from oppression. The first Government grant to national education was also made in 1833; and in that year the New Ecclesiastical Commission had already begun the reform of evils that had survived the Reformation. In that very year also Parliament had opened India to Christian Missionary activity.

So much for the envenomed darts! And all this makes us wonder whether we have ever the right to say, 'Grant us thy help till backward they are driven'. Our human judgments are so blind that it is wise to listen to a voice that says, 'Judge not'.

Sapphic feet, but wrongly divided, 11 11 11. 5.

MUSIC. CHRISTE DU BEISTAND is Löwenstern's original melody to his own words in *Geistliche Kirchen und Hauss-Musik* (Breslau 1644), where it is no. 17 of the 'Symbola und Oden'. The melody is as at present except for one or two slight alterations of rhythm.

ISTE CONFESSOR (ROUEN) is a Rouen 'church melody' (see 28). The alternative version (descant) by Harvey Grace was written especially for the enlarged *Songs of Praise* (1931).

THANKSGIVING

350 Now thank we all our God.

M. Rinkart, 1586–1649. *Tr. C. Winkworth.*

Nun danket alle Gott
  Mit Herzen, Mund, und Händen,
Der grosse Dinge tut
  An uns und allen Enden;
Der uns von Mutterleib
Und Kindesbeinen an
Unzählig viel zu gut
Bis hieher hat getan.

'The German *Te Deum*' was composed by Martin Rinkart, during the horrors of the Thirty Years War, when his little town of Eilenburg in Saxony was sacked once by the Austrians and twice by the Swedes. Doubtless it was in the 1st edition (1636) of his *Jesu Herz-Buchlein*; for it is in the extant edition of 1663, where it is entitled 'Grace', *Tisch-Gebetlein.* It is also in J. Crüger's *Praxis* (1648). The story connecting it with the Peace of Westphalia (1648), which closed the war, is therefore untrue. But Rinkart had been a hero in his little town of Eilenburg in Saxony. Pestilence and famine followed as usual in the wake of war: during the plague he is said to have buried 4,480 persons. Then came the Swedish army, demanding 30,000 thalers. Rinkart gathered his flock and said, 'Come, my children; we can find no mercy with men: let us take refuge with God'. His prayers and his labours availed, and the tribute was reduced, first to 8,000 and then to 2,000 thalers only. The Lutheran Bible includes the Apocrypha; and *Nun danket* is founded on Ecclesiasticus l: 22–4, the 3rd verse being in the original a paraphrase of the *Gloria Patri.* Miss Winkworth's translation appeared first in her *Lyra Germanica* (2nd series, 1858), and later in her *Chorale Book for England* (1863). The hymn has of course been sung at innumerable great public occasions, in Germany and England and America.

Iambic, 6 7. 6 7. 6 6. 6 6.

MUSIC. NUN DANKET is from J. Crüger's *Praxis Pietatis Melica* (see 24), where it is set to the German original of the present words as follows:

The tune, which is probably by Crüger himself, is found with the hymn in almost all German collections down to the present day, with slight modifications of form; that here given is the one in general use to-day, the arrangement being an adaptation to four parts of Mendelssohn's six-part setting in his *Lobgesang*.

The alternative version (descant) by Geoffrey Shaw appeared in the *Descant Hymn-Tune Book* (Book I, 1925).

The tune is sometimes attributed to Rinkart himself, and a picturesque story describes the simultaneous origin of words and melody during the Thirty Years War; there seems, however, to be no reason for the ascription except the velleities of romance. It has now become a recognized hymn of thanksgiving in national crises.

351 O praise ye the Lord! *Sir H. W. Baker*, 1821–77.

This paraphrase of Psalm 150 in a very useful musical metre, was written for the 1875 edition of *Hymns Ancient and Modern*, of which Baker was the editor.

Iambic, 5 5. 5 5. 6 5. 6 5. Occurs also in 618.

MUSIC. LAUDATE DOMINUM, by H. J. Gauntlett, appeared in *Hymns Ancient and Modern* (revised edition 1875), where it was set to the hymn 'O worship the King'. The tune strongly resembles 'Houghton' by the same composer, and both give the impression of having been formed on the model of 'Hanover' (618); but, whatever its source may have been, it is itself an energetic, candid tune, of simple and solid construction.

PART VI

FOR CHILDREN

THE 18th century had not arrived at the understanding of children: indeed the rudiments of child psychology only begin to appear in hymns towards the end of the 19th. Dr. Watts has suffered for this, often being remembered, not as the fine poet he was, but as a priggish old pedagogue, scowling uncomprehendingly at the young. He certainly could rub it in:

My thoughts on awful subjects roll,
 Damnation and the dead:
What horrors seize the guilty soul
 Upon a dying bed!

Then swift and dreadful she descends
 Down to the fiery coast,
Amongst abominable fiends,
 Herself a frightful ghost.

There endless crowds of sinners lie,
 And darkness makes their chains:
Tortured with keen despair they cry,
 Yet wait for fiercer pains.

Not all their anguish and their blood
 For their old guilt atones,
Nor the compassion of a God
 Shall hearken to their groans.

Yet Mr. W. T. Brooke (Julian's *Dictionary*, p. 220) assures us that 'Watts is mild compared with some contemporary theologians'. An aged lady assured a friend of ours that she had to learn these verses as a child. But the more subtle horror of Mrs. Alexander's hymn, written as late as 1848, is almost as bad in another way:

Within the churchyard, side by side,
 Are many long low graves . . .
Full many a little Christian child,
 Woman, and man, lies there . . .
They cannot hear our footsteps come,
 They do not see us pass . . .
They cannot rise and come to Church
(*dim*) With us, for they are dead.

This was in her *Hymns for Little Children*. Of course, the idea was to frighten children into being good. The excellent Dr. Watts has left it on record that he did not really believe the things he often wrote about hell. But his *Divine and Moral Songs for Children* (1715) must needs end everything with an improving tag. So with the lines, as famous as a proverb:

How doth the little busy bee
  Improve each shining hour,
And gather honey all the day
  From ev'ry opening flower.

How skilfully she builds her cell!
  How neat she spreads her wax!
And labours hard to store it well
  With the sweet food she makes.

In works of labour and of skill
  I would be busy too;
For Satan finds some mischief still
  For idle hands to do.

There is a moral, too, but a gentle one, to another famous lyric of his. They are all in danger of being forgotten except for a line or two, generally misquoted. Watts's books for children were the most popular text-books for religious education seventy years ago, just as there are folk still alive who can remember his *Logic* as a valued text-book at Oxford:

Let dogs delight to bark and bite,
  For God hath made them so;
Let bears and lions growl and fight,
  For 'tis their nature too.

But, children, you should never let
  Such angry passions rise;
Your little hands were never made
  To tear each other's eyes.

Let love through all your actions run,
  And all your words be mild,
Live like the blessed Virgin's Son,
  That sweet and lovely child.

Nowadays we note the story of the rude little boys and Elisha as an example of undeveloped ethical ideas. Not so Dr. Watts:

When children in their wanton play
  Served old Elisha so,
And bade the prophet go his way,
  'Go up, thou bald-head, go!'

God quickly stop'd their wicked breath
  And sent two raging bears,
That tore them limb from limb to death,
  With blood and groans and tears!

The minatory note is not absent either from the Wesleys' *Hymns for*

Children (1763), and the attempt to prevent them being childlike continues:

Let heathenish boys
In their pastimes rejoice,
  And be foolishly happy in play;
Overstocked if they are,
We have nothing to spare,
  Not a moment to trifle away.

'Suffer the little children!' In few things is the uniqueness of Jesus Christ more conspicuously revealed. The ancients were not interested in children, and there is nothing in their literature that shows any understanding or love; but what is more astonishing is that there is nothing in Christian literature either, until quite modern times. There is a flash of rare insight in Wesley's 'Gentle Jesus' (356) from the same book, but little else; and lines like this (for children) abound:

Come, Holy Ghost, thy grace impart,
  Reveal thy dying Deity.

While for lads of about 16 an earlier hymn-book, attractively called *War with the Devil* (1676), matter like this had been considered suitable:

The blessed Virgin's hallowed womb
  Received the Godhead from on high!
He left for that contracted Room
  The chrystal palace of the sky!
    His heavenly hoast,
    In wonder lost,
With silent harps admiring stood;
    Till Gabriel's tongue
    Divinely sung
The triumphs of a Saviour's Blood.

Indeed a glance at much later books will reveal the same inability to understand child-nature. Mrs. Carey-Brock's *The Children's Hymn Book* (1881) was the leading book in the last century, published by the S.P.C.K. and revised by Bishops Walsham How and Oxenden and by John Ellerton; yet it expects children to sing 'Just as I am, poor, wretched, blind', and much more introspective meditation of like nature. And not many collections for the young even in the present century are free from quantities of equally unsuitable matter.

Even accomplished versifiers like Dr. Neale were not at their best with children. He wrote a hymn, 'Christian children, hear me', for the *Churchman's Companion*, which contained the lines,

How elect your
Architecture.

This was omitted when the hymn was toned down for the *People's*

Hymnal (edited by Dr. R. F. Littledale in 1867); but the following couplets can still be culled from it (350):

He had many a fervent
Happy baby servant.

Many a baby martyr
Who rejoiced to barter.

Some day, some day, we too
Your bright home will flee to.

Lauded day by day be
Cyriac, victor baby.

Of course, it is not fair to blame a writer for not noticing that ribald men might twist his simple meaning, as in 'His watch . . . the little Levite kept'; but the ponderous phraseology of 'Hush'd was the evening hymn' and suchlike productions makes parody almost excusable. Such nursery directness as this, from Masters' *Hymns for Little Children* is at the other extreme, and perhaps is an unconscious reaction:

Waste not precious time in dressing;
Be alert, alive, awake!

The truth seems to be that our grandparents thought of children as troublesome creatures who had to be smacked and kept in their place, and that therefore they mishandled even serious themes, as for instance this typical verse of 1842 which still occurs in the *Church Hymnal* of 1917:

God is in heaven. Can he see
When I am doing wrong?
Yes, that he can! He looks at me
All day and all night long.

William Blake seems to have been the first to adopt a different method with children—and Blake's ideas generally took a hundred years to win acceptance.

352 A little child on the earth has been born.

Old Flemish Carol. Tr. R. C. Trevelyan.

Mr. Trevelyan translated this old Flemish carol ('Er is een kindeken geboren op d'aard) for the *Oxford Book of Carols* (1928, no. 74). We would remind the reader at the beginning of this Part that the hymns and carols are for little children, hymns for older children being included among those for adults, since it is found in practice that there is very little distinction.

Irregular.

MUSIC. A LITTLE CHILD is the traditional Flemish melody to the original carol of which the above words are a translation. The present setting, by Professor Julius Röntgen, appeared in the *Oxford Book of Carols* (1928). It is an artless little tune, thoroughly in accord with the innocence of the words.

353 Away in a manger, no crib for a bed. *Anon.*

This pretty little song has been ascribed to Luther, although it is not to be traced in any of his works, and nothing less like the hymns of that pioneer can well be imagined.

Anapaestic, 11 11. 11 11.

MUSIC. CRADLE SONG was composed for this hymn by W. J. Kirkpatrick, in an American book towards the end of last century; but the exact date and title of this work cannot be ascertained. It is here newly arranged by R. Vaughan Williams. Kirkpatrick assisted in the compilation of some fifty collections of hymn-tunes, to which, and to others, he contributed many melodies of his own. The present is a good example of his unsophisticated style.

354 Daisies are our silver. *Jan Struther.*

Written for our book.

Trochaic, 6 5. 6 5.

MUSIC. GLENFINLAS, by K. G. Finlay, appeared in *Songs of Praise* (1925), set to 'Summer suns are glowing'. It is an excellent little pentatonic tune, well within the grasp of quite young children.

355 Father, we thank thee for the night. *Rebecca J. Weston.*

Rebecca Weston has not been traced: this hymn seems to be her only known work: it appeared in *The Tonic Sol-fa Course* (O. Ditson & Co.) to a tune by the editor of that book, the Rev. D. Batchellor, and the poem may have been written for that collection.

L.M.

MUSIC. WAINWRIGHT, by Richard Wainwright, comes from *A Collection of Hymns, with appropriate Symphonies and Accompaniments, as originally composed for the Children of the Liverpool Blue Coat Hospital* (*c.* 1790). There it is set to the hymn, 'My God, and is thy table spread', and named 'Newmarket'. The original form of the 1st line is as follows:

but the present regularity of rhythm is more suited to childish capacities.

356 Gentle Jesus, meek and mild. *C. Wesley*, 1707–88.

When Charles Wesley published his *Hymns for Children* (1763) he had already written many such, which were scattered through other works. A second edition appeared in 1767, with the words *And Others of Riper Years* added to the title. The work was never popular, and with the exception of 'Gentle Jesus', contains hardly a hymn known to modern collections outside the Wesleyan Methodist Church. John Wesley, in a Preface of 1790, wrote:

'There are two ways of writing or speaking to children: the one is, to let ourselves down to them; the other, to lift them up to us. Dr. Watts has wrote in the former way, and has succeeded admirably well, speaking to children as children, and leaving them as he found them [!]. The following hymns are written on the other plan; they contain strong and manly sense, yet expressed in such plain and easy language, as even children may understand. But when they do understand them, they will be children no longer, only in years and stature.'

One feels that Dr. Watts had all the same been more successful with his 'I thank the goodness and the grace', and ' 'Tis the voice of the sluggard'. Wesley's surviving children's hymn has, however, been learnt at their mother's knee by all succeeding generations of children. The various forms in use are selected from 14 verses; for 'Gentle Jesus' had seven verses, and 'Lamb of God' had the same number.

Mr. John P. Gough used to tell a story of the search for unfortunate children. A visitor found a ladder pushed through the ceiling of an empty room; it led into an attic; at the corner he saw a boy of about 10, huddled on some shavings. He drew from the terrified little creature the story that his mother was dead, that he had thieved for his father until he went to a mission school and was told that stealing was wrong. So he had refused to steal; and his father had covered him with bruises. Then he said, 'Shall I sing you a little hymn?' and he sang, 'Gentle Jesus', and 'Fain I would to thee be brought'. When the visitor came back a little later to take the child away, the ragged little body lay quietly on the shavings. 'Suffer me to come to thee' had been fulfilled.

Trochaic, 7 7. 7 7.

MUSIC. GENTLE JESUS was composed for this hymn by Martin Shaw, in *Additional Tunes and Settings in use at St. Mary's, Primrose Hill* (1915). It is an aptly simple tune, very easily learned by small children.

357 God my Father, loving me. *G. W. Briggs.*

Written for *Songs of Praise for Boys and Girls* (53), 1930.

Trochaic, 7 7. 7 7.

MUSIC. VIENNA, by J. H. Knecht, appeared in his and J. F. Christmann's *Vollständige Sammlung . . . vierstimmiger choral-melodien für das neue Wirtembergische Landgesangbuch, &c.* (Stuttgart, 1799), where it is set to 'Ohne Rast und unverweilt'. The melody is as at present, except that the 2nd note of the 3rd line is flattened. The present version, however, seems the better, as the other introduces a touch of sophistication, very slight perhaps, but inappropriate to the clarity of the rest of the tune.

358 God who made the earth. *Sarah Betts Rhodes* (1870).

Written by Mrs. Rhodes, *née* Bradshaw, the wife of a Sheffield merchant, for the Sheffield Sunday School Festival, 1870; printed in the *Methodist Sunday School Hymn Book* (1879).

Trochaic and iambic, 5 6. 6 4. Unique.

MUSIC. PLATT'S LANE was composed by Miss Evelyn Sharpe for this hymn in *Songs of Praise for Boys and Girls* (1930). It is an easy, unaffected tune, with a lack of finality about the close which aptly illustrates the words.

359 God whose name is love. *Florence Hoatson.*

The words were specially written by Miss Hoatson for the tune, at the request of Mr. Carey Bonner for his *Child Songs*, 1908 (no. 139).

Trochaic, 5 5. 5 5. Unique.

MUSIC. HASLEMERE is an arrangement, by Martin Shaw, of a tune which is found in John Curwen's *Songs and Tunes for Education* (1861), where it is set to the words 'Brightly glows the day, night has fled away', and is headed 'German'. It appeared to the present words in *Child Songs* (vol. i, 1908), edited by Mr. Carey Bonner, who then gave it its present name, 'Haslemere', as he was at that time spending a holiday there, and headed it 'German Air'. The German original has not been identified. Internal evidence suggests that it is a traditional cradle song or 'nursery' air, which was heard by John Curwen during his travels in Germany; he introduced many German tunes in his song books, and possibly the present melody was a popular oral one, which had not before been noted in print.

360 Hark! a hundred notes are swelling. *G. W. Briggs.*

Written for *Songs of Praise for Boys and Girls* (12), 1930. The words and tune are by the same writer, as in 194, 243, 572.

Trochaic, 8 3. 8 3. 7 7. 8 7. Unique.

MUSIC. SPRINGTIME was composed by G. W. Briggs for his words. The tune is rather more elaborate than most of those in this section, but, owing to the recurrence of the 2nd bar, not difficult for children to learn and remember.

361 I love God's tiny creatures. *G. W. Briggs.*

Written for *Songs of Praise for Boys and Girls* (59), 1930.

D.C.M.

MUSIC. BILSDALE was composed by Gordon Slater especially for the enlarged *Songs of Praise* (1931). This is a pleasant but comparatively complex tune, suitable rather for older children than for classes of the very young.

362 In another land and time. *Eleanor Smith.*†

This hymn, by an American author, has not been traced. The word 'little' has been so overworked in children's hymns that we have reduced its use as much as possible: here we have taken out the word before 'baby'.

Trochaic, 7 7. 7 7. It is noticeable how many hymns for children are trochaic.

MUSIC. FARNABY is adapted from an English traditional melody by R. Vaughan Williams, and appeared in the *English Hymnal* (1906).

363 Jesus, friend of little children. *Walter J. Mathams.*

Composed at 24 Chalmers St., Edinburgh, in May 1882, at the request of the Psalms and Hymns Committee of the Baptist Union, for their *Psalms and Hymns for School and Home*. Since then it has appeared in many books (often, as here, in a selection only), British, American, and in the Dominions. It has been done into Welsh, and is a great favourite with the children of the Congo and the west coast of Africa.

Trochaic, 8 5. 8 3. Unique.

MUSIC. WESTRIDGE was composed by Martin Shaw for *Songs of Praise for Boys and Girls* (1930). It is a straightforward tune, easily mastered by children of all ages.

364 Jesus, tender shepherd, hear me. *Mrs. Mary Duncan*, 1814–40.

Written in 1839, printed in the *Memoir*, by her mother, Mrs. Lundie, 1841. In 1842 all the hymns she had made three years before were published as *Hymns for my Children*. Mrs. Duncan, who lived in the Scottish country parish of Cleish, exercised an extraordinary fascination on all who met her, through her fine intellect and lovable character. 'If', wrote Duncan Campbell, 'the Memoir of M'Cheyne was one of the "aids to the devout life" of Scotland in the last generation, the Memoir of Mary Lundie Duncan was another, unfolding as it did the aspirations of a soul so lofty and pure.'

Trochaic, 8 7. 8 7.

MUSIC. SHIPSTON is an arrangement, from the collection of Miss L. E. Broadwood, of the air of a Warwickshire ballad, and appeared in the *English Hymnal* (1906).

365 Little drops of water. *Mrs. J. A. Carney*† (1845).

This tiny hymn has led to some controversy and prolonged research. The authorship was claimed for Dr. Ebenezer C. Brewer, who wrote a 'Little Drops of Water' in 1848; but it was at last discovered that the real text was published by Mrs. Carney in the Boston Primary School Reader (1845). Brewer had merely taken—in fact he had stolen—Mrs. Carney's idea and her 1st verse, 'adding thereto four inferior verses of his own'. By a fortunate chance the hymn first got to England through a book published in Manchester, 1855, which had copied Mrs. Carney's proper version from a reprint in the *American Juvenile Magazine*. Bishop Bickersteth added a last verse about angels to the reprint in the *Hymnal Companion* (1876), but this carried on the proper text: he indexed it as by Brewer, but unconsciously he killed Brewer's copy of it, which had been gaining ground. Thring, in the *Church of England Hymn Book* (1880–2), added two more verses about angels 'in the sky', and a doxology. All this makes one feel that it is very difficult to write a good short hymn, and that the forgotten primary-school teacher had something like an inspiration.

A few alterations do occur, however, in most books: we have changed 'heathen' to 'other', omitting the original 2nd and 4th verses, and adding a new doxology. The original text (but with another doxology added) is in *E.H.* 600.

Trochaic, 6 5. 6 5.

MUSIC. CAMBER was composed by Martin Shaw especially for this hymn in the enlarged *Songs of Praise* (1931). It is a gentle, fluent little tune with an attractive interchange of accent in the last two lines.

366 Loving Shepherd of thy sheep. *Jane E. Leeson*, 1807–82.

From her *Hymns and Scenes of Childhood* (1842), in three verses of eight lines. The verse beginning 'Bought with blood' is generally omitted.

Trochaic, 7 7. 7 7.

MUSIC. INNOCENTS is found in the *Parish Choir* (vol. iii, no. 59, Nov. 1850), under the name 'An Ancient Litany'. It has not been definitely traced to an earlier source, but in a manuscript collection of tunes by Joseph Smith of Halesowen, Birmingham, there is one bearing a close resemblance to 'Innocents', and it is possible, though by no means certain, that this is the original of the tune. Smith's melody is entitled 'The Sun', and the 1st and 3rd lines are virtually identical with the corresponding lines of the present tune; but, as the alternate lines differ, the resemblance is quite possibly a coincidence, since the phrase is not, in itself, of an unusual kind.

367 O dear and lovely Brother. *S.P.*

Written for *Songs of Praise for Boys and Girls* (72), 1930, by the editor. A little philosophy is wrapped up in ver. 2.

Iambic, 7 6. 7 6.

MUSIC. BULSTRODE was composed by Miss Evelyn Sharpe especially for this hymn in the enlarged *Songs of Praise* (1931). It is a serene little tune, with a slight suggestion of traditional folk-song.

368 Once in royal David's city. *Mrs. C. F. Alexander*, 1823–95.

Mrs. Alexander heard some god-children of hers telling one another how dreary the Church Catechism seemed to them. So she set herself to write verses which should make the meaning plain—'Do no sinful action' (the baptismal promise), 'All things bright' ('I believe in God'), 'There is a green hill' ('was crucified'), are three of these; and this is another ('And in Jesus Christ . . . born'). They appeared first in her *Hymns for Little Children* (1848).

Trochaic, 8 7. 8 7. 7 7.

MUSIC. IRBY, by H. J. Gauntlett, was written for this hymn in *Hymns for Little Children . . . Set to music with piano accompaniment, by H. J. Gauntlett* (1858), and has since become one of the best known children's hymn-tunes, always associated with these words.

369 Remember all the people. *P. Dearmer.*

Written at the request of the Church Missionary Society for their children's magazine, *The Round World*, and reprinted a few months later in *Songs of Praise for Boys and Girls* (1 Jan. 1930).

Iambic, 7 6. 7 6. D.

MUSIC. IN DER WIEGEN is from D. G. Corner's *Geistliche Nachtigal* (Vienna, 1649), where it is set to 'Ein kindlein in der Wiegen'. The present arrangement, by Martin Shaw, with a translation of the original carol, appeared in the *Oxford Book of Carols* (1928). As befits the original words, it is a most ingenuous tune, of the cradle-song type, and is evidently a traditional melody, considerably older than the above work.

370 Saviour, teach me, day by day. *Jane E. Leeson*, 1807–82.

Like 366, from Miss Leeson's *Hymns and Scenes of Childhood* (1842). The original 4 verses of 8 lines are here reduced to 4 verses of 4 lines.

Trochaic, 7 7. 7 7.

MUSIC. WHITE LADIES ASTON was composed by Sir Ivor Atkins especially for this hymn in the enlarged *Songs of Praise* (1931). It is a graceful, fluent tune, in slow triple time, very simple in structure, and easy to sing for children of any age.

371 Sing to the Lord the children's hymn.

R. S. Hawker of Morwenstow, 1803–75.

Robert Stephen Hawker spent his life in the then remote and wild Cornish village, for the children of which he wrote our hymn. The story of the parson-poet's work there is unique in the history of modern England. 'It was the work', said Mr. J. A. Noble, 'not of an ordinary parish priest, but of a missionary among wrecking, smuggling, superstitious savages, upon whom his influence was not simply meliorative and educational but radically transforming.'

From his *Poetical Works* (1879), in seven verses, three being here omitted.

C.M.

MUSIC. ST. HUGH is an arrangement, from the collection of Miss L. E. Broadwood, of the air sung to an English ballad on the legend of St. Hugh of Lincoln. It appeared in the *English Hymnal* (1906). It is a very cheerful, straightforward tune, with an attractive air of resoluteness.

372 The shepherds had an angel. *Christina Rossetti*, 1830–94.

In her *Poetical Works* (1904) this is entitled, 'A Christmas Carol. For my god-children', and dated 1856. It was included in the *Sunday School Hymnary* (1905).

Iambic, 7 6. 7 6. 7 6; and as often with this poet slightly irregular.

MUSIC. BERWICK STREET, by Martin Shaw, appeared in *Songs of Praise for Boys and Girls* (1930). It is a dainty tune, with a light, lively rhythm; suitable and appealing to quite young children.

373 The wise may bring their learning. *Anon.*

Entered as anonymous in the *Congregational Church Hymnal* (1887) and the *Hymnal Companion* (1890).

Iambic, 7 6. 7 6. D.

MUSIC. IN MEMORIAM was composed by Sir John Stainer for the hymn 'There's a friend for little children', in the following circumstances. The committee engaged on the music of *Hymns Ancient and Modern* (1875) were meeting at the Langham Hotel, London; and, when this hymn came up for consideration it was found that, though they had several tunes before them, none was satisfactory. It was suggested that a new tune might be written by one of the committee, and Sir Henry Baker proposed that Sir John Stainer should retire to Sir Henry's bedroom, and try what he could do. Sir John complied with the suggestion, and in a very short time returned with the present tune, which was at once adopted. It is here very slightly adapted to fit the present words.

374 Thou who once on mother's knee. *F. T. Palgrave*, 1824–97.

From Professor Palgrave's *Hymns* (1867–70), dated 1863–7.

Trochaic, 7 7. 7 7. 7 7.

MUSIC. VOLLER WUNDER comes from *Geistliche Andacht-Lieder Herrn Paul Gerhard . . . gesetzt von J. G. Ebeling* (Berlin, 1666, 1667). This collection was published in 10 parts, each containing 12 hymns, the present melody being set, in part 4, to the hymn, 'Voller Wunder, voller Kunst'. It is a very beautiful tune, unpretentious, yet full of emotional significance, while remaining perfectly simple and easily understood by children.

375 Through the night thy angels kept.

William Canton, 1845–1926.

From his *The Comrades* (1902), first reprinted in the *English Hymnal* (1906). Besides writing many charming books for children, Mr. Canton compiled the huge *History of the British and Foreign Bible Society*. (Cf. 379, 519.)

Trochaic, 7 7. 7 7.

MUSIC. BOYCE, by W. Boyce, is found in *A Collection of Melodies for the Psalms of David, According to the Version of Christopher Smart, A.M. &c.* (1765), where it is set to Psalm 4, 'To the call of pressing need'. This collection contains tunes by various composers, including several by Boyce (cf. 452). He was not only a very important figure in 18th-century church music, both for his own compositions and his collection of earlier masters, *Cathedral Music* (1760), but he also produced much excellent work in almost all contemporary forms of composition, and as a writer of 'secular' music is not yet appreciated at his true value. So far as it is possible to classify musicians by nationality, he was a supremely 'English' composer. The present tune is an excellently plain, direct one, in a familiar manner, but most solid and satisfactory.

376 To God who makes all lovely things. *J. M. C. Crum.*

From *The Winchester Hymn Supplement*, 1922.

L.M.

MUSIC. DANIEL is an arrangement, by Martin Shaw, of an Irish traditional melody. It appeared in *Songs of Praise for Boys and Girls* (1930).

377 When a knight won his spurs, in the stories of old.

Jan Struther.

Written for our book to carry the tune.

Anapaestic, 7 4. 7 4. Unique.

MUSIC. STOWEY is an arrangement, for *Songs of Praise*, of an English traditional melody collected by Cecil Sharp in Somerset.

378 When lamps are lighted in the town.

(*The Ships.*) *M. M. Penstone*, 1859–1910.

From *The Sunday Kindergarten*, 1909. In *Songs of Praise for Boys and Girls* (89), 1930.

C.M.

MUSIC. BUTLER is an arrangement, by Martin Shaw, of an English traditional melody, and appeared in *Songs of Praise for Boys and Girls* (1930).

379 When the herds were watching.

(*Nativity.*) *William Canton*, 1845–1926.

From his book *The Comrades* (1902).
Trochaic, 6 5. 6 5. D.

MUSIC. GAMBLE is an adaptation, by Martin Shaw, of a melody in John Gamble's *Ayres and Dialogues for one, two and three voices* (1659). This was Gamble's second collection, the first being *Ayres and Dialogues* (1656). The present arrangement appeared in *Songs of Praise for Boys and Girls* (1930). Gamble was a renowned lute player of his day, and many of his songs obviously were composed with a fairly elaborate accompaniment in mind, though in the printed copies only melody and bass are found; some, however, like the original of the present tune, are simple melodies, in a popular manner; he was clearly influenced by the style of Henry Lawes.

380 Winter creeps. (*Winter.*) *S.P.*

From *Songs of Praise for Boys and Girls* (15), 1930. Written for the tune.

Cretic (– ◡ –), 3 3. 3 3. 3 3. 3 3; but set down in the music as 6 6. 6 6. It is entirely different from the trochaic 6 6. 6 6 of 570.

MUSIC. SUO-GÂN is an arrangement, by Martin Shaw, of a Welsh traditional cradle-song which appeared in *Songs of Praise for Boys and Girls* (1930); the name is the Welsh word for 'Lullaby', and the tune is found in Edward Jones's *Musical Relicks of the Welsh Bards, &c.* (music ed., 1800), headed 'The Lullaby Song, as sung by Welsh nurses, &c.', and set to the words 'Hwi, hwi, plentyn bach, hwi, hwi, druân bach'. The melody is of the simplest possible form, consisting of three notes only.

CAROLS

The carols which now follow (381 *to* 385) *were chosen by a committee of school teachers, who considered a small collection to be necessary for little children, in addition to those others in this Part which are of the nature of carols.*

381 From out of a wood did a cuckoo fly. *O.B.C. from the Czech.*

The *Birds Carol* is a free translation, by the editor, of a folk carol taken from a particularly poor and shabby little Czech girl, who asked her teacher, Miss Jakubičuva, at Polička (in the hills between Bohemia and Moravia) if she would like to hear a little song she knew. Thus, in the Christmas of 1921, this little gem was discovered, 'Žežulka z lesa vylitla, kuku'. First printed in the *Oxford Book of Carols* (103), 1928.

Anapaestic and iambic, 10 2. 10 2. 8 8 6. Unique.

MUSIC. THE BIRDS is an arrangement, by Martin Shaw, of the tune obtained from the same source as the words. The present version appeared in the *Oxford Book of Carols* (1928). It is an attractive, gay tune of a type found in the folk melodies of many European countries.

382 Hush! my dear, lie still and slumber.

(*Cradle Song.*) *Isaac Watts*, 1674–1748.

This 'exquisite cradle hymn' received high praise from the Oxford Professor of Poetry, Palgrave (cf. 374). It appeared first in Watts's *Divine and Moral Songs* (1715) (wherein there also appeared 'How doth the little busy bee', 'Let dogs delight to bark and bite', and 'Whene'er I take my walks abroad'). The seven verses in the *Oxford Book of Carols* (130) are here reduced to four.

Isaac's father was a schoolmaster, and taught his son. The boy could not help always tagging rhymes; this annoyed his father so much that he threatened to flog him, whereat Isaac cried out:

> O father, do some pity take,
> And I will no more verses make.

Trochaic, 8 7. 8 7.

MUSIC. NORTHUMBRIA is an arrangement, by Martin Shaw, of a traditional carol tune, sung to these words, and noted in Northumberland by R. Vaughan Williams. The present version is part of a fuller arrangement which appeared in the *Oxford Book of Carols* (1928). It is a very short but individual tune, and not one of the more common types found in English folk melodies; its brevity and the second phrase give it something of the character popularly associated with Russian folk-song.

383 Little Jesus, sweetly sleep, do not stir.

(*The Rocking Carol.*) *Czech. Tr. O.B.C.*

A translation by the editor of the touching little Czech carol, 'Hajej, nynjej'. First printed in England, and in English, in the *Oxford Book of Carols* (87).

10 7. 8 8. 7 7. Unique, of course: trochaic and Cretic; but the first line might be printed as three lines, 7 3 3, since there are marked pauses. The whole stanza then is 7 3 3. 7. 8 8. 7 7.

MUSIC. ROCKING is an arrangement, by Martin Shaw, of the tune generally sung in Czechoslovakia to this carol, having been, like 381, contributed by Miss Jakubičuva. The present version appeared in the *Oxford Book of Carols* (1928). It is an easy, unpretentious tune, but more characteristic of its country of origin than 'The Birds', both in rhythm and structure; it acquires a curious attractiveness from the little echoed phrase at the end of the 1st line.

384 The first Nowell the angel did say. *Old Carol.*

Three verses from the nine in the *Oxford Book of Carols* (27). The text of all folk-songs varied with the singer; the 1st verse here is that taken down by William Sandys, *Christmas Carols Ancient and Modern* (1833), with 'three' altered to 'certain'. As the traditional words have got the Gospel account wrong (for the shepherds did not see a star), and children should not be taught mistakes of that kind, we have altered the first couplet of ver. 2, and have followed it by a couplet from ver. 3 in the original. Our ver. 3 is also from Sandys's text. The text in Davies Gilbert's *Collection of Christmas Carols* is earlier (1822), but is from a rougher source. The carol cannot be later than the 17th century.

The French word 'Noël' is supposed to come from the Provençal 'Nadal', a corruption of the Latin *Natalis*, birthday; there is perhaps also an association with *novella*, news (neuter plural of *novellus*), whence, through Italian and Old French, the word 'novel'.

An irregular form of the Long Measure.

MUSIC. THE FIRST NOWELL is the traditional tune to the above carol, as found in W. Sandys's *Christmas Carols* (1833). It is not later than the 17th century, at least, and probably originated as a descant to another melody (v. *Folk-Song Society's Journal* (vol. vii), though it is now one of the best known of all English carols. The present arrangement, by Martin Shaw, is part of a fuller version in the *Oxford Book of Carols* (1928).

385 Unto us a boy is born! *15th-cent. Carol. Tr. O.B.C.*

Puer nobis nascitur,
rector angelorum,
in hoc mundo pascitur
dominus dominorum.

The words of this are in a 15th-century Trier MS. which also preserves the melody. There are many variants, which are given by Zahn, Dreves, and Baümker; and also a German version, 'Uns ist geborn ein Kindelein', is printed by Spangenberg, 1544, in the Mainz *Cantual* (1605), and elsewhere. The translation by the editor is from the *Oxford Book of Carols* (92). It is a curious fact that 19th-century writers shrank from translating *puer* literally: 'boy' was avoided, as was 'baby'. But 'child' and 'babe' were considered to be correct. The rollicking Latin text, from which we have transcribed the lines above, is in F. J. Mone, *Lateinische Hymnen des Mittelalters* (vol. i, 1853).

Trochaic, 7 6. 7 7; but the tune is more than that, and in any case the metre is unique.

MUSIC. OMEGA AND ALPHA (PUER NOBIS NASCITUR) is an arrangement, by Geoffrey Shaw, of the melody to the above words, as it is given in *Piae Cantiones* (1582): see 4. There are many variants of the original tune, which is to be found with the words in the Trier MS. The present version is part of a fuller arrangement, with varied accompaniment for each verse, which appeared in the *Oxford Book of Carols* (1928): cf. 33, part II (ii).

SUNDAY KINDERGARTEN

386 (I) Good day to you all, good day to each one.
(*Greeting.*) *S.T.*

These verses for a Sunday Kindergarten were made (where not otherwise stated) by the editor, in collaboration with Martin Shaw, for the book of nursery rhymes, &c., which they produced with the title *Song Time*, in 1915. Some are slightly altered here.

Trochaic, 5 5. 6 5. Unique.

386 (II) Here we come with gladness. (*Collection March.*)
Julia H. Johnston.

In *Child Songs*, 1908 (no. 115).

Trochaic, 6 5. 6 5.

386 (III) We wish you many happy returns of the day. (*Birthdays.*) *S.T.*

Unique! 12 12. 8 10. The pedantic prosodist might analyse the familiar birthday greeting of l. 1 as an amphibrach, followed by two trochees, an iamb, and one anapaest: ∪ – ∪ | – ∪ | – ∪ | ∪ – | ∪ ∪ – |.

386 (III) Who has seen the wind? (*For use when there is no Birthday.*) *Christina Rossetti.*

From *Sing-Song* (1872).
Trochaic, 5 5. 8 6. D. Also unique.

386 (IV) Our babies' names are on the roll. (*The Roll.*) *S.T.*

Iambic, 8 8. 8 6.

386 (V) Praise him, praise him, all his children praise him! *S.P.V.*

Based on Mr. Carey Bonner's *Child Songs*, No. 148. The inveterate tendency of adults to sing children's hymns (to which we have already referred, see e.g. 131, 444) has extended farther; and it was at the earnest request of a dean that we so altered these lines as to make them inclusive of grown-up people.

Also unique, 10 (trochaic) 6 (Cretan). Saintsbury in his *Manual of Prosody* (p. 268), 1910, doubts whether the Cretan or amphimacer (– ∪ –) ever occurs as an actual foot in English rhythm; but it occurs here certainly in 'He is love'.

386 (VI) Good-bye! Our school is over. *S.T.*

This iambic 7 6. 8 6. with refrain is also of course peculiar to our book.

MUSIC. GREETING, OPPIDANS MEWS, BIRTHDAY are all by Martin Shaw and appeared in *Song Time* (1915).

FAIRLIGHT, by Geoffrey Shaw, appeared in *Songs of Praise for Boys and Girls* (1930).

CHILDREN ALL, MANOR STREET, GOOD-BYE are also by Martin Shaw and from *Song Time.*

The tunes are all easy and attractive, suitable for, and enjoyable by, very young as well as older children.

Part VII

PROCESSIONAL

Processions of ministers and choir seem to have disappeared in England after the Reformation, except for great and rare public occasions, such as coronations, an important funeral or other function, or the procession of the Knights of the Garter at Windsor. So much was this the case that Wren wished to build St. Paul's on the plan of a Greek cross because, there being no processions, a long nave was not needed. In parish churches the little processions of utility alone continued, as at baptisms, weddings, and funerals; and (also without choristers) the out-door processions at Rogationtide. The natural human instinct reasserted itself in church during the 19th century, and how natural it is was shown by the large use of processions among Trade Unions and the Salvation Army. The Great Lancashire Sunday School processions may have arisen soon after the establishment of Sunday Schools early, that is, in the 19th century. Village out-door processions are also an old custom among Methodists.

It is sometimes forgotten that parts of the processional hymns can be used as ordinary hymns for occasions other than those of a procession—just as some ordinary hymns are serviceable for processional use.

387 Of the Father's heart begotten. (*Christmastide.*)

Prudentius, b. 348. *Tr. Roby Furley Davis.*

Corde natus ex parentis ante mundi exordium,
alpha et O cognominatus, ipse fons et clausula
omnium quae sunt, fuerunt, quaeque post futura sunt,
saeculorum saeculis.

From the *Cathemerinon* of Prudentius(see 37), in the poem 'Da puer plectrum'. This fine hymn is in the York and Hereford Breviaries, and in other breviaries abroad.

Our version is from the *Hymns of Prudentius*, translated by R. Martin Pope and R. F. Davis. First reprinted in the *English Hymnal* (1906).

Trochaic, 8 7. 8 7. 8 7 7. Unique.

MUSIC. divinum mysterium appeared, set to the present words, in the *Hymnal Noted* (part ii, 1856), headed 'from a MS. at Wolfenbuettel of the XII century'. The melody was certainly in use, from the 13th century, to the words 'Divinum mysterium', but the 'Wolfenbuettel MS.' has not been identified, and it is probable that Helmore, the editor of the *Hymnal Noted*, took the tune from *Piae Cantiones* (1582) [see 4]. He misread the rhythm of the melody at several points, and his mistake was followed by the editors of subsequent collections, the correct form, as at present, being first given in the new edition of *Hymns Ancient and Modern* (1904). This form, besides being correct, is certainly superior to the spurious version; it shows the characteristic triple metre, and slightly unsymmetrical rhythm of phrase, which marks many of the early measured tunes; it must not be sung too slowly.

388 From the eastern mountains.

(*Epiphany.*) *G. Thring*, 1823–1903.

Written in 1873, and first published in his *Hymns and Sacred Lyrics* (1874).

Trochaic, 6 5. 6 5. D.

MUSIC. LAUS TIBI CHRISTE is an arrangement of a German processional melody, which is found in a manuscript written towards the end of the 14th century to the words 'Eya der grossen Liebe'. It is, however, certainly older than this, being the melody proper to the Latin hymn 'Laus tibi, Christe, qui pateris'. It became attached particularly to German translations of the third stanza, 'Ach du arme Judas', and to imitations and travesties of these words. Many versions of the tune are found in various collections, both Catholic and Protestant, the earliest printed form seeming to be that found in J. Gutknecht's *Gantz newe geystliche teutsche Hymnus, &c.* (Nürnberg, 1527), where it is set to one of the imitations mentioned above, 'Ach wir armen Menschen', as follows:

389 Hail thee, Festival Day! blest day that art hallowed for ever.

(*Festivals.*) *Bp. Venantius Fortunatus*, *c.* 530–609. *Cento, S.P.V.*

Salve, festa dies, toto venerabilis aevo,
qua Deus infernum vicit et astra tenet:
ecce renascentis testatur gratia mundi
omnia cum Domino dona redisse suo.

Venantius Honorius Clementianus Fortunatus, the author of *Vexilla Regis* (130), seldom rises to the rugged grandeur of that poem, among the mass of hymns, *vers de societé*, and a Life of St. Martin in hexameters, which have survived; he represents indeed 'the last expiring efforts of the Latin muse in Gaul' to retain something of the 'old classical culture amid the advancing tide of barbarism'. In the poem, 'Tempora florigero rutilant distincta sereno', from which 'Salve festa dies' is taken, he rises again to a worthy level; and the fact that a poem containing so much feeling for nature became the chief processional hymn does great credit to the Medieval Church (cf. 21). It is found as early as the *Echternach Gradual*, *c.* 1000, and, especially in the cento for Easter, in most British and Continental Processionals during the Middle Ages. There are many versions for other festivals (winter feasts being excluded), some of which contain nothing from Fortunatus but the opening line. The Sarum and York

Processionals have Salves for Easter, Ascension, Whitsunday, Dedication Festival, Corpus Christi, the Visitation, and the Name of Jesus, in some of which little of Fortunatus is left. Translations of those for our greater festivals (the first four of these) are in the *English Hymnal*, 624, 628, 630, 634), done by various hands. Here we have revised these, and have put selected verses together, printing the choruses for the four festivals. As the verses themselves are meant to be sung by chanters (the chorus only being sung by the people), it is easy for the appropriate verses to be selected or marked in the chanters' books.

For Cranmer's letter about 'Salve, festa dies', see p. ix.

Elegiac. See below, 390.

MUSIC. PLAINSONG is the melody proper to this hymn from the *Sarum Processional* and the *Sarum Gradual*, arranged by J. H. Arnold for *Songs of Praise* (1931).

390 Welcome, Day of the Lord, the first and the best of the seven.

(*For any Sunday.*) *P. Dearmer.*

The Dean of Liverpool, Dr. Dwelly, asked the editor to write a hymn for use on a Sunday, with the Lord's Day for its theme, in elegiac couplets, so that it could be sung to either of our tunes. The hymn is long enough for a simple Sunday procession, but is not too long for other use.

Elegiac, like 389. In this example the metre is kept almost uniform in dactylic accent. In 389, a marked spondee (e.g. 'Hail thee') sometimes takes the place of a dactyl (– ∪ ∪), as in classical verse. An elegiac couplet is a hexameter line followed by a pentameter. The Greek and Latin form (in quantity, of course) of the hexameter is:

– ∪∪ | – ∪∪ | – ∪∪ | – ∪∪ | – ∪∪ | – –
or – – | or – – | or – – | or – – | |

And of the pentameter:

– ∪ ∪ | – ∪ ∪ | – || – ∪ ∪ | – ∪ ∪ | –

(*Also with spondaic variants.*)

These classical metres are rarely used in English (Southey's *Vision of Judgment* and Longfellow's *Evangeline* are examples) and then are mainly in dactyls. Trochees – ∪, or even pyrrhics ∪ ∪, are often substituted for spondees, e.g. Southey's:

– ∪ ∪ – ∪ – ∪ ∪ – ∪ – ∪ ∪ – ∪
(*Hex.*) 'Twas at that | sober | hour, when the | light of | day is re|ceding.

Here are examples of the scansion of our hymns:

– – – ∪ ∪ – – – ∪ ∪ – ∪ ∪ – ∪
(*Hex.*) Hail thee, | Festival | Day! || blest | day that art | hallowed for | ever.

– ∪ ∪ – ∪ ∪ – – ∪ ∪ – ∪ ∪ –
(*Pent.*) Day when the | Church, like a | bride, || welcomes the | help-mate of | all.

– ∪ ∪ – ∪ ∪ – ∪ ∪ – ∪ ∪ – ∪ ∪ – ∪
(*Hex.*) Lo, the fair | beauty of | earth, || from the | death of the | winter a | rising!

— — — ∪ ∪ — ∪ — ∪ ∪ — ∪ ∪
(*Hex.*) Welcome, | Day of the | Lord, || the | first and the | best of the |
— ∪
seven,

— ∪ ∪ — ∪ — — ∪ ∪ — ∪ ∪ —
(*Pent.*) Day whereon | Christ a|rose, || brought us the | promise of | life.

In this hymn (390) the verses, apart from the chorus, are linked by internal rhymes, which are leonine in their general effect.

MUSIC. SALVE FESTA DIES was composed by R. Vaughan Williams for the previous hymn and is found in the *English Hymnal* (1906); the rhythm there of the 3rd and 16th bars being syncopated on the last two beats, whereas in this new *Songs of Praise* version these follow the regular form of the rest. It is a vigorous, broad tune, with a genial, progressive rhythm.

391 Holy Spirit, make us strong! (*Whitsuntide.*)

Martin Moller (1584), *from* Veni, sancte Spiritus. *S.P.V.*

This, which is practically a new hymn, using Moller's version of 'Veni, sancte Spiritus' and Miss Winkworth's translation in *Lyra Germanica* as framework, was written in order to provide a modern hymn to the Holy Spirit for processional use, to Corner's tune, which is proper to 'Heiliger Geist, du Tröster mein', by Martin Moller (*Meditationes sanctorum Patrum*, 1584).

Trochaic, 7 7 7. 4; but with the Alleluyas repeated, it is thus 7 7. 7 4. 4. 4. Unique.

MUSIC. HEILIGER GEIST is an arrangement, by Henry G. Ley, of a melody found in both D. G. Corner's collections, *Gross Catolisch Gesangbuch* (1631), and *Geistliche Nachtigall der Catholischen Teütschen, &c.* (Vienna, 1648). The arrangement is from no. 3 of *Six Short Anthems . . . by Henry G. Ley* (1927).

392 At the name of Jesus. *Caroline M. Noel, 1817–77, and others.*

Miss Noel, like Charlotte Elliott (253), was a great sufferer; she also wrote a hymnal for invalids, *The Name of Jesus, and other verses for the Sick and Lonely*, in the 1870 edition of which this hymn appeared, as 'In the name of Jesus'. The text is in the *English Hymnal* (368). We have altered some words, omitted her ver. 2 ('At his voice creation') as a little recalcitrant in theology, and added a new doxology.

Trochaic, 6 5. 6 5. D.

MUSIC. KING'S WESTON was composed by R. Vaughan Williams for this hymn in *Songs of Praise* (1925). It is a solid tune, in triple time, with a strongly stressed rhythm, and a characteristic exchange of accent in the last two lines; it is a dignified, but not a solemn tune, and must not be sung too slowly.

393 City of Peace, our mother dear.

(*The Psalm of Sion.*) *Cento from W. Prid*‡ (1585).

Selected and slightly altered verses from the delightful free version of the passage in the Meditations of St. Augustine, beginning '*Mater Hierusalem, civitas sancta Dei. . . . Felix anima mea, semperque felix in saecula, si intueri meruero gloriam tuam, beatitudinem tuam, pulchritudinem tuam, portas et muros tuos, et plateas tuas, et mansiones tuas multas, nobilissimos cives tuos, et fortissimum regem tuum Dominum nostrum in decore suo. Muri namque tui ex lapidibus preciosis, portae tuae ex margaritis optimis.* The fine passage, it will be seen, owes much to the description of the New Jerusalem in Rev. 21, &c. The whole is too long for quotation here, but is printed in Julian's *Dictionary*, p. 580. This, together with Damiani's hymn, 'Ad perennis vitae fontem', which at the time was thought by many to be Augustine's, is certainly the source of the hymn by W. Prid, and seems to have been also the source of the more famous one by 'F.B.P.', 395. Many perhaps will prefer Prid to F.B.P. One is indebted to the other; but it is impossible to say which hymn was the earlier. Prid's is dated 1585, and the 2nd edition is 1593. The title is: '*The Glasse of vaine-glorie: Faithfully translated (out of S. Augustine his booke, intituled Speculum peccatoris) into English by W. P., Doctor of the Lawes. Printed at London by John Windet dwelling at the signe of the white Beare, nigh Baynard's Castle, 1585.*' The changes from the original are: ver. 1, l. 1, from 'O mother dear Hierusalem, Jehovah's throne on High'; ver. 6, l. 3, from 'glorious seat'; ver. 10, l. 4, from '(I mean)'; ver. 11, l. 1, from 'O mother dear Hierusalem'; ver. 13, l. 2, from 'My gives', l. 4, 'Of Cedar'.

C.M.

MUSIC. STALHAM is an arrangement, by R. Vaughan Williams, of a folk-song noted by E. J. Moeran at Sutton, Norfolk. Miss A. G. Gilchrist (*Folk-Song Journal*, vii. 14) considers that the shape of the tune suggests that it is a traditional version of a modal psalm-tune.

DUNSTAN is an arrangement for *Songs of Praise*, by R. Vaughan Williams, of an English folk-song.

EARDISLEY is an arrangement of yet another folk-tune, which was contributed by Miss Andrews to the *English Hymnal* (1906). The tune is evidently the original of the adaptation by Sir Arthur Sullivan, known as 'Noel' (76).

394 Forward! be our watchword. *H. Alford*,† 1810–71.

The son of J. G. Wood, the eminent parson-naturalist, in his *Life* of his father, says that this was written for the festival of the Canterbury Diocesan Choral Union, 1871, on the text, 'Speak unto the children of Israel that they go forward', Exod. 14 : 15. Dr. Alford did not want to have a procession, but 'by dint of much perseverance my father carried his point, and then incontinently followed up his victory by suggesting that the Dean himself should write a processional hymn for the occasion and compose the music also! The Dean, at first, was a little overcome by the audacity of the proposal, but finally consented; and shortly afterwards my father received a very admirable hymn with the Dean's compliments. This, however, good as it was, was by no means the kind of hymn which he wanted; and so he wrote off again to the Dean, pointing out that the hymn, while excellent in its way, was not at all adapted to be sung upon the march. Would he kindly go into his Cathedral, walk slowly along the course which the procession would take, and compose another hymn as he did so? The good old Dean was not in the least offended by the unhesitating rejection of his work, and did as he was bid; and the result was the grand hymn beginning "Forward! be our watchword". . . . The manuscript reached my father with a humorous little note to the effect that the Dean had written the hymn and put it into its hat and boots; and that my father might add the coat and trousers for himself. On looking at the music, he found, accordingly, that only the treble and bass had been supplied by the composer.'

'Jehovah' occurred in vv. 1, 2, and 3, and is here changed to 'our Captain', 'the Spirit', 'Almighty'; vv. 2 and 3 (in *E.H.* 642) are omitted.

Trochaic, 6 5. 6 5, *ter*. Occurs also in 397.

MUSIC. BLENCATHRA was composed by Sir Arthur Somervell for this hymn in *Songs of Praise* (1925). It is a bold, energetic tune with a well-marked, forward rhythm and a straightforward design, easy to learn, and invigorating to sing.

395 Jerusalem, my happy home.

'F.B.P.' (late 16th or early 17th cent.)

See 393. As this only existed in manuscript (British Museum, Add. MS. 15225) till it was printed (much corrupted, and incomplete) in *The Son of Mary* (1601), the presumption is that it is later than Prid's version, 1585: there is copying in certain places (e.g. ver. 10 in both hymns), and the general style is the same. W. T. Brooke, in Julian's *Dictionary*, who dates it 'the latter part of the 16th or the beginning of the 17th century, thinks that there may have been an earlier version of the MS. and the 1601 print, now lost. Prid may also be indebted to that unknown source. 'F.B.P.' was probably a Papist; but the statement in some quarters to-day (e.g. *The Westminster Hymnal*) that the hymn was by a Jesuit, Anderton, alias J. Brerely 'Pater' (which would make the initials 'J.B.', or at best 'J.B.P.' is an invention.

The great subsequent popularity of some of the verses is due to their being reprinted as broadsides—showing the people's craving for hymns at a time when congregations were limited to the metrical psalms.

1. There is a broadside version by David Dickson (1583–1660), which was very popular in Scotland in the 17th century (reprinted in H. Bonar's *New Jerusalem*, 1852): this began, 'O mother dear, Jerusalem', and continued as in ver. 1. It combines parts of Prid and F.B.P.

2. A contemporary broadside in England, which is in the Rawlinson Collection, may be dated *c.* 1660. This begins with ver. 1, and continues with vv. 2 and 4 slightly changed; it then leaves the original with three verses adapted from those prefixed to several editions of the Bible in the early part of the 17th-century beginning:

> Heaven is the spring where waters flow
> To quench our heat of sin,
> There is the tree where truth doth grow
> To lead our lives therein.

After these three stanzas it goes on in typical broadsheet fashion:

> God still preserve our Royal King,
> Our Queen likewise defend,
> And many happy joyful days
> Good Lord unto them send.
>
> Thus to conclude I end my song
> Wishing health, wealth, and peace;
> And all that wish the Commons good,
> Good Lord their wys [ways] increase.

3. The popularity of the hymn is shown by the way in which a verse or two appears in the old broadsheet carols, and in those taken down by

folk-song collectors in recent years, e.g. 'O fair, O fair Jerusalem', *Oxford Book of Carols*, 46, ver. 3. Our village people must have everywhere known the first verse at least in some form by heart. As Bonar says in his edition of the *New Jerusalem*: 'It offers us neither polish nor ornament . . . but the ploughman at his plough, the weaver at his loom, the traveller on his journey, the schoolboy loitering along, the children round the hearth, the hunted martyr in his hiding place, have all chanted the rude old melody, and found utterance through it to the home-sick longings of their souls.' In Dickson's broadside, however, the melody was to be one of 'the common tunes of the Psalms'; and the broadside of *c.* 1660 is headed 'to the Tune of "O man in desperation"'. The F.B.P. MS. has 'to the tune of Diana', of which the bass part, and that only, has been recently discovered.

4. William Burkitt's cento of 1693 in *An Help and Guide to Christian Families* is reprinted in Julian, p. 582, where a version of 1725 and others are described. See under 74.

5. There were other versions; but the only important one is that by Joseph Bromehead in the Eckington Collection (*Psalms and Hymns . . . Sheffield*, 1795. See Julian, p. 1656). This book was reprinted by James Montgomery at his *Iris* office in 1802; and Montgomery included 'Heaven', as it was styled, in his *Christian Psalmist* (1825); thus the version came to be mistakenly connected with his name. This short hymn of seven verses was the one that came into common use in the 19th-century hymnals. Four verses of it are in *Hymns Ancient and Modern*, 236 (vv. 1, 2, 3, but in ver. 4, l. 2 is altered from 'My soul still pants for thee'); and another verse, not in Bromehead, is added by the Compilers, 'O Christ, do thou my soul prepare'. The verses omitted from *Hymns Ancient and Modern* are here given, to make Bromehead complete:

3 O when, thou city of my God,
Shall I thy courts ascend;
Where congregations ne'er break up,
And Sabbaths have no end?

4 There happier bow'rs than Eden's bloom,
Nor sin nor sorrow know;
Blest Seats! thro' rude and stormy scenes
I onward press to you.

5 Why should I shrink at pain and woe,
Or feel, at death, dismay?
I've Canaan's goodly land in view,
And realms of endless day.

The delicious couplet in ver. 3 is from Burkitt. It will be seen that a book of some size would be needed for all the versions.

C.M.

MUSIC. ST. AUSTIN is an arrangement, by R. Vaughan Williams, from the *English Hymnal* (1906) of an English traditional melody, known as a folk-song, and also as a carol melody.

SOUTHILL is an arrangement, from the *English Hymnal* (1906), of another English traditional melody, contributed by A. Foxton Ferguson.

NEWBURY is an arrangement, from the collection of Miss Arkwright, of the traditional melody to the Christmas carol 'There is six good days set in a week'.

ST. NICHOLAS is from Israel Holdroyd's *Spiritual Man's Companion* (1753), the 5th edition of this work, which was first published in 1724.

396 O Father above us, our father in might.

(*Onward ever.*) *P. Dearmer.*

Onward Ever was written in collaboration with Martin Shaw, in order to provide in a new musical form something for those occasions when a very long processional hymn is needed, especially for children; though, as we have more than once pointed out, adults have a way of taking up children's hymns. As the footnote sets forth at some length, the verses were made so that they could be sung in sections or as short hymns.

11 11. 11 9. The refrain is trochaic—7 2 (enumerated as 9 in the music); the verses themselves (11 11 11) are better scanned as amphibrachs (∪ – ∪) than as anapaests (∪ ∪ –), if the structure of the line is considered:

∪ – ∪ ∪ – ∪ ∪ – ∪ ∪ –
O Father | above us, | our father | in might.

Unique.

MUSIC. MADDERMARKET and ALDEBY were composed by Martin Shaw for this hymn in *Songs of Praise for Boys and Girls* (1930). The two tunes are complementary, the second being a kind of variation, in the minor, of the first; both show the natural, sincere simplicity which marks so many of this composer's melodies.

397 Onward, Christian soldiers! *S. Baring-Gould*, 1834–1924.

Baring-Gould was in charge of a mission at Horbury Bridge, near Wakefield, Yorkshire, in 1865, and he wrote this for a Sunday School feast, when the children went in procession, with cross and banners, from one village to another. He wrote it for a tune arranged from the slow movement in Haydn's Symphony in D, no. 15; but it owed much of its popularity to Sullivan's tune, for which Holst now offers a stirring substitute. One verse, beginning

What the Saints established
That I hold for true,
What the Saints believed
That believe I too—

is usually omitted, 'certainly', says Julian, 'to the advantage of the hymn'. The undisguised reference in the chorus to a processional cross distressed many folk in the last century; and some editors, being unaccustomed to poetry and not seeing the lines, 'With the cross of Jesus Going on before', can have legitimate use as metaphor, altered them. It is indeed said that long ago a bishop, when a procession in one of his churches was about to start, pointed to the cross, and said, 'Leave that behind'; whereupon the choirmen conspired to end each chorus with the words 'Left behind the door'.

Baring-Gould was thinking of his happily united children when he wrote in ver. 3, 'We are not divided'; and the line has been objected to: one hymn-book even substituted 'Though divisions harass'. But at the present day, when unity is becoming real among British Christians, there can be nothing better than for us to assert that we are not divided—and to behave accordingly.

In the days of the Moody and Sankey revivals, Mr. Moody always refused to give out this hymn, protesting, 'We are a fine lot of soldiers!' On the other hand, Mr. F. R. Barry in his *Relevance of Christianity*, 1931 (p. 273), says, 'There is nothing in the whole world that the Church of God should less resemble'.

Trochaio, 6 5. 6 5, *ter*, as in 394.

MUSIC. PRINCE RUPERT is an adaptation of the old English march, 'Prince Rupert's March', which is found in *Bellerophon* (*Gesangh der Zeeden*, Amsterdam, 1648), *The Dancing Master* (1650, &c.), and other collections. It was named after the famous Cavalier cavalry-leader. The present version, by Gustav Holst, is slightly extended; the original march contained only the verse melody, the refrain being adapted from another traditional tune. It appeared in *Songs of Praise* (1925).

398 The God of Abraham praise.

T. Olivers,‡ 1725–99 *Based on the Yigdal.*

Olivers, a poor orphan who became a blacksmith's apprentice, was converted by hearing a sermon by Whitefield; he finally joined John Wesley, became one of his preachers—riding, it is said, over 100,000 miles in 25 years (John Wesley himself never rode less than 4,500 miles *in one year*)—helped him to edit the *Arminian Magazine*, but his lack of education unfitted him for the work—'as corrector of press', his 'errata were insufferable'. About 1770 he heard the chorister Leoni (Meyer Lyon) sing the Yigdal, or doxology of the thirteen articles of the Hebrew faith, at the Great Synagogue, Duke's Place, London. Shortly after, he showed this hymn to a friend, saying: 'Look at this—I have rendered it from the Hebrew, giving it as far as I could a Christian character, and I have called on Leoni the Jew, who has given me a synagogue melody to suit it. Here is the tune, and it is called "Leoni".' The hymn was published as a tract, *A Hymn to the God of Abraham*, undated, but the 4th edition is 1772. After 8 editions it passed into Wesley's *Pocket Hymn-book for the Use of Christians of all Denominations*. Oliver's paraphrase remains extremely Hebrew, his original text is furnished with a Bible reference to nearly every line; and to its Jewish original it owes that 'majestic style' which surprised Montgomery (who was ignorant of its source) to find in 'an unlettered man'. Of the original 12 verses we print vv. 1 (combined with 2), 5, 6, 7, 9, 10, 12. The full original text, without the alterations which we, in common with other editors, have made, is printed in Julian, with the text of the *Yigdal*, pp. 1149–50.

Henry Martyn, the great missionary to India, wrote in his *Diary* (29 July 1805), when he was waiting for the ship that was to take him to the East, that he was much engaged in learning this hymn: 'As often as I could use the language of it with any truth, my mind was a little at ease. There was something peculiarly solemn and affecting to me in this hymn and particularly at this time. The truth of the sentiments I knew well enough. But, alas, I felt that the state of mind expressed in it was above mine at the time, and I felt loath to forsake all on earth.' The brave man was suffering from his separation from Miss Lydia Grenfell. He was only 24 at the time; and he was only to live seven more years.

Iambic, 6 6. 8 4. D. Unique.

MUSIC. LEONI was obtained by Olivers from Meyer Lyon, as is stated above. It has been said that Olivers wrote his words to fit the music, but from his above remark it would seem that this is not the case. The melody is probably of the 17th century. Hymn and tune became popular through their inclusion in the Wesleyan collections, the *Pocket Hymnbook for the use of Christians of all Denominations* (1785), and the *Sacred Harmony, or a choice Collection of Psalm and Hymn Tunes, &c.* (1789).

PART VIII
VERSES AND DOXOLOGIES
GRACES AND OTHER VERSES

THE result of not printing any forms of grace in so many of our hymnals has been that at many gatherings, when a grace was needed, none could be remembered. There is a convenience also in here including a few other short verses.

399 Day by day. *St. Richard of Chichester, c.* 1197–1253.

This little prayer is printed on a card published by Skeffington, and dated as received at the British Museum on 18 Mar. 1915, where it is described as 'Partly—at least—by St. Richard, Bishop of Chichester, A.D. 1245–53'.

Irregular.

MUSIC. STONETHWAITE was composed by Sir Arthur Somervell for these words in the enlarged *Songs of Praise* (1931). The tune solves in a very natural and musical fashion the rather difficult problem set by the unusual metrical scheme of the words; it flows simply and melodiously without obtrusion of its skilful manipulation.

400 Dear Father, keep me through this day. *G. W. B.*

Written for *Prayers for Little Children* (1930)

C.M.

MUSIC. STRASSBURG is from Rihel's *Psalmen, geystliche Lieder und Gesänge, &c.* (Strassburg, 1578), where it is set to 'Nun schlaf, mein liebes Kindelein'. The last line there runs:

The present form is found in the *Strassburger Gesangbuch* (1616), and in many other collections.

It is, as befits the lullaby to which it was originally set, a soothing, simple tune of small compass, with a gentle, running rhythm: a very attractive, unsophisticated little melody.

401 Enrich, Lord, heart, mouth, hands in me.
George Herbert,† 1593–1633.

From his poem 'Trinitie Sunday' in *The Temple* (1633), where the 1st line is, 'Enrich my heart, mouth, hands in me'. The vocative, 'Lord', comes from the 1st line of the poem, 'Lord, Who hast form'd me out of mud'. Of George Herbert as a child, his biographer, Isaak Walton, wrote: 'The beauties of his pretty behaviour and wit shined and became so eminently lovely in this his innocent age, that he seemed to be marked out for piety, and to become the care of Heaven, and of a particular good angel to guard and guide him.'

Herbert's poems were published in *The Temple* the year after his death.

He had given the manuscript to his executor on his death-bed, with the humble request that he would ask Mr. Nicholas Ferrar to look at it, 'and then, if he can think it may turn to the advantage of any dejected soul, let it be made public'.

Iambic, 8 8 8. Also occurs in 142.

MUSIC. WULFRUN was composed by G. W. Briggs for these words in *Hymns for Little Children.* The tune obtains an effect of tranquillity by great regularity of the rhythmic and melodic pattern.

402 Here a little child I stand. *Robert Herrick*, 1591–1674.

From 'Another Grace for a Child' in *Noble Numbers* (1647). The word 'paddock', as we have noted in the text, is a generic one for both toads and frogs, and there has a certain convenience of its own.

Trochaic, 7 7. 7 7. 7 7.

MUSIC. PADDOCKS was composed by Geoffrey Shaw for these words in *Song Time* (1915). This tune is rather less simple than some of those already drawn from the above collection, but it is not so complex as to be either out of accord with the words, or difficult for children's voices.

403 Our Father, for our daily bread. *G. W. B.*

Written for the small edition of *Songs of Praise* with prayers, called *Prayers and Hymns for Use in Schools*, 1930.

Iambic, 8 8. 8 8 8.

MUSIC. PACHELBEL (WAS GOTT THUT) is an adaptation of a melody by Severus Gastorius which appeared first in *Auserlesenes Weimarisches Gesangbuch* . . . (Weimar, 1681), set to the hymn 'Was Gott thut'. This was written by S. Rodigast for Gastorius, during the latter's illness, in 1675, and the tune was composed by Gastorius, after his recovery. Its original form was as follows:

It is a good tune, but, like so many others of its kind, has been considerably altered both in rhythm and melody, by being forced into the usual chorale pattern.

404 Thank you for the world so sweet. *E. Rutter Leatham.*

First published anonymously in *Child Songs*, Part I, 1908.

Trochaic, 7 7. 7 7.

405 We thank thee, loving Father. *Anon.*

Representative bodies of teachers were consulted when the original *Songs of Praise* (1925) was being tested, together with *Prayers and Hymns for Use in Schools* which immediately followed it: and this hymn was asked for by them.

Iambic, 7 6. 7 6.

DOXOLOGIES, ETC.

During the 19th century the convenient custom of printing a separate collection of doxologies gradually died out. They can be found in many Free Church books, but the Methodist *Hymns*, for example, of 1877 is without them. There is a good collection of 33, in various metres, in the American *Hymnal of the Protestant Episcopal Church* of 1882, 11 in the *Hymnal Companion* of 1890, and 7 in the *Psalter in Metre*, Church of Scotland, 1924; but most other collections had dropped the practice. It is, however, a convenience to be able to add doxologies to hymns of different metres, especially to a hymn with a great tune which may need lengthening when it is used at the end of a service or for a procession; and there are occasions when a doxology is sung by itself, as at children's services, or in order to replace such a trivial sentimentality as the so-called 'Vesper Hymn'.

If there had been room, we should have included here certain verses which make admirable doxologies, such as 'How great a being, Lord, is thine' (526, ver. 4). They are noted in the list of the doxology verses at the end of this part; but many in that list may be overlooked unless it is carefully studied.

406 All praise and thanks to God (350).

The last verse of 350 is repeated here, for convenience among the Doxologies.

407 Be, Lord, the happy guide. *G. D.*

Written by Geoffrey Dearmer for us, to provide a doxology to the music of 'O Seigneur', 696, this tune by its solemnity and weight being particularly suitable for a doxology of one stanza.

Iambic, 6 6 7. 6 6 7. D. Unique in this double form.

408 From all that dwell below the skies. *I. Watts* (1719).

This, the classic of English doxologies, appeared first as a paraphrase of Psalm 117 (the shortest chapter in the Bible) in Watts's *Psalms of David* (1719).

L.M.

409 Honour and glory, power and salvation. *Laurence Housman.*

In order to provide a doxology in the Sapphic metre, this, the last verse of Mr. Housman's translation of *Iste Confessor* (*E.H.* 188), is printed here.

Sapphic, 11 11. 11 5.

410 I to the hills will lift mine eyes. (Ps. 121.)
Scottish Psalter, 1650.

The metrical Psalm 121 is well loved by Scotsmen, among whom it is associated with the tune 'French' (called also 'Dundee'). We have taken the first two quatrains of the four in the *Scottish Psalter*. In England people are not so accustomed to the bold inversions that are familiar across the Border, but there is a fine manly swing about the style, as in the two last quatrains also:

> The Lord thee keeps, the Lord thy shade
>   On thy right hand doth stay;
> The moon by night thee shall not smite,
>   Nor yet the sun by day.
>
> The Lord shall keep thy soul; he shall
>   Preserve thee from all ill.
> Henceforth thy going out and in
>   God keep for ever will.

C.M.

411 I will arise and to my Father go. *J. C. Earle*, 1821–99.

From his book of poems, *Light leading into Light* (1875).
Iambic, 10 10. 10 10.

412 In God rejoice! his good endures. *A. G.*

Written to provide a doxology, based on philosophical conceptions rather than on the traditional formula, which could be sung to 'St. Patrick'.

413 Praise God, from whom all blessings flow (25).

This, with 408, the most famous of doxologies, is printed separately here, though it is of course included in Ken's Morning and Evening Hymns, 25 and 45.

We thus have a doxology for L.M. Tunes. Tunes in C.M. and S.M. are provided for in 416 and 417.

414 Praise the Lord of heaven; praise him in the height.
T. B. Browne, 1805–74.

Chosen, principally for the music, from the hymn in *E.H.* 534, a paraphrase of Psalm 148, by Thomas Brierly Browne of Mellington (not Wellington, as in Julian's *Dictionary*) who is not to be confused with Thomas Edward Brown, the Clifton master, who translated some German hymns, but gained his real distinction as the Manx poet.

Trochaic, 11 11. 11 11. in the music of 388, set out as 6 5. 6 5. D.

415 Through north and south and east and west. *S.P.* (157).

Written to supply a doxology for the glorious 'Easter Alleluya' tune; and at the same time to allow of 'Let us rejoice' (157) being lengthened for processional or other use. It is a doxology suitable also for Missionary gatherings.

416 To Father, Son, and Holy Ghost (449).

The C.M. doxology from the *New Version* (1696) of English metrical psalms, as in 449, 'As pants the hart'.

417 To thee, who makest all. *S.P.* (601).

The S.M. doxologies were rather uncouth. The *New Version* has:

To God the Father, Son,
  And Spirit, glory be;
As 'twas, and is, and shall be so
  To all eternity.

This was not very successfully polished in the *Hymnal Companion:*

To God the Father, Son,
  And Spirit ever blest,
The One in Three and Three in One,
  Be endless praise addrest.

A modern doxology to this metre being asked for, we have printed this from 601, 'O Holy Spirit, God'.

418 Worship, honour, glory, blessing (624).

For convenience it seemed worth while to print this also separately from 624, 'Praise the Lord! Ye heavens, adore him'.

PART IX

CANTICLES, ETC.

IN the Free Churches, and often at Anglican gatherings when there are no Prayer Books at hand, a collection of the English canticles with a few Psalms is useful; and we are given the opportunity of including the later canticle of St. Francis. In this way also a service on the lines of Morning or Evening Prayer can be improvised, if the reader has a Bible and Prayer Book and the congregation has *Songs of Praise*.

419 Venite. O come, let us sing unto the Lord. *Ps.* 95.

Many a battle-field resounded with the *Venite*, for it was the war-song of the Knights Templars.

The psalm originally ended as we end it here—'the sheep of his hand'. But some later editor spoilt its noble character (it is one of the finest) by adding minatory verses of a discouraging nature; so that, instead of ending with the note of loving confidence, the new end dragged on to a reminder of the Jews in the Wilderness who 'should not enter into my rest'. There have always been teachers who considered that everything, even a Parable, is better if it ends with a threat, and who do not see that such editing spoils the poetic shape as well as the religious strength of the original. The attempted Revision of the Prayer Book in 1927–8 was therefore right in dividing off this addition.

420 Te Deum. We praise thee, O God. *4th or 5th century.*

'*The Psalm Te Deum, or the Canticle of Ambrose and Austin*' is the description in the old Breviaries, the legend being that at the baptism of Augustine by Ambrose the two saints were inspired to improvise the canticle, singing the verses in alternation. It is not later than the 6th century: Morin has attributed it (i.e. our Parts I and II) to Niceta of Remesiana, a friend of Prudentius (cf. 37) and a missionary bishop in Dacia at the end of the 4th century; but the temptation to find an author is strong, and it is best to suspend judgment, noting that there are still reasons against a unity of authorship. The *Te Deum* is not found in any service book before the time of the monks of St. Benedict, who introduced it for the night service, called Mattins, on certain days. In the Sarum Breviary it was sung on Sundays and festivals, except in Advent, and from Septuagesima till Easter.

The *Te Deum* really consists of the two parts only which we print. But certain suffrages ('O Lord, save thy people', &c.), sometimes sung after the canticle, came to be written as if they were part of it. Thus the strong ending of the original ('in glory everlasting') was lost, and the hymn was drawn out to end in a plaintive anti-climax—in the first person singular—*non confundar in aeternum*, 'May I never be confounded'. By another mistake (a fortunate one) *munerari*, 'rewarded', was often written, *numerari*, 'numbered', and this was the rule in printed editions of the Breviary from 1491 onwards; this more modest aspiration is also that of the Prayer Book version.

As would be expected from its date, the *Te Deum* is not very original, but is drawn largely from the Apostles' Creed, the Preface, *Sanctus*, and *Gloria in excelsis* of the Liturgy. (The suffrages of the appended Part III, which we omit, are from the Psalms—28: 10; 144: 2; 138: 2; 123: 3; 33: 21; 31 : 1—with the characteristic addition of 'Vouchsafe, O Lord, to keep us this day without sin'.)

To whom is the canticle addressed? There is confusion here also. If it is addressed to Christ throughout, the words *aeternum Patrem* in the Latin of ver. 2 are without parallel in Latin forms as applied to the Second Person of the Trinity; but if the first 13 verses are addressed to the Father, and the rest to the Son, then the canticle has a dual character which is very unusual.

Shakespeare, following Holinshed, in *King Henry the Fifth*, iv. 8, makes the King say after his victory:

> Do we all noble rites:
> Let there be sung *Non nobis* and *Te Deum*.

Non nobis (Ps. 115) had its beautiful Peregrine Tone; but the plainsong of the *Te Deum* was, as it still is, a patchwork, the confusion being increased by the inevitable bathos produced by the inappropriate juxtaposition of the concluding suffrages; and the difficulty has pursued modern composers. It is doubtless the feeling that the *Te Deum* lacks unity, and that its verses are curt and uneven in English, which is causing modern hymns to replace it for great occasions of praise and thanksgiving.

421 Benedicite. O all ye works of the Lord. *Apocrypha.*

Arranged here to suggest different ways in which it may be sung. This great canticle is printed as the ninth book of the Apocrypha: it was part of the Septuagint, the Greek version of the Old Testament, where it was inserted, as the Song of the three 'Children' in the burning fiery furnace, in Daniel 3, between vv. 23 and 24. A paraphrased exposition of Psalm 148, it had been used as a hymn in the Jewish Church; and in Christendom was commonly sung among the morning Psalms. As it was used at Lauds (the service which followed immediately after Mattins in the Breviaries), it came naturally into the Prayer Book as an alternative to the *Te Deum*, and was ordered in the Book of 1549 for use in Lent. It is perhaps most suitable for the Septuagesima season, and for such occasions as harvest festivals.

422 Benedictus. Blessed be the Lord God of Israel.
Luke 1: 68–80.

As with the other Scriptural canticles, the text is that of the Prayer Book, which is taken from the Great Bible of 1539, and not from the Authorized Version of 1611. The Sarum Breviary called it 'The psalm *Benedictus*', or the Song of the Prophet Zacharias; the Prayer Book calls it a hymn and gives the reference to Luke 1: 68.

423. Jubilate. O be joyful in the Lord, all ye lands. *Ps.* 100.

Jubilate is the famous Hundredth Psalm, of which the metrical version is 'All people that on earth do dwell' (443), with its tune from the *Old*

Version and therefore called 'The Old Hundredth'. It will be noticed that the word translated 'fear' ('him serve with fear') in the English version of 1560 is 'gladness' in v. 1 of the Prayer Book prose version. Mrs. Ford in *The Merry Wives of Windsor* probably meant the 'Old Hundredth' when she said, 'They do no more adhere and keep place together than the Hundredth Psalm to the tune of "Greensleeves"' (which tune is in the *Oxford Book of Carols*, 28). Longfellow mentions the psalm in the hexameter—from *Evangeline*, 'Singing the hundredth psalm, that grand old Puritan anthem'.

424 Magnificat. My soul doth magnify the Lord. *Luke* 1: 46–55.

In the East, i.e. in the Greek, Russian, and kindred Churches, *Magnificat* is sung with the morning canticles; and, in the west of Europe, one of the earliest instances of its use is in the service of Lauds, very early in the morning (the Lauds office of Aurelian, *c.* A.D. 540, in Migne, *Pat. Lat.* lxviii. 393). It seems to us by nature an evening canticle, only because since the time of St. Benedict's monks it has been sung in our part of the world at Vespers.

425 Cantate. O sing unto the Lord a new song. *Ps.* 98.

Cantate Domino was added as an alternative to the *Magnificat* in the Second Prayer Book, 1552; it was doubtless chosen because in the Latin rite it had been one of the Psalms for Lady Day and for Christmas.

'Wherever the pursuits of the inner life have been most largely conceived', wrote Gladstone, 'the Psalms have towered over every other vehicle of general devotion. . . . We have a conspicuous illustration of their office in the fact that of 253 citations from the Old Testament found in the pages of the New, no less than 116 are from the single book of Psalms, and that a similar proportion holds with most of the early Fathers.'

426 Nunc dimittis. Lord, now lettest thou thy servant depart in peace. *Luke* 2: 29–32.

The 'Song of Symeon' was inserted for Evening Prayer in the First Prayer Book, 1549, being taken from the late evening service of Compline. It was one of the earliest songs from the Bible to be used in the worship of the Christian Church.

427 Deus Misereatur. God be merciful unto us, and bless us. *Ps.* 67.

Added, like 425, as an alternative at Evensong, in the Prayer Book of 1552. The brothers, Cyril and Methodius, were sent in 863 by the Greek Emperor to Moravia in order to translate the Scriptures into Slavonic, for which purpose they made the Cyrillic alphabet, still used in Russia and Bulgaria. As a result of troubles with the German clergy, who were jealous of their success, they paid two visits to Rome. On the second, Pope John VIII told Methodius that the words of this Psalm ('O let the nations rejoice', &c.) had convinced him that God had not intended the Scriptures to be used only in Hebrew, Greek, and Latin; he therefore agreed to the Greek Liturgies being translated into Slavonic, so long as only Greek or Latin were used for the actual celebration. Fortunately for the Slav nations, this restriction was not accepted.

428 Dominus regit me. The Lord is my shepherd. *Ps.* 23.

This is included because it is the most loved and most used of all the Psalms. Our hymns 653, 654, and 656 are paraphrases of it.

St. Francis sang ver. 4 when he went alone, bare-headed, and barefoot to convert the Sultan. He was warned that he was going to certain death, since a price had been set by the Saracens upon every Christian head; but his sincerity so impressed the Sultan that he was courteously treated and sent safely back.

Ver. 2 is quoted in one of Heine's last poems. Ruskin tells us that he learnt Ps. 23 first of the psalms, at his mother's knee, and that she gave him this, with Psalms 1, 8, 12, 14, 15, 19, and 24, as the solid foundation for all life and learning. Edward Irving recited it in Hebrew on his deathbed, when he had been deprived for heretical views by the presbytery of Annan, 1833, after having been driven from Regent Square Chapel in 1832 on account of his approval of 'speaking with tongues'.

The 23rd Psalm has many other associations in history. Bishop Hooper, who refused to fly when Mary came to the throne, saying, 'I am thoroughly persuaded to tarry, and to live and die with my sheep', wrote an 'Exposition' of its comfort from his 'pad of straw' in a 'vile and stinking chamber' of the Fleet Prison. In the persecution of the Covenanters, in 1681, the two 'honest worthy lasses', Isabel Alison and Marion Harvie, sang Psalm 84 to the tune of 'Martyrs' on the scaffold; and, when a priest was forced upon them, 'Come, Isabel,' said Marion, who was but 20 years old, 'let us sing the Twenty-Third Psalm'; and they drowned the voice of the curate until they were hanged.

Bishop Montgomery, when he was Secretary of the Society for the Propagation of the Gospel, told a story about this Psalm:

'One of our priests was out on the track. He saw on the roadside a little boy herding sheep, and in the distance a small farmsteading. Having asked the boy's name, he then said: "Would you mind me asking if you ever said a prayer in your life?" "Never, guv'nor," was the reply. "Have you ever read your Bible?" "Never seen one, guv'nor." "Has your father or mother got one?" "None in the house at all, sir." "Then," said the man, "I shall be back here next year. Will you do me a favour and learn five words for me, '*The Lord is my shepherd*'?" The boy agreed, and went over the words on *his fingers*, and the man said: "One thing more, when you come to the last finger but one, which reads 'my', *crook that finger*."

'A year later the missionary came to the farm again, "Are you the man who taught him some words?" asked the mother. "Yes. How is he?" "Dead. He went out after the sheep, and there was a blizzard. We could not find him till next day. I think he must have remembered what you taught him; for he lay dead in the snow with his fingers held the way you said."'

429 Miserere mei, Deus. Have mercy upon me, O God. *Ps.* 51.

The most famous of the so-called Penitential Psalms, so famous that Dante, in the 32nd Canto of the *Paradiso* mentions David, not by his name, but simply as 'he who for grief at his fall said "Miserere mei" '.

The *Miserere* is red with the blood of martyrs: Lord Ernle, in *The*

Psalms in Human Life, describes the execution of Savanarola, who began a commentary on it, for, when his left arm had been broken by the Pope's agents, his right arm was left intact so that he could sign his 'confessions'; of Sir Thomas More and of Lady Jane Grey who recited it on the scaffold, as also did Lady Jane's father, the Duke of Suffolk. Egmont and Horn, the founders of Dutch liberty, when Alva had treacherously delivered them to the Council of Blood, were beheaded at Brussels, and Egmont recited the Psalm. So did Wolfgang Schuch, the Lutheran, when he was burnt alive at Nancy in 1525, the year the Inquisition was set up in France; so did two Huguenots of the 18th century, the venerable Jacques Roger at his execution in 1745, and the youthful François Benezet in 1752.

There are other associations; but we can here mention only one, which links the *Miserere* with the metrical psalter. George Wishart, the beloved master of John Knox, sang, on the night when he was taken, Wedderburn's version of the Psalm:

> Have mercy on me now, good Lord,
> After thy great mercie;
> My sinful life does me remord,
> Which sore has grievèd me.

He was burnt at the Castle Wynd of St. Andrews in 1546, having first kissed his executioner's cheek in token of forgiveness.

The psalm must have been written by some prophet poet, who saw that sacrifices were not desired by God, and said, 'thou delightest not in burnt offerings'. Some later redactor, feeling this to be heretical, added the curious last verse (which we omit) directly contradicting it—'then shalt thou be pleased . . . with the burnt offerings and oblations: then shall they offer young bullocks upon thine altar'. Thus the *Miserere*, like the *Venite* and the *Te Deum*, ends in common use with an anticlimax.

430 Dilexi, quoniam. I am well pleased. *Ps.* 116.

The Churching Psalm. Being in the second part of the Hallel, this was probably sung by our Lord and his Apostles after the Last Supper. Ver. 9 was the antiphon for the funeral psalms; and was said by many in their dying moments. Ver. 9 was often engraved on chalices, as on that of John Paston in 1464. With vv. 14–16 ('Behold, O Lord . . . thou hast broken my bonds in sunder') St. Augustine resolved to lead a new life.

It was put to a different use at the Relief of Lucknow, 1857, when 'Quaker' Wallace of the 93rd went into the Secundrabagh, says an eye-witness, 'like one of the Furies . . . plainly seeking death, but not meeting it'. He shouted or sang the Scottish version of Psalm 116:

> I love the Lord, because my voice
> And prayers he did hear:
> I while I live will call on him,
> Who bowed to me his ear.

and at every line he fired with his rifle, or thrust with his bayonet.

431 Gloria in excelsis. Glory be to God on high. *Greek, c. 4th cent.*

This was translated for the Prayer Book of 1549 from the original Greek, and not from the Latin of the Vulgate and Missal, which reads, not 'goodwill towards men', but '*pax hominibus bonae voluntatis*', 'peace to men of goodwill'. It was originally a hymn for morning prayer of the Greek Church, not later than the 4th century, and possibly as early as the 2nd. Translated, it was sung at Rome, by the Pope only, on Sundays and festivals in the 6th century, and did not come into general use till the 11th. By a fine inspiration Cranmer moved it from the beginning to the end of the Liturgy in the Prayer Book, 1549.

432 Let us now praise famous men. *Ecclesiasticus* 44.

The first 15 magnificent verses of this chapter from the Apocrypha are often read at memorial services. The passage is here made into a canticle by the selection of vv. 1, 3, 4 (lines 1 and 2), 5, 7, 9 (first three lines) and 14, from the Authorized Version.

MUSIC. FAMOUS MEN (Canticle), by R. Vaughan Williams, appeared in separate form in 1923. It is a broad, majestic tune, very typical of the composer, especially in the characteristic phrase of the 4th bar of the melody, which occurs, in various forms, throughout the canticle. It lies well within the compass of all voices, as also within the easy apprehension of any congregation.

433 *We believe:* God is spirit.

Drawn up, by Dr. H. D. A. Major, in order to give a statement of the Christian faith in words taken entirely from the Gospel according to St. John, and forming in themselves a canticle of much beauty.

MUSIC. GOD IS SPIRIT was composed for this canticle by Martin Shaw for the enlarged *Songs of Praise* (1931). It is in chant form, or rather in the usual style of the responses in the liturgy.

434 The Song of the Creatures. O most high, almighty.

St. Francis (1225). *Tr. Matthew Arnold.*

The famous Song of the Creatures, often called 'The Canticle of the Sun'—'Cantico di fratre sole, laude delle creature'—is well worthy to be included with the old canticles of the Church. Towards the end of his life in the year 1225, St. Francis was seated at table in his monastery at San Damiano after a long conversation with St. Clare. They had barely begun to eat, when he fell into an ecstasy. When he came to, he cried, 'Laudato sia il Signore!', 'Praised be the Lord'. He had composed the Song of the Creatures:

Altissimu omnipotente bon signore,
Tue so le laude, la gloria e l'honore et onne benedictione
Ad te solu, altissimu, se confanno,
Et nullu homo ene dignu te mentovare.
Laudatu si', mi signore, cum tucte le tue creature,
Spetialmente messor lu frate sole,
Lo quale lu jorno allumeni per nui;
Et ellu è bellu e radiante cum grande splendore:
De te, altissimu, porta significatione.

His joy had come back, as great as ever before his illness. 'For a whole week he forgot to say his usual services, and passed his days repeating the Canticle.'

Jorgensen (*St. Francis of Assisi*, 308–9), following the *Speculum Perfectionis* among its chapters 100, 101, 120, and 123, arrives at a different account from that of Paul Sabatier above (which is from *Vie de S. François d'Assise*, 1926): Francis lay at San Damiano depressed by his blindness, plagued by field-mice, probably from the straw walls of his hut, who ran over his face day and night; and in his illness and misery he composed his masterpiece.

Part II. Next year, 1226, in the great pain of his last illness, he was taken to the bishop's palace at Assisi. The bishop, 'the irritable Guido, always at war with some one', had quarrelled with the podestà of the city, and had excommunicated him; the podestà responded by boycotting the bishop. St. Francis was miserable. Then he had an inspiration. He wrote the two verses about pardoning one another (in Part II), and invited the podestà to the court-yard of the palace; at his arrival, the bishop was induced to go out with two of the brothers, who said, 'Brother Francis has made to the glory of God a canticle, which he begs you to hear devoutly'. The two then sang the Canticle with the new verses added. The podestà, who seems to have behaved very well, listened reverently for his great love of Francis; and then wept copiously. Then he said that he would pardon the bishop even if he had murdered his brother; he threw himself at the bishop's feet, and said he was ready to do his will 'for the love of Jesus Christ and of his servant Francis'. The bishop took his hand, saying, 'In my position I ought to be humble; and as I am naturally too quick to anger, you must forgive me'.

The 3rd verse of Part II was made when the physician told him that he could not live beyond the autumn. 'Welcome, Sister Death!' he cried, in accents of intense happiness; and, later in the day, he called the brothers together, and made them sing the Canticle. When they were just about to begin the Doxology (which had been part of the original song), he stopped them, and sang the new verse, the song of death. This in the original is longer; for Francis shared with his age the terrible belief of the Two Deaths, the first, the death of the body; and the Second Death, which only some could escape, the unending torment of the lost:

> Praised be my Lord for our sister, the death of the body, from whom no man escapeth. Woe to him who dieth in mortal sin. Blessed are they who are found walking by thy most holy will, for the Second Death shall have no power to do them harm.

The translation by Matthew Arnold (1822–88) is from his essay on 'Pagan and Medieval Religious Sentiment' in *Essays in Criticism* (1st series, 1865).

MUSIC. ALL CREATURES, by Martin Shaw, was originally composed for use in the Guildhouse (1926). It is partly founded on a Parisian Tone, which is set to vv. 1, 2, 4, 5, &c., and an original melody, in the same manner, set to vv. 3, 6, 9, &c.; the composition thus forms a consistent whole of two alternating sections.

BOOK II

PART X

GENERAL

435 A brighter dawn is breaking. *E.H.*

Written for the *English Hymnal* (1906), because there were no words for the tune. Originally made for Easter because there was a dearth of cheerful Easter tunes, the hymn has come to be sung at other seasons also, and is therefore now included in this part.

Iambic, 7 7. 7 7. Although there are many trochaic examples of 7 7. 7 7, there are no other in iambics, which bring double rhymes. This is therefore unique.

MUSIC. SELNECKER (NUN LASST UNS GOTT DEM HERREN) is from N. Selnecker's *Christliche Psalmen* (1587), where it is set to the hymn 'Nun lasst uns Gott dem Herren' as follows:

In J. Crüger's *Praxis Pietatis Melica* (1649), it appears in triple time throughout, and in a less monotonous form; the present is one of many variants which appear in later collections.

436 A safe stronghold our God is still.

Martin Luther, 1483–1546. *Tr. Thomas Carlyle.*

Ein' feste Burg ist unser Gott,
  Ein' gute Wehr und Waffen.
Er hilft uns frei aus aller Not
  Die uns jetzt hat betroffen.
    Der alte böse Feind
    Mit Ernst er es jetzt meint:
    Gross' Macht und viele List
    Sein' grausam' Rüstung ist:
    Auf Erd'n ist nicht sein's Gleichen.

Carlyle, who made this marvellous translation, as if he were an English Luther of another age, said of 'Ein' feste Burg' that it was 'like the sound of Alpine avalanches, or the first murmur of earthquakes'. Heine called it 'The Marsellaise of the Reformation'; though this is rather like calling Cicero the Chauncey Depew of ancient Rome. 'The greatest hymn', says the *Handbook to the Church Hymnary* (1927), 'of the greatest man in the greatest period in German history.' Dr. Bernhard Pick, in his *Dr. Martin Luther's Hymn of the Reformation* (1897), printed 80 translations of it in 53 languages: he notes how many Huguenots, 'in the time of their bloody persecutions between 1560 and 1572 died joyfully as martyrs with this hymn upon their lips'. Carlyle in the article in *Fraser's Magazine* (1831), accepted the tradition that Luther wrote it for the Diet at Worms, 16 April 1521, and sang it as he entered the town—the last a picturesque exaggeration by Heine, who wrote, 'The old cathedral trembled at these new notes, and the ravens were startled in their hidden nests among the towers'. This seemed natural; for Luther had said to Spalatin, two days before, what was much the same as ver. 3 of the hymn: 'Though there were as many devils in Worms as there are tiles on the roofs, I will go there nevertheless':

Und wenn die Welt voll Teufel wär'
Und wollt' uns gar verschlingen,
So fürchten wir uns nicht zu sehr
Es soll uns doch gelingen.
Der Fürst von dieser Welt,
Wie sauer er sich stellt,
So tut er uns doch nicht:
Das macht, er ist gericht,
Ein Wörtlein kann ihn fällen.

But there is no valid evidence for dating the hymn before its publication, and it is not included in the 21 hymns which he published in 1524. He wrote 37 in all, and this seems to be among the later ones: an appropriate time would be the persecution in south Germany, 1527, when the Bavarian pastor, Leonard Kaiser, was burnt alive; or else the Diet at Speyer, 1529, when the famous protest was made: 'In matters concerning the honour of God, and the salvation of our souls, every man must stand alone before God and give account of himself.'

Luther knew what he was about. 'It is my intention', he had said in his letter to Spalatin, 'to make German psalms for the people—spiritual songs, that is, whereby the word of God may be kept alive in them by singing. We are seeking therefore everywhere for poets.' Hymns do indeed shape the religion of the people, as we in England, now emerging painfully from the strange religions of the 19th century, have good reason to know. In Germany nothing is more striking than the contrast between the manly courage of Luther's hymns and the self-centred pietism that became the characteristic note of hymns and chorales (see 442). From that weakness German Protestantism has not even yet recovered.

'Ein' feste Burg' first appeared in Klug's *Gesangbuch* (Wittenberg, 1529). The heading is 'Der xxxxvi Psalm. *Deus noster refugium et virtus*'. But, although words of Psalm 46 occur, it is used as little more than a motto, the imagery throughout being entirely original. With its magnificent tune it quickly spread. Luther sang it daily at Coburg; Coverdale translated it ('Our God is a defence and tower') in 1539; Melanchthon, Jonas, and Cruciger in their banishment from Wittenberg, 1547, were cheered by hearing a little girl singing it as they came into Weimar. Gustavus Adolphus had it sung by the whole army before the Battle of Leipzig, 1631; and in 1882 it was sung by the thousands assembled on the field of Lützen, 'as by one man' (as it had been before the battle itself, the last he was to fight); and at countless other commemorations and celebrations. There are many stories. The Elector, John Frederick, imprisoned by the Emperor Charles V in 1547 at Augsburg during the Schmalkaldic War, was visited by the deposed ministers of Augsburg: he asked them, 'Has the

Emperor banished you from Germany?' They answered, 'Yes'. 'Has he banished you from heaven?' 'No.' 'Then', said he, 'fear nothing: *Das Reich muss uns doch bleiben!*' Again, in 1720 there was a remarkable revival in Moravia, which was persecuted; David Nitschmann's house was broken into by the police, but the people who were gathered there, nothing dismayed, broke out into singing, 'Und wenn die Welt voll Teufel wär'.' Nitschmann was imprisoned with special severity, but escaped, was afterwards made a bishop, and in 1735 joined the Wesleys in their mission to Savannah. The first line, 'Ein' feste Burg ist unser Gott', is inscribed on the Luther monument at Wittenberg. It is indeed the true national hymn of Germany.

Iambic, 8 7. 8 7. 6 6. 6 6 7. It is remarkable that so famous a hymn and tune should be in a metre unique in this book.

MUSIC. EIN' FESTE BURG was composed by Martin Luther for his own hymn. It is to be found in *Kirchen Gesenge* (Nürnberg, 1531), and in the 1535 edition of Klug's *Geistliche Lieder* (Wittenberg, 1st ed. 1529—not extant). In both of these the melody is as follows:

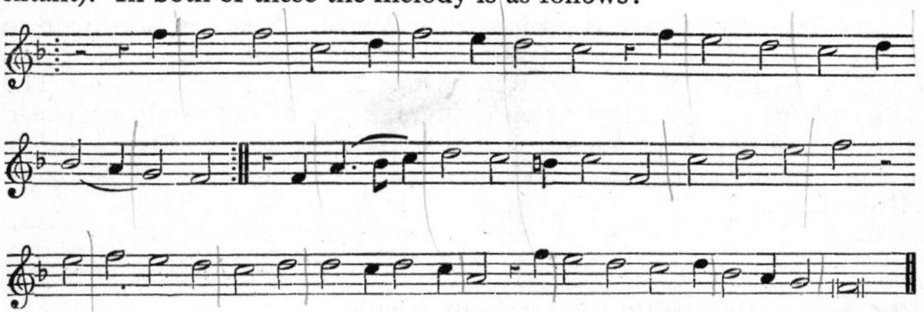

The present version is that adopted by J. S. Bach in his cantata on this chorale and elsewhere, and by subsequent composers, but, owing to the prosody of the English translation, the second note of the 6th line is doubled. It has become the most famous of German chorales.

437 Abide with me; fast falls the eventide.

H. F. Lyte, 1793–1847.

This beautiful poem, as J. Ellerton pointed out long ago in the folio edition of *Church Hymns* (1881), is not an evening hymn; for 'there is not throughout the hymn the slightest allusion to the close of the natural day'. It is really a poem for one in his last illness. But the misunderstanding of it fell in with the custom, then extremely common, of being sentimental at the Evening Service; and people did not notice much what the words were, so long as the tune suited their mood. Nor apparently is it true that Lyte wrote it about himself when his own death was approaching. A letter was published in the *Spectator* for 3 Oct. 1925, by Mr. T. H. Bindley, stating that it was written in 1820, when 'Lyte, as a young clergyman, was staying with the Hores at Pole Hore, near Wexford. He went out to see an old friend, William Augustus Le Hunte, who lay dying, and who kept repeating the phrase "Abide with me". After leaving the bedside, Lyte wrote the hymn and gave a copy of it to Sir Francis Le Hunte, William's brother, amongst whose papers it remained. . . . These details were given me some years ago by Sir George Ruthven Le Hunte, grandson of William Augustus, and I have recently had them confirmed by members of his family.' The story in his daughter's Preface to Lyte's *Remains* (1850) can be adjusted to this. She said, with a good many words, merely that, when Lyte knew that his end was not far off, he announced, to the alarm of his family, that he would preach once more to his people. He did so; and beyond a natural exhaustion suffered no harm. In the evening of that day, he gave a written copy of the hymn to a relative, together with an air of his own composition. She does not say that the hymn had been just written by him, though her style of writing might well lead one to imagine that it was. The manuscript of the sermon is dated 'Lower Brixham. Sept. 4, 1847'; and he died on the following 20 Nov. The text of the hymn was first published in the *Remains* of 1850. There are, however, variations between this text, that of a facsimile of the author's manuscript, and the *Miscellaneous Poems* of 1868. The chief of these variants is, in ver. 1, 'the darkness thickens', the others being small. The original has eight verses. We follow the generally accepted text.

Iambic, 10 10. 10 10.

MUSIC. EVENTIDE was composed by W. H. Monk for this hymn in *Hymns Ancient and Modern* (1861). The alternative version (descant), by R. Vaughan Williams, was written for *Songs of Praise* (1925). The famous tune has, since its first publication, become inseparably associated with the words; the composer is said to have written it in ten minutes, and it certainly gives the impression of having been conceived as a complete whole.

438 All as God wills, who wisely heeds.

J. G. Whittier, 1807–92.

From his poem, 'My Psalm', beginning at stanza 11, in Whittier's *The Panorama, and other Poems* (1856); brought to England by Garrett Horder in *Congregational Hymns* (1884).

C.M.

MUSIC. STRACATHRO, by Charles Hutcheson, is from his *Christian Vespers* (Glasgow, 1832). The tune does not quite maintain the excellence of its 1st line, being slightly weakened by a halt in the middle; it remains, however, a very beautiful and significant melody.

439 All creatures of our God and King.

W. H. Draper, based on St. Francis.

Written during the time (1899–1919) when Mr. Draper was Rector of Adel, Yorkshire, for a Schoolchildren's Whitsuntide Festival at Leeds, the exact year of which he does not remember. The hymn shapes the thoughts of the Canticle into a fine musical form for singing, omitting, however, the 'brother' and 'sister' element.

Iambic, 8 8. 4 4. 8 8, and Alleluyas. Occurs also in 157.

MUSIC. ST. FRANCIS, by G. W. Briggs, was written for this hymn in *Hymns for Use in Schools*. It is a cheerful tune, with a vigorous rhythm, in triple time, and a straightforward melody with something of the character of the early psalm-tunes.

440 All hail the power of Jesus' name.

E. Perronet (1780), *and others*.

In the *Gospel Magazine* for Nov. 1779 appeared the tune 'Miles Lane' together with the 1st verse of 'Crown him': in the April number the remaining verses were added, which rang the changes on the rhymes to 'Lord of all'. Immortality was the inevitable result. But editors have always had to intervene. We print the 1st verse as in the original; so also the first half of our ver. 2, and the whole of ver. 4. But Perronet printed the following delicious quatrain as the opening verse for his second instalment in April 1780:

> Let high-born seraphs tune the lyre,
> And as they tune it, fall
> Before his face, who tunes their choir,
> And crown him Lord of all.

This must have been remarkable in the old days of 'lining' the hymns, when the parish clerk read out, 'Let high-born seraphs tune the lyre', and the congregation sang the line; then he read out, 'And as they tune it, fall'. . . . But such anomalies were common when lining was practised: in Scotland the congregation would be greeted by the contradictory assertion from Psalm 50, 'Our God shall come, and shall no more'; and, having disposed of this, would receive the paradoxical challenge, 'Be silent, but speak out'.

The next stanzas, familiar in many versions, were generally retained—those on the morning stars, the martyrs, the seed of Israel, the heirs of David, that beginning 'Sinners', and the conclusion 'Let every tribe'. But many plain men have wondered what was the meaning of 'Extol the stem-of-Jesse's rod'. The fact is that Perronet, who was no mean poet and who also wrote a fine satire that aroused the hottest anger of his chief, John Wesley, had an inspiration, doubtless brought about by 'Miles Lane'; but, as generally happens with worse poets, could not keep to the level of his first *afflatus*. The whole idea is, however, magnificent; and the best tribute we can pay is to transfer it from the 18th to the 20th century. This we have tried to do.

John Wesley admired Perronet and was anxious to hear him preach, but Perronet was determined that he should not. One day, seeing the younger man among his audience, Wesley tried to force his hand by announcing publicly that Mr. Perronet would preach next morning. Perronet was obliged to comply, though he felt sure that Wesley was concealed somewhere about the building. So he went into the pulpit and said: 'I am compelled by the respect I have for Mr. Wesley to occupy his place. I am entirely inadequate to the task; but, for all that, I will give you the best sermon that has ever been delivered. He thereupon read out the Sermon on the Mount, and concluded the service. Many years later a missionary in India, named E. P. Scott, went to visit one of the murderous tribes in the mountains; he insisted on taking his violin with him; after two days' travel he was suddenly surrounded by the people he sought, who pointed their spears at his breast. Expecting instant death, he shut his eyes, and began singing 'All hail the power', playing 'Miles Lane' on his fiddle. When he ventured to open his eyes, he found the tribesmen grinning with delight. He settled among them and worked with them for two years with memorable results.

C.M., but not when it is sung!

MUSIC. MILES LANE was printed in the *Gospel Magazine* (Nov. 1779), with one verse of the hymn, but without author's or composer's name. Shortly afterwards the tune appeared in the Rev. Stephen Addington's *Collection of Psalm Tunes* (1780), under the name 'Miles's Lane', William Shrubsole being given as the composer. The present form of the 2nd line is that commonly sung to-day, the original tune has the key-note as the last note of this line. The alternative version (descant), by Edgar C. Robinson, was written especially for the enlarged *Songs of Praise* (1931).

The tune suffered much at the hands of various early editors, but it now almost invariably appears in approximately its original form, which is certainly superior to any of the altered versions.

441 All hail to the Power that giveth men might. *B. R.*

Written to carry the tune, and to add a short hymn to those, once so few in number, about Almighty God.

Anapaestic, 10 10. 10 10. There are many Iambic 'tens' among our hymns; but in anapaests the rhythm is unique. It is further marked by a caesura in the middle of each line, followed by an iamb, the last couplets having internal rhymes. It might thus be set out as 5 5. 5 5. 5 5. 5 5.

MUSIC. ST. JOSEPH, by J. Parry, appeared in Stephen's *Ail Lyfr Tonau ac Emynau* (Wrexham, 1879). It is a sturdy tune, the long downward scale in lines 2 and 4 giving a strong air of resolute purpose to the melody.

442 All my hope on God is founded.

J. Neander, 1650–80. *Pr. Y.H.* (*Robert Bridges*).

Meine Hoffnung stehet feste
Auf dem unerschaffnen Gott:
Er ist ja der Treuste, Beste,
Der mir beisteht in der Noth.
Er allein
Soll es seyn
Den ich nur von Herzen mein'.

It is important to remember that Bridges, in the *Yattendon Hymnal* (1899), as in this example, does not really translate his German originals, but uses them merely for suggestion, not only paraphrasing freely, and omitting many verses, but also adding new verses of his own. Thus, although the individualistic note of the post-Luther German pietism is here retained in the opening stanzas, the hymn is on the whole on a wider and more modern note, and in line with his final mature thought in the *Testament of Beauty*. Neander, who died of a decline at the age of 30, was the first important German hymnist after the great Reformers. There was thus a gap, during which the tone of religion was changing. Neander was converted, *c.* 1670, by Under-Eyck, who was a recognized leader of the Pietists. Nevertheless, although many of his hymns are of a subjective cast, the most famous are triumphant outbursts of praise, a glorious example of which is 626, 'Praise to the Lord, the almighty, the King of creation', which is quite free from the 'Covenant Theology' of 17th-century Pietism. His hymns, 19 of the tunes being by himself, were published in 1680, the year of his death, at Bremen, as *Joachimi Neandri*

Glaub- und Liebesübung: auffgemuntert durch einfältige Bundes Lieder und Danck-Psalmen. Oddly enough, 'Meine Hoffnung', which consisted of 5 verses, was styled 'Grace after Meat'.

Trochaic, 87. 87. 337. Unique.

MUSIC. MEINE HOFFNUNG in *A und Ω. Joachimi Neandri Glaub- und Liebesübung*, 1680, is stated by Neander to be a melody already known, but it has not been found in any earlier collection, and may therefore have been a traditional melody. It is there set to the hymn 'Meine Hoffnung stehet feste', and the cadences of lines 2 (4) and 7 and the first notes of lines 5 and 6 are syncopated 𝅗𝅥. ♩, the penultimate note of line 2 (4) being E. The present form is that adopted by J. S. Bach in one of his Church Cantatas. The tune is a strong and individual one, but has lost some of its force of character by the change of the original rhythm, especially in the short 5th and 6th lines.

443 All people that on earth do dwell.

W. Kethe, Daye's Psalter (1560–1), *and the Scottish Psalter of* 1650.

'"The Old Hundredth" of the *Old Version*', says Lord Ernle in *The Psalms in Human Life*, 'composed by William Kethe, a friend of John Knox, and set to the music of Louis Bourgeois, survives all the changes of thought and fashion that the progress of four centuries has witnessed.' It must have been familiar to Shakespeare and all the great Elizabethans, for it appeared in the *Psalter* of John Daye or Day, 1560–1, and in the *Anglo-Genevan Psalter* of 1561. It is not in the full *English Psalter* of 1562 (the *Old Version*, or 'Sternhold and Hopkins'); but it reappeared in the *Appendix* to the edition of 1564, and in the body of 'Sternhold and Hopkins' in 1565, since when it has been printed in all the metrical psalters and in most hymn-books during 370 years. Kethe is said to have been a native of Scotland; but nothing is really known about him till he appears as a refugee, first at Frankfort and then at Geneva, during the Marian persecution. In 1563 he was chaplain to the forces, and he held for some time the Dorsetshire living of Childe Okeford.

There were also L.M. versions of the 100th Psalm in the older English Psalters. These contained the word 'mirth', instead of 'fear' (cf. the Prayer Book prose version, 'gladness', in 423). The word 'gladness' correctly represents the Hebrew: Knox's friend, wishing to be dour, unwarrantably changed it to 'fear'. The Scottish Church, however, subsequently made good. The *Scottish Psalter* of 1564 (1565) did indeed, like the English, keep to Kethe's version; but the *Scottish Psalter* of a century later, 1650, altered the word to 'mirth'. This amendment we have accepted, at the urgent solicitation of friends, and also indeed 'with gladness'. We have not, however, used the other changes of this Scottish version. That of ver. 2, l. 1, 'Know that the Lord', is hardly an improvement on Kethe. Nor have we used the alteration of 'folk' to 'flock' in ver. 2. It is quite possible that 'folck' was originally a printer's error; but it is just the right word; and without it the Hebrew is imperfectly rendered; for the literal translation is 'his *people* and the flock of his pasture', or 'of his shepherding' (S. R. Driver, *The P. B. Version of the Psalms*). By preserving Kethe's 'folk' we keep the idea of 'his people', while the rest of the couplet expresses that of the shepherding.

As to the authorship, Julian discusses, in his *Dictionary*, the possibility of it being by Sternhold or Hopkins, and concludes from the style, the L.M. metre, and the history of Kethe, that it is not, and that 'its correct subscription is therefore "W. Kethe, 1560–1" '. Moreover, the verdict of time is against both Sternhold and Hopkins; for none of their metrical psalms have survived into modern hymnals. The doxology, rather modern in diction, but now the one in common use, is a 19th-century adaptation of the C.M. doxology in the *New Version* ('Tate and Brady'), which is printed as 416.

The Old Hundredth, owing much of its character to the virile strength of the psalm, and indeed of the whole Psalter in whose ideas the Reformers were then steeped, is the chief example among hymns of perfect simplicity of expression; nor is it for this in any way the less a great poem. A hymn indeed is either poetry or it is nothing.

There are, however, other hymns and other songs which are popular without being so simple in expression; and it was a mistake, very prevalent a few decades ago, to think that only well-known words are good for common use. For an unfamiliar word ceases to be so where it is often used—a truism! but a truism that was forgotten. 'Rock of ages' is not a very simple poem; the 'herald angels' must have sounded almost precious at first, and 'risen with healing in his wings' cannot have been very clear to a village congregation; Ken's Morning Hymn was not prevented from becoming popular by containing lines like 'Reflect all heaven's propitious way'; and there was never any need to alter Milton's

> The hornèd moon to shine by night,
> 'Mid her spangled sisters bright,

which is a delight even to little children. (See also under 82, 598, and 648.)

See also 521, 598.

L.M.

MUSIC. OLD HUNDREDTH was composed or adapted by L. Bourgeois for Psalm 134 in the *Genevan Psalter* of 1551. The original form of the last line was as follows:

The tune was attached to Kethe's version of Psalm 100 in the Genevan *Fourscore and Seven Psalms of David* and in Daye's *Whole Book of Psalmes*, both of which were published in 1561.

The alternative version (fa-burden) by John Dowland appeared in *Ravenscroft's Psalter* (1621).

The simpler alternative version (fa-burden), also by John Dowland, is from *Este's Psalter* (1592); there, in the first three lines, the first and last notes only are semibreves.

This is probably the most famous of all psalm-tunes, whether early or late.

444 All things bright and beautiful.

Mrs. C. F. Alexander,‡ 1823–95.

This, as we have mentioned in 174, is from Mrs. Alexander's *Hymns for Little Children* (1848). It has also become one of the most popular of adults' hymns, especially since Martin Shaw discovered our present delightful tune. The original contained the appalling verse:

The rich man in his castle,
  The poor man at his gate:
God made them high and lowly,
  And ordered their estate.

She must have forgotten Dives, and how Lazarus lay 'at his gate'; but then she had been brought up in the atmosphere of a land-agent on an Irish estate. The *English Hymnal* led the way in obliterating this verse from the Anglican mind. But how admirable is the song as a whole, and how excellently carried out! Lines like 'The ripe fruits in the garden' are perfect examples of good poetry in its simplest form.

Since grown-up people, very rightly, insist more and more on singing this hymn, and since they do not play every day in the meadows, and since even in Ireland it is not easy everywhere and on every day to gather rushes, we have ventured for the sake of the sincerity to those who now sing this delightful hymn, to make a small alteration in ver. 5, 'for our play', and 'To gather', instead of:

The meadows where we play,
  The rushes by the water,
We gather every day.

7 6. 7 6, and refrain. But not really a simple metre: in the refrain which opens the song the first line is trochaic, but the second changes to iambic; and so with the last couplet of the refrain. The rest, however, is purely iambic; hence the peculiar swing round as the refrain keeps coming in. Unique.

MUSIC. ROYAL OAK is an arrangement, by Martin Shaw, of an English traditional melody. It first appeared, set to these words, in separate sheet-form (1915). It is a brisk, unison melody, very characteristic of 17th- and 18th-century popular tunes, with a cheerful, dancing rhythm, simple and unelaborate, which makes it perfectly adapted to the artless nature of the words.

445 All things which live below the sky.

Edward J. Brailsford, 1841–1921.

First published in the *Methodist School Hymnal* (1911).

C.M.

MUSIC. JACKSON, by T. Jackson, appeared first in his *Twelve Psalm Tunes and Eighteen Double and Single Chants . . . composed for Four Voices* (1780), where it is set to Psalm 47. In Miller's *Sacred Music* (1800) the tune is called 'Byzantium'. Slight variations, chiefly of rhythm, are found in some collections. The tune is given a lively, almost jovial character by the recurrence of the little figure on the third syllable of the text, and thereby accords well with the present words.

446 And did those feet in ancient time.

Jerusalem. *William Blake*, 1757–1827.

First appeared in the Preface to *Milton*, written and etched, 1804–8. The poem ends with the text: 'Would to God that all the Lord's people were prophets. Numbers, xi. ch., 29 v.'

The preface to the poem says:

> 'Rouze up, O young Men of the New Age! set your foreheads against the ignorant Hirelings! For we have Hirelings in the Camp, the Court & the University, who would, if they could, for ever depress Mental and prolong Corporeal War. Painters! on you I call. Sculptors! Architects!' . . .

This wonderful prophetic outburst (it might have been written yesterday) was in the minds of those responsible for the *English Hymnal* thirty years ago; but clearly it would not become a hymn to any D.L.M. tune, and it was reluctantly dropped till 1930, when it was printed without number at the beginning of that book. What had happened in the meantime was that Parry had made a tune so exalted, and fitting so marvellously with the words, that Blake's *Jerusalem* had become possible for an ordinary congregation. The history of the emergence of the lines from the mass of Blake's poems is this: In the eighteen-eighties and nineties, a small monthly paper was edited (and paid for) by Stewart Headlam, the chairman of a Christian Socialist society called the Guild of St. Matthew. The circulation was only about 300; but the readers were keen and able men, and a good many others saw the fiery little paper from time to time (including such young writers as Bernard Shaw). Under the title, the paper bore the unvarying motto, in thick print, 'I will not cease from mental fight'—to the end of the poem. In this way many people came to know it by heart, and it became, unconsciously the motto of a far larger number of reforming spirits. When, in the midst of the War, 1916, Women's suffrage was passed by a 7 to 1 majority in the British House of Commons, and became law, a great service of thanksgiving was held in the Albert Hall, London. Sir Hubert Parry, who was a strong suffragist, composed the tune 'Jerusalem' for the now universally known lines. Blake's *Jerusalem* then speedily attained the position of a new national anthem. For the British are lovers of poetry, when they can get it.

On the centenary anniversary of Blake's death, 12 Aug. 1927, *The Times* well said:

> 'It has become almost a second National Anthem—nay, if it be not disloyal to say so, it has come to stand for something that the National Anthem fails to express: the private loyalty to some Little England—the white and secret "Albion" of Blake's imagination—upon which public loyalty to the larger England of the National Anthem depends. . . . "Jerusalem", in fact, has become the hymn for those special occasions on which the private Englishman . . . finds the need for expression, impossible in his own words, and at the same time too subtle in reference for the formal statement, adapted to all occasions, of the National Anthem.'

The *Handbook to the Church Hymnary* (1927, p. 270) admirably sums up Blake's prophetic message:

> 'His passion was to set men free from everything that imposed restraint on thought and conduct, whether in politics, literature, religion, art, or ordinary convention, so that the creative urge of personality, which he regarded as the divine in man, might express itself freely and fully. He was the unsparing enemy, therefore, of all social evils that tended to repress personality or destroy it—poverty, starvation, harlotry, the gambling passion, misery in all forms—at a time when these things stirred in few breasts the spirit of revolt; and he dreamt and sang of a new Jerusalem from which these things should be banished.'

(See also 461.)

D.L.M.

MUSIC. JERUSALEM was written by Sir Hubert H. Parry in 1916, and published in separate form in the same year, in the circumstances related below.

It was suggested to Sir Hubert Parry by Dr. Robert Bridges that he should write 'suitable simple music to Blake's stanzas—music that an audience could take up and join in'. Parry agreed, and gave the manuscript of 'Jerusalem' to Sir Walford Davies with the words, 'Here 's a tune for you, old chap. Do what you like with it.' After the first singing in the Albert Hall, it was adopted by the Federation of Music Competition Festivals as the National Hymn of that movement, and is now almost invariably sung at these festivals.

Writing to *The Times* of 27 Aug. 1927, Sir Walford Davies says:

'Sir Hubert Parry gave me the manuscript of this setting of Blake's "Jerusalem" one memorable morning in 1916. It may have been very late in 1915, but I do not think it was. We looked at it long together in his room at the Royal College of Music, and I recall vividly his unwonted happiness over it. One momentary act of his should perhaps be told here. He ceased to speak, and put his finger on the note D in the second stanza where the words "O clouds unfold" break his rhythm. I do not think any word passed about it, yet he made it perfectly clear that this was the one note and one moment of the song which he treasured. . . . I copyrighted it in the composer's name and published it in 1916. We needed it for the men at that time. It is indeed good to know that Dame Millicent Fawcett needed and had asked for it for the women too. I know Dr. Bridges specifically wanted every one of us to sing it, and this is happily coming true.'

Parry's tune combines, in an unusual degree, musical excellence with popular appeal.

447 And didst thou love the race that loved not thee?

Jean Ingelow, 1820–97.

A cento from the poem on 'The Love of Christ', in her *Poems* (1863). The selection first appeared in the *Congregational Church Hymnal* (1887).

Iambic, 10 10. 10 6. Unique.

MUSIC. MUNDAYS, by Martin Shaw, was written for this hymn in the enlarged *Songs of Praise* (1931). It is a deeply felt and unaffectedly moving tune, of which the effect is much the same even with a considerable variation of pace; thus the emotional significance of it is inherent in the melodic progressions themselves, and is not due to a definite ratio of speed—though, naturally, the variation must be within reasonable limits. This is a rather uncommon quality in a melody of this kind, and is a fair test of its essential, not adventitious, expressiveness. It need scarcely be said, however, that there is always a 'best' speed, which in this case is slightly on the fast side of moderate.

448 Angels holy, high and lowly. *John Stuart Blackie*,† 1809–95.

Professor Blackie published this paraphrase of the Benedicite (421) in the *Inquirer* (1840); it subsequently appeared in H. Bonar's *Bible Hymn Book* (1845); and it was reprinted in Blackie's *Lays and Lyrics of Ancient Greece* (1857), in seven stanzas. A few lines were omitted and the refrain was elaborated to fit the Flemish tune 'Flanders', in the *Oxford Book of Carols* (160), 1928; and from that book we have taken it.

Trochaic, 8 7. 8 7. 8 7. 7 7. Unique.

MUSIC. FLANDERS is an arrangement, by Martin Shaw, of the traditional Flemish melody 'De Dryvoudige Geboorte'. It appeared to the present words in the *Oxford Book of Carols* (1928). This is a fine swinging melody, with a robust marchlike rhythm, and the characteristic quaver movement often found in the melodies of the Low Country; it should be compared with the Dutch tunes 'De Boodschap' (226) and 'Vruechten' (169).

449 As pants the hart for cooling streams. (Ps. 42.)
N. Tate and N. Brady. New Version (1696).

By Nahum Tate or Nicholas Brady, or both, this appeared in the *New Version of the Psalms* (to use the full title), 1696. As it there appears in six double verses of four lines, it is obvious that our familiar verses are selections, though unaltered. Some of the omitted parts in our grandfathers' copies of Tate and Brady are too racy to be omitted here. After our vv. 1 and 2 are these:

Tears are my constant food, while thus
  Insulting foes upbraid:
Deluded wretch! where's now thy God?
  And where his promised aid?

I sigh, whene'er my musing thoughts
  Those happy days present,
When I with troops of pious friends
  Thy temple did frequent.

Our ver. 3 is followed by:

My soul's cast down, O God, but thinks
  On thee and Zion still;
From Jordan's banks, from Hermon's heights,
  And Mizar's humbler hill.

One trouble calls another on,
  And gath'ring o'er my head,
Fall spouting down, till round my soul
  A roaring sea is spread.

From which one may guess, what is indeed true, that there was little more in the *New Version* than in the *Old* (see 44) that was worthy to survive. From the *New* we have also 'Through all the changing scenes', 677, while Sternhold and Hopkins provide only one, *The Old Hundredth*, 443, which is by neither Sternhold nor Hopkins. These two official Psalters seem like national disasters. There were indeed an enormous number of metrical psalters (Julian annotates 326) and the translators include Queen Elizabeth, Lord Bacon, Philip Sidney, Fairfax, and many other poets and theologians; and, though an untiring genius might have made a fair collection out of all these, few of them stand out as conspicuously good. There are, however, a number of fine metrical psalms (some are mentioned below), but these are for the most part very free paraphrases.

But what is left of 'As pants the hart' is very good. And it is an improvement on the Old Version, which begins:

Like as the hart doth breathe and bray,
  The well-springs to obtain,
So doth my soul desire alway
  With thee Lord to remain.

In the Scottish Psalter also the deer emulates the less graceful animal:

> Like as the hart for water-brooks
> in thirst doth pant and bray.

C.M.

MUSIC. MARTYRDOM appeared first on single sheets at the end of the 18th century, the original form being in common time. It is first found in triple time in R. A. Smith's *Sacred Music sung in St. George's Church, Edinburgh* (1825), where it is headed 'Old Scottish Melody', and the harmony is stated to be 'by Mr. Smith'. It also appeared in *The Seraph, a selection of Psalms and Hymns* (Glasgow, 1827), edited by J. Robertson, in triple time, and with a footnote stating 'the above tune "Fenwick" or "Martyrdom", and by some called "Drumclog", was composed by Mr. Hugh Wilson, a native of Fenwick'.

The publication of the tune by R. A. Smith led to a legal dispute as to its ownership, but abundant evidence was produced to show that Wilson was without doubt the composer. Many years ago a writer in *The Psalmodist* said, 'I well remember the day it ("Martyrdom") was first sung in St. George's, Edinburgh, for Dr. Thomson then said to me, "O, man! I could not sing for weeping".'

The tune was certainly worth a dispute, for it would be a credit to any composer; on the other hand, if, as it seems, R. A. Smith was responsible for re-writing it in triple time, a large part of the credit must be his, since the beauty of the melody is immensely enhanced by the change.

The alternative version (fa-burden), by Geoffrey Shaw, appeared in the *Tenor Tune Book* (1917).

Metrical Psalms

For the subject in general see pp. x–xv. It is sometimes assumed because of the official version that no good metrical psalms are possible. Yet some are very good indeed. Such are the three famous paraphrases of Psalm 23 (653, 654, 656), Christopher Smart's 521, 'Hosanna! Music is divine', Milton's delicate C.M. version, 525, 'How lovely are thy dwellings fair'; 605, 'O Lord, in me there lieth nought', probably by Lady Pembroke; 618, 'O worship the King'; 623, 'Praise, my soul, the King of heaven'; 624, 'Praise the Lord! Ye heavens adore him'; 628, 'Pray that Jerusalem may have'; 658, 'The Lord will come'; 659, 'The spacious firmament'.

Several others are more or less based on Psalms. Montgomery called 'Hail to the Lord's Anointed' (87) an imitation of Psalm 72; 500, 'Glorious things', and 545, 'Jesus shall reign', are also really based on Psalms 87 and 72; 'Praise to the Lord, the Almighty, the King of creation' (626) is founded on Psalms 103 and 150; and Smart's 690, 'We sing of God' ('He sung of God'), has the very spirit of Psalm 104.

We may add here that the smallest hymn-book in common use was the *gantier*, a French metrical psalter, which was so called because in the days of persecution the Huguenot women concealed it in one of their gloves.

450 Awake, awake to love and work!

G. A. Studdert-Kennedy, 1883–1929.

A selection from a poem 'At a Harvest Festival' first published in *The Sorrows of God, and other Poems* (1921).

Iambic, 8 6. 8 6. 8 6. Occurs also in 454.

MUSIC. BRUNSWICK. See 297.

451 Awake, our souls! away, our fears!

I. Watts, 1674–1748.

From his *Hymns and Spiritual Songs* (1707), where it is headed 'The Christian Race', and is in five verses, as here.

L.M.

MUSIC. SAMSON is an adaptation of the chorus, No. 31, in Handel's oratorio, *Samson*, to the words, 'Then round about the starry throne'. The adaptation is considerable, being patched from various parts of the chorus.

452 Before thy feet I fall.

Sir Ronald Ross, 1857–1932.

A cento from the stanzas published in his volume *In Exile*. The occasion was a memorable one. Ross had been toiling for years with a rusty microscope in tropical heat to investigate the cause of malaria, which has killed many millions every year and destroyed the health of millions more, and which was more destructive to European workmen in hot countries than a war. He followed up his investigations on the *anopheles* mosquito, and on 21 Aug. 1897 made his final discovery, the result of which has been that the microbe of malaria, 'the mighty small', can be destroyed by clearing away or sealing up the stagnant water where the larvae of the mosquito live. On the evening of his great discovery, he scribbled part of his triumphant and grateful hymn. Seldom before has a great scientific discoverer celebrated his achievement in verse.

Iambic, 6 6. 6 6.

MUSIC. KINGSLAND, by W. Boyce, is found in Bond's *The Psalms of David* (1791), where it is named 'Rockingham'. The construction is here very exactly balanced, but slightly unusual, the analogy lying between the 1st and 4th, and the 2nd and 3rd lines, the former two moving downward, and the latter upward (inverted); thus weakness is avoided, for though two lines, the 2nd and 3rd, follow each other in almost exactly similar motion, the tendency to 'feel' a four-lined tune of this kind as divided into two sections is so strong, that the psychological stress is thrown not on the internal parallelism, but on the contrary motion in each 'section'. The tune itself is a good, fluent melody, in triple time, not especially characteristic of the individual composer, but typical of its period.

453 Believe not those who say.

Anne Brontë,† 1820–49.

By Anne, 'Acton Bell', the sister who wrote *Agnes Grey*. From '*Wuthering Heights, and Agnes Grey*. By Ellis and Acton Bell. A new edition, revised, with . . . a Selection from their Literary Remains. By Currer Bell, 1850.' The poem is in 10 stanzas, of which we omit the 3rd and 4th, 6th and 7th; and we have altered the 1st line of the last stanza from 'What matter, if thy God approve', replacing the note of interrogation at the end of the previous stanza with a comma.

D.S.M.

MUSIC. LLANLLYFNI is from *Gemau Mawl* (D. Jenkins, 1890). Though the composition of it is attributed to the Rev. John Jones of Talysarn, it is really by David Jenkins, who wrote the tune on the remarkable intonations of Mr. Jones's voice in preaching.

454. Beyond, beyond that boundless sea.

Josiah Conder, 1789–1855.

First published in his *Star of the East* (1824); included in Curtis's *Union Collection* (1827), and in Conder's own *Congregational Hymn Book* (1836), which contained 56 of his hymns. An editor and a voluminous writer, he represented the best liberal evangelicalism of his age, and the modernization of English hymnody owes much to him.

Iambic, 8 6. 8 6. 8 6.

MUSIC. ARABIA is found in William Holford's *Voce di Melodia, a collection of congregational Psalm and Hymn Tunes, &c.* (*c.* 1820), where it is attributed to 'Cole' and named 'Arabia', being set to the hymn 'To thee, my Saviour and my Lord'. There were two William Coles—the first published *The Psalmist's Exercise* (1760?), but this tune is not found there; the second 'William Cole of Colchester' published, in 1795, a volume containing a morning and evening service and several anthems, and contributed hymns and chants to various collections; the latter is probably the composer of the present tune. The tune is also found, without name of composer, in Joshua Done's *Selection of Psalm and Hymn Tunes, &c.* (1830), and elsewhere is assigned to 'W. Wilson'; there was a W. Wilson who published a dictionary of music in 1830, but nothing further seems to be known about him. The attribution to William Cole of Colchester seems most probable.

455 Blest are the pure in heart. *J. Keble*, 1792–1866, *and others*.

This popular little hymn is a cento made at different times. Vv. 1 and 3 are from the *Christian Year* (1827) (The Purification, in 17 stanzas), with a line in ver. 3 altered—'for his cradle and his throne'. Vv. 2 and 4 are from the *New Mitre Hymn Book* (1836), and may have been written either by the editor, W. J. Hall, or the co-editor, Edward Osler. Keble authorized the text as it stands. He was too good a writer of English to confuse purity with the specific virtue of chastity, as is so often done in the use of this hymn.

S.M.

MUSIC. FRANCONIA is from *Harmonischer Lieder-Schatz*, oder *Allgemeines Evangelisches Choral-Buch . . . gestellet von Johann Balthasar König* (Frankfurt a. M., 1738), where it is set to the hymn 'Was ist, das mich betrübt?' The original melody, which may be by König himself, runs as follows:

The present tune was arranged from this by the Rev. W. H. Havergal, and published in his *Old Church Psalmody* (1847). The adaptation has been skilfully made by the omission of ll. 3 and 5 of the original, the alteration of the last line confirming the structural analogy (by inversion) of the alternate lines. It has become, in its new form, one of the best known Short Metre tunes.

456 Blest be the day when moved I was.

P. B. Clayton, based on John Bunyan.

'The Working Member's Hymn' was published in the *Toc H Journal* (Aug. 1926).

Mr. Clayton, who earned the popular and now universal name of 'Tubby Clayton' during the War (when he served as chaplain at Talbot House—on the telephone 'Toc H'—in Poperinghe), has continued his work in the great organization of young men known by the old name of Toc H. This manly and bracing hymn is a brief summary or application of the *Pilgrim's Progress*.

C.M.

MUSIC. TIVERTON is from *A Selection of Psalm and Hymn Tunes, from the best authors, in three and four parts: adapted principally to Dr. Watts's Hymns and Psalms, and to Dr. Rippon's Selection of Hymns, by John Rippon, D.D.* (*c.* 1795). The composer's name is given as '— Grigg', without any Christian name. His identification with the Rev. Joseph Grigg, the hymn-writer, is purely conjectural.

457 Book of books, our people's strength.

P. Dearmer.

Written for the tune in order to express the modern appreciation of the Bible. It appeared first in the original *Songs of Praise* (1925).

Trochaic, 7 8. 7 8. 8 8. Unique.

MUSIC. DESSAU (LIEBSTER JESU), by J. R. Ahle, comes from *Neue geistliche auf die Sonntage durchs gantze Jahr gerichtete Andachten* . . . (Mühlhausen, 1664), where it is set to the hymn 'Ja, er ists, das Heil der Welt', in the following form:

Later German collections contain many variants of the melody set to Clausnitzer's hymn 'Liebster Jesu, wir sind hier'. The present form is that adopted by Bach in his *Choralgesänge*. The tune has been reduced to the usual chorale formula, not altogether to its advantage, though it has suffered less in the process than some. There is a grave tranquillity in the present form which is very attractive.

458 Breathe on me, Breath of God.

Edwin Hatch, 1835–89.

Dr. Hatch, University Reader in Ecclesiastical History at Oxford, was a scholar of world reputation, in whose learning, said Harnack (who translated his Bampton Lectures on *The Organization of the Early Christian Churches*, 1881, into German), 'that of England's great old theologians, Ussher and Pearson, lived to me again'. The hymn was first published in a privately printed leaflet called *Between Doubt and Prayer* (1878). S.M.

MUSIC. CARLISLE, by C. Lockhart, was originally set to 'Come, Holy Spirit, come', in the *Lock Hospital Collection, edited by Martin Madan* (2nd ed., 1769), and named 'Invocation'. The 1st line of the original tune runs:

The alternative version (descant), by Sydney H. Nicholson, was written especially for the enlarged *Songs of Praise* (1931).

Lockhart, who was blind, was the first organist of the above hospital, and gained a reputation as a trainer of children's choirs; he published some of his tunes separately in sheet form, in 1791, 'Carlisle' being among the number. This tune, which is a fine dignified example of his ability, soon won, and has always retained, a well-merited popularity.

459 Brief life is here our portion.

Bernard of Cluny, 12th cent. Tr. J. M. Neale.

Hic breve vivitur, hic breve plangitur, hic breve fletur;
Non breve vivere, non breve plaudere, retribuetur.

Like 'Jerusalem the golden', 198, part of Bernard of Cluny's *Hora Novissima.* The other Bernard, the saint of Clairvaux, thundered against the luxury of Cluny, which was near Macon, and the most magnificent monastery in France. His voice found an echo in the monk who wrote the fierce and bitter satire which begins 'Hora novissima', and which he styled *De Contemptu Mundi*, and headed with the text, 'Little children, it is the last time'. St. Bernard had asked, in his *Letter to Guillaume de Saint-Thierry*, if all the gilding and all the attractions of the senses were to secure 'the admiration of fools or the offerings of the simple. . . . Doth the root of this lie in covetousness, which is idolatry? do we but seek a gift? . . . The Church is resplendent in her walls, beggarly in her poor; she clothes her stones in gold, and leaves her children naked.' The unknown monk of the church upon which the saint had heaped phrases like these, noted the contrast. His own abbot lived in princely state; the wealth and luxury of Cluny were famous; hundreds of lesser convents owed allegiance to it. And outside its great walls were poverty, filth, oppression, and disease. So he pondered alone, and wrought this marvellous satire on the whole crazy business, consoling himself with his incredible ingenuity in getting six rhymes into every couplet. Consoling himself also by prefacing his description of contemporary foulness with those pictures of the heavenly perfection which have kept his name alive: 'Hora novissima, tempora pessima', he begins, 'The world is very evil'; and in the 2nd quatrain:

Curre, vir optime; lubrica reprime, praefer honesta,
Fletibus angere, flendo merebere caelica festa.

Neale's version seems flat beside this; but then it is untranslatable:

Arise, arise, good Christian, Let right to wrong succeed;
Let penitential sorrow To heavenly gladness lead.

And we barely catch a trace of the satire that is coming in his:

> And now we watch and struggle, And now we live in hope;
> And Sion in her anguish With Babylon must cope.

It is far stronger in the original:

> Spe modo vivitur, et Sion angitur a Babylone;
> Nunc tribulatio, tunc recreatio, sceptra, coronae.

Iambic, 7 6. 7 6.

MUSIC. DEVONSHIRE is an arrangement of a North Devon folk-song from Miss L. E. Broadwood's collection, and appeared in the *English Hymnal* (1906). It is a characteristic tune in one of the usual narrative ballad rhythms.

ST. ALPHEGE, by H. J. Gauntlett, was written for this hymn in the *Church Hymn and Tune Book* (1852), and has since then been closely associated with these words, and with 'The voice that breathed o'er Eden'; owing to the latter connexion the previous beautiful tune was chosen for the present hymn.

460 Bright the vision that delighted. *Bishop R. Mant*, 1776–1848.

Based on Isaiah 6: 1–3, this first appeared in his *Ancient Hymns* (1837), when he was Bishop of Down and Dromore. It is, however, not a translation, as 203 is. Two quatrains are omitted, as in most books.

Trochaic, 8 7. 8 7.

MUSIC. LAUS DEO (REDHEAD No. 46) is from *Church Hymn Tunes, ancient and modern, for the several seasons of the Christian Year . . . selected, composed, and edited by Richard Redhead* (1853). It is said to be an adaptation of a German original, and is headed 'German Choral' in the *Merton Tune Book* (1863), but this has not been identified.

The alternative version (descant), by Percy Whitlock, was written especially for the enlarged *Songs of Praise* (1931).

The tune is now very well known, and almost invariably associated with the present hymn.

461 Can I see another's woe. *William Blake*, 1757–1827.

From *Songs of Innocence*, etched in 1789. The poem is called 'On another's Sorrow', and is in nine stanzas. See also 446.

Speaking of 'the three fore-runners', Mozart, Burns, and Blake, Sir Henry Hadow says, in his *Oxford Treasury of English Literature*, iii. 213, that of the three,

> 'Blake exercised at the time the least influence. He was flouted as a madman, his mysticism was ridiculed, his poetry was decried, his engravings were cynically dismissed as "good to steal from"; not until our own day has he come to his reputation and been acknowledged at his true value. His exquisite sensitive genius is too delicate for the hand of criticism: you must take it and be enriched or leave it and be impoverished.'

Trochaic, 7 7. 7 7.

MUSIC. GALLIARD is an adaptation, by Martin Shaw, of a melody in John Dowland's *The First Booke of Songs or Ayres* (1597), and appeared in *Songs of Praise* (1925). The original melody, for voice and lute, ran as follows:

The tune has a great, simple charm, and is an excellent specimen of the less elaborate side of Dowland's genius.

462 Can you count the stars that brightly.

Johann Wilhelm Hey (1837). *Tr. H. W. Dulcken.*

This was written for children by Hey, court preacher at Gotha, who wrote many poems for them; his chief collection, *Fabeln für Kinder* (1833 and 1837), was several times translated into English: at the end of each of these two series was a 'Serious Appendix' and these also were translated twice separately, in 1853 and 1857. There have been several versions of 'Weisst du wie viel Sternlein stehen', and we give here one of our own. We have made two hymns in the rare metre, repeating the tune from 158, so that it can be learnt with a simpler setting by children.

Trochaic, 8 7. 8 7. 8 8. 8 7. Unique.

MUSIC. TREFAENAN is a unison version of the traditional Welsh melody, which is found in a harmonized version set to 158, and appeared in *Songs of Praise for Boys and Girls* (1930).

463 Children of the heavenly King.

J. Cennick, 1718–55.

This, the most popular of Cennick's hymns, and the only survivor in our book, appeared in his collection with the remarkable title, *Sacred Hymns for the Children of God in the Days of their Pilgrimage*, 1742, in 12 verses. Cennick was of Quaker stock, but brought up in the English Church; he joined Wesley, left him for Whitefield, and left Whitefield for the Moravians; and it was said of him after his death, that 'he has again joined those with whom he began his Methodist itinerancy; they all sing together now'.

Trochaic, 7 7. 7 7.

MUSIC. MELLING, by John Fawcett, is from *A New Set of Sacred Music* (1822 (?)), where it is set to the present hymn. In the original the last line of the words is repeated, the following line of music occurring between the present 3rd and 4th lines (original key B♭):

The tune is in the tradition of the more elaborate melodies popularized by the Methodists during the 18th century; the varied repeat of the last line being especially characteristic.

464 Christ is our corner-stone.

J. Chandler, based on Angularis fundamentum, *7th cent.*

Chandler's translations have been gradually disappearing in recent years; but this one is of use because it carries tunes for which there are not enough texts. It is based on the Dedication Hymn, 'Angularis fundamentum', of which Neale's translation in the metre proper to the tune is given above, 190, II.

Iambic, 6 6. 6 6. 8 8.

MUSIC. RAMOTH, by J. R. Jones, appeared in its present form in Ieuan Gwyllt's *Llyfr Tonau Cynulleidfaol* (1859). This seems to be an abbreviated form of the original tune, which probably made its first appearance in a Welsh magazine; research, however, has not yet succeeded in tracing this original. The tune is named after a hill-side chapel not far from the village of Llanfrothen, where Jones was minister.

HAREWOOD, by S. S. Wesley, appeared first in C. D. Hackett's *National Psalmist* (1839), where it is set to 'Rejoice, the Lord is King'. In the original form of the melody the last note of the 3rd line and the 1st of the 4th are equal semibreves.

465 Christ, of all my hopes the ground. *R. Wardlaw*, 1779–1853.

Dr. Wardlaw, a doughty controversialist of his time, and a Congregationalist, edited a hymn-book for Scottish use in 1803, *A Selection of Hymns for Public Worship*. This hymn was printed in the *Supplement* to the 5th edition, 1817.

Trochaic, 7 7. 7 7.

MUSIC. LONG MYND was composed by R. S. Thatcher for this hymn in the enlarged *Songs of Praise* (1931). It is an exceedingly simple tune, with a small compass, and a sincere, innocent expressiveness.

466 Christian, do you see him. *P. Dearmer.*

The tune was printed in the *English Hymnal* to replace an old one, but the hymn itself was not wanted for *Songs of Praise*. In order to help if possible to reduce the lack of hymns about Jesus Christ, in his actual person and life, 568 and 611 were added, with some others, including this, which was written by the editor for the tune.

Trochaic, 6 5. 6 5. D.

MUSIC. GUTE BÄUME BRINGEN, by P. Sohren, is from his edition of *Praxis Pietatis Melica* (1668), where it was set to the hymn 'Gute Bäume bringen, Früchte guter Art'. In the original melody the penultimate note of line 6 is G, and the last line runs:

467 Christian, seek not yet repose. *Charlotte Elliott*, 1789–1871.

From her *Morning and Evening Hymns for a Week*, printed in 1836 for sale on behalf of a benevolent institution in Brighton. In six verses, it was appointed for Wednesday, the text being 'Watch and pray, that ye enter not into temptation'.

Trochaic, 7 7. 7 3. Occurs also in 348.

MUSIC. ROBYN is an adaptation, by Geoffrey Shaw, of a melody by William Cornysshe which is found in an early 16th-century manuscript containing part-songs by various composers, including Henry VIII (B.M. Add. 31922). The present tune is from a three-part composition, being adapted from the following extracts from two parts:

and

Cornysshe was court musician to Henry VIII, and enjoyed great popularity; his compositions were both secular and ecclesiastical, but he had an especial gift for setting cheerful words, such as some of Skelton's poems, to suitably gay music, usually for three voices. These part-songs vary in length from a few bars to quite considerable compositions such as 'Ho, jolly Rutterkin'. The original of the present tune is a good example of medium length.

468 City of God, how broad and far. *S. Johnson*, 1822–82.

From *Hymns of the Spirit* (1864). One of the exceptionally fine hymns from America which did not come into general use in England till they were introduced by the *English Hymnal* in 1906.

C.M.

MUSIC. RICHMOND appeared in *Carmina Christo* (1792), which was edited by the Rev. Thomas Haweis and contained original hymns by him. This tune was set to his words 'O thou, from whom all goodness flows', and in its original form had florid repeats before the final line.

It is a characteristic 18th-century tune, in triple time; allowing for the difference of rhythm the 3rd line is identical with the 3rd line of 'Carlisle' (458). The present melody is one of the best of its type. The alternative version (fa-burden), by Martin Shaw, appeared in the *Tenor Tune Book* (1917).

469 Close by the heedless worker's side.
G. A. Studdert-Kennedy, 1883–1929.

From *Lighten our Darkness: some less rough Rhymes by a Padre* (1925). Studdert-Kennedy had a piercing originality in showing to others the facts of religious experience.

Iambic, 8 4. 8 4. 8 4. Occurs also in 582.

MUSIC. EXON was composed by Thomas Armstrong for this hymn in the enlarged *Songs of Praise* (1931). The structure of this tune is noticeable in that, in spite of its length, it is composed of two phrases only, the first extending to the end of the fourth bar, the second being, in a sense, a contracted imitation of the first. The sense of continuity, thus obtained, accords well with the feeling of the poem.

470 Come, kindred, upstand in the valour of Jesus.

P. B. Clayton.

First used at the Birthday Thanksgiving Service, held at All Hallows, Barking, near the Tower of London, in 1923.

There are many hymns that begin with the word 'Come'. One which we do not include is 'Come, thou Fount of every blessing', by Robert Robinson (*c.* 1758), which contains this, of which Dr. Rendel Harris says (rather mercifully) that all the rhymes may be challenged while all the reasons are unchallengeable:

Teach me some melodious sonnet
  Sung by flaming tongues above.
Praise the mount: I'm fixed upon it,
  Mount of God's unchanging love.
Here I raise my Ebenezer,
  Hither by thy help I'm come,
And I hope by thy good pleasure
  Safely to arrive at home.

Anapaestic, 12 11. 12 11. Unique.

MUSIC. WAS LEBET, WAS SCHWEBET is from a manuscript chorale book, *Choral-Buch vor Johann Heinrich Reinhardt*, written at Üttingen between 21 June and 22 July 1754, where it was set to the hymn 'Was lebet, was schwebet, was Odem nur hat'. This manuscript contains many melodies not found elsewhere, which were probably taken from old manuscripts or song-books now lost sight of. The original melody, being attached to a hymn with the metre 11. 11. 11. 11, has a semibreve for the two minims at the end of lines 1 and 3. It is a robust melody, in triple time, strongly stressed by repeated notes on the first two beats of the bar, in a manner typical of many traditional popular songs; it is possible that the tune is actually an adaptation of such a song.

471 Come, labour on! *Jane Borthwick*, 1813–97.

From her *Thoughts for Thoughtful Hours* (1859), in seven verses of six lines: in her edition of 1863 the seven verses were made into five-line stanzas. It was included in Thring's *Church of England Hymn Book* and the *Hymnal Companion*. 'Gentlest and most unselfish of mortals that I have met', as the writer of a memoir of her said, she wrote under the initials, H.L.L., her chief book being called *Hymns from the Land of Luther* (1854), and she was somewhat vexed when Dr. C. Rogers revealed her identity to the world in his *Lyra Britannica*.

After the stressed opening word each verse is iambic, 4 10. 10 10 4. Unique.

MUSIC. SALONICA, by J. S. Scott, was written especially for this hymn in the *Public School Hymn Book* (1919). Its name is due to the fact that it was composed in 1917, on the eve of Mr. Scott's departure for Salonica, on active service. It is a direct unison melody, with a progressive marching rhythm; a straightforward, vigorous tune excellently suited to the structure and spirit of the words.

472 Come, let us join our cheerful songs. *I. Watts*, 1674–1748.

From his *Hymns and Spiritual Songs* (1707). One of the most widely esteemed of Watts's compositions, this is generally printed without ver. 4, which begins, 'Let all that dwell above the sky'.

C.M.

MUSIC. CHEERFUL, by Martin Shaw, appeared in *Additional Tunes and Settings in Use at St. Mary's, Primrose Hill* (1915). It is a sturdy tune, which fully lives up to its name.

473 Come, my soul, thy suit prepare. *J. Newton*,† 1725–1807.

'John Newton, clerk, once an Infidel and Libertine', to quote the epitaph he composed for himself, contributed this, when he was Vicar of Olney, to the famous *Olney Hymns*, which he edited with his friend Cowper in 1779. It was in seven verses. Spurgeon used to have one or two verses sung very softly before the main prayer of the service at the Metropolitan Tabernacle. See also under 2.

Trochaic, 7 7. 7 7.

MUSIC. LOUEZ DIEU was the melody set to Psalm 136 in the complete *Genevan Psalter* of 1562. The present is its original form. It has nothing in common with the sober, introspective melodies common in this psalter; it is an energetic, plain tune, in the Mixolydian mode, but individualized by the admirable change of rhythm in the 2nd line.

474 Come, my way, my truth, my life. *George Herbert*, 1593–1633.

From *The Temple*, 1633. Some hymns seem at first sight more suited to private use, or to use in the home, than to singing in church. But that depends a good deal on the character of the music; and many which began at home have come to be much loved in church also.

Trochaic, 7 7. 7 7.

MUSIC. TUNBRIDGE, by J. Clark, appeared in Playford's *The Divine Companion: or, David's Harp new tun'd, &c.* (1709), where it is headed 'An Hymn set by Mr. Jer. Clarke, for Two Voices', and set to the hymn 'How uneasie are we here'. This must not be confused with the tune of the same name which is probably the original of 'Rockingham'. The present tune is a rather grave, four-square melody of a familiar type, but with an unusual melodic progression in line 3, which makes it most attractive.

475 Come now, all people, keep high mirth. *A. G.*

Written in order to bring in certain aspects of religion, in words that would make available another tune in this metre.

Iambic, 8 7. 8 7. 8 8 7.

MUSIC. MELCHIOR (LOBT GOTT), by M. Vulpius, appeared in his *Ein schön geistlich Gesangbuch, &c.* (Jena, 1609), where it is set to the hymn 'Lobt Gott den Herrn, ihr Heiden all'. It is a forcible, swinging melody, in triple time, with a spirited expression of confident cheerfulness, and most invigorating to sing.

476 Come, O thou Traveller unknown. *C. Wesley*,† 1707–88.

'Wrestling Jacob' is by many considered the greatest of Charles Wesley's hymns; but its length has often caused it to be overlooked. Here we print only 4 verses, out of the original 14, which were first published in the *Hymns and Poems* of 1742. Julian says, 'though a poem of great power and finish, it is unsuited to public worship'. Isaac Watts, on the other hand, says, 'that single poem, "Wrestling Jacob", is worth all the verses I have written myself': James Montgomery noted how 'with consummate art he carries on the action of a lyrical drama'; and Dean Stanley wrote in Ward's *English Poets* (iii. 258) that it was 'not only a hymn but a philosophical poem filled with depth and pathos'. No one, however, now dares to print the last line but one as in the original, 'To me, to all, thy bowels move'.

The subject was repeatedly preached on by Charles Wesley. A fortnight after his death, John gave out the hymn before a sermon. When he reached the lines,

My company before is gone,
And I am left alone with thee,

he burst into tears and covered his face with his hands, while the whole congregation wept with him. The same verse was quoted by Dr. Stanley at the unveiling of the memorial to the Wesleys in Westminster Abbey, in 1876, shortly after the death of his own wife.

Iambic, 8 8. 8 8. 8 8.

MUSIC. DAVID'S HARP, by Robert King, is set to Miles Smyth's version of Psalm 101 in Playford's *The Divine Companion: or, David's Harp new tun'd* (1st ed. 1701). This is a very beautiful tune, and out of the rut of common hymn-tune types of the period. Robert King was a well-known song-writer during the first years of the 18th century, and the present tune is a good example of his suave and significant melodic gift. The last two lines, especially, are beautifully expressive.

477 Come, ye people, raise the anthem.

J. Hupton (1805), *and others*.

Job Hupton, in the *Gospel Magazine* (1805), published a hymn of 13 verses, and signed it 'Ebenezer', in the odd manner of those days. The 1st verse is:

Come, ye saints, and raise an anthem,
Cleave the skies with shouts of praise,
Sing to him who found a ransom,
Th' Ancient of eternal days—
In your nature
Born to suffer in your place.

Neale, in an article on hymns in the *Christian Remembrancer* (1863), remarking that a hymn with some merit might be made out of crude materials, re-wrote seven of Hupton's verses; and the experiment, appearing in the *People's Hymnal* (1867), passed into popularity. Its text will be found in the *English Hymnal*, 380. When *Songs of Praise* was being produced, it was felt that the confusion with 'Come, ye faithful, raise the strain' might be avoided; and 'others' felt themselves in rather the same position towards Neale that he had been towards Hupton. As Hupton had been already moved out of the reign of George III, there seemed a good opportunity for establishing him in the era of George V; and the *Songs of Praise* version is the result.

Trochaic, 8 7. 8 7. 8 7.

MUSIC. NEANDER, by J. Neander, is from his *A und Ω. Glaub- und Liebesübung* . . . (Bremen, 1680), where it is set to the hymn 'Unser Herrscher, unser König', in the following form:

The form, in common time throughout, dates from the end of the 17th century, with slight variations of the last line.

The alternative version (descant), by Alan Gray, appeared in his *A Book of Descants* (1920).

This famous tune is now, almost invariably, associated with the present words.

478 Cometh sunshine after rain.

P. Gerhardt (1656). *Tr. C. Winkworth.*‡

Auf den Nebel folgt die Sonn',
Auf das Trauern Freud' und Wonn',
Auf die schwere, bitt're Pein
Stellt sich Trost und Labsal ein:
  Meine Seele, die zuvor
  Sank bis an des Todes Thor,
  Steigt gen Himmel nun empor.

Paul Gerhardt (1607–76) was the greatest German hymnist after Luther, and he marks the transition from the objective to the subjective religion of Germany. Our 57, 89, 128 ('O sacred head') are based on him, and 479 is a free translation. This is one of his best, and in a fine metre for musical purposes; but sunshine came little to poor Gerhardt; he struggled long in exclusion from ministerial work, on a question of principle. His last years were clouded; and the description on his portrait at Lübbe describes him as '*Theologus in cribro Satanae versatus*' ('a divine strained in the sieve of Satan'. The more praise for his cheerful faith! Miss Winkworth's translation, here somewhat altered, was in her *Lyra Germanica* (1st series, 1855).

Trochaic, 7 7. 7 7. 7 7 7. Unique.

MUSIC. IN NATALI DOMINI is the melody, probably of the 14th century, originally attached to the Latin hymn 'In natali domini gaudent omnes angeli'. Its earliest printed form seems to be in *Ein Gesangbuch der Brüder in Behemen und Merherrn, &c.* (Nürnberg, 1544), where it is set to 'Da Christus geboren war' as follows:

It is found in the Andernach song-book, *Catholische Geistliche Gesänge . . . Von der Fraternität S. Cecilie zu Andernach* . . . (Cölln, 1608), set to the original Latin hymn, with a German translation, in the following form:

on which the present version is based, with emendations from a variant, set to 'Als Maria die Jungfrau schön', in *Alte Catholische Kirchengesäng, &c.* (Cöln, 1619). Other variants are found in several collections, both Catholic and Protestant. The splendid Dorian tune is thoroughly characteristic of its period in rhythm and feeling.

479 Commit thou all thy griefs.

P. Gerhardt, 1607–76. *Tr. J. Wesley*, 1703–91.

Befiehl du deine Wege
  Und was dein Herze kränkt,
Der allertreusten Pflege
  Des, der den Himmel lenkt:
Der Wolken, Luft, und Winden
  Giebt Wege, Lauf, und Bahn,
Der wird auch Wege finden,
  Da dein Fuss gehen kann.

A quite free translation of Gerhardt's great hymn, which appeared in Crüger's *Praxis* (1646), this was published in the Wesleys' *Early Hymns and Sacred Poems* (1739). There is a more literal rendering in A. R. MacEwen's *Life of Principal Cairns*. The 12 stanzas were reduced by Wesley to 8, of which we give what seem to be the 4 best. It will be remembered that in Germany hymns are sung slowly, and often one hymn is divided and used in sections throughout the service.

'Befiehl du deine Wege' was sung when the foundation-stone was laid of the first Lutheran church at Philadelphia, 1743. Queen Luise of Prussia, when the kingdom was downtrodden by Napoleon, wrote in her diary, 5 Dec. 1806, some verses from Goethe's *Wilhelm Meister*; and then, drying her tears, sang this hymn to her harpsichord. 'The most comforting of all his hymns', Lauxmann says, 'it is surrounded by a cloud of witnesses.'

D.S.M.

MUSIC. DINBYCH, by Joseph Parry, appeared in his *Llyfr Tônau Cynulleidfaol Cenedlaethol Cymru* (1887–92). The tune is here slightly abridged from the form in which it appears in the above collection, which contains several hundred tunes, and was published in serial parts during the six years of its production.

480 Crown him upon the throne. *A. F.*

Three or four hymns on the theme 'Crown him' have been written, of which the famous original is 'All hail the power of Jesus' name', 440. One of these became popular in Anglican circles; but, as it was not felt that this hymn was good, though the motive was a good one and had won favour, the editor undertook to write a new hymn in the same metre, so that it could be sung to the tune here given.

D.S.M.

MUSIC. ICH HALTE TREULICH STILL is from Schemelli's *Musikalisches Gesangbuch* (Leipzig, 1736). It is believed to be an original melody by J. S. Bach, but the attribution is not certain, and the internal evidence does not altogether support it.

481 Dear Lord and Father of mankind. *J. G. Whittier*, 1807–92.

The Church of England hymn-books of the 19th century ignored the beauty of Whittier's work, as also that of other New England poets and hymn-writers, perhaps because Whittier was a Quaker, Longfellow and others Unitarians—and Lowell because he was an American. At the same time a mass of bad work was included whose only merit was that it set forth the ideas of various church parties. This is from Whittier's *The Brewing of Soma* (1872). In the poem he describes the pagan custom of drinking the intoxicating Indian *soma* in order to have communion with the deity; and in our stanzas he praises the quiet spiritual converse with God, as against sensuous excitement in worship.

Iambic, 8 6. 8 8 6, i.e. C.M. with an added penultimate line. Unique.

MUSIC. REPTON, by Sir Hubert Parry, is from his oratorio *Judith* (1888), where in Scene ii, a dialogue between Meshollemeth and a Child, it is sung by the former to the words beginning 'Long since in Egypt's plenteous land'. The tune is typical of the composer in its broad melody, and especially in the elliptical rhythm of the last three lines. In its present form it makes a fine, strong unison tune.

NICOLAUS (LOBT GOTT), by Nicolaus Hermann, is first found in *Ein Christlicher Abentreien, &c.* (Leipzig, 1554), set to the words 'Kommt her, ihr Lieben Schwesterlein' as follows:

and later in *Die Sontags Evangelia, &c.* (Wittenberg, 1560), set to Hermann's own hymn 'Lobt Gott, ihr Christen, alle gleich'.

The present version is J. S. Bach's.

482 Enduring Soul of all our life. *E. Sherman Oakley*, 1863–1934.

Written by Mr. Oakley, Principal of Ramsay College, Almora, N. India, and contributed to Dr. John Hunter's *Hymns of Faith and Life* (1885), from whence it passed to the *Public School Hymn Book* (1903). C.M.

MUSIC. CROWLE appeared in *A Book of Psalmody, &c.* by James Green (5th ed. 1724), where it is anonymous, and set to Psalm 1. It does not seem traceable in any earlier collection, and its attribution in later publications to, among others, Dr. Maurice Greene seems to rest on no good grounds.

483 Enter thy courts, thou word of life. *Y.H.* (*Robert Bridges*).

Composed for the Tallis tune in the *Yattendon Hymnal* (1899).
Iambic, 8 4. 8 6. D. Unique.

MUSIC. FIFTH MODE MELODY, by Thomas Tallis, is from *The Whole Psalter translated into English metre, &c.* (see 45). It is a notable tune with a very individual rhythm, and a lofty air of resolution imparted to it by the strong initial phrase and nobly sustained throughout its considerable length.

484 Eternal Father, who didst all create.

Y.H. (*Robert Bridges*).

A sonnet from the *Growth of Love* (1876), this expresses in noble language the more personal feelings of the author of the *Testament of Beauty* (1930) and is less on the traditional lines of hymnody than his work in the *Yattendon Hymnal* (1899). It follows the clauses of the Lord's Prayer.

In the musical enumeration, iambic 10 10. 10 10. 10 10, i.e. sonnet form with the last couplet omitted in the musical enumeration because of the repetition in the tune of the last two lines. Metrically a single stanza of 14 decasyllables. In the sonnet the rhymes may be arranged in varying ways: here they are: *abba*, *abba*, *cdcd*, *ee*. See the Note on Prosody, pp. xxix–xxxi, and cf. 22, 622.

MUSIC. DECREE is an arrangement, by Martin Shaw, of a traditional English melody, and appeared in *Songs of Praise*. It is an admirable tune, imposingly dignified, and of great emotional power, especially in the deeply expressive 3rd line.

485 Eternal Ruler of the ceaseless round.

J. W. Chadwick, 1840–1904.

'The smoke of battle hung over the mighty hosts for six days, while the North remained in a state of suspense bordering on agony; but Grant wrote to the Government at Washington, "I propose to fight it out on this line, if it takes all summer".' In the midst of this slaughter and hate,

Chadwick wrote his song of peace and goodwill—'Hymn written for my Divinity-School Graduation'—19 June 1864, at the Divinity School, Cambridge, Mass., shortly before his ordination to the Second Unitarian Church, Boston. From *A Book of Poems* (1876), this is another of the American hymns that were overlooked in England; and we owe the wider extension of this and others of them to Garrett Horder (*Congregational Hymns*, 1884).

Iambic, 10 10. 10 10. 10 10, with the rhymes *ababcc*.

MUSIC. SONG 1. See 296.

486 Everything changes. *S.P. from Goethe.*

Written in collaboration with Dr. Martin Shaw, to provide a new musical form, and to express the philosophy of the supreme values.

Dactylic, with trochaic refrain, 5 5. 6 5. 8 7. 8 7. Unique.

MUSIC. GUN HILL, by Martin Shaw, appeared in *Songs of Praise for Boys and Girls* (1930). It is an easy 'natural' tune of the attractively extrovert type characteristic of much of this composer's music, with a beautiful change of the rhythmic scheme in the refrain.

487 Father, hear the prayer we offer.
Mrs. L. M. Willis (1864), *and others.*

Another American hymn, this was written by Mrs. Willis as 'Father, hear the prayer I offer' for *Hymns of the Spirit*, by S. Longfellow and S. Johnson (see e.g. 16, 468), it was re-written (for it contained a fine motive), probably by S. Longfellow. In England it was printed in Horder's *Worship Song* (1905) and in the *English Hymnal* (1906).

Trochaic, 8 7. 8 7.

MUSIC. GOTT WILL'S MACHEN, by J. L. Steiner, appeared in *Newes Gesangbuch Auserlesener Geistreicher Liedern, &c.* (vol. ii, Zurich, 1735 [vol. i, 1723]), set to the hymn 'Gott wills machen, dass die Sachen gehen'. The present is the original form of the melody.

488 Father in heaven who lovest all. *Rudyard Kipling.*

From *Puck of Pook's Hill* (1906): a boy's hymn which is fit also for adults.

L.M.

MUSIC. LLANGOLLEN (LLEDROD) is a Welsh melody from *Llyfr Tonau Cynulleidfaol* (1859). It is a cheerful, vigorous tune with an unusual and spirited rhythm.

489 Fierce raged the tempest o'er the deep.
G. Thring, 1823–1903.

Based on Mark 4:39, this was written in 1861, and published in Thring's *Hymns Congregational and Others* (1874), and in his *Church of England Hymn Book* (1880), of which Julian wrote in 1891: 'Its literary standard is the highest', and 'it will be difficult to find its equal and impossible to name its superior'.

Iambic 8 8. 8 3; but the refrain is an amphimacer, – ⏑ –. Unique.

MUSIC. WHITE GATES was composed by R. Vaughan Williams for this hymn in the enlarged *Songs of Praise* (1931). The tune has rather an 18th-century 'feel' about it; the phrase in the 3rd line, however, has a turn very characteristic of the composer, and, by its reference to the previous line, makes the melody excellently terse and compact.

490 Fierce was the wild billow. *J. M. Neale*‡, 1818–66.

This is based on the same text as the other 'Fierce' hymn, 489. From *Hymns of the Eastern Church*, 1862. Whether Neale was joking when he attributed this to St. Anatolius, or whether, in his obsession for old Greek hymnists, he had forgotten that this was his own, we do not know; but no Greek original has ever been found, and there is nothing of the sort in St. Anatolius of Constantinople (the absence of interest in the events of our Lord's life being one of the major phenomena of Greek and Latin hymnody, as it is of Byzantine and Medieval pictorial art). Moreover, the only hymnist of the name of Anatolius lived in the 8th century, and not, like Anatolius of Constantinople, in the 5th.

Congregations used to be puzzled by the 'Wail of Euroclydon' in ver. 2. Who was Euroclydon? Only a learned blunder of Neale's. St. Mark does not make the mistake of calling the fierce local squalls on the lake of Galilee by this name. The 'euroclydon' or 'euraquilo' is indeed mentioned in Acts 27:14; but it was a north-east wind from the mountains of Crete. 'Euros' is the south-east wind, and 'aquilo' the north wind, so that 'euraquilo' was probably a sailor's name for a local 'tempestuous wind' such as buffeted the ship of St. Paul off Cape Matala. We have changed the line to 'Wail of the hurricane'; we have also altered in ver. 1 'God of Gods' to 'Lord of Lords'.

Dactylic, 6 4. 6 4. D. Unique, and delightful for music. Lines like 'Trembled the mariners' are perfect dactyls, comparatively rare in English verse.

MUSIC. ST. ISSEY is an arrangement of an English traditional melody. It is found in the *Fitzwilliam Virginal Book*, and many collections of *c.* 1600 and later. It was immensely popular in the 16th and 17th centuries, being frequently mentioned in plays and other writings of that time. The tune is probably of the 15th century, as the Priory of Walsingham, to which the pilgrimages referred to in the original song were made, was destroyed in 1538. The present arrangement appeared in the *English Hymnal* (1906).

491 Fight the good fight with all thy might.

J. S. B. Monsell, 1811–75.

This of course has nothing to do with the Army or Navy, but is based on 1 Tim. 6:12, passing on to 2 Tim. 4:7–8. Dr. Monsell, in his *Hymns of Love and Praise* (1863), put it down for Trinity 19; but it has little application to the Epistle, Eph. 4:17–32, which is about being renewed in the spirit, and practising the social virtues. James Montgomery in 1834 had written a hymn beginning 'Fight the good fight', but it went on differently.

L.M., with an internal rhyme in each first line.

MUSIC. DUKE STREET. See 298. The alternative version (descant), by Alan Gray, appeared in his *A Book of Descants* (1920).

MONTESANO, by John Law, appeared in *Songs of Praise* (1931). It is a fluent tune, in triple time, to which the regularity of the rhythmic scheme gives great force and decision, making it admirably adapted to the present hymn.

Both these tunes, on the grounds of quality of melody and of suitability to the words, are infinitely superior to the poor tune usually associated with this hymn; it is to be hoped that the latter will finally drop out of use.

492 Fill thou my life, O Lord my God. *Horatius Bonar*, 1808–89.

From his *Hymns of Faith and Hope* (3rd series, 1866). Dr. Bonar was a Calvinist and was all his life much occupied with the Second Advent, an interest which appeared in much of his work. He threw off his hymns in the most casual way, and seemed to be taken up with other things: 'One said of him that he was always visiting, another that he was always preaching, another that he was always writing, another that he was always praying.' (Cf. under 607.)

C.M.

MUSIC. ABBEY is one of the twelve Common Tunes in *The CL Psalms of David, &c.* (A. Hart, Edinburgh, 1615). It is in the usual psalm-tune manner, but gains some individuality from the effect of determination given by the rising inflexion of the first three lines.

493 For mercy, courage, kindness, mirth. *Laurence Binyon.*

In his *Collected Poems* (1932) this is in the group of poems written between 1914 and 1920.

Trochaic, 77.77, irregular, because the first couplet begins with iambs.

MUSIC. LEW TRENCHARD is an arrangement, by S. Baring-Gould, of a traditional English melody, collected by him, which appeared in the *English Hymnal* (1906). It is a very simple little tune, not especially characteristic of folk-melodies in its present form, except in the formation of the 3rd line out of part of the 2nd, which is a common feature; but, in its ingenuousness and candour, most appealing and attractive.

494 For the beauty of the earth. *F. S. Pierpoint*,† 1835–1917.

From O. Shipley's *Lyra Eucharistica* (2nd ed. 1864), in eight verses. We have altered in the refrain, 'Christ our God to' into 'Father, unto'.

Trochaic, 77.77.77, the last couplet being the refrain.

MUSIC. ENGLAND'S LANE is an adaptation, by Geoffrey Shaw, of the traditional English melody, and appeared in the *Public School Hymn Book* (1919).

495 For the might of thine arm we bless thee, our God, our fathers' God. *C. Silvester Horne*, 1865–1914.

Silvester Horne wrote this stirring song for use at Whitefields Tabernacle, London, and it was included in the *Fellowship Hymn Book*

(1909). It was suggested to him by Mrs. Hemans's 'Hymn of the Vaudois Mountain Christian', which begins:

For the strength of the Hills we bless thee,
  Our God, our Fathers' God;
Thou hast made thy people mighty
By the touch of the mountain sod,
Thou hast fixed our ark of refuge
Where the spoiler's feet ne'er trod,
For the strength of the hills we bless thee,
  Our God, our Fathers' God.

Silvester Horne made less use of the three remaining stanzas, which are mainly inspired by mountain scenery.

Anapaestic 14. 14. 14. 14, slightly irregular. With such long lines there is inevitably a marked caesura, e.g. after 'we bless thee'. This—apart from elegiac hymns, &c., 'Irregular' in our Metrical Index—is the hymn with the second longest lines in our book; and, curiously enough, that with the longest lines comes next, 496. Unique.

MUSIC. CORMAC is an arrangement, by Martin Shaw, of a traditional Irish melody in the *Feis Ceoil Collection of Irish Music*. The structure of this tune is typical of a large class of Irish folk-tunes, being built of two recurring lines in the form *abba*, with the middle line usually, as here, slightly varied the second time. The present tune also has the triple repeat of the tonic at the cadence, which, however, is not typically Irish, as is often popularly supposed. The melody, as a whole, is a fine one, with a wide, expressive sweep of contour.

496 From glory to glory advancing, we praise thee, O Lord.

Liturgy of St. James, Tr. C. W. Humphreys.

The opening words, here paraphrased, of the Litany of Dismissal in the Greek Liturgy of St. James, sung by the deacon, before the priest goes from the Lord's Table to the sacristy. Included in the *English Hymnal* (1906).

Anapaestic, 14. 14. 14. 15. The longest in our Metrical Index, which includes elegiacs, &c. as 'Irregular'. Cf. 495. Unique.

MUSIC. SHEEN, by Gustav Holst, appeared in the *English Hymnal* (1906), set to the present hymn. It is a broad, flowing tune in triple time, with skilful control of the long rhythm of the individual phrases, and a finely pliant and sensitive melodic line.

497 Gather us in, thou love that fillest all.

George Matheson, 1842–1906.

Unlike any other missionary hymn, and full of originality, this is from his *Sacred Songs* (1890), written in that year at Row in Dumbartonshire with the other contents of the book.

Iambic, 10 10. 10 10. 4. Unique.

MUSIC. BILLESLEY, by Michael Mullinar, was composed especially for these words in *Songs of Praise*, and appeared also in sheet form (1927). It is a brisk, straightforward tune, with a regular, vigorous rhythm well adapted to the nature of the words.

498 Gird on thy sword, O man, thy strength endue.

Robert Bridges, 1844–1930.

The last section (vii) of 'A Hymn of Nature: an Ode written for Music. The music composed by Sir Hubert Parry, performed at the Gloucester Festival, 1898', included in *Later Poems* (1912).

Iambic, 10 10. 10 10.

MUSIC. CHILSWELL, by Gustav Holst, is from his anthem 'Man born to toil' (1927). It is a firm, shapely tune with a progressive continuity of phrase, showing slightly, perhaps, the influence of the 16th-century English school of composers, both in the free manipulation of the rhythm, and in the insistence on the B♭, the *fa fictum* of the older theorists. It is also a characteristically compact tune, with an easy melodic flow.

499 Glad that I live am I. *Lizette Woodworth Reese.*

From *A Handful of Lavender* (1891). This delightful little song was meant for children; but hearty adults insist, very rightly, on making it their own. It is good to become as little children. Walter de la Mare, in a facsimile typewritten letter pasted into *Selected Poems* (1926), says of the author:

'She belongs to no particular school; she belongs to herself . . . open this book at random, and the accents of one voice, the colouring of one mind, the presence of a definite sensibility, and the dreaming and reverie of one single imagination are instantly evident. . . . Every work of art is a revelation of one human spirit's living and vivid interest in these things (life, humanity, and what we call nature). Here is hers: revealing her courage, simplicity, insight, downrightness, tenderness, and consuming zeal.'

Irregular, 6 5. 6 5.; a line of dactyls, followed by spondees in most cases.

MUSIC. WATER-END, by Geoffrey Shaw, was composed for this hymn in *Songs of Praise* (1925). It is a bright, unaffected tune, excellently suited to the rhythm and character of the words.

500 Glorious things of thee are spoken. *J. Newton*, 1725–1807.

This famous hymn is really based on Psalm 87, although in the *Olney Hymns* (1779) (see 473) it is styled, 'Zion, or the City of God, Isa. 33: 20, 21'. Originally in five verses, this is often made into a cento, and the following verse (with its awkward rhyme of 'banner' with 'manna') re-written:

Round each habitation hovering,
  See the cloud and fire appear,
For a glory and a covering,
  Showing that the Lord is near:
Thus deriving from their banner
  Light by night and shade by day,
Safe they feed upon the manna
  Which he gives them when they pray.

The fact is that this verse is not so good as the rest; and the hymn is much better without both it and the other verse which the curious can find in *Church Hymns* (1871), beginning:

Blest inhabitants of Zion,
  Washed in the Redeemer's Blood!
Jesus, whom their souls rely on,
  Makes them kings and priests to God.

Such phrases, in our three verses, as 'solid joys' are delightfully redolent of 18th-century matter-of-factness—in the days when matter was thought to be solid.

Trochaic, 8 7. 8 7. D.

MUSIC. AUSTRIAN HYMN was composed by Joseph Haydn for Hauschka's national hymn 'Gott erhalte Franz den Kaiser', which was first performed on the Emperor's birthday, 12 Feb. 1797. Haydn afterwards used it as the theme for the variation movement in his String Quartet, No. 77, known, in consequence, as the 'Kaiserquartett'. The melody is founded on a Croatian folk-tune. In English collections the tune is first found in Edward Miller's *Sacred Music*, &c. (1802).

The alternative version (descant), by T. H. Ingham, was written for *Songs of Praise* (1925).

501 God be in my head. *Sarum Primer*, 1558.

First published as a hymn, so far as we know, in the *Oxford Hymn Book* (1908). Prefixed as a motto to the book, as well as set to music for hymn 207, this modest little jewel from a Sarum Primer of 1558—a very late date—(It has, however, been found in a Book of Hours of 1514) became rapidly popular, as very simple things often do; and it has since passed from one book to another. It seems generally to be used as a short anthem on the occasions when such an interlude is required.

Irregular, practically in rhythmical prose.

MUSIC. CONSTANTIA was composed by R. O. Morris for this hymn in the enlarged *Songs of Praise* (1931).

DAVID was composed by G. W. Briggs for this hymn in *Hymns for Use in Schools* (1930).

Of these two tunes, the first is, perhaps, slightly the more difficult: both, in their various ways, however, are apt to the form and spirit of the words.

502 God is love: his the care. *A. F.*

Written for the original *Songs of Praise* (1925) for the young and reprinted in *Songs of Praise for Boys and Girls* (1930). It was devised to convey if possible some fundamental theology in a simple form, and also to fit the carol tune of 'Personent hodie'.

Cretan and trochaic, 6 6 6. 6 6. 5 5. 3. 9 (the last four numbers representing the refrain). The cretan or amphimacer feet being the first and third—'God is love', cf. 325. Unique.

MUSIC. THEODORIC is an arrangement, by Gustav Holst, of the melody from *Piae Cantiones* (1582) [see 4]. It appeared first in *Songs of Praise* (1925), and in the *Oxford Book of Carols* (1928), 78. It is a very strong Dorian tune, with a steady unflinching rhythm, and a remarkable air of triumphant resolution in the refrain, very captivating and enjoyable to sing.

503 God moves in a mysterious way. *W. Cowper*, 1731–1800.

There is no basis for the legend that Cowper had been prevented from committing suicide, when he wrote what the *Handbook to the Church Hymnary* well calls 'this profound hymn'. For some time it appeared in various places as anonymous, until Newton, who had first published it in his *Twenty-six Letters on Religious Subjects; to which are added Hymns &c. by Omicron* (1774), set the matter at rest in the *Olney Hymns* (Bk. III, 1779). It rapidly became popular, and for long has appeared in every hymnal; it has been also more than once published in Latin versions.

It is related that during the Cotton Famine in Lancashire of 1865, a mill-owner called his people together, and told them that the mill must be closed. Bitter silence fell upon the workers; and then the tension was broken by the ringing voice of a girl, and the words she sang were from this hymn: 'Ye fearful saints, fresh courage take'. Confidence and hope came back.

C.M.

MUSIC. LONDON NEW is one of the 31 Common Tunes in *The Psalmes of David, &c.* (Hart's heirs, Edinburgh, 1635), where it is called 'Newtoun' and the 3rd line runs:

This form occurs in many Scottish books down to about 1820, principally in those issued in the east and north of Scotland. The present form appeared in Playford's *Psalms and Hymns in solemn Musick* (1671) and in all subsequent English collections, as well as in those published in the west of Scotland. After the publication of R. A. Smith's *Collection* (1825), this form seems to have become universal. Another variation in the melody is the substitution, at the 4th note of the 2nd line, of either the 6th or the 4th of the scale for the 5th. This peculiarity is found in the *Supplement to the New Version of the Psalms* (1708); in some editions of Playford; in Chalmers's *Collection* (Aberdeen, 1748 or 1749); and in one or two other books published in the north of Scotland.

The alternative version (fa-burden), by Martin Shaw, appeared in the *Tenor Tune Book* (1917).

504 God, who created me. *H. C. Beeching*, 1859–1919.

A hymn for boys, this first appeared in Beeching's *In a Garden, and other Poems* (1895).

Irregular, 6 6. 6 6. D.

MUSIC. PRAYERS was composed by R. H. Milford for this hymn in *Songs of Praise* (1925). It is a bright tune, in triple time, and minuet rhythm, with something of the elegant refinement that befits this form.

505 Good cheer! *S.P., based on Abp. Trench.*

Trench's noble lines (in his *Poems*, 1865) were not written for a hymn; and the present writer had never succeeded in getting them sung as they were written, though they were printed for this use in several leaflets and little books. They begin:

Let all men know that all men move
Under a canopy of love,
As broad as the blue sky above;
That doubt and trouble, fear and pain,
And anguish, all are shadows vain;
That death itself shall not remain.

Lines 3 and 4 in ver. 2 also are taken from Trench's poem; and the last verse is his but for a few words. The great Welsh tune, 'Braint', had to be included in our book; and we therefore arranged this hymn to carry it with the necessary addition of the opening words, 'Good cheer'.

Spondaic-iambic, 2. 8 8 8. 8 8, the spondee being the first two words. Unique.

MUSIC. BRAINT is a Welsh air from *Llyfr Tonau Cynulleidfaol* (1859), harmonized by David Evans. This is a remarkably fine Dorian tune, with an individual rhythm, and a quite exceptional significance of phrase, especially in the 2nd (4th) line. Of its kind it is a tune of the first rank. It will stand the severe test of considerable variation of speed without change of character.

GLAN'RAFON, by David Davies, appeared in Stephen's *Llyfr Tonau ac Emynau* (1868). Though less striking than the previous tune, this is a most interesting and attractive melody.

506 Gracious Spirit, dwell with me. *T. T. Lynch*, 1818–71.

This first appeared in the *Rivulet* (1855) which provoked the Rivulet Controversy and shook the foundations of puritanism (cf. 21). Lynch chose the title 'Rivulet' because 'Christian poetry is indeed a river of the water of life, and to this river my rivulet brings its contribution'. The hymn, which appeared in six stanzas, was included in the *Baptist Psalms and Hymns* (1858); until now it has been little known in the Church of England, though it has long been popular in the Free Churches.

Trochaic, 7 7. 7 7. 7 7.

MUSIC. JESU, JESU, DU MEIN HIRT, by Paul Heinlein, is from the Nürnberg *Gesangbuch* (1676), where it is set to the hymn 'Jesu, Jesu, du mein Hirt'. The present is the original form of the melody. It is a good tune of the normal chorale pattern.

507 Gracious Spirit, Holy Ghost.

Bishop Christopher Wordsworth, 1807–85.

From his *Holy Year* (1862), where it is put for Quinquagesima, the Epistle being 1 Cor. 13. Some of the eight verses are not very good, and few hymnals have printed them all. *Hymns Ancient and Modern* and the *English Hymnal* give six verses. We have reduced them to five, by omitting that one which hardly does justice to St. Paul's statement that hope and faith 'abide' as well as charity:

Faith will vanish into sight;
Hope be emptied in delight;
Love in heaven will shine more bright;
Therefore give us love.

The *Church Hymnary* also omits our last verse, 'From the gold', &c.; but it includes the poor verse, 'Though I as a martyr bleed', and the following, with its unfortunate false accent on 'Without' in the last line:

Faith that mountains could remove
Tongues of earth or Heaven above,
Knowledge, all things, empty prove
Without heavenly love.

But some bad verses have to be included anyhow. The fact is that Christopher Wordsworth, an admirable bishop but no poet, was at a particular disadvantage in setting himself the impossible task of changing the peerless rhythmical prose of the Authorized Version into verse. And ought we not to recover for common speech the proper meaning of the irreplaceable word 'charity', instead of giving it up? Compare 'Though I speak with the tongues of men and of angels, and have not charity . . .', with 'Tongues of earth or heaven above . . . Without heavenly love!'

Trochaic, 7 7 7. 5. Also in 47.

MUSIC. CAPETOWN, by F. Filitz, is from *Vierstimmiges Choralbuch herausgegeben von Dr. F. Filitz* (Berlin, 1847).

The alternative version (fa-burden), by H. Goss Custard, was written for the enlarged *Songs of Praise* (1931).

The tune was originally set in the above work to the hymn 'Morgenglanz der Ewigkeit'; it is now commonly associated, in England, with the above words, and in some collections is found with the last line in this form:

but this seems to be rather forcing the sentiment.

508 Guide me, O thou great Redeemer.

W. Williams, 1717–91. *Tr. P. and W. Williams*.‡

William Williams wrote in Welsh 'Guide me, O thou great Jehovah', for *Halleluiah*, his first book of hymns, 1745. The 1st verse was published in English, with the 2nd in part—by Peter Williams the commentator—in *Hymns on Various Subjects* (1771). The 2nd and 3rd verses were translated either by William himself or by his son, John Williams, afterwards Principal of Trevecca College, which was referred to when the hymn appeared in a leaflet (1772) as, *A favourite Hymn sung by Lady Huntingdon's Young Collegians*. There were four verses in this, and five in the Welsh version. We have altered, in ver. 1 from 'Jehovah', in accordance with our rule; and in ver. 3, from 'Death of deaths'.

A curious example of hymn-mangling occurs in the *Hymn Book of the Friends of the Rational Order of Society*, where there are many other quaintly altered hymns. These people were called Owenites, because they were disciples of the early Socialist reformer, Robert Owen; they began our hymn thus:

Guide us, Truth, thou star refulgent,
Travellers through a darksome land;
We are weak, but thou art mighty
To support our social band;
Lead us onward,
Bending to thy high command.

But William Williams himself could write queer verses, as in this expansion of the Song of Songs:

Hark! the voice of my Beloved,
  Lo! he comes in greatest need,
Leaping on the lofty mountains,
  Skipping o'er the hills with speed,
    To deliver
Me unworthy from all woe.

Trochaic, 8 7. 8 7. 4 7.

MUSIC. LLANILAR is a Welsh melody found in its present form in Ieuan Gwyllt's *Llyfr Tonau Cynulleidfaol* (1859). Like 'Ramoth' (464, i) this is stated to have been abbreviated by the editor, and probably appeared in its original form in some Welsh monthly magazine, but this has not yet been traced. As it stands it is a fine, sturdy tune with a strongly marked character in the last two lines, and of a very remarkable quality throughout.

CAERSALEM, by R. Edwards, appeared in Parry's *Peroriaeth Hyfryd* (1837). This is not so strong a tune as the previous one, and the similarity of the 5th line in both provides a just measure of comparison, the effect, in the 2nd tune, being weakened by the return, in the 3rd bar, to the *motif* of the 1st bar, whereas, in the former tune, the 3rd bar reinforces the impression both by the continuation of the rising movement in the 1st note and the variation of the previous phrases in the rest of the bar. The present tune, however, is in itself an admirable one.

509 Happy are they, they that love God.

Y.H. (Robert Bridges), based on C. Coffin (1736).

O quam juvat fratres, Deus,
unum quibus Christus caput
vitale robur sufficit,
uno moveri spiritu.

Dr. Bridges seems to have been so dissatisfied with the translation of this by Chandler (*Hymns of the Primitive Church*, 1837), which he found in use at Yattendon Church ('O Lord, how joyful 'tis to see'), that he turned to the Latin; and then, being still unsatisfied, he did what many others have done, altered so much that he made a new hymn. He paraphrased most freely vv. 1, 2, and 3 (leaving hardly any of the original), omitted ver. 4 altogether, and added two verses entirely his own (our 4 and 5).

C.M. But the 1st line of each verse falls into two halves, each beginning with a trochee.

MUSIC. BINCHESTER, by William Croft, is set to Psalm 96 in Playford's *The Divine Companion* (2nd ed. 1709). The melody, in triple time, is indeed 'happy' both in rhythm and melody, a characteristic which Dr. Bridges stressed in the words he wrote for it.

510 Hark, my soul! it is the Lord. *W. Cowper*, 1731–1800.

Cowper's hymn had been written at Huntingdon, *c.* 1765, and first appeared in Maxfield's *New Appendix* (1768). It was in the *Olney Hymns* (1779). Young people nowadays sometimes turn against the 'she bear' hymn; but that is because it has been associated with a tune that sentimentalized it in a horrible way. It is really a simple poem, intimate, sincere, and clean. Gladstone did it into Italian, 'Senti, senti, anima mea', and J. W. Hales into Latin, 'Audin'? adest Dominus'.

Trochaic, 7 7. 7 7.

MUSIC. FREUEN WIR UNS, by Michael Weisse, appeared in his *Ein New Gesengbuchlen* (Behmen, 1531), set to the hymn 'Freuen wir uns all ein'. The melody is as the present, except that the penultimate note is a semibreve; the crotchet is found in *Ein Gesangbuch der Brüder in Behemen und Merherrn, &c.* (1544). It is an incisive Aeolian tune, with a steadily moving rhythm; it is serious, but not solemn, and must not be sung too slowly.

511 Hark what a sound, and too divine for hearing.

F. W. H. Myers, 1843–1901.

Frederick Myers's splendid poem, *St. Paul*, from which these stanzas are taken, was first published, as a small volume, in 1867.

Iambic, 11 10. 11 10, involving thus double rhymes throughout.

MUSIC. ST. OSYTH, by Thomas Wood, appeared in *Songs of Praise* (1925). It is a lucid tune with a briskly moving rhythm and march-like melody of a remarkably smooth and graceful continuity.

512 Hast thou not known, hast thou not heard.

I. Watts (1745), *and others.*

Our three verses, except the last quatrain of ver. 2, are in the *Scottish Paraphrases*, originally published 1745–51, and still in use. They come from Watts's 'Whence do our mournful thoughts arise?', in his *Hymns and Spiritual Songs* (1707). The Scottish version—Paraphrase 22 (from Isa. 11: 27 to the end)—begins, 'Why pour'st thou forth thine anxious plaint?' We include vv. 2, 3, 5, 6, 7 from this, except that the origin of our ver. 2, last quatrain, we have not yet traced: it is neither in the paraphrase nor in Watts; but it conforms well to a fine, brave hymn, 'comforting' in the original sense of that word.

D.C.M.

MUSIC. OLD 107TH appeared in the *Genevan Psalter* set to Psalm 107 as follows:

The present form is from the 1635 edition of the *Scottish Psalter*, where it is set to the same psalm. It is a noble tune, with a modal flavour, and a wide, majestic sweep of phrase; the later version is, as can be seen, near enough to the earlier to preserve all its original character.

513 He that is down needs fear no fall. *John Bunyan*, 1628–88.

The song, in Part II of the *Pilgrim's Progress* (1684), which the shepherd boy sang:

> 'Now as they were going along and talking, they espied a Boy feeding his Father's Sheep. The Boy was in very mean Cloaths, but of a very fresh and wellfavoured Countenance, and as he sat by himself he Sung. Hark, said Mr. *Great-heart*, to what the Shepherd's Boy saith. So they hearkened and he said, *He that is down, needs fear no fall*. . . . Then said their *Guide*, do you hear him? I will dare to say, that this Boy lives a merrier Life, and wears more of that Herb called *Hearts-ease* in his Bosom than he that is clad in Silk, and Velvet.'

The curious thing is that Bunyan, great imaginative writer as he was, wrote little poetry except this and the Pilgrim Song (515); for the introductions and other verses in the *Pilgrim's Progress* are not put together as if he imagined for a moment that they were poems.

C.M.

MUSIC. WARWICK, by Samuel Stanley, is marked as a new tune 'never before published', in *Sacred Music. . . . An Appendix to Dr. Watts's Psalms and Hymns, by Edward Miller, Mus. Doc.* (1802). It is also found in Stanley's own *24 Tunes in four parts* (1802), set to Psalm 23, 'The Lord himself, the mighty Lord'. Miller's 'never before published' must not be taken too seriously, as it is sometimes appended to tunes found in considerably earlier collections; in the present case, however, as both publications belong to the same year, the priority cannot be great in either instance. The tune is an example of the rather ornamental style of the period applied to the traditional psalm-tune manner.

514 He wants not friends that hath thy love.

R. Baxter,† 1615–91.

A cento, first introduced in 1906 by the *English Hymnal*, from a poem in his *Poetical Fragments* (1681) called 'The Resolution', headed, 'Written when I was silenced and cast out', dated 3 Dec. 1603, and beginning, 'Lord, I have cast up the account'. We have had to alter, in ver. 2 of this stately hymn, 'In the communion of saints', because the word is no longer pronounced as four syllables.

L.M.

MUSIC. CAMERONIAN MIDNIGHT HYMN is a Scottish hymn melody, as arranged in the *English Hymnal* (1906). It is a grandly stirring tune with a splendid sturdiness of rhythm and melody, and a very characteristic turn of phrase in the 3rd line.

515 He who would valiant be. *J. Bunyan* (1684), *and others*.

When Mr. Valiant-for-Truth met Christiana and Mr. Great-heart towards the end of their journey, he told them how his father and mother had tried to dissuade him by setting forth the dangers of the pilgrimage, and how he had still believed what Mr. Tell-true had said, 'and that carried me beyond them all'. Mr. Great-heart said, 'Then this was your Victory, even your Faith. *Valiant*. It was so, I believed and therefore came out, got into the Way, fought all that set themselves against me, and by believing am come to this Place.' Then follows the poem, *Who would true Valour see*. There is a space on either side of the poem; and at its conclusion the episode of the Enchanted Ground begins.

In 1904, we who were working at the *English Hymnal* felt that some cheerful and manly hymns must be added to the usual repertory; and this song sprang to mind. It was a daring thing to add the song to a hymn-book, and it had never been attempted before. To include the hobgoblins would have been to ensure disaster; to ask the congregation of St. Ignotus, Erewhon Park, to invite all to come and look at them, if they wished to see true valour, would have been difficult. But when with the help of the marvellous folk-tune which Vaughan Williams had discovered, we had made a great hymn, it became easy for our imitators to complain that we had altered the words. We felt that we had done rightly; and that no one would have been more distressed than Bunyan himself to have people singing about hobgoblins in church. He had not written it for a hymn, and it was not suitable as a hymn without adaptation. When, in 1923, Mrs. Meynell, than whom no better judge then existed, published her anthology, *The School of Poetry*, she included the Pilgrim Song in our version.

Here is the original:

Who would true Valour see,
Let him come hither;
One here will Constant be,
Come Wind, come Weather.
There's no Discouragement,
Shall make him once Relent,
His first avow'd Intent,
To be a Pilgrim.

Who so beset him round,
With dismal Storys,
Do but themselves confound;
His strength the more *is,*
No Lyon *can him fright,*
He'll with a Gyant *Fight,*
But he will have a right,
To be a Pilgrim.

Hobgoblin, *nor foul* Fiend,
Can daunt *his Spirit:*
He knows, he at the end,
Shall Life Inherit.
Then Fancies fly away,
He'll fear not what men say,
He'll labor Night and Day,
To be a Pilgrim.

That Bunyan would never have sanctioned the unaltered form as a hymn may be illustrated by considering the literary associations of the word 'hobgoblin'. The word does not occur in the Bible (nor in the *Metrical Psalter*)—nor does 'goblin' either—whereas 'giant', of course, does. That the word 'hobgoblin' was even then hardly in the rank of serious diction is shown by the fact that it is found only twice in Shakespeare, and then in playful, fairy connexions (*Midsummer-Night's Dream*, II. i, and *Merry Wives*, V. v: hobgoblins in fact occurred, as they do here, with 'Fairies black, grey, green, and white, Moonshine revellers and shades of night'; and they were not mentioned in a serious religious connexion at that time, any more than now. 'Goblin', which has been substituted in one recent version, has little more dignity: it also goes with fairies and owls (e.g. *Comedy of Errors*, II. ii), and is used as a designation of Puck (*Midsummer-Night's Dream*, III. ii); and though in *Hamlet* it is once used with grisly effect in a serious connexion (the grisliness of the grotesque), 'Be thou a spirit of health, or goblin damned?' (I. iv), it retains its common meaning, 'With, ho! such bugs and goblins in my life' (V. ii), throughout Shakespeare and throughout English literature.

Nor does Bunyan put it into the mouth even of the brave Mr. Valiant—who was not given to braggadocio. The poem is an invitation to the reader, if he wishes to see what courage really is, to contemplate the heroes of the story, Pilgrim, Valiant, and the others.

The song does not occur in the 1st edition of *Pilgrim's Progress* ('Printed for *Nath. Ponder* at the *Peacock* in the *Poultrey* near *Cornhill*, 1678'): it came to him afterwards, and seems to have summed up his reflections on the whole book. He dropped it into the second part as a kind of prelude to the conclusion. He did not weave it into the narrative, or put it into the mouth of one of his characters, as he did with his other lyrics: it is placed after Mr. Valiant's discourse, because his name makes it appropriate there; but it is not sung by him. It is indeed an admirable description of the book as a whole, and quite meaningless as a hymn. To sing it thus is to go against the whole intention of the words, and against Bunyan himself; but it has proved possible to enshrine its noble spirit and most of its diction in a real hymn which has quickly become a national possession.

Iambic, 6 5. 6 5. 6 6 6. 5; but set down for the music as 11 11. 12 11. Unique.

MUSIC. MONKS GATE, from the *English Hymnal* (1906), is an arrangement, by R. Vaughan Williams, of the melody of a Sussex folk-song, especially adapted for this hymn in the circumstances noted above.

516 Heavenly Father, may thy blessing. *W. Charter Piggott.*

This wise hymn was written for *Songs of Praise*, primarily for the young, and at the same time to carry the first tune which was associated with such use in the *English Hymnal*. Such, however, is the wealth of melodies that we have now added a second.

Trochaic, 8 7. 8 7. D.

MUSIC. PLEADING SAVIOUR is from the *Plymouth Collection of Hymns and Tunes* (New York, 1855), edited by Henry Ward Beecher, the musical editors being John Zundel and the Rev. Charles Beecher. It is of the type, reminiscent of traditional folk-song, which is sometimes found in negro 'spirituals', and was, later, strongly evident in American revivalist hymn-books.

ENGADINE is an adaptation of a melody from Frizzoni's *Canzuns Spirituaelas davart Cristo Jesu, il bon pastur, &c.* (Cellerina, 1765), where it is set to no. xxxvii, 'Cantain á Gesu nos chaer Segner', a hymn for Ascensiontide. In the original the 3rd beat of the 1st bar of line 6 is D (not E), and the rhythm has been slightly adapted to fit the present metre. Several tunes of this kind are to be found in this collection, and appear to be founded on traditional popular melodies.

517 Help us to help each other, Lord. *Charles Wesley*, 1707–88.

In the *Collection of Hymns for the use of the People called Methodists*, by the Rev. John Wesley, M.A.—in other words, *The Methodist Hymn Book*—there is a group of hymns (from *Hymns and Sacred Poems*, 1749), 501–4, beginning, 'Jesus, great Shepherd of thy sheep'; in this group occurs 'Try us, O God, and search the ground' (503), and 'Jesus, united by thy grace' (504), not indexed by Julian. From 503, vv. 3, 5, and 504, ver. 4, we have made this beautiful and much needed little cento.

C.M.

MUSIC. DUNFERMLINE is one of the twelve 'common tunes' in *The CL Psalms of David, &c.* (Andro Hart, Edinburgh, 1615). Its first appearance in an English book is in Ravenscroft's *Whole Book of Psalms* (1621), where it is classified in the index among the Scottish tunes.

The alternative version (descant), by Robin Milford, was written for the enlarged *Songs of Praise* (1931).

518 Here in the country's heart. *Norman Gale.*

From *A Country Muse* (New Series, 1893).

Dactylic, the 2nd and 4th lines being trochaic, 6 5. 6 5. Unique.

MUSIC. OAKRIDGE LYNCH, by Martin Shaw, appeared in *Songs of Praise* (1925). The tune is written in one long phrase, with an expressive extension of the rhythm in the second half of it. It is a simple, tranquil melody in complete harmony with the spirit of the words.

519 Hold thou my hands! *W. Canton*, 1845–1926.

Canton had been to a Gilbert and Sullivan opera, and he found the words of Phoebe's Song ringing in his ears: 'When I went to bed late last night, the words, "Hold thou my hands" kept floating about in my mind, and then there grew upon me the most perplexing half-recollection of a lovely air. I could not remember it quite, but it simply haunted me. Then somehow the words seemed to grow into it and out of it. . . . Well, it was from the *Yeomen of the Guard.*' He published it in *Good Words* (May 1893), and in *The Invisible Playmate* (1894), one of his many child books. 'Hold thou my hands' first appeared as a hymn in the *English Hymnal* (1906). Cf. 375.

Iambic, 4 8. 8 4. Unique.

MUSIC. MISERERE MEI is an adaptation of a melody in *Seven Sobs of a Sorrowful Soule for Sinne, &c., by William Hunnis* (1583), where it is set to some Poetical Meditations called 'The Widow's Mite', beginning 'Ah, helples wretch! what shall I doo?' The original tune runs as follows:

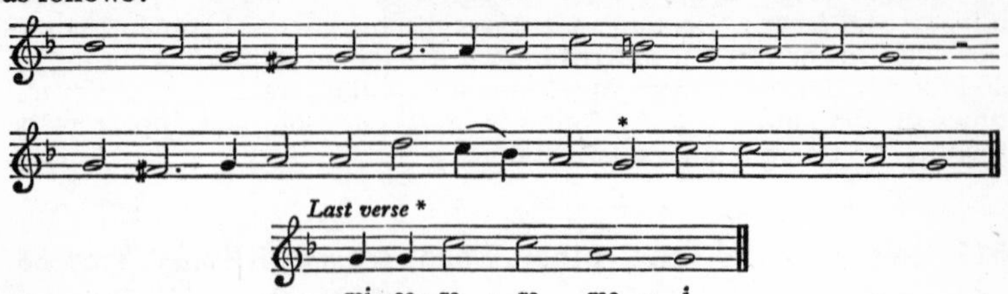

The present arrangement appeared in the *English Hymnal* (1906). The tune is from the same source as 'Hunnys' (108), and shows the same quality of unaffected sincerity, but it is a more original melody with a peculiar expressiveness in the sharpened 3rd of the 2nd line.

520 Holy Spirit, truth divine. *Samuel Longfellow*, 1819–92.

Henry Wadsworth Longfellow (Samuel's famous brother) also wrote several hymns, none of which however have quite secured themselves, although they have been included in different collections, and 'Tell me not in mournful numbers' nearly succeeded. Samuel, on the other hand, who was a Unitarian minister, wrote this and five others (e.g. 16 and 532) which have promise of immortality. This one first appeared in *Hymns of the Spirit*, edited by Samuel Johnson (cf. 468) and himself. Ver. 6 alludes to Numbers 21: 17.

Trochaic, 7 7. 7 7.

MUSIC. HARTS is from *Sixteen Hymns as they are Sung at the Right Honourable the Countess of Huntingdon's Chapel in Bath.* Set to Music by *Benjn. Milgrove* (1769?). It is No. 15 in that collection, and is set as under to the hymn 'Brethren, let us join to bless', with the addition of a 'Hallelujah', which has now been dropped.

A note at the beginning of the book says, 'The Men that sing the Air must rest where 'tis written the Women to sing this part alone, and begin where the word Altogether is written'. The whole setting is given here, as an excellent example of a type of hymn which was much popularized by the nonconformist bodies in the 18th century.

521 Hosanna! Music is divine. *Christopher Smart*, 1722–71.

This splendid paraphrase of Psalm 147, first printed in Christopher Smart's *Translation of the Psalms of David* (1765), may be compared with our extract from the *Song to David*, 690. In 1759 he was shut up in an asylum—apparently because he was too open in his religion: at least Dr. Johnson said: 'I do not think he ought to be shut up. His infirmities were not noxious to society. He insisted on people praying with him; and I'd as lief pray with Kit Smart as any one else. Another charge is that he did not love clean linen; and I have no passion for it.' Garrick gave a performance for his benefit, and, when these *Psalms* were published in 1765, among the long list of subscribers were printed the names of Gray, Cowper, Akenside, Churchill, Sterne, Smollett, and Hogarth. He was indeed much loved, in spite of his infirmities, which caused his life to end in the debtor's prison of the King's Bench: his biographer of 1791 notes his deep religious absorption, which caused him to write kneeling, his charm in conversation, his improvident liberality. Would that another *New Version* of the psalms by him had supplanted Tate and Brady!

Our stanzas 1, 2, 3, and 5 are from his 'Psalm 147'; our fourth is from his 'Psalm 104'.

The metre, 8 8 6. D. is interesting. Mr. Edmund Blunden, in his Preface to the 1924 edition of the *Song to David*, says: 'There is such speed, such definition in the making of the verse, as to stamp the stanza form, though many have used it, as Christopher Smart's.' It occurs also (besides the companion 690) in 604.

MUSIC. ERFURT (ALLGÜTIGER, MEIN LEBELANG), by G. P. Weimar, is from his *Choral-melodien Buch* (Erfurt, 1803), where it is set to the hymn 'Allgütiger mein Lebelang (Preisgesang)'. In the original form of the tune the 5th line is not a replica of the 4th, as here, but is varied as follows:

It is an attractive tune, with an excellent sense of continuity, and an air of tranquil assurance.

522 How are thy servants blest, O Lord!

J. Addison,‡ 1672–1719.

Addison was justified in claiming (as Stopford Brooke notes in his *English Literature*, p. 125), 'I have brought philosophy out of closets and libraries, schools and colleges, to dwell in clubs and assemblies, at tea-tables and in coffee-houses'. He made a great mystery about his hymns in the *Spectator*; but the rival claims once made are now deserted. In the *Spectator* for 20 Sept. 1712 is an Essay on 'The Wonders of the Deep', which begins:

'Great painters do not only give us Landskips of Gardens, Groves, and Meadows, but very often employ their Pencils upon Sea-pieces. I could wish you could follow their example. If this small Sketch may deserve a Place among your Works, I shall accompany it with a Divine Ode, made by a Gentleman upon the conclusion of his travels.'

At the end of the essay is our hymn, signed 'C.' Macaulay, in the *Edinburgh Review* (July 1843), gives the explanation. Addison in 1700 went for a tour in the Mediterranean; and, off the Ligurian coast, a storm arose:

'The captain of the ship gave up all for lost, and confessed himself to a capuchin who happened to be on board. The English heretic, in the meantime, fortified himself against the terrors of death with devotions of a very different kind. How strong an impression this perilous voyage made on him appears from the Ode, "How are thy servants blest, O Lord", which was long after published in the *Spectator*.'

When he was breathing his last in Holland House, Addison sent for his dissolute step-son, bidding him come and see how a Christian could die.

The original is in ten stanzas, the past tense in the first person singular being used throughout. Cf. 656, 659, 694.

C.M.

MUSIC. KILMARNOCK, by Neil Dougall, appeared in *Parochial Psalmody: A New Collection of the Most Approved Psalm Tunes. . . . By J. P. Clarke, Second edition* (1831). This seems to be the earliest collection in which the tune was printed, but it was certainly circulated in manuscript for some time previously. In 1854 the composer issued *Poems and Songs by Neil Dougall, with a Memoir of the Author*. The following passage occurs in the Memoir:

'One day R. A. Smith and the late John Taylor, who was then Precentor in the Middle Parish Church, Greenock, paid him (Dougall) a visit. . . . After some conversation Smith said, "Anything new doing, Mr. Dougall? no scraps to divert us?' Mr. Dougall went to a drawer and brought the first few scraps of paper he could lay his hands on. Smith took up one, and hastily humming it over, said, "A very pretty melody; and what do you call it?" "It's not christened yet," was the answer; "but do you observe anything peculiar about it?" "I do," said Smith; "it is on the Caledonian scale, the same as 'Morven'." "Yes; the same as your tune." "No, no; not my tune," said Smith. "Will you oblige me with a copy of your nameless tune?" "With pleasure," said the composer, "and we'll christen't 'Kilmarnock';" and this ended the conference.'

523 How blest are they whose hearts are pure.

W. H. Bathurst, 1796–1877.

Bathurst retired from his rectory in 1852. He had translated the *Georgics of Virgil* in 1849 and had published all his 206 hymns and 141 metrical psalms in his *Psalms and Hymns for Public and Private Use*, 1831; 2nd edition, 1842.

C.M.

MUSIC. GLENLUCE is No. XX of the Common Tunes in the *Scottish Psalter* of 1635. The original form of the melody begins on A, the 3rd of the scale.

524 How happy is he born and taught. *Sir H. Wotton*,‡ 1568–1639.

The delightful original of this, published in *Reliquiae Wottonianae*, with a Memoir by Isaak Walton, 1651, could not possibly be sung as a hymn without alteration. We omit two stanzas, and differ from Robert Bridges, in *The Chilswell Book of English Poetry*, in reading, ver. 2, l. 4, 'public fame or private breath' for 'princes' love or vulgar breath'; ver. 3, l. 2, 'goods' for 'gifts'; ver. 4, l. 3, 'freed' for 'free'; l. 4, 'yet' for 'he'. For ver. 3, ll. 3, 4, Bridges has:

And entertains the harmless day
With a well-chosen book or friend.

Bridges says that his text is based on 'what would seem the best authority among many variants, some of which are probably the author's own corrections'. Our variants are more suited to congregational use.

L.M.

MUSIC. KENT, by J. F. Lampe, appeared in *Hymns on the great festivals and other occasions by Charles Wesley* (1746), where it is set to the hymn 'Sinners obey the Gospel word'. No composer's name is given in this work, but in the 2nd edition (1753) it is stated that the book may be obtained at 'Mr. Lampe's lodging', and Wesley, in a letter, refers to 'Mr. Lampe's tunes' with approbation; the attribution to Lampe, therefore, of the music in the above work is very probable. Lampe was a bassoon-player who migrated to England from Germany at the age of 21, and became well known as a composer of vocal and stage music. He edited various collections of contemporary songs, and, after coming under the influence of Charles Wesley, probably wrote many of the tunes which were introduced among his followers, and was partly responsible for the more ornate style of hymn melody popularized by them. The present tune, however, is in a more sedate manner.

525 How lovely are thy dwellings fair! Ps. 84. *J. Milton*, 1608–74.

There are 19 versions of Psalms in Milton's *Poems, &c. upon Several Occasions* (1673). This version of Psalm 84 was written April 1648, and in the volume of 1673 was grouped among 'Nine of the Psalms done into Metre, wherein all but what is in a different Character, are the very words of the Text, translated from the Original'. That is to say, the adjectives, 'pleasant' and 'bright' (vv. 1 and 5), and the lines 'Where thou dost dwell so near' and 'With joy and gladsome strength' (vv. 1 and 4) are not represented in the original Hebrew; and Milton prints ver. 4, l. 3, thus:

'*Till* all before *our* God *at length*'.

We have chosen six stanzas out of the original twelve.

Compare with this simple and lovely thing the average metrical psalms, Tate or Brady's complete Ps. 42, as an instance of the best (and see on this 449, and also 443). But though the *Old* and *New Versions* were often doggerel, they were never sloppy; and they had nothing in common with the 'invalid hymns' which were so popular in the latter half of the last century. See also 677.

C.M.

MUSIC. DURHAM, in Ravenscroft's *Whole Booke of Psalms* (1621), is set to Psalms 28 and 76, and marked as a 'Northern Tune'. It is included among the Common Tunes in the 1635 edition of the *Scottish Psalter*.

526 How shall I sing that majesty. *John Mason*, *c.* 1645–94.

The whole weakness of Victorian hymnody may be summed up in the fact that this great hymn, and a hymn it is about God, had not even come into the enormous index of Julian's *Dictionary* of 1891, although 400,000 hymns had been examined. So far as Julian could discover, when he included it in his *A New Supplement* of 1907, it had only then appeared in the *English Hymnal* of the previous year. John Mason had published it in his *Spiritual Songs* (1683).

For John Mason, Rector of Water Stratford, see also 675. About a month before his death he had a vision of Jesus wearing a glorious crown, and with an aspect of unutterable majesty. He spoke about this, and preached a sermon, 'The Midnight Cry', proclaiming the nearness of approach of the second Advent. A report spread that this would be at his own village: Water Stratford was crowded with people, who brought in furniture and provisions; extraordinary scenes of singing, leaping, and dancing took place, and in the midst of the excitement the old man passed away, still testifying that he had seen the Lord, and that it was time for the nations to tremble; but his last words were, 'I am full of the loving-kindness of the Lord'. Oddly enough, the only pregnant event which history records of 1694 is the founding of the Bank of England.

D.C.M.

MUSIC. OLD 137TH was the tune set to that psalm in the *Anglo-Genevan Psalter* (1556), and in all subsequent English and Scottish Psalters. It is a good example of the standard psalm-tune style of its period.

527 How sweet the name of Jesus sounds.

J. Newton,† 1725–1807.

This famous hymn, based on the Song of Songs, 1 : 3, 'Thy name is as ointment poured forth', was contributed by Newton to the *Olney Hymns* (1779). It was because of the reference to the beautiful Hebrew love-song, then thought to represent Christ and his Church, that he used the word 'husband' in ver. 4. As we cannot defend it, we have altered it to 'brother'. An interesting example of the change in our religious atmosphere is given by the verse which all hymn-books now omit:

> By thee my prayers acceptance gain,
> Although with sin defiled:
> Satan accuses me in vain,
> And I am owned a child.

C.M.

MUSIC. ST. BOTOLPH, by Gordon Slater, appeared in *Songs of Praise for Boys and Girls* (1930), set to the hymn 'Dear Father, keep me through this day'; at Lincoln Cathedral, where the composer is Organist and Master of the Choristers, it is sung to 'Jesu, the very thought of thee'. It is an easy, flowing tune, in triple time, with a gentle suavity well suited to the nature of the present poem.

ST. PETER is from A. R. Reinagle's *Psalm Tunes for the Voice and the Pianoforte* (1830), where it is set to Psalm 118. It is named after the church in Oxford of which the composer was organist.

The alternative version (fa-burden), by Edgar C. Robinson, was written for the enlarged *Songs of Praise* (1931).

The tune is now closely associated with the present words.

528 I bind unto myself to-day.

Attr. to St. Patrick, c. 372–466. *Tr. Mrs. C. F. Alexander.*

As the chief certain thing about St. Patrick seems to be that he was a Britisher, so the certain thing about his Breastplate seems to be that he did not write it. Scholars are now convinced that in its present form it is not earlier than the 8th century. See K. Meyer, *Ancient Irish Poetry* (1913, pp. 25, 111). Further, the meaning is not what we suppose, but a wilder thing than our well-kempt congregations know: 'To-day I arise by the strength of heaven, light of sun, shine of moon, splendour of fire, swiftness of wind', and so on.

The story thus appears to be unfounded, that Patrick lighted his beacon before that of King Leary, and that, when the king drove up to the Hill of Slane to put the saint to death, Patrick sang the 20th Psalm, following it with the 'Lorica' or Breastplate. It is sometimes called 'The Deer's Cry', because Leary's ambushed soldiers are said to have mistaken Patrick and his men for wild deer—which sounds almost more improbable.

In its complete form the Lorica is at once a war-song, an incantation, and a creed. Mrs. Alexander's spirited translation was made for St. Patrick's Day, 1889, and was printed in leaflet form, and also in the Appendix to C. H. H. Wright's *Writings of St. Patrick* (1889). Mrs. Alexander's opening lines, 'I bind unto myself to-day', are a mistranslation of the Irish, 'To-day I arise'; and the rest is a free rendering with expansions of her own; but after all one does not need to be too near to the incantations of the Dark Ages. A closer rendering of great interest by Professor

R. A. S. Macalister is given in the *Church Hymnary*, 505. Mrs. Alexander's full version is in the *English Hymnal*, 212—nine verses, divided into two parts. We have reduced this to five verses differently arranged, eliminating the traces of white magic, and retaining the grandeur of the main part of the song.

Part I and Doxology, L.M. and D.L.M. Part II, trochaic, 8 8. 8 8. D.

MUSIC. ST. PATRICK is from Dr. George Petrie's *Irish Melodies*; it is said to be an old Irish setting of 'Jesu dulcis memoria'. It is a remarkably impressive tune, in triple time, with a smooth, dignified contour, and a characteristic traditional touch in the melodic curve of the 3rd line.

MORLEY is also a traditional Irish melody, here harmonized by C. Burke, this version having originally appeared in sheet form for mixed voices in 1922. This is again a stately tune, in triple time, but with a resolute rhythm, which gives the melody a very different cast from that of the previous one, and accords perfectly with the change of rhythm and feeling in the words.

The two tunes, which, by their consistence of quality and contrast of character, form a well-balanced whole, have, of late years, become closely associated with the present words.

529 I heard the voice of Jesus say. *H. Bonar*, 1808–89.

From his *Hymns Original and Selected* (1846). Many have admired this hymn, including Bishop Fraser of Manchester and Bishop Bickersteth, who edited the *Hymnal Companion*. It is based on John 1: 16, 'Of his fullness have all we received, and grace for grace'. Deeply felt, however, though the words are, it is difficult to imagine anything more remote in tone from that quiet, profound passage. The hymn suffered from a somewhat gushing tune, but Vaughan Williams rescued it from that in 1906.

D.C.M.

MUSIC. KINGSFOLD is an arrangement of the melody of a folk-song from the collection of Miss L. E. Broadwood. It appeared in the *English Hymnal* (1906). It is a modal tune of great dignity and significance, very characteristic of a large class of the folk-tunes which have been collected during the last forty odd years.

530 I know not what the future hath. *J. G. Whittier*, 1807–92.

Most of Whittier's poems are rather long, written apparently without any thought of their being sung as hymns. This, which is pre-eminently an old person's meditation on trust in God, is from 'The Eternal Goodness', written in 1865, and included in *The Tent on the Beach, and Other Poems* (1867), beginning with stanza 16.

C.M.

MUSIC. CULROSS is one of the Common Tunes in the *Psalms of David* (Hart's heirs, Edinburgh, 1634).

531 I learned it in the meadow path. *Lucy Larcom*, 1826–93.

Another New Englander, Miss Larcom, collaborated with Whittier in *Child Life in Poetry* (1871), and other children's books. She began as an elementary school teacher. This memorable statement of the Christian outlook upon the world was published in her *Collected Poems* (1885).

L.M.

MUSIC. CROMER, by J. A. Lloyd, appeared in the *Norwich Tune Book* (1844).

532 I look to thee in every need. *S. Longfellow*, 1819–92.

It has been pointed out before that the rise in America of the Inner Health movement, of which Christian Science is the best-known manifestation, was due to the fact that current forms of religion had ignored the effect of religious faith and trust upon mental and bodily health. It is significant that here we have an American hymn which expresses that idea—so essential a part of the Gospels—as early as 1864, when *Hymns of the Spirit* was published; still more significant that the hymn itself was ignored: it was not included in the *Hymnal* of the Protestant Episcopal Church in America, in 1882, nor did it come into use in England till Garrett Horder's *Worship Song* (1905) and the *English Hymnal* (1906).

Iambic, 8 6. 8 6. 8 8.

MUSIC. O JESU, by J. B. Reimann, appeared in *J. B. Reimanns Org. v. Hirschb. Sammlung alter und neuer Melodien Evangel. Lieder, &c.* (1747), set to the hymn 'O Jesu, warum legst du mir'. In the original the first and last notes of each line are semibreves.

533 I praised the earth, in beauty seen.

Bishop R. Heber, 1783–1826.

One of Heber's less-known hymns, though Lord Selborne says (*Hymns, their History and Development*, 1892), 'It may be ranked with Addison's "The spacious firmament on high" as of nearly equal excellence': this appeared in the posthumous collection of 1827.

No one had a better right than Heber to pen these sweet but sad lines, for there was no one less for this world. Even when he was a schoolboy his parents had to sew up his money in his pockets to prevent him giving it all away to the first poor man he saw. When he was a parson every crying child and every sick person attracted him like a magnet; and he came to death's door through his devotion during a local pestilence. Yet the intellect which had served him so brilliantly at Oxford was given no rest; he spent seven hours a day in reading, writing, and prayer; and he read of the child-wives and the widows in India; and there he went—to work himself out in three years.

Iambic, 8 8. 8 8. 8 8.

MUSIC. GESIUS (HEUT' TRIUMPHIRET), by B. Gesius, is from *Geistliche deutsche Lieder, &c.* (Frankfurt, 1601), where it is set to the hymn 'Heut triumphieret Gottes Sohn' as follows:

The present version is J. S. Bach's, and the original form of the melody has been fairly closely preserved. In rhythm the tune conforms to a large number of others belonging to this period, but the melody is more unusual in form, and has an attractive individuality of its own.

534 I sought thee round about, O thou my God.

Thomas Heywood,‡ *c.* 1650.

Tom Heywood (he said, 'I hold he loves me best who calls me Tom') was one of the best loved and the most prolific of the Elizabethans; apart from the 220 plays in which he claimed 'either an entire hand or at the least a main finger', his principal work was a huge gallimaufrey, as Mr. Crosse calls it, of heroic couplets, lyrics, and prose—full of out-of-the-way learning—called *The Hierarchie of the blessed Angells* (1635), 'Theologicall, Philosophicall, Poeticall, Historicall, Apothegmaticall, Hierogriphicall and Emblematicall Observations'. There are 11 more stanzas after our selection. We have selected 3 stanzas out of 11, and have altered ver. 1, l. 5, from 'I am not; I enquired'; ver. 2, l. 1, 'And now'; l. 7, 'Thou in thy mercy, justice, truth'; l. 8, 'thou com'st nearest'.

Iambic, 10 4. 10 4. 10 4. 10 10. Unique.

MUSIC. MONK STREET was written by Gustav Holst especially for this hymn in *Songs of Praise*. The words have set a problem to the composer, not only by the very unusual metrical scheme, but also by the running over of the sense from one line to other in varying ways and degrees; when a uniform setting is in question, as in a hymn-tune, this can only be met by a compromise which will adjust, as well as may be, the conflicting claims of the various verses. The present melody finds a solution in a structure consisting of two long phrases, each embracing two overlapping lines; the first phrase being repeated for the first two pairs, and again, with an initial extension, for the last longer pair, while the second phrase, both by its position and by its mainly inverted movement, balances the complete melody. Apart from these technical considerations, the tune itself is a broad, satisfying melody, with a firm, progressive rhythm.

535 Immortal, invisible, God only wise.

W. Chalmers Smith, 1824–1908.

We have pointed out how little there was about God in the old hymn-books, and yet this brilliant and conspicuous hymn had been ready for inclusion since 1867, when it was printed in Dr. Smith's *Hymns of Christ and the Christian Life*; and since it was brought into use, with its buoyant tune, in the *English Hymnal*, it has been one of the most popular of hymns. To Garrett Horder belongs the credit of first introducing it into England—in his *Congregational Hymns* (1884).

Anapaestic, 11 11. 11 11.

MUSIC. ST. DENIO is a Welsh melody, known in Wales as 'Joanna', and based on a folk-tune 'Can Mlynedd i 'nawr' (*c.* 1810). It first appeared as a hymn-tune in *Caniadau y Cyssegr* (1839), edited by John Roberts (Henllan), where it is named 'Palestina'. It is a straightforward tune, in triple time, which, however, gains a rather strange flavour from the impression, given by the 1st line, of its being in D flat rather than in A flat, the G♮ feeling like a modulation; and, though the rest of the tune is most indubitably in the key, this initial effect seasons the whole melody.

536 Immortal love for ever full. *J. G. Whittier*, 1807–92.

This lovely hymn about Jesus Christ was also little known in the Church of England of the 19th century, outside the circle which used the *Hymnal Companion*, to which book belongs the credit of including it in the edition of 1890. It is a selection from the long poem of 35 stanzas, 'Our Master', in Whittier's *The Panorama, and Other Poems* (1856). When some one, speaking of Puritan New England, said, 'But you, Sir, could never have been a Puritan and a Calvinist,' he answered, 'Nay, thee are right! the world is much too beautiful, and God much too good. I never was of that mind.'

C.M.

MUSIC. BISHOPTHORPE (or ST. PAUL'S) has not been traced earlier than Edward Miller's *The Psalms of David for the use of Parish Churches* (1790), where the tune is named 'Bishop Thorpe', and ascribed to Jeremiah Clark. It may be an adaptation by Dr. Miller. It is a captivating tune, very characteristic of its century in the grace and suavity of the flexible melodic contour.

537 In Christ there is no East or West. *John Oxenham.*

In the *Selected Poems of John Oxenham* (1924) this much-needed hymn is the last of the group written between 1900 and 1913.

C.M.

MUSIC. ST. BERNARD is from *Neues . . . Kirchen und Hauss Gesang der . . . Tochter Sion* . . . (Cologne, 1741), where it is set to one of the hymns in praise of the Virgin Mary in the following form:

In *Heil- und Hülfs-Mittel zum thätigen Christenthum* (1767) the melody runs as follows:

This form is also found in *Cantica Spiritualia* (vol. ii, Munich, 1847), from which book the present tune was probably arranged. It seems to have first appeared thus in *Easy Hymn Tunes with the words in full, adapted for Catholic Schools, &c.* (1851), where it is set to the hymn, 'Jesus, the very thought of thee', and headed 'Hymn of St. Bernard'. The adaptation was possibly made by John Richardson, and the tune has been attributed to him in several collections.

538 In our work and in our play. *W. Charter Piggott.*

Mr. Charter Piggott wrote these admirable verses for *Songs of Praise* to provide a substitute for *E.H.* 596, suitable for the young in years or mind.

Trochaic, 7 7. 7 7.

MUSIC. BATTISHILL is adapted from a melody in *Twelve Hymns; the Words by the Rev. Charles Wesley, M.A., late student at Christ Church, Oxford; set to music by Jonathan Battishill* (1765). The original tune, which was set to the hymn 'Jesus, Lord, we look to thee', ran as follows:

The original tune is an excellent, unexaggerated example of the 'new style' of Methodist hymn-tunes introduced in the 18th century; the present abridgement and adaptation is more in accordance with the taste of to-day.

539 It fell upon a summer day. *Stopford A. Brooke*, 1832–1916.

From Dr. Stopford Brooke's *Christian Hymns* (1881), in ten verses, from which we have selected eight.

Iambic, 8 8. 8 6.

MUSIC. FITZWILLIAM is an arrangement, by R. Vaughan Williams, of an English traditional melody, and first appeared in the *English Hymnal* (1906).

540 Jesus, good above all other. *E.H.*

Written originally for children, by the editor of the *English Hymnal* (1906), to carry the carol tune 'Quem pastores laudavere'. In ver. 3, 'by thine altar' is now everywhere changed, because its mystical intention was not understood

Trochaic, 8 8 8. 7. Also in 340.

MUSIC. QUEM PASTORES LAUDAVERE is the melody of a German carol from a 14th-century manuscript. The present version, by R. Vaughan

Williams, is in the *English Hymnal* (1906), and, with the original words, in the *Oxford Book of Carols* (1928). Its first appearance in print seems to be in V. Triller's *Ein Schlesich singebuchlein aus Göttlicher schrifft, &c.* (Breslau, 1555), where it is set to the Latin words and a German hymn, 'Preis sei Gott im höchsten Throne' (which is not a translation of the Latin). It is found in many later collections, both Catholic and Protestant, with slight variants, but mainly in its present form, except that the last bar of each line is almost invariably syncopated thus ♩𝅗𝅥 It was one of the carols often sung, at Christmastide, during the ceremonies round the crib in the churches (see 700).

541 Jesus, Lord, we look to thee. *Charles Wesley*, 1707–88.

Four lovely verses from a hymn, not indexed by Julian (cf. 517), but belonging to the group beginning 'God of love, that hear'st the prayer', *Methodist Hymn Book* (508), and there numbered 509, and beginning 'Jesus, Lord, we look to thee'. We here include vv. 1, 3, 4, 5. Originally in the Wesleys' *Hymns for those that Seek and those that Have Redemption* (1747).

Trochaic, 7 7. 7 7.

MUSIC. PEACEFIELD is an arrangement, by David F. R. Wilson, of an ancient Irish lullaby, and first appeared in the *Irish Hymnal* (Dublin, 1919). Mr. Wilson, who is Rector of Donnybrook and Precentor of St. Patrick's Cathedral, Dublin, writes as follows:

'This lullaby, which I named after my mother's homestead in Co. Armagh, is the first air which I ever heard and never forgot. It was sung over my cradle to "Hush a bye baby on the tree-top". An old folk-tune like this has many variants; one is given in the Petrie Collection of Ancient Irish Music, no. 1016. When the Musical Committee of the Irish Hymnal asked for "a simpler tune" to Miss Havergal's children's hymn, "Now the daylight goes away', I hummed this old air, which pleased them and must have pleased many editors since, as it has been used in many hymnals published in Great Britain and America.'

542 Jesus, lover of my soul. *Charles Wesley*, 1707–88.

Written in 1740 (in his *Hymns and Sacred Poems*), though not included in the *Methodist Hymn Book* till nine years after his death, this continued from 1797 throughout the 19th century to express the intimate convictions of the religious public. Henry Ward Beecher, for instance, in the middle of the century said, 'I would rather have written that hymn than to have the fame of all the kings that ever sat upon the earth'. The opening must have been suggested by Wisdom 11: 26, 'But thou sparest all; for they are thine, O Lord, thou lover of souls', which is a larger and finer idea than that of the hymn. There are many legends about the composition —that a sea-bird flew to Wesley in a storm, that he himself was in a storm, that a dove took refuge from a hawk in his room, that the occasion was his own escape from a threatening mob in England, or that he made it while hiding in Ireland under a hedge from his enemies; and they are mere legends. It is more likely that the hymn was connected with the great spiritual change that he underwent in 1738, since it was printed two years after that date. John Wesley, in his *Journal*, 25 Sept. 1767, relates that William New, 'one of the first Methodists in Bristol who always walked as became the Gospel', had the hymn sung to him on his death-bed.

It has been noted that, in the 1st verse 36 out of 46 words are monosyllables; in the 2nd, 37 out of 46; in the 3rd, 36 out of 45: with all this simplicity, as Professor Saintsbury has said in his *History of English Prosody*, ii. 531, 'the mere word-music is fingered throughout in the most absolutely adequate manner'.

The last verse, beginning 'Wilt thou not regard my call?' is generally omitted. The history of other changes is curious. Many have objected to 'lover' in l. 1—probably because it looks wrong with a capital letter, though it is perfectly right as a divine attribute; some books changed it, even to the dreadful sibilant line, 'Jesu, Saviour of my soul'. Many objected to the 'nearer waters'; and Dr. Julian devotes nearly half a column to explaining this inspired poetic epithet by an analysis of the behaviour of waves in some local kinds of storm. The prize must, however, be given to Dr. Kennedy's *Hymn Book* of 1863:

Jesu*s*, *Refuge* of *the* soul,
  To thy sheltering arms we fly;
While the *raging billows* roll,
  While the *tempest's roar* is high.

In these 4 lines there are (not counting the opening word) 6 alterations —11 words—all made by different persons at different dates. It did not always occur to the compilers of hymnals that a little understanding of poetry is necessary for their work. In this case, Dr. Julian could find 'in the whole range of hymnody', 'no stanza or portion of a stanza which has undergone so many alterations'. And it is difficult to imagine the state of mind of those editors who could argue, as one did, that 'if the waters rolled at all, they would all do so, and not merely the waves in the immediate neighbourhood'.

And all the time no one seems to have noticed the serious difficulty of the 3rd verse:

Thou, O Christ, art all I want;
  More than all in thee I find:
Raise the fallen, cheer the faint,
  Heal the sick, and lead the blind.
Just and holy is thy name;
  I am all unrighteousness;
False and full of sin I am;
  Thou art full of truth and grace.

Regarded from the mere technical side of formal theology, the last 4 lines of this verse can with difficulty be cleared of the unpleasant heresy of the Total Depravity of Man; even the Ninth of the Forty-nine Articles, in condemning Pelagianism, is content to say that man 'is very far gone from original righteousness, and is of his own nature inclined to evil'. From the point of view of pure Christianity the objection is stronger; it is unlike the teaching of Christ to speak like this about sin, or even rhetorically to accuse oneself of being all unrighteousness; from that of modern psychology, it is dangerous to teach people to say that they are false and full of sin. We have therefore omitted this verse also. For the probable reason why John Wesley omitted the hymn altogether from the Methodist *Collection* of 1780 see under 127.

Because of ver. 1 the hymn has been popular among sailors; and a story is told of a ship that went on the rocks in the English Channel: the crew took to the boats and were lost, but the empty ship stood out the storm; and, when she was boarded, a hymn-book was found in the captain's cabin with a pencil in it and a mark against this verse. The story has often been told of another ship, burnt in the Channel. The father of one little family was rescued, but the mother and babe were lost. A vessel, however, sailing from Newport, Mon., sighted an object that looked like a piece of wreckage. A boat was sent to investigate; as the crew drew near they heard 'Jesu, lover of my soul' very softly sung: the mother was clinging, hidden, to the wreckage with her little child.

The following story appeared first in the Annotated Edition of the *Book of Common Praise* (1909):

'A party of Northern tourists were on the deck of an excursion steamer, on the Potomac, one summer evening in 1881. One of the party, who had a remarkable voice, began to sing hymns to the others. When he had sung two verses of "Jesu, lover of my soul", a stranger made his way from the outskirts of the crowd: "Beg your pardon, sir, but were you actively engaged in the late war?" "Yes, sir, I fought under General Grant." "Well," the first speaker continued, "I did my fighting on the other side, and I think I was very near you one bright night eighteen years ago this month. It was much such a night as this. If I am not mistaken, you were on guard-duty. We of the South had sharp business on hand. I crept near your post of duty, my weapon in my hand; the shadows hid me. Your beat led you into the clear light. As you paced back and forth you were singing that same hymn. I raised my gun and aimed at your heart—and I had been selected for the work because I was a sure shot. Then out upon the night floated the words:

Cover my defenceless head
With the shadow of thy wing.

Your prayer was answered. I couldn't fire after that. And there was no attack made upon your camp that night. I felt sure, when I heard you singing this evening, that you were the man whose life I was spared from taking." The singer grasped the hand of the Southerner and said: "I remember the night very well, and the feeling of depression with which I went forth to my duty. I knew my post was one of great danger. I paced my lonely beat, thinking of home and friends and all that life holds dear. Then the thought of God's care came to me with peculiar force, and I sang the prayer of my heart and ceased to feel alone. How the prayer was answered I never knew until this evening." '

Trochaic, 7 7. 7 7. D.

MUSIC. ABERYSTWYTH, composed or adapted by Joseph Parry, appeared in *Ail Lyfr Tonau ac Emynau* (1879).

The alternative version (descant), by Alan Gray, appeared in his *A Book of Descants* (1920).

This has become one of the best known of all Welsh hymn-tunes, and needs no comment.

543 Jesus, meek and gentle. *G. R. Prynne*, 1818–1903.

From his *The Hymnal suited for the Services of the Church* (1858). Because of its slightness the hymn was commonly thought to be for children, for whom such material was considered suitable; but the author stated later that it was not written specially for them.

In this part of our book are several of those hymns which are sometimes held open to objection as constituting what German theologians have called 'Jesus worship'. The theological or liturgical question involved does not concern us here; but it is important to notice that the typical hymns of this type are addressed to a divine idea, and often show little or no interest in the actual historical Jesus. This can be tested by substituting some other name, such as 'Buddha' for that of our Lord. It is the major tragedy of Christian history that, with all the wealth of devotion which was poured out, the interest in the life of Christ was almost confined to the Church festivals, and apart from the Nativity, the Passion, and the Resurrection, there was little notice of the life, character, and teaching of the Redeemer. In pictorial art the change began after the cycle of the Catacombs, with Constantine and the Byzantine mosaics; and Christian literature faithfully reflects the same change. Our next hymn, 544, offers a curious illustration of this.

Trochaic, 6 5. 6 5.

MUSIC. BELSIZE, by Martin Shaw, appeared in *Additional Tunes and settings in use at St. Mary's, Primrose Hill* (1915). It is a very simple, but appealing tune, exactly expressive of the spirit of the words.

544 Jesus, priceless treasure.

J. Franck, 1618–77. *Tr. C. Winkworth.*‡

Jesu, meine Freude,
Meines Herzens Weide
  Jesu, meine Zier;
Ach, wie lang, ach lange
Ist dem Herzen bange
  Und verlangt nach dir!
Gottes Lamm, mein Braütigam,
Ausser dir soll mir auf Erden
Nichts sonst Liebers werden.

Franck's hymn appeared in Peter's *Andachts Zymbeln* (1655) in seven verses. It was printed with Crüger's melody in his *Praxis*, in 1653. It was modelled on a love-song by Alberti, 'Flora, meine Freude, meiner Seelenweide'. Many older Lutherans thought that its depth of spiritual experience unfitted it for congregational use; just as Christopher Wordsworth objected for a similar reason to 542, 'Jesu, lover of my soul'. Peter the Great, of all people, had it translated into Russian, and it was also done into Esthonian. Miss Winkworth's translation, which we have endeavoured slightly to improve, was in her *Chorale Book for England* (1863).

Trochaic, 6 6 5. 6 6 5. 7 8 6. Unique.

MUSIC. JESU MEINE FREUDE is an adaptation of a German traditional melody in J. Crüger's *Praxis Pietatis Melica* (ed. of 1653), where it is set to 'Jesu, meine Freude, meines Herzens Weide' as follows:

Variants are found in several later collections, the present version of melody and harmony being J. S. Bach's.

It is a superbly dignified and intense tune, and certainly one of the finest of all German chorales.

545 Jesus shall reign where'er the sun. *I. Watts*, 1674–1748.

This glorious song, now wearing a tune adequate to its exalted spirit, is the earliest notable hymn for oversea missions, and is prophetically modern in tone. Indeed, it is significant that it rarely found its way into hymn-books in the 18th century. It comes from Part II of his version of Psalm 72, in his *Psalms of David* (1719), and shows his determination to treat David as if he were a Christian (see p. xvii). Really it is, as he said, one of 'the Psalms of David imitated in the language of the New Testament'. The original excellent 2nd and 3rd verses are generally omitted, and often the 4th also:

Behold the Islands with their kings,
And Europe her best tribute brings;
From north to south the princes meet
To pay their homage at his feet.

There Persia glorious to behold,
There India shines in eastern gold;
And barbarous nations at his word
Submit and bow, and own their Lord.

For him shall endless prayer be made,
And praises throng to crown his head;
His name like sweet perfume shall rise
With every morning sacrifice.

And before the last verse is:

Where he displays his healing power,
Death and the curse are known no more;
In him the tribes of Adam boast
More blessings than their father lost.

In his *Methodist Hymn Book Notes* (1883), G. J. Stevenson relates how King George of the South Sea Islands gave a new constitution to the people:

'Under the spreading branches of the banyan trees sat some thousand natives from Tonga, Fiji, and Samoa, on Whitsunday, 1862, assembled for divine worship. Foremost amongst them all sat King George himself. Around him were seated old chiefs and warriors who had shared with him the dangers and fortunes of many a battle. . . . It would be impossible to describe the deep feeling manifested when the solemn service began by the entire audience singing Dr. Watts' hymn, "Jesus shall reign".'

'Peculiar honours' means honours appropriate to the various peoples who bring them.

L.M.

MUSIC. TRURO. See 337, ii. The alternative version (fa-burden), by Geoffrey Shaw, appeared in the *Tenor Tune Book* (1917).

546 Jesus, so lowly. *Edith Williams.*

This was contributed by Miss Williams to our book.

Dactylic, 5 4. 5 4. Unique.

MUSIC. SWANWICK was composed, by Martin Shaw, for this hymn in the enlarged *Songs of Praise* (1931). It is a very exactly balanced and proportioned little tune, and in perfect correspondence with the innocent simplicity of the words.

547 Jesu! the very thought of thee.

c. 12th cent. Tr. E. Caswall (1858).

Dulcis Jesu memoria
dans vera cordi gaudia:
sed super mel et omnia
ejus dulcis praesentia.

There is no doubt that the earlier manuscripts begin as above, and not with the familiar 'Jesu, dulcis memoria'.

A selection from Caswall's translation of the whole poem in his *Masque of Mary* (1858). It is not by St. Bernard. Doubt was thrown upon the authorship more than 250 years ago by Mabillon. Bernard of Clairvaux was born in 1091, and, while a few verses were added later, the poem itself has been found in a manuscript of the 11th century. This manuscript was ascribed in the *Revue du Chant Grégorien* (x. 147) to an abbess; but, although the poem is strikingly feminine 'in the honeyed sweetness' of its affection, this ascription has been shown to be a mistake by Reginald Vaux, in *The Church Quarterly Review* (Apr. 1929). Mr. Stephen Gaselee, in the *Oxford Book of Medieval Latin Verse*, 1928, suggests that judging from the nationality of the best manuscripts, the author may possibly be of English origin. But we really know nothing and are not likely to know.

As a matter of fact St. Bernard, though he did speak of the Lord as 'honey in the mouth', was not the man to write such carefully composed verses. He disliked art, and spoke in scathing terms about the architecture of churches (which after all was still simple enough in the 12th century); he hated rich ceremonial; and when he wrote some verses for the Victorines of Paris, he deliberately wrote them 'so that they would not scan, though they lent themselves to chanting'.

It is a long way from the clinging amenities of the *Jubilee Rhythm* (or *Joyful Rhythm*), as it was called, to Livingstone in the wilds of Africa; yet he wrote: 'The hymn of St. Bernard, on the name of Christ, although in what might be termed dog-Latin, pleases me so: it rings in my ears as I wander across the wide, wide wilderness.' But people's minds were much influenced by the belief that it was by Bernard—indeed the popular notion of him is just that he was a medieval saint who wrote a famous hymn. Some of the verses are weaker than others; there is a certain poverty of thought; it 'eddies round its subject'; and, as Archbishop Trench said: 'With all the beauty of the stanzas in particular, the composition, as a whole, lies under the defect of a certain monotony and want of progress.'

The best perhaps of all the manuscripts, Mr. Gaselee considers, is in the Missal of Lesnes Abbey (near Greenwich), written between 1178 and 1220, and now in the Victoria and Albert Museum. He considers that originally it was a meditation on the Holy Communion and not on the Holy Name.

It came late into liturgical use. When an office of the Holy Name was instituted, it was included in certain Breviaries, Sarum, *c.* 1495, Paris, 1498, but not in the Roman till 1568. At one time its 42 verses were expanded to 50 for use as a rosary. See also 547.

C.M.

MUSIC. KING'S NORTON, by Jeremiah Clark, appeared in Playford's

The Divine Companion: or, David's Harp new tun'd, &c. (1709), where it is set to 'No songs of Tryumph now be sung', and headed 'An Hymn for Good-Fryday'. It is a most attractive tune, with a very characteristic sequence in the 3rd line; the whole melody is reminiscent of many of this composer's small pieces for the harpsichord.

WINDSOR is first found, set to Psalm 116, in the *Booke of the Musicke of M. William Damon . . . conteining all the tunes of David's Psalmes, &c.* (1591). The Rev. H. Parr, however, has suggested, with probability, that the tune is an adaptation of the one set to chapter iii in Christopher Tye's *Actes of the Apostles* (1553), of which the treble runs as follows:

In *Este's Psalter* (1592), the tune, harmonized by G. Kirby, is set to the same psalm, and is classified among 'those tunes newly added in this booke', the melody being as follows:

In this edition the tune is nameless, but in three subsequent issues it is called 'Suffolk Tune'. The name 'Windsor', by which it is generally known in England, is found in *Ravenscroft's Psalter* (1621), where it is included, in the Index, among 'English tunes', and called 'Windsor or Eaton'. In Scotland it first appeared in the *Scottish Psalter* of 1615, among the Common Tunes, headed 'Dundie Tune', the form of the melody being as at present except that the 7th of the scale is not sharpened, and the penultimate note of the 2nd line is the 4th in place of the 2nd.

The alternative version (descant), by Harold E. Darke, was written especially for the enlarged *Songs of Praise* (1931).

548 Jesu! the very thought is sweet!

(*Sarum Gradual*, 1527.) *Cento from* Jesu, dulcis memoria (547).
Tr. J. M. Neale‡ (1854).

See 547 for '*Jesu dulcis*' or '*Dulcis Jesu*', and the question of authorship. This translation is in the proper metre of the original—Long Measure—of the cento, forming *The Rosy Sequence*, which appeared with its music in the *Sarum Gradual*, on the eve of the Reformation, 1527. Neale published it as no. 44 in his *Hymnal Noted* of 1654, and in a shorter form, with three other verses after the first two, as no. 43. It consists of the first seven and the last two verses of the older manuscripts, before they were increased to 44 in the 13th and to 49 and 51 by the 15th century. Here is the Latin last verse of the original (our ver. 9) from the earlier MSS.:

Jam prosequamur laudibus
Jesum, hymnis et precibus,
ut nos donet caelestibus
cum ipso frui sedibus.

L.M.

MUSIC. THE ROSY SEQUENCE is an arrangement, by J. H. Arnold, of the melody from the *Sarum Gradual* (1527, 1528, and 1532), which was sung to the hymn 'Christe, redemptor omnium' during Mattins of Christmas Day and throughout Christmastide, on the Feast of the Circumcision, and vacant days between Christmas and Epiphany. It was also used for 'Martyr Dei qui unicum' of a Feast of one Martyr, 'Coelestis formam gloriae' of the Transfiguration, 'Jesu, dulcis memoria' at Mattins of the Feast of the Holy Name, 'Christe Redemptor omnium' of All Saints, and 'Jam lucis orto sidere' of Prime from the Octave of Christmas until Epiphany. It is a very late but attractive tune on the borderland between plainsong and later measured music.

549 Jesus, thou joy of loving hearts. *Pr. Ray Palmer* (1859).

Jesus dulcedo cordium,
fons veri, lumen mentium,
excedit omne gaudium
et omne desiderium.

The most popular of the forms in which 'Jesu, dulcis memoria' (547, 548) appears, as well as the least medieval, this cento (vv. 4, 3, 16, 24, 10 of the 12th-century manuscript in the Bodleian) appeared in the American Andover *Sabbath Hymn Book* (1858). It is indeed a very free paraphrase: compare, for instance, the Latin above with ver. 1 and with Caswall's 547, ver 8. Still more striking is the difference between Ray Palmer's 2nd verse:

Thy truth unchanged hath ever stood;
  Thou savest those that on thee call:
To them that seek thee thou art good,
  To them that find thee, all in all.

and:

Jesu spes paenitentibus,
quam pius es petentibus,
quam bonus te quaerentibus—
sed quid invenientibus!

which Neale more closely renders in 548, ver. 3:

Jesus, the hope of souls forlorn,
How good to them for sin that mourn;
To them that seek thee, O how kind;
But what art thou to them that find?

Neither Palmer nor Caswall is very successful in the last verses. In the Latin (some versions of which end 'tua pasce dulcedine', while the original line 2 is replaced by the inferior 'nos tuo replens lumine') it is one of the best:

> Mane nobiscum, domine,
> mane novum cum lumine,
> pulsa noctis caligine,
> mundum replens dulcedine.

But Palmer's hymn as a whole, stronger and more intellectual as it is, deserves the popular preference which has been given it.

L.M. The rhymes are alternate and not coupled as in the Latin.

MUSIC. PLAINSONG, from the *Sarum Antiphonal*, is, strictly, the proper melody to the Christmas hymn 'Christe, redemptor omnium'. It was, however, from an early date, associated also with the present hymn. Several variants of the melody are found, but in English uses the differences are only slight. It is an extraordinarily attractive, suave melody, not solemnly impressive like some of the other great plainsong tunes, but with a beautifully smooth line, and an expression of tranquil loveliness.

JESU, DULCIS MEMORIA is the melody proper to this hymn in *Catholische Geistliche Gesänge* (Andernach, 1608) (see 130).

550 Jesus, these eyes have never seen. *Ray Palmer*, 1808–87.

This, an original hymn, is also by Dr. Ray Palmer, the last words heard upon whose lips were the concluding lines, 'When death these mortal eyes shall seal'. It also appeared in the *Sabbath Hymn Book* (1858), and like other American hymns, owes its introduction in common use in England to the *English Hymnal*. Dr. Duffield, in his *English Hymns* (1888), gives Palmer's own account of how it was written:

> 'He was preparing a sermon which had Christ for its special theme. Needing a volume from his closed book-case, he rose and opened the door, when the book appeared first in his hand. At once it occurred to him that in some such way the face of Christ would be unveiled to us: and the thought so filled his heart that he turned to his desk and composed the hymn.'

C.M.

MUSIC. OSBORNE is an adaptation of a melody by Henry Carey, entitled 'An Elegiac Ode to the Memory of that sober Ingenious Youth Mr Richard Osborne. Educated by the Author, and lamented by all. He died Dec. 22, 1736, aged 19'. It appears in a large album of miscellaneous airs by Carey and others (1737?), in which there is also found 'Strephon's Request, a song set to Music by the late Mr Richd Osborne'. The present melody is set to words by Carey beginning 'Where is my soul's chief Comfort flown'; in the original the first note is in the octave above, and the first two lines are repeated.

551 Jesus, where'er thy people meet. *W. Cowper*, 1731–1800.

One of John Newton's devices for keeping up the people's interest in the prayer-meeting at Olney was to provide a new hymn every Tuesday. In April 1769 they moved, he tells us, 'to the great room in the Great House. It is a noble place, with a parlour behind it, and holds 130 people conveniently.' For this occasion two hymns were written, Newton's 'Great

Shepherd of thy people,' and Cowper's 'Jesus, where'er thy people meet' (*Olney Hymns*, 1779). The line 'Thy former mercies here renew' is an open reference to the move; and another is too topical and, to us (with its ingenious reference to 'stretch forth the curtains of thy habitations' in Isa. 54: 2) too quaint to be included:

Behold, at thy commanding word
We stretch the curtain and the cord.
Come thou and fill this wider space,
And bless us with a large increase.

The Old Testament was so sacred a thing that the danger of laughter emerging did not occur to men at that time. Nowadays few would know, for instance, that the following oddity by C. Wesley (Wesley's *Hymns*, 1877, &c., 231) seemed grave to him because it is based on Gen. 32: 10:

With my pastoral crook
I went over the brook,
And behold: I am spread into bands.

L.M.

MUSIC. SIMEON, by Samuel Stanley, appeared in his *Twenty-four Tunes in four parts, &c.* (Birmingham, 1802), where it is set to Dr. Watts's hymn, 'Jehovah reigns, his throne is high'.

552 Judge eternal, throned in splendour.

Henry Scott Holland, 1847–1918.

The only hymn, so far as we know, that Dr. Holland ever wrote, this embodied the two chief interests of his fruitful life—social reform and missionary work. It appeared in the Christian Social magazine which he edited, *The Commonwealth* (July 1902), and was included in the *English Hymnal* in 1906.

Trochaic, 8 7. 8 7. 8 7.

MUSIC. RHUDDLAN is an arrangement, from the *English Hymnal* (1906), of the Welsh traditional melody 'Dowch i'r Frwydr' (Come to battle). It is found in Edward Jones's *Musical Relicks of the Welsh Bards, &c.* (music ed., 1800), and various other collections. The 4th note of the tune is frequently A.

553 King of glory, King of peace.

George Herbert, 1593–1633.

So much was George Herbert overlooked by compilers in the 19th century that this is not even in the index of first lines in Julian's *Dictionary* of 1891. The *Wellington College Hymn Book* (1902) and the *English Hymnal* (1906) gave him the opportunity of including it in the *New Supplement* to the *Dictionary* in 1907. From *The Temple* (1633). Like so many of his time, Herbert was a musician, and sang his songs to the lute or viol.

Trochaic, 7 4. 7 4. D. The same metre as the Easter hymn and its cognate 149 and 172.

MUSIC. GWALCHMAI, by J. D. Jones, appeared in Stephen's *Llyfr Tonau ac Emynau* (1868), of which Jones was also part-editor. It is a good resolute tune, of a pattern often found in Welsh hymn-tunes, but with a melody of a more general character, and of a type associated with many of the Easter hymns, owing to the short lines which suggest an 'Alleluya'.

554 Lead, kindly Light, amid the encircling gloom.

J. H. Newman, 1801–90.

Newman had been ill in Sicily, and his servant thought he would die, but he made the strange answer, 'I shall not die, for I have not sinned against the light'. When at last he got off in an orange-boat, he wrote these lines: in the 1873 edition of his *Apologia* he says: 'Then it was I wrote the lines, "Lead, kindly Light", which have since become well known. We were becalmed a whole week in the straits of Bonifacio.' He himself said, 'they are not a hymn, nor are they suitable for singing; and it is that which at once surprises and gratifies me, and makes me thankful, that, in spite of their having no claim to be a hymn, they have made their way into so many collections.' On another occasion he said to G. Huntington, 'But, you see, it is not the hymn, but the tune, that has gained the popularity'. This was no doubt little short of the truth; Dykes seized a certain mood of his age, and the hymns that he set became popular to a huge extent and his tunes still survive in many quarters. When Froude wrote his *Short Studies* in the eighteen-seventies he could say with truth that it was then the most popular hymn in the language.

In J. T. Fowler's *Life of Dr. Dykes* it is stated that 'Dr. Dykes's friends remember his telling them that the tune to "Lead, kindly Light" came into his head while walking through the Strand in London'. The Rev. George Huntington relates the following incident:

> 'I had been paying Cardinal Newman a visit. . . . I happened to mention his well-known hymn "Lead, kindly Light". . . . I ventured to say, "It must be a great pleasure to you to know that you have written a hymn treasured wherever English-speaking Christians are to be found; and where are they not to be found?" He was silent for some moments, and then said with emotion, "Yes, deeply thankful, and more than thankful"; then after another pause, "But you see it is not the hymn, but the tune, that has gained the popularity! The tune is Dykes's, and Dr. Dykes was a great master." '

No one knows what the last two lines mean: Newman told a correspondent that 'I am not bound to remember my own meaning'. Five interpretations were given in *Notes and Queries* (1880). J. Mearns, after a close study, came to the conclusion that he must have been thinking of the guardian angels who would smile on him again. Most people of course thought of those whom they had lost by death. The angel faces seem to be like the night pilgrims of another hymn, once all too popular, of which Ellerton said: 'We inquire in vain into the meaning of the "Pilgrims of the Night".'

Nor is it known what 'kindly light' itself means. Mearns concluded that it meant the Inward Light of conscience, 'kindly' being used in the Elizabethan sense of 'implanted' or 'innate'. Probably to most the phrase meant just the divine guidance. On the other hand, we have been assured that it means Christ as the Light of the World. Newman was justified in answering as he did: 'There must be a statute of limitation for writers of verse, or it would be quite tyranny if in an art which is the expression, not of truth, but of imagination and sentiment, one were obliged to be ready for examination on the transient states of mind which came upon one when home-sick, or sea-sick, or in any other way sensitive or excited.' (*Letter to Dr. Greenhill*, 18 Jan. 1879.) The popular idea was doubtless vague, but it was not this. No doubt the very fact that the hymn expressed an emotional mood rather than any activity of thought helped on its popularity, as did the emotional effect of the short lines.

Iambic, 10 4. 10 4. 10 10. Unique.

MUSIC. ALBERTA was composed by William H. Harris for this hymn in the enlarged *Songs of Praise* (1931). This is a fine melody with an excellent sense of climax, in the gradually rising contour of the phrases, and the expressive return of the last line; it merits general acceptance as an alternative to the well-known tune which follows.

LUX BENIGNA was written by J. B. Dykes for this hymn and appeared first in *Psalms and Hymns for the Church, School, and Home edited by the Rev. D. T. Barry, B.A. With accompanying Tunes from the Parish Tune Book* (1867), where it is named 'St. Oswald'. It is in the key of G, and the harmony differs slightly from that of the present version, which appeared in *Hymns Ancient and Modern, Appendix* (1868).

555 Lead us, heavenly Father, lead us.

J. Edmeston, 1791–1867.

From his *Sacred Lyrics* (Set 2, 1821). A hymn written 'for the Children of the London Orphan Asylum', in three verses as here. One of the triadic hymns, expressing well the spirit of religious trust, though without much originality, it is in a useful metre which fits some good tunes. From the *Baptist Psalms and Hymns* of 1858 it has passed into most hymnals.

Trochaic, 8 7. 8 7. 8 7.

MUSIC. LEWES, by J. Randall, was first published in sheet form about 1774, set to the hymn 'Mighty God, while angels bless thee', and, later, in the composer's *Collection of Psalm and Hymn Tunes* (1794). The tune is a good specimen of a type common during its period, the last two lines being especially characteristic. A pleasant swing is imparted to the whole tune by the first phrase, and the rhythm throughout has an excellent sense of continuity.

MANNHEIM is from *Vierstimmiges Choralbuch herausgegeben von Dr. F. Filitz* (Berlin, 1847), where it appears in the following form:

The present adaptation appeared in *Congregational Church Music* (1853), and, in this form, the tune has become closely associated with the present words.

556 Let all the world in every corner sing.

George Herbert, 1593–1633.

This is the only hymn of George Herbert's that partly escaped the neglect of the 19th-century books. It was not in *Hymns Ancient and Modern*

(1861), but was included in 1875; in the new 1904 edition it was still the only example of his sacred poetry; but the *Second Supplement* of 1916 added 'King of glory', which had been already in the *English Hymnal* (1906). Even 'Let all the world' was not in the *Hymnal Companion*, nor in *Church Hymns*, till 1903.

Herbert called it 'Antiphon', because he intended a chorus to sing, 'Let all the world in every corner sing, My God and King'. It was published in *The Temple*, 1633, the year after his death. (See 401.)

Iambic, 10 4. 6 6. 6 6. 10 4. Unique.

MUSIC. HIGH ROAD, by Martin Shaw, appeared in *Additional Tunes and settings in use at St. Mary's, Primrose Hill* (1915). It has an excellent rhythmic and melodic lilt, to which the repetitions in the four middle lines add a feeling of spontaneous exultation, thoroughly in keeping with the exuberance of the words; it is a very cheerful and captivating tune.

557 Let saints on earth in concert sing.

C. Wesley (1759), *and others.*

Since this is a curious and extreme example of the 'cooking' of a hymn, with successful results, it may be of interest to print the original as it is in the *Methodist Hymn Book:*

Come, let us join our friends above
That have obtained the prize,
And on the eagle wings of love
To joys celestial rise:
Let all the saints terrestrial sing,
With those to glory gone;
For all the servants of our King,
In earth and heaven, are one.

One family we dwell in him,
One church, above, beneath,
Though now divided by the stream,
The narrow stream of death:
One army of the living God,
To his command we bow;
Part of his host have crossed the flood
And part are crossing now.

Ten thousand to their endless home
This solemn moment fly;
And we are to the margin come,
And we expect to die:
His militant embodied host,
With wishful looks we stand,
And long to see that happy coast,
And reach the heavenly land.

Our old companions in distress
We haste again to see,
And eager long for our release,
And full felicity:
Even now by faith we join our hands
With those that went before;
And greet the blood-besprinkled bands
On the eternal shore.

Our spirits too shall quickly join,
Like theirs with glory crowned,
And shout to see our Captain's sign,
To hear his trumpet sound.
O that we now might grasp our guide!
O that the word were given!
Come, Lord of hosts, the waves divide,
And land us all in heaven!

This, first published in the Wesleys' *Funeral Hymns* (1759), was completely changed in the Appendix to the 6th edition of Cotterill's *Selection of Psalms and Hymns* (1815) (it may thus be the work of James Montgomery, who contributed 50 hymns to Cotterill's famous 8th edition) (see 71). This is the version now in so many books.

Ver. 1 was altered in Cotterill from 'The saints on earth and all the dead' to 'The saints on earth and those above'. But our familiar first two lines are not from Cotterill, but from Murray's *Hymnal* (1852); and vv. 4 and 5 are also from Murray, who went back to Wesley's original; while the last line of all is from the 1st edition of *Hymns Ancient and*

Modern (1861). In other words, the first couplet is from Murray; the next couplet of ver. 1, and the whole of vv. 2 and 3, are from Wesley; and vv. 4 and 5 (except the last line) are from Murray.

C.M.

MUSIC. DUNDEE (or FRENCH) is one of the twelve Common Tunes appearing in *The CL Psalmes of David, &c.* (A. Hart, Edinburgh, 1615), and is there called 'French Tune'. Its first appearance in an English Psalter is in Ravenscroft's *Whole Booke of Psalms* (1621), where it is named 'Dundy' and indexed among the 'Scottish Tunes'. The alternative version (fa-burden) is Ravenscroft's in the latter work. The melody has always enjoyed great popularity, and has become one of the best known of the psalm-tunes of the middle period.

558 Let the whole creation cry. *Stopford A. Brooke*, 1832–1916.

When Stopford Brooke left the Church of England because it was too dogmatic for him (and at the same time with much the same convictions, Haweis, thought it right to remain where he was), he compiled *Christian Hymns* (1881) for his congregation. In this collection appeared our hymn (in 10 verses), an imitation of Psalm 148, and, as Julian says, 'of special merit'.

Trochaic, 7 7. 7 7. D.

MUSIC. SALZBURG appeared anonymously in the 19th edition of *Praxis Pietatis Melica* (1678), but in the 24th edition (1680) has attached to it the initials J. H., which are known to stand for Jakob Hintze. It was set to the hymn 'Alle Menschen müssen sterben', which was written for the funeral of a Leipzig merchant in 1652 and printed with music by J. Rosenmüller. Owing to this the present tune has sometimes been attributed to Rosenmüller, but the two melodies are totally different. The present version of Hintze's tune is from J. S. Bach's *Choralgesänge*, and is slightly altered from the original, which was 8 7 8 7. 8 8 7 7, the 1st line ending:

the other long lines having for

The alternative version (fa-burden), by Geoffrey Shaw, was written especially for the enlarged *Songs of Praise* (1931).

559 Life of ages, richly poured. *S. Johnson*, 1822–82.

This excellent thing is from Samuel Johnson's and Samuel Longfellow's youthful venture, *Hymns of the Spirit* (1864). Owing to the identity of their Christian names a fellow student suggested that they should call it 'The Sam Book'.

Trochaic, 7 7. 7 7.

MUSIC. KEINE SCHÖNHEIT HAT DIE WELT is from *Heilige Seelenlust oder Geistliche Hirten-Lieder . . . von Johann Angelo Silesio, Und vom Herren Georgio Josepho mit aussbundig schönen Melodeyen geziert . . . Breslau* (1657), where it is set to Scheffler's hymn 'Keine Schönheit hat die Welt'.

The original melody, at the end of the 1st and beginning of the 2nd lines, ran on thus:

and the F is not sharpened until the cadence.

It is a simple tune, in a fluent triple measure, which has a great, ingenuous charm.

560 'Lift up your hearts!' We lift them, Lord, to thee.

H. Montagu Butler, 1833–1918.

Written by Dr. Montagu Butler for the *Harrow School Hymn Book* (1881), when he was Head Master there, this passed to the *Public School Hymn Book* (1903) and to the *English Hymnal* (1906). A little heavy for schoolboys, its fine moral passion makes it too good a hymn to be missed by adults. It is not down in *Songs of Praise* for Lent, the list there being already long, but it is suitable for such use.

Iambic, 10 10. 10 10.

MUSIC. FFIGYSBREN is a Welsh melody, generally known in Wales as 'Clod'. It first appeared in R. Mills's *Caniadau Seion* (1840). It is a tune of the simplest and most economical construction, both melodically and rhythmically; but, when sung rather slowly, the melody has a remarkable effect of frugal strength.

561 Lo, in the wilderness a voice.

P. Dearmer.

Written because of a request for a hymn on the conception of the divine judgment, and in this form to help the Music Editors.

Iambic, 8 7. 8 7. 8 8 7.

MUSIC. ALLEIN GOTT IN DER HÖH' SEI EHR' is from *Geistliche Lieder auffs new gebessert und gemehrt* . . . (Leipzig, 1539), where it is set to the hymn 'Allein Gott in der Höh' sei Ehr', Nicolaus Decius's version of the 'Gloria in excelsis', as follows:

This tune is adapted from an Easter Gloria found in the Lutheran *Deutsch Evangelisch Messze* (1524), but probably of earlier date, all the tunes in this work being, almost certainly, of pre-Reformation origin.

Variants appear in various later collections, and many settings have been made by Bach, Mendelssohn, and others. The tune has lost something in expressiveness by its adaptation to the general chorale form, and by the substitution of stepwise movement for the leap from G to B♭ in the 2nd,

5th, and last lines; but it makes up for this by the relentless determination which, in its present form, seems to impel its simple and broadly majestic phrases.

562 Lord Christ, when first thou cam'st to men.

W. Russell Bowie.

Dr. Russell Bowie is the Rector of Grace Church in the City of New York, and the author of *The Master: A Life of Jesus Christ* (1928).

Iambic, 8 7. 8 7. 8 8 7.

MUSIC. WÄCHTERLIED is an arrangement of the German 16th-century melody of a song beginning 'Wolauf, wolauf mit lauter stimm', which is found in C. Egenolf's *Reutterliedlein* (Frankfurt, 1535) as follows:

Both words and music were adapted (along with several other popular songs) to religious purposes by J. Walther in his *Gesengbuchlein* (1551), where the melody appears thus:

and variants occur in later collections. It has become, in the present form, a fine tune, in the grand manner, with the strong individuality of the original still persisting through the adaptation.

563 Lord, my weak thought in vain would climb.

Ray Palmer,† 1808–87.

Like 550, this was first published in the *Sabbath Hymn Book* (1858). Ray Palmer, although he did not write between 1843 and this date, is said to have composed more hymns than any other American writer, but it should be 'male writer' to exclude Mrs. Van Alstyne (see under 54). He is described as 'a wise teacher and a simple and devout-minded Christian. He was a healthy, cheerful, buoyant man, loved by everybody who knew him.' He wrote this deeply-thought hymn specially to meet the difficulties about free will which Calvinists had accentuated in Puritan New England.

L.M.

MUSIC. DER TAG BRICHT AN is from M. Vulpius's *Ein schön geistlich Gesangbuch, &c.* (Jena, 1609), where it is set to the hymn 'Der Tag bricht an, und zeiget sich', and the melody is as at present except that the first beats of the 3rd bar and the last beats of the 5th bar are syncopated thus ♩. ♪ The melody, which does not seem to be found in any earlier collection, may be by Vulpius himself. It is a tune of great dignity, with an undercurrent of very great emotional significance, which links it with the grandest of the 'passion' chorales; it is a most moving and impressive melody.

564 Lord of all being, throned afar. *O. Wendell Holmes*, 1809–94.

This fine poem about Almighty God was first published by Oliver Wendell Holmes in the *Atlantic Monthly* (Dec. 1859), at the conclusion of his famous *Professor at the Breakfast-Table*, and thus introduced: 'Peace to all such as may have been vexed in spirit by any utterance these pages may have repeated! They will doubtless forget for the moment the difference in the hues of truth we look at through our human prisms, and join in singing (inwardly) this hymn to the source of the light we all need to lead us, and the warmth which alone can make us brothers.'

Holmes was Professor of Anatomy at Harvard for 35 years: as a physician and man of letters he is the direct succession of Sir Thomas Browne, and both men were profoundly interested in theology. In the midst of the huge popularity of his *Autocrat of the Breakfast-Table*, and other books, he said rather wistfully of his hymns: 'It would be one of the most agreeable reflections to me if I could feel that I had left a few worthy to be remembered after me.' Let us hope that we have helped a little towards the fulfilment of his wish.

L.M.

MUSIC. UFFINGHAM appeared in Playford's *The Divine Companion: or, David's Harp new tun'd, &c.* (1701), where it is set to the hymn 'Sleep, downey Sleep, come close mine eyes', and headed 'An Evening Hymn. Set by Mr. Jer. Clarke'. It is a beautiful tune in the best 17th-century manner, very smooth and 'vocal', but deeply expressive; it is certainly one of Clark's finest tunes, and especially characteristic of him is the particular emotional relation between the 2nd and 3rd lines, and the leap of a 6th in the last line before the cadence, and between lines 1 and 2 (cf. 474 and others).

565 Lord of all hopefulness, Lord of all joy. *Jan Struther.*

As I write this I am lately returned from a service of university students, who have speedily made it their favourite. It is indeed a lovely example of the fitting together of thought, words, and music. It was written to bring the tune into *Songs of Praise*.

Anapaestic, 10 11. 11 12. Unique.

MUSIC. SLANE is a traditional Irish air, from Joyce's *Old Irish Folk Music and Songs*. It is here arranged by Martin Shaw for *Songs of Praise*.

566 Lord of all majesty and might. *G. W. Briggs.*

This thoughtful hymn was written in order to provide a Christian expression of our thought about God in an age of scientific knowledge.

Iambic, 8 8. 8 8. 8 8.

MUSIC. VATER UNSER, in *Geistliche Lieder* (Leipzig, 1539), is set to Luther's version of the Lord's Prayer 'Vater unser im Himmelreich', the melody being as at present, except that the first and last notes of each line are semibreves, and there are no passing notes in lines 3 and 6. In the *Anglo-Genevan Psalter* (1558) it is set to a similar English metrical version of the Lord's Prayer by Dr. Richard Coxe. This version and tune were included in many of the later English and Scottish Psalters. In the *Anglo-Genevan Psalter* (1561) the tune is set to Kethe's version of Psalm 112. This adaptation appears also in the complete English and Scottish Psalters, 1562 and 1564, and was continued in most later editions. Hence the tune came to be known as 'Old 112th'.

It was a favourite tune of John Wesley. He once said to some Yorkshire friends, 'If you want to hear pure psalmody you must go to Fulneck and hear the Moravians sing "Think on thy Son's so bitter death" '—which was sung to this chorale.

The alternative version (descant), by Sydney H. Nicholson, was written especially for the enlarged *Songs of Praise* (1931).

567 Lord of health, thou life within us. *B.R.*

Written by the editor for the stirring tune in an unusual metre.

A five-line stanza, trochaic, 8 7. 8 7 7. Unique.

MUSIC. IL BUON PASTOR is adapted from a melody in *Canzuns Spirituaelas davart Cristo Gesu, il bon pastur, &c.* (Cellerina, 1765), where it is set to hymn lxxxix 'Rovain pur tuots per la grazia'. The original tune begins on the dominant *below*, and, at the end of lines 3 and 4, has ♩ ♩ for 𝅗𝅥 This extensive collection contains, among well-known chorales and tunes derived from other sources, many melodies which seem, from internal evidence, to be derived from popular songs, both traditional and contemporary; they are, like the present tune, of a cheerfully vigorous cast, or, like 'Engadine' (see 516), of a suave, flowing character, but both kinds have in general a certain distinguishing quality which seems to point to a common local origin.

568 Lord of the strong, when earth you trod.

Donald Hankey, 1884–1916.

Another of the formerly rare hymns about Jesus Christ (cf. 543), this is by the 'Student in Arms'—who became famous for his essays, originally printed in the *Spectator*, during the War, and was killed in 1916.

Iambic, 8 8. 8 8. 8 6. Unique.

MUSIC. RISBY was composed by J. B. Rooper for this hymn in *Songs of Praise* (1925). The tune is an independent one, rather out of the common run of hymn-tunes, with a fluent rhythm, and a firm sense of continuity throughout, which makes it well adapted to the structure of the individual verses of the present poem.

569 Lord, thou who gav'st me all I have. *Eleanor Farjeon.*

Miss Farjeon, well known for her charming *Nursery Rhymes of London Town*, wrote this at our request for a hymn on the human need for God.

Iambic, 8 8. 8 8. 8 10. Unique.

MUSIC. NEED was composed by Harry Farjeon for this hymn in the enlarged *Songs of Praise* (1931). The tune, with its changes of time, may appear, at first sight, a little difficult for congregational singing; but the rhythm falls in naturally with that of the words, and is quite easy to grasp and remember, while the melody is attractively natural and vocal.

570 Lord, thy word abideth. *Sir H. W. Baker*,† 1821–77.

Written for *Hymns Ancient and Modern* (1861), and included in the *Hymnal Companion* (1870) and in *Church Hymns* (1871). (Cf. 660.)

Trochaic, 6 6. 6 6. Unique.

MUSIC. RAVENSHAW is in Michael Weisse's *Ein New Gesengbuchlen* (1531), the earliest German hymn-book of the Bohemian Brethren, where it is set to the hymn 'Menschenkind, merk eben', as follows:

The melody, however, is older than this, having been associated with the Latin hymn 'Ave Hierarchia, caelestis et pia'. It has been set by Bach in his *Choralgesänge* to the hymn 'Gottes Sohn ist kommen'.

The present adaptation was made by W. H. Monk for *Hymns Ancient and Modern* (1861), and has become closely associated with the present words.

The alternative version (fa-burden), by E. T. Cook, was written especially for the enlarged *Songs of Praise* (1931).

571 Lord, when the wise men came from far.

Sidney Godolphin (*cento*), 1610–43.

Arthur Clutton Brock, in his *Essays on Art* (1919), wrote:

'The art of mankind is the offering of its wise men, it is the adoration of the Magi, who are one with the simplest in their worship—

"Wise men, all ways of knowledge past,
To the Shepherds' wonder come at last."

But they do not lose their wisdom in their wonder. When it passes into wonder, when all the knowledge and skill and passion of mankind are poured into the acknowledgement of something greater than themselves, then that acknowledgement is art, and it has a beauty which may be envied by the natural beauty of God himself.'

Sidney Godolphin's poem, from which our cento is taken, is in the Malone MS., and is printed in Mr. Saintsbury's *Caroline Poets* (vol. ii, 1906).

L.M.

MUSIC. ST. VENANTIUS, a Rouen 'church melody' (see 28), appeared in the *English Hymnal* (1906).

572 Lord, who thyself hast bidden us to pray. *G. W. Briggs.*

This, on the theme, not otherwise provided for, of 'day by day', was contributed first to our book.

Iambic, 10 4. 10 4. Unique.

MUSIC. ST. MARTIN was composed by G. W. Briggs for his hymn in the enlarged *Songs of Praise* (1931). It is a grave tune, rather in the style of the older psalm-tunes, with a variation of rhythm in the long lines, which naturally follows the structure of the poem.

573 Love divine, all loves excelling. *C. Wesley*, 1707–88.

It is noticeable how few of the earlier hymns dwell upon the thought of God as love. The popularity in recent years of this fine hymn of Wesley's is probably due to the fact that it does address God in this way. This was in the curiously named *Hymns for those that seek and those that have Redemption in the Blood of Christ* (1747). The *Wesleyan Hymn Book* of 1780 omitted one verse, and in this form the hymn is everywhere printed, as it is here. The omitted verse is:

Breathe, O breathe thy loving Spirit,
 Into every troubled Breast,
Let us all in thee inherit,
 Let us find that Second Rest:
Take away our *Power* of sinning,
 Alpha and Omega be,
End of Faith as its Beginning,
 Set our Hearts at Liberty.

Trochaic, 8 7. 8 7. D.

MUSIC. MORIAH is a Welsh melody, probably derived from the same original as *Gwalia* (see 54).

EXILE is an arrangement, made by Martin Shaw for the enlarged *Songs of Praise* (1931), of a traditional English melody, sung to various words. William Chappell, in his *Popular Music* (1859), states that it was widespread in England at that period, and that he had received copies of versions from many districts, the present form being found in Somerset and the south-west of England generally. It is a beautiful tune, very smooth and expressive, and with a cadence characteristic of many Somerset and west of England folk-tunes. In its present version it is so remarkably appropriate, both melodically and emotionally, to the words that it might have been especially composed for this poem.

574 Love of the Father, Love of God the Son.

12th cent. Pr. Y.H. (*Robert Bridges*).

Amor patris et filii,
veri splendor auxilii,
totius spes solatii,
O indeficiens piorum
lux et praemium justorum,
sublevator perditorum.

Robert Bridges wrote the words specially to carry the peculiarities of the beautiful tune in the *Yattendon Hymnal* (1899). They are only based on the Latin hymn, which is found in a 12th-century manuscript from Thame Abbey, Oxon., now in the British Museum (*Burney*, 357, f. 15 b). Nearly every line is Bridges' own; even the first is speedily left, as can be seen by the above (which is in Mone, p. 236). The original is a hymn to the Holy Spirit, expressing the idea, afterwards formulated by St. Thomas Aquinas, that the love of the Father and the Son *is* the Holy Spirit—an idea which is not very acceptable to modern philosophy; indeed, as Dr. W. R. Matthews says: 'The abstract statement that the Third Person in the Holy Trinity is the relation between the other two is, on the face of it, unsatisfactory, since the religious value of belief in the Holy Spirit is not in any way preserved by such a conception, and moreover the statement itself is not even logically respectable. It depends upon the unacceptable notion that the relation between two terms is itself a third term' (*God in Christian Thought*, p. 195). We had best therefore take the hymn as addressed simply to God, which doubtless was what Bridges intended. And this brings us back to our note on 573.

Iambic, 10 10. 10 10.

MUSIC. SONG 22, by Orlando Gibbons, appeared in the *Hymns and Songs of the Church* (1623) (see 29). It was set to a paraphrase of Hezekiah's Prayer in Isaiah 37, and is sometimes known as 'Hezekiah'. It is a lovely tune, one of the finest of those in the above work; the emotive force of the first two lines is especially noticeable, due, partly, to the prevalence of the rising leap of a 4th in the melody. The tune is, in every way, worthy of Gibbons's genius.

575 Made lowly wise, we pray no more.

F. L. Hosmer, 1840–1929.

Written in 1879, and first printed in the *Christian Register* (Boston) that year, with the title 'The Larger Faith', it was published in Hosmer's *The Thought of God* (1885). At first it was printed as 'We pray no more, made lowly wise', which was less suitable for singing. It abounds in his felicitous expression of incisive thoughts.

C.M.

MUSIC. BLACKBOURNE is marked 'Fish' in Ralph Harrison's *Sacred Harmony* (vol. i, 1784), and is believed to have been composed by J. Fish, a Lancashire musician. See Dr. John Brown's *Jeems the Doorkeeper*. Jeems was the doorkeeper of Broughton Place Church (Edinburgh) when Dr. John Brown's father was there. Jeems for many years had appropriated 7 tunes to the days of the week for 'family prayers', and these 7, and no others, were regularly used in rotation; 'Blackbourne' was allocated to Saturday. Jeems had many eccentricities.

576 Make me a captive, Lord.

George Matheson, 1842–1906.

Dr. Matheson wrote two hymns on this theme of surrender. It is a difficult theme with its temptation to exaggeration in a denial of the will.

The other, 'O Love that wilt not let me go', was received with extreme enthusiasm in Scotland some half century ago, when the 'invalid hymn' still dominated the popular mind—and the tune was as much liked as the words. But 'much controversy has raged' about this in recent years, says the *Handbook to the Church Hymnary*, both as to words and tune in Scotland. Matheson wrote it, he tells us, as in automatic writing: 'I felt myself rather in the position of one who was being dictated to than of an original artist. I was suffering from extreme mental distress, and the hymn was the fruit of pain.' It was indeed particularly apposite for one who was losing his eyesight. The present hymn, our 'Make me a captive, Lord', is stronger and more virile; and it does not overstress the sense of infirmity. It first appeared in his *Sacred Songs* (1890).

S.M.

MUSIC. ZACHARY is an arrangement, by Martin Shaw, of a tune which was long in use at St. Agnes, Kennington Park, but only one manuscript copy of the melody was found there in the organ loft by Harvey Grace, and without any evidence of its origin. The melody in its present form appeared in the *Tenor Tune Book* (1917). Some recent correspondence in the *Musical Times* seems to establish its French origin, and it is found as the theme of an organ work by Guilmant.

577 Mercy thou art, Creator, Friend! *S.P.*

Written for *Songs of Praise* to encourage charity in the place of bitterness and party-spirit.

C.M.

MUSIC. NORWICH is from Ravenscroft's *Whole Booke of Psalmes* (1621), where it is headed 'Norwitch Tune' and set by John Milton, senior, to Psalms 5, 55, and 102. It is classed in the Index among the 'English Tunes'. The present is the original form of the melody, which is in the strict tradition of the psalm-tunes of the middle period.

578 Mine eyes have seen the glory of the coming of the Lord.

Mrs. Julia Ward Howe, 1819–1910.

The history of this stirring hymn is curious. First the words were written because the tune of 'John Brown' was so good; next the present tune was written because the new words were so good. John Brown was an intensely religious man, of the old Puritan tradition, who thought that slavery could not be abolished without violent means. On 16 Oct. 1859 he made his famous attack, with only 18 men, on the arsenal at Harper's Ferry. He captured the town and the arsenal, but next day was in turn attacked by a force of United States marines, wounded, and taken prisoner. He was tried on a charge of 'treason and conspiring and advising with slaves and other rebels, and murder in the first degree'. But Emerson defended him with the prophecy that the martyrdom of this saint would make 'the gallows glorious like the cross'. On 2 Dec. he was hanged. On that day H. W. Longfellow wrote in his diary, 'This will be a great day in our history, the date of a new revolution.' It came in 1861; and the abolitionists of the North sang the famous marching song:

John Brown's body lies a-mouldering in the grave,
 But his soul goes marching on.

Mrs. Howe was also an ardent abolitionist, one of the most distinguished of American women, a pioneer of the suffrage movement, who preached in Unitarian pulpits, and was a leader in peace and humanitarian movements. She was the only woman member of the American Academy of Arts and Letters, owing her election to the fame of this hymn, which came out in the *Atlantic Monthly* (Feb. 1862). It had been written in

1861, at the outbreak of the Civil War. She was at Washington, and heard the Union troops singing 'John Brown's body'. The thrilling tune deserved better and more permanent words, and James Freeman Clerke suggested that she should write them. 'I will,' she said; the words came to her that night, and she jotted them down before daybreak.

The next stage is in England. During the War, Mr. A. R. Reynolds, a master at Merchant Taylors' School, a publicist, and one of the original committee of the *English Hymnal*, said: 'These words are much too fine for the "John Brown" tune; and we need the hymn in these times'; so he asked Martin Shaw to write a new tune for Mrs. Howe's words; and words and tune together were published in *The Treasury* for Dec. 1915. After the War they were published in the League of Arts *Motherland Song Book*, and the words only in a little *Canson Book*, by the composer and the present editor; and the hymn became very popular at Dr. Maude Royden's Guildhouse in Eccleston Square, London.

There is one other curious thing. The excellent 6th verse, 'He is coming like the glory', is not in the original; nor in the hymn as it is in *The Treasury of American Sacred Song*. No one knows who wrote it.

Irregular, but the form is three fourteeners, followed by a line of three iambic feet (14 14 14. 6). The fourteener is the metre of Chapman's Homer, much used in early and middle English. It can be split into C.M., and is in fact a form of the old ballad metre.

MUSIC. BATTLE SONG was composed, as is noted above, by Martin Shaw. It is a bold march tune, with a regular progressive rhythm, and a strongly marked melody in full accord with the nature of the words.

579 More lovely than the noonday rest. *Eleanor Farjeon.*

Written by Miss Farjeon for *Songs of Praise*, at our request for a hymn about rest.

Iambic, 8 4. 8 4. 10 10. Unique.

MUSIC. FOUNTAINS ABBEY was composed by Gordon Slater for this hymn in the enlarged *Songs of Praise* (1931). It is a fittingly quiet and equable tune, with a pleasant freedom of rhythm, which conforms, in a natural, easy fashion, both with the structure and the spirit of the poem; a very fluent, attractive tune.

580 My faith looks up to thee. *Ray Palmer*, 1808–87.

Ray Palmer wrote this as long ago as 1830, when he had just left Yale at the age of 21. Afterwards he said: 'I gave form to what I felt, by writing, with little effort, the stanzas. I recollect I wrote them with very tender emotion and ended the last lines with tears.' For this very reason it is not a hymn to be used too often. Its concise beauty will be the better appreciated when we remember that he wrote it in youth, looking forward to the life he had not yet begun as a Congregationalist minister. It appeared in *Spiritual Songs for Social Worship* (1831), when the editors, Dr. T. Hastings and Dr. Lowell Mason (who composed its first tune, 'Olivet'), asked him (as he was walking with the manuscript in his pocket-book) to contribute to their book. Mason said to him about this time: 'Mr. Palmer, you may live many years and do many good things, but I think you will be best known to posterity as the author of "My faith looks up to thee"'

—which has proved to be true. It was long, however, before it was well known in the Church of England: Thring first included it in his *Church of England Hymn Book* (1880); it was in the *Hymnal Companion* of 1890; and the *English Hymnal* helped to spread its use in 1906.

Iambic, 6 6 4. 6 6 6. 4, the metre of the National Anthem and of 303.

MUSIC. DENBIGH is a Welsh hymn melody from *Llyfr Tonau Cynulleidfaol* (1859). It is extremely exact in structure; the first two lines, parallel in movement, being answered by the inverted movement of the 4th and 5th lines, the 6th line being a contraction into one phrase of the first two lines, while the last is virtually a repetition of the 3rd, these also being inversions of their respective precursors. This exactitude, combined with the great regularity of the rhythm, gives a most resolute air to a solemn and dignified tune.

581 My God, how wonderful thou art. *F. W. Faber*,‡ 1814–63.

This simple, deeply felt hymn had 11 verses when it appeared in Faber's *Jesus and Mary* (1849). To Faber belongs the once rare distinction of making a hymn about God, as he did also in 188.

C.M.

MUSIC. WESTMINSTER, by James Turle, appeared, under the name 'Birmingham', in *The Psalmist: A Collection of Psalm and Hymn Tunes . . . edited by Vincent Novello* (Part II, 1836). This collection was issued in four parts, each containing a hundred tunes, between 1835 and 1844. This well-known tune is now closely associated with the present words.

582 My God, I thank thee who hast made.
A. A. Procter,† 1825–64.

Adelaide Anne Procter, the daughter of 'Barry Cornwall', was once a very popular poet; although little of her work has now survived, these three verses express a true thought so simply and so well that they seem to deserve a place in our hymnals. In the original, however, there are five stanzas, and the poem in that form is not free from weakness. She began, 'I thank thee, O my God, who made'; and her last line was, 'On Jesu's breast'. Bishop Bickersteth, in his note in the *Hymnal Companion*, where it afterwards appeared, says that it is 'most useful for the visitation of the sick'. The verses, however, that specially fits it for this use is hardly true of normal life ('I thank thee more that all our joy is touched with pain'); and we have, we think, improved the hymn by confining it to the three best verses.

Iambic, 8 4. 8 4. 8 4. Also in 469.

MUSIC. SEVERN was composed by Herbert Howells for this hymn in the enlarged *Songs of Praise* (1931). It is a vigorous unison tune, with a straightforward rhythm and an expansive melody which excellently expresses the mood of the words.

583 My God, my Father, make me strong.
Frederick Mann, 1846–1928.

This is an example, like 578, of an original being replaced by both new words and a new tune.

There is a well-known hymn, 'My God and Father, while I stray', from Charlotte Elliott's *Invalid's Hymn Book* (1835), which marked the then common idea that the petition in the Lord's Prayer is a cry of resignation (instead of a prayer that the divine will may be carried out in the world), and therefore summed up the major sorrows of life as constituting God's will. To stop this, without depriving church-goers of the shape of hymn they were used to, Mr. Mann wrote this, which has come speedily to the fore. Its cheerful optimism is the finer because he suffered under many disabilities, and few would have envied his apparently unsuccessful lot. Mr. Harold Anson wrote of this brave and good man in the *Guild of Health Quarterly* (Aug. 1928):

'The Guild has lost one of its wisest, holiest, and humblest supporters in the passing away of Frederick Mann. He was at one time a Free Church Minister, and later on, a very wise and able Chaplain of Claybury Asylum. He was also at one time Vicar of Temple Ewell. He had a very wide experience of psychical research.... His hymn "My God, my Father, make me strong", written, I believe, first at the suggestion of one of our members, is well known to all listeners-in to St. Martin's services. As Chairman of the Croydon Branch of the Guild, and as a member of our Council, he was indefatigable up to the end of his long life.'

Rabbi Akiba in the Talmud was once journeying, and had with him a lamp, an ass, and a cock. At nightfall he vainly sought shelter in a village. 'All that God does is well,' he said, and proceeded to the forest. There he lit his lamp, but the wind blew it out. 'All that God does is well,' he repeated. The ass then escaped, and was devoured by wild beasts; at this he said the same words. Then the fowl flew away; and he said them again. In the morning he perceived that the enemy's troops had passed that way, and the village was destroyed. If the lamp had burned, or if the ass had brayed, or if the cock had crowed, he would have been noticed and slain.

Iambic, 8 8. 8 4.

MUSIC. MEYER (ES IST KEIN TAG). See 289.

584 My Lord, my Life, my Love.

Y.H. (*Robert Bridges*), *based on I. Watts.*

Here again one seems to see Dr. Bridges beginning with an old hymn, and, finding it not up to his standard, gradually coming to re-write it for the village church at Yattendon whose choir he was training. He wrote: 'My adaptation was made in ignorance of its authorship and must stand on its merits.' When it had become widely known through the *English Hymnal*, James Mearns noted in Julian's *New Supplement* (1907), that it 'is much superior to its original', 'My God, my life, my love', in Watts's *Hymns and Spiritual Songs* (1707).

S.M.

MUSIC. SONG 20, by Orlando Gibbons, was set to a metrical version of Isaiah 12 in *The Hymnes and Songs of the Church* (1623) [see 29].

585 My soul, there is a country.

Henry Vaughan the Silurist, 1622–95.

This exquisite lyric is from *Silex Scintillans* (Part II, 1655). Of Vaughan and Traherne (for whom see also 294 and 651) Sir Henry Hadow says, in the *Oxford Book of English Literature* (iii. 11):

'Vaughan and Traherne touch strings which no hand set vibrating again until Wordsworth: they are at one with him in their devotion, their passionate receptivity, their living sense of the immanence of God in nature: the difference is that they are absorbed in the ecstasy which after long and painful labour he learned to control. . . . It was Vaughan and Traherne who, in a questioning age, stood forth as prophets.'

Iambic, 7 6. 7 6.

MUSIC. CHRISTUS DER IST MEIN LEBEN is from *Ein schön geistlich Gesangbuch . . . Durch Melchiorem Vulpium Cantorem zu Weymar* (Jena, 1609), where it is set to the hymn 'Christus der ist mein Leben', as follows:

The present form of lines 3 and 4 is found in the 1662 edition of Crüger's *Praxis Pietatis Melica*.

The version here given is from J. S. Bach's *Choralgesänge* (1769).

It is a simple but lovely tune, permeated with a feeling of gentle serenity, yet with a deep undercurrent of emotional significance. It is a perfect tune for the present poem.

586 Nearer, my God, to thee. *Sarah F. Adams*, 1805–48.

This, if one reads it steadily, is a long way above the level of the normal popular hymn of the last century, and really free from crawling sentimentality when one dissociates it from the familiar air of Dykes. Even the 'stony griefs' (which Matthew Arnold used to cite as illustrative of hymnic failure) have a certain force in their over-compression; and we have put back vv. 4 and 5, which the *English Hymnal* omitted—only starring them to show that the hymn is a good one without them. Mrs. Adams wrote the hymn (based of course on Gen. 28 : 10–22) in 1840 for the *Hymns and Anthems* (1841) compiled by W. H. Fox for his congregation at the well-known Unitarian South Place Chapel. She was, as Robert Browning said, 'a very remarkable person'; Leigh Hunt called her a 'rare mistress of thought and tears'. Her elder sister, Eliza, had inspired a boyish love in Browning and is supposed to have been the original of *Pauline*. It was said that when the *Titanic* sank on 14 Apr. 1912, and 1,635 passengers (W. T. Stead among them) were lost, the band played the tune as the ship went down; but some doubt has been since thrown upon this.

Two little stories were told during the American Civil War. Bishop Martin of the Methodist Episcopal Church was driven from his home by the Union soldiers, and was wandering alone and miserable in the wilds of Arkansas, when he heard some one crooning 'Nearer, my God, to thee'. He followed the sound to a log-cabin and found a solitary old woman, singing to herself, in such poverty as he had never known. A new faith came to him, and he lost his fears. The other story is of a drummer-boy who was picked up with his arm torn off by a cannon ball after the battle of Fort Donelson, and who died as he gently sang 'Nearer to thee'.

Dactylic, 6 4. 6 4. 6 6 4. Unique.

MUSIC. ROTHWELL, by Geoffrey Shaw, appeared in *Additional Tunes and settings in use at St. Mary's, Primrose Hill* (1915).

LIVERPOOL, by John Roberts (Ieuan Gwyllt), is from his *Llyfr Tonau Cynulleidfaol* (1859).

The first is a very sympathetic modal tune, with a strong initial impulse in the firm downward movement of the 1st line, and a most sensitive rhythmical ellipsis in the 3rd and 4th lines, which gives an added emotional effect to the regular beat of the succeeding phrases.

The second is likewise a solid, powerful tune, and of a modal cast. A comparison of these two melodies shows that, while both are equally well balanced and proportioned, this result is obtained in the first mainly by the exactly placed contrast of rhythm, and in the second by the counterpoise of contrary movement. Both are moving tunes, but without any trace of mawkishness, and thus conform perfectly with the true sentiment of the words.

HORBURY, by J. B. Dykes, appeared in *Hymns Ancient and Modern* (1861). In J. T. Fowler's *Life of Dr. Dykes* it is stated: 'On June 1st, 1859, Dr. Dykes visited the Rev. John Sharp at Horbury, and preached there.' During this visit he wrote the present tune to the hymn 'Nearer, my God, to thee', naming it after its place of origin.

587 Never weather-beaten sail more willing bent to shore.

T. Campian, 1567–1620.

Thomas Campian (sometimes spelt 'Campion') was a physician whose music is still a delight, and who wrote his own charming words for his tunes. From *Two Bookes of Ayres*, undated, but probably 1613.

Trochaic, 13 13. 15. 13. A curious metre. Unique.

MUSIC. WEATHER-BEATEN SAIL, by Thomas Campian, is from the first book of his *Two Bookes of Ayres. The First contayning Divine and Morall Songs: the Second, Light Conceits of Lovers . . .* (London, 1613), where it is set to his present poem. Campian's harmony has been slightly adapted in the last line, which in the original runs thus:

It is a beautiful tune for a beautiful poem, the two forms of expression so perfectly coinciding that it can be imagined that both were conceived simultaneously as complementary aspects of the one idea.

588 No coward soul is mine. *Emily Brontë*, 1818–48.

One of the great poems in the English language; indeed there have been critics who have given it the first place. The late Lord Haldane was never tired of quoting it. It is also a condensed statement of a whole philosophy of religion. From the same source as 453.

Iambic, 6 10. 6 10. Unique.

MUSIC. GLYNTHORPE, by Geoffrey Shaw, appeared in *Songs of Praise* (1925). It is an attractive, individual tune, sturdily built on a very close correspondence of the alternate lines, the analogy of the 2nd and 4th being by inversion, thus varying without weakening the structure; the melody has a graceful curve, and a powerfully expressive quality especially in the last line.

589 Not always on the mount may we. *F. L. Hosmer*, 1840–1929.

Written in 1882, and published in the *Chicago Unity* (1884), this was revised and included in Hosmer's first series of *The Thought of God* (1885).

L.M.

MUSIC. WHITEHALL, by Henry Lawes, is from George Sandys's *A Paraphrase upon the Divine Poems* (1638), where it is set to Psalm 8 (see hymn 22). The tune is in the traditional manner of the psalm-tunes of the middle period, but there are several distinctive turns in the shape of the melody which make it characteristic of its composer—especially in the 3rd line, and the first five notes of the 4th—and give the tune an agreeable personality of its own.

590 Not with a choir of angels without number.
Sir Edmund Gosse, 1849–1928.

Gosse wrote two fine poems, 'Old and New, I. B.C.; II. A.D.', representing the feelings of pagan and Christian, in his book of poems, *On Viol and Flute* (1873). This is from the second.

Iambic, 11 6. 11 6. D. Unique.

MUSIC. BERRY DOWN, by Ernest Bullock, appeared in *Songs of Praise* (1925). It is a broad, unison tune, with a very free rhythm and extension of phrase; it requires a little intelligence for its apprehension, but is not of any great difficulty and will repay the slight effort needed to make it familiar.

591 Now in life's breezy morning. *Ernest Myers*, 1844–1921.

This beautiful little poem on truth was written by Ernest, the brother of Frederick Myers (see 511), and published in his *Poems* (1877).

Iambic, 7 6. 7 6.

MUSIC. MAGDALENA is a German traditional melody of the 16th century, as arranged in the *English Hymnal* (1906).

592 Now join, ye comrades true! *P. Dearmer.*

Written, after vainly asking others to embark in the difficult metre, to carry the remarkable Welsh tune.

Iambic, 6 6. 8 6. 8 6. 8 8 6, with internal rhymes that really reduce the eight-syllabled to four-syllabled lines—6 6. 4 4 6. 4 4 6. 4 4 4 4 6. Unique.

MUSIC. GLAN GEIRIONYDD is a Welsh melody, harmonized by David Evans. The melody was written by the Rev. Evan Evans (Ieuan Glan Geirionydd), and first appeared in a Welsh periodical. It was first published in book form in *Geirionydd* (1862), under the name 'Hiraeth Cymro'. It is an animated melody, with a lively but resolute rhythm, and a spirit of festal triumph, which is well represented by the poem to which it is set; a dynamic tune, and most inspiring to sing.

593 O Christ who holds the open gate. *John Masefield.*

From the Poet Laureate's *The Everlasting Mercy* (1911).

L.M.

MUSIC. GONFALON ROYAL, by Percy Buck, appeared in *The Public School Hymn Book* (1919), where it was set to the hymn 'Lord of all being, throned afar'. It was originally written for the boys at Harrow, as a setting of 'Vexilla Regis prodeunt', and is a suitably bold melody with a steady, marching rhythm, the effect of unflinching determination being enhanced by the way the tune, so to speak, returns upon itself throughout.

594 O for a faith that will not shrink.
W. H. Bathurst, 1796–1877.

From his *Psalms and Hymns* (1831); included in most of the later 19th-century books. An interesting example of improvement by the omission of a harsh verse is to be found in the original ver. 4:

That bears unmov'd the world's dread frown,
  Nor heeds its scornful smile;
That sin's wild ocean cannot drown,
  Nor its soft arts beguile.

C.M.

MUSIC. ROCHESTER, by C. Hylton Stewart, appeared first in a separate sheet-form (1924). It is a graceful buoyant melody, in triple time, rather in the 18th-century tradition of such tunes, moving mainly by step, and very easy and vocal in character.

595 O for a thousand tongues to sing. *C. Wesley*, 1707–88.

First in the *Methodist Hymn Book* stands this fine hymn; but its original (in 18 verses) began, 'Glory to God, and praise, and love', and was headed 'For the Anniversary Day of One's Conversion' in Wesley's *Hymns and Sacred Poems* (1740), having been composed on the anniversary of Charles's great spiritual change, which had been 21 May 1738. Conyers made a cento in his *Psalms and Hymns*, 1767, beginning with 'O for a thousand'. John Wesley rearranged it for the *Wesleyan Hymn Book* (1780), beginning with ver. 7 ('O for a thousand'), putting the 1st verse at the end, and writing the new 2nd line, 'My dear Redeemer's praise'. The idea of thus commencing with the 7th verse came, it is supposed, from the man to whom he owed the spiritual change, Peter Böhler, the Moravian missionary and mystic. It is difficult for men of to-day to realize the attraction that the word 'blood' had for the old writers (cf. 125). In the following verse, which we omit, much objection was taken to the word 'cancelled', because many did not like the idea of getting away so easily from sin; but the metaphor of blood was so securely established that none felt any difficulty in the rest:

He breaks the power of cancelled sin,
He sets the prisoner free;
His blood can make the foulest clean;
His blood availed for me.

C.M.

MUSIC. O GOD OF LOVE is from Playford's *The Divine Companion, &c.* (1709), where it is headed 'A Hymn made for Christmas-Day, B.R.', and set, for two voices, to the words 'O God of Love, who rules above'. It appears also in subsequent editions; the initials B.R. probably stand for Benjamin Rogers. It is a simple, flowing tune, in triple time, with a suave melody, characteristic rather of the past 17th than of the beginning 18th century.

596 O God of Bethel, by whose hand.

P. Doddridge (1736), *and others.*

A very composite hymn with a curious history, which may be shortly summarized by saying that the present form is by Philip Doddridge (1736), *Scottish Translations and Paraphrases* (1745), J. Logan (1781), and *Scottish Paraphrases* (1781). To this may be added a further change in *Hymns Ancient and Modern*, which included it in 1889, and reverted to Orton's text of 1755, with 'O God of Jacob'.

Ours is the Scottish version, which, says the *Handbook to the Church Hymnary*, 'holds a place in the affections of all Scotsmen second only to "The Lord's my shepherd".' 'O God of Bethel' is surely better than the versions that have substituted Abraham, Israel, or some other patriarch, for the significant name that bases the hymn on Gen. 28: 20–2, of which it is in fact a paraphrase.

The last Scottish verse, however, is generally omitted in England:

Such blessings from thy gracious hand
Our humble prayers implore;
And thou shalt be our chosen God,
And portion evermore.

The chief complication is that there are two Doddridge versions, the Rooker MS. (1736) and the Orton MS. (1755). Logan published his version in his *Poems* (1781), claiming the hymn as his own; but, as he was only seven years old when Orton in 1755 published Doddridge's hymns, this was not true: Logan only changed certain words, and added a verse of his own which has not survived. In the same year the *Scottish Translations and Paraphrases* was issued, with the form in our book, and the 5th verse as above.

Some of our best hymns are composite. When people like such a hymn, or are used to it, they call it a composite production; otherwise they may call it a garbled version.

The earliest Doddridge version only differed in ver. 1 by having 'Israel' instead of the far better 'people'. The second is inferior; so is the third, which runs:

If thou thro' each perplexing Path
  Wilt be our constant Guide,
If thou wilt daily Bread supply,
  And Raiment wilt provide.

C.M.

MUSIC. BURFORD is set to Psalm 42 (new version) in *A Book of Psalmody, containing Variety of Tunes for all the Common Metres of the Psalms in the Old and New Versions, and others for Particular Measures . . . by John Chetham* (1718). Here no names are given either of tunes or composers, but in Gawthorn's *Harmonia Perfecta* (1730) this tune is called 'Burford', though other names are given to it in various collections.

It has often been ascribed to Purcell, but only in books dating from the end of the 18th century onwards, and there seem to be no authoritative grounds for the attribution; the earliest being, apparently, in Edward Miller's *The Psalms of David* (1790), where it is headed 'said to be Purcells'. It is a very good tune, in triple time, of a kind frequently found during its period, but without any definite characteristics which would enable an ascription to be made on internal evidence; there is certainly nothing especially 'Purcellian' in it.

597 O God of truth, whose living word.

Thomas Hughes, 1822–96.

The only hymn written by the author of *Tom Brown's Schooldays*, this was given by him to Mrs. Norton for the *Lays of the Sanctuary* (1859), three years after the famous story appeared. 'It is obviously suggested', wrote John Ellerton, 'by Mr. Maurice's sermon on "The Word of God conquering by Sacrifice" in his volume on *The Doctrine of Sacrifice*.'

C.M.

MUSIC. MARTYRS is one of the twelve Common Tunes in *The CL Psalmes of David* (A. Hart, Edinburgh, 1615). Its first appearance in England seems to be in *Ravenscroft's Psalter* (1621), where it is classed among the 'Scottish Tunes' and is in triple time. Playford and other English editors follow Ravenscroft in this respect. In the 1615 edition the tune is in minims throughout with the exception of the first and last notes of each line. In the subsequent editions, including the harmonized one of 1635, the semibreves are introduced, as at present, in the first and last lines. In all the old books, both Scottish and English, the tune is in the Dorian mode, as here, but many editors have introduced changes into the tune in order to force it into the modern minor mode.

Burns refers to this tune in 'The Cottar's Saturday Night' as 'plaintive "Martyrs", worthy of the name'. There is a tradition, adopted by Sir Walter Scott in *Old Mortality*, that the Covenanters entered the battle of Drumclog, on 1 June 1679, singing the 76th Psalm to this tune. Dr. Alexander Smellie, also accepting the tradition, gives a spirited description of the scene in his *The Men of the Covenant*.

The alternative version (fa-burden), by Martin Shaw, appeared in *Additional Tunes and settings in use at St. Mary's, Primrose Hill* (1915).

598 O God, our help in ages past. *I. Watts*,‡ 1674–1748.

Let us call this 'Watts's Ninetieth', to put it by the side of its companion, the Old Hundredth. From his *Psalms of David* (1719), where it is in nine verses, it was printed by John Wesley in his *Collection of Psalms and Hymns* (1737), who altered the opening from 'Our God, our help', to 'O God, our help'. If it is the greatest hymn in our language—and few would put any above it—this would be another example of the futility of such principles as that translations are inferior to originals; for both the Old Hundredth and Watts's Ninetieth are translations of translations. They succeed, with Milton, Christopher Smart, and a few more, where thousands of other metrical psalms have failed. Perhaps it is true that translations fail when they seek to be literal through ingenuity, and only triumph when they are free. But even this has an exception in Milton's 525.

Mr. F. J. Gillman, in the *Evolution of the English Hymn*, 1927 (p. 209), comparing Watts's Ninetieth with 'When I survey', says:

'They both, in a superlative degree, reveal the characteristic features of his best work—its simple strength, its transparency, its hold upon the common mind, its straightforwardness, its accentual and punctuative perfection, and its faithfulness to Scripture. The first has become the great ceremonial hymn of the English nation, and if nothing else had come from his pen, it justifies its author's memorial in Westminster Abbey. The other is more personal and has more passion.'

Watts's heading for the hymn was, 'Man frail and God eternal'. It is one of the most 'broad' hymns in the Church, and could be sung by men of all the religions in the British Empire—indeed it has been said that it could be addressed by a pious agnostic to his First Cause or to the Absolute. If Watts had been a Unitarian, it would doubtless have been amended; 'to make it definitely Christian', as was done with Mrs. Adams's 'Nearer, my God, to thee', in book after book. Watts had written the hymn about 1714, shortly before the death of Queen Anne, at that time of acute national anxiety about the succession, which is described in the closing chapters of Thackeray's *Esmond*. The references to it in literature must be very many. Charlotte Brontë, for instance, uses it effectively in chapter 24 of *Shirley*. Perhaps our readers will send the editor any other examples of the use of this or other famous hymns?

The omitted stanzas, as Julian says, being unequal to the rest, impede the grandly sustained flow of thought; and in its commonly accepted form of six verses the hymn is seen to the fullest advantage. No one has interfered with it for a hundred years; but Toplady in 1776 made a curious combination of it with Tate and Brady in 10 verses. Translated into many languages, its use among our own people is universal.

Notice how much, even in such a simple poem as this, there is of metaphor and simile: the opening couplet and the 3rd stanza are statements of fact (couched in perfect phrase), but practically all the other lines are either metaphor or simile, or both. (See also under 82, 443.)

Popularity in Hymns

There is some interest in noting the change in the popularity of hymns. Watts's Ninetieth never reached the first ten on a vote; but the Old Hundredth had the second place in a symposium in *John o' London's Weekly* (5 Dec. 1925), though it had not been included in the 19th-century lists. A symposium, for instance, of 1885 began with 'Rock of ages' (perhaps due to Mr. Gladstone's well-known preference), then 'Jesu, lover of my soul', 'Just as I am', 'Eternal Father, strong to save', and 'When I survey'.

The popular taste was not good, and was much influenced by a depraved musical habit: the clientèle consulted was uncertain, too; sometimes it consisted mainly of those who had not been to church for half a century, sometimes of a particular section of church-goers—as in 1887, when the *Sunday School Times* elicited only four hymns with more than 3,000 votes —'Rock of ages', 'Abide with me', 'Jesu, lover', and 'Just as I am'; or when a plebiscite of the Anglican clergy, organists, and others in Canada, 1906, insisted on the inclusion of 'There is a fountain filled with blood', undeterred by the fact that the second line ends with the word 'veins'. On this occasion also 'The Church's one foundation' actually headed the list.

In 1925, only 'Abide with me', 'Jesu, lover', and 'When I survey' remained at the top, while, besides the Old Hundredth, 'Lead, kindly Light', and 'God moves in a mysterious way' had got in. Even 'On the Resurrection morning' had in 1925 one admirer who put it first, Miss Fay Compton. General Booth, on the other hand, put 'Just as I am' first, while Arnold Bennett gave the highest places to 'When I survey', and 'God moves in a mysterious way', adding with some truth, 'Most good hymns are spoilt by bad tunes, and most good tunes are spoilt by bad hymns'. To-day the scale of preference is changing rapidly.

Dr. Jowett once asked a tea-party of Balliol and other dons to jot down a small list of the best hymns: they each returned with one hymn only, 'O God, our help', which each had felt to fulfil all the conditions of a perfect hymn.

C.M.

MUSIC. ST. ANNE appeared in *A Supplement to the New Version of Psalms by Dr. Brady and Mr. Tate . . . The Sixth Edition, corrected and much enlarged* . . . (1708), where it is set, under its present name, to Psalm 42. It is there in two parts, treble and bass, the melody being exactly as here given except that the last line runs:

It is indexed as a new tune, and, like all the other tunes in the book, is anonymous. There is, however, good reason to think that William Croft was concerned in the book's production, and this tune has been generally attributed to him, this view being supported by the fact that he was then organist at St. Anne's, Soho. It is assigned to him in Philip Hart's *Melodies Proper to be sung to any of yᵉ versions of the Psalms of David* (*c.* 1720), and in John Church's *An Introduction to Psalmody* (1723), both these editors being contemporaries of Croft, and the latter master of the choristers of Westminster Abbey while Croft was organist there. It also appears in A. Barber's *Book of Psalms*, but not before the 7th edition of 1715, where it is named 'Leeds', and has attached to it the name 'Mr Denby'; this, however, is probably the name only of the arranger of the tune in the book, the setting here being in four parts with melody in the tenor, and with a different modulation in line 3. The first line of the tune is a stock phrase during the 17th and 18th centuries; for example, it is the initial phrase of two tunes by Henry Lawes in Sandys's *Paraphrase* (1637), of the first chorus in Handel's 6th Chandos Anthem, 'O praise the Lord' (1734), and is the theme of Bach's famous organ fugue in E♭, which has therefore received, in England, the nickname of 'St. Anne's fugue'.

The alternative version (fa-burden), by Martin Shaw, appeared in *Additional Tunes and settings in use at St. Mary's, Primrose Hill* (1915).

599 O happy band of pilgrims. *J. M. Neale*, 1818–66.

No more like a Greek hymn than it is like Milton, this, with the rather too emotional 'Safe home, safe home in port', and 'Art thou weary', was included in *Hymns of the Eastern Church* (1862), with a note, 'This is merely a cento from the Canon of SS. Chrysanthus and Daria' (cf. 490). In a later edition he said they would be transferred to an appendix. There is not a line in the Canon that corresponds, the resemblance being little more than that both are connected with the Christian religion.

Iambic, 7 6. 7 6.

MUSIC. CHERRY TREE is the traditional melody of the carol known as 'The Cherry Tree Carol', and beginning 'Joseph was an old man'. It was one of the most popular carols, and was printed in broadsides in all parts of England. This version, by Martin Shaw, with two other traditional tunes and the original words, may be found in the *Oxford Book of Carols* (1928), where there is also the following note: 'The whole story of carol-music is summed up in an incident related by Baring-Gould: about 1865 he was teaching carols to a party of mill-girls in the West Riding; and amongst them that by Dr. Gauntlett—"St. Joseph was a walking"—when they burst out with "Nay! we know one a great deal better nor yond"; and, lifting up their voices, they sang.'

Amyas Leigh sings this carol at Smerwick Fort in Charles Kingsley's *Westward Ho!* ch. ix.

600 O heavenly Beauty, lovelier far. *Edgar Allison Peers.*

This hymn was written for the twenty-fifth anniversary of the University of Liverpool, by Mr. Peers, who is Professor of Spanish in that University. It was suggested by, but not translated from, a hymn by St. Teresa.

Iambic, 8 8. 8 8 8.

MUSIC. O JESULEIN SÜSS appears first in *Auserlesene Catholische Geistliche Kirchengesäng, &c.* (Cologne, 1623), where it is set to the hymn 'Ist das der Leib, Herr Jesu Christ', as follows:

In *New bezogene Christliche Seelenharfe, &c.* (1650), it is set to the hymn 'Komm heiliger Geist, mit deinem Genad', in the following form:

while in S. Scheidt's *Tabulatur Buch* (Görlitz, 1650) it is found to the hymn (or carol) 'O Jesulein süss, O Jesulein mild' in the form here given. It appears in many later collections, both Catholic and Protestant, the most interesting variant being the melody set to the hymn 'O heiliger Geist, O heiliger Gott' in Vopelius's *New Leipziger Gesangbuch, &c.* (Leipzig, 1682), which is rather a derivative than a variant.

The present arrangement is to be found, with a translation of 'O Jesulein süss', in the *Oxford Book of Carols* (1928).

The tune, in triple time, is of a type especially associated with early German carols (cf. 700, &c.), but it is an extraordinarily attractive specimen of its kind.

601 O Holy Spirit, God. *P. Dearmer.*

Written for this book, in order to provide a hymn on the Holy Spirit which children could sing, and which should touch on other aspects of the working of the Eternal Spirit, as well as those enumerated in the Whitsuntide hymns.

S.M.

MUSIC. DRUMCONDRA, by David F. R. Wilson, was composed for the *Irish Hymnal* (Dublin, 1919). Mr. Wilson, who is Rector of Donnybrook and Precentor of St. Patrick's Cathedral, himself states that it 'is very reminiscent of old Irish folk-songs, of which the composer is a devoted lover'.

602 O life that makest all things new. *S. Longfellow*, 1819–92.

Written in 1874 and published in his posthumous *Hymns and Verses* (1904), this is another fine American hymn which is but recently come into English use. The subject is unity by freedom, and the more immediate occasion is that of assembly, either for an ordinary service or for the beginning of a session or term.

L.M.

MUSIC. HERONGATE is an arrangement, by R. Vaughan Williams, of a folk-tune sung in Essex, and appeared in the *English Hymnal* (1906). The tune is in a familiar triple rhythm and very economical in construction, the last line being a repetition of the 1st, with one note changed, while the 3rd line is formed partly from the 1st and partly from the 2nd; the partial repetition of the 2nd line to make the 3rd, especially as here, the formation of the 1st bars of the 3rd line from the last bars of the 2nd, is very characteristic of a large number of English folk-songs. The present tune has a very quiet and tender charm.

603 O Lord and Master of us all. *J. G. Whittier*, 1807–92.

Like 536, this is a selection from the poem, '*Our Master*'—beginning at the 15th stanza—which appeared in his *The Panorama, and Other Poems* (1856), the original being in 35 stanzas.

C.M.

MUSIC. WALSALL is first found in *A Choice Collection of Psalm Tunes by W. Anchors* (*c.* 1721). In this and other 18th-century books it is anonymous, but towards 1800 it, like 'Burford' (596), begins to be ascribed to Purcell. There seems, however, to be no authority whatever for the attribution, and the tune itself, though a very satisfactory example of its kind, exhibits no especially Purcellian traits.

604 O Lord, how happy should we be. *J. Anstice*,† 1808–36.

Anstice, who was Professor of Classical Literature at King's College, London, died at the age of 28. During his last illness, he dictated this and his other hymns to his wife in the afternoons. He gave up his brighter morning hours to his pupils up to the very day of his death, and it was in the afternoon that he suffered most the oppression of his illness. Gladstone, who had been more deeply influenced by him at Oxford than by any one else, says in his *Diary*, 'Read to my deep sorrow of Anstice's death on Monday. His friends, his young widow, the world can spare him ill.'

Iambic, 8 8 6. D.

MUSIC. SONG 18, by Orlando Gibbons, is set to a metrical paraphrase of a passage from the Song of Solomon in the *Hymnes and Songs of the Church* (1623) [see 29]. It is an adequate, well-made tune, simpler and less passionate than some of the deeply-felt melodies in the above book, but with a tranquil beauty of its own.

ADVENT is from the *Plymouth Collection of Hymns and Tunes* (New York, U.S.A., 1855), edited by Henry Ward Beecher, the music edition being by John Zundel and the Rev. Charles Beecher. It is one of several tunes headed 'Western Melody' in that work, all of which give the impression of being based on, or imitative of, popular traditional melodies.

605 O Lord, in me there lieth nought.

Sir Philip Sidney, 1554–86, *and Mary Sidney*, *Lady Pembroke*, 1561–1621.

From *The Psalmes of David, Translated into Divers and Sundry Kinds of Verse, More rare and Excellent For the Method and Varietie, Than any yet hath been done in English. Begun by the noble and learned gent, Sir* PHILIP SIDNEY, *Knt., and finished by the Right Honorable The* COUNTESS OF PEMBROKE, *his Sister. . . . In the reign of James the First.* Mary, 'the Subject of all Verse', died in 1621; and of the two is reckoned the more excellent poet. This paraphrase of Psalm 139 is probably by her; Julian (p. 1057) gives the reasons which now lead to the opinion that Sidney wrote only the first 43. Ruskin in *Fors Clavigera*, Letter XXXV, 'Songs of Songs', deals with Sidney's love-poems; and his and his sister's translation of the Psalms are referred to and sometimes quoted in *Fors*. Ruskin also published in vol. ii of *Bibliotheca Pastorum*: 'Rock Honeycomb. Broken Pieces of Sir Philip Sidney's Psalter. Laid up in store for English Homes. With a Preface and a Commentary by the Editor [of BP., i.e. Ruskin]. In Two Parts. Part I. 1877.' Part II never appeared. Dr. Garrett Horder introduced this example into his *Worship Song* (1905).

Iambic, 8 8. 4 4. 8. 8 8 (unique), or 8 8. 8 8. 8 8.

MUSIC. LEICESTER (or BEDFORD), by John Bishop, is from *A Sett of New Psalm Tunes in Four Parts by John Bishop, Organist of the College at Winton* (*c.* 1700), where it is called 'Bedford', and set to Psalm 112; this name has now, however, been irrevocably taken possession of by Weale's famous tune (114). The present melody is of a familiar type, but very solid and satisfying, with a slow, hammerlike pulse, to which the passing crotchets, far from lightening the texture, seem to give an added weight; the general effect is of massive pomp.

606 O Lord of hosts, all heaven possessing.

E. H. Plumptre, 1821–91.

A hymn primarily for school use written and published in *Lazarus, and Other Poems* (1864). How good the 3rd stanza is, with its thought—'Renew the primal awe of youth'!

Iambic, 9 8. 9 8. 8 8. Unique.

MUSIC. NEUMARK is from G. Neumark's *Fortgepflanzter Musikalisch-Poetischer Lustwald* (Jena, 1657), where it was set to his hymn 'Wer nur den lieben Gott lässt walten'. The present is the original form of the melody, which is also found in duple time, and, in the latter form, has been set by Bach and Mendelssohn, among others. The innate stability of the tune is proved by the fact that in either form it is equally strong and imposing, and that its individual character also remains but little changed—no mean test for the inherent quality of any melody.

607 O love of God, how strong and true. *Horatius Bonar*,† 1808–89.

From his *Hymns of Faith and Hope* (1857). James Bonar, who was joint editor of the *Scottish Free Church Hymn Book*, contributed a paradoxical estimate of Horatius Bonar to the *Dictionary of Hymnology* (1891) (p. 161), which is worth quoting: 'Dr. Bonar's scholarship is thorough and extensive; and his poems display the grace of style and wealth of allusion which are the fruit of ripe culture . . . although, in reading them we meet with feeble stanzas, halting rhythm, defective rhyme, meaningless iteration.' (Cf. under 492.)

L.M.

MUSIC. HYMNUS EUCHARISTICUS, by Benjamin Rogers, is from the composer's manuscript in the Library of Christ Church, Oxford, where it is set to the hymn, 'Te Deum Patrem colimus'. It is sung on May Day morning from the tower of Magdalen College, Oxford.

O AMOR QUAM EXSTATICUS is a Mode i melody, which is said to be old French, but has not yet been traced to its source. The title is the first line of a hymn attributed to Thomas à Kempis. The present setting, by Basil Harwood, appeared in the *Oxford Hymn Book* (1908).

608 O love who formest me to wear.

J. Scheffler, 1624–77. *Tr. C. Winkworth.*‡

Liebe, die du mich zum Bilde
  Deiner Gottheit hast gemacht;
Liebe, die du mich so milde
  Nach dem Fall mit Heil bedacht;
Liebe, dir ergeb ich mich,
  Dein zu bleiben ewiglich.

From *Heilige Seelenlust* (1647), in seven verses; the translation is from *Lyra Germanica* (2nd series, 1858), where it begins, 'O Love who formedst me to wear'.

Iambic, 8 8. 8 8. 8 8.

MUSIC. LAMBETH, by S. Akeroyde, is from Playford's *The Divine Companion: or, David's Harp new tun'd* (1701), where it is set to the hymn 'Dear Saviour, Oh! what ails this heart?' It is headed 'An Hymn for Good Friday, Set by Mr. Akeroyde', and is for two voices. The composer was well known as a song-writer during the first years of the 18th century, numerous examples of his art appearing in collections and on single sheets at this period; the present hymn is a specimen of his earlier style, belonging by character rather to the 17th than the 18th century. Especially characteristic is the change of rhythm in the 4th line, with a consequent alteration of stress also in the last line. It is a very quiet, attractive tune.

609 O sing to the Lord now, his greatness. *A. G.*

Because a new hymn was asked for on the divine protection, this was written to be sung to a famous Welsh tune in an uncommon metre.

Anapaestic, 9 8. 9 8. D. Unique.

MUSIC. CRUGYBAR is a Welsh melody from *Moliant Seion* (1883), here harmonized by David Evans. It is an interesting tune, with an unusual rhythm which gives it a very distinct individuality of its own; the melody, though not strictly confined to the scale, is mainly pentatonic, and this, combined with the strong pulse of the syncopation, gives a rude vigour to the whole tune which invests it with a kind of primitive grandeur.

610 O sometimes gleams upon our sight.

J. G. Whittier, 1807–92.

This compact and inspiring little hymn is taken from *The Chapel of the Hermits* (1852), a long poem of 94 stanzas. The cento was first made in the *Hymns of the Spirit* (Boston, 1864).

L.M.

MUSIC. ILLSLEY, by John Bishop, is from his *A Sett of New Psalm Tunes in Four Parts by John Bishop, Organist of the College at Winton* (*c.* 1700), where it is set to Psalm 100. Variants of the last line are found in different collections; in the original it is as follows:

The alternative version (descant), by Harvey Grace, was written especially for the enlarged *Songs of Praise* (1931).

Bishop's book had some success, since it passed through three editions, and the present tune is a good example of the fine quality of its contents—splendidly 'singable' melodies, very firmly constructed in the full tradition of the solidly majestic style of this class of tunes.

611 O son of man, our hero strong and tender. *Frank Fletcher.*

The hymn was written for Charterhouse about 1924, and was used there for some time before it appeared in any publication. At Charterhouse they sing it to a special tune of their own written by R. S. Thatcher.

Iambic, 11 10. 11 10. In the music it is Double, the tune running to eight lines.

MUSIC. LONDONDERRY. See 230.

612 O source divine, and life of all. *John Sterling*, 1806–44.

A noble and remarkably 'modern' hymn, this was written in 1840, in a longer form beginning 'When up to nightly skies', which Dr. Martineau included in his *Hymns* (1873), and Dr. Horder in his *Congregational Hymns* (1884). Our cento was first printed in *Hymns of the Spirit* (1864), by S. Longfellow and S. Johnson.

L.M.

MUSIC. MONTGOMERY appears in several collections from the middle of the 18th century onwards and is attributed to various composers, but none of these ascriptions is certain. The position is as follows. In T. Call's *Tunes and Hymns as they are used at the Magdalen Chapel* (1762) the tune is anonymous; in T. Chapman's *Musical Companion, &c.* (1772) it is attributed to W. Champness; in R. Harrison's *Sacred Harmony* (Part II, 1784) it is anonymous; in Seeley's *Devotional Harmony* (1806) it is attributed to J. Stanley; in W. Russell's *Psalms, &c. for the Foundling Chapel* (1809) it is attributed to S. Jarvis, and named 'Burton'. Champness, therefore, seems to have a slightly better claim than the others, as being the earliest. The tune itself does not give much indication of any especial authorship; it is an agreeable, fluent melody, in triple time, of a kind that was produced in large numbers during the 18th century and after (cf. the next hymn), most of them excellent tunes, but not markedly characteristic of any individual composer.

613 O sweeter than the marriage-feast.
S. T. Coleridge, 1772–1834, *and another.*

The only way to make a hymn of Coleridge's immortal lines from *The Ancient Mariner* (1798) was to shape them into the normal ballad metre form of the poem as a whole. This arrangement first appeared in an article by Geoffrey Dearmer in the *London Mercury* for Nov. 1923. Coleridge's original stanzas are:

O sweeter than the marriage-feast,
'Tis sweeter far to me,
To walk together to the kirk
With a goodly company!

To walk together to the kirk,
And all together pray,
While each to his great Father bends,
Old men, and babes, and loving friends,
And youths and maidens gay!

Farewell, farewell! but this I tell
To thee, thou Wedding Guest!
He prayeth well who loveth well
Both man and bird and beast.

He prayeth best, who loveth best
All things both great and small;
For the dear God who loveth us,
He made and loveth all.

C.M.

MUSIC. HARINGTON (RETIREMENT), by H. Harington, is from T. Williams's *Psalmodia Evangelica* (1789); it was originally written as a glee, and published separately as 'Retirement. A Glee for three voices' (London, 1775 (?)), hence its second name. As it stands, the tune belongs to the same type as 'Montgomery' (see the previous hymn), and is of the same high quality; the final cadence, in the last two bars, is identical in these two hymns, and may be found also in many others, evidence of the generic style mentioned in the previous note.

614 O thou in all thy might so far. *F. L. Hosmer*, 1840–1929.

Written in 1876, and printed in the New York *Enquirer*, this flawless poem, one of the completest expressions of religious faith, was published in Hosmer's *Thought of God* (2nd series, 1894), and is only beginning to be included in hymnals.

C.M.

MUSIC. RELIEF is from John Fawcett's *A New set of Sacred Music, &c.* (1822?), where it is set to the hymn 'Dear refuge of my weary soul', as follows:

The tune, especially in its original form, is an excellent example of the persistence of the style introduced by Lampe, Milgrove, and other composers of the Wesleyan and kindred Methodist bodies during the 18th century, of which several examples have already been met with in the present collection; indeed, the ornamental elaboration was often carried much further during the first half of the 19th century, and the above version is a comparatively staid specimen of the type. The present, pruned form, when sung rather slowly, makes a very good tune.

615 O thou not made with hands. *F. T. Palgrave*, 1824–97.

Palgrave, whose hymns are marked by originality of thought and great beauty of diction, said that his object was 'to try and write hymns which should have more distinct matter, thought, and feeling than many in our collections offer, and so perhaps be of a little use and comfort to readers'. He was indeed successful; and nowhere better than in this classic, which goes to the very heart of the Christian religion. From his *Hymns* (1867); included in Horder's *Congregational Hymns* (1884), *Primitive Methodist Hymnal* (1887) (as 'City not made'), *English Hymnal* (1906).

Iambic, 6 6. 6 6. 6 6.

MUSIC. OLD 120TH is found in William Damon's *The Psalmes of David in English meter, &c.* (1579), and in the revised edition of this work published in 1591, but not in the majority of the English Psalters before Este's *Whole Book of Psalmes* (1592), where it is set by Giles Farnaby. In *Ravenscroft's Psalter* it is called an 'Italian tune', but from its likeness to the 'Old 77th' (81st) (*v.* 216), it might be thought to be an adaptation from the latter. The present form of the melody is that in *Este's Psalter*, except that in the latter the first two notes of lines 3, 4, and 5 are syncopated thus:

616 O thou that movest all, O Power.

A. Mary F. Robinson (*Madame Duclaux*).

In this magnificent ode by Mary F. Robinson, who became Madame Darmesteter, and later, Madame Duclaux, the thought of the Eternal Spirit is extended beyond the normal range of the Whitsuntide hymns, many of which do not go further than the classical description of the six (not seven) gifts of the Spirit in Isa. 11 : 2, and most of which derive from one another. In her *Collected Poems* (1902) this is the last of the 'Songs of the Inner Life'.

Iambic, 9 8. 9 8. D. Also in 265.

MUSIC. HENHAM was composed, by Martin Shaw, for this hymn in the enlarged *Songs of Praise* (1931). It is a broad unison tune, slightly influenced, perhaps, by a certain type of Irish traditional melody, but not in any 'precious' or archaistic sense; it has a wide sweep and continuity of phrase, and a sustained dignity excellently expressive of the large scope of the words.

617 O world invisible, we view thee.

Francis Thompson, 1859–1907.

This poem, which had not received the author's final revision, was first published posthumously in Mr. Wilfrid Meynell's *Selected Poems of Francis Thompson* (1908). In the original *Songs of Praise* (1925), this, together with one or two others, was called a 'choir song', to suggest that it would probably not prove to be suitable for ordinary congregational use.

The distinction, which was found to be applicable in so few cases, has been dropped in the present edition; but there are a few hymns which are more suitable for singing at home, or for singing by the choir alone in church; and this is probably one of them.

Iambic, 9 8. 9 8. Irregular.

MUSIC. PIMLICO ROAD was composed, by Martin Shaw, for this hymn in *Songs of Praise* (1925). It is a free unison melody, which immediately intimates the comprehensive mood of the whole tune by the candid expansiveness of the first phrase, and is in complete accord with the sentiment of the poem. The varied form of the tune, set to the last verse, should, if possible, not be omitted, since the long E♭ of the penultimate line sums up, as do the words at this point, the emotional significance of the whole.

618 O worship the King. *Sir Robert Grant*,‡ 1779–1838.

This simple, straightforward, and manly hymn was published in Henry Bickersteth's *Christian Psalmody* (1833), the year before Grant became Governor of Bombay. It is of course based on the magnificent 104th Psalm—too free to be called merely a paraphrase. Moreover, it is based on the version of Kethe (see 443) in the *Anglo-Genevan Psalter* of 1561 (which will be found in the *Old Version*, bound up with 17th-century Prayer Books). A comparison of Kethe with our first two verses may be interesting:

My soule praise the Lord,
  speake good of his Name,
O Lord our great God
  how doest thou appeare,
So passing in glorie,
  that great is thy fame,
Honour and maiestie
  in thee shine most cleare.

His chamber beames lie
  in the clouds full sure,
Which as his chariot,
  are made him to beare.
And there with much swiftness
  his course doth endure:
Upon the wings riding,
  of winds in the aire.

The word 'the' before 'deep thunder-clouds' is always added to make the line singable; and the sibilance of 'Shall lisp to thy praise', generally altered as in our version. We have also accepted the less important but familiar improvement on 'Thy humbler creation' in the last verse.

Iambic, 5 5. 5 5. 6 5. 6 5. Also in 351.

MUSIC. HANOVER first appeared in *A Supplement to the New Version of Psalms by Dr. Brady and Mr. Tate, &c. The Sixth edition, corrected and much enlarged* (1708), where it is set to the version of Psalm 67 beginning 'Our God, bless us all with mercy and love', and headed 'A New Tune to the 149th Psalm of the New Version, and the 104th Psalm of the Old'. No name is given either of hymn or composer, but William Croft is thought to have had a hand in the production of the book, and this tune has been attributed to him, mainly on this ground (cf. 'St. Anne', 598). It has also, since about the end of the 18th century, been frequently ascribed to Handel, but for this ascription the evidence is even more uncertain: Handel did not come to England until 1710, and it is, at least, unlikely that he should have contributed to an English collection of 1708, and the earliest name given to the tune seems to be 'St. George's', not 'Hanover', so that this latter name cannot be regarded as evidence in Handel's favour. In all collections contemporary with both Croft and Handel the tune seems to be anonymous, ascription to either being found only a considerable time after their respective deaths. Thus it is anonymous in Broome's *Choice Collection* (*c.* 1728), Gawthorn's *Harmonia Perfecta* (1730), *The Foundery Collection* (1742), Riley's *Parochial Music Corrected* (1762), Wesley's *Sacred Melody* (1765), and others. In Turle and Taylor's *The People's Music Book* (1844), it is attributed to Handel in the text, but to Croft in the Index, with a note: 'This Tune has been ascertained to be the composition of Dr. Croft, by satisfactory evidence, since the page in which it is contained was printed.' What this 'satisfactory evidence' was, however, is not revealed. On the whole, the attribution to Croft seems probable, but it cannot be regarded as certain. The famous tune has long been closely associated with the present words.

The alternative version (fa-burden), by Harvey Grace, appeared in *The Tenor Tune Book* (1917).

619 Oft in danger, oft in woe.

H. Kirke White (1806), *and others* (1812–33).

About the year 1805 a brilliant undergraduate, who was shortly to die of consumption, aggravated by overwork (but not before he had made himself a place in literature as a poet), sat in the examination room at Cambridge. The son of a butcher at Nottingham, he had won the attention of Southey, who afterwards wrote his *Life*. When he had finished his mathematical paper, he occupied the remaining time in writing ten lines of a hymn beginning:

> Much in sorrow, oft in woe,
> Onwards, Christians, onward go,
> Fight the fight, and, worn with strife,
> Steep with tears the bread of life.
>
> Onward, Christians, onward go,
> Join the war, and face the foe:
> Faint not—much doth yet remain,
> Dreary is the long campaign.
>
> Shrink not, Christians—will ye yield?
> Will ye quit the painful field?

Here was the commencement of a typical invalid hymn; and he wrote no more. But after his early death at Cambridge (he lived from 1785 to 1806), Dr. William Bengo Collyer (the author of the once popular 'Great God, what do I see and hear?') published, in 1812, his *Hymns partly Collected* (979 of them, with eight choruses and four doxologies); and in this he included 'Much in sorrow', completed by six now forgotten lines of his own.

In 1827 Mrs. Ebenezer Fuller-Maitland (Bethia was her Christian name) compiled *Hymns for Private Devotion*. In this Henry Kirke White's fragment appeared with the omission of his last four depressing lines; instead of 'Faint not', the hymn went on, 'Will ye flee in danger's hour?', thus concluding with the 16 admirable lines, as in our version. These were by Mrs. Fuller-Maitland's daughter, Frances Sara, afterwards Mrs. John Colquhoun. The story was that the mother showed the fragment to her daughter, saying that it was a pity it was not finished, and that the daughter, a girl of 14, took it to her room, and 'presently brought it back with the 14 lines completed'. But there were 16 lines; and the girl was certainly 18. Mrs. Colquhoun republished them afterwards in her *Rhymes and Chimes* (1876).

There is a further stage. In 1833 E. Bickersteth included it in his *Christian Psalmody*, altering the 1st verse to 'Oft in danger, oft in woe', and making the other changes in ver. 1 which are familiar in England, and are in our text. Some books, however—and that is the worst of alterations—while accepting Bickersteth's elimination of the tears, retained the 'Much' of the opening line. This is the form in the *Church Hymnary*; and in any collection the index must be consulted for both possible first lines.

Trochaic, 7 7. 7 7.

MUSIC. UNIVERSITY COLLEGE, by H. J. Gauntlett, appeared in the *Church Hymn and Tune Book, edited by W. J. Blew and H. J. Gauntlett* (1852). The tune has become one of the most widely known of all hymn-tunes, and is now almost invariably associated with the present words.

620 Our Father, while our hearts unlearn.

O. Wendell Holmes, 1809–94.

This most felicitously expressed and Christian hymn has not as yet been included in many books (with the honourable exception as so often, of Horder's *Worship Song*), apparently because it was thought the 2nd line might be read, 'the Creeds (which wrong thy name)'; but, although Dr. Wendell Holmes would no doubt have been ready to say this about the so-called Athanasian Creed, he is here merely stating the undisputed fact that certain forms of the various religions in the world do wrong the name of God. He wrote it for an anniversary of the Boston Young Men's Christian Union, 1893; and it was published in his *Complete Poetical Works* (1895).

C.M.

MUSIC. BALFOUR is a Scottish hymn melody, as arranged by Geoffrey Shaw for the *Public School Hymn Book* (1919). Of large mould, the rugged but beautifully poised melodic line gives this tune an immense rocklike stability.

621 Our God, to whom we turn.

Edward Grubb.

From Mr. Grubb's *The Light of Life: Hymns of Faith and Consolation* (1925).

Iambic, 6 7. 6 7. 6 6. 6 6. The metre of 350, 'Now thank we all'.

MUSIC. DARMSTADT (O GOTT, DU FROMMER GOTT), by Ahasuerus

Fritsch, is from his *Himmels-Lust und Welt-Unlust, &c.* (Jena, 1679), where it is set to the hymn 'Die Wollust dieser Welt', as follows:

Many variants are found in later collections, the following, from the *Geistreiches Gesangbuch, &c.* (Darmstadt, 1698), showing its form midway in its development:

The present version is from J. S. Bach's *Vierstimmige Choralgesänge* (1765–9), virtually the same form of the melody being found at the same date in Nicolai's *Vollständiges Choralbuch, &c.* (1765). Through all its transformations this splendid tune has retained the sturdy independence of its character, and, in its final version has become one of the finest and most stately of German chorales.

622 Poor Soul, the centre of my sinful earth.

W. Shakespeare, 1564–1616.

Shakespeare's Sonnets were probably written between 1591 and 1594, and were published in 1609. This is Sonnet CXLVI. 'Fooled by' in line 2 is Malone's conjectural filling-up of a blank in the 1609 edition.

Tens in sonnet form. See 22.

MUSIC. CONGLETON is first found in the *Psalms of David, by Robert Goodridge* (1684), where it is set to Psalm 67, and attributed to 'Mr. Michael Wise'. It is one of seven tunes at the end of the above work, in two parts, 'to which all the psalms may be sung as directed'. The present version is from the *Standard Psalm Tune-book* (1852).

Michael Wise was one of the most celebrated musicians of his day, and held several important posts, which are detailed in the biographical notes. He was also a great 'character' of his time, with a strong sense of humour, and an unfortunately hasty temper, which finally led to his death; for, during a quarrel with a watchman, he received a blow on the head which killed him. He was an excellent musician, with a very pure, original gift of melody, as is exemplified by the present tune; cast, as it is, in the pattern of the period, it still shows his very great individual talent.

623 Praise, my soul, the King of heaven. *H. F. Lyte*, 1793–1847.

Goss's tune, little known till the present century, has made this hymn deservedly popular in recent years. The text, a free paraphrase of the 103rd Psalm, it is one of the most successful of the simpler renderings, and may be compared with Grant above (618), and with Milton, Christopher Smart, and others who are described under 449. It was published in Lyte's *Spirit of the Psalms* (1834), and is more jubilant than are his other renderings. He printed it in five verses, with ver. 4 bracketed; and this verse is generally omitted, as with us.

Trochaic, 8 7. 8 7. 8 7.

MUSIC. PRAISE, MY SOUL was composed by Sir John Goss for this hymn, and appeared in the *Supplemental Hymn and Tune Book, compiled by the Rev. R. Brown-Borthwick. Third edition with new Appendix* (1869). It is there given for voices in unison with a varied organ accompaniment for each of five verses, and also in four-part vocal harmony, the latter in E major. The present version is a combination of part of the first setting with the second.

624 Praise the Lord! Ye heavens, adore him.

I. *Foundling Hospital Coll.* (*c.* 1801).
Part II by *E. Osler*, 1798–1863.

I. Of unknown authorship, the earliest appearance of this famous hymn was in a four-page tract which is found pasted into the book used at the then fashionable chapel of the Foundling Hospital in London, now recently demolished: the book was called *Psalms, Hymns, and Anthems of the Foundling Hospital*; and the hymn is stuck in some copies of the Music Edition of 1796, and of the Words Edition of 1801. When it was printed and pasted in we do not know; but it seems to have been after 1801, when it would naturally have been put into both editions at the same time. There are five hymns in the tract, which was '*For Foundling Apprentices, attending Divine Service to return Thanks*'. It is headed, 'Hymn from Psalm cxlviii. Hayden.'

II. Osler's stanza appeared in Hall's *Mitre Book* (1836). In Cooke and Denton's *Church Hymnal* (1852) it was printed with the Foundling Hospital verses. In 1906 the *English Hymnal* brought back this convenient arrangement, and, by making Osler's verse a separate part, provided longer and shorter forms of the hymn, and three excellent doxologies besides.

Trochaic, 8 7. 8 7. D.

MUSIC. PRAISE, by Geoffrey Shaw, appeared in *Additional Tunes and settings in use at St. Mary's, Primrose Hill* (1915). It is a bold, unison tune, in triple time, with a strong modal feeling, and a very broad swinging rhythm.

625 Praise to the Holiest in the height. *J. H. Newman*, 1801–90.

From his *Dream of Gerontius*, which was written in 1865, and printed in *Verses on Various Occasions* (1868). The repetition of the 1st verse at the end was done in order to make it into a hymn, when it was included in the 1868 *Appendix* of *Hymns Ancient and Modern.* In the original poem it is sung by the 'Fifth Choir of Angelicals'; very soon, thanks to the Dykes tune, it was being sung by most choirs of evangelicals also and appeared in many hymn-books. Next to 'Rock of ages', it was Gladstone's favourite hymn. It depends, however, for its subject upon the doctrine that Adam fell through eating a certain fruit in the Garden of Eden, thereby ruining the whole human race: that idea it treats with delicacy and grace; but the meaning of the hymn seems to be gone unless the legend is accepted as historical fact.

C.M. (arranged as D.C.M. for the tune).

MUSIC. FIRST MODE MELODY is the first of the nine tunes by Thomas Tallis in *The Whole Psalter translated into English Metre, &c.* (see 45).

626 Praise to the Lord, the Almighty, the King of creation.

J. Neander, 1650–80. *Tr. C. Winkworth, S.P.V.*

Lobe den Herren, den mächtigen König der Ehren,
Meine geliebete Seele, das ist mein Begehren;
  Kommet zu Hauf,
  Psalter und Harfe, macht auf,
Lasset den Lobgesang hören.

This magnificent song of praise, perhaps the finest there is, when we consider the tune, and certainly the finest production of Neander (cf. 442), is founded on Psalms 103: 1–6 and 150, and was published in his *Glaub- und Liebesübung* (Bremen, 1680) with the tune. We have altered Miss Winkworth's translation (in her *Chorale Book for England*, 1863), which indeed is seldom used unchanged. The music requires more stress where we have altered (ver. 1) 'All ye' to 'Come ye', and (ver. 3) 'What the Almighty' to 'All the'. Similarly in ver. 2, we read 'All that is needful', instead of 'How thy heart's wishes' or 'How thy entreaties'. Ver. 3, 'If with his love he befriend', is not an altogether satisfactory thought, and is not true to the original ('Der dir mit Liebe begegnet'), and we have changed it to 'He who with love doth befriend thee'.

How much the hymn is loved by Germans is illustrated by the fact that A. von Roon had it sung at the great thanksgiving service on 9 Jan. 1871.

Dactylic, 14 14. 4. 7. 8. Unique.

MUSIC. LOBE DEN HERREN appeared first in *Ander Theil des Erneuerten Gesangbuchs, &c.* (Stralsund, 1665), this being the second volume of the Stralsund song-book, the first having appeared in 1654. In this work the melody is set to the hymn 'Hast du denn, Liebster', as follows:

but it was transferred in 1680 to Neander's hymn, and has since then been universally associated with it.

Many variants are found in subsequent collections, the present form being that given with Miss Winkworth's translation, in the *Chorale Book for England* (1863).

627 Praise we the Lord, who made all beauty. *Steuart Wilson.*

From the *Oxford Book of Carols* (164) (1928). Mr. Steuart Wilson wrote the words for the French carol tune.

Dactylic, 9 8. 9 8. 9 8. Unique.

MUSIC. FRAGRANCE is the traditional French tune to the carol 'Quelle est cette odeur agréable'. The tune has long been well known in England through having been introduced as the setting of a chorus in Gay's *Beggar's Opera* (1728).

628 Pray that Jerusalem may have. *Scottish Psalter* (1650).

This strong and lovely thing is an example of a unity between words and music, involving in this case the original setting also, with the melody in the tenor. It was first in this form in the *English Hymnal*, where the practice of singing fa-burden verses, now so popular, was first introduced; but we felt that the scope of the setting would be improved by having five verses instead of three. The cento is pieced together solely with the view of making a good modern hymn, the Psalms chosen from being in this order, 122, 133, 116. Scotsmen rightly love their rugged old Psalter, but much of it could not now be introduced for the first time; for instance, the verse which follows our 2nd stanza is (Ps. 133):

Like precious ointment on the head
that down the beard did flow,
Ev'n Aaron's beard, and to the skirts
did of his garments go.

To get a good ending we have gone back to Ps. 116 for the last verse. Our vv. 1, 3, and 4 are (as in *E.H.* 472) from the Scottish Ps. 122.

C.M.

MUSIC. YORK is one of the twelve Common Tunes in *The CL Psalmes of David, &c.* (A. Hart, Edinburgh, 1615), where it is named 'The Stilt'. In Ravenscroft's *Whole Book of Psalmes* (1621) it appears four times. The two versions here given are from the latter work, the first being by John Milton, senior, and the second (fa-burden) by Simon Stubbs. It became a most popular tune in England, possibly owing to the swinging, rather bell-like character of the first phrase; according to Sir John Hawkins it was sung as a lullaby by 'half the nurses in England', and he adds 'the chimes of many country churches have played it six or eight times in four and twenty hours from time immemorial'. The name 'The Stilt' has been a puzzle to some commentators, but it was given to the tune because of the 'striding' effect of the swinging phrase already mentioned; it does rather suggest the action of stepping over obstacles.

629 Pray when the morn is breaking.

Mrs. J. C. Simpson (1831), *and others.*

The original, now over a century old, is not really very good. Indifferently qualified poets often have an excellent idea, and start off triumphantly with it, but cannot keep up to their original level. This tendency to droop will be noticed in many once well-known hymns, as well as the manner in which unskilled writers mix up good lines with bad ones, and also do not know when to finish. Miss Jane Cross Bell, at the age of 20, had a very excellent idea, which she contributed to the *Edinburgh Literary Journal* in 1831, clad in verses of unequal merit. She reproduced them, reduced to three stanzas, in her *April Hours* (1838). 'Go when the morning shineth' became popular; we found a good tune for it in 1905 (*E.H.* 473), and two friends improved it; but it seemed when *Songs of Praise* was in making that something more could be done for a hymn that sets forth the idea of prayer in a quite simple way, better perhaps than any other. As a new Dictionary of Hymnody may possibly one day be compiled, we should perhaps give the names of the 'others' in this work: they are, Stephen Gwynn, Mabel Dearmer, Jan Struther, and the editor.

Iambic, 7 6. 7 6. D.

MUSIC. MEIRIONYDD, by William Lloyd, is from a manuscript book of tunes formerly in his possession, where it is called 'Berth'. The present form is slightly altered from the original. It is a straightforward tune on the pattern of many Welsh hymn-tunes, but the form differs somewhat in that the last two lines are not, as in the majority of such melodies, simple repeats of the first two, but varied imitations of them; it has a four-square, easy rhythm and a general character of unaffected vigour.

630 Prayer is the soul's sincere desire. *J. Montgomery*, 1771–1854.

This great hymn, which, like 629, teaches the principle and practice of prayer with truth and power, would have been lost to 19th-century Anglicans but for the *Hymnal Companion* and *Church Hymns*. James Montgomery wrote it in 1818 for Edward Bickersteth's *Treatise on Prayer*, and it was included in the famous 8th edition of Cotterill's *Selection* (1819). Montgomery made a few alterations in subsequent reprints. Presumably it has been omitted from several important books because it consists in the main of a series of statements; but so does the *Magnificat*; and its last verse is a beautiful direct petition, whereas the *Magnificat* is a statement throughout, as also are some other great psalms and hymns.

C.M.

MUSIC. WIGTOWN is one of the Common Tunes in the *Psalmes of David* (Hart's heirs, Edinburgh, 1635). This tune, though of the usual type, has more individuality than many of these 'common tunes', mainly owing to the 1st and 3rd lines, which have a greater significance than is found in the phrases that generally compose these particular psalm melodies; they are mostly good plain tunes, but not highly differentiated or expressive as befits their 'common' use.

631 Rejoice, O land, in God thy might. *Y.H.* (*Robert Bridges*).

Quite short hymns are a very precious part of our church song when they come near to perfect execution; and this has been deservedly loved since the *English Hymnal* took it over from the *Yattendon Hymnal* (1899), where the words were written for Tallis's Canon, which Dr. Bridges found, intelligibly edited for the first time by Harry Ellis Wooldridge.

L.M.

MUSIC. WAREHAM, by William Knapp, is from *A Sett of New Psalm Tunes and Anthems, in Four Parts by William Knapp* (1738), where it is set to Psalm 36, vv. 5–10, with the heading 'For the Holy Sacrament', the melody being as follows:

Another form, in common time, is found in Knapp's later book *New Church Melody, &c.* (1754), where it is called 'Blandford Tune', and set to Psalm 139 as follows:

The alternative version (descant), by Geoffrey Shaw, appeared in the *Descant Hymn-Tune Book* (Book I, 1925).

The tune gained almost immediate popularity, and has deservedly retained it ever since; it is a remarkably smooth melody, moving throughout by step except between the 5th and 6th notes. The original form, in triple time as here given, is undoubtedly far superior to the reconsidered version.

632 Rejoice! The Lord is King. *C. Wesley*, 1707–88.

One of the three Wesley hymns for which Handel composed tunes, this first appeared in J. Wesley's *Sacred and Moral Poems* (1744), and then in Wesley's *Hymns for our Lord's Resurrection* (1746), in seven verses. How good in its simplicity is the opening, with lines like 'Mortals, give thanks and sing!'

Iambic, 6 6. 6 6. 8 8.

MUSIC. GOPSAL, by G. F. Handel, was written for this hymn, and is from the same source as 'Cannons' (see 337, i). It is named after Gopsal House, near Ashby-de-la-Zouche, the residence of Charles Jennens, who compiled the libretto of the *Messiah*, and is a fine characteristic tune, which seems to bear out S. Wesley's remark in a letter to his wife at the time of his discovery of the tunes: 'my dear father's poetry must have highly delighted Handel.'

633 Ring out, wild bells, to the wild sky.

Alfred Tennyson, 1809–92.

Stanzas taken from *In Memoriam*, which was published in 1850, and had been written at intervals from 1833 onwards.

The *In Memoriam* metre is the normal L.M., but with the rhymes grouped *abba*, which produces an impressive 'circular' movement. It was first used by Ben Jonson, Lord Herbert of Cherbury, and George Sandys in the 17th century.

MUSIC. DEUS TUORUM MILITUM is a Grenoble 'church melody' (see 28). The present arrangement appeared in the *English Hymnal* (1906).

634 Ring out, ye crystal spheres!

John Milton, 1608–74.

These glorious stanzas are the 13th, 14th, and 15th of Milton's *Ode on the Morning of Christ's Nativity*, which is in 27 stanzas and was begun on Christmas Day, 1629, when he was still at Cambridge. He reached in the Nativity Hymn, says Professor Saintsbury, 'almost the maximum of majesty in concerted measures'; and Hallam calls this Ode 'perhaps the finest in the English language'. The imagery of the 'crystal spheres' is taken from the Ptolemaic astronomy—vast concentric shells bearing the heavenly bodies, and making as they move the music of the spheres.

Iambic, 6 6 10. 6 6 10. 8 12. Unique.

MUSIC. RING OUT was composed by Geoffrey Shaw for this hymn in *Songs of Praise* (1925). It is an excellent tune, with a vigorous swinging rhythm, which fulfils satisfactorily the requirements of the rather unusual scheme of the words, and at the same time makes an easy, attractive melody for congregational singing. It should be sung fairly fast, and without too strong a stress on the accents, so that the rhythmic continuity of the long phrases may obtain its full value.

635 Rise up, O men of God!

W. P. Merrill.

Our text is as in the revised *Church Hymnary*, 1927.

S.M.

MUSIC. FALCON STREET (SILVER STREET), by Isaac Smith, is from his *A Collection of Psalm Tunes in Three Parts: &c.* (*c.* 1770), where it is called 'Silver Street', and appears as follows:

Isaac Smith, who was for some time clerk to the Alie Street Meeting-House in Goodman's fields, wrote a preface which was evidently based on bitter experience; he commends the use of a pitch-pipe to avoid 'shrieking on the high notes or growling on the low ones', and particularly urges the necessity of weekly practice of the chosen hymns. He had already abandoned his clerkship for commerce when he published the above work, possibly because he was unable himself to enforce these rules. The present tune, and the famous 'Abridge' (see 100), were his most successful melodies, and have always been popular.

636 Rock of ages, cleft for me. *A. M. Toplady*,† 1740–78.

The main idea of this famous hymn is from the marginal rendering of Isa. 26: 4, 'In the Lord Jehovah is the rock of ages'; perhaps also, 'I will put thee in a cleft of the rock' (Exod. 33: 22), and 1 Cor. 10: 4, 'and that Rock was Christ'. It appeared first in the *Gospel Magazine* (which Toplady, then Vicar of Broadhembury, edited), March 1776, at the end of an article called, '*A remarkable calculation Introduced here for the sake of the Spiritual Improvements subjoined. Questions and answers relating to the National Debt.*' First, Toplady points out that the National Debt is so large that the Government will never be able to pay it off (he could not see our modern Budgets!). Then he proceeds to a 'Spiritual Improvement', on the ground that a man 'never rises to the mark of legal sanctity', and therefore breaks God's laws 'every second of our sublunary duration'. Then the unfortunate reader is led to calculate how many sins each human being, at different ages, will have been guilty of for every day, half-day, hour, minute, or second. Taking the last as the true rate, and unconsciously letting us off the extra days of the leap-years, he proceeds:

> 'Our dreadful account stands as follows: At ten years old each of us is chargeable with 315 millions and 360,000 sins. At twenty, with 630 millions and 720,000. At thirty, with 946 millions and 80,000. . . . At eighty, with 2,522 millions and 880,000.'

The conclusion of course follows that the debt can only be paid (for the elect minority) by the blood of the Crucifixion. Upon this conspicuous example of the sin obsession the hymn is based; and it is printed after his 'calculation', under the heading, 'A living and dying PRAYER for *the* HOLIEST BELIEVER in the World'. Yet 'Rock of ages' was not precise enough for some: the *Hymn Book* of the Plymouth Brethren altered it to:

> Rock of ages, hid in thee,
> Where can condemnation be?

In common with most editors, we are content with one alteration—that in ver. 4, from 'When my eye-strings break in death'.

Toplady had already printed the first couplet, with that beginning 'Foul, I to the fountain', in the *Gospel Magazine* for Oct. 1775; and he repeated the whole hymn (altering in ver. 4 'Whilst' to 'While', and 'tracts' to 'worlds') in his *Psalms and Hymns* (1776). It did not win popularity till after 1830; then, when Toplady's controversial volumes were forgotten and his Calvinism already on the wane, it rose to a pinnacle of esteem, not among the simple alone. Overwrought with the idea of sin as it is, the universal need of the divine help is expressed with a passionate intensity that has caused it to survive the ideas which gave it birth.

It is strangely unlike any other hymn; although its thought is but the common form of its age, and the very phrase 'Rock of ages' was well known as a title of the Saviour long before Toplady's day. It has been criticized more than once: John Hudson, for instance, wrote in the *National Review* (Aug. 1888):

'It seems a medley of confused images, and accumulated, if not misapplied metaphors—"cleft rock", "riven side", "to thy cross I cling", "to the fountain fly". What is the precise meaning of "*double* cure"? Is the curative agent or the thing cured *double*? i.e. does it refer to "water and blood", or "guilt and power" of sin? And surely to cleanse from power is an odd expression! The hymn does not make clear to the reader whence the writer took his idea. "Rock of ages" is generally supposed to be taken from the marginal reading of Isa. 26: 4, rendered by the Revisers, "In the Lord Jehovah is an everlasting rock", the idea being stability. But the second line, "Let me hide myself in thee", would seem to be suggested by some such verse as Isa. 32: 2, "The shadow of a great rock in a weary land", or by the incident in Moses' life recorded in Exod. 32: 22, "I will put thee in a cleft of the rock, and will cover thee with my hand". Whereas, again, the heading of the hymn, "That rock was Christ", would seem to imply an allusion to the history of the Israelites described in Exod. 17: 5, 6; Num. 20: 11, and referred to in 1 Cor. 10: 4.' [And there are other possible references —Ps. 78: 15; Exod. 33: 22; Isa. 2: 10; John 19: 34; John 5: 6.]

All this is evidence that a popular hymn need not be simple. 'Anything far-fetched', wrote a very able critic in 1892, 'ingenious, or subtle, whether of imagery or phraseology, still more, anything bordering on bombast, would impede, instead of assisting, the uplifting of the singer's heart'; and, he added, 'hymns must be chaste, simple, subordinated to the thought, capable of quick apprehension by the average mind'. There is much truth in this; yet a hymn may become popular by some heart-piercing quality which overrides its faults.

Against the adverse criticisms we may place Professor Saintsbury's verdict, 'Every word, every syllable, in this really great poem has its place and meaning.' There may be here some influence of early associations, to which we are all subject; but the intensity of religious passion has surely endued Toplady with a power beyond his normal gifts: there is such vigour of unconscious art—the violence of the opening cry, the sweeping negatives of the 2nd and 3rd verses, the growing exultation of the last, and the quiet return at the end, in a changed tone of gentle confidence, to the opening words. It may be questioned whether we ought to sing the hymn to-day; but it remains a notable monument of the religion which gripped our fathers. Even so broad-minded a man as the Prince Consort had taken it to his heart, and repeated it constantly on his death-bed, saying 'if in this hour I had only my worldly honours to depend upon, I should be poor indeed'. So it was with Mr. Gladstone, as with countless other men: when it was sung in Westminster Abbey at the funeral of this 'very old and honourable and wearied warrior', Mr. A. C. Benson, who was present, reflects: 'To have written words which should come home to people in moments of high, deep, and passionate emotion, consecrating, consoling, uplifting . . . there can hardly be anything worth better doing than that.'

And, with all this, Toplady was a man of peculiar and imperfect character, fanatical in a gross Calvinism, and most difficult to deal with. His torrent of scurrilous pamphlets caused John Wesley to write (24 June 1770) to Merryweather: 'Mr. Augustus Toplady I know well; but I do not fight with chimney-sweepers.' Yet when the same Mr. Augustus lay dying at the age of 38, and a friend suggested that he would recover, he replied, 'No, no. I shall die. For no mortal could endure such manifestations of God's glory as I have done, and live.'

We have only to add that the story of his making the hymn when he took refuge in the cleft rock of Burrington Combe in the Mendips, was invented about the year 1850—perhaps by some one who thought that one little lie would hardly count among a total of 2,522,880,000 sins.

Trochaic, 7 7· 7 7· 7 7·

MUSIC. CHRISTOPHER (IHR GESTIRN') is from C. Peter's *Andachts Zymbeln, &c.* (Freiburg, 1655), where it is set to the hymn 'Ihr Gestirn, ihr hohlen Lüfte' as follows:

The present is an adaptation of a form found in later collections.

REDHEAD NO. 76, by Richard Redhead, is from his *Church Hymn Tunes, Ancient and Modern* (1853). It is also known as 'Petra'. It has become very closely associated with the present words.

637 Say not, 'The struggle nought availeth'.

Arthur Hugh Clough, 1819–61.

'Nothing can be more perfect in form, or stronger or surer in matter,' said T. H. Ward in his *English Poets* (iii. 549), pointing out 'the note of certainty, without which the poet, whatever else he may have, can have no message to mankind.' This poem was written in 1849, Russell Lowell, who knew him, said: 'We have a foreboding that Clough, . . . dying before he had subdued his sensitive temperament to the sterner requirements of art, will be thought a hundred years hence to have been the truest expression in verse of the moral and intellectual tendencies, the doubt and struggle towards settled convictions, of the period in which he lived.' Palgrave collected his *Poems* in 1863, and his widow published his *Poems and Prose Remains* in 1869.

Iambic, 9 8. 9 8.

MUSIC. WEISSE (GOTTLOB, ES GEHT NUN MEHR ZUM ENDE) appears in many German collections from about the middle of the 18th century onwards, but its actual source remains unknown. The earliest form yet traced seems to be that in a manuscript entitled *Sammlung alter und neuer mit orgelmässigen Bässen versehene Melodien . . . von Johann Gottlieb Wagnern* (1742), where it runs as follows:

Zahn, however, thinks that the date, 1742, is added in a different hand from the rest of the manuscript. The first appearance of the tune in print is in *J. B. Reimanns Org. v. Hirschb. Sammlung alter und neuer Melodien, &c.* (1747), where the form differs in many respects from the above, and several variants are found in later books.

The present version is from J. S. Bach's *Vierstimmige Choralgesänge* (1769).

ESSEX is an arrangement, by R. Vaughan Williams for *Songs of Praise*, of an English traditional melody.

638 Shall God not share. *G. W. Briggs.*

This thoughtful hymn was written for the fine, unusual tune, and contributed to *Songs of Praise*.

Iambic, 4 4. 11. 4 4. 11. Unique.

MUSIC. WIR CHRISTENLEUT appeared in the Dresden *Gesangbuch* (1593), where it is set to the hymn 'Wir Christenleut haben jetzund Freud' as follows:

Various forms of the melody are found in subsequent collections, both German and English, the present adaptation being by J. S. Bach. Like so many others, which have already been encountered, this tune has been forced into the general mould of the German chorale, but, in this case, has gained as much as it has lost. It is a robust melody, which has won a certain attractive liveliness from the regularity of the rhythm in the later version, and is, at the same time, a most solid and satisfying tune.

639 Sing a song of joy, praise our God with mirth.

Thomas Campian, 1567–1620.

From *Two Bookes of Ayres* (undated, but probably 1613) by the physician, Thomas Campian (or Campion), who was a popular London physician in the reign of Elizabeth, died five years before the accession of Charles I, and was buried in St. Dunstan's, Fleet Street. His position among both the musicians and the poets of a great era is of recent recognition. He wrote both in Latin and English, caught the very spirit of Catullus in such lyrics as 'My sweetest Lesbia', and made original songs, all of which are good, and some, like 'There is a garden in her face', matchless.

This peculiar metre is trochaic-iambic, 10. 14, the 1st line of each stanza being trochaic and the 2nd iambic. Unique in this book, and probably elsewhere. Campian was fond of such cunningly combined iambic and trochaic metres, as in his well-known 'Rose-cheeked Laura, come', unrhymed there, as often in his lyrics.

MUSIC. SONG OF JOY is from the first book of Thomas Campian's *Two Books of Ayres, The First contayning Divine and Morall Songs: the Second, Light Conceits of Lovers . . .* (London, 1613), where it is set to his present poem. Campian's alto and tenor parts have here been extensively adapted. The tune is a simple one, without the deep feeling of 'Weather-beaten sail' (587), or the remarkable beauty of contour of that melody; but it is completely in accord with the nature of the words, for which a more elaborate setting would be unsuitable. The whole composition, words and music, has a great, unaffected charm.

640 Sing praise to God, who spoke through man. *P. Dearmer.*

An attempt to extend this type of hymn to the larger view of the prophetic function. As has been already noted, the debt of Christianity to Hellenism as well as to Hebraism is never remembered in hymnody.

Iambic, 8 7. 8 7. 8 8 7.

MUSIC. NUN FREUT EUCH is from *Etlich Cristliche Lyeder Lobgesang und Psalm, &c.* (Wittenberg, 1524), where it is set to the hymn 'Nun freut euch lieben Christengmein', as follows:

and has remained associated with these words ever since. The present version is J. S. Bach's. It is a most stately tune in the 'grand' style of the German chorales, and has been but little altered from its original form, being one of the early melodies on which the tradition of this style was based.

641 Soldiers of Christ, arise. *C. Wesley*, 1707–88.

One is constantly reminded that the two Wesleys, like Dr. Watts, were eminent scholars and quite unlike the admirable but unlearned men, like Olivers (398), who contributed so much to the hymnody and other work of Methodism. The mastered simplicity of this, its faultless technique, its sagacity in the use of imperfect rhymes, are signs of high accomplishment. Originally in 32 verses (16 eight-line stanzas), it first appeared in *Hymns and Sacred Poems* (1749). Toplady made a cento of 16 four-line verses in 1776; for his admiration of the Wesleys survived his fierce controversial opposition to them in the interests of Calvinism. The original title was 'The whole Armour of God', and it is based of course on Eph. 6: 10–18. There are some fine quatrains among the omitted ones, for instance:

But, above all, lay hold
  Of faith's victorious shield,
Armed with that adamant and gold
  Be sure to win the field.

S.M.

MUSIC. FROM STRENGTH TO STRENGTH was composed by E. W. Naylor for use in Emmanuel College Chapel about 1902, in which year it was first printed in sheet form. It has since then appeared in several publications. It is a fine, robust tune, in a suitable march rhythm, and with a very careful attention to the due accentuation of the words.

ST. ETHELWALD, by W. H. Monk, was also composed for this hymn, and appeared in *Hymns Ancient and Modern* (1861).

642 Soldiers of the cross, arise!

Bishop W. Walsham How, 1823–97.

It is interesting to compare this excellent straightforward hymn with the last, 641, from which its opening is partly taken, and to notice how the Bishop uses familiar epithets whereas Wesley, for all his simplicity, gives distinction to every verse. But the actuality and practical directness of Walsham How's appeal give it a real value. It was first printed in Morrell and How's *Psalms and Hymns* (1854), in seven verses. Dr. How made some changes when it appeared in *Church Hymns* (1871).

Trochaic, 7 7. 7 7; but Double in the music.

MUSIC. MÜLLER is an arrangement of a melody from *Koralbok for den Norske Kirke* (1928), where it is attributed to J. M. Müller; but it is not to be found in his extensive collection *Neu aufgesetztes, vollständiges . . . Psalm- und Choral-Buch, &c.* (1719, 2nd issue, enlarged, 1735–6), or in the appendix of 1741. It is a plain, straightforward tune, of a familiar pattern, and a very sound and favourable specimen of its kind.

643 Sometimes a light surprises. *W. Cowper*, 1731–1800.

'This brilliant lyric', as Palgrave calls it in his *Treasury of Sacred Song* (353), is surely the sweetest and most characteristic of Cowper's hymns. It was published in four stanzas in the *Olney Hymns* (1779, Bk. III), and headed 'Joy and Peace in Believing'. The reference in ver. 3 is to Hab. 3: 17. Regretfully often, a stanza is omitted in the making of collections such as ours, for the sake of obtaining a wider use of the hymn itself. Here is the original 3rd verse:

It can bring with it nothing
  But he will bear us through;
Who gives the lilies clothing
  Will clothe his people too.
Beneath the spreading heavens,
  No creature but is fed;
And he who feeds the ravens
  Will give his children bread.

Iambic, 7 6. 7 6. D.

MUSIC. LLANGLOFFAN is a Welsh melody from *Hymnau a Thônau* (1865).

RHYDDID is also a Welsh melody from John Parry's *Peroriaeth Hyfryd* (1837).

Both tunes are of the same formal design, which is typical of the majority of Welsh hymn melodies; the second is a rather more individual tune, in rhythm as well as in melodic outline, but both show a characteristically strong and clear definition of draughtsmanship.

644 Songs of praise the angels sang.

J. Montgomery,† 1771–1854.

We cannot but feel a certain pleasure in commenting on this hymn, which James Montgomery printed in his *Christian Psalmist and Original Hymns* (1825), after it had been published in Cotterill's 8th edition (see 71) of his *Selection* (1819). Originally headed 'God worthy of all Praise', which was changed in 1825 to 'Glory to God in the highest', the reference to Luke 2: 13–14 being obvious, while the 1st verse also alludes to Job 38: 7, 'The morning stars sang together, and all the sons of God shouted for joy'—one of the finest couplets in one of the greatest poems in the world.

In accordance with our rule, we have changed in ver. 1:

When Jehovah's work begun,
When he spake, and it was done,

where also the convenient modern usage of confining 'begun' to the past participle renders the original confusing. Some hymnals have altered the 1st line to 'Songs of praise the angels sing'; but we have resisted this temptation to assert that the angels are thus engaged.

Trochaic, 7 7. 7 7. D.

MUSIC. RILEY, by Martin Shaw, appeared in *Additional Tunes and settings in use at St. Mary's, Primrose Hill* (1915). It is a brisk, cheerful tune, of simple and economical construction, with a spontaneous effect due to the frequent recurrence of the 1st phrase, and the four-square nature of the rhythm; it has an agreeable, unemotional candour which aptly expresses the plain factual character of the words.

645 Spread, still spread, thou mighty word.

J. F. Bahnmaier, 1774–1841. *Pr. S.P.*

Walte, walte nah und fern,
  Allgewaltig Wort des Herren,
Wo nur seiner Allmacht Ruf
  Menschen für den Himmel schuf.

In the 19th-century Bahnmaier, German individualist Pietism has passed into a zeal for education and for foreign missions. This fine hymn was translated by Frances Cox, H. J. Buckoll, Catherine Winkworth (*E.H.* 552), and others; but we felt that more could be made of it by a freer and more modern use of the original; and the editor attempted this new paraphrase.

Trochaic, 7 7. 7 7.

MUSIC. GOTT SEI DANK appeared first in J. A. Freylinghausen's *Geistreiches Gesangbuch* (Halle, 1704), where it is set to the hymn 'Gott sei Dank in aller Welt'. In some subsequent collections the melody is slightly simplified, but the present is the original form.

646 Stand up, stand up for Jesus. *G. Duffield,*† 1818–88.

When Dr. Duffield, a Presbyterian, preached the funeral sermon for Dudley Atkins Tyng, rector of the Church of the Epiphany, Philadelphia, to an immense concourse, he chose as his text Eph. 6: 14, and concluded by reciting, not Wesley's hymn on that passage, but a poem which he had just composed: this was 'Stand up, stand up for Jesus'. The reason was that Tyng's dying words had been, 'Tell them to stand up for Jesus', which he had sent as a message to the Young Men's Christian Association. That was in 1858. The Sunday before, Tyng had preached a great sermon in Jayne's Hall to 5,000 men: his text was Exod. 10: 11.

'Hence', wrote George Duffield, 'the allusion in the third verse of the hymn. The following Wednesday, leaving his study for the moment, he went to the barn-floor, where a mule was at work on a horse-power, shelling corn. Patting him on the neck, the sleeve of his silk study gown caught in the cogs of the wheel, and his arm was torn out by the roots. His death occurred in a few hours.' (*From a leaflet printed by George Duffield at Detroit, 1883.*)

Further information is given in *English Hymns* (1888) by his son, Samuel W. Duffield, who describes it as the most widely circulated of American hymns, and 'the most stirring of the greater American hymns'. Dr. Duffield was pleasantly indifferent about it at first: the superintendent of the Sunday School had it printed as a leaflet; then a stray copy found its way into a Baptist newspaper; and so it became more widely known, first in *The Psalmist* (1858), and then in other American hymnals.

The whole story sets one asking whether we are as good as our fathers were. Duffield says, 'I knew young Tyng as one of the noblest, bravest, *manliest* men I ever met.' He died before the Civil War of 1861 had accomplished the destruction of slavery; and it was because he had suffered much persecution in the pro-slavery days for his courageous persistency in pleading the cause of the oppressed, that his thoughts turned at the end, in his pain, to the splendour of courage, and he sent the message which begins our hymn.

The full text is in *Lyra Sacra Americana* (1868). We have omitted the original 5th verse, and in ver. 2 have altered 'God of battles' to 'God of freedom'.

Iambic, 7 6. 7 6. D.

MUSIC. LITTLE BADDOW, by C. Armstrong Gibbs, was one of three tunes written, in 1929, especially for Charterhouse School. It was then in more elaborate form, with a varied arrangement of the different verses. In its present form it appeared in *Songs of Praise* (1931); a virile, unison melody with an incisive march rhythm, and a very effective variation of tune and mode in the last verse.

MORNING LIGHT, by G. J. Webb, appeared in *The Odeon: A Collection of Secular Melodies, designed for adult singing schools and for social music parties, by G. J. Webb and Lowell Mason* (Boston, 1837), where it was set to a song beginning ''Tis dawn, the lark is singing'. It is first found as a hymn-tune in the *Wesleyan Psalmist* (1842), and has been universally associated with the present words.

647 Stern daughter of the Voice of God!

W. Wordsworth, 1770–1850.

'Many and many a time have I been twitted', wrote the poet Wordsworth, 'by my wife and sister for having forgotten this dedication of myself to the stern lawgiver.' He wrote it in 1805, and thus was open to its silent reminder for 45 years. We have taken stanzas 1, 3, 5, and 6 from the 'Ode to Duty'.

Iambic, 8 8. 8 8. 8 8. 8 12. Unique.

MUSIC. SANTWAT is an adaptation, by Martin Shaw, of a Manx melody from W. H. Gill's *Manx Songs* (1896), and appeared in *Songs of Praise*. It is a very remarkable and fascinating tune with a beautiful rhythmic inflexion in the last line.

648 Strong Son of God, immortal Love.

Alfred Tennyson, 1809–92.

Taken, like 633, from *In Memoriam.* Tennyson never deliberately wrote a hymn. When Dr. Warren, the President of Magdalen, and afterwards Professor of Poetry at Oxford, asked the reason, he replied, 'A good hymn is the most difficult thing in the world to write. In a good hymn you have to be both commonplace and poetical.' That was a Victorian idea; and it partly accounts for the bad hymnody of the time. What could be less commonplace than Blake's *Jerusalem*, for instance?—or even *Rock of ages*, which, whatever its defects, is not commonplace, although its ideas are those of its age and circle. (See also our notes on 82, 443, 598.)

In Memoriam metre, i.e. L.M. (8 8. 8 8) with peripheral and central rhymes, *abba*.

MUSIC. SONG 5, by Orlando Gibbons, is from *The Hymnes and Songs of the Church* (1623) [see 29], where it appears in the following form:

In the present version the rhythm has been slightly simplified, but without detriment to the noble intensity of this splendid tune.

649 Sunset and evening star.

Alfred Tennyson, 1809–92.

Like Browning's *Epilogue*, and Clough's 'Say not, the struggle' (637), this delicate work of art is always printed at the end of the author's poems. Tennyson's son wrote:

'*Crossing the Bar* was written in my Father's eighty-first year, on a day in October (1889) when we came from Aldworth to Farringford. Before reaching Farringford he had the moaning of the bar in his mind, and after dinner he showed me this poem written out. I said: "That is the crown of your life's work." He answered: "It came in a moment." He explained the "Pilot" as "that Divine and Unseen who is always guiding us". . . . A few days before my Father's end (1892), he said to me, "Mind you put *Crossing the Bar* at the end of all my poems".'

It is perhaps needless to add that the conception of the Divine Pilot is mystical rather than nautical, and that criticisms based on the latter assumption need not be taken very seriously.

Irregular iambic.

MUSIC. GILLAM, by Geoffrey Shaw, appeared first in separate sheet-form (1915), as it is here given. It is a plastic, unison melody, with a modal feeling emphasized by the Ambrosian 4th of the cadence, and a fine continuity of phrase; the long contour is broken only once by a leap of an octave in the middle of its curve, which thereby stresses the quiet serenity of the tune's general character, completely expressing the quality of the poem. It is grateful to sing and, musically, most attractive.

650 Sweet day, so cool, so calm, so bright.

George Herbert, 1593–1633.

There are no commonplace expressions in this lovely poem from Herbert's *Temple* (1633)—'Sweet rose, whose hue, angry and brave', for instance—but the thought of this particular lyric is in truth so directed that it is more likely to be used as an anthem or home-song than in an ordinary congregational way. Izaak Walton introduces it into the *Compleat Angler* (1653) thus:

'*Piscator*. And now, scholar! my direction for thy fishing is ended with this shower, for it has done raining. And now look about you, and see how pleasantly that meadow looks; nay, and the earth smells as sweetly too. Come, let me tell you what holy Herbert says of such days and showers as these; and then we will thank God that we enjoy them.'

Iambic, 8 8. 8 4.

MUSIC. GAZA is an adaptation, from the *Public School Hymn Book* (1919), of an ancient Jewish melody.

651 Sweet Infancy!

Thomas Traherne, 1637–74.

Traherne, the son of a Hereford shoemaker, afterwards rector of Credenhill, near Hereford, and chaplain to Sir Orlando Bridgman, Lord Keeper in the Cabal Ministry of 1667, published two unimportant books during his lifetime, and was completely forgotten, until Mr. Bertram Dobell published his manuscript *Poems* in 1903 and his *Centuries of Meditations* in 1908, with the passage which became at once famous, beginning, 'The corn was orient and immortal wheat'. Since then he has ranked high among the choice band of lyrical poets which the 17th century produced. The preoccupation that dominates his work is the remembrance of the idyllic happiness and spiritual insight of childhood. This song also is not for ordinary use (though one never knows what hymns congregations will take to their hearts), but rather for occasions when people listen rather than sing. In its praise to God for the gift of a human soul it is at the opposite extreme to the vermicular type of hymn, mentioned under 188. See also under 585.

Iambic, 4. 8 4. 4 8. Unique.

MUSIC. ESKDALE was composed by Jane Joseph for this hymn in *Songs of Praise* (1925). It is an interesting example of a tune strongly under the influence of an earlier period, yet avoiding any affected archaism by the transfusion of this influence through the individuality of the composer; the tune, in fact, could not have been written in quite its present form during the first half of the 17th century, neither would the composer have produced such a tune to-day had she been unaware of the music of that date. The tune, therefore, without 'preciousness', is completely adapted to Traherne's poem, and at the same time is a natural and attractive melody in itself.

652 Teach me, my God and King. *George Herbert*, 1593–1633.

When John Wesley went to America as a young man, he was charged before the Grand Jury at Savannah in 1737, the first item in the list of grievances being that he made alterations in the Metrical Psalms, and the second was his 'introducing into the church and service at the Altar compositions of psalms and hymns not inspected or authorized by any proper judicature'. These psalms and hymns were at first a manuscript collection, but they were published the same year as a roughly printed little volume of 74 pages—his first hymn-book—*A Collection of Psalms and Hymns, Charles-town, 1737*. Half the pieces are by Watts, 2 from Addison, 7 from J. Austin, and 6 adapted from George Herbert; while none are by Charles Wesley (who had returned to England), 5 are by his father, Samuel, and 5 by Samuel jun., his brother, and 5 translated from the German by John himself.

It was characteristic of Wesley's cultured mind that he appreciated Addison and Herbert; but characteristic also of this classical era that he altered 'Teach me, my God and King' as follows:

Ver. 1 unaltered from the *Temple*. Ver. 2, 'Not rudely as a beast' (omitted by us) he was obliged to regularize. He wrote instead a very good new verse:

To scorn the sense's sway,
  While still to thee I tend:
In all I do be thou the way,
  In all be thou the End

He then proceeds:

A man that looks on glass,
  On that may fix his eye;
Or unopposed may through it pass
  And heaven behind descry.

All may of thee partake;
  Nothing so mean can be
But draws, when acted for thy sake,
  Greatness and worth from thee.

If done to obey thy laws,
  Even servile labour shines;
Hallow'd all toil, if this the cause
  The meanest work divine.

This is the long-sought stone
  That all converts to gold;
For that which God for his doth own
  Cannot for less be told.

'Tincture', says Palgrave, in his *Treasury of Sacred Song*, may refer to the *Elixir* regarded as a cleansing or transmuting liquid. But the more obvious sense will be, 'if coloured or tinged with this thought, *For God's sake*'.

S.M.

MUSIC. SANDYS is found in *Christmas Carols Ancient and Modern . . . by William Sandys* (1833), where it is given as the traditional air to the words 'A child this day is born'. A more elaborate setting, by Geoffrey Shaw, may be found, with the original words, in the *Oxford Book of Carols* (1928).

653 The God of love my shepherd is.

Ps. 23. *George Herbert*, 1593–1633.

Sir Edward Fry once wrote that though our forefathers thought they believed all Scripture to be equally the work of God, they showed in many unconscious ways that they considered some parts much better than others. That has been the case with the 23rd Psalm. So many versions have appeared that all the best ones cannot be included, and we have, for instance, to risk the anger of Scotsmen by omitting 'The Lord's my shepherd, I'll not want'. It was a pity that later hymnists have added to the plethora; but a new one, 'Jesus, my Shepherd, here I know', by R. O. Assheton was included, not only in *Church Hymns* (1903) but also in the *People's Hymnal* compiled for St. Martin's-in-the-Fields as late as 1924.

Surely two versions stand above all others—Herbert's and Addison's; and they are so entirely different that there is no competition; and Herbert's exquisite version may be safely crowned as the best ever made.

C.M.

MUSIC. UNIVERSITY is found in Pieter Hellendaal's *A Collection of Psalms for the Use of Parish Churches, &c.* (Cambridge, 1780), where it is attributed to Dr. Collignon, at that time Professor of Anatomy in the University. It also appears in *A Collection of Psalm and Hymn Tunes* (Cambridge, 1794) where it is anonymous and has therefore been often assigned to the editor, F. Randall. As Randall, however, was also a contributor to the earlier book, it seems probable that the attribution to Collignon is correct, or, at least, that Randall was not the composer. The attribution, in Vincent Novello's *The Psalmist* (Part iv, 1842), to 'Chas. Hague, Mus.Doc.' can scarcely be considered, as Hague was born in 1769, and was therefore only eleven years old when the tune was published.

The alternative version (fa-burden), by Martin Shaw, appeared in the *Tenor Tune Book* (1917).

654 The King of love my shepherd is.

Ps. 23. *Sir H. W. Baker*, 1821–77.

This is probably the best hymn that Baker wrote; and he may have liked it perhaps best himself, for the last words heard upon his lips were 'Perverse and foolish oft I strayed' and the rest of the third verse. Yet one cannot help wishing that he had paraphrased some other Psalm for *Hymns Ancient and Modern* in 1868; for Herbert's lovely version has been unknown to the majority of church-goers, owing to this being put in its place. In part it is a recast of Herbert in a different metre; in part it is an introduction of ideas which were beginning to stir people in 1868, but which would have surprised David.

Iambic, 8 7. 8 7.

MUSIC. ST. COLUMBA is a traditional Irish melody from the *Petrie Collection* (1855), where it is said to be the melody of a hymn sung at the dedication of a chapel. Several adaptations of the tune are found in various hymnals. The present version is, with one change of harmony at the end of the 1st line, from the *English Hymnal* (1906), and gives the original form of the melody.

DOMINUS REGIT ME was composed by J. B. Dykes for this hymn in the Appendix to *Hymns Ancient and Modern* (1868); it was sung at his funeral on 28 Jan. 1876.

655 The Lord is in his holy place. *W. C. Gannett*, 1840–1923.

William Channing Gannett, the author of this admirable hymn, belonged to the younger generation of New England sacred poets; he edited with F. L. Hosmer *The Thought of God in Hymns and Poems* (1885), and the 2nd series in 1894. This was written for the dedication of a church in Chicago, 1875, and published in the 1st series of the collection.

D.C.M.

MUSIC. OLD 44TH appeared first in the *Anglo-Genevan Psalter* (1558), set to Psalm 44, and was retained in all subsequent English and Scottish Psalters. The present form is that found in *Este's Psalter* (1592), but it shows very little change throughout its career, and the frequency of alternative settings proves that it was always a favourite. Its general shape and character, and especially the 5th and 6th lines, suggest that it was originally an old ballad tune.

656 The Lord my pasture shall prepare.

Ps. 23. *J. Addison*, 1672–1719.

Addison's famous version, a delightful example of the classically embroidered style of the 'Augustan' age, was introduced in the *Spectator* (26 July 1712) with these words:

'David has very beautifully represented this steady reliance on God Almighty in his twenty-third psalm, which is a kind of pastoral hymn, and filled with those allusions which are usual in that kind of writing. As the poetry is very exquisite, I shall present my readers with the following translation of it.'

The article was on Divine Providence, and was signed 'C': the authorship of this and Addison's other hymns is, however, now undisputed. The combination of pastoral beauty with the majestic grace of the age gives this hymn a special place, with his companion, 'The spacious firmament'; and both are very happily married to their music.

Iambic, 8 8. 8 8. 8 8.

MUSIC. SURREY, by Henry Carey, appeared in John Church's *Introduction to Psalmody* (1723), where it is headed 'Psalm the 23rd, Paraphras'd by Mr. Addison, set to Musick by Mr. H. Carey,' and is found among the 'entirely new' pieces at the end of the book. Carey's music is in two parts, treble and figured bass, the melody being as follows:

The present version is a later elaboration, found in several subsequent collections; in *An Abridgment of the new version of the Psalms, &c.* (1777) it is named 'Yarmouth'. It is a beautiful tune which became immediately popular and has deservedly remained so ever since.

657 The Lord of Heaven confess.

Ps. 148. *George Wither*, 1588–1667.

We have touched on George Wither's personality already (176); he stands out for us as a pioneer of the modern hymnal before Watts, as well as a writer who deserves the 'somewhat whimsical and rather contagious enthusiasm' bestowed upon him by Charles Lamb. Here are three verses from his vivid, hammering paraphrase of the psalm most used after the 23rd, to wit the 148th. It is from his *The Psalms of David translated into lyrick verse* (1632), following up his attempt of 1623 to launch a new version in the place of Sternhold and Hopkins (p. xv). It was a pity that he failed to move the authorities. This particular paraphrase, however, of Psalm 148 is printed as an alternative rendering in the Scottish Psalter.

'P.M.', one of the old Psalter measures that went beyond the original C.M., L.M., and S.M. Iambic, 6 6. 6 6. 4 4. 4 4 (in the music enumerated as 6 6. 6 6. 8 8).

MUSIC. CROFT'S 136TH is from Playford's *The Divine Companion: or, David's Harp new tun'd, &c.* (1709), where it is headed 'A Psalm Set by Mr. William Crofts. Psalm cxxxvi'. The present is the original form of the melody, with the extension of the rhythm in the last two lines, which adds greatly to the individuality and force of the whole. It is a splendidly solid tune, in every way worthy of the great talents of its composer.

The alternative version (fa-burden), by Geoffrey Shaw, was written especially for the enlarged *Songs of Praise* (1931).

658 The Lord will come and not be slow.

J. Milton (*cento*), 1608–74.

Milton translated Psalms 114 and 136 when he was 15 (1623); but this cento—from Psalms 82: 4, 85: 1–3, and 86: 5–6—comes from a later collection. Moved by the stress of the Civil War, Milton in 1648, when he was 40, translated *Nine of the Psalms done into Metre*, choosing the appropriate Psalms 80 to 88. These were translated direct from the original, the Hebrew words being printed in the margin, and every English word not in the Hebrew being in italic. Later on, in 1653, he translated Psalms 1 to 8 (first printed in the edition of his *Poems*, 1673) without this scrupulous Puritan literalism.

This priceless cento looks like the work of Garrett Horder, *c.* 1884. It appeared in his *Worship Song* (1905) and in the *English Hymnal* (1906).

C.M.

MUSIC. COLESHILL is really a variant of 'Windsor' (547, ii). Its earliest appearance seems to be in the 1st edition of William Barton's *Book of Psalms in Metre* (1644), where there is a 'London long tune, proper for solemn ditties, and used everywhere', which, allowing for obvious misprints, closely resembles 'Coleshill'.

It is then found, according to H. E. Dibdin's *Standard Psalm Tune Book* (1851), in Edmund Ireland's *Tunes of the Psalms in Two Parts* (York, 1699) as follows:

and in Ireland's *The Most Useful Tunes of the Psalms* (1713) the melody, named 'Hull Tune', is the same except for some differences in rhythm.

The present form occurs first in the *Psalms of David in Metre . . . By William Barton, M.A. And Set to the best Psalm Tunes . . . By Thomas Smith* (Dublin, 1706), where it is called 'Dublin Tune', but the melody is a mere string of minims, thus:

Finally in *A Collection of Psalm Tunes in Four Parts, Fitted to the Old or New Versions* (London, 1711), the tune is named 'Coleshill', and set to Psalm 116 as follows:

The connexion with 'Windsor' (called in Scotland 'Dundee') is recognized in Thomas Moore's *Psalm Singer's Delightful Pocket Companion* (Glasgow, 1762), where the melody makes its first appearance in a Scottish collection, and is accompanied by the note 'Sing Dundee Bass and Counter to this Tune'. It is a magnificent tune, and, in its present version, possibly the greatest of all psalm-tunes.

659 The spacious firmament on high.

Joseph Addison, 1672–1719.

'If this be not poetry,' said Lord Selborne, 'I do not know what it is; and to prove that it is song, and soul-stirring song too, it is only necessary to hear it, as I often have, heartily sung to an appropriate tune,' the only appropriate tune being of course 'Addison's'. Unfortunately this 'very perfect and finished composition, taking rank among the best hymns in the English Language', as he said, was excluded from the most widely used hymn-book in the 19th century, and a generation grew up that knew it not.

Like 656, it was signed 'C' when it first appeared in the *Spectator* (23 Aug. 1712). It comes at the close of the Essay on *Faith and Devotion*—discussing the best means of confirming faith in the mind of man, which ends:

'The Psalmist has very beautiful strokes of poetry to this purpose, in that exalted strain:

"The heavens declare the glory of God; and the firmament showeth his handiwork. One day telleth another; and one night certifieth another. There is neither speech nor language; but their voices are heard among them. Their sound is gone out into all lands; and their words into the ends of the world." As such a bold and sublime manner of thinking furnishes very noble matter for an ode, the reader may see it wrought into the following one: *The spacious firmament, &c.*'

There was a certain gentleman of the name of Knightly, who was fond of boasting of his ancestry. Sir William Harcourt, who was a wit as well as a statesman, and whose own descent was particularly illustrious, said that he always reminded him of the lines, 'And Knightly to the listening earth Repeats the story of his birth.'

D.L.M.

MUSIC. LONDON (or ADDISON'S), by John Sheeles, is from his *Skylark* (*c.* 1720), where it is set to Addison's paraphrase of Psalm 19, 'The spacious firmament on high'. In this publication Sheeles set to music all Addison's hymns from the *Spectator*, but none of the other tunes seems to have come into general use. The present tune, which is an excellent one, was popularized by the Methodists, whose adoption of it probably led to its inclusion in *Harmonia Sacra*, whence it found its way into other collections.

660 The Spirit of the Lord revealed. *G. W. Briggs.*

This, like 457, sets forth the profound character of the Bible in the light of the knowledge acquired during the last hundred years. Hymns like 'Lord, thy word abideth' have become a little inadequate, dating, as they do, from a time when the light of scientific biblical study had not penetrated beyond a very small circle of scholars in this country; and therefore most hymnists were confined to generalities of a not very impressive character. This was written also to carry the very noble German tune.

Iambic, 8 6. 8 6. 6 8. 8 6. Unique.

MUSIC. WOLDER (AUS MEINES HERZENS GRUNDE) is found in D. Wolder's *New Catechismus Gesangbüchlein, &c.* (Hamburg, 1588), set to the hymn 'Herzlich thut mich erfreuen' as follows:

Several variants are found in later collections. The tune is probably a traditional one, considerably older than Wolder's book.

661 Thee will I love, my God and King. *Y.H.* (*Robert Bridges*).

Dr. Bridges wrote this for the inimitable Genevan tune in its peculiar metre; and it first appeared in the *Yattendon Hymnal* (1899). It is interesting to notice how a past master of the craft is not afraid to use well-worn rhymes like 'pleasure' and 'treasure' when he needs and can legitimately use them.

The reader will have often noticed how the musical excellence of a hymnal depends upon the ability of writers to compose new poetry in unusual metres. Many of the very finest tunes were formerly excluded from collections because there were no words to bring them into use.

Iambic, 8 9. 8 9. D. Unique.

MUSIC. PSALM 138 is the original form of the tune set to Psalm 138 in the *Genevan Psalter*. The present version is adapted from Goudimel's setting (see 50).

CROSSINGS, by Armstrong Gibbs, was one of three tunes written, in 1929, especially for Charterhouse School. In its original form the setting was more elaborate, with varied accompaniments and arrangements of the vocal parts for the different verses. It appears here in a unison version; it is a vivid tune, in a forceful triple measure, with a finely balanced contrast of keys giving it an unusual and ardent intensity.

662 Then welcome each rebuff. *Robert Browning*, 1812–89.

Stanzas 6, 9, 10, and 32 of *Rabbi Ben Ezra*, which appeared in Browning's *Dramatis Personae* (1864).

Iambic, 6 6 10. 6 6 12. Unique.

MUSIC. ST. GABRIEL is an adaptation, by R. Vaughan Williams, for *Songs of Praise*, of a German hymn melody of the 17th century. The tune is very characteristic of its period, but not especially of its nationality, being of a type, both rhythmically and melodically, which is frequently found in English music of that time, particularly in songs, with lute or other accompaniment, such as those of Henry Lawes and his school; it is of a kind more common in secular solo songs than in church music of that date, and may be derived from such a composition, or from a traditional air. It forms, here, an exceptionally attractive setting for the present words.

663 There are a myriad means, O Lord. *Geoffrey Dearmer.*

Written for the original *Songs of Praise* (1925).

Iambic, 8 6. 8 6. 8 8.

MUSIC. O JESU, by J. B. Reimann, is from *J. B. Reimanns Org. v. Hirschb. Sammlung alter und neuer Melodien Evangel. Lieder, &c.* (1747), where it is set to the hymn 'O Jesu, warum legst du mir'. In the original tune the first and last notes of each line are semibreves. It is a tune of a simple, familiar pattern, but with a certain quiet dignity, and a particular emotive trait in the phrase of the 5th line, which gives it a distinctive, and very appealing, quality.

664 There is a book who runs may read. *J. Keble*, 1792–1866.

A rich gift of Keble's to the Church, which will be long remembered when the controversies that gathered round him are forgotten, was his realization of the religious character of Nature. He brought the inspiration of Wordsworth into our public worship; and Septuagesima Sunday, when the First Lessons are the first two chapters of Genesis, was the right place for this poem in the *Christian Year*, with the text from Rom. 1 : 20, 'The invisible things of him from the creation of the world are clearly seen, being understood by the things that are made'. The original 12 verses were written in 1819 and came out in *The Christian Year* (1827).

C.M.

MUSIC. TALLIS' ORDINAL ('9th Tune') is from *The Whole Psalter translated into English metre, &c.* (see 45), where it is set to the version of 'Veni Creator Spiritus' which appears in the Prayer-book Ordinal. It is the last of the nine tunes by Tallis, but its very close resemblance to 'This endris Nyght' (72) can scarcely be fortuitous, since the whole tune is an adaptation to common time of the first two lines of the carol melody, the 4th line being merely a repetition of the 2nd in the tonic.

The alternative version (fa-burden), by Geoffrey Shaw, appeared in the *Tenor Tune Book* (1917).

665 There is no sorrow, Lord, too slight.

Mrs. Jane Crewdson, 1809–63.

Published in *A Little While* (1860), by Mrs. Thomas Crewdson, *née* Jane Fox, and included by Dr. Benjamin Hall Kennedy (the author of the *Public School Latin Grammar*) in his *Hymnologia Christiana* (1863), this little hymn found many friends through its inclusion in the 1903 edition of *Church Hymns*, in the *Church Hymnary* and other collections. We use Kennedy's slight alterations, though whether they were made in consultation with the author or not we do not know. She wrote originally, in ver. 2, l. 3, 'For he who bore'; and she began ver. 4 with 'Life's woes without'. Also the 1st verse, 'There's not a grief, however light', is generally omitted.

C.M.

MUSIC. ELGIN is one of the 15 Common Tunes in *The Psalms of David, &c.* (Edward Raban, Aberdeen, 1625).

666 There's a wideness in God's mercy. *F. W. Faber*, 1814–63.

As we said under 188, Faber was one of those unequal writers who have a difficulty in getting under way. He spoilt this otherwise altogether praiseworthy hymn with the line, 'Souls of men, why will ye scatter?' when he published it in his *Oratory Hymns* (1854). By beginning, as several collections have done, with 'There's a wideness', we may give an impression of universalism that was not in his mind, but at least we have an impressive and coherent hymn.

Trochaic, 8 7. 8 7. D.

MUSIC. LLANSANNAN is a Welsh melody from *Aberth Moliant* (1873). It is a strong, sober tune, with a steady marching rhythm; though the form of the tune differs from that of many of the Welsh hymn melodies, the 'feeling' of it is characteristic; from the 5th line onwards there is a very distinct likeness to 'Goldschmidt (O der alles)', which illustrates the prevalence of this type of phrase, as was remarked in the notes on that tune (217).

667 There's heaven above, and night by night.

Robert Browning, 1812–89.

The strength of Calvinism, and of the Augustinianism of which it is a form, is its affirmative side—the absolute conviction of safety in the love of God. Browning describes both the good and the bad sides (the bad led him at first to group it with *Porphyria's Lover* under 'Madhouse Cells') in *Johannes Agricola in Meditation*. This was first published in 1836 in the *Monthly Repository*, then included in *Bells and Pomegranates, III*, Dramatic Lyrics (1842); *not* included in *Men and Women* (1855); but transferred to that section in the Collected Works at some later date.

But the date of its first appearance, 1836, makes it wrong to speak of it as part of a group written from 1840 onwards. We have printed the first 15 lines as vv. 1 to 3 of our hymn, and taken the concluding 5 lines for our last verse. The sense of entire communion with God, and of reliance upon his will, have seldom been so finely expressed.

Iambic, 8 8. 8 8 8. The verses happen to be very amenable to musical treatment.

MUSIC. ICH FAHR DAHIN is an arrangement, by J. Brahms, of the German traditional melody to the words 'Ich fahr dahin, wenn es muss sein'. It is found in the *Locheimer Liederbuch*, a manuscript of 1452–60, in the Dorian mode, and a free triple rhythm, with the heading 'Ritters Abschied'. The present version is no. 2 in vol. ii of Brahms's *Deutsche Volkslieder* (1864), where it is set to the original words and headed 'Abschiedlied'. The present form of the melody is close to that found in the above book, though the notation in the manuscript is, in some places, uncertain, and has been interpreted in various ways, especially as regards the rhythm. The present metrical scheme is, however, characteristic of the period of the melody, and is probably correct.

668 They all were looking for a king.

George MacDonald, 1824–1905.

These enchanting verses from George MacDonald's volume, *A Threefold Cord, Poems by Three Friends* (1883), have not, so far as we know, been used as a hymn before. Set to a very happy tune, they have proved a great success in more than one church within our knowledge where they are being sung.

Iambic, 8 8. 8 6, i.e. L.M. without the last foot.

MUSIC. CHILDHOOD appeared in *A Students' Hymnal* (University of Wales, 1923), set to the hymn 'It fell upon a summer day'. It is one of the tunes attributed in that hymnal to the 'University of Wales', and of these the editor, Sir Walford Davies, states in his preface that they were 'composed by a small community of minds. In two cases no less than five melodists took an essential part in a four-line tune.' The collaboration has here produced a very happy result.

669 Those who love and those who labour follow in the way of Christ.

G. D.

A paraphrase made for *Songs of Praise* of some of the *Agrapha*, or sayings purporting to come from Jesus which are outside the canonical Gospels. Some few *agrapha* are certainly authentic, as, for instance, the saying preserved in Acts 20: 35, when St. Paul tells the presbyters of Ephesus to remember the words of the Lord Jesus, 'It is more blessed to give than to receive'. Others are probably authentic, others doubtful in various degrees, and others spurious. In the hymn therefore such words as 'Jesus said' are not used; but the sayings are put dramatically into the mouth of the present Lord, as in many hymns. The motive of the first two verses is the now famous *Logion 5*, from the Oxyrhynchus papyri discovered by Grenfell and Hunt in 1897:

> 'Jesus said, Wherever there are two, they are not without God; and wherever there is one alone, I say, I am with him. Raise the stone and there thou shalt find me; cleave the wood and there am I.'

The last verse is based on *Logion 1*, discovered in 1903:

'Jesus saith, Let not him who seeks . . . cease until he finds, and when he finds he shall be astonished; astonished he shall reach the kingdom, and having reached the kingdom he shall rest.'

There is another version of this in the *Logion* quoted by St. Clement of Alexandria from the lost 'Gospel according to the Hebrews' (*Strom.* ii. 9, 45):

'He that seeketh shall not stop until he finds; when he hath found he shall wonder, and when he hath wondered he shall reign, and when he hath reigned he shall rest.'

Scholars vary as to the possible authenticity and the date of the Oxyrhyncus *Logia*. They may be of the 1st or 2nd century: *c.* 140 seems the latest probable date. The actual papyri are of the 3rd century.

Trochaic. 8 7. 8 7. D.

MUSIC. ALTA TRINITA BEATA is an adaptation of a melody in a manuscript collection of 'Laudi Spirituali' at Florence (Bibl. Naz. II. i. 122), the original being as follows:

These hymns had their origin during the latter half of the 13th century, when a religious movement started in Italy which is thus described in the *Oxford History of Music* (vol. ii, part ii, p. 303):

'In 1260 there arose in Umbria a religious mania of a most fanatical kind. Terrified at the awful results of the bloody wars between Frederick II and the Papacy and anxious to propitiate, as they thought, a wrathful and avenging deity, the people turned to flagellation as a penance for their sins. Young and old, rich and poor, united together in procession and wandered through the country, inflicting on each other the ghastly torments which they considered necessary and singing as they went. In the south of Italy the movement was checked, but in the north it had more success. Crossing the Alps, it spread over France, Austria, and Germany, and even reached as far as Poland. The mania which had inspired these processions naturally died down in time, but the singing which had been a feature of the penance persisted and was kept up by lay brotherhoods known as *Disciplinati di Gesú Cristo*. Neither brotherhoods nor the singing of Italian hymns were new inventions (they can in fact be traced back to the eleventh century), but it was the outbreak of flagellation and the subsequent reaction which were largely responsible for the widespread popularity of *Laudi spirituali*, as these hymns were called, at the end of the thirteenth century.'

The style of these hymns was founded upon plainsong, but was considerably influenced also by the manner of the popular songs of the time. The original form, as given above, of the present tune, is a good average specimen of the type, though some were more elaborate, and, in their later developments, approximated more and more to the secular songs known as 'villanelle'.

The present version is due to Burney, who, in his *History of Music*, gave what purported to be a transcript of the melody in the Florentine manuscript; with his usual carelessness in such matters, however, he apparently misread, or failed to realize, a change of clef in the manuscript, and therefore invented a large part of his 'version', since his note of the transcript would be unintelligible. This seems the kindest explanation of his travesty of the original tune; though he was also quite capable of 'improving' the melody into what he considered it ought to have been, being without even the rudiments of an historic sense. Burney was an amusing writer, but as a faithful researcher or an intellectually honest critic he cannot be given a high place.

As it stands, however, the tune, from a purely musical point of view, is a very good one; Burney's ability as a musician was considerable, and the present melody, though evidence of his habitual negligence as an historian, is an excellent instance of his high capacity as a composer.

670 Thou art my life; if thou but turn away.

Francis Quarles, 1592–1644.

More than one hymn has been written on the theme of John 14: 6, for instance, the late Bishop Doane's 'Thou art the way: to thee alone', which was done about 1824, and is a good hymn; but one hardly needs more than one about the same subject—and how much better is the finely wrought hymn of Francis Quarles! It was first published in his *Emblemes* (Bk. III, vii), 1635.

Iambic, 10. 10. 10. Unique.

MUSIC. LÖWENSTERN (HEUT' IST, O MENSCH), by M. A. von Löwenstern, is no. 18 of his 'Geistliche Oden' in *Geistliche Kirchen- und Hauss-Music, &c.* (1644), where it is set to the hymn 'Heut ist, O Mensch, ein grosser Trauertag', the melody being as at present. In the original, however, this tune is linked with another, the poem being divided into three parts, of which the first and third are sung to the present tune, and the second to the companion melody, so that the whole may be said to be in 'aria form'. In later collections the tunes are found, with some variation, both together and separately.

671 Thou hidden Love of God, whose height.

G. Tersteegen, 1697–1769. *Tr. J. Wesley*, 1703–91.

Verborgne Gottes Liebe du
  O Friedensreich so schöne,
Ich seh von ferne deine Ruh
  Und innig dahin sehne;
Ich bin nicht stille wie ich soll,
Ich fühl es ist dem Geist nicht wohl,
  Weil er in dir nicht stehet.

There was a 'Pilgerhütte' near Mühlheim, where Tersteegen the

Quietist and mystic, belonging to no Church and founding no sect, used to direct 'awakened souls' He was a great leader among the 'Stillen im Lande', and he published a book, *Geistliches Blumengärtlein* (1729), which placed him with Neander at the head of German hymnody. John Wesley printed his translation of 'Verborgne Gottes Liebe' in his first hymn-book, the *Charles-town Collection* (1737), omitting 2 from the original 10 stanzas. Yet, even so, it was too long for English congregations, who do not divide a hymn into separate verses for use throughout a service, as is done in Germany. Even when reduced to 4 verses, as here, this classic is seldom sung, and for many stands as part of an anthology of sacred poetry. Dr. Oliver Wendell Holmes (564, 620) said once that it was the greatest hymn in the English language, and Emerson agreed.

Tersteegen, 'a gentle, heaven-inspired soul', as Frances Cox said, 'whose hymns are the reflection of a heavenly happy life', called this hymn 'the longing of the soul quietly to maintain the secret drawings of the Love of God': Wesley, in translating the last couplet of ver. 1, evidently had in mind Augustine's saying, 'Thou hast made us for thyself, and restless is our heart until it find its rest in thee.'

Iambic, 8 8. 8 8. 8 8. i.e. L.M. with two additional lines: not the metre, it will be observed, of the German original.

MUSIC. NEW 113TH, by William Hayes, appeared in his *Sixteen Psalms . . . set to music for the use of Magdalen Chapel in Oxford* (*c.* 1774), where it is set to Merrick's version of Psalm 134. William Hayes was appointed to the chair of music in Oxford in 1741, and was succeeded by his son, Philip, who also published a book of psalm-tunes with an almost identical title. The present tune is one of the suave melodies, in triple time, which are typical of the middle period of the 18th century; the majority of them are good tunes, but, with a few outstanding exceptions, are not much individualized.

672 Thou Judge by whom each Empire fell. *P. Dearmer.*

Written in the attempt to express what is felt to be the truth about the idea of judgment, and also because there were not enough hymns to carry the great tunes in this metre.

Iambic, 8 7. 8 7. 8 8 7.

MUSIC. LUTHER'S HYMN (NUN FREUT EUCH) appeared in *Geistliche Lieder* (Wittemberg, 1535), set to Luther's 'Nun freut euch lieben Christengemein'. This hymn, however, was already associated with another tune (see 640), and the present melody was early transferred to Ringwaldt's hymn 'Es ist gewisslich an der Zeit', since when it has been always connected with ideas of doom and judgment rather than, as originally, with those of joy and mirth. In England, where it was introduced towards the end of the 18th century, this association of ideas was continued and it was for long wedded to the words 'Great God, what do I see and hear'. The tune has been popularly known as 'Luther's Hymn', but there is no evidence of its being his composition.

The present form differs from the original in some respects, especially in lines 5 and 6, which ran as follows:

673 Thou long disowned, reviled, oppressed.

Eliza Scudder, 1821–96.

Miss Scudder, a niece of Dr. Sears (76), was a Boston Unitarian who joined the Protestant Episcopal Church, and who contributed several hymns to Longfellow's and Johnson's *Hymns of the Spirit* (1864) (see 16). This, with two others, was also included in Dr. Martineau's *Hymns* (1873). An apostrophe of this kind, if it is real poetry, can take a place among hymns; God is really addressed in the character of truth, which is his nature and his manifestation.

C.M.

MUSIC. MANCHESTER, by Robert Wainwright, is first found in Langdon's *Divine Hymns* (1774), where it is set to Psalm 103. The tune varies slightly in different collections, but only to the extent of a greater or lesser introduction of passing notes. Robert was the son of John Wainwright, the composer of the famous 'Yorkshire (or Stockport)' (73), and was noted for his skill as an organist; he is said to have remained a fine performer, even after the dislocation of some of the fingers of his left hand by a rival. This tune is anonymous in the above work, but is found under its present name in Ralph Harrison's *Sacred Harmony* (1784); it is in triple time, but less smooth than most of its type, being, in fact, somewhat angular, and with a curious insistence on the upper tonic, which gives it a strange and attractive individuality.

674 Thou true Vine, that heals the nations. *T. S. N.*

Based on John 1. 5, because a hymn was asked for on the True Vine, which, it will be noticed in our *Table of Hymns Arranged* (p. 860 in the music edition), follows, as the subject of Easter IV, the themes of the Good Shepherd and the Bread of Life. As with 672 and other hymns, the subject was cast in this metre because there were not enough hymns to the great tunes which belong to the rhythm.

Trochaic, 8 7. 8 7. D.

MUSIC. ZUM FRIEDEN is one of the tunes attributed to J. S. Bach in Christian Schemelli's *Musicalisches Gesangbuch* (Leipzig, 1736), which contains many tunes with the figured bass by Bach, some of the melodies also being by him, while others which do not seem to be found previously are ascribed to him. The present tune is one of the latter, and internal evidence, especially the last two lines, would seem to support the attribution.

675 Thou wast, O God, and thou wast blest.

John Mason, *c.* 1645–94.

John Mason, 'enthusiast' as he has been called, 'the glory of the Church of England', as his Nonconformist friend, Richard Baxter, called him, came to our rescue when we wanted another hymn on the subject of Almighty God, which should also carry Tallis's 'Third Mode Melody'. This splendid homage, which is taken from his *Songs of Praise*, our precursor of 1683, should be compared with 526. Probably his hymns were used in public worship; and if so, they are among the earliest so used (see under 526). His *Songs of Praise*, with its additions, passed through 20 editions. Baxter says of him:

'The frame of his spirit was so heavenly, his deportment so humble and obliging, his discourse of spiritual things so weighty, with such apt words and delightful air, that it charmed all those who had any spiritual relish.'

Neglected for more than two centuries, he will surely now come to his own; for these two hymns of his are mighty contributions to the filling of that deficiency which is noticed in the Preface to the new *Hymns Ancient and Modern* of 1904:

'It is often urged as an objection to Christian hymn-books, that so great a proportion of the hymns contained in them are addressed to our Blessed Redeemer, rather than to the Father to Whom He brings us. The defect lies largely with the composers of our hymns, and not with the compilers of the collections.'

D.C.M.

MUSIC. THIRD MODE MELODY is the third of the nine tunes by Tallis in Parker's *The Whole Psalter, &c.* (1567) (see 45). The alternative version (fa-burden) is Tallis's own setting, with the rhythm slightly simplified, the following being the original form of the melody:

It is a remarkable tune, with a nobility and solid grandeur which make it the finest of those in the above work, and, indeed, place it among the greatest melodic conceptions of Tallis's genius. It is the theme of R. Vaughan Williams's *Fantasia* for strings, where the supreme beauty of the tune is given its full value.

676 Though lowly here our lot may be. *William Gaskell*, 1805–84.

William Gaskell would have been well content to be remembered as the husband of the beautiful and famous author of *Cranford*; it was he who urged her to begin to write when she was overwhelmed by the death of her little son—and the result in 1848 was *Mary Barton*. But he was himself a very distinguished person, with a niche in the *Dictionary of National Biography*; Professor of English History and Literature at Manchester New College, of which he became the Secretary, and a famous Unitarian minister at Cross Street Chapel, he characteristically printed one of his few publications, *Lectures on the Lancashire Dialect*, as an appendix to the fifth edition of his wife's first novel. A pioneer with her of social reform, he wrote this hymn some time before 1860, when it was printed in Miss E. Courtauld's *Psalms, Hymns, and Anthems*. Thence it passed to other books, including the *Congregational Church Hymnal* (1887) (one suspects through Horder's influence), the *Public School Hymn Book* (1903), and Horder's *Worship Song* (1905). We should be ungrateful if we did not somewhere point out how much the best hymnody owed to Unitarians in the last century, and how much Anglican collections lost at that time by ignoring them.

C.M.

MUSIC. ASCENDIT, by F. D. Morice, is found in the *Rugby School Hymn Book* (1896). The tune is an adaptation of a traditional German students' song.

677 Through all the changing scenes of life.

Ps. 34. *N. Tate and N. Brady* (*New Version*, 1696).

The reader may care to look up other notes about metrical psalms, under 449, 525: this is regarded as perhaps the most successful in 'Tate and Brady' (but there were not many successes): it appeared in the *New Version* (1696), in 18 verses; and many are the centos that have been made from it.

H. Leigh Bennett well said in a contribution to Julian's *Dictionary*, p. 922:

'For the worship of the masses certain grand and simple psalms are unequalled. The indirect influence of the long tutelage of the Psalter must not be lost sight of. It gave to our earlier hymns a severity, a breadth, an objective tone, and a wide and deep base in natural religion. Nowhere is the glory of God in his works so magnificently exhibited as in the Psalms. . . . Nowhere is the jubilance of praise, unchecked by the chilling and irrelevant thought—true and sad as it is—of the sinfulness and inadequacy of our utterance, so majestic. These characteristics are impressed deeply on Watts; and they are of abiding value, as a counterpoise to the morbid emotion, effeminacy, self-consciousness, and anatomy of motives, which make some modern hymns so sickly.'

C.M.

MUSIC. WILTSHIRE, by Sir G. Smart, appeared first in his *Divine Amusement* (*c.* 1795), where it was set to Psalm 48. In later publications the melody was slightly altered by the composer himself.

The alternative version (descant), by Geoffrey Shaw, appeared in the *Descant Hymn-Tune Book* (Bk. I, 1925).

678 Through the night of doubt and sorrow.

B. S. Ingemann, 1789–1862. *Tr. S. Baring-Gould.*

'Dr. Littledale', wrote Baring-Gould, 'asked me to look through the Danish Hymnal and see if any merited translation. This was when he was editing the *People's Hymnal* (1867). I did three or four from the Danish, among them Ingemann's hymn.' We have preserved Baring-Gould's text as he wrote it, omitting the last two verses.

Ingemann has not the fame with us of Hans Andersen; but his historical romances, to the making of which he was led by the influence of Walter Scott, are read by all Danish youth, and his hymns and songs are sung in every Danish home—which is perhaps why 90 per cent. of the Danish people are members of the national Church. On his 70th birthday the children of Denmark gave him a golden horn ornamented with figures from his poetry: subscriptions were limited to a halfpenny each child.

Trochaic, 8 7. 8 7.

MUSIC. MARCHING, by Martin Shaw, appeared first in *Additional Tunes and settings in use at St. Mary's, Primrose Hill* (1915). It is a vigorous tune, with a square march rhythm, solidly constructed of two long phrases, each embracing two lines of text, the movement of the second being mainly an inversion of that of the first, and preserving the general equilibrium of the whole; the steady, progressive character of the melody is perfectly adapted to the nature of the words.

679 Thy heaven, on which 'tis bliss to look.

Thomas Moore, 1779–1852.

This useful little hymn by the famous Irish poet, Tom Moore, comes from his *Sacred Songs* (1816), and consists of stanzas 4, 6, and 7 of a seven-stanza poem beginning 'The turf shall be my fragrant shrine'.

L.M.

MUSIC. DAS WALT' GOTT VATER is found in Daniel Vetter's *Musicalische Kirch- und Haus-Ergötzlichkeit* (vol. ii, Leipzig, 1713), where it is set to the hymn 'Das walt' Gott Vater und Gott Sohn' as follows:

The present arrangement is J. S. Bach's in his *Choralgesänge* (1769). It is a good, compact tune in the full chorale tradition, the changes in the later version being only slight, and not of a kind to alter its original character.

680 Thy Kingdom come! on bended knee.

F. L. Hosmer, 1840–1929.

We have referred already on p. 172 to the other hymn beginning with the same three words, which was all we had in the 19th century to express that petition of the Lord's Prayer. Fortunately in 1891 Frederick Hosmer wrote one of the noblest hymns in the language; and this does express the eternal hope of the Prayer. He made it for the Commencement of the Meadville Theological School, Pennsylvania, and included it in the Second Series of *The Thought of God* (1894). In England it appeared in Horder's *Worship Song* (1905) and in the *English Hymnal* (1906).

C.M.

MUSIC. IRISH appeared first in *A Collection of Hymns and Sacred Poems* (Dublin, 1749), where it is found at the end of the volume among the 'Tunes adapted to the foregoing Hymns'. It is there given without name of tune or composer, but in Ashworth's *Collection of Tunes* (*c.* 1760) it is called 'Irish Tune', no doubt as having appeared in the former work. It is also found in Isaac Smith's *A Collection of Psalm Tunes, &c.* (*c.* 1770), and was for a long time attributed to Smith in consequence, but the ascription rests on no other grounds, and is incorrect. The Dublin collection is thought, with some reason, to be the work of John Wesley, as he was in that town in 1749, and accompanied by J. F. Lampe, who may have edited the music, as he did that of other publications by Wesley; it is unlikely, however, that Lampe was the composer of the tune, as it shows none of the characteristics of his known compositions. On the other hand the melody belongs to the type of smooth, triple-time tunes, of which a very large number appeared during the 18th century—mostly excellent tunes, but with so strong a family likeness that their attribution, on internal evidence alone, to any particular composer is impossible. The tune certainly gives no indication of an Irish origin, and must, for the present, remain anonymous.

681 To God, the everlasting, who abides.

J. Addington Symonds, 1840–93.

Though it could be found in the conclusions of a philosopher like Hegel, very few thinkers had expressed clearly the great generalization of the triad of supreme values, Goethe (486) and this hymn being exceptions, until Arthur Clutton-Brock made it clear, as we have noted under the paraphrase of Goethe; though, since then, it has been repeated so often as to incur the danger of a reaction.

The work of that accomplished man, John Addington Symonds, was in great part given to the study of art, and his *History of the Italian Renaissance* (1876–85) remains a standard work. This is from 'An Invocation' in *Many Moods* (1878).

Iambic, 10 10. 10 10.

MUSIC. SONG 24, by Orlando Gibbons, is from *Hymnes and Songs of the Church* (1623), where it is set to a paraphrase of Lam. 1 (see 29).

682 To Mercy, Pity, Peace, and Love. *William Blake*, 1757–1827.

What were the hymns that Blake sang on his death-bed? For he kept on singing, rapturously, and all his songs were in praise of God; and sometimes he would stop and say to his wife, 'Not mine, not mine'; for they came to him, and he claimed no copyright. We do not know what they were—only that just before he died 'his countenance became fair, his eyes brightened, and he burst out singing of the things he saw in heaven'. Few of our forefathers would have cared. Oceans of sickly rubbish and seas of innocuous commonplace receive annotation among the 20,000 hymns thus honoured in Julian's original *Dictionary* of 1891; but 'Blake' does not occur even in the far more wide-sweeping index. In the *Appendix*, Part II, however, tacked on the end there is a note that 'Can I see another's woe' was included in Martineau's *Hymns* (1873); and in the *New Supplement* (1907), the appearance of 'To Mercy, Pity' in the *English Hymnal* of the previous year is noted with a twinge of pain: 'It is certainly difficult to call it a hymn at all, or to assign it to any special purpose.' Yet how few hymns sum up the Good News of Jesus so perfectly! And few are now more popular. See our Introduction, p. xxiii.

Blake called it, in *Songs of Innocence* (1789), 'The Divine Image'. In *Songs of Praise* we have omitted the last verse:

And all must love the human form,
  In heathen Turk, or Jew;
Where Mercy, Love, and Pity dwell,
  There God is dwelling too.

Not because it is not utterly and sublimely true, but because we found it was sometimes misunderstood in the Council schools, when the original *Songs of Praise* began to be used for general education.

C.M.

MUSIC. EPSOM is found in Arnold's *The Compleat Psalmodist* (1756), where it is named 'Epsom Tune'; the melody is as here given except that the end of the 1st and 4th lines is syncopated thus ♩ 𝅗𝅥 𝅗𝅥, and the last note of the 2nd line is a minim only— 𝅗𝅥 not 𝅗𝅥 . 𝅗𝅥

It is a good tune in the direct descent from the older psalm-tunes, both in manner and form of phrase; if the melody be read in duple time it will be seen that all the phrases can be paralleled from any of the 16th- and early 17th-century psalters, but its style has also a grace and lucidity typical of its period.

The alternative version (descant), by Stanley Marchant, was written especially for the enlarged *Songs of Praise* (1931).

683 To the Name that is salvation. *P. Dearmer.*

Written to provide another hymn about God, on the lines of a hymn, and for a tune already familiar.

Trochaic, 8 7. 8 7. 8 7.

MUSIC. ORIEL. See 190, ii. The alternative version (descant), by Alan Gray, appeared in his *A Book of Descants* (1920).

684 To thee whose eye all nature owns.

Thomas Hardy, 1840–1928.

From the august chorus at the end of *The Dynasts*. We have ventured to head it 'Magnificat', in order to make clear at once the reference in the last line of the first stanza.

In the Preface to his *Late Lyrics* (1922) Hardy wrote:

> 'What other purely English establishment than the Church, of sufficient dignity and footing, and with such strength of old association, such architectural spell, is left in this country to keep the shreds of mortality together?
>
> 'It may be a forlorn hope, a mere dream, that of an alliance between religion, which must be retained unless the world is to perish, and complete rationality, which must come, unless also the world is to perish, by means of the interfusing effect of poetry—"the breath and finer spirit of all knowledge; the impassioned expression of science", as it was defined by an English poet.'

The 'English poet' was Wordsworth.

L.M.

MUSIC. DEO GRACIAS is the English 15th-century (probably *c.* 1415) melody of the song celebrating the victory of Agincourt, 'Our King went forth to Normandy'. It is found in a manuscript in the Pepysian Collection, Magdalene College, Cambridge, and also in one in Trinity College Library, Cambridge, with a descant throughout, and a long florid cantilena at the beginning and end to the words 'Deo gracias anglia redde pro victoria', but these are probably additions by some academic composer, as is also, possibly, the flourish which seems to end the actual tune:

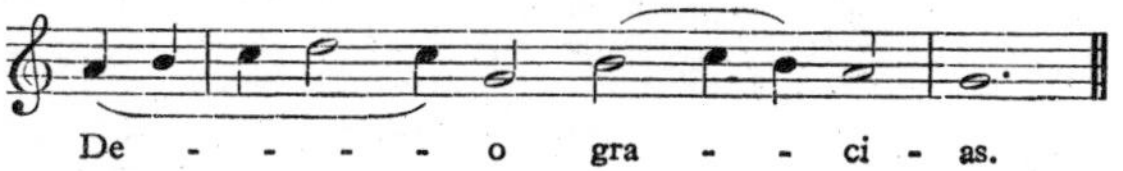

but which involves reading the tune in a different mode. The original tune was probably a popular one, since official celebration of the victory in song was apparently forbidden by the king; Hollinshed, quoting and translating Thomas de Elmham, states that the king ordered that 'no ditties should be made and sung by Minstrels or others' (seu per Citharistas vel alios quoscunque) . . . 'for that he would whollie have the praise and thankes altogether given to God' (cf. under 420). It is a magnificently direct and stirring tune, with a vehement dignity, and a remarkable expression of triumphant pride.

685 To us in Bethlem city. *Cölner Psalter*, 1638. *Pr. O.B.C.*

This paraphrase of the folk-carol appeared first in the *Oxford Book of Carols*; the original was first printed in the *Cölner Psalter* (1638).

Iambic, 7 6. 7 6. 4 6, but 'Eia' may be taken as a spondee. Unique.

MUSIC. EIA, EIA (ZU BETHLEHEM GEBOREN) is the traditional melody of the above carol, as it is found in *Nordsterns Führer zur Seeligkeit* (1671). The earliest appearance of the tune in print seems to be in the *Cölner Psalter* (1638), and other variants are to be found in the *Strassburgischer Gesangbuch* (1679), the *Neu-Vollkommen-Catholisches Gesangbuch Strassburger Bischthums, &c.* (1703), and later books. It is a simple, frank tune, with a spontaneity due to the frequent recurrence of the second line cadence, which gives it an attractive air of innocent gaiety.

686 Up to those bright and gladsome hills.
Ps. 121. *Henry Vaughan the Silurist*, 1622–95.

This gem, a paraphrase of the 121st Psalm, is from Vaughan's *Silex Scintillans; or Sacred Poems and Private Ejaculations. By Henry Vaughan, Silurist* (London, 1650). (See also under 294 and 585.)

MUSIC. MELROSE is No. xxiv of the 31 Common Tunes in the *Psalmes of David, &c.* (Hart's heirs, Edinburgh, 1635), where it is headed 'Melros Tune'. It is of the normal pattern of these common tunes, but gains an agreeable individuality from the sequential nature of the phrase forming the first two lines, which gives the whole melody a curious air of purposeful firmness.

687 Wake, O wake, for night is flying!
P. Nicolai, 1556–1608. *Tr. S.P.*

Wachet auf! ruft uns die Stimme
Der Wächter sehr hoch auf der Zinne;
Wach auf, du Stadt Jerusalem!
Mitternacht heisst diese Stunde,
Sie rufen uns mit hellem Munde:
Wo seid ihr klugen Jungfrauen?
Wohl auf, der Braüt'gam kommt!
Steht auf, die Lampen nehmt!
Hallelujah!
Macht euch bereit
Zur Hochzeitfreud;
Geht ihm entgegen—es ist Zeit.

There is no other hymn like this, surely the grandest and most thrilling both in words and music—and both words and music by the same man. 'The King of Chorales' was composed thus: Nicolai was pastor at Unna in Westphalia when the terrible pestilence raged there from July 1597 to Jan. 1598, during which over 1,300 people died. In the intervals between burying, perhaps 30 folk in one day, his thoughts turned, through that of death, to God and to the eternal Fatherland. In the Preface (10 Aug. 1598) to *Frewden-Spiegel*, in the Appendix to which the chorale first appeared, he says:

> 'There seemed to me nothing more sweet, delightful, and agreeable, than the contemplation of the noble, sublime doctrine of eternal life. . . . I gave to my manuscript the name and title of *Mirror of Joy*, and took this, thus composed, to leave behind me (if God should call me from the world) as the token of my peaceful, joyful, Christian departure, or (if God should spare me in health) to comfort other sufferers.'

One thinks of the pastor, looking out from his parsonage window upon the too familiar churchyard, then wrapping himself in prayer, till this immortal work of inspiration and of art came white-hot from his soul. And all the time he pleased himself and honoured a friend and old pupil, Count William Ernst, by making it a reversed acrostic! W(*achet*); v. 2, Z(*ion hört*); ver. 3, E(*hr und Preis*), i.e. E.Z.W., Ernst zu Wallenstein.

There have been many translations, neither Miss Winkworth's nor Miss Cox's being quite satisfactory, while that in Mendelssohn's *St. Paul* spoils the 1st line, which has to be sung 'Sleep, Ers, wake'. Professor Birkett made an admirable version in the *English Hymnal* (12); but we were compelled by our advisory committee to attempt yet another, so as to transfer the phraseology more evidently to the present day. 'Hosianna' is the fine word in the German (and in the original Hebrew itself) for Hosanna, which had by New Testament times come to mean what has been plumply called 'a holy hurrah'.

Trochaic-iambic, lines 1 and 4 being trochaic, 8 9 8. 8 9 8. 6 6 4. 4 4 8. Unique, of course. Note Nicholai's use of assonance, which can so greatly extend the scope of verse, as in the 1st couplet—'Stimme', 'Zinne'.

MUSIC. WACHET AUF appears in Nicolai's *Frewden Spiegel des ewigen Lebens, &c.* (Franckfurt am Mayn, 1599), set to the above hymn; the tune is probably by Nicolai himself, and its original form was as follows:

Zahn suggests that there are some false rhythms here caused by misprints and that at (1) the note should be dotted, at (2) the rest should be omitted, and at (3) the note should be a semibreve. These 'corrections', however, seem unnecessary considering the date at which the tune was written, before music had submitted to 'the tyranny of the bar-line'; if the melody is sung freely and naturally the rhythm perfectly fits that of the words.

The glorious tune rapidly became popular, and settings have been made by various composers, two of the best known being 'Sleepers, wake' in Mendelssohn's *St. Paul*, and J. S. Bach's cantata on this theme, the present version being from the latter work.

688 We love the place, O God. *W. Bullock* (1854), *and others.*

The highly condensed form used in this hymn taxes the skill of the most consummate poets, who in fact generally avoid it. Unfortunately a young sailor-missionary in Canada, William Bullock, used it in 1827 for a little hymn which happened just to fit in with new interest in ecclesiology that was already beginning to arise. Bullock became Dean of Nova Scotia, and in 1854 included his hymn in a little book, *Songs of the Church*. It was not good enough for use; but by 1860 the interest in the significance of church arrangements had enormously increased and Sir H. W. Baker very naturally endeavoured to improve it for the forthcoming *Hymns Ancient and Modern*. Nothing more was required in that era but a tune sufficiently trivial and doleful. Others have also tried to reshape it; for few hymnals have found it possible to discard it altogether.

Yet its origin is striking. A young naval officer, ordered to survey the coast of Newfoundland, is so horrified at the condition of the settlers that he resigns his commission, and returns to Newfoundland as a missionary. At a small place called Trinity Bay he builds a humble mission chapel, and for its consecration he writes this little hymn. Seventy years afterwards, a church was built on the same site and the hymn was sung again, and Bullock's original sermon was read to the people.

Iambic, 6 6. 6 6. (set to 6 6. 6 6. D. in the music). It will be noticed that the traditional Short Measure has two syllables more in the 3rd line (6 6. 8 6); this makes a more ordered expression possible, and by giving a gathering power in the longer line, makes 'S.M.' an adequate form for even august themes. But in 6 6. 6 6. there is so little room that it is really an ejaculatory metre. It lends itself with regrettable ease to parody. One has been lately going the rounds which contains the verse:

> We love the Vicar's pram:
> For there with tender care
> The latest little lamb
> Is wheeled to Morning Prayer.

MUSIC. ANNUE CHRISTE is from F. D. Aynes's edition of La Feillée's *Nouvelle Méthode . . . du Plain Chant* (Lyons, 1808). This edition of the work, which was first published in 1745 and was frequently augmented, contains some melodies not found in either previous or later issues. The present melody, like all the rest throughout the various impressions of the book, shows an approximation of the plainsong to measured music, both in rhythm and, to a considerable extent, in the form of the phrases; it should, however, be sung freely without insistence on the similarity of the melodic groups.

689 We saw thee not when, far away. *A. F.*

'Successive alterations', wrote J. H. Gurney (who had been responsible in 1851 for the last of them), 'have left nothing of the original composition remaining but the first four words and the repeated words.' The same thing has happened again in 1931; but even the repeated words have now gone. The fact is that about a hundred years ago a young lady had a good idea, and, as so often happens, did not know quite how to carry it through. Her name was Anne Rigby, she married a parson called Richter; and a hymn of hers has been traced to a book called *Songs of the Valley*, compiled by the Misses Carus Wilson in 1834; the hymn began, 'We have not seen thy footsteps tread'. It was something new; for it was about the actual Jesus Christ of whom we read in the Gospels. And it is well done—a better poem than after Buckoll, Gurney, and others had got to work on it, and had produced, 'We saw thee not when thou didst tread' (1838), and then after another version in 1842, 'We saw thee not when thou didst come' in 1851. These can be seen in some form in most hymnals, and compared with the original in Julian's *Dictionary*, pp. 1242–3. Our friends did not feel that we ought to use any of them, and therefore the editor was bidden to begin again.

Iambic, 8 8. 8 8. 8 8.

MUSIC. FARMBOROUGH, by Arthur S. Warrell, appeared first in *Songs of Praise* (1931). It is a broad, dignified tune, with robust, straightforward rhythm, and a very purposeful air due to the frank tonic movement of the beginning of the 1st and 3rd lines and its inversion in the 5th; well poised and direct, it makes a stimulating tune to sing.

690 We sing of God, the mighty source.

Christopher Smart,† 1722–71.

Kit Smart 'struck the stars' in the *Song to David*, as Mr. Edmund Blunden says in his edition of 1924; later he says:

'So schooled into himself, and taking flame at the psalms which hymn God's millions in air, earth, and water, he at length gathered many moments of vision into one panorama. "A Song to David" needs the slightest preliminary. Its daring rapture, glowing picture, rich and rare words, chime and answer of stanza are beyond dispute; its imperfections are rose-marks. The splendour seems Hebraic in origin, but the soil, the sun and rain of the poem are English.'

Fortunately, in order to make some of the stanzas into a hymn, we have only had to alter the opening words, from 'He sung' to 'We sing'. Our cento consists of stanzas 18, 84, 21, 76, 78, out of the 86 which make up the poem. It is difficult to avoid quoting from the rich ore that had to be passed over. We will content ourselves with a tribute to the Psalmist which is apposite for us:

Great, valiant, pious, good, and clean,
Sublime, contemplative, serene,
  Strong, constant, pleasant, wise!
Bright effluence of exceeding grace;
Best man! the swiftness and the race,
  The peril and the prize!

Compare 'Hosanna! music is divine', 521; and see the note about Metrical Psalters, under 449.

Iambic, 8 8 6. D. See 521.

MUSIC. MAGDALEN COLLEGE, by W. Hayes, appeared in his *Sixteen Psalms . . . set to music for the use of Magdalen College Chapel in Oxford* (1774), where it is set to Merrick's version of Psalm 122. This is probably Hayes's best-known tune, and is a fine, strong melody which deserves its continued popularity (see 671).

691 We thank thee, Lord, for this fair earth.

Bishop G. E. L. Cotton, 1813–66.

Inserted at the request of a former Head Master, this is much loved in several public schools, and probably was inspired by the scenery round Marlborough, where Dr. Cotton was himself Head Master in 1852, and until he became Bishop of Calcutta. He also wrote the fine collect, 'O God, who hast made of one blood all the nations of men'; and a collect is a prose poem.

L.M.

MUSIC. NEW SABBATH, by H. Phillips, is found in Done's *Selection of Psalm and Hymn Tunes* (1830). It is a felicitous tune, in triple time, with a certain animation of rhythm, and belongs rather to the type of tune which was popularized in the 18th century by the Wesleyans and Methodists, though it is not so elaborate in ornamentation as many of those melodies were in their original form. It has a very pleasant air of ingenuous good spirits.

692 We thank you, Lord of Heaven. *Jan Struther.*

Christopher Smart, we fancy, would have appreciated this hymn, which was written for *Songs of Praise*, that the tune 'Abendlied' might not be lost.

Iambic, 7 7. 7 7 6. D. Unique. It will be noticed that a complete system of assonance is carefully wrought into this lyric: e.g. 'greet us', 'delight us'; 'meadows', 'shadows'; while each stanza is keyed up by a rhyming conclusion.

MUSIC. ABENDLIED (DER TAG MIT SEINEM LICHTE), by J. G. Ebeling, is from *Pauli Gerhardi Geistliche Andachten, &c.* (1666–7), which was published in ten sets of a dozen each, the present melody being from the third dozen, *Das Dritte Dutzet Geistliche Andacht-Lieder, &c.*, set to the hymn 'Der Tag mit seinem Lichte'. The tune is an unpretentiously cheerful one, its general character and, especially, the short repeated phrases, giving rather the impression that it is founded on, or imitative of, a traditional popular song; its bright, almost festive air is most attractive, and remarkably well-suited by the present words.

693 What conscience dictates to be done.

Alexander Pope, 1688–1744.

The marvellous workmanship of the *Essay on Man* expounds a rather shallow deistic philosophy that does not lend itself to hymnody; but Pope put at the conclusion of the *Essay*, which was published in 1738, a paraphrase of the Lord's Prayer in 13 stanzas, from which this cento is taken. Warburton, in his Preface to the 1748 edition of the *Essay*, says that as some passages had been 'unjustly suspected of a tendency towards Fate and Naturalism', Pope had 'composed that Prayer as the sum of all, to show that his system was founded in Free-will and terminated in Piety'. 'To give all this the greater weight and reality, the Poet chose for his model The Lord's Prayer, which of all others best deserves the title prefixed to his Paraphrase.' The title is *The Universal Prayer*.

C.M., arranged for the music as D.C.M.

MUSIC. OLD 30TH is found in Thomas Este's *Whole Book of Psalmes* (1592), where it is set to Psalm 30 by John Farmer. The present version is an adaptation of Farmer's arrangement. It is a most impressive and stately tune, in the traditional manner of the early psalm-tunes, but with considerable originality of phrase, and a greater sense of continuity than is frequently found in these eight-lined melodies, many of which fall into two distinct halves, as if two four-lined tunes had been run together without much attempt at coherence; the present melody, however, 'feels' like a complete whole, and is undoubtedly one of the finest and most imposing of the tunes of this kind.

694 When all thy mercies, O my God.

Joseph Addison, 1672–1719.

Also, like 659, signed 'C', this concludes the Essay on 'Gratitude' in the *Spectator* for 9 Aug. 1712. It is prefixed by the following words:

'I have already obliged the public with some pieces of divine poetry which have fallen into my hands; and as they have met with the reception which they deserve, I shall, from time to time, communicate any work of the same nature which has not appeared in print, and may be acceptable to my readers.'

The Broadsheet was modified in later editions: 'communicated to' being substituted for 'obliged', and 'which have fallen', &c., and 'which they deserve', omitted. Apparently the secret had got out.

It is a remarkable fact that Addison had noticed that lack of hymns to Almighty God which we have more than once commented upon. Earlier in this Essay he says:

'Most of the works of the pagan poets were either direct hymns to their deities, or tended indirectly to the celebration of their respective attributes and perfections. . . . One would wonder that more of our Christian poets have not turned their thoughts this way, especially if we consider, that our idea of the Supreme Being is not only infinitely more great and noble than what could possibly enter into the heart of a heathen, but filled with everything that can raise the imagination, and give an opportunity for the sublimest thoughts and conceptions.'

From his 13 stanzas we have taken numbers 1, 5, 6, 8, 11, and 13.

C.M.

MUSIC. BELGRAVE, by W. Horsley, appeared in *National Psalmody. . . . A Collection of Tunes. . . . The Music harmonized, arranged, and adapted by B. Jacob* (1817), where it is set to Psalm 16. 'My lot is fallen in that blest land', and is noted in the index as a new composition. Horsley was one of the founders of the Philharmonic Society, and an intimate friend of Mendelssohn; he is probably best known to the general public by his hymn-tune 'Horsley' (131), written for the children of the Royal Female Orphan Asylum, where he was organist for many years. The present tune, in triple time, is of a familiar type, but rather less suavely uneventful than many, owing to the frequency of fairly wide leaps in the melody, which, while remaining excellently 'vocal', give it a great individual strength.

695 When by fear my heart is daunted. *P. Dearmer.*

Another hymn on confidence in God was demanded, and another hymn to carry a fine tune which was still unprovided for.

Trochaic, 8 7. 8 7. 8 7.

MUSIC. ARDUDWY, by Ieuan Gwyllt (John Roberts), appeared in *Llyfr Tonau Cynulleidfaol* (*Ychwanegiad*) (1870). It is a strong tune, with a slight unexpectedness in its phrases, which gives it an agreeably independent character, although the 5th line is of a type found in many Welsh tunes; the last line has a fine, resolute sweep, and imparts a vehement decisiveness and confidence to the whole melody.

696 When morning gilds the skies.

19th cent. Tr. E. Caswall and others.

Bei frühen Morgenlicht
Erwacht mein Herz und spricht.
  Gelobt sei Jesus Christus!
So sing ich früh und spät,
Bei Arbeit und Gebet,
  Gelobt sei Jesus Christus!

This hymn, by an unknown German author, is an example of a hymn being popularized by a bad tune: indeed both the new *Hymns Ancient and Modern* of 1904 and the *English Hymnal* of 1906 endeavoured to wean the public by changing the metre (reading 'praisèd' at the end of each verse), and offering a good Genevan psalm-tune instead. The German author of the words is unknown; but, as they have been traced to 1828 by Julian (who has found another German form in a collection of 1855), they evidently belong to the *hochpunkt* of the German sentimental movement; nor was Caswall the man to brace them. His first version appeared in Formby's *Catholic Hymns* (1854), and was changed a good deal afterwards by himself and others: in the end he ran it into 18 three-line verses. An attempt has here been made to increase the more manly side, which of course is borne out by the music.

Now (reading 'praisèd') iambic, 6 6 7. 6 6 7. D. Unique; but other words are supplied in the Doxology, 407.

MUSIC. O SEIGNEUR, composed or adapted by L. Bourgeois, appeared in the *Genevan Psalter* of 1551, set to Psalm 3, replacing the melody attached to this psalm in earlier editions. In the *Anglo-Genevan Psalter* of 1561 it was slightly adapted to fit Kethe's version of Psalm 122, and this association was continued in the complete *English Psalter* of 1562, and the *Scottish Psalter* of 1564. This is a superbly robust and ardent tune, which maintains an excellent sense of continuity throughout its considerable length; it falls, rhythmically, into four long phrases, each comprising three lines of the present words, and should be sung fairly fast for the perfect appreciation of its extraordinarily vigorous and stimulating quality.

697 When on my day of life the night is falling.

J. G. Whittier, 1807–93.

Included because a hymn was demanded for old age, and the gentle serenity of Whittier's lines seemed to fill the need very completely: his death indeed, at the age of 86, was not less calm and full of love than his life had been. He wrote them in 1882, when he was 75; and they were published in *The Bay of the Seven Islands, and Other Poems* (1883). Next year Garrett Horder included them in his *Congregational Hymns*.

Iambic, 11 10. 11 6. Whittier generally uses the more common metres. Unique.

MUSIC. STANSTEAD was composed by S. L. Russell especially for this hymn in the enlarged *Songs of Praise* (1931). It is a most attractive unison tune, with a naturally free rhythm, very well adapted to the stresses of the words, and a candidly expressive melody: an excellent and truly original tune.

698 When through the whirl of wheels, and engines humming.

G. A. Studdert-Kennedy, 1883–1929.

This original and moving hymn was written by Studdert-Kennedy for the Industrial Christian Fellowship, for which he used to go about preaching to the crowds of men who knew him from the War, and loved him; and it was first printed as one of the Fellowship leaflets. It is included in the volume of his collected poetry, *The Unutterable Beauty* (1927).

Iambic, 11 10. 11 10, but it has a special character from the powerful dactylic opening of each line.

MUSIC. LOMBARD STREET, by F. G. Russell, appeared in separate sheet form for the Industrial Christian Fellowship, and was first published in the *Hymnal for Canadian Youth* (1929). Russell was a great admirer of Studdert-Kennedy, and set several of his poems to music in various forms.

699 Where is thy God, my soul? *T. T. Lynch*, 1818–71.

We may remind ourselves of the historic importance of Lynch, and of the 'Rivulet Controversy', by consulting 297. This sound and vigorous hymn appeared in that very *Rivulet* (1st ed., 1855).

S.M.

MUSIC. ST. BRIDE appeared in *Parochial Harmony: consisting of a Collection of Psalm Tunes, &c. by William Riley* (1762), where it was set to the new version of Psalm 130, and headed 'St. Bridget's Tune, by Mr. Sam[l]. Howard'.

The alternative version (fa-burden), by Geoffrey Shaw, appeared in the *Tenor Tune Book* (1917).

Samuel Howard was a very popular song-writer of his day, and composed much music for the theatre and for public entertainments at the various 'Gardens' round London. The present tune, however, like all those in Riley's book, is in the strict psalm-tune style, and therefore shows less of the composer's individual style. It became popular and was included in *An Abridgment of the new version of the Psalms, &c.* (1777), under the name 'Bridget', set to Psalm 134, and is found in many collections down to the present time, its high quality being thoroughly deserving of its wide and continuous use.

700 Who within that stable cries. *A.F.*

The carol tune impelled us to make a new hymn based on 'Who is he in yonder stall', which is near the metre of the carol and was written probably by an American divine, B. Russell Hanby (1833–67), and published in *The Dove* (Chicago, 1866). The tune was adapted in *E.H.* 612; but we have now taken the opportunity of framing words which involve no alteration of the charming but complicated tune.

The 1st quatrain is iambic, 7 8. 7 11, but the 3rd line is trochaic, and there are tripping extra syllables. Similarly with the 1st couplet of the refrain, which has tripping dactyls: then the 3rd line ('We will praise') is trochaic, the 4th, iambic; and the last two lines trochaic again. The whole refrain being 10 9. 7 4. 4. 10. Of course, unique.

MUSIC. RESONET IN LAUDIBUS is a German carol melody probably of the 14th century. It is found set to various words, both Latin and German, the earliest being 'Resonet in laudibus', and 'Joseph, lieber, Joseph mein'. The latter carol is in a manuscript at Leipzig university (*c.* 1500), and, like 'Resonet in laudibus', was sung during the ceremonies, or mystery plays, performed in church round the crib; it was frequently coupled with the 'Magnum nomen Domini', which was sung to a section of the present tune, and is closely connected in form and nature with other Christmas songs such as 'Quem pastores', 'In dulci jubilo', 'Nunc angelorum' and others. It is found, with some variants, in many collections, virtually the present form, but with some slight rearrangement of the order of the sections, being found in Klug's *Geistliche Lieder zu Wittenberg, &c.* (1543). There is an English translation of 'Joseph, lieber' in the *Oxford Book of Carols*, 77.

701 Ye holy angels bright. *R. Baxter* (1681), *and others.*

There used to be confusion about this well-known hymn, and various names were given in connexion with its present form; but it is really Baxter's original in his *The Poor Man's Family Book* (1672), and in his *Poetical Fragments* (1672), re-written by J. Hampden Gurney in his Lutterworth *Church Psalmody* (1838). It came into general use through the S.P.C.K. *Church Hymns* (1871). The last two verses are not in Baxter at all, and seem to be Gurney's own. The author of *The Saint's Rest* calls his paraphrase, 'A Psalm of Praise to the tune of Psalm cxlviii': there are 16 cheerful verses, the first two being:

Ye holy angels bright,
Which stand before God's throne,
And dwell in glorious light,
Praise ye the Lord, each one!
You were so nigh,
Fitter than we
Dark sinners be,
For things so high.

You blessed souls at rest,
Who see your Saviour's face,
Whose glory, ev'n the least,
Is far above our grace,
God's praises sound
As in his sight
With sweet delight,
You do abound.

It is interesting to notice how religious ideas move: even a century ago, 'dark sinners' was too much for the reviser. But there is a real inspiration of joy in the original, which is a little weakened in the familiar version, good as it is.

In the old Psalters this would have been called 'P.M.' (Peculiar Measure), the name given to a few settings that were not in the normal C.M. or S.M. It is iambic, 6 6. 6 6. 4 4 4 4, enumerated in the music as 6 6. 6 6. 8 8.

MUSIC. DARWALL'S 148TH appeared in Aaron Williams's *New Universal Psalmodist* (1770), where it was set to Psalm 148. It is one of the 150 tunes composed by the Rev. H. Darwall for the complete metrical psalter, some of which appeared in various late 18th-century collections, though the majority remained unpublished, and are contained in two manuscript copies made by the composer himself. The present tune is sometimes stated to have been first used in Walsall parish church, of which Darwall was vicar, at the opening of a new organ by Green; this, however, seems to be incorrect. In the *Gentleman's Magazine* (1800) an account is given of this ceremony, in which the psalm is stated to be the 150th, and as the date is given as 1773, and the 148th had appeared in Williams's book in 1770, there seems no reason for supposing that the 150th is a misprint, especially as the vicar's text was drawn from this psalm. The present tune originally began on the dominant thus:

but the alteration to the tonic was made early in its printed career.

The alternative version (fa-burden), by Martin Shaw, appeared in the *Tenor Tune Book* (1917).

702 Ye servants of the Lord. *P. Doddridge*,† 1702–51.

The very learned Dr. Doddridge was a product of the happy time in which a first-rate scholar could know pretty well all there was to know. Just as John Wesley found time—incredible as it seems—to write handbooks of wide utility on many subjects (including physic), just as Watts produced the standard text-book on logic, so the gentle Doddridge taught his classes of 200 candidates for the Congregationalist ministry Hebrew Greek, algebra, trigonometry, logic, philosophy, and theology. Our hymn, 'The Active Christian', was first printed in Job Orton's posthumous edition of *Hymns founded on Various Texts* (1755). In the original the penultimate line is, 'And raise that fav'rite servant's head'; but this was too much, even a hundred years ago, and compilers began to alter 'favourite' to 'faithful', which, said Dr. Alford, 'is more a matter of duty than of choice'.

S.M.

MUSIC. ST. MICHAEL (OLD 134TH) is derived from the tune composed or adapted by L. Bourgeois for Psalm 101 in the *Genevan Psalter* (1551), where it appears as follows:

and was adapted, in the *Anglo-Genevan Psalter* of 1561, to Psalm 134, thus:

In subsequent editions the 4th and 5th notes are G, as in the original; the B's here may, therefore, be a misprint. This form was retained in all editions of the *Scottish Psalter*, but from 1562 onwards the *English Psalter* has the 3rd line as at present, and, until 1577, the 4th line thus:

after which date it appears as follows:

After 1595 the tune seems to have dropped out of use, until it was revived by W. Crotch in his *Psalm Tunes* (1836), who is probably responsible both for the present ending and the name 'St. Michael'.

The alternative version (fa-burden), by Martin Shaw, was written especially for the enlarged *Songs of Praise* (1931).

703 Zeal of the Lord, for ever burning. *S.P.*

Based on the great Messianic 9th chapter of Isaiah, with special reference to the 7th verse, and on the story of the Sower in Mark 4 (Matt. 13), this was written for the magnificent but exceedingly intricate rhythm of Bach's tune.

Iambic, 9 8. 9 8. 9 9 8. 9 9 8, with both single and double rhymes four times repeated, *abacddcaac*. Unique.

MUSIC. DESSLER (WIE WOHL IST MIR), melody and bass by J. S. Bach, is found in the *Anna Magdalena Notenbuch* set to the hymn 'Wie wohl ist mir, O Freund der Seelen'. The *Notenbuch* is a manuscript collection, written by Anna Magdalena Bach, of various tunes and small pieces of music, mostly by J. S. Bach; it is most beautifully and clearly written, and gives the impression of having been very much a 'labour of love'. The present tune is a most interesting and individual composition, with some very characteristic touches, for instance the little figure which makes its first appearance in the 11th bar, and its subsequent use, and the generally economical construction of the whole melody. The poise of the formal relations of the phrases, what may be called the ratio of the melodic proportions, is noteworthy; it is largely responsible for the emotional significance of this extremely expressive tune.

APPENDIX

1. *MUSIC.* COBBOLD, by 'S.M.W.V.R.', is an alternative tune to the hymn 'Sing, brothers, sing and praise your King' (164); it is a composite melody, the rhythm of the last line being here slightly adapted. Of a very bold and strenuous character, in a strongly accented triple time, it is particularly well suited to the expansive spirit of the words.

2. *MUSIC.* GORRAN, an alternative tune to the hymn 'Lead, kindly Light' (554), was composed by Ronald Dussek for *Songs of Praise*. It is an excellent tune which gains a fine continuity by treating each of the first two pairs of lines as virtually one phrase; this, besides its good musical effect, is also in accord with the metrical scheme of the poem, with its overlapping lines, and allows a more natural accentuation of the words, especially in the last two verses. The result is also enhanced by the first half of the tune being in unison.

3. AMEN

At the end of the Music Edition some settings of Amen are printed, for use at the close of a service in places where such musical elaboration is practised. Otherwise Amens are not printed, except for the Doxologies, 406–18. The chief use of the word is RESPONSIVE: thus it was among the ancient Jews. When the priest or reader said a prayer or doxology alone, the people's part was to respond by saying Amen, meaning, *So be it*. St. Paul mentions a similar custom among Christians in 1 Cor. 14 : 16, when he asks one who wishes to pray 'with tongues' unintelligibly—How shall the plain man 'say the Amen at thy giving of thanks'? The INITIAL use of the word—'Amen I say unto you', translated *Verily*, has been called 'an idiom of Christ', being only found in the sayings of the Lord. There is a similar use, but FINAL, when the word is used by a speaker in solemn confirmation of what he has already said, *So it is*; and fourthly, a SUBSCRIPTIONAL use, when it practically equals *Finis*: this last does not occur in the Old Testament, nor in the best texts of the New, except when there is another reason, as when an Epistle ends with a prayer or doxology. This subscriptional use was thus a later one; and it has a curious parallel in the habit among copyists of ending a manuscript with '99', these figures being the numerical equivalent of the Greek letters for Amen. A modern example of this use was the custom which grew up in some quarters, about seventy years ago, of adding it, rather tediously, to all hymns, as if it merely meant, *This is the end* (see p. 499). For ending doxologies with it there is a continuous tradition; though even with these it is not essential, its primary use being as a response by the people to words said by the reader.

MUSIC. The seven following settings vary in elaboration, and are therefore variously suited to different occasions. Roughly speaking, iii is the simplest, the rest increasing in complexity in their numerical order from i to vii. None, however, is of much difficulty, and all are attractive to sing.

(i) by G. W. Briggs, for 4 voices.
(ii) by William Byrd, for 5 voices.
(iii) by John Holmes, for 4 voices.
(iv) by Robert Ramsay, for 4 voices.
(v) by Thomas Tallis, for 5 voices.
(vi) by William Byrd, for 3 trebles.
(vii) by Orlando Gibbons, for 4 voices.

BIOGRAPHICAL AND HISTORICAL NOTES ON AUTHORS, COMPOSERS, SOURCES, ETC.

Note: Dates of death have been inserted up to 1951, but otherwise biographies have not been brought up to date.

* Denotes that the tune in question has a Fa-burden, Descant, or alternative harmonization.

ABELARD (ABAILARD), PETER (Le Pallet, 1079–1142, St. Marcel), was the son of a noble Breton house, and became a Lecturer in the Cathedral School at Notre-Dame, Paris, where he had enormous influence and numbered over fifty future archbishops and bishops among his pupils. Here began his passionate attachment to Héloïse, the niece of Fulbert, a wealthy canon. The pair fled to Brittany, where a son was born, and they were privately married. Fulbert then employed ruffians to mutilate Abelard in an atrocious manner; the victim retired to the Abbey of St. Denis as a monk, while Héloïse took the veil. Abelard's fame as a teacher increased, and the hermitage he built himself at Nogent became a noted theological school, which he called The Paraclete. On his taking charge of the Abbey of St. Gildas, The Paraclete was made a religious house for women under the charge of Héloïse. Finally, at the instance of Bernard of Clairvaux, Abelard was found guilty of heresy by a council at Sens and by the Pope. He died on his way to defend himself at Rome, and was buried by Héloïse. Their ashes are now in the Pére-Lachaise Cemetery in Paris. Abelard founded an all-important movement in philosophy and is perhaps the only theologian of the Middle Ages who appeals to the modern spirit to-day.

As a hymn-writer he was little known until last century, when several of his poems were discovered in the Vatican, and a number of others in the Royal Library at Brussels.

200. *O what their joy and their glory must be.*

ADAM OF ST. VICTOR (? 1172–92, Paris) was named 'Briton' by contemporaries, but it is uncertain whether he was English or Breton. Educated in Paris, entered, *c.* 1130, the Abbey of St. Victor then near, later in, Paris, where he remained till his death. He was the most prolific of Latin hymnists. A complete edition of his extant hymns was published by M. Gautier in 1858, and a selection is to be found in Archbishop Trench's *Sacred Latin Poetry*.

291. *Joy and triumph everlasting.*

ADAMS, SARAH FLOWER (Harlow, 1805–48, London), second daughter of Benjamin Flower, editor of the *Cambridge Intelligencer* and the *Political Review*: 1834, married William Bridges Adams; 1840–1, contributed 13 hymns, including 'Nearer, my God, to thee', to *Hymns and Anthems, &c.*, edited by the Rev. William Johnson Fox, minister at South Place Religious Society, Finsbury; 1841, published *Vivia Perpetua*, a dramatic poem in five acts; 1845, *The Flock at the Fountain*, catechism for children, interspersed with hymns. Contributed much prose and verse to the journal *The Monthly Repository*, edited by Fox.

586. *Nearer, my God, to thee.*

ADDERLEY, Hon. JAMES GRANVILLE (1861–1942), is the fifth son of the first Baron Norton. Educated at Eton and Christ Church, Oxford, he was Head of Oxford House, Bethnal Green, 1885–6, ordained in 1888, became Head of the Christ Church Oxford Mission, 1887–93, afterwards held various charges in London and Birmingham, and is now rector of St. Edmund's, Lombard Street. He was select preacher at Oxford, 1917–19, and at Cambridge in 1919. His most important publications are *Stephen Remarx* (1893), *In Slums and Society* (1916), *Old Seed on New Ground* (1920), and *Comprehensive Religion* (1930).

269. *Father, we greet thee, God of Love, whose mercy.*

ADDISON, JOSEPH (Milston, Wiltshire, 1672–1719, London), son of Lancelot Addison, rector of Milston and afterwards dean of Lichfield, was educated at Charterhouse (where he had as fellow-pupil his friend Richard Steele) and at Queen's and Magdalen Colleges, Oxford. Intended for the ministry, he turned instead to literature and politics, attached himself to the Whig interest, and found a patron in Charles Montague, afterwards Lord Halifax. His early literary efforts included an address to Dryden, a translation of part of Virgil's *Georgics*, and an account of the greatest English poets. In 1699 his political friends secured for him a pension with a view to foreign travel; and he visited France, Italy, Austria, Germany, and Holland. In the following reign a laudatory poem on Marlborough's victory at Blenheim brought him preferment to various successive offices of state. The fall of the Godolphin Ministry in 1710 gave him leisure for the composition of the Essays on which his fame mainly rests. Most of these were contributed to the *Tatler*, the *Spectator*, and the *Guardian*, in all of which he collaborated with his friend Steele. The best of his work is in the *Spectator*. Those years saw also the production of his tragedy *Cato*, which, mainly for political reasons, was successful beyond its deserts. The accession of George I brought Addison again into favour and office. In 1716 he married Charlotte, Countess of Warwick. His hymns were all contributed to the *Spectator*.

522. *How are thy servants blest, O Lord.*
656. *The Lord my pasture shall prepare.*
659. *The spacious firmament on high.*
694. *When all thy mercies, O my God.*

AHLE, JOHANN RUDOLPH (Mühlhausen, Thuringia, 1625–73, Mühlhausen), was educated at the Universities of Göttingen and Erfurt. In 1646 he was appointed cantor at St. Andreas's Church, and director of the musical school, at Erfurt. Soon he became known as one of the most radical reformers of church music in his time. In 1649 he accepted the post of organist of St. Blasius's Church, Mühlhausen, was elected to the town council in 1655, and was made Burgomaster in 1661. He published *Compendium pro tonellis*, a treatise on singing; *Geistliche Dialogen*; *Thüringischen Lust-Gartens*; *Neue Geistliche Chorstücke*; *Neuverfaste Chor-Musik* (motets), &c.

457. DESSAU (LIEBSTER JESU).

AINGER, ARTHUR CAMPBELL, M.A. (Blackheath, 1841–1919, Eton), son of a vicar of Hampstead and prebendary of St. Paul's, was educated on the foundation at Eton, and at Trinity College, Cambridge, where he won a first class in the Classical Tripos, 1864. Till 1901 he was an assistant master at Eton. He published the spirited and beautiful

Carmen Etonense and the well-known *Vale*, both set to music by Sir Joseph Barnby; *Eton Songs*; a section on Fives in *The Badminton Library*; a volume of *Memories of Eton Sixty Years Ago* (1917); and, with H. G. Winkle, M.A., an *English-Latin Verse Dictionary*.

300. *God is working his purpose out.*

AKEROYDE, SAMUEL (late 17th century). Nothing is known of this musician's life except that from 1687 onwards he was musician in ordinary to James II and William III. He was a popular song-writer and many of his compositions are found in various contemporary collections such as D'Urfey's *Third Collection of Songs* (1685), *The Banquet of Music* (1688), *Thesaurus Musicus* (1693–6), *The Gentleman's Journal* (1692–4), &c., while many of his hymn-tunes are found in *The Divine Companion* (1701, &c.).

346, 608. LAMBETH.

ALBERT, HEINRICH (Lobenstein, Voigtland, 1604–51, Königsberg), attended the Gymnasium at Gera, and afterwards became a pupil of his distinguished uncle Heinrich Schütz at Dresden, later also of Stobäus. At the desire of his parents he abandoned the study of music, and went to Leipzig to study law. Thence he set out with an embassy for Warsaw, but on the way was taken prisoner by the Swedes, and was not able to return until 1628, after suffering many hardships. The profession of law had little interest for him, and in 1632 he was glad to abandon it on his appointment as organist of the cathedral of Königsberg. His chief work was a collection of arias in eight volumes, to many of which he wrote the words. The preface contains an exposition by him of the principles of music.

32. GOTT DES HIMMELS.
32. *Now the morn new light is pouring.*

ALEXANDER, CECIL FRANCES (Miltoun House, Co. Tyrone, 1823–95, The Palace, Londonderry), daughter of Major Humphreys, married the Rev. William Alexander, who in 1896 became bishop of Armagh and Primate of All Ireland. Before marriage she published *Verses from Holy Scripture*, and *Hymns for Little Children* (1848), her most famous book, which ran into 100 editions. Later books were *Moral Songs*, *Narrative Hymns*, *Hymns Descriptive and Devotional*, *&c.*; and a posthumous collected edition, *Poems by Cecil Frances Alexander*.

131. *There is a green hill far away.*
174. *The eternal gates lift up their heads.*
217. *Jesus calls us! o'er the tumult.*
368. *Once in royal David's city.*
444. *All things bright and beautiful.*
528. *I bind unto myself to-day.*

ALFORD, HENRY, D.D. (London, 1810–71, Canterbury), was son of the rector of Aston Sandford. Educated at the Grammar School, Ilminster, and Trinity College, Cambridge, he served as curate to his father at Winkfield, Wilts., also at Ampton; became vicar of Wymeswold, Leicestershire, then incumbent of Quebec Chapel, London, and, finally, in 1857, dean of Canterbury. He was a Fellow of his college, and Hulsean Lecturer. *The Contemporary Review* was started and for some time edited by him.

Among his works were an edition of Homer; a volume of *English Descriptive Poetry*; *A Dissuasive against Rome*; a volume on *The Queen's English*; and various volumes of sermons. He wrote much poetry also, was greatly interested in hymnology, and himself wrote and translated many hymns, including a series for Sundays and Holy Days throughout the year. These were published in *Psalms and Hymns* (1844), *The Year of Praise* (1867), *Poetical Works* (1868), and other volumes. His *magnum opus* was his *Greek Testament*, which took its place as the standard critical commentary of the later 19th century. He was a member of the New Testament Revision Company.

9. *Come, ye thankful people, come.*
250. *In token that thou shalt not fear.*
394. *Forward be our watchword.*

ALINGTON, Cyril Argentine (Ipswich, 1872–), is the son of the Rev. H. G. Alington of Candlesby, Lincolnshire. Educated at Marlborough and Trinity College, Oxford, he became a Fellow of All Souls, and assistant master at Marlborough and Eton. From 1908 to 1916 he was Head Master of Shrewsbury, then Head Master of Eton, and in 1933 Dean of Durham. Chairman of the Head Masters' Conference in 1924–5, and elected an Hon. Fellow of Trinity College, Oxford, in 1926, he was for some time examining chaplain to the Bishop of Lichfield, and select preacher to Oxford University in 1909–10 and 1928–9, and has been chaplain to the King since 1921. His publications are many, including poetry, essays, theological works, and novels.

154. *Good Christian men, rejoice and sing.*
164. *Sing brothers, sing, and praise your King.*

AMBROSE, St. (Trier, 340–97, Milan), the greatest bishop in his day of the Western Church, was the son of a prefect of Gaul. He studied law, and was early appointed governor of the district of Northern Italy in which is situated the city of Milan. In the conflict between Catholics and Arians he displayed such courage and wisdom that on the death of the Bishop of Milan in 374 he was elected bishop by acclamation, and, though only a catechumen, was baptized and consecrated forthwith. As bishop he showed himself at once gentle and firm. Ambrose's greatest service to the Church was the improvement he effected in its musical services. He seems to have been the first to introduce in the West the practice of antiphonal singing, besides being himself a hymn-writer of distinction. Grimm calls him 'the Father of Church Song'. There is no foundation for the belief (at one time widely accepted) that he was the author or part-author of the *Te Deum*.

33. *O splendour of God's glory bright.*
44. *Creator of the earth and sky.*
51. *O Trinity of blessèd light.*

ANATOLIUS (?) probably lived in the 8th–9th century; said to be a pupil of Theodore of the Studium (759–826), but he is too late to be identified with any of the other historical figures of the same name, since he mentions martyrs of the early 7th century. More than a hundred hymns of his are extant, all, however, short.

490. *Fierce was the wild billow.*

ANCHORS, William (early 18th century), published *A Choice Collection of Psalm-Tunes, Hymns, and Anthems* in 1720.

603. WALSALL.

ANDERNACH is a little town in the district of Coblenz on the Rhine, once a Roman fortress, afterwards a residence of the Merovingian kings, which gave its name to a Gesangbuch produced there in 1608 by the Guild of St. Cecilia, under the title *Catholische Geistliche Gesänge*. This book represented a departure from the plainsong type of tune in favour of others of a more popular kind. It contained Latin hymns with German translations, and original German hymns also.

130. ANDERNACH. 305. TRES MAGI DE GENTIBUS.
478. IN NATALI DOMINI.

ANSTICE, Joseph, M.A. (Madeley Wood, Shropshire, 1808–36, Torquay), was educated by his uncle at Enmore Rectory, Bridgwater, at Westminster School, and at Christ Church, Oxford. He gained the Newdigate Prize in 1828 for a poem on *Richard Cœur de Lion*, and a Double First Class two years later. During his Oxford days, according to Lord Morley, he was the friend who influenced Gladstone most. At the age of 22 Anstice was appointed Professor of Classical Literature at King's College, London. Within three years his health failed, and he died at the age of 28. He had published his English Prize Essay on *The Influence of the Roman Conquest upon Literature and the Arts at Rome*; and *Selections from the Choice Poetry of the Greek Dramatic Writers, translated into English Verse*. His 52 hymns were printed for private circulation—*Hymns by the Late Joseph Anstice, M.A.* (Bridgwater, 1836).

604. *O Lord, how happy should we be.*

AQUINAS, Thomas (Aquino, 1227–74, Fossa Nuova), was the son of a Count of Aquino and was closely related to several of the reigning families of Europe. At an early age and in spite of family opposition, he joined the Dominican order, and studied under Albertus Magnus at Cologne and afterwards at Paris, where at the Pope's request he defended his Order with great success in its controversy with the University on liberty of teaching. His life was one of extraordinary industry, his public service and tedious journeys on behalf of his Order being only equalled by his immense literary activity. He refused all ecclesiastical preferments and rewards. Summoned by the Pope to attend the Council of Lyons on the differences between the Greek and Latin Churches, he died before reaching the Council. Thomas's philosophy aims at gathering together all known science into a single system, a condensed summary of which is given in his *Summa Theologiae*, still the standard theological text-book of the Roman Church.

277. *O Saviour victim.*
279. *Thee we adore, O hidden Saviour.*
280. *Therefore we, before him bending.*

ARKWRIGHT, John Stanhope (London, 1872–), is the eldest son of J. Hungerford Arkwright, Lord-Lieutenant of Herefordshire. Educated at Eton and Christ Church, Oxford, was Newdigate Prizeman in 1895, became a barrister, and sat in Parliament for Hereford 1900–12, and is Chief Steward of the City of Hereford. His publications include *The Last Muster* and *The Supreme Sacrifice, and other poems in time of War*.

293. *O valiant hearts, who to your glory came.*

ARMSTRONG, THOMAS, D.Mus. (Peterborough, 1898–), son of A. E. Armstrong, also a musician, was educated at the Choir School, Chapel Royal, St. James's, King's School, Peterborough, Keble College, Oxford (organ scholar), and the Royal College of Music (Wesley Exhibitioner). He has held posts as sub-organist at Peterborough Cathedral, Manchester Cathedral, as organist of St. Peter's, Eaton Square (1923), Exeter Cathedral (1928), and in 1933 was appointed to Christ Church, Oxford. During the War he served with H.M. Forces from 1917 to 1919. Among his musical publications are many songs, part-songs, and anthems; he has also contributed much to periodical literature, and published two volumes of criticism, *Strauss's Tone-poems* and *Mendelssohn's 'Elijah'*.

469. EXON.

ARNOLD, JOHN (Essex, 1720–92?), is known by two publications, *The Essex Harmony*, a collection of songs and catches for 2, 3, 4, and 5 voices, and *The Compleat Psalmodist* (1756), which contained instruction in the singing of church music, and a large number of psalm- and hymn-tunes, chants, &c. Both books passed through several editions, some of them bearing a slight change of title.

682. EPSOM.

ARNOLD, MATTHEW (Laleham, 1822–88, Liverpool), was the son of Dr. Thomas Arnold. Educated at Rugby, Winchester, and Balliol College, Oxford, he was Newdigate Prizeman in 1843, and became a Fellow of Oriel College in 1845. He was first a master at Rugby, private secretary to the Marquis of Lansdowne in 1847, and became an inspector of schools in 1851. He was distinguished both as poet and critic, but his poetry is the more enduring. His publications began with *The Strayed Reveller and other Poems* (1849) and ended with the second series of *Essays in Criticism* (1888); a collected edition of his poetry was published in three volumes in 1885. Other important works were *On Translating Homer* (1861–2), *Culture and Anarchy* (1869), and *Literature and Dogma* (1873).

213. *Servants of God, or sons.*
434. *O most high, almighty, good Lord God.*

ATKINS, Sir IVOR ALGERNON, Mus.Doc., F.S.A., F.R.C.O. (Cardiff, 1869–), son of Frederick Atkins, was educated at Roath and privately; in 1890 he was appointed assistant organist of Hereford Cathedral; 1893, organist and choirmaster of the Collegiate Church of Ludlow; since 1897 has been organist and master of the choristers of Worcester Cathedral, and since 1899 conductor of the festivals of the Three Choirs at Worcester, and also conductor of several choral societies in that county. He was knighted in 1921. Among his compositions are *Hymn of Faith* (1905), festival settings of the Magnificat and Nunc Dimittis, and many anthems, part-songs, songs, &c.

*323. WORCESTER. 370. WHITE LADIES ASTON.

ATTWOOD, Thomas (London, 1765–1838, Chelsea), was the son of a trumpeter, viola player, and coal merchant. As a chorister in the Chapel Royal, he came under the notice of the Prince of Wales, afterwards George IV, and was sent abroad by him to study, first in Italy, then in Vienna under Mozart, one of whose favourite pupils he became. In 1796 he was appointed organist of St. Paul's Cathedral and composer to the Chapel Royal; in 1841, organist of George IV's private chapel at Brighton; in 1823, one of the first professors of the Royal Academy of Music on its foundation; and in 1836, organist of the Chapel Royal. In early life he was much engaged in dramatic composition, and did not till comparatively late begin to write church music. In this, however, he showed marked originality, and in many respects may be called 'the father of modern church music'. He was one of the first musicians in this country to recognize the genius of Mendelssohn, who dedicated to him his three Preludes and Fugues for the organ. He wrote many songs and glees, one song, *The Soldier's Dream*, long retaining its popularity; many sonatas; and services, anthems, chants. A volume of his church compositions, containing 4 services, 8 anthems, and 9 chants, was published about 15 years after his death.

181. VENI, CREATOR (ATTWOOD).

AUBER, Harriet (London, 1773–1862, Hoddesdon), was one of the daughters of James Auber, whose grandfather, Pierre Auber (Aubert), of Ecquetat in Normandy, came to England in 1685, as a Huguenot refugee after the Revocation of the Edict of Nantes. Most of her life was spent in the quiet villages of Broxbourne and Hoddesdon, Hertfordshire. In *The Spirit of the Psalms* (1829), she endeavoured to put 'elegance' and 'poetic language' into versions of certain selected psalms, hoping that these would displace from use the often far from poetic versions of Tate and Brady. Some of them did find their way into hymn-books in England and America; Mr. Spurgeon in particular made considerable use of them in his Metropolitan Tabernacle collection. Miss Auber's volume included also a selection of hymns of literary quality, by various writers; and among a number of contributions from her own pen was the one exquisite lyric by which her name survives.

182. *Our blest Redeemer, ere he breathed.*

AUSTIN, John (Walpole, Norfolk, 1613–69, London), was educated at St. John's College, Cambridge, became a Roman Catholic, and entered Lincoln's Inn to study for the Bar. Later he became a private tutor, and finally settled down to literature as a career. His works include *The Christian Moderator*, *Reflections upon the Oaths of Supremacy*, and *Devotions in the Antient Way of Offices containing Exercises for every day in the Week* (1668), the latter containing 39 hymns in this first edition, four more being added in later issues.

19. *Hark, my soul, how everything.*
205. *Hail, glorious spirits, heirs of light.*

BACH, Johann Christoph (Arnstadt, 1642–1703, Eisenach), was the eldest son of Heinrich Bach. In 1665 he became organist at Eisenach, and seems to have remained there till his death. He may have succeeded Pachelbel as court organist in 1678, but this is not certain, though for the last years of his life he had apartments and stabling in the ducal mint. He was a remarkable musician, a bold harmonist, and an excellent composer, especially of vocal music. He was a second cousin of J. S. Bach.

32 (ii). ST. LEONARD.

BACH, JOHANN SEBASTIAN (Eisenach, 1685–1750, Leipzig), belonged to the most musical family ever known. They were of peasant stock, and Bach himself was an embodiment of the simple personal and domestic virtues and the deep religious sentiment most characteristic of his race. He was trained in the choir schools of Ohrdruf and Lüneburg, and held official positions at Arnstadt, Mühlhausen, Weimar, and Anhalt Cöthen, before he settled finally in Leipzig as cantor of the famous Thomas School and director of music in the Thomas and Nicholas Churches. With the exception of opera, he handled every type of musical form with unequalled mastery. He was the greatest organist of his own time; both as a player and as a composer for that instrument, he 'stands at the summit of human achievement'. What Palestrina was to the Roman Church, Bach became to Protestantism. He had immense physical and mental energy, and poured out works that were prodigal not only in quantity, but in fertility of ideas, variety of sentiment, and inimitable perfection. He left many vocal works, including motets, masses, about 200 cantatas (verse anthems), and two great *Passions*, the *St. Matthew* and the *St. John*. He reharmonized the standard German chorales, embodying many of them in his *Passions*. A collection of those chorales was published posthumously as *Vierstimmige Choralgesänge* (1765–9). Bach not only consummated the music of the previous period, but also pointed out the path which all subsequent music has followed, consciously or unconsciously. Schumann wrote, 'To him music owes almost as great a debt as a religion owes its Founder'.

*42. CALVISIUS (ACH BLEIB BEI UNS).
*57. INNSBRUCK.
60. RINKART (KOMMT SEELEN).
*90. WIE SCHÖN LEUCHTET DER MORGENSTERN.
93. CRASSELIUS.
*99. HERZLIEBSTER JESU.
*123. DRESDEN (SO GIEBST DU).
*128. PASSION CHORALE.
*135. ST. THEODULPH (VALET WILL ICH DIR GEBEN).
*139. SEBASTIAN (JESU MEINES GLAUBENS ZIER).
150. CÖTHEN (EINS IST NOT).
*156. WITTENBERG (ES IST DAS HEIL).
*159. HERMANN (ERSCHIENEN IST DER HERRLICH TAG).
194. DANK SEI GOTT IN DER HÖHE.
264. NICHT SO TRAURIG.
*277. ERHALT' UNS, HERR.
*278. ACH GOTT UND HERR.
480. ICH HALTE TREULICH STILL.
*481. NICOLAUS (LOBT GOTT).
*533. GESIUS (HEUT' TRIUMPHIRET).
*544. JESU, MEINE FREUDE.
*558. SALZBURG.
*566. VATER UNSER.
*585. CHRISTUS DER IST MEIN LEBEN.
621. DARMSTADT (O GOTT, DU FROMMER GOTT).
*637. WEISSE (GOTTLOB, ES GEHT NUN MEHR ZUM ENDE).
*638. WIR CHRISTENLEUT.
*640. NUN FREUT EUCH.
674. ZUM FRIEDEN.
*679. DAS WALT' GOTT VATER.
*687. WACHET AUF.
703. DESSLER (WIE WOHL IST MIR).

BAHNMAIER, JONATHAN FRIEDRICH (Oberstenfeld, 1774–1841, Owen), son of J. C. Bahnmaier, Town Preacher at Oberstenfeld, studied at

Tübingen, and became assistant to his father in 1798. In 1806 he became Diaconus at Marbach, and in 1810 at Ludwigsberg. In 1815 he was appointed Professor of Education and Homiletics at Tübingen, but being obliged to resign his post, was, in 1819, made decan and town preacher at Kirchheim-unter-Teck, where he remained until his death. He was on the committee which compiled the Württemberg *Gesangbuch* of 1842. He wrote many hymns, most of which were published in his *Christliche Blätter aus Tübingen*.

645. *Spread, still spread, thou mighty word.*

BAIRSTOW, Sir EDWARD C., Mus.D., F.R.C.O. (Huddersfield, 1874–1946), son of James O. Bairstow, a clothing manufacturer, was educated privately and became in 1893 pupil and assistant of Sir F. Bridge and organist of All Saints, Norfolk Square; in 1899 organist of the parish church, Wigan, in 1906 of the parish church, Leeds, since 1913 organist and master of the choir of York Minster, and since 1929 Professor of Music in Durham University. From 1901 onwards he has been the conductor of many musical societies, both choral and orchestral, and is examiner to the Associated Board of the Royal College and Royal Academy of Music, and to the Royal College of Organists. His publications include songs, part-songs, church and organ music.

*114. BEDFORD.

BAKER, Sir HENRY WILLIAMS, Bt., M.A. (London, 1821–77, Monkland), was the son of Vice-Admiral Sir Henry Loraine Baker, Bt., and was educated at Trinity College, Cambridge. Ordained in 1844, he became vicar of Monkland, near Leominster, in 1851. In 1859 he succeeded to the baronetcy. He was the chief promoter of *Hymns Ancient and Modern*, and from the first, for twenty years was chairman and acknowledged leader of the Committee responsible for the preparation and development of that epoch-making book, to which he contributed translations from the Latin, and many original hymns. He published *Family Prayers for the Use of those who have to work hard*, and a *Daily Text Book* for the same class.

351. *O praise ye the Lord.*
570. *Lord, thy word abideth.*
654. *The King of love my shepherd is.*

BARING-GOULD, SABINE, M.A. (Exeter, 1834–1924, Lew Trenchard), in early life lived much in Germany and France, was educated at Clare College, Cambridge, and ordained in 1861. He became curate of Horbury, with special charge of the mission at Horbury Bridge, in 1864; two years later, perpetual curate of Dalton, near Thirsk; in 1871, rector of East Mersea, Colchester; and in 1881, having in the meanwhile succeeded his father in the estate of Lew Trenchard, Devon, he exercised his privilege as squire and patron by presenting himself to the living there as rector. He was a man of an extraordinary range of interests, and of inexhaustible versatility and industry; and he was said to have more works attached to his name in the British Museum catalogue than any other writer of his time. He wrote a long series of the *Lives of the Saints*; *A Study of St. Paul*; *The Origin and Development of Religious Belief*; books of travel in Iceland, Brittany, and southern France; works on Germany and its Church;

histories of the Caesars and Napoleon Bonaparte; popular books on antiquarian subjects, such as the *Book of Were-Wolves* and *Curious Myths of the Middle Ages*; and a very large number of novels, many of which, such as *Mehalah*, *John Herring*, *Richard Cable Lightshipman*, *Mrs. Curgenven of Curgenven*, enjoyed a large degree of popularity. He was a keen collector of folk-songs, of which he edited two valuable collections, *Songs of the West* and *A Garland of Country Song*.

49. *Now the day is over.*
397. *Onward, Christian soldiers!*
678. *Through the night of doubt and sorrow.*
49. EUDOXIA.

BARNBY, Sir JOSEPH (York, 1838–96, London), became a chorister in York Minster, and was an organist and choirmaster at 12 years of age. After studying at the R.A.M., he served as organist at St. Michael's, Queenhithe; St. James the Less, Westminster; St. Andrew's, Wells Street, where his choir reached a degree of efficiency second to none in London; and at St. Anne's, Soho, where he established annual recitals of Bach's Passion Music (*St. Matthew* and *St. John*). From 1875 to 1892 he was precentor and director of musical instruction at Eton College. From 1861 to 1876 he was musical adviser to Novello, Ewer & Co., who in 1867 established for him what became known as Barnby's Choir. Later, he conducted the Royal Choral Society. In 1892 he became Principal of the Guildhall School of Music, and was knighted. His published work includes an oratorio, *Rebekah*, part-songs, vocal solos, a series of *Eton Songs*, many services and anthems, and 246 hymn-tunes, which were published in one volume after his death. He edited five hymn-books, of which the most notable was the *Hymnary* (1872).

95. CANTATE DOMINO.

BARTHÉLÉMON, FRANÇOIS HIPPOLYTE (Bordeaux, 1741–1808, London), was the son of a French Government officer in the colonial department, and an Irish lady of a wealthy Queen's County family. Entering the army, he became an officer in Berwick's Regiment in the Irish Brigade. Here, however, he made the acquaintance of the Earl of Kellie, a musical enthusiast, who induced him to leave the army and adopt music as his profession. He came to England in 1765, and became one of the most distinguished violinists of his time. In that year he was appointed leader of the band at the opera, and in 1770 at Marylebone Gardens. He wrote much music for the theatre and the public gardens, but little for the Church. His works include dramatic pieces, quartets for stringed instruments, and preludes for the organ.

25. MORNING HYMN. 207. BALLERMA.

BATHURST, WILLIAM HILEY, M.A. (Cleve Dale, Mangotsfield, near Bristol, 1796–1877, Lydney Park), was son of the Rt. Hon. Charles Bragge, M.P. for Bristol, who assumed the name of Bathurst on succeeding to his uncle's estate of Lydney Park, Gloucestershire. Educated at Winchester and Christ Church, Oxford, where he graduated in 1818, he took Orders, and was presented by his kinsman, Earl Bathurst, to the rectory of Barwick-in-Elmet, near Leeds. Doctrinal difficulties arising out of the Prayer Book, and especially the baptismal and burial services, led to his resignation of the living in 1852. He then retired into private life at Darley Dale, near Matlock. In 1863 he succeeded to the family estate. He published *A Translation of the Georgics of Virgil* (1849); *Metrical Musings*; and *Psalms and Hymns for Public and Private Use* (Leeds, 1830).

523. *How blest are they whose hearts are pure.*
594. *O for a faith that will not shrink.*

BATTISHILL, Jonathan (London, 1738–1801, Islington), was chorister of St. Paul's, then deputy to Dr. Boyce as organist of the Chapel Royal, and, later, organist of St. Clement, Eastcheap, and Christ Church, Newgate Street. He sang at Charles Wesley's concerts, and was for some time conductor (harpsichord) at Covent Garden Theatre, composing much music for theatrical and concert performance; later wrote church music almost exclusively; was renowned for his extraordinary musical memory. He is buried near Boyce in the crypt of St. Paul's.

538. BATTISHILL.

BAX, Arnold Edward Trevor (London, 1883–), son of Alfred Ridley Bax, F.S.A., was educated privately and at the Royal Academy of Music, which he entered in 1900. He first appeared publicly as a composer in 1903, and since 1908 his works have been often found in the programmes of all the principal London concerts. His output has been large, and includes virtually all contemporary forms of musical composition except opera. He is one of the most important musicians of his generation.

107. WONDER.

BAX, Clifford (London, 1886–), the third son of Alfred Ridley Bax, F.S.A., was educated privately, and then studied art at the Slade School and Heatherley's. Later, he lived much abroad in Germany, Belgium, and Italy; finally, he gave up painting for literature, especially dramatic work. His first play to be publicly produced was the *Poetasters of Ispahan* (1912); since 1923 he has been concerned in many productions in several of which music has played an important part, for instance *Midsummer Madness* (music by Armstrong Gibbs) in 1924, *Mr. Pepys* (1926), and *Waterloo Leave* (1928), both with music by Martin Shaw. He has also published, besides his plays, books of poems, essays, and a volume of memoirs, *Inland Far* (1925).

329. *Turn back, O Man, forswear thy foolish ways.*

BAXTER, Richard (Rowton, 1615–91, London), one of the ablest as well as most devoted among the Puritan clergy, was brought up by his maternal grandfather, and educated at Wroxeter School, but never attended a University. After a short experience of Court life, his strong religious convictions led him to study divinity. Ordained to the ministry, he served successively at Bridgnorth and Kidderminster. During the Civil War he attached himself to the Parliamentary army, but rebuked Cromwell for assuming supreme power in the State, and defended the old Monarchy. For a short time after the Restoration he held the office of King's Chaplain, and took part in the Savoy Conference, 1661, one result of which was his *Reformed Liturgy*. After the Act of Uniformity he was subjected to much intermittent annoyance, culminating in his trial before Jeffreys in 1685. Released after a two years' mild imprisonment, he passed the remaining four years of his life in peace and honour.

Among his 'books enough to fill a cart' (Jeffreys), the three which take first rank are *The Saints' Everlasting Rest* (1650); *The Reformed Pastor* (1656); and *The Call to the Unconverted* (1657). Of great biographical interest are his *Reliquiae*, containing a narrative of his life and times. His poetical works are of less merit.

105. *Lord, it belongs not to my care.*
288. *Christ who knows all his sheep.*
514. *He wants not friends that hath thy love.*
701. *Ye holy angels bright.*

BEECHING, Henry Charles, D.D. (Bexhill, 1859–1919, Norwich), was educated at the City of London School and Balliol College, Oxford. After a curacy at Mossley Hill, Liverpool, he became rector of Yattendon, Berks., in 1885, and so continued till 1900; he was select preacher at Oxford, Cambridge, and Dublin; Clark Lecturer in English Literature at Cambridge, 1900; chaplain of Lincoln's Inn and Professor of Pastoral Theology, King's College, London, 1900–3; in 1902 he became a canon of Westminster; and in 1911 dean of Norwich. He was one of the authors of *Love in Idleness* and *Love in a Looking-Glass*; wrote *In a Garden, and Other Poems*; published, besides sermons, *Lectures on Poetry*, *Religio Laici*, *The Grace of Episcopacy*, *Pages from a Private Diary*, &c.; and edited Milton, Herbert, Vaughan, Daniel, Drayton, Tennyson's *In Memoriam*, also *Lyra Sacra*, *A Paradise of English Poetry*, and *A Book of Christmas Verse*.

504. *God, who created me.*

BELL, George Kennedy Allen, D.D. (Hayling Island, 1883–), bishop of Chichester, was educated at Westminster and Christ Church, Oxford, won the Newdigate Prize (1904), and became Senior Student (Fellow) of his college. He was ordained in 1907 and became a curate at Leeds, 1907–10. He was examining chaplain to the Bishop of Wakefield 1910–16, resident chaplain to the Archbishop of Canterbury 1914–24, dean of Canterbury 1924–9, assistant secretary Lambeth Conference 1920, and episcopal secretary Lambeth Conference 1930, a member of the Archbishop's Conference on Social and Industrial Problems 1917, and in 1925 was Olaus Petri Lecturer to the University of Upsala. Publications: *Poems of Life and Death*; *The War and the Kingdom of God* (1915), and other works on social and religious problems.

242. *Christ is the King! O friends rejoice.*

BELL, Maud Alma (London, 1868–), daughter of George William Bell, Barrister, was educated at the Francis Holland School for a year, privately, and at various art schools. Miss Bell, who is an artist of distinction, has held four exhibitions of her water-colours of London; during the War she worked under the Ministry of Health, and also for Serbian Relief. In 1924 she published *London Songs*.

330. *Father all-seeing, friend of all creation.*

BENSON, Edward White, D.D. (Birmingham, 1829–96, Hawarden), was educated at King Edward's School, Birmingham, and at Trinity College, Cambridge, where he was a scholar, and graduated as senior optime, first class Classical Tripos, and was Senior Chancellor's Classical Medallist, becoming Fellow of his College. He left Cambridge to be an assistant master at Rugby, but in 1859 went as Head Master to Wellington College until 1872, and thence to Lincoln as Chancellor of the Cathedral. He left Lincoln for Truro in 1877 to be first bishop of that diocese; in 1883 he proceeded to Canterbury as Primate of All England. He contributed to the *Dictionary of Christian Biography* and was the author of *Work, Friendship, and Worship*; *Boy Life*; *Sundays in Wellington College*; and *Singleheart*. He edited the *Rugby School Hymn Book* and the *Wellington College Chapel Hymn Book* (1860), (1863), and (1873), and translated various Latin and Greek hymns and composed a few original ones. His great work, *Cyprian: his Life, his Times, his Work*, was published posthumously.

35. *The splendours of thy glory, Lord.*

BERNARD of Cluny (12th century), sometimes called 'of Morlaix' erroneously, from his supposed birthplace, but more accurately 'of Cluny' from the great abbey of which he became a monk, is said to have been of English extraction by Pitseus (*De Scriptoribus Angliae*); but there is no real evidence. Of him, unlike his great contemporary Bernard of Clairvaux, practically nothing is known save his authorship of the poem *De Contemptu Mundi*, from which the well-known hymns undernoted are taken.

198. *Jerusalem the golden.*
459. *Brief life is here our portion.*

BIANCO da Siena (Anciolina- ? , 1434, Venice). Little is known of his life. In 1367 he joined a religious order founded by John Columbinus of Siena, and is said to have spent the latter part of his life at Venice. His hymns (*Laudi Spirituali*) were published in 1851, and some of them have been translated into English by Dr. Littledale.

177. *Come down, O Love divine.*

BICKNELL, Clarence (1842–1918), was educated at Trinity College, Cambridge, where he took his B.A. degree in 1865. In 1866 he became curate of St. Paul's, Newington, and from 1872 until his retirement was rector of Stoke, Market Drayton.

136. COME, FAITHFUL PEOPLE.

BIGG, Charles, D.D. (Manchester, 1840–1908, Oxford, was educated at Manchester Grammar School and Christ Church, Oxford, where he won the Hertford Scholarship and the Gaisford Prize, and became Senior Student and classical tutor of his college. He became an assistant master at Cheltenham College, and thence went as Head Master to Brighton College. From 1887 to 1901 he was hon. canon of Worcester and also rector of Fenny Compton, Leamington. In 1901 he was elected Regius Professor of Ecclesiastical History at Oxford. Publications: *The Christian Platonists of Alexandria*; *Neoplatonism*; and was editor of *St. Augustine's Confessions*; the *De Imitatione*; *Law's Serious Call*; a *Commentary on the Epistles of Peter and Jude*; *The Doctrine of the Twelve Apostles*; and *Wayside Sketches in Ecclesiastical History*.

44. *Creator of the earth and sky.*

BINYON, Laurence, LL.D. (Lancaster, 1869–1943), was educated at St. Paul's School and Trinity College, Oxford (Newdigate Prize, 1890). He received the honorary LL.D. degree from Glasgow University, and became Keeper of Prints and Drawings at the British Museum, retiring in 1933. Among his many publications are: *The Praise of Life* (1896); *The Death of Adam and other poems* (1904); *The Secret* (60 poems) (1920); *Sophro the Wise* (1927); *A Laurence Binyon Anthology* (1927), &c.

493. *For mercy, courage, kindness, mirth.*

BISHOP, John (? 1665–1737, Winchester), a composer of the Purcellian school, became temporary organist and lay clerk of King's College, Cambridge, in 1687; organist of Winchester College in 1695; and in 1729 organist of Winchester Cathedral. He was buried in the cloisters of the College, where his epitaph describes him as 'Vir singulari probitate, integerrima vita, moribus innocuis, musicaeque scientiae bene peritus, qui, postquam huic Collegio per XLII. annos sedulo inserviisset, ad Caelestam Choram placide migravit, decimo nono die Decembris, anno Dom. 1737, Aetat. 72.' (A man of unexampled honesty, purest life, blameless morals, and of excellent skill in music, who, after serving this College diligently for 42 years, passed tranquilly to the Celestial Choir on the 19th of December A.D. 1737, aged 72.)

605. LEICESTER (or BEDFORD). 610. ILLSLEY.

BLACKIE, John Stuart, LL.D. (Glasgow, 1809–95, Edinburgh), was educated at Marischal College, Aberdeen, and Edinburgh University, resided on the Continent for a time, was called to the Bar in 1834, appointed Professor of Latin in Marischal College, and in 1850 Professor of Greek in the University of Edinburgh. He was for some time editor of the *Sunday Magazine* in succession to Dr. Guthrie. Publications: translations of *Faust* (1834), and *Aeschylus* (1850); *Pronunciation of Greek* (1852); *Lyrical Poems* (1860); *Homer and the Iliad*, 4 vols. (1869); *Lays and Legends of Ancient Greece* (1857); and *Songs of Religion and Life* (1876).

448. *Angels holy, high and lowly.*

BLAKE, William (Carnaby Market, London, 1757–1827, Strand, London), was son of a hosier, engraver by training and profession, and poet and painter of remarkable original force. In 1783 appeared his *Poetical Sketches*, poems written between the ages of 12 and 20; thereafter the greater number of his published works were produced by a process of his own, 'Illuminated Printing', in which the text and embellishments were etched, in relief, on copper, from which impressions were taken in monochrome, and tinted by hand in water-colour. It was a laborious process and very few copies of any work were produced. His principal publications were *The Songs of Innocence and of Experience* (1793–4), but mostly issued five or six years later, and some of his 'Prophetic Books' such as *Jerusalem*, *The Book of Thel*, *The Marriage of Heaven and Hell*, and designs for *The Book of Job*, &c.; most of his works, however, remained in manuscript till many years after his death. Many paintings, chiefly in water-colour, also exist, including various allegorical subjects and a superb series illustrating Dante. The mainspring of his life and thought was a combination of a passionate love of liberty and the worship of beauty.

446. *And did those feet in ancient time.*
461. *Can I see another's woe.*
682. *To Mercy, Pity, Peace, and Love.*

BODE, JOHN ERNEST, M.A. (London, 1816–74, Castle Camps, Cambridgeshire), was educated at Eton, Charterhouse, and Christ Church, Oxford, where he was the first winner of the Hertford Scholarship. He was a Student (Fellow) and tutor of Christ Church for six years; then, in 1847, became rector of Westwell, Oxfordshire, and, later, of Castle Camps, Cambridgeshire. He was Bampton Lecturer in 1855, and in 1857 contested, unsuccessfully, the Chair of Poetry in Oxford, basing his claims on a volume of *Ballads from Herodotus, with an Introductory Poem* (1853). He published also *Short Occasional Pieces*, and *Hymns from the Gospel of the Day for Each Sunday and Festivals of our Lord.*

255. *O Jesus, I have promised.*

BOHEMIAN BRETHREN.—This body originated with the Calixtine or Utraquist section of the followers of the reformer John Hus. The chief demands of this community were for (1) the unrestricted preaching of God's word; (2) Communion in both kinds, the laity to receive the cup (*calix*) as well as the bread (*communio sub utraque specie*); (3) the apostolic poverty and moral purity of the clergy; (4) strictness of Church discipline. The Brethren separated from the Utraquists in 1467. They called themselves Jednota Bratrská, which they rendered into Latin as Unitas Fratrum. Their chief concern was to secure practical Christianity, the fulfilling of the law of Christ in daily life and conduct—whence they were sometimes called 'Fratres legis Christi'. Their spiritual leader about 1490 was Brother Lucas, who gave the body its organization and its first hymn-book and catechism. When the Reformation began, they were among the first to welcome it, and they sent ambassadors to Luther to see how far community of doctrine and discipline was possible. One of these was Michael Weisse (q.v.), whose translations from the Bohemian hymns in his *Ein New Gesengbuchlen* (1531) had a considerable influence on the early Lutheran hymnody. The history of the Brethren was much chequered by persecution from without and strife and division within. The last remnants of them found a refuge in Saxony and a new beginning (see Zinzendorf) in 1725.

11. CORNFIELDS. 142. BOHEMIA (O MENSCH SIEH).
214. MIT FREUDEN ZART. 225. STETTIN (NUN SEHT).

BONAR, HORATIUS, D.D. (Edinburgh, 1808–89, Edinburgh), was the son of a solicitor of Excise, and educated at the High School and the University of Edinburgh. He became missionary-assistant in Leith, and in 1838 was ordained at Kelso, in charge of the new North Parish there. In 1843 he entered the Free Church, and was for a time part-editor of the *Border Watch*, and, later, editor of the *Journal of Prophecy*; 1855–6, visited Egypt and Palestine; 1866, became minister of the Chalmers Memorial Free Church, Grange, Edinburgh; 1883, was elected Moderator of the General Assembly of his Church. He was an indefatigable writer of hymns, among his publications being *Songs for the Wilderness*, *The Bible Hymn Book*, *Hymns Original and Selected*, *The Desert of Sinai*, *Hymns of Faith and Hope*, &c.

270. *Here, O my Lord, I see thee face to face.*
492. *Fill thou my life, O Lord my God.*
529. *I heard the voice of Jesus say.*
607. *O Love of God, how strong and true.*

BORTHWICK, JANE LAURIE (Edinburgh, 1813–97, Edinburgh), was the elder daughter of James Borthwick, manager of the North British Insurance Office, Edinburgh. Along with her sister Sarah (Mrs. Findlater, q.v.) she published, in four series (1854, 1855, 1858, and 1862), *Hymns from the Land of Luther*, 69 of the translations being from her own pen, and 53 from Sarah's. The title of this book supplied the initials—H. L. L.—over which many of her hymns appeared in the *Family Treasury*. These were collected and published in 1857 as *Thoughts for Thoughtful Hours*. A further collection of translations, under the title *Alpine Lyrics*, consisting of a selection of the poems of Meta Heusser-Schweitzer, was published in 1875.

471. *Come, labour on!*

BOURGEOIS, LOUIS (Paris, *c.* 1510– ?), was an adherent of Calvin, and followed him to Geneva in 1541. The Consistory appointed him cantor in one of the churches there, and in 1545 master of the choristers in succession to Guillaume Franc. They also entrusted him with the duty of providing music for the metrical psalter, then under gradual preparation. A partial psalter appeared in 1542. In this Bourgeois made alterations in some of the tunes hitherto in use, and replaced some of the old tunes with others quite different. He seems to have been concerned in the music of all editions of the psalter appearing within the following fifteen years. In 1547 there was printed at Lyons *Pseaulmes cinquante de David Roy et Prophete, traduictz en vers françois par Clement Marot, et mis en musique par Loys Bourgeoys à quatre parties, à voix de contrepoinct égal consonnante au verbe. Tousiours mord envie.* This volume seems to embrace the whole of Bourgeois's work on the psalms to this date. It is not certain whether the melodies were composed by Bourgeois, or merely arranged by him in four-part harmony. Towards the end of 1551 he was thrown into prison for making unauthorized alterations in certain well-known tunes. Calvin, albeit remonstrating with him, secured his release after 24 hours. But other troubles followed, and finally, failing to induce his employers to allow the introduction of part-singing into public worship, he left Geneva and returned to Paris. From 1561, when he was still there, he vanishes from history. He had found in use at Geneva a psalter with about 30 tunes; he left one with 85, many of them, probably, his own. The alterations for which he was imprisoned ultimately received official sanction and passed into general use. Dr. Robert Bridges says, 'Historians who wish to give a true philosophical account of Calvin's influence at Geneva ought probably to refer a great part of it to the enthusiasm attendant on the singing of Bourgeois's melodies.'

50. NUNC DIMITTIS.
56 (i). LES COMMANDEMENS DE DIEU.
121. MON DIEU, PRÊTE-MOI L'OREILLE.
265. RENDEZ À DIEU
291. PSALM 42.
347. L'OMNIPOTENT.

BOURNE, George Hugh, D.C.L. (St. Paul's Cray, Kent, 1840–1925), son of the Rev. R. B. Bourne, was educated at Eton and Christ Church, Oxford; B.A. 1863; B.C.L. 1866; D.C.L. 1871. He took Holy Orders in 1863, and the same year became curate of Sandford-on-Thames Subsequently he became Head Master of Chardstock College, and in 1886 warden of that school at St. Edmund's, Salisbury, whither it had been transferred.

274. *Lord, enthroned in heavenly splendour.*

BOWIE, Walter Russell, D.D. (Richmond, Virginia, 1882–), was educated at Hill School, Pottstown, Pa., and Harvard University, and became rector of Grace Church, New York. He has published, *The Children's Year*, *The Master of the Hill*, *Sunny Windows*, *The Inescapable Christ*, *A Life of Jesus*, *When Jesus was Born*, and some shorter works.

562. *Lord Christ, when first thou cam'st to men.*

BOYCE, William, Mus.Doc. (London, 1710–79, London), was the son of a cabinet-maker, and became a chorister of St. Paul's. In his youth his hearing became impaired, but this did not lessen the ardour of his studies. He became organist of several London churches; conductor of the Three Choirs of Gloucester, Worcester, and Hereford; Composer to the Chapel Royal; Master of the King's Band; one of the organists of the Chapel Royal. His deafness so increased that he had to give up teaching and relinquish some of his offices. He then employed himself in collecting and editing materials for the work by which he is best known, *Cathedral Music, being a Collection in score of the most valuable and useful compositions for that service by the several English masters of the last two hundred years* (1760). He published 46 anthems, 5 services, 8 symphonies, 12 sonatas, duets and songs, including *Heart of Oak*, and music for the theatre. An amiable man, of blameless life, and an excellent musician, he may be regarded as the last of the old English school of church composers. He was buried in a vault under the centre of the dome of St. Paul's.

375. BOYCE. 452. KINGSLAND.

BOYLE, Ina (Enniskerry, Co. Wicklow, 1889–), daughter of the Rev. W. F. Boyle, studied privately, first with Charles Wood, then with P. C. Buck and C. H. Kitson in Dublin, and finally with R. Vaughan Williams in London. Among her published compositions are *Soldiers at Peace*, for chorus and orchestra, performed in Ireland; *The Magic Harp*, a rhapsody for orchestra, which won a Carnegie Award, and has been frequently performed in London and elsewhere; a set of *Gaelic Hymns*, for unaccompanied choir, performed by the Oriana Madrigal Society in 1931; and several songs and anthems, &c.; many considerable works still remain in manuscript.

240. ENNISKERRY.

BRADBY, Godfrey Fox, M.A. (1863–), son of the Rev. E. H. Bradby, D.D., former Head Master of Haileybury College, was educated at Rugby and Balliol and became an assistant master at Rugby from 1888 to 1920, in which year he retired. His publications are: *The Great Days of Versailles*; *About Shakespeare and his Plays*; *About English Poetry*;

Christianity and Common Sense, &c.; a few novels; and *Hymns without Tunes*.

296. *Where is death's sting? We were not born to die.*

BRADY, Nicholas (Bandon, 1659–1726?). Received the degree of D.D. from Dublin University for services rendered to the Protestant cause and became prebendary of Cork. He was educated at Westminster and Christ Church, Oxford, and Trinity College, Dublin, was an active supporter of William III, and three times saved his native town from being put to the fire. He became a chaplain to the King and, 1702–5, incumbent of Stratford-on-Avon, and held many appointments. He published several volumes of sermons, a tragedy, *The Rape, or the Innocent Impostors*, and *A poetical translation of the Aeneid of Virgil* (4 vols.); and, with Nahum Tate, the *New Version of the Psalms* (1696). Pope had Tate and Brady in mind when, in the *Essay on Criticism*, he wrote,

And ten low words oft creep in one dull line.

449. *As pants the hart for cooling streams.*
677. *Through all the changing scenes of life.*

BRAHMS, Johannes (Hamburg, 1833–97, Vienna), son of Johann Jakob Brahms, studied first with O. Cossel, and later with the renowned Marxsen of Altona. His main study at this early period was the pianoforte, and as a pianist he made appearances at concerts in 1848, 1849, and 1850. In 1853 he accompanied Eudard Remcuyi, the gipsy violinist, on a tour, during which Brahms met Joachim, who encouraged and helped him by introductions to Liszt and Schumann, from which time his fame became established. He held three appointments during his life, 1854–9 as court director of music to the Prince of Lippe-Detmold, 1862–3 as conductor of the Singakademie in Vienna, 1872–5 as conductor to the Gesellschaft der Musikfreunde. Apart from these his life was devoted to the production of music, in composition or performance, and passed without other than domestic events. He composed in all forms of music except opera, and the list of his work contains 121 opus numbers.

*667. ICH FAHR DAHIN.

BRAILSFORD, Edward John (Birmingham, 1841–1921), son of C. J. Brailsford, was educated at Didsbury College for the Wesleyan Ministry. He first held office at Bangor and Carnarvon, 1863, and later held important appointments at Liverpool, London, Bolton, Ilkley, Edinburgh, &c.

445. *All things which live below the sky.*

BREMNER, Robert (Edinburgh, 1720–89, London), was a music publisher, first in Edinburgh, and, later, with head-quarters in London. He published many collections of Scottish music, and a very successful little book, *The Rudiments of Music*. After his removal to London he extended his business, and published a very large quantity of all kinds of music; his Scottish collections remain, however, the most important.

320. ABERDEEN.

BRIDGES, Matthew (Maldon, Essex, 1800–94, Quebec), the younger son of John Bridges of Wallington House, Surrey, published *Jerusalem regained, a Poem*, in 1825, and in 1828 a book on *The Roman Empire under Constantine the Great*. He entered the Roman Church in 1848, and spent the latter part of his life in Canada. His later publications were: *Babbicombe, or Visions of Memory, and Other Poems* (1842); *Hymns of the Heart* (1847); *The Passion of Jesus* (1852); and *Popular Ancient and Modern Histories*.

254. *My God, accept my heart this day.*

BRIDGES, Robert (Seymour), M.A., M.B., F.R.C.P. (Walmer, Kent, 1844–1930, Boar's Hill, Oxford), son of a Kentish squire, was educated at Eton and Corpus Christi College, Oxford (Hon. Fellow). On leaving the University he travelled on the Continent and in the East, then studied medicine at St. Bartholomew's Hospital, London. On qualifying, he became casualty physician there, and physician at the Great Northern Hospital, and also carried on general practice. He gave up practice in 1882, and settled at Yattendon in Berkshire, and devoted himself to literature, in which he had already made his mark as a poet of unusual and highly distinctive gifts. He was appointed Poet Laureate in 1913. He was a scholar of great learning, both in ancient and modern letters, and a highly skilled and cultivated musician. His *Eros and Psyche* is dedicated to the celestial spirit of Henry Purcell, and in *The Christian Captives* he introduces the music of Anerio and Allegri. He wrote an oratorio, *Eden*, which Sir C. V. Stanford set to music. And his *Yattendon Hymnal*—issued in instalments (words and music) of 40 pages, till the 100 hymns were completed in 1899—is, both in words and music, easily the most distinguished of individual pioneer contributions to modern hymnody.

33. *O splendour of God's glory bright.*
50. *O gladsome light, O grace.*
57. *The duteous day now closeth.*
99. *Ah, holy Jesus, how hast thou offended.*
128. *O sacred head, sore wounded.*
179. *Come, O creator Spirit, come.*
208. *Rejoice, ye dead, where'er your spirits dwell.*
245. *Christ hath a garden walled around.*
291. *Joy and triumph everlasting.*
324. *The King, O God, his heart to thee upraiseth.*
442. *All my hope on God is founded.*
483. *Enter thy courts, thou word of life.*
484. *Eternal Father, who didst all create.*
498. *Gird on thy sword, O man, thy strength endue.*
509. *Happy are they, they that love God.*
574. *Love of the Father, Love of God the Son.*
584. *My Lord, my Life, my Love.*
631. *Rejoice, O land, in God thy might.*
661. *Thee will I love, my God and King.*

BRIGGS, George Wallace (1875–   ), was a scholar of Emmanuel College, Cambridge, where he took a first class in the Classical Tripos in 1897. For six years he was a chaplain in the Royal Navy; 1909–18, vicar of St. Andrew's, Norwich; 1918, rector of Loughborough, and, later, canon of Leicester; 1920, select preacher, Cambridge. He is a Proctor in Convocation of Canterbury, and has served on many committees of the Church Assembly; is widely involved in educational work, especially in publication of books of prayers and hymns for schools, and was a sub-editor of *The Little Bible*, and author of several articles in the Appendix of that work.

194 (ii). LOUGHBOROUGH. 243. LOUGHBOROUGH COLLEGE.
360. SPRINGTIME. 401. WULFRUN. 439. ST. FRANCIS.
501 (ii). DAVID. 572. ST. MARTIN. App. 3 (i). AMEN.

60. *Christ is the world's true light.*
109. *Lord, who hast made me free.*
194. *Our Father, by whose servants.*
243. *For the brave of every race.*
266. *Come, risen Lord, and deign to be our guest.*
275. *O God, in whom we live and move.*
337. *Lord, in the hollow of thy hand.*
357. *God, my Father, loving me.*
360. *Hark! a hundred notes are swelling.*
361. *I love God's tiny creatures.*
400. *Dear Father, keep me through this day.*
403. *Our Father, for our daily bread.*
566. *Lord of all majesty and might.*
572. *Lord, who thyself hast bidden us to pray.*
638. *Shall God not share.*
660. *The Spirit of the Lord revealed.*

BRIGHT, William, D.D. (Doncaster, 1824–1901, Oxford), was educated at University College, Oxford, and became a Fellow of his college. Ordained in 1848, he became theological tutor at Glenalmond College, Perthshire; tutor of University College, Oxford; hon. canon of Cumbrae Cathedral, 1865–93; canon of Christ Church, Oxford, and Regius Professor of Ecclesiastical History, 1868. Among his historical works were: *A History of the Church from the Edict of Milan to the Council of Chalcedon* (1860); *Chapters of Early English History* (1877); he also edited *Eusebius' Ecclesiastical History* (1872); *Socrates' Ecclesiastical History*; and a *Latin Version of the Prayer Book*. His poetical works were: *Athanasius, and Other Poems, by a Fellow of a College* (1858); and *Hymns and Other Poems* (1866).

24. *At thy feet, O Christ, we lay.*
41. *And now the wants are told that brought.*
237. *He sat to watch o'er customs paid.*
261. *And now, O Father, mindful of the love.*

BRONTË, Anne (Thornton, near Bradford, 1819–49, Haworth), sister of Charlotte and Emily, and daughter of the Rev. Patrick Brontë, B.A., vicar of Haworth, Yorkshire. Joint author with her sisters of a book of *Poems* (1846); author of *Agnes Grey* (1847); *The Tenant of Wildfell Hall* (1847); (pseudonym, Acton Bell).

453. *Believe not those who say.*

BRONTË, Emily Jane (Thornton, 1818–48, Haworth, Yorkshire), sister of the above, collaborated with her sisters in *Poems by Currer, Ellis and Acton Bell* (1846), taking the pseudonym Ellis Bell.

She is regarded by many as the ablest of the three illustrious sisters. She published *Wuthering Heights* in 1848, the year of her death.

588. *No coward soul is mine.*

BROOKE, Stopford Augustus, LL.D. (Glendoen, Letterkenny, Donegal, 1832-1916, Ewhurst, Guildford), was educated at Kingstown,

Kidderminster, and Trinity College, Dublin. On taking Orders, in London in 1857, he accepted a curacy at St. Matthew's, Marylebone; then another at St. Mary Abbott's, Kensington. From 1862 to 1865 he was chaplain to the British Embassy in Berlin. Returning to London, he took a lease of St. James's (proprietary) Chapel, York Street, then derelict, and in a short time crowded it to the doors. His *Life and Letters of F. W. Robertson* (1865) took rank at once as a classic biography, and brought him great reputation, which was enhanced by his first volume of *Sermons* (1869), and his *Theology in the English Poets*. He was now one of the foremost of London preachers, and in 1867 was appointed chaplain to the Queen. Her Majesty was eager to give him a canonry of Westminster, but his liberal views made the appointment impossible. On the expiry of the lease of St. James's Chapel, his services were transferred to Bedford Chapel, which was proprietary also, and there he ministered till his retirement in 1894. In 1880 he resigned his Orders, and thenceforward he occupied an independent position, retaining in the main the Church of England service, but having close relations with the Unitarians. At this time he prepared for his congregation a collection entitled *Christian Hymns*, containing some fine compositions of his own, along with many standard hymns freely altered to suit his doctrinal position. After his retirement from the ministry, through ill health, he preached and lectured from time to time, but for the most part devoted himself to literary work.

539. *It fell upon a summer day.*
558. *Let the whole creation cry.*

BROOKS, PHILLIPS, D.D. (Boston, 1835–93, Boston), studied at Harvard, where he was deeply influenced by the works of Emerson and Theodore Parker. On graduating he tried teaching, in the Boston Latin School, but proved 'a conspicuous failure'. He then studied at the Episcopal Theological Seminary at Alexandria, Virginia. Ordained in 1859, he became rector of the Church of the Advent, Philadelphia; then of Holy Trinity, Philadelphia; then of the famous Trinity Church, Boston; and finally, in 1891, after refusing the office of preacher at Harvard, professorships, and the assistant bishopric of Pennsylvania, he was elected bishop of Massachusetts. He was one of the most distinguished of modern preachers.

79. *O little town of Bethlehem.*

BROWNE, Sir THOMAS (London, 1605–82, Norwich), was educated at Winchester and the Hall (now Pembroke College), Oxford, and took his B.A. degree in 1626. He practised medicine in Oxfordshire, Shipden Hall, Yorkshire, and Norwich. He wrote many scientific and antiquarian works, but his *Religio Medici* is his best-known book.

58. *The night is come like to the day.*

BROWNE, THOMAS BRIERLY (1805–74), published, among other works, a volume entitled *The National Bankruptcy and other Poems* (1844), which contained the subjoined stanza.

414. *Praise the Lord of heaven; praise him in the height.*

BROWNING, ROBERT (London, 1812–89, Venice), was educated at Peckham, and privately, he then studied Greek at University College, London, 1829–30. While still in early youth he composed a number of poems. Published *Pauline* (1832), produced *Paracelsus* (1835), and therewith attracted the notice of Carlyle, Wordsworth, Dickens, and other men of letters. His tragedies *Strafford* and *A Blot in the 'Scutcheon* were produced by Macready. He published *Sordello* (1840) and subsequently many other poems now famous. He was made an Hon. M.A. of Oxford in 1868, and Hon. LL.D. of Edinburgh University in 1864. He was buried in Westminster Abbey.

6. *The year's at the spring.*
662. *Then welcome each rebuff.*
667. *There's heaven above, and night by night.*

BRYAN, Joseph (*c.* 1620), contributed 22 Psalms to the collection of Psalms by the co-workers, Francis Davison, Christopher Davison, Richard Gipps, T. Carey, and J. Bryan. Little else is known about him.

121. *To my humble supplication.*

BUCK, Percy Carter, Mus.Doc. (West Ham, Essex, 1871–1947), was educated at the Guildhall School of Music and the Royal College of Music. He became organist of Worcester College, Oxford, 1891; of Wells Cathedral, 1895; of Bristol Cathedral, 1900; musical director of Harrow School, in succession to Eaton Faning, 1901; Professor of Music, Trinity College, Dublin, 1910–20; first Cramb Lecturer, Glasgow University, 1923; since 1925, King Edward VII Professor of Music, University of London; and is musical adviser to the L.C.C. He has published three organ sonatas; several choral works and school songs; two organ manuals; *Unfigured Harmony* (1911); *Acoustics for Musicians* (1918).

148 (ii). MONT RICHARD.
247. MARTINS.
593. GONFALON ROYAL.

BUCKOLL, Henry James, M.A. (Siddington, near Cirencester, 1803–71, Rugby), was educated at Rugby and Queen's College, Oxford. On graduating in 1826 he became an assistant master in his old school, and is believed to have been the first editor of the Rugby School *Collection of Hymns*. In 1893 he edited a *Collection* for Rugby parish church; in 1842 published *Hymns Translated from the German*, taken from Bunsen's *Versuch eines allgemeines Evangelischen Gesang- und Gebetsbuch* (1833); and in 1850, with Dean Goulburn, a new edition of the Rugby School *Collection*, in which 14 of his own hymns appeared.

32. *Now the morn new light is pouring.*
333. *Lord, behold us with thy blessing.*

BULLOCK, Ernest, Mus.Doc. (Wigan, 1890–), son of Thomas Bullock, was educated at Wigan Grammar School and privately, and received his musical training from Dr. E. C. Bairstow (q.v.) at Leeds parish church, where he became assistant organist, and organist of St. Mary, Micklefield, and Adel Church in 1906; in 1912 he became sub-organist of Manchester Cathedral; from 1915 to 1919 served in H.M. forces as Captain and Adjutant, after which he was appointed organist, in 1919, of St. Michael's College, Tenbury, and from 1919 to 1928 of Exeter Cathedral. Since 1928 he has been organist and master of the choristers of Westminster Abbey. He has published songs, part-songs, and church and organ music.

*46. AR HYD Y NOS. *216. OLD 81ST (OLD 77TH). 590. BERRY DOWN.

BULLOCK, WILLIAM, D.D. (Prettiwell, Apex, 1798–1874, Halifax, Nova Scotia), was educated at Christ's Hospital, then entered the Royal Navy. While serving under his brother, Admiral Frederic Bullock, on a survey of the coast of Newfoundland, he resolved to take Holy Orders and to become a missionary in that colony, and served there for 32 years under the Society for Propagating the Gospel. He became dean of Nova Scotia, at Halifax, where he published in 1854 his *Songs of the Church.*

688. *We love the place, O God.*

BUNYAN, JOHN (Elstow, 1628–88, London), was the son of a tinker, and educated at the village school. The autobiographical *Grace Abounding* gives some account of his early life and spiritual struggles. He served for a short term in the Parliamentary army, and later joined a religious community founded by John Gifford, and became an itinerant preacher. After the Restoration he was imprisoned until 1671, in which time he wrote many pamphlets, and in 1675, during a second term of mild imprisonment, began *The Pilgrim's Progress*, which, printed in 1678, won a position perhaps second only to the Bible. He later published *The Holy War* (1682) and the second part of *The Pilgrim's Progress* (1684). He was buried in Bunhill Fields.

513. *He that is down need fear no fall.*
515. *He who would valiant be.*

BURKITT, FRANCIS CRAWFORD, F.B.A., D.D. (London, 1864–1935), was educated at Harrow and Trinity College, Cambridge, Wrangler (1886); First class Theological Tripos, 1888. He won may academic distinctions, and later he has received honorary degrees from the Universities of Edinburgh, Dublin, St. Andrews, and Oxford. Since 1905 he has been Professor of Divinity in Cambridge University, where in 1926 he became a Fellow of Trinity College. Author of many linguistic and theological works, he wrote *Three Hymns for Whitsuntide*, composing both the words and the music.

183. *Our Lord, his Passion ended.*

BURLEIGH, WILLIAM HENRY (Woodstock, Connecticut, 1812–71, Brooklyn), was descended on his mother's side from Governor Bradford of the *Mayflower*. Brought up on a farm at Plainfield, Connecticut, he went in 1837 to Pittsburg, Pennsylvania, and was apprenticed to the printing trade. Then journalism claimed him. He published *The Christian Witness* and *The Temperance Banner*, being an enthusiastic reformer. In 1843 he became editor of *The Christian Freeman*, an abolitionist journal, at Hartford, Conn. Thereafter he spent some years at Syracuse as editor, lecturer, and secretary of the New York State Temperance Society. His last appointment was as harbour-master of New York. In religion he was a Unitarian. His *Poems*, collected from periodicals, were published in 1841, and in an enlarged edition in the year of his death. His wife, Mrs. Celia Burleigh, wrote his *Life*, and added a number of his poems to it.

102. *Lead us, O Father, in the paths of peace.*

BURROUGHS, EDWARD ARTHUR, M.A., D.D. (Kingstown, Co. Dublin, 1882–1934), son of Preb. W. E. Burroughs, was educated at Harrow and Balliol College, Oxford, where he won the Hertford and Craven Scholarships, and many other distinctions. He was Fellow and tutor of Hertford College; was select preacher at Cambridge, 1915, and at Oxford, 1916; canon of Peterborough and chaplain to the King, 1917–22; dean of Bristol, 1922–6, and became bishop of Ripon in 1926. Among his many publications are *Faith and Power*; *A Faith for the Firing Line*; *The Patience of God*; *Latin Culture*, &c.

343. *Lord God, from whom all life.*

BUTLER, HENRY MONTAGU (Gayton, Northamptonshire, 1833–1918, Cambridge), son of Dr. George Butler, Head Master of Harrow, was educated at Harrow and Trinity College, Cambridge, where he won many prizes, and, in 1855, became a Fellow of his college. In 1856 he was private secretary to William Francis Cooper, and also to the royal commission for rebuilding the National Gallery. After a year's travel he became a curate at Great St. Mary's, Cambridge, but shortly afterwards, in 1859, was elected Head Master of Harrow. In 1885 he was appointed dean of Gloucester, and in 1886 became Master of Trinity College, Cambridge, where he remained till his death, being Vice-Chancellor in 1889–90. Among his publications were *Ten Great and Good Men*; *Some Leisure Hours of a Long Life*; volumes of sermons, &c.

560. *'Lift up your hearts!' We lift them, Lord, to thee.*

BYRD, WILLIAM (? Lincoln, 1542–1623, London), was one of the most illustrious figures of an age in which the musical glory of this country was at its height. Part of his training he received from Tallis, with whom he was associated in the sole right, granted to them by royal patent, to print music and ruled music paper—a venture which landed both in heavy loss. About 1563 he became organist of Lincoln Cathedral, and in 1569 a member of the Chapel Royal. After the Reformation he stood out as a Papist, and though allowed to continue in office in the Chapel Royal, he was often in trouble because of his religion: it is on record that his wife was arraigned on a charge of proselytizing, and that his family were excommunicated for at least seven years. He wrote much for the Roman services. He was an organist of distinction, and one of the first of the great madrigalists, but it is his religious music that establishes his title to be accounted one of the greatest of English composers.

App. 3 (ii) & (vi). AMEN.

BYROM, JOHN (Kersall, near Manchester, 1692–1763, Manchester), son of a Manchester tradesman of good family, was educated at Merchant Taylors' School and Trinity College, Cambridge, of which he became a Fellow in 1714. In 1716 he travelled abroad and studied medicine at Montpellier, but never practised or took a medical degree. Until his fortunes improved by succession to the family estates, Byrom maintained himself by teaching a system of shorthand of his own invention, which attained considerable popularity. His poems were first published in 1793.

73. *Christians, awake.*
111. *My spirit longs for thee.*

CALVISIUS, SETH (Gorsleben, 1556–1615, Leipzig), was born of poor parents, but succeeded in obtaining an education at the Magdeburg Gymnasium, and the Universities of Helmstedt and Leipzig. In 1581 he was appointed repetent at the Pauliner Church, Leipzig, in 1582 cantor at Schulpforte, and in 1594 cantor and Schulcollege at the Thomasschule and music director at the Thomaskirche of that city. He was an astronomer and chronologer, besides being a musician, but music was his first love, and for her sake he refused the Chair of Mathematics at Wittenberg in 1611. He wrote treatises on the theory of music and published several collections of his own and others' music, the most important being *Hymni sacri latini et germanici* (1594), and *Harmonia cantionum a M. Luthero . . . compositarum* (1597).

42 (i). CALVISIUS (ACH BLEIB BEI UNS).

CAMPBELL, JANE MONTGOMERY (Paddington, London, 1817–78, Bovey Tracey, South Devon), was a daughter of the rector of St. James's, Paddington, and taught singing to the children of her father's parish school. At Bovey Tracey she gave valuable help to the Rev. Charles S. Bere in the compilation of his *Garland of Songs, or an English Liederkranz* (1862), and his *Children's Chorale Book* (1869). To these she contributed a number of excellent translations. She published also *A Handbook for Singers*, embodying the musical exercises she had made use of in her work among London children.

14. *We plough the fields, and scatter.*

CAMPBELL, THOMAS (Glasgow, 1777–1844, Boulogne), was educated at the Glasgow Grammar School. His literary fame no longer rests on his poem *The Pleasures of Hope*, or even on *Gertrude of Wyoming*, but on his battle-poems, 'Of Nelson and the North', 'Hohenlinden', 'Ye Mariners of England', and in a lesser degree on the ballads, 'Lord Ullin's Daughter' and 'The Maid of Neidpath'. He wrote a *Life of Mrs. Siddons*, and a *Life of Petrarch*. In 1832 he founded the Polish Association to interest Englishmen in the welfare of Poland. He was buried near Goldsmith in Westminster Abbey.

321. *Men of England, who inherit.*

CAMPIAN, THOMAS, M.D. (Witham, Essex, *c.* 1575–1619, London), physician, poet, dramatist, musician, was of French descent, his father having been organist in a Paris church for many years. He studied at Cambridge and abroad, left Gray's Inn and the law for medicine, received his degree from some foreign university, and practised his profession in London to the end of his life. But he found time to write four masques, many fine lyrics, and much good music. In 1595 he published a small book of Latin elegiacs and epigrams; in 1602 *Observations on the Art of English Poesie*, in which he disparaged 'the childish titillation of riming' and advocated unrhymed verse; in 1606–7 the first of his masques, before James I at Whitehall; in 1610, he being now a recognized authority on music, *Two Bookes of Ayres*, being songs with accompaniments many of them to music of his own; then in 1612–13, *A New Way of making foure parts in Counterpoint, by a most familiar and infallible rule, with some other Discourses on the Theory of Music.*

124. BABYLON'S STREAMS.
587. WEATHER-BEATEN SAIL.
639. SONG OF JOY.

587. *Never weather-beaten sail.*
639. *Sing a song of joy.*

CANTON, William (Isle of Chusan, off coast of China, 1845–1926, Hendon), spent the greater part of his childhood in Jamaica. He was educated in France. His first book of poems was *A Lost Epic, and Other Poems*. For many years journalism engaged Canton, as sub-editor and leader-writer on the *Glasgow Herald*, then as sub-editor of the *Contemporary Review*. He acted also as manager of Isbister & Co., publishers. His best-known books were *The Invisible Playmate*; *W. V., her Book and Various Verses*; *In Memory of W. V.*; *Children's Sayings*; and *A Child's Book of Saints*. He also published *The Crusader, Poems of Old and New*; *A Child's Book of Warriors*; and *The Story of Elizabeth of Hungary*. He spent years on the monumental centenary *History of the British and Foreign Bible Society*, in four volumes, and for more popular use wrote also *The Bible and the Anglo-Saxon People* and *The Bible Story*.

375. *Through the night thy angels kept.*
379. *When the herds were watching.*
519. *Hold thou my hands.*

CAREY, Henry (? 1692–1743, Clerkenwell), is said to have been the son of George Saville, Marquis of Halifax, and of a schoolmistress. His chief occupation was that of teaching in boarding schools and private families. He was a prolific author of burlesques, farces, ballad operas, and vivacious poems and songs, the best known being *Sally in our Alley*. His musical knowledge was slight, but he had a high inventive faculty, and composed successfully the music for a number of his songs. He was only incidentally a writer of church music. The authorship of *God save the King* has been attributed to him, but without sufficient grounds. He collected and published his songs in 1740—*The Musical Century, One Hundred English Ballads on various important Occasions*; and his dramatic works appeared in 1743.

550. OSBORNE. 656. SURREY.

CARLYLE, Joseph Dacre, B.D. (Carlisle, 1758–1804, in Syria), was sometime Professor of Arabic at the University of Cambridge, and afterwards vicar of Newcastle-on-Tyne. In 1799 he went with the Earl of Elgin to Constantinople to examine the literary treasures in the Public Library and extended his journey to Asia Minor and the Islands of the Archipelago. He published *Specimens of Arabian Poetry* (1796); and Susanna Maria Carlyle published in 1805 his *Poems suggested chiefly by scenes in Asia Minor, Syria, &c.* His hymns are in J. Fawcett's *Psalms and Hymns*.

108. *Lord, when we bend before thy throne.*

CARLYLE, Thomas (Ecclefechan, 1795–1881, Chelsea), second son of a stonemason, was educated at Annan Academy and the University of Edinburgh. He began study for the ministry, but abandoned this, tried schoolmastering, and then the law, finally settling down to literature as a profession. His subjects included history, biography, politics, criticism, poetry, philosophy and religion, and, in later life, he became one of the greatest literary figures of the Victorian age. In 1865 he was elected Lord Rector of the University of Edinburgh, and in 1874 was offered the G.C.B. or a baronetcy, with a pension, but declined the honour. A burial in Westminster Abbey was also offered, but, in accordance with his wishes, he was buried in his native village. His best-known works are *Sartor Resartus*; *Frederick the Great*; *Heroes and Hero-Worship*; and *The French Revolution*.

34. *So here hath been dawning.*
436. *A safe stronghold our God is still.*

CARNEY, JULIA ABIGAIL, *née* FLETCHER (Boston, 1823–1908), was a contributor to various periodicals, and for some time a teacher in a Boston (U.S.A.) Primary School. Her main claim to fame, however, seems to be the subjoined hymn.

365. *Little drops of water.*

CARPENTER, EDWARD (Brighton, 1844–1929, Guildford), was educated at Brighton College and Trinity Hall, Cambridge, with an interval of some months in Germany. In 1870 he was ordained, and became curate to Frederick Denison Maurice, but shortly afterwards, feeling himself unfitted for the Church, left it, and devoted himself to lecturing. He was much influenced by Walt Whitman, and from 1881, for some ten years, worked as a manual labourer. His life thereafter was devoted to social reform and the furtherance of democratic ideas, both by his writings, lectures, and in more practical ways. His chief publications were *Narcissus and other Poems* (1873); *Towards Democracy* (1883), and the complete edition (1905); *Civilization, its Cause and Cure* (1889); *Love's Coming-of-Age* (1896); *The Intermediate Sex* (1908); *My Days and Dreams* (1916), &c.; and very many pamphlets, magazine articles, &c.

316. *England, arise! the long, long night is over.*

CASWALL, EDWARD, M.A. (Yately, Hants, 1814–78, Edgbaston, Birmingham), son of a vicar of Yately, was educated at Marlborough and Brasenose College, Oxford. Taking Orders, he became perpetual curate of Stratford-sub-Castle, Wilts., in 1840, but in 1847 resigned his living and was received into the Roman Church. On his wife's death in 1850 he became a priest and entered the Oratory of St. Philip Neri, at Edgbaston, under Newman, where he remained for the rest of his life. He also engaged himself to translate the early Latin hymns in the Roman Breviaries, and published *Lyra Catholica* (1849); *The Masque of Mary, and other Poems* (1858); *A May Pageant and other Poems* (1865); and *Hymns and other Poems* (1863).

84. *Bethlehem, of noblest cities.*
547. *Jesu, the very thought of thee.*
696. *When morning gilds the skies.*

CENNICK, JOHN (Reading, 1718–55, London), belonged to a family of Quakers, but was brought up in the Church of England. His name (originally Cennik) proclaims him of Bohemian stock. At one time a land-surveyor at Reading, he became acquainted with the Wesleys, and was appointed by John Wesley teacher of a school for colliers' children at Kingswood, and subsequently the first lay preacher among the Methodists. Parting from the Wesleys on doctrinal grounds, he came for a time under the influence of Whitefield, but ultimately joined the Moravian Brethren, in whose service he spent some time in Germany and North Ireland.

463. *Children of the heavenly King.*

CHADWICK, JOHN WHITE, M.A. (Marblehead, Massachusetts, 1840–1904, Brooklyn, New York), graduated at the Divinity School, Cambridge, Mass., in 1864, and received the M.A. degree from Harvard in 1888. He was minister of the Second Unitarian Church, Brooklyn, N.Y., from 1864. He wrote a *Life of Theodore Parker* and a *Life of William Ellery Channing*; was a frequent contributor of poems to periodicals like *Harpers' Magazine*; and published *A Book of Poems* (1876); *In Nazareth Town, and Other Poems* (1883); *A Legend of Good Poets* (1885); *A Few Verses* (1900); and his *Sermons*, issued in successive series.

485. *Eternal Ruler of the ceaseless round.*

CHANDLER, JOHN, M.A. (Witley, Godalming, Surrey, 1806–76, Putney), was educated at Corpus Christi College, Oxford. Ordained in 1831, he succeeded his father as patron and vicar of Witley. He produced *The Hymns of the Primitive Church, now first Collected, Translated and Arranged* (1837); and *Hymns of the Church most Primitive, Collected, Translated and Arranged for Public Use* (1841)—the previous work revised and altered. He wrote also a *Life of William of Wykeham* and *Horae Sacrae, Prayers and Meditations from the Writings of the Divines of the Anglican Church, with Introduction* (1854); and many sermons and tracts. See also under 35.

464. *Christ is our corner-stone.*

CHAPMAN, T. (18th century), published *The Young Gentleman and Ladies' Musical Companion* (2 vols., 1772 and 1774), which contained a variety of hymn-tunes, &c., by different composers.

612. MONTGOMERY.

CHATFIELD, ALLEN WILLIAM, B.A. (Chatteris, 1808–96, Much Marcle), son of a vicar of Chatteris, was educated at Charterhouse and Trinity College, Cambridge, where he graduated in 1831 with first class classical honours. Ordained in 1832, he became vicar of Stotfold, Bedfordshire, and, in 1848, of Much Marcle, Herefordshire. His most notable work was his rendering into Greek, in various metres, of the Litany, the Te Deum, and other parts of the English Church Offices. He published also *Songs and Hymns of the Earliest Christian Poets, Bishops and Others, translated into English Verse* (1876).

106. *Lord Jesus, think on me.*

CHESTERTON, GILBERT KEITH (Kensington, 1874–1936), was educated at St. Paul's School, London. He attended classes at the Slade School of Art, but, beginning to contribute art criticisms and reviews to the *Bookman* and the *Speaker*, found his way into journalism. He has been one of the most vivacious, versatile, and provocative figures in that field ever since. There is no more effective critic of other people's beliefs, but he is curiously uncritical in the exposition and defence of his own. Long a pillar of orthodoxy, he became a Roman Catholic under the influence of the ultramontane Hilaire Belloc. In the teeth of history he was persuaded that the medieval 'ages of faith' were Europe's halcyon age, and that only a return to the Roman obedience would destroy what remains of Puritanism and bring 'merrie England' back, and that the resuscitation of the medieval trade-guild system is the cure for modern industrial ills. His

Short History of England is really a perversion of history in support of these odd prepossessions.

308. *O God of earth and altar.*

CHETHAM, John (*c.* 1700–63, Skipton), was a musician and clergyman who became master of the Clerk's School, Skipton, in 1737, and curate of Skipton two years later. *A Book of Psalmody, all set in four parts* was published by him in 1718. It was very widely adopted, ran through many editions, and continued in use for a century and a half. It is surmised that he may have himself composed some of the anonymous tunes in the first edition that are not traceable to any other source.

120 (i). WIRKSWORTH. 596 BURFORD.

CLARK, Jeremiah (London, *c.* 1670–1707, London), was a chorister of the Chapel Royal under Dr. John Blow; organist of Winchester College (1692–5); organist of St. Paul's (1695), and vicar choral (1705); joint organist, with Croft, of the Chapel Royal (1704). He was of a melancholy and sensitive temperament, which is reflected in his expressive and delicate music, and he died by his own hand. He wrote operatic and instrumental music, a cantata, songs, and many anthems and psalm-tunes.

175. ST. MAGNUS (NOTTINGHAM).
228. BROCKHAM.
474. TUNBRIDGE.
536. BISHOPTHORPE (or ST. PAUL'S).
547 (i). KING'S NORTON.
564. UFFINGHAM.

CLARK, Thomas (Canterbury, 1775–1859, Canterbury), was a cobbler by trade and a musician by talent. He was leader of psalmody first in the Wesleyan Church, Canterbury, then in a church which was originally anabaptist, and worshipped in the dilapidated monastery of the Blackfriars, which had been purchased for this purpose by Peter de la Pierre, a surgeon from Flanders. The congregation came to be called General Baptists, but by Clark's time they had drifted into Unitarianism: they were dissolved in 1913. Clark was a prolific composer of hymn-tunes, publishing over 20 sets of them. He reharmonized the 2nd edition of *The Union Tune Book* for the Sunday School Union in 1842. A revision of it in 1854 contained between 40 and 50 tunes by him. He arranged also a *Union Harmonist* in 1841.

35. CREDITON. 252. WARSAW.

CLAUDIUS, Matthias (Reinfeld, near Lübeck, Holstein, 1740–1815, Hamburg), the son of a Lutheran pastor, was educated at Jena, and lived at Wandsbeck, near Hamburg. He studied theology with a view to the ministry, but turned to law and languages. He became a journalist, and for some years edited the *Wandsbeck Messenger*. In 1776 he was appointed one of the Commissioners of Agriculture and Manufactures of Hesse Darmstadt, and, a year later, editor of the official newspaper there, but afterwards renounced his position and returned to Wandsbeck to edit the *Messenger*. In 1788 he was appointed by the Crown Prince of Denmark auditor of the Schleswig-Holstein Bank at Altona. In 1815 he retired to his daughter's home at Hamburg, where he died. His fugitive pieces appeared as *Asmus omnia sua secum portans, oder Sämmtliche Werke des Wandsbecker Bothen* (1774). Examples of his work will be found in Longfellow's *Poets and Poetry of Europe*.

14. *We plough the fields, and scatter.*

CLAYTON, Philip Thomas Byard, M.A., M.C., F.S.A. (Queensland, 1885–), youngest son of the late R. B. B. Clayton, was educated at St. Paul's School and Exeter College, Oxford. Curate of Portsea 1910 to 1914, and during the War, Brigade Chaplain to the 6th Division, he founded Talbot House, Poperinghe, and has been since 1915 Padre of Toc H. Amongst his publications we have *The Work of a Great Parish*, and *Plain Tales from Flanders*. He has also done much current social and religious writing for *The Times*.

456. *Blest be the day when moved I was.*
470. *Come, kindred, upstand in the valour of Jesus.*

CLOUGH, Arthur Hugh (Liverpool, 1819–61, Florence), was educated at Chester, Rugby, where he won distinction as scholar and athlete, and Balliol College, Oxford. He became a Fellow of Oriel, but, owing to religious scruples, resigned his Fellowship, and was for some time Warden of University Hall, London. In 1850 he resigned this post also, and went to America, where he took pupils at Cambridge, Massachusetts, did much literary work, and became intimate with Emerson and his circle. In 1853 he returned to England to take up an examinership in the Education Office, married, and continued his official duties until 1859, when his health failed. Travel in Greece, the Pyrenees, and Italy failed to restore him, and he died in Florence of paralysis, induced by malaria. He was rightly considered by his contemporaries to be one of the most brilliant intellects of his time, but died before attaining the full control of his powers. His *Poems* were collected by F. T. Palgrave in 1863, and his *Poems and Prose Remains* by his widow in 1869.

637. *Say not, 'The struggle nought availeth'.*

COBBOLD, William (Norwich, 1559/60–1639, Beccles), was born in the parish of St. Andrew, Norwich, and was organist of Norwich Cathedral from before 1599 until 1608, after which date he became a 'singing-man'. He harmonized many of the tunes in *Este's Psalter* (1592), the only other known music by him being two madrigals and an anthem.

43. OLD 18TH.

COFFIN, Charles (Buzancy, 1676–1749, Paris), succeeded the historian Rollin, in 1712, as principal of the College of Dormans-Beauvais, and in 1718 was rector of the University of Paris. *The Paris Breviary* (1736), for which book he was mainly responsible, contained a large number of his hymns, and he himself, in the same year, published 100 hymns in *Hymni Sacri Auctore Carolo Coffin*, with a preface explaining his object in writing them. See also under 35.

35. *The splendours of thy glory, Lord.*
67. *On Jordan's bank the Baptist's cry.*
68. *The advent of our God.*
509. *Happy are they, they that love God.*

COLERIDGE, Samuel Taylor (St. Mary Ottery, Devonshire, 1772–1834, Highgate, London), was educated at Christ's Hospital and Jesus College, Cambridge. For a time he enlisted as a private in the army, but was soon discovered and restored to his friends. He was one of the most brilliant and versatile intellects of his day, but ill health and his consequent addiction to opium, combined with an unfortunate marriage to prevent the true fulfilment of the extraordinary powers shown in some of his metaphysical speculations, and the famous poems, such as *The Ancient Mariner*, *Kubla Khan*, &c. From 1795, for three years, he lived at Nether Stowey, in the constant companionship of the Wordsworths. From 1813 to 1834 he lived with his friend Gilman at Highgate. Among his publications, besides his *Poems* (1794) and (with Wordsworth) *Lyrical Ballads* (1798), were *Table Talk* and *Notes on Shakespeare and the Dramatists* (edited by his daughter); *Biographia Literaria*; *Lay Sermons*; *Confessions of an Inquiring Spirit*.

613. *O sweeter than the marriage-feast.*

CONDER, Josiah (Aldersgate, London, 1789–1855, St. John's Wood, London), was the son of an engraver and bookseller. At 15 he became assistant in his father's bookshop. In his 17th year he began a long correspondence with Ann and Jane Taylor, and he joined them and others in publishing, five years later, *The Associate Minstrels*. For 20 years he owned and edited the *Eclectic Review*; he edited also the *Patriot* newspaper. Among his many works were—*The Modern Traveller*, a compilation in 30 volumes which cost him seven years' labour; a *Dictionary of Ancient and Modern Geography*; a *Life of Bunyan*; *Protestant Nonconformity*; *Sacred Poems*, *Domestic Poems*, *Miscellaneous Poems*; *The Choir and the Oratory, or, Praise and Prayer*; *Hymns of Praise, Prayer, and Devout Meditation* (a collection of his poems and hymns personally revised, but published after his death). For the Congregational Union he edited their first official hymn-book, *The Congregational Hymn Book, A Supplement to Dr. Watts's Psalms and Hymns*, which contained 62 of his own hymns.

264. *Bread of heaven, on thee we feed.*
454. *Beyond, beyond that boundless sea.*

COOK, Edgar T., Mus.B., F.R.C.S. (Worcester, 1880–   ), son of Edgar Cook of Worcester, was educated at Worcester Royal Grammar School, and privately. In 1898 he became organist of Newland, Malvern, in 1904 assistant organist of Worcester Cathedral, and since 1907 has been organist and director of the music of Southwark Cathedral. In 1914 and 1921 he was President of the London Society of Organists; he is also a member of the council and examiner for the Royal College of Organists, and professor of choir training, organ accompaniment, and theory at the Royal College of Music, and is Hon. R.C.M. and L.R.A.M. His publications include many anthems, services, part-songs, and organ music.

*570. RAVENSHAW.

CORNER, David Gregor (Hirschberg, Silesia, 1587–1648, Vienna), studied in Breslau, Prague, and Gratz; in 1618 he became Pfarrer in Rötz, and later in Maulbronn; in 1627 entered the Benedictine Order; and from 1638 till his death was rector of the University of Vienna. His fame rests on his two great collections *Geistliche Nachtigall* and the *Gesangbuch* (1631), both of which passed through several editions during the 17th century: these contained tunes derived from various sources, but none, apparently, of his own composition.

8. SOLL'S SEIN.
138 (ii). CORNER (CHRISTI MUTTER STUND VOR SCHMERZEN).
217 (i). OMNI DIE. 369. IN DER WIEGEN. 391. HEILIGER GEIST.

CORNYSSHE, WILLIAM (? *c.* 1465–1523, London), was, during the first quarter of the 16th century, pageant master, composer, and dramatist to Henry VIII. He was also a poet, and often appeared as an actor in the performances he directed at the Court. Many of his secular part-songs, and some church music are extant; some of the former are found in a contemporary manuscript now in the British Museum (Add. 39122); two are printed in Sir John Hawkins's *History*, and one in the *Oxford Choral Songs*. Most of his music that has survived is still in manuscript in various libraries.

467. ROBYN.

COSIN, JOHN (Norwich, 1594–1672, London), was educated at Caius College, Cambridge, took Holy Orders, and was appointed chaplain to the Bishop of Durham. He subsequently became prebendary of Durham, and archdeacon of the East Riding of Yorkshire. Other preferments followed, and in 1640 he became Chancellor of the University of Cambridge and dean of Peterborough. At this point, however, his fortunes suffered eclipse. His *Collection of Private Devotions* had already been severely criticized by the Puritans, and one of their number, whom Cosin had treated with severity, succeeded in inducing the Long Parliament to deprive him of his benefices. He retired to France and remained there till the Restoration, when he was restored to active life and became bishop of Durham. During his episcopate he spent large sums on the cathedral, on the library, and on various works of charity. A man of much liturgical knowledge, he took part in the final revision of the *Book of Common Prayer* (1662), in which is incorporated his translation of the *Veni, Creator Spiritus.*

178. *Come, Holy Ghost, our souls inspire.*

COTTON, GEORGE EDWARD LYNCH, D.D. (?1813–66, Calcutta), was educated at Westminster and Trinity College, Cambridge. From 1837 to 1852 he was a house master at Rugby under Arnold and Tait and appears in *Tom Brown's Schooldays* as 'the young master'. In 1858 he became Bishop of Calcutta. He founded schools for European and Eurasian children. He died by drowning in the River Ganges.

691. *We thank thee, Lord, for this fair earth.*

COURTEVILLE, RAPHAEL (London ?–1772, London), was the son of a chorister of the Chapel Royal, and was trained as one of the children of the Chapel. In 1691 he became organist of St. James's, Piccadilly, and, according to the church records, held the post for 81 years. Other instances of equally long tenure are known, and it is not therefore necessary to assume, as have some writers, that he was succeeded at some date by his son, without the fact being noted in the records. He was the reputed author of the *Gazetteer*, a paper written in defence of Sir Robert Walpole's administration, and received the nickname of 'Court-evil'. He wrote *Memoirs of Lord Burleigh*, was associated with Purcell in composing music for D'Urfey's opera *Don Quixote*, and composed songs, violin and flute sonatas, and much other music.

96. ST. JAMES.

COWPER, WILLIAM (Berkhampstead, 1731–1800, East Dereham), the greatest English poet of his age, was son of a chaplain to George II, whose father was a Judge of Common Pleas, and whose elder brother became

Lord Chancellor and first Earl Cowper. After education at Westminster School he was articled to an attorney and called to the Bar in 1754. On his being offered, through his kinsman, Major Cowper, the post of Clerk to the Journals of the House of Lords, the dread of appearing before the House to stand an examination so affected a mind already wounded by cruelty at a preparatory school that he lost his balance, and was never thereafter entirely free from deep melancholy. After undergoing treatment in a private asylum, he found a home at Huntingdon in the family of the Rev. Morley Unwin, whose wife became his lifelong friend and guardian. On the death of Mr. Unwin he removed with the family to Olney, where their friend, the Rev. John Newton, was curate. Here Cowper collaborated with Newton in strenuous parochial and evangelistic work, and also in the production of what became known as the *Olney Hymns*. A means of brightening the poet's outlook in life was afforded by the arrival of Lady Austen, a widow who came to reside at Olney, and at whose instigation Cowper began his greatest poem, *The Task*. A more ambitious, though not equally successful literary venture, was a translation of Homer, in which he was encouraged by another good friend, his cousin Lady Hesketh. In spite of these and other distractions, the depression of spirits returned and never again left him except for brief periods. With Mrs. Unwin, now an invalid, he removed to East Dereham, in Norfolk, where she died in 1796, and the poet's death followed in 1800.

112. *O for a closer walk with God.*
503. *God moves in a mysterious way.*
510. *Hark, my soul! it is the Lord.*
551. *Jesus, where'er thy people meet.*
643. *Sometimes a light surprises.*

COX, Frances Elizabeth (Oxford, 1812-97, Oxford), was one of the best-known translators of German hymns. She was indebted to Baron Bunsen for guidance as to those most worthy of being translated; and she published *Sacred Hymns from the German* (1841), and *Hymns from the German* (1864).

115. *O let him whose sorrow.*
155. *Jesus lives! thy terrors now.*
210. *Who are these like stars appearing.*

CREIGHTON, Mandell, D.D. (Carlisle, 1843–1901, London). Elected Fellow of Merton College, Oxford, 1866, vicar of Embleton, Northumberland, 1875. In 1884 he became the first Professor of Ecclesiastical History at Cambridge, in 1891 bishop of Peterborough and afterwards of London, 1896. His chief publications were *Simon de Montfort*; *History of the Papacy during the Reformation Period*; and *Queen Elizabeth*.

284. *O thou, who gavest power to love.*

CREWDSON, Jane, *née* Fox (Perranarworthal, Cornwall, 1809–63, Summerlands, Whalley Range, Manchester), married Thomas D. Crewdson, a Manchester manufacturer, in 1836. Always delicate, she was long a confirmed invalid. She published *Aunt Jane's Verses for Children* (1851); *Lays of the Reformation and Other Lyrics* (1860); *The Singer of Eisenach*; and *A Little While, and Other Poems* (1864).

665. *There is no sorrow, Lord, too slight.*

CROFT (or CROFTS, as he sometimes wrote), WILLIAM, D.Mus. (Nether Eatington, now Ettington, Warwickshire, 1678–1727, Bath), was born of good family, became one of the children of the Chapel Royal under Dr. Blow; organist of St. Anne's, Soho, and gentleman extraordinary of the Chapel Royal, 1700; joint-organist of the Chapel Royal with Jeremiah Clark, 1704, and sole organist, 1707; organist of Westminster Abbey and composer to the Chapel Royal, 1708; D.Mus. Oxon., 1713. In earlier life he composed for the theatre and also wrote sonatas, songs, and odes; but he became absorbed in sacred music and made for himself in this field one of the greatest names in English musical history. It is believed that his cathedral music was one of the models of Handel's 'high sacred style' in his oratorios. But his tunes give him widest fame. They are 'of importance historically, as they are the earliest examples of the English psalm-tune as distinguished from the Genevan; they require quicker singing, and the glorious rhythmical impulse of "Hanover" and its triple measure marked at once a distinct originality'. In *Divine Harmony* he published a collection of the words of anthems with a brief historical account of English Church music; and in *Musica Sacra*, thirty anthems and a Burial Service of his own composition. His epitaph in Westminster Abbey concludes, 'Having resided among mortals for fifty years, behaving with the utmost candour . . . he departed to the heavenly choir . . . that being near, he might add to the concert of angels his own HALLELUJAH.'

192. EATINGTON. 287. ST. MATTHEW. 509. BINCHESTER.
598. ST. ANNE. 618. HANOVER. 657. CROFT'S 136TH.

CROSSMAN, SAMUEL, B.D. (*c.* 1624–83, Bristol), was educated at Pembroke College, Cambridge, where he graduated in arts and took his B.D. in 1660. He was one of the ejected ministers of 1662, but soon afterwards conformed and became one of the King's chaplains, was appointed prebendary of Bristol, 1667, and for a few weeks before his death was dean of Bristol. He published the *Young Man's Monitor* and the *Young Man's Meditation*, both in 1664, various Sermons and Poems.

127. *My song is love unknown.*
197. *Jerusalem on high.*

CRÜGER, JOHANN (Grossbriesen, near Guben, Prussia, 1598–1662, Berlin), the celebrated composer of chorales, was educated at the Jesuit College of Olmütz, and at the school of poetry at Regensburg. He travelled through Austria, Hungary, Bohemia, and arrived at Berlin in 1615. There he was tutor in the family of Colonel Christoph von Blumenthal for five years, and then he finished his theological studies at the University of Wittenberg. He became cantor of the Lutheran Cathedral of St. Nicholas, Berlin, in 1622, and founded its celebrated choir. There he continued till his death, writing on the theory and practice of music, and publishing many concertos and motets, and a collection of Magnificats; but he is chiefly known now as composer of some of the most famous and favourite chorales. These appeared in his *Praxis Pietatis Melica* (1644), which appeared in countless editions, and 'constituted the main stream of Lutheran hymnody in the middle of the seventeenth century'. As a tune-writer he was of the first rank, and as an editor no less eminent.

He preserved much fine material already in existence, and called other composers to his aid.

24. RATISBON (JESU, MEINE ZUVERSICHT). 87. CRÜGER.
99. HERZLIEBSTER JESU. 186 (ii). HERR, DEINEN ZORN.
267. SCHMÜCKE DICH. 350. NUN DANKET.
544. JESU MEINE FREUDE.

CRUM, JOHN MACLEOD CAMPBELL, M.A. (nr. Knutsford, Cheshire, 1872–), was educated at Eton and New College, Oxford. He was domestic chaplain to the Bishop of Oxford; was rector of Farnham, 1913–20, and is now a canon of Canterbury. He has published: *Road mending on the Sacred Way* (1924), and *What mean ye by these Stones* (1926).

220. *On the moorland of life God's shepherd is seen.*
376. *To God who makes all lovely things.*

CUNNINGHAM, FRANCIS (early 19th century), published two collections, *A Selection of Psalm Tunes, adapted to a selection of psalms and hymns extracted from various authors* (1826), and *A Selection of Psalm Tunes, designed to assist public worship* (1834).

266. BIRMINGHAM.

CUSTARD, HENRY GOSS, Mus.Bac. (St. Leonards-on-Sea, 1871–), studied for some time with E. H. Lemare, and held several important posts in London, including the honorary organistship of the Royal Philharmonic Society. Since 1917 he has been organist of the new Cathedral at Liverpool.

*507. CAPETOWN.

DAMON (or DAMAN), WILLIAM (*c.* 1540–*c.* 91), was organist of the Chapel Royal under Queen Elizabeth. The book by which he is best known, a collection of the Psalms in four parts, which he had prepared for the use of his friend John Bull, citizen and goldsmith of London, was published by John Day under the title: *The Psalmes of David in English meter, with notes of four parts set unto them by Guilielmo Damon*, 1570. The tunes used are, with one or two exceptions, those which had appeared in previous books—the *Anglo-Genevan Psalter* of 1556, the *English* of 1562, and the *Scottish* of 1564. There are four books, one for each part, and the harmony is simple note against note. This simple harmony was apparently not thought worthy of Damon's reputation and ability, and he withdrew it and destroyed the remaining copies, so that it is now extremely rare. He then set himself to revise the harmonies, and in 1591 a second and more elaborate edition was published with this title, *The former* (*second*) *Booke of the Musicke of M. William Damon, late one of her majesties Musitions: contayning all the tunes of David's psalms as they are ordinarely soung in the Church, most excellently by him composed into 4 parts.* The work is in eight books, the first four of which have the melody in the tenor, and the second four in the Cantus.

106. SOUTHWELL. 547 (ii). WINDSOR.

DARBYSHIRE, JOHN RUSSELL, D.D. (Birkenhead, 1880–1948), was educated at Birkenhead School, Dulwich College, and Emmanuel College,

Cambridge. He took a first class in the Classical Tripos 1902, and in the Theological Tripos 1904, achieving several further academic distinctions. He has held various appointments in Cambridge, Liverpool, Manchester, and Sheffield, and has been bishop of Glasgow and Galloway since 1931. Publications: *The Christian Faith and some alternatives*; *Our Treasury of Prayer and Praise.*

142. *At eve, when now he breathed no more.*
218. *Who dreads, yet undismayed.*
241. *Great is their joy who hide their own.*
286. *Life and health are in the name.*

DARKE, HAROLD EDWIN, Mus.Doc., F.R.C.O. (Highbury, London, 1888–   ), was educated at the Royal College of Music, where he gained scholarships for organ and composition, and won the Tagore Gold Medal. In 1906 he became organist of Emmanuel Church, West Hampstead, and, later, of St. James's, Paddington, and assistant at the Temple Church. In 1916 he was appointed to St. Michael's, Cornhill, where the organ and choral recitals instituted by him soon became famous. In 1919 he joined the staff of the Royal College of Music, and in 1925 founded the City of London Choral Union. His compositions include songs, part-songs, organ, piano, and chamber music, and several settings for chorus and orchestra.

41. CORNHILL. *200. REGNATOR ORBIS. *547 (ii). WINDSOR.

DARWALL, JOHN, B.A. (Haughton, Staffordshire, 1731–89, Walsall), was educated at Manchester Grammar School and Brasenose College, Oxford, where he graduated in 1756. He became curate, and in 1769 vicar, of Walsall, Staffs. He wrote hymns and poetical pieces, and was an enthusiastic amateur musician. He composed a tune for each of the 150 metrical psalms. Few of these were published, but some are found in late 18th-century tune-books and in Dr. Mann's *Church of England Hymnal.* They were written in two parts only, treble and bass. He published two volumes of pianoforte sonatas; *A Christmas Hymn and Tune*; *A Charity Hymn and Tune*; and *A Hymn, to which is prefixed a biographical notice.*

701. DARWALL'S 148TH.

DAVIES, Sir HENRY WALFORD, Mus.Doc., LL.D. (Oswestry, Shropshire, 1869–1941), became a chorister of St. George's, Windsor, in 1882; assistant organist to Sir Walter Parratt there, 1885–90; a teacher of counterpoint, Royal College of Music, 1895; conductor, London Bach Choir, 1903–7, and of the London Church Association, 1901–13; organist of the Temple Church, 1890–1919; Professor of Music, University College of Wales, Aberystwyth, from 1919; Chairman, National Council of Music, University of Wales, from 1919; Gresham Professor of Music, 1924; organist of St. George's, Windsor, and master of music to the King, 1927. He was knighted in 1922. He has been a great inspiring force as director of music in the Welsh University and schools, as adjudicator at musical festivals all over the country, and as conductor of community singing. His works include an oratorio, *The Temple*; cantatas, *Three Jovial Huntsmen*; *Everyman*; *Ode on Time*; *Five Sayings of Jesus*; *Song of St. Francis*; *Songs of a Day*; *Noble Numbers*. He is author of *Music and Christian Worship*, and has edited the *Fellowship Song Book*, *Fifty-Two Hymn Tunes*, and *Hymns of the Kingdom* and *A Students' Hymnal.*

79 (ii). CHRISTMAS CAROL.

DAVIS, ROBY FURLEY, M.A. (Nottingham, 1866–), was educated at St. John's College, Cambridge, where he took his degree in 1888, and has since held various appointments as classical master, &c. He has edited and annotated several classical authors, and was co-translator with R. Martin Pope of the *Hymns of Prudentius* (1905).

387. *Of the Father's heart begotten.*

DAY (DAYE or DAIE), JOHN (Dunwich, Suffolk, 1552–84, Walden, Essex), was one of the earliest of music printers. He used as his device a sleeper awakened by one who points to the rising sun, with the punning motto, 'Arise, for it is Day'. He was a zealous supporter of the reformed religion, and suffered imprisonment for his loyalty to it; for a time also he had to live abroad. 'There are very few of our earlier printers to whom both literature and typography are more deeply indebted' (Dibdin). He printed the 1st edition of what is known as *Queen Elizabeth's Prayer Book*; the 1st edition of *Foxe's Book of Martyrs*; the first Church music book in English, *Certaine Notes set forth in foure and three parts to be song*; Archbishop Parker's translation of the Psalms, the first by one person of the whole Psalter in English metre; in 1562, the 1st edition of the complete Metrical Psalter known as the Old Version, with the old proper tunes; and in 1563, *The Whole Psalmes, in foure partes, which may be sung to all musical instruments*, Tallis being a contributor—probably the earliest psalter in which the proper tunes were harmonized.

43. OLD 18TH.
176. OLD 22ND.
188. ST. FLAVIAN.
195. OLD 25TH.
216. OLD 81ST (OLD 77TH).
235. TALLIS' LAMENTATION.
329. OLD 124TH.
526. OLD 137TH.
443. *All people that on earth do dwell.*

DEARMER, GEOFFREY (London, 1893–), son of Dr. Percy Dearmer (q.v.), was educated at Westminster School, abroad, and at Christ Church, Oxford; and served in Gallipoli and France during the War. Among his publications are *St. Paul*, a drama; and two volumes of poems.

193. *Sing, all good people gathered.*
222. *'To Damascus!' Paul had shouted.*
224. *When Judas did his Lord reject.*
663. *There are a myriad means, O Lord.*

DEARMER, PERCY, D.D. (London, 1867–1936), was educated at Westminster School, abroad, and at Christ Church, Oxford, and from 1901 to 1915 was vicar of St. Mary the Virgin, Primrose Hill. He was secretary of the London branch of the Christian Social Union, 1891–1912, and is chairman of the League of Arts. After much service abroad during the War, he became in 1919 Professor of Ecclesiastical Art in King's College, London, and Lecturer in Art, and in 1931 canon of Westminster. Among his publications are: *The Parson's Handbook*; *The Sanctuary*; *Body and Soul*; *Highways and Byways in Normandy*; *The English Carol Book* (with Martin Shaw); *The Art of Public Worship*; *The Power of the Spirit*; *The Legend of*

Hell. He was secretary of the Committee that prepared the *English Hymnal*, and acted as editor of that epoch-making book; he edited also *Songs of Praise* (1925 and 1931), with the co-operation, in the music, of R. Vaughan Williams (q.v.) and Martin Shaw (q.v.), and the present handbook.

59. *Ah! think not, 'The Lord delayeth'.*
91. *In Asia born, from Asia hailed.*
98. *Now quit your care.*
158. *Life is good, for God contrives it.*
212. *Prophets, teachers, true recorders.*
214. *Virtue supreme, thy mighty stream.*
238. *Angels and ministers, spirits of grace.*
244. *Unknown and unrewarded.*
262. *As the disciples, when thy Son had left them.*
292. *Now thy earthly work is done.*
302. *Servants of the great adventure.*
369. *Remember all the people.*
390. *Welcome day of the Lord.*
396. *O Father above us, our father in might.*
457. *Book of books, our people's strength.*
466. *Christian, do you see him?*
561. *Lo, in the wilderness a voice.*
592. *Now join, ye comrades true.*
601. *O Holy Spirit, God.*
640. *Sing praise to God, who spoke through man.*
672. *Thou Judge by whom each Empire fell.*
683. *To the Name that is salvation.*
695. *When by fear my heart is daunted.*

DIX, Leopold L. (Dublin, 1861-1935), was educated at a private school and at Trinity College, Dublin. He is a solicitor by profession. He composed many arrangements of Irish and other tunes for the *Irish Hymnal* of the Church of Ireland, and has published: *Quintet from, and Introduction to, the 3rd Act of The Meistersingers (Wagner), arranged for String Orchestra*; *17 Hymn Tunes*; songs, piano pieces, &c.

*268. ST. SECHNALL.

DIX, William Chatterton (Bristol, 1837–98, Clifton), was the son of William John Dix, a Bristol surgeon, who wrote the *Life of Chatterton* the poet, a book of *Pen Pictures of Popular English Preachers*, and other works. He was educated at the Grammar School, Bristol, for a mercantile career, and became manager of a marine insurance company in Glasgow. Some of his hymns are found in most modern hymn-books. They were published in *Hymns of Love and Joy* (1861); *Altar Songs, Verses on the Holy Eucharist* (1867); *A Vision of All Saints* (1871); *Seekers of a City* (1878).

13. *To thee, O Lord, our hearts we raise.*
83. *As with gladness men of old.*
260. *Alleluya, sing to Jesus.*

DODDRIDGE, Philip, D.D. (London, 1702–51, Lisbon), was the son of a London merchant. His paternal grandfather was a clergyman ejected from his living under the Act of Uniformity, and his mother's father a Lutheran pastor, who fled from Bohemia to England to escape persecution. Philip was the youngest of a family of 20, most of whom died young. Declining an offer from the Duchess of Bedford to educate him for the Church of England, he studied under Jennings for the dissenting ministry, and succeeded his preceptor at Kibworth in 1723. In 1729 he accepted a charge at Northampton, which included the care of a seminary. There he remained for 22 years. In 1751, worn down by consumption, he vainly sought health by a voyage to Lisbon, where he died. Doddridge wrote many theological works, the most notable being the *Rise and Progress of Religion in the Soul*, which went through many editions and was translated into a number of languages. His hymns were posthumously published by his friend Orton.

62. *Hark the glad sound! the Saviour comes.*
596. *O God of Bethel, by whose hand.*
702. *Ye servants of the Lord.*

DOLES, Johann Friedrich (Steinbach, Franconia, 1715–97, Leipzig), was a pupil of J. S. Bach at the Thomasschule, Leipzig. After 14 years as cantor at Freiburg, he became director of the Thomasschule himself. He was an admirable teacher, and enjoyed a great reputation among musicians of his time. He was not of the spirit of his great master, however: 'he wrote in a sentimental quasi-operatic style', Fuller-Maitland says, 'and the high standard of Bach's time was lost and lowered during his tenure of office'. Among his publications were: *The Forty-Sixth Psalm* set to music; *Melodien zu Gellerts Geistlichen Oden*, for four voices, with accompaniment; *Vierstimmiges Choralbuch, oder harmonische melodien Sammlung für Kirchen* (1785).

2. DA CHRISTUS GEBOREN WAR.

DOMETT, Alfred (Camberwell Grove, 1811–87, London), Colonial statesman and poet. Entered at St. John's College, Cambridge, 1829; barrister of the Middle Temple, 1841; migrated to New Zealand, 1842. Robert Browning, his friend, lamented his departure in *Waring* (1842). M.P. for Nelson 1855, Prime Minister of New Zealand 1865; returned to England, 1871; was made a C.M.G. 1880. Publications: *Ranolf and Amohia, a South Sea Day Dream* (1872); *Flotsam and Jetsam* (1877); and some official publications.

77. *It was the calm and silent night.*

DONNE, John, D.D. (London, 1573–1631, London), was educated as a Roman Catholic, but at 19 years of age he became an Anglican. He was for a time secretary to Lord Chancellor Ellesmere. He took Orders in accordance with King James's wish and became a famous preacher. He was chosen in 1617 to be preacher of Lincoln's Inn, and became dean of St. Paul's, 1621. He was buried in St. Paul's. In 1610 he published the *Pseudo-Martyr*, a work he had undertaken to furnish the King with arguments wherewith to confute the English Romanists, who had declared they were martyrs; in 1611 he further published *An Anatomy of the World*, of which only two copies are known to exist; *The Progress of the Soul* (1612); and several other works. He was one of the earliest and certainly the greatest of the poets of the 'metaphysical school', but has only of late years been appreciated at his true value. His *Poems* were posthumously published in 1633.

123. *Wilt thou forgive that sin, where I begun.*

DORR, Julia Caroline Ripley (Charleston, South Carolina, 1825–1913, Vermont), daughter of William Young Ripley, married, in 1847, Seneca R. Dorr, and her first poem was published a year or two later in the *Union Magazine*. From 1848 onwards she wrote much. Her publications were chiefly novels and stories such as *Sybil Huntingdon*, *Lanmere*, &c.; and poetry such as *Poems* (1871), *Afternoon Songs* (1885), &c.

290. *How can I cease to pray for thee?*

DOUGALL, Neil (Greenock, 1776–1862, Greenock), was the son of a shipwright who was impressed into national service and died in Ceylon when Neil was 4 years old. The boy went to school till he was 15, then took to a seafaring life. Three years later, an accident during the firing of a salute deprived him of his right arm and his eyesight. After some study of music he took up the teaching of singing. For 45 years he conducted successful singing-classes, and for 60 gave an annual concert in Greenock. He published a small volume of poems in 1854, and wrote about a hundred psalm- and hymn-tunes.

522. KILMARNOCK.

DOWLAND, or Douland, John, Mus.Bac. (Westminster, 1562–1626, London), graduated with Thomas Morley in 1588. It has been said that he was of Irish parentage, and that the family name originally was Dolan or O'Dolan, but without good grounds. He was a celebrated lutanist and 'a touring virtuoso'; about 1585 he made a musical tour through Germany, France, and Italy, and acquired a great reputation in these countries: his works were printed all over the Continent, and his success there was greater than in his own country. In 1598 he was appointed lutanist to the King of Denmark, and was liberally treated by him, his salary of 500 dalers being as much as a minister of state at that time received. But he was prodigal in an extreme degree; and, the king's patience becoming exhausted, he returned to England, dismissed, in 1606. Six years later he received the only appointment he seems to have held in this country, as one of the King's Musicians for the Lutes. Both in composition and in performance his music was characterized by a rare grace and tenderness; hence the lines in which Richard Barnfield immortalized him:

> Dowland to thee is deare, whose heavenly touch
> Upon the Lute doeth ravish humaine sense.

He published three *Bookes of Songs or Ayres*, and a fourth collection under the title *A Pilgrim's Solace*, all with accompaniments for lute and viol da gamba. He harmonized some of the tunes in *Este's Psalter*, and contributed also to Sir William Leighton's *The Teares or Lamentacions of a Sorrowful Soule*.

*443. OLD HUNDREDTH. 461. GALLIARD.

DOWNTON, Henry, M.A. (Pulverbatch, Shropshire, 1818–85, Hopton), was son of the sub-librarian of Trinity College, Cambridge, where he graduated in 1840. Ordained in 1843, he became perpetual curate of St. John's, Chatham; and in 1857 English chaplain at Geneva. Returning to this country in 1873, he became rector of Hopton, Suffolk. He translated Naville's *Lectures on Modern Atheism* (1865); and his familiarity with the hymnody of the Swiss and French Churches enabled him to render a number of their hymns effectively into English. They are included in his *Hymns and Verses, Original and Translated* (1873).

1. *For thy mercy and thy grace.*

DRAPER, William Henry, M.A. (Kenilworth, 1855–1933), was educated at Keble College, Oxford. Ordained in 1880, he acted as curate of St. Mary's, Shrewsbury; vicar of Alfreton; vicar of the Abbey Church, Shrewsbury; rector of Adel, Leeds; was Master of the Temple, London, 1919–30, and thereafter vicar of Axbridge. He has published *Hymns for Holy Week*, translations from hymns of the Greek Church; *The Victoria Book of Hymns* (1897); *The Way of the Cross*; translated Petrarch's *Secretum* (1911); and edited *Seven Spiritual Songs by Thomas Campion* (1919), and *Hymns for Tunes by Orlando Gibbons* (1925).

439. *All creatures of our God and King* (tr.).

DRYDEN, John (Aldwinkle, Northamptonshire, 1631–1700, London), poet and chief literary figure of the Restoration era, came from an old north country family which took the parliamentary side in the Civil War. The first verses to bring Dryden fame were his *Heroic Stanzas* on the death of Cromwell; yet he soon afterwards welcomed the royal exile in *Astræa Redux*, and in 1670 was made Poet Laureate. For a number of years after the Restoration his work consisted mainly of plays, many of them coarse even for that not too refined age. His true genius, however, lay in his use of the heroic couplet for purposes of satire, as shown in *Absalom and Achitophel* and elsewhere. On the accession of James II he became a Roman Catholic, and he did not change at the Revolution. He also produced translations of Juvenal, Virgil, Boccaccio, and other poets.

181. *Creator Spirit, by whose aid.*

DUFFIELD, George, jun., D.D. (Carlisle, Pennsylvania, 1818–88, Detroit), son of Dr. Duffield of Detroit, was educated at Yale and Union Seminary, New York, for the Presbyterian ministry. Ordained in 1840, he held charges at Brooklyn; Bloomfield, New Jersey; Philadelphia; Adrian, Michigan; Galesburg, Illinois; Saginaw City, Michigan; Ann Arbor and Lansing, Michigan. His later years were spent at Bloomfield, New Jersey.

646. *Stand up, stand up for Jesus!*

DUNCALF, Henry (18th century), was organist of St. Bartholomew's, London.

256. ST. BARTHOLOMEW.

DUNCAN, Mary, *née* Lundie (Kelso, 1814–40, Cleish, Kinross-shire), was daughter of the Rev. Robert Lundie, parish minister of Kelso. She went to school in London, and early showed a talent for verse. In 1836 she married the Rev. William Wallace Duncan, minister of Cleish. Her hymns, written for her own children between July and December 1839, were published in a *Memoir* by her mother in 1841, and in the following year were issued separately—23 in number—as *Rhymes for my Children*.

364. *Jesus, tender Shepherd, hear me.*

DYKES, John Bacchus, M.A., Mus.Doc. (Hull, 1823–76, St. Leonards-on-Sea), was a son of a banker, and grandson of a well-known evangelical clergyman, in Hull. 'Bacchus' was the Christian name of his maternal grandfather. John's talent for music developed early; he played the organ in his father's church at the age of 10. Educated at Wakefield, to which the family home had been removed, and at St. Catharine's College, Cambridge, he helped as an undergraduate, along with William Thomson, afterwards Lord Kelvin, to found the University Musical Society. After taking Orders in 1847, he was licensed to the curacy of Malton, but two years later proceeded to Durham to be a minor canon and was, soon after, precentor in the Cathedral there. In 1861 Durham University conferred on him his doctorate, and a year later he became vicar of St. Oswald's in the same city, where he remained until the break-down of his health in 1875. He published various sermons and writings on liturgics, wrote several services and a number of anthems which are much in use; but he is best known by his hymn-tunes, of which he wrote about 300.

140. ST. CROSS. 187 (i). NICAEA.
554 (ii). LUX BENIGNA. 586 (iii). HORBURY.
654 (ii). DOMINUS REGIT ME.

EARLE, John Charles (London, 1821–99, London), was educated at St. Edmund Hall, Oxford, where he graduated in 1842. He was a hymnologist of some note, and a contributor to Julian's *Dictionary of Hymnology*. Among his publications were *Maximilian and other poems* (1868); *The Palace of Theobalds* (1869); *A First and a Second Hundred Sonnets* (1871); *Light leading unto Light* (1875); *The Forty Days* (1877); *The Master's Field* (1878), &c.

411. *I will arise and to my Father go.*

EBELING, Johann Georg (Lüneburg, 1637–76, Stettin), in 1662 succeeded Johann Crüger as cantor of St. Nicholas Cathedral, Berlin, and as director of music at the College of St. Nicholas there. In 1668 he became Professor of Music at the College of St. Charles (Carolinen Gymnasium), Stettin. He published *Archaeologiae Orphicae, sive antiquitates Musicae* (1675); *Pauli Gerhardi Geistliche Andachten, bestehend in 120 Liedern mit 6 Singstimmen, 2 violinen und general-bass* (1666–7).

89. BONN (WARUM SOLLT ICH). 374. VOLLER WUNDER.
692. ABENDLIED (DER TAG MIT SEINEM LICHTE).

EDMESTON, James (Wapping, London, 1791–1867, Homerton, London), was an eminent London architect and surveyor. Among the pupils trained by him was Sir G. Gilbert Scott. He joined the Church of England early in life, and was latterly churchwarden of St. Barnabas's Church, Homerton. He was a constant visitor at the London Orphan Asylum, and he found there the inspiration of many of his children's hymns. His *Cottage Minstrel* was written in successful response to an advertisement offering a prize of £20 for 50 simple hymns suitable for cottage meetings. Edmeston wrote over 2,000 hymns, many of which he published in *Sacred Lyrics*, *Infant Breathings*, and several other works. It was his regrettable practice to write a hymn every Sunday and read it at family worship.

54. *Saviour, shed an evening blessing.*
555. *Lead us, heavenly Father, lead us.*

EDWARDS, John David (? 1805–85, Llanddoget Rectory, Denbighshire), was vicar of Rhosymedre, Ruabon; he wrote a considerable quantity of music, but is chiefly known by the tune below.

127 (ii). RHOSYMEDRE.

EDWARDS, Robert (Mostyn, Flintshire, 1797–1862, Liverpool), went to Liverpool as a young man and became a carter in the employ of the Bridgewater Trustees, who managed the canal system between Liverpool, Manchester, and Runcorn. Later in life he was promoted to the position of superintendent of the carting department. He was passionately fond of music, and for many years was precentor in Bedford Street Calvinistic Methodist Chapel. He was a very modest man, and though he composed tunes, took no steps to make them known. During his absence from Bedford Street Chapel on one occasion, owing to illness, some one discovered the tune *Caersalem* in his desk; the choir practised it, and sang it as a surprise for him on his return. But for this, it might never have been known.

508 (ii). CAERSALEM.

ELLERTON, John, M.A. (London, 1826–93, Torquay), was educated at King William's College, Isle of Man, and at Trinity College, Cambridge. At the University he was deeply influenced by Frederick Denison Maurice, and he did not identify himself with any party in the Church. In 1860 he became vicar of Crewe Green and domestic chaplain to Lord Crewe. While there he was vice-president of the Mechanics' Institution, reorganized its educational work, and himself conducted classes in English and Scripture History. He also organized one of the first choral associations of the Midlands, which met for many years at Nantwich. In 1872 he became rector of the secluded parish of Hinstock, Shropshire, and in 1876 came to London as rector of Barnes. The heavy burden of this large and populous parish broke him down, but after a year abroad he was able, in 1885, to accept the quiet charge of White Roding, Essex. His work as a hymnologist was of the first importance. He was chief compiler and editor of *Church Hymns* and the *Children's Hymn Book*, and assisted the committee of *Hymns Ancient and Modern*, both in 1875 and 1889. He edited or assisted in editing *Hymns for Schools and Bible Classes*, the *Temperance Hymn Book*, the *London Mission Hymn Book*; and his advice was sought in the compiling of the last edition of *Hymnal Companion to the Book of Common Prayer*. His *Notes and Illustrations of Church Hymns* appeared in the folio edition in 1881. His own hymns were published in 1888 as *Hymns, Original and Translated*.

39. *Behold us, Lord, a little space.*
53. *Saviour, again to thy dear name we raise.*
56. *The day thou gavest, Lord, is ended.*
141. *Throned upon the aweful tree.*

ELLIOTT, Charlotte (Clapham, 1789–1871, Brighton), was a granddaughter of the Rev. Henry Venn, the famous evangelical divine, author of a book long valued on the *Whole Duty of Man*. In her youth she wrote humorous poems, but a grave illness in 1821, which made her permanently an invalid, made serious impressions on her which were deepened in the following year by the influence of César Malan, the evangelist, of Geneva. Her hymns appeared in *Psalms and Hymns*, edited by her brother, the Rev. Henry Venn Elliott of Brighton (1835–9); and in her own *Hours of Sorrow cheered and comforted* (1836); *Hymns for a Week* (1839); *The Invalid's Hymn Book* (1834—41); and *Thoughts in Verse on Sacred Subjects* (1869). She lived with her father for 32 years at Clapham; the later years were spent at Torquay and Brighton.

253. *Just as I am, without one plea.*
467. *Christian, seek not yet repose.*

ELLIOTT, EBENEZER (Rotherham, Yorkshire, 1781–1849, Barnsley), lived for most of his life in Sheffield, where he was in the iron trade, and many of his poems appeared in a newspaper in that town. Among his publications were *Corn Law Rhymes* (1831), in consequence of which he gained the name of 'The Corn Law Rhymer'; and *Poems* (1834).

314. *When wilt thou save the people?*

ELVEY, Sir GEORGE JOB, Mus.Doc. (Canterbury, 1816–93, Windlesham, Surrey), was baptized in the Presbyterian Chapel, Canterbury. He was educated as a chorister in the Cathedral. From 1835 to 1882 he was organist and master of the boys at St. George's Chapel, Windsor, and as such had charge of the music in connexion with many events of importance in the Royal House. He was knighted in 1871. Much sacred music was composed by him, oratorios, *The Resurrection*, *The Ascension*, *Mount Carmel*; a festival march, &c.; and he contributed tunes to *Hymns Ancient and Modern* and other collections. He was buried outside the west front of St. George's Chapel.

9. ST. GEORGE.

ESTE (EST, EASTE, EAST), THOMAS (1540?–1608?), a famous printer and music publisher, appeared first as a music printer in 1587, with *Sonnettes and Songs made into musick of fyve parts. By William Burd.* This is supposed to be identical with the undated edition of Byrd's *Psalmes, Sonets, and Songs of Sadness and Pietie* (1588). In the latter year, Este's *Musica Transalpina*, a collection of Italian madrigals, laid the foundation of the splendid school of English madrigalists. In 1591 he printed the new edition of Damon's *Psalmes*, published by William Swayne. In the edition of the psalter printed by Este in 1592 the tunes were harmonized by ten eminent composers of the time, including Richard Allison, Giles Farnaby, John Douland, John Farmer, and George Kirbye. This psalter is probably the earliest example in which the parts are printed on opposite pages instead of in separate books.

43. OLD 18TH. 82 (i). WINCHESTER OLD. 105. CHESHIRE.
176. OLD 22ND. 197 (i). OLD 136TH. 216. OLD 81ST (OLD 77TH).
547 (ii). WINDSOR. 615. OLD 120TH. 655. OLD 44TH.
693. OLD 30TH.

ETT, CASPAR (near Landsberg, 1788–1847, Munich), was a distinguished Bavarian musician who from 1816 onwards was organist of the Michaeliskirche, Munich. He made a special study of church music from the 16th to the 18th century, and gathered large collections of it, which went on his death to the Munich Library. He published, in 1840, *Cantica Sacra*, containing many tunes of his own modelled on the older chorales.

190 (ii), 683. ORIEL.

EVANS, David, Mus.Doc. (Resolven, Glamorganshire, 1874–1948), was educated at Arnold College, Swansea, and University College, Cardiff, and graduated at Oxford. For a time he was organist and choirmaster of Jewin Street Welsh Presbyterian Church, London. Since 1903 he has been Professor of Music at University College, Cardiff; he is now the senior Professor of the University of Wales. At Cardiff he has organized a large department of music, in which all branches of the art are taught. He is a leading adjudicator at the National Eisteddfod, where his compositions constantly appear as test pieces or as concert items. His splendid collection of standard tunes, published as *Moliant Cenedl*, reflects his just discrimination and catholicity of taste, and has greatly influenced and enriched subsequent hymn collections. His editorship of *Y Cerddor*, a literary journal devoted to the cause of music in Wales, has made a deep and lasting impression upon the life of the Principality. He has been a prolific composer of choral and orchestral works, the best known of which are *The Coming of Arthur*, a cantata for chorus and orchestra; *Llawenhewch yn yr Ior* (Rejoice in the Lord); *Deffro mae'n Ddydd*, a Welsh choral ballad; *Bro Bugeiliaid*, a children's cantata. He has written a large number of anthems, services, hymn-tunes, songs, &c. He was one of the representatives of Wales on the Joint Revision Committee of the *Church Hymnary*, and also chairman of the sub-committee of experts responsible for the editorship of the music.

47. TON-MÂN.	54. GWALIA.	69. MALDWYN.
193 (i). CAERLLEON.	233. PISGAH.	*242. LLANGOEDMOR.
*270. ERFYNIAD.	283. CHARTERHOUSE.	339. YN Y GLYN.
*505 (i). BRAINT.	*592. GLAN GEIRIONYDD.	609. CRUGYBAR.

EVEREST, Charles William, M.A. (East Windsor, Connecticut, 1814–77, Waterbury, Conn.), graduated at Trinity College, Hartford, Conn., in 1838, was ordained in 1842, and for 31 years thereafter was rector of the Episcopal Church, Hampden, near New Haven. During that time he also managed successfully an important school; and he was agent for a number of years of the Society for the Increase of the Ministry. He published *Visions of Death, and Other Poems*, in 1833.

119. *'Take up thy cross,' the Saviour said.*

EWING, Alexander (Old Machar, Aberdeen, 1830–95, Taunton), was the son of Alexander Ewing, M.D., lecturer on surgery at Marischal College, Aberdeen. He was a skilled musician, playing well on violin, 'cello, and cornet. He was closely identified with the Haydn Society of Aberdeen and the Harmonic Choir. One evening, after the practice of this choir, he approached Carnie, told him that he had tried his hand at writing a hymn-tune, and, offering copies of the voice-parts, asked that the choir should sing it over. This was done, and his one tune was launched on its long and popular career. Ewing left Aberdeen about 1853, joined the Army Commissariat Department in 1855, on the outbreak of the Crimean War, and attained the rank of lieutenant-colonel. He subsequently served in South Australia and China. Returning to England in 1867 he married Juliana Horatia Gatty, authoress of many well-known books for children.

198 (i). EWING.

FABER, Frederick William, D.D. (Calverley, Yorkshire, 1814–63, London), was educated at Shrewsbury, Harrow, and Balliol and University Colleges, Oxford. He was elected a Fellow of University in 1837. In 1838 he published *The Ancient Things of England*, vindicating the Church of England as against the Roman Church, and, after taking Orders, was for three years rector of Elton, Huntingdonshire. His views, however, changed, and he finally entered the Roman Church, and formed in Birmingham, with eight others, a community called 'Brothers of the Will of God'. In 1848 this brotherhood joined the Oratory of St. Philip Neri, under Newman, and in 1849 Faber established a branch of that order in London, which developed into the Brompton Oratory. He wrote many theological and devotional books, but is best known by his hymns, of which he wrote 150.

140. *O come and mourn with me awhile.*
188. *Most ancient of all mysteries.*
581. *My God, how wonderful thou art.*
666. *There's a wideness in God's mercy.*

FARJEON, Eleanor (London, 1881–), was educated privately, and is a writer of stories, poems, and music. Among her publications are *Nursery Rhymes of London Town*; *Faithful Jenny Dove*; *Singing Games from Arcady*; *Tomfooleries*, &c., and musical settings of the *Nursery Rhymes*, &c. She is sister to Harry Farjeon (q.v.).

11. *Fields of corn, give up your ears.*
30. *Morning has broken.*
569. *Lord, thou who gav'st me all I have.*
579. *More lovely than the noonday rest.*

FARJEON, Harry (Hohokus, New Jersey, 1878–1948), was born of English parents, and came to England at a very early age. After private study with Sir Landon Ronald and John Storer, he entered the Royal Academy of Music, where he gained several prizes and distinctions, and joined its professorial staff in 1903. He has written operettas, suites for orchestra, chamber music, songs, and much pianoforte music.

569. NEED.

FARMER, John (*fl.* 1591–1601). Nothing is known as to either the date or place of Farmer's birth or death. He was an important madrigal composer of the Elizabethan period who made very skilful settings for four voices of the old church psalm-tunes, and was the author of *Divers and Sundry waies of two parts in one to the number of fortie upon one playn Song*, of which work only one copy is known to be extant.

*693. OLD 30TH.

FAWCETT, John (Wennington, Lancashire, 1789–1867, Bolton), was a shoemaker who left his trade to follow the profession of music at Bolton-le-Moors. He published *A New set of Sacred Music, in three parts*, in *c.* 1822, and followed it with five collections of psalm- and hymn-tunes under the titles, *Miriam's Timbrel*; *Melodia Divina*; *Harp of Zion*; *The Cherub Lute*; *Voice of Devotion*. He also produced *Music for Thousands, or, The Vocalist's Manual*; an oratorio, *Paradise*; and much other music. Melling is about a mile and a half from Fawcett's birthplace.

463. MELLING. 614. RELIEF.

FILITZ (or FIELITZ), FRIEDRICH, Ph.D. (Arnstadt, Thuringia, 1804–76, Munich), resided in Berlin, 1843–7, and for the rest of his life in Munich. He edited *Vierstimmiges Choralbuch zu Kirchen- und Hausgebrauch*; a book of four-part tunes for the *Allgemeine Gesang- und Gebetbuch* of von Bunsen, who was his friend; and collaborated with Erk in bringing out a collection of the chorales of the most distinguished masters of the 16th and 17th centuries.

507. CAPETOWN. 555 (ii). MANNHEIM.

FINLAY, KENNETH GEORGE (London, 1882–), son of the late Prof. D. W. Finlay, Aberdeen University, was educated at Robert Gordon's College, Aberdeen, and Merchiston Castle School, Edinburgh. He was a Member of the Institute of Naval Architects, and, until 1928, held various positions of responsibility in connexion with shipbuilding. In 1928 he decided to devote himself altogether to music, and after a year at the Royal College of Music, and another at the Teachers' Training College, Jordanhill, Glasgow, has been, since 1930, a teacher of class-singing in Irvine under the Ayr County Council. He has published papers dealing with Safety of Life at Sea in the *Transactions* of the I.N.A.; hymn-tunes which have appeared in many collections, a cantata *The Saviour's Birth* (1928), and many unaccompanied choral works and educational part-songs.

354. GLENFINLAS.

FLETCHER, FRANK, M.A. (Atherton, Manchester, 1870–), was educated at Rossall School and Balliol College, Oxford. At the University he had a brilliant career, winning the Craven, Ireland, and Derby Scholarships. He was assistant master at Rugby, 1894–1903; master of Marlborough College, 1903–11; and has been Head Master of Charterhouse School, Godalming, since 1911.

611. *O Son of Man, our hero strong and tender.*

FLETCHER, PHINEAS (Cranbrook, Kent, 1582–1650, Hilgay, Norfolk), son of Dr. Giles Fletcher and cousin of John Fletcher the dramatist, was educated at Eton and King's College, Cambridge; took Holy Orders in 1621, and held the living of Nilgay for nearly 29 years. He wrote *The Purple Island* (1633), an allegorical poem after the manner of Spenser, and *The Locustes or Apollyonists*, a satire against the Jesuits.

125. *Drop, drop, slow tears.*

FORTUNATUS, VENANTIUS HONORIUS CLEMENTIANUS (*c.* 530–609), was a native of Italy, though he spent most of his time in Gaul. He studied at Milan and Ravenna with the object of excelling as a rhetorician and poet, after which he travelled in various parts of France. Eventually he attached himself to Queen Radegundis, who had left her husband, Clothaire II, the Frankish king, to found the nunnery of Ste Croix at Poitiers. Under her influence he took Holy Orders and was afterwards elected bishop of Poitiers.

129. *Sing, my tongue, the glorious battle.*
130. *The royal banners forward go.*
389. *Hail thee, Festival Day!*

FOSS, HUBERT JAMES (Croydon, 1899–   ), was educated at Bradfield College. Since 1921 he has been musical editor of the Oxford University Press (H. Milford); from 1922 to 1923 he was music critic of the *New Witness*, and in 1923 of the *Daily Graphic*. He has contributed many articles to the periodical press. Among his musical publications are *Seven Poems by Thomas Hardy . . . for baritone, male chorus, and piano* (1925); *Six Songs from Shakespeare* (1929); and many single songs, part-songs, &c.

170 (ii). CROYDON.

FOUNDERY COLLECTION. This was the first Methodist hymn-book with tunes and appeared as *A Collection of Tunes, set to Music, as they are commonly Sung at the Foundery* (1742). The Foundery was an old state cannon-foundry, abandoned after a destructive explosion in 1716, and bought by Charles Wesley, in 1739, as the site of the first Methodist meeting-house in London. This collection, which was extremely badly printed and arranged, did not reach a 2nd edition, and is now very rare; a facsimile reprint was published in 1882.

160. SAVANNAH (or HERRNHUT). 343. MILITES.

FOUNDLING HOSPITAL COLLECTION. This was a collection of hymns and anthems written for Captain Coram's famous foundation (1738), where the training of the children in singing was, from the first, made an especial feature; it was published as *Psalms, Hymns and Anthems of the Foundling Hospital* (1774), and subsequent augmented editions were also issued. The Hospital owed much, in its early years, to the support of Handel, who presented it with an organ, on the completion of the chapel in 1750, and also gave annual recitals there of the *Messiah*, for the benefit of the Institution.

184. *Spirit of mercy, truth, and love.*
624. *Praise the Lord! Ye heavens, adore him.*

FRANCIS OF ASSISI (Assisi, 1182–1226, Assisi) was the son of a well-to-do merchant in that city. Until the age of 25 he showed no religious inclinations, but, after a severe illness at this time, he established himself in a cell outside the city, and there formed an order of men sworn to poverty and renunciation of the world, whom he sent out by couples to preach the Gospel and relieve distress. The order developed with great rapidity, was sanctioned by the Pope; and two others were established, one for women, by Clare, and a third for persons of both sexes, who took no vows of poverty, but followed certain rules of life and conduct. St. Francis's love for animals, birds, and all nature is famous. Though his order soon lost its original character, his influence was enormous; no saint is more esteemed to-day.

434. *O most high, almighty, good Lord God.*
439. *All creatures of our God and King.*

FRANCK, JOHANN (Guben, Brandenburg, 1618–77, Guben), the son of an advocate, was educated at Guben, Cottbus, Stettin, and Thorn, and then at Königsberg, the only university not disorganized by the shattering effects of the Thirty Years War. There he was greatly influenced by Simon Dach, Professor of Poetry. After some experience of travel, he settled as an advocate in his native town, where he became a councillor, in 1651 burgomaster, and in 1671 deputy from the town to the Landtag of Lower Lusatia. He was a notable poet in his day. To a modern taste his secular poetry seems diffuse and artificial, but his hymns are on a much higher level—simple, earnest in spirit, and compact and massive in form. He marks the transition from the objective form of church song prevalent till his time, to the more individual and mystical type: his leading idea is the union of the soul with its Saviour. His 110 hymns were published at Guben in 1674 under the title *Geistliche Sion.*

267. *Deck thyself, my soul, with gladness.*
544. *Jesus, priceless treasure.*

FRANCK, JOHANN WOLFGANG, M.D. (? 1641–88), practised his profession of medicine and composed music in Hamburg. He wrote a number of *Geistliche Lieder*, chiefly settings of Heinrich Elmenhorst's hymns. Little of his life is known, but it is believed that he repaired to Spain in 1688, and there met his death by poisoning.

255 (i). KOMM SEELE.

FREYLINGHAUSEN, JOHANN ANASTASIUS (Gandersheim, Brunswick, 1670–1739, Halle), son of the burgomaster of Gandersheim, studied at Jena, but, attracted by the preaching of A. H. Francke and J. J. Breithaupt, the Pietist leaders, removed to Erfurt, and then followed them to Halle. There he became colleague to Francke, first in the Glaucha Church, then in St. Ulrich's. Marrying Francke's daughter, he assisted his father-in-law as director of the Paedagogium and the Orphanage in Halle, and in 1727 succeeded him in that office as well as in the full charge of St. Ulrich's. Under him these institutions reached their highest prosperity. Freylinghausen was a musician also, and some 22 melodies are attributed to him; his fame, however, rests chiefly on his two great collections, the *Geistreiches Gesangbuch den Kern alter und neuer Lieder . . . in sich haltend, &c.* (1704), and *Neues Geistreiches Gesangbuch, &c.* (1714). The former contained 683 hymns and 173 melodies, the latter 815 hymns, and 154 melodies, a complete augmented edition being issued in 1741. More than half these melodies were new, or, at least, do not seem to be found in any earlier publication.

27. MORGENGLANZ DER EWIGKEIT.
77. FREYLINGHAUSEN (MACHT HOCH DIE THÜR).
139. SEBASTIAN (JESU MEINES GLAUBENS ZIER).
292. PRESSBURG (NICHT SO TRAURIG).
645. GOTT SEI DANK.

FRITSCH, AHASUERUS (Mücheln, Saxony, 1629–1701, Rudolfstadt). His early youth was lived during the troublous period of the Thirty Years War; his native town was besieged and he and his family suffered. His education was greatly interrupted by poverty: by making sacrifices, however, and by hard work he was able to present himself in 1650 before the learned Jurisprudist Struve for study. In 1657 he became tutor to the young Earl Albert Anton von Schwarzburg-Rudolfstadt; his character made him admired by that family, and he received various preferments. He was a prolific writer on antiquarian, legal, and sacred subjects. He also made collections of hymns, and while very careful to name the author, he usually omitted mention thereof where the poem was his own.

621. DARMSTADT (O GOTT DU FROMMER GOTT).

FYLEMAN, Rose (Nottingham, 1877–), was educated privately and at University College, Nottingham. For some years she was a school teacher, but later studied singing both abroad and at the Royal College of Music. Since 1903 she has been engaged in teaching, lecturing, singing, and writing. She has contributed much to periodical literature, and also published many volumes of plays, stories, and poems for children, such as *Fairies and Chimneys* (1918); *Eight Little Plays for Children* (1924); *Letty* (1926); *Fifty New Nursery Rhymes* (1931), &c.

3. *Lift your hidden faces.*

GALE, Norman (Kew, 1862-1942), was educated privately and at Exeter College, Oxford. For some years he was a schoolmaster, but success in literature led him to adopt this as his profession; and for 13 years he was occupied as a reviewer, a publisher's reader, and contributor to various periodicals. After this period he returned once more to teaching, combining the activities of a coach with those of a free-lance journalist. During the War he acted as supplementary master at Rugby School, remaining there for seven years, since when he has lived in retirement at Bexhill. Among his publications are 3 volumes of verse for children, 5 volumes of other poetry, 3 volumes of 'Cricket Songs', and 4 volumes of prose.

518. *Here in the country's heart.*

GAMBLE, John (died in 1687), was a violinist, pupil of Ambrose Blyland, and one of the violins to Charles I; he also performed in the theatres, and was cornet player in the Chapel Royal. In 1656 he published *Ayres and Dialogues to be sung to the Theorbo Lute or Bass Viol*, and a second collection in 1659. In 1662 he set the songs in *Aqua Triumphalis*, a pageant by John Tatham. He lost all his property in the Great Fire of London.

379. GAMBLE.

GANNETT, William Channing (Boston, U.S.A., 1840–1923, New York), son of Dr. Ezra Stiles Gannett, was educated at Harvard and the Divinity School, Cambridge, U.S.A. In 1868 he became a Unitarian minister, and in 1889 was appointed pastor of the Unitarian Church at Rochester, N.Y. His publications included *A Year of Miracle* (1882); *The Thought of God in Hymns and Poems*, with F. L. Hosmer (q.v.) (1886); *The Childhood of Jesus* (1890); *Francis David* (1914), &c.

655. *The Lord is in his holy place.*

GASCOIGNE, George (Westmorland, *c.* 1525–77, Stamford), heir of Sir John Gascoigne, was educated at Trinity College, Cambridge. He entered the Middle Temple as a law student before 1548, transferred to Gray's Inn 1555, but left it shortly afterwards. In 1557–8 he represented Bedford in Parliament, returned to Gray's Inn 1565, and there, a year later, produced two plays, *The Supposes* from the Italian of Ariosto, and *Jocasta*, an adaptation from Euripides. In 1572 he was returned member for Midhurst, but did not sit, owing to objections that were raised. He served in Holland under William of Orange and was made a captain, but was taken prisoner and sent back to England. When, in 1575, Queen Elizabeth visited Kenilworth he was charged by Leicester to devise the masques and entertainments. He published *The Steele Glas* (1576), and contributed to various miscellanies.

38. *You that have spent the silent night.*

GASKELL, William, M.A. (Latchford, near Warrington, 1805–84, Manchester), studied at Glasgow University and Manchester College, York. Becoming a Unitarian minister, his one and only charge was Cross Street Chapel, Manchester. He became Professor of English History and Literature in Manchester New College, and his denomination conferred its highest honours upon him. At Owens College and a Working Men's College he conducted classes with much acceptance and success. He published sermons, tracts, memoirs, lectures on the Lancashire dialect, &c., and a number of hymns, which were contributed to the Rev. Dr. J. R. Beard's collection of Hymns by Unitarians. His wife was the famous authoress of *Cranford*, &c.

676. *Though lowly here our lot may be.*

GATTY, Nicholas Comyn, B.A., Mus.Doc. (Bradfield, near Sheffield, 1874–1946), was educated at Downing College, Cambridge, and after leaving Cambridge spent three years at the Royal College of Music, holding an exhibition for composition, under Stanford. Until his appointment as musical critic to the *Pall Mall Gazette*, 1907–14, he held various musical posts in London, among them organist to the Duke of York's Royal Military School. He has composed the short operas *Greysteel* (1906), *Duke or Devil* (1909), and *The Tempest*, a choral setting of Milton's *Ode on Time* (1905), a pianoforte concerto, a string-quartet, orchestral variations, choruses, &c. He further assisted the editors of two editions of *Grove's Dictionary of Music and Musicians*.

152. MIDHURST.

GAUNTLETT, Henry John, Mus.Doc. (Wellington, Shropshire, 1805–76, Kensington), became, at the age of nine, organist of his father's Church at Olney, Buckinghamshire. His father destined him for the law, and articled him to a solicitor. This profession he followed till 1844, when he gave it up to devote himself to music. He was organist in turn of St. Olave's, Southwark; Christ Church, Newgate Street; Union Chapel (Dr. Allon's), Islington; and St. Bartholomew the Less, Smithfield. The Archbishop of Canterbury conferred on him the degree of Mus. Doc., he being the first recipient of such a degree from that source for 200 years. He edited many hymn-books, and himself wrote a vast number of tunes, some of which were of excellent quality and have taken their place among the most familiar hymn-tunes. His most important work, however, was in the reform of church music, both by raising the standard of quality, as by his *Gregorian Hymnal* (1844), and his *Gregorian Psalter* and *Bible Psalter*, and by mechanical improvements in English organs.

151. ST. FULBERT. 155. ST. ALBINUS. 351. LAUDATE DOMINUM.
368. IRBY. 459 (ii). ST. ALPHEGE. 619. UNIVERSITY COLLEGE.

GELLERT, CHRISTIAN FÜRCHTEGOTT (Haynichen, Saxony, 1715–69, Leipzig), son of a country clergyman who was also a poet, studied at Meissen and Leipzig with some thought of the Church, but experiment proved him too timid for the preacher's calling. He took a degree in the faculty of Belles Lettres, and became first a lecturer on poetry and eloquence, and then Professor of Philosophy, in Leipzig University. He co-operated with some friends in a periodical called *Bremer Beiträge*, in which his *Tales and Fables*, long popular in Germany, first appeared. He composed comedies, wrote *Consolations for Valetudinarians* out of his own experience of poor health and melancholy; *Didactic Poems*; *Moral Poems*; *Letters*; and, in 1757, *Spiritual Odes and Songs*.

155. *Jesus lives! thy terrors now.*

GERHARDT, PAUL (Gräfenhainichen, Saxony, 1607–76, Lübben, Saxe-Merseburg), son of a burgomaster of his native town, spent most of his life amid the distractions and disasters of the Thirty Years War. He studied at Wittenberg for the Lutheran ministry, but was a man of 45 before he received his first ecclesiastical appointment, to the pastorate of a small village called Mittenwalde. Before that, he had been tutor in the household of Andreas Berthold, a Chancery advocate in Berlin, whose daughter he married. From Mittenwalde his hymns began to attract attention, and were quickly adopted into the hymn-books of Brandenburg and Saxony. They had already made him famous when, in 1657, he was called as third 'diaconus' of St. Nicholas Cathedral, Berlin. In 1664, on his refusing to subscribe to the Elector Friedrich Wilhelm I's edict restraining freedom of speech on disputed points between the Lutheran and Reformed Churches, he was deposed from office, and interdicted from performing any of his functions even in private. In 1668 he was appointed archdeacon of Lübben, where he remained until his death. His hymns appeared in Crüger's *Geistliche Kirchenmelodian* (1649) and *Praxis Pietatis Melica* (1656).

57. *The duteous day now closeth.*
128. *O sacred head, sore wounded.*
478. *Cometh sunshine after rain.*
89. *Hearts at Christmas time were jolly.*
479. *Commit thou all thy griefs.*

GERMANUS, ST. (Constantinople, 634–734, Constantinople). A Greek hymn-writer, and great defender of the Icons. He was ordained in the town of his birth and subsequently became bishop of Cyzicus. He was present at the Synod of Constantinople 712, at which the Monothelite heresy was restored. In later life, however, he condemned it, and was Patriarch of Constantinople in 715. Driven from the see because he had dared to defend icons against the Emperor Leo the Isaurian, he died soon after.

70. *A great and mighty wonder.*

GESIUS, OR GESE, BARTHOLOMÄUS (Muncheberg in Brandenburg, *c.* 1555–1613 *or* 1621, Frankfort-on-the-Oder), was first a student of theology, then a cantor at Frankfort-on-the-Oder from about 1595 till he died. His works cover the whole area of the liturgical music of the older Lutheran Church, the most important of them being his *Passion according to St. John* for two to five voices.

194 (i). DANK SEI GOTT IN DER HÖHE.
533. GESIUS (HEUT' TRIUMPHIRET).

GIARDINI, Felice (Turin, 1716–96, Moscow), was trained as a chorister in Milan Cathedral, but made his fame as a violinist. In 1750 he visited England, and obtained a great success in London, becoming leader at the Italian Opera, and, later, impresario. After a long residence in England, he went to Naples in the train of Sir William Hamilton, British Ambassador to the Sardinian Court, but on his return, five years later, failed to retrieve his former popularity. A visit to Moscow did nothing to restore his fortunes, and he died in that city in poverty and distress.

303. MOSCOW.

GIBBONS, Orlando, Mus.Doc. (Oxford, 1583-1625, Canterbury), was a son of one of the Cambridge Waits, and belonged to a family of musicians. He joined the choir of King's College, Cambridge, in 1596; became organist of the Chapel Royal, London, 1604; King's musician for the virginals, 1619; organist, Westminster Abbey, 1623. He was one of the greatest of the polyphonic writers. He wrote the tunes for Wither's *Hymns and Songs of the Church* (1623) [p. xv]. These beautiful tunes, some of which were long kept in use in mutilated forms, and others dropped from use altogether, are returning now to the favour which is their due. Commanded by Charles I to attend him in Canterbury Cathedral on the occasion of his marriage with Henrietta Maria of France, Gibbons was seized with apoplexy and died there; he is buried in the Cathedral, where his epitaph describes him as 'a man of integrity, whose manner of life and sweetness of temper vied with that of his art'.

29. ANGEL'S SONG (SONG 34). 103. SONG 24. 125. SONG 46.
134. SONG 13. 204. SONG 67. 261. SONG 4.
296. SONG 1. 485. SONG 1. 574. SONG 22.
584. SONG 20. 604 (i). SONG 18. 648. SONG 5.
681. SONG 24. App. 3 (vii). AMEN.

GIBBS, Cecil Armstrong, Mus.Doc. (Great Baddow, 1889–), was educated at Winchester and Trinity College, Cambridge, where he took his B.A. in 1911, Mus.Bac. 1913, and Mus.Doc. 1931. Since 1921 he has been a professor at the Royal College of Music, becoming Hon. A.R.C.M. in 1928. Among his compositions are a *Symphony* (1931), string quartets, and works for chorus and orchestra. He has also written for the theatre, including Music to the Cambridge Greek Play (1921 and 1933); Maeterlinck's *Betrothal* (1921); *Midsummer Madness* (1924); and *The Blue Peter* (1923), which received a Carnegie Award. In addition he has published over 60 solo songs, and some 50 part-songs, &c.

81. DANBURY. 646 (i). LITTLE BADDOW. 661 (ii). CROSSINGS.

GILDING, Edmund (? –1782, London), was organist of St. Martin's, Ludgate, and of St. Edmund King and Martyr, when he contributed to Riley's *Parochial Harmony* in 1762; also, at one time, of St. Giles's, Cripplegate. Subsequently he was organist of the Parish Clerks' Company (*c.* 1765).

120 (ii). ST. EDMUND.

GILLETT, George Gabriel Scott, B.A. (Hawley, Hants, 1873–1948), son of the Rev. E. A. Gillett, was educated at Westminster School and Keble College, Oxford. Ordained in 1898, he held curacies for some years in London and Brighton; was successively domestic chaplain to Earl Beauchamp and to Viscount Halifax, and from 1913 to 1925 worked in

South Africa. He is now editorial secretary to the Society for the Propagation of the Gospel. His publications include *The Claims and Promise of the Church* (1909); *Religion and Politics* (1911); *A Garden of Song* (1922), and contributions to periodical literature, &c.

139. *It is finished! Christ hath known.*

GODOLPHIN, SIDNEY (Godolphin, Cornwall, 1610–43, Chagford), son of Sir William Godolphin, was educated at Exeter College, Oxford, and later entered one of the Inns of Court. After some foreign travel he was, in 1628, elected member of Parliament for Helston, and sat also in the Short and Long Parliaments of 1640. He raised a troop in Cornwall in the Royalist cause and was regarded by his superiors as a valuable and promising leader, but was killed in a skirmish. He wrote several poems which were posthumously published in various miscellanies.

571. *Lord, when the wise men came from far.*

GOSS, Sir JOHN, Mus.Doc. (Fareham, Hants, 1800–80, Brixton Rise, London), was the son of the organist of Fareham. He was trained as one of the children of the Chapel Royal, and as a pupil of Thomas Attwood. In 1838 he succeeded Attwood as organist of St. Paul's. He sang for a time in opera, but left it early to devote his powers to church music. He was made one of the composers of the Chapel Royal in 1856, was knighted in 1872, and made Mus.Doc. by Cambridge in 1876. He had a very individual gift of melody and great technical accomplishment, and was second only to S. S. Wesley among the English church composers of his period. There is a cenotaph to his memory in the crypt of St. Paul's. He edited *Parochial Psalmody* (1826); *Chants, Ancient and Modern* (1841); the music of Mercer's *Church Psalter and Hymn Book* (1856); and wrote (1833) *An Introduction to Harmony and Thorough Bass.*

623. PRAISE, MY SOUL.

GOUDIMEL, CLAUDE (Besançon, *c.* 1505/10–72, Lyons), probably went to Paris in 1549, at least he makes his first appearance then as a composer of Chansons published by Du Chemin of Paris. In 1557 he lived in Metz and associated himself with many of the Huguenots there. In 1568 Goudimel returned to Besançon, going on later to Lyons, where he perished in the massacre of the Huguenots, St. Bartholomew's Day, 27 Aug. 1572. Goudimel's music appears in many of the psalm books published in various languages throughout the 17th and 18th centuries. In 1554 Du Chemin published five masses composed by Goudimel.

*50. NUNC DIMITTIS. *208. PSALM 93.
*210 (ii). PSALM 146. *661 (i). PSALM 138.

GRACE, HARVEY, Mus.Doc. (Romsey, 1874–1944), studied under Dr. Madeley Richardson at Southwark Cathedral. Since 1916 he has been the editor of the *Musical Times*, and since 1931 organist and director of the choir of Chichester Cathedral. Among his publications are *Ludwig van Beethoven*; *The Organ Works of Rheinberger*; *A Musician at Large*; *A Handbook for Choralists*; *The Complete Organist*; *French Organ Music, Past and Present*; *The Organ Works of Bach*; and many organ pieces, songs, and part-songs, &c.

*250. ST. STEPHEN. *349 (ii). ISTE CONFESSOR (ROUEN).
*610. ILLSLEY. *618. HANOVER.

GRANT, Sir ROBERT (Bengal, 1779–1838, Dalpoorie, Western India), was a son of Charles Grant, sometime M.P. for Inverness, Director of the East India Company, and Indian philanthropist. Educated at Magdalen College, Oxford, of which he became a Fellow, he was called to the Bar in 1807, and became King's Serjeant in the Court of the Duchy of Lancaster and one of the commissioners in bankruptcy. Entering Parliament in 1808, he represented in succession the Elgin Burghs, Inverness Burghs, Norwich, and Finsbury. In 1831 he was made a Privy Councillor. In 1833 he carried through the Commons a Bill for the emancipation of the Jews. He was made Judge Advocate General in 1832, and Governor of Bombay in 1834, being knighted on this occasion. As a memorial of his governorship, a medical college was erected, bearing his name. His hymns were contributed to the *Christian Observer*, and to H. V. Elliott's *Psalms and Hymns* (1835). His brother, Lord Glenelg, collected and published twelve of them in 1839.

618. *O worship the King.*

GRAY, ALAN, LL.B., LL.M., Mus.Bac., Mus.Doc. (York, 1855–1935), educated at St. Peter's School, York, and Trinity College, Cambridge, was at first intended for the Law, but having studied with Dr. E. G. Monk he thereafter devoted himself entirely to music; was appointed musical director at Wellington College 1883, and in 1892 succeeded Villiers Stanford as organist of Trinity College, Cambridge, and conductor of the Cambridge Musical Society till 1912. His chief musical publications are *The Widow of Zarephath*; *Arethusa*; *The Legend of the Rock Buoy Bell*; *The Vision of Belshazzar*; *A Song of Redemption*; many important compositions for the organ, and *A Book of Descants* in which the following arrangements appear.

*97. HEINLEIN.
*189 (ii). BUCKLEBURY.
*197 (ii). CHRISTCHURCH.
*199. TANTUM ERGO (WEBBE).
*211. OLD 104TH.
*303. MOSCOW.
*477. NEANDER.
*491 (i). DUKE STREET.
*542. ABERYSTWYTH.
*683. ORIEL.

GREATOREX, WALTER (Mansfield, 1877–1949), son of H. E. Greatorex, a bank manager, was educated at Derby School and St. John's College, Cambridge, and is director of Music at Gresham's School, Holt.

299. WOODLANDS.

GREEN, JAMES (*c.* 1690–*c.* 1750), was an organist in Hull, who edited *A Book of Psalm Tunes, with variety of Anthems in four parts*. Appearing in 1724, this book passed through many editions, the title of which became *A Book of Psalmody, containing Chanting Tunes for the Canticles and the reading Psalms, with Eighteen Anthems and a variety of Psalm Tunes in four parts* (1731). Green composed many hymn-tunes. Latterly he lived in London and acquired fame as a bell-ringer; he had a belfry of his own on the top of his house.

39. FERRY. 120 (i). WIRKSWORTH. 482. CROWLE.

GREENWOOD, JOHN (*floruit c.* 1790–*c.* 1840), was a musician and teacher in Leeds. He published *A Selection of Antient and Modern Psalm Tunes* (Leeds, 1825); *Modulus Sanctus, a Collection of Sacred Music*

(Leeds, 1828); and *Psalmody harmonised in score, with accompaniment for organ and pianoforte* (Halifax, 1838).

284. AFFECTION.

GREGORY, St. (Rome, 540–604, Rome), surnamed the Great (Pope Gregory I), was born of a Roman family distinguished for public service and piety. He himself became praetor of the city of Rome at an early age, but finally renounced his position and devoted himself and his fortune to monasticism. He dispatched, as Pope, missionaries to all parts of the empire, the incident ('Non Angli sed angeli') which led to his sending Augustine to England being too well known to need repetition. His reform of church music led to his name being attached to the system of plain-chant which he made obligatory throughout the Western Church, and perfected by means of the school of singing founded by him in Rome.

28. *Father, we praise thee, now the night is over.*

GREITER, Matthäus (*c.* 1500–52), was originally a monk and singer in Strassburg Minster, but in 1524 became a Protestant and devoted his musical powers to the service of the Lutheran Church. In 1528 he was appointed assistant pastor of St. Martin's Church, and, later, of St. Stephen's. In 1548 he founded a choir school. Four years later he died, it is said, of the plague. He was an accomplished musician, as several extant settings of German songs show. He contributed seven psalm-lieder to the *Strassburger Kirchenamt* (1525), and is credited with six of the chorale melodies. Four of these tunes were used in the early *French Psalter* published at Strassburg in 1539, and all these were transferred to the *French Genevan Psalter* in 1542.

246. PSALM 68.

GRIGG, ? . This composer is frequently identified with the Rev. Joseph Grigg, the hymn-writer; but this is pure assumption. No details of his life survive. Three tunes by him appeared in *A Selection of Psalm and Hymn Tunes arranged by John Rippon, D.D.* (*c.* 1795). In that book no Christian name is given.

456. TIVERTON.

GUIDETTI, Giovanni (Bologna, 1532–92, Rome), was a pupil of Palestrina, who having been commissioned by Gregory XIII to revise the Services of the Roman Church, delegated part of the labour to his pupil Guidetti, because he had intimate knowledge of the manuscripts in St. Peter's and other churches of Rome. The work which occupied him from 1576 to 1581 was published in 1582—*Directorium chori . . . opera Joannis Guidetti Bononiensis*, &c. For ten years Guidetti had the right of sale. He had done all the drudgery, leaving to Palestrina only the polishing up and revising.

37 (i). AETERNA CHRISTI MUNERA.

GURNEY, Archer Thompson (? 1820–87, Bath), was called to the Bar, but took Orders, and held among other appointments the British Chaplaincy at Paris. He wrote several volumes of poems, now forgotten.

152. *Christ is risen! Christ is risen!*

GURNEY, Dorothy Frances, *née* Blomfield (London, 1858–1932, London), was a granddaughter of Bishop Blomfield, of Chester and London. Her father, Frederick George Blomfield, was rector of St. Andrew Undershaft, London. She published two volumes of *Poems*.

283. *O perfect Love, all human thought transcending.*

GURNEY, John Hampden, M.A. (London, 1802–62, London), son of Sir John Gurney, a baron of the Court of Exchequer, was educated at Trinity College, Cambridge, and after some study of law, turned to the Church. He became curate of Wyclif's old parish of Lutterworth, and was chaplain of the poor-law Union there. In 1847 he was rector of St. Mary's, Bryanstone Square, Marylebone, London, and in 1857 a prebendary of St. Paul's. He took a deep interest in the Religious Tract Society and the S.P.C.K. Two collections of hymns were made by him—one for Lutterworth in 1838, the other for Marylebone in 1851.

10. *Fair waved the golden corn.*

GWYLLT, Ieuan (John Roberts) (Tanrhiwfelen, near Aberystwyth, 1822–77, Vron, near Caernarvon), after a variety of occupations was ordained to the ministry of the Calvinistic Methodist Church in 1859, and held pastoral charges first near Merthyr, then at Capel Coch, Llanberis, until 1869, when he retired. He did a great work as a reformer of congregational singing. He was the founder of the great institution known in Wales as the *Gymanfa ganu*, or singing festival, for the encouragement of the writing of hymns and hymn-tunes. Ieuan Gwyllt's *Llyfr Tonau Cynulleidfaol* (Book of Congregational Tunes, 1859), the recognized tune-book of the Calvinistic Methodists, was epoch-making. He also edited the monthly musical magazine *Y Cerddor Gymreig*.

218. MOAB. 586 (ii). LIVERPOOL. 695. ARDUDWY.

HADLEY, Patrick (Cambridge, 1899–), was educated at Winchester and Pembroke College, Cambridge. After war service 1917–18, he studied at the Royal College of Music, and joined the staff there in 1925. His publications include *Nightfall*, for solo, male chorus, and orchestra; *The Trees So High*, a symphonic ballad for orchestra, with baritone solo and chorus; and songs with piano or chamber orchestra accompaniment.

311. PEMBROKE.

HANDEL, George Frederick, originally Georg Friedrich Händel (Halle, 1685–1759, London), was son of the surgeon to Duke Augustus of Saxony. His extraordinary musical gifts early made themselves apparent, but the father, intending him for the legal profession, tried to repress them. Ultimately, through the intervention of the Duke of Saxe-Weissenfels, the boy was allowed to take lessons from Zachau, organist of the Cathedral. In 1702 he entered the University of Halle, but in the following year repaired to Hamburg, joined the band of the theatre as a violinist, and in 1705 produced his first opera, *Almira*. In 1707 he went to Italy, and during some years there won many triumphs. Returning to Germany, he became chapelmaster to the Elector of Hanover, afterwards George I of Great Britain and Ireland. A first visit to England in 1710 made this country so attractive to him that in 1713 he returned to it and finally made it his home. For nearly 30 years his genius, which was essentially dramatic, was concentrated almost wholly on operatic composition. During one interval he was chapelmaster to the Duke of Chandos, at Cannons, nine miles from London. Here Handel composed for the Duke's private chapel the Chandos Te Deums and Anthems, and in 1720 his first oratorio *Esther*. *Acis and Galatea* was also produced at Cannons. A long operatic war waged between him and his rival Buononcini (see 73) ended in the bankruptcy of both in 1737. Paralysis induced by this blow partially disabled him, yet subsequently he discharged all his obligations. The disaster led him to abandon opera and concentrate his genius upon the oratorios, which, for 150 years, made him supreme in England. After the *Messiah*, composed in 24 days, swept Dublin with enthusiasm on its first performance there in 1741, till blindness befell him in 1753, he lived happily in the sunshine of popular favour. His productiveness was inexhaustible: he wrote over 40 operas, 7 English oratorios, 3 English serenatas, 4 odes, besides Psalms, Te Deums, and other minor works. Most of his instrumental works were for the organ, in the playing of which he was a master, and for the harpsichord, his favourite instrument.

110. SOLOMON. 297. BRUNSWICK. 337 (i). CANNONS.
450. BRUNSWICK. 451. SAMSON. 632. GOPSAL.

HANKEY, DONALD WILLIAM ALERS (Brighton, 1884–1916, at the Battle of the Somme), was educated at Rugby, and in 1901 passed into Woolwich. There he gained the prize for the best essay on the lessons of the South African War. After two years at Woolwich he received his commission (1903) and joined the Royal Garrison Artillery, Sheerness. In 1904 he embarked on a troopship bound for Ceylon *en route* for Mauritius. He was not satisfied with himself as a soldier, and wished to take Orders. A year and ten months spent in Mauritius deepened this dissatisfaction. On his return to England in 1906 he worked at the Rugby Mission. In 1907 he resigned his commission, travelled on the Continent, and in October matriculated at Corpus Christi College, Oxford. He left Oxford in 1910, and in 1911 went to the Leeds Clergy School. In 1912 he travelled steerage to Australia and returned in 1914, lived in Bermondsey, and there wrote *The Lord of All Good Life*. In May 1915 he crossed to France. His chief publications are: *Religion and Common Sense*; *The Cross*; *The Lord of All Good Life*; *A Student in Arms* (2 series); *Passing in June*, &c.

568. *Lord of the strong, when earth you trod.*

HARDY, THOMAS, O.M., LL.D., Litt.D., &c. (near Dorchester, 1840–1928, Dorchester), was educated in Dorchester and at King's College, London. He studied architecture under Sir A. Blomfield, and was a prizeman of the Royal Institute of British Architects, 1863. He practised for some years, but later, after the success of his first novel *Desperate Remedies* (1871), abandoned architecture to devote his whole time to literature. Among his other novels are *Under the Greenwood Tree*; *Far from the Madding Crowd*; *The Return of the Native*; *Tess of the d'Urbervilles*; *Jude the Obscure*, &c.; while among his volumes of poetry are *Wessex Poems*; *The Dynasts*; *Satires of Circumstance*; *Time's Laughing-Stocks, and other poems*, &c.

684. *To thee whose eye all nature owns.*

HARINGTON, Henry, M.D., M.A. (Kelston, Somersetshire, 1727–1816, Bath), was educated at Queen's College, Oxford, where he took his degree in 1748. At Oxford he was a member of the Musical Society, and, while in practice as a physician at Bath and Wells, established a musical society there: he was also, at one time, mayor of Bath. He published three collections of *Glees*, in 1770, 1785, and 1797; numerous separate glees; and many songs and anthems.

613. HARINGTON (RETIREMENT).

HARRIS, William Henry, M.A., D.Mus. (London, 1883–   ), was educated at St. David's and the Royal College of Music; organist of Christ Church Cathedral, Oxford, 1928–33; conductor of the Oxford Bach Choir since 1926. He was at one time assistant organist at Lichfield Cathedral, and organist at New College, Oxford, 1919–28, and is now organist of St. George's Chapel, Windsor. Publications: a setting of the *Hound of Heaven, for baritone solo, chorus and orchestra*, a Carnegie award piece; church music, songs, part-songs, &c.

*84. STUTTGART. 554 (i). ALBERTA.

HARRISON, Ralph (Chinley, Derbyshire, 1748–1810, Manchester), was son of a Presbyterian (Unitarian) minister. Educated at Warrington Academy, he became assistant minister of the Presbyterian Chapel, Shrewsbury, 1769; and minister of Cross Street Chapel, Manchester, 1771. When Manchester Academy was established in 1786, he was appointed classical tutor in it. He published *Institutes of English Grammar*, geographical manuals, &c.; and after endeavouring in vain to induce others to undertake the task, compiled *Sacred Harmony* (2 vols., 1784–91), a collection of psalm-tunes, ancient and modern, for use in the Manchester district. Included in it were some tunes of his own composition.

25 (Part III). WARRINGTON. 575. BLACKBOURNE.

HARRISON, William (*fl. c.* 1620), was one of the distinguished company of musicians who contributed arrangements of the psalm-tunes to Ravenscroft's *Whole Book of Psalms* (1621). Little else is known of his life.

*171. LINCOLN.

HARVEY, Patrick Eugene Lawrence (London, 1910–   ), was a choir-boy at St. Mary's, Primrose Hill, where he received his first organ lessons from Geoffrey Shaw. Later he studied at the London Academy of Music, and in 1928 gained an organ scholarship at Keble College, Oxford. In 1932 he was appointed a tenor lay clerk to Armagh Cathedral. He has published *A Short Mass in Unison*.

*131. HORSLEY.

HARWOOD, Basil, M.A., D.Mus. (Woodhouse, Olveston, Gloucestershire, 1859–1949), was educated at Charterhouse and Trinity College, Oxford. He held posts successively as organist of Trinity College, Oxford; St. Barnabas, Pimlico; Ely Cathedral; Christ Church, Oxford; also as precentor of Keble College, and as Choragus of the University of Oxford. He was musical editor of the *Oxford Hymn Book* (1908). His published works include anthems, hymn-tunes, church services, organ works; a cantata, *Song on May Day Morning*; and a motet, *Jesus, Thy boundless love to me.*

255 (iii). THORNBURY. *607 (ii). O AMOR QUAM EXSTATICUS.

HASSLER, HANS LEO (Nuremberg, 1564–1612, Frankfurt), came of a musical family in the Joachimsthal, and studied at Venice under Andrea Gabrieli, organist of St. Mark's. In 1585 he was given a home in the house of the Fuggers, the great merchant princes and art patrons of Augsburg. He was appointed musical director there in 1600, but a year later accepted the post of organist in the Frauenkirche in Nuremberg. In 1608 he entered the service of the Elector of Saxony. Accompanying that prince to the Diet at Frankfurt in 1612, he died there. His works included *XXIV Canzonetti a 4 voci*; *Cantiones Sacrae de praecipuis festis totius anni, 4, 5, 8, et plurium vocum*; *Concentus ecclesiasticae*; *Madrigali*; *Cantiones novae*; *Sacri Concentus* for 5 to 12 voices; 4-part Psalms and Songs; and 5 collections of German and Latin secular songs. Many of his chorales were published in the Hizler (Strassburg) *Chorale Book.* He was the most eminent organist of his day.

128. PASSION CHORALE.

HATCH, EDWIN, D.D. (Derby, 1835–89, Oxford), was educated at King Edward's School, Birmingham, and Pembroke College, Oxford. At the University he was closely associated with Burne-Jones, William Morris, and Swinburne. By the time he took his degree he was already contributing largely to reviews and magazines on a wide range of subjects. His parents were Nonconformists, but he took Orders in the Church of England and for a time worked in an east-end parish in London. In 1859 he accepted an appointment as Professor of Classics in Trinity College, Quebec. Returning to Oxford in 1867, he became Vice-Principal of St. Mary's Hall; in 1880, Bampton and Grinfield Lecturer; in 1883, rector of Purleigh, Essex; in 1884, University Reader in Ecclesiastical History; in 1888, Hibbert Lecturer.

458. *Breathe on me, Breath of God.*

HATTON, JOHN (Warrington, ? –1793, St. Helen's), resided in St. Helen's, in the township of Windle, in a street whose name he gave to the one tune by which his name is known. His funeral sermon was preached in the Presbyterian Chapel, St. Helen's.

298 [491 (i)]. DUKE STREET.

HAVERGAL, FRANCES RIDLEY (Astley, 1836–79, Caswall Bay, near Swansea), was the youngest child of the Rev. W. H. Havergal (q.v.), the pioneer of reform in metrical psalmody. She began to write verses at the age of seven, and her poems were soon admitted to *Good Words* and other religious periodicals. Her health was delicate, and systematic study had to be discouraged in her childhood; she studied for a time at Düsseldorf. So far as her strength allowed, she threw herself energetically into religious and philanthropic work; she wrote incessantly, and composed music also. Her collected *Poetical Works* were published in 1884, and a volume of *Memorials* contained a partial autobiography.

257. *Take my life and let it be.*

HAVERGAL, William Henry, M.A. (High Wycombe, Buckinghamshire, 1793–1870, Leamington), was educated at the Merchant Taylors' School and St. Edmund Hall, Oxford. Ordained in 1816, he served two curacies in Gloucestershire, and in 1829 became rector of Astley, near Bewdley. A carriage accident, in which he sustained concussion of the brain and had his eyesight permanently injured, compelled him to resign his living. He devoted his enforced leisure to the pursuit of the study of music, and began publishing anthems and services. He reprinted *Ravenscroft's Psalter* in 1844, and in 1847 issued his influential work, *Old Church Psalmody*. In these works he drew attention to the classical school of English ecclesiastical music, and did much to purify metrical psalmody. In 1842 he was able to resume clerical duty, as rector of St. Nicholas, Worcester, and in 1845 he received an honorary canonry in the Cathedral there. Impaired health compelled him to accept in 1860 the quiet living of Shareshill, near Wolverhampton, and in 1867 he resigned and retired to Leamington. Lowell Mason, in 1852, described the musical service in Havergal's church as excellent in all particulars, and far in advance of anything that he heard in England. Havergal wrote about a hundred hymns, published about fifty musical works, and issued also two volumes of *Sermons on Historical Subjects from the Old and New Testaments* (1853); *A History of the Old Hundredth Psalm Tune, with Specimens* (1854); *A Hundred Psalm and Hymn Tunes* (1859), of his own composition; and *Fireside Music*, a collection of songs, carols, rounds, &c.

455. FRANCONIA.

HAWEIS, Thomas, LL.B., M.D. (Truro, 1734–1820, Bath), studied medicine for a time, but eventually resolved to read for Holy Orders, and went to Christ Church, Oxford, subsequently to Magdalen. He held the curacy of St. Mary Magdalen's Church at Oxford, and was at one time assistant to Martin Madan at the Lock Hospital, London. Later he became rector of All Saints, Aldwinkle, Northamptonshire, and chaplain to Lady Huntingdon's chapel at Bath. He published a collection of hymns entitled *Carmina Christo, or Hymns to the Saviour*, which was a companion to the *Select Collection of Hymns* compiled by the Countess of Huntingdon for use in the chapels of her Connexion, and was often bound up with it. Haweis became manager of Lady Huntingdon's chapels. He was the most musical of her chaplains and composed tunes published after her death as *Original Music suited to the various metres*.

117. *O thou from whom all goodness flows.*
468. RICHMOND.

HAWKER, Robert Stephen (Plymouth, 1804–75, Plymouth), was the grandson of Dr. Hawker, of Christ Church, Plymouth, author of some *Morning and Evening Portions*, famous in their day. His studies at Oxford, where he entered Pembroke College in 1823, were interrupted by lack of means; a wealthy marriage, however, enabled him to return to college, and he gained the Newdigate Prize in 1827. In 1834 he became vicar of Morwenstow, Cornwall, where many tales were told of his eccentricity. He published several volumes of poems: *Tendrils* (1821); *Ecclesia* (1840); *The Quest of the Sangraal* (1863); and *Cornish Ballads* (1869).

371. *Sing to the Lord the children's hymn.*

HAYDN, Franz Josef (Rohrau, Austria, 1732–1809, Vienna), was the son of a master wheelwright. He was taught music first, at the age of six, by a relative, J. M. Frankh of Hainburg, but at eight years old was admitted to the Cantorei of St. Stephen's in Vienna, where he received no instruction in composition, but taught himself. On the breaking of his voice he was thrown on his own resources for some years, and continued to study while making a living in any way that presented itself. By 1756 his name began to be known as performer and teacher; and in 1759 he was appointed music director to Count Ferdinand Maximilian Morzin, and in 1761 became second Kapellmeister to Prince Paul Anton Esterhazy, with which family he remained happily for the rest of his life. With a good band at his service, Haydn devoted himself freely to composition, and produced a continuous stream of all kinds of music, virtually inventing many of the musical forms, such as the symphony, sonata, and string quartet, which have obtained ever since. In 1791 Haydn paid a visit to England, which was repeated in 1794, both sojourns being a great success. During his later years Haydn was the most famous and universally honoured musician in Europe, and no man ever deserved his renown better. He wrote over 100 authenticated symphonies, 22 operas, 4 oratorios, and an immense quantity of instrumental quartets, trios, sonatas, &c.

500. AUSTRIAN HYMN.

HAYES, William, D.Mus. (Gloucester, 1706–77, Oxford), was trained as a chorister in Gloucester Cathedral, and served as organist in St. Mary's, Shrewsbury; Worcester Cathedral; and Magdalen College, Oxford, where he remained for 43 years up till his death. In 1741 he was appointed Professor of Music in the University. It is doubtful whether he ever delivered any lectures during his occupancy of the Chair, but he was active in other ways. He published *Twelve Ariettas or Ballads and Two Cantatas* in 1735; a setting of Collins's *Ode on the Passions*; *Circe, a Masque*; many anthems, which are still popular with choirs; *Sixteen Metrical Psalms selected from Merrick's Version*, set to music for use in Magdalen College Chapel; and other vocal and instrumental music.

20 (671). NEW 113TH. 690. MAGDALEN COLLEGE.

HEBER, Reginald, D.D. (Malpas, Cheshire, 1783–1826, Trichinopoly, India), came of an old Yorkshire family, and was educated at the Grammar School, Whitchurch, privately at Neasden, and at Brasenose College, Oxford, where he won the Newdigate Prize with a poem on *Palestine*. He won a fellowship at All Souls, and after two years' travel in eastern Europe, became rector of the family living at Hodnet, Shropshire, an estate inherited by his father. In 1812 he was appointed a prebendary of St. Asaph; in 1815 was Bampton Lecturer; in 1822 became preacher at Lincoln's Inn, and in the same year was offered the bishopric of Calcutta. After two refusals he accepted; but the incessant travelling demanded by the extent of this see, which at that time included the whole of British India, broke down his health, and he died suddenly, of apoplexy, in Trichinopoly. In 1811 he had begun the publication of his hymns in the *Christian Observer*, and, in conjunction with Dean Milman, projected a series of hymns to meet the requirements of the Christian year, which was published in 1827 as *Hymns written and adapted to the Weekly Church Service of the Year.*

21. *When spring unlocks the flowers.*
46 (i). *God that madest earth and heaven.*
85. *Brightest and best of the sons of the morning.*
187. *Holy, holy, holy! Lord God Almighty!*
216. *The Son of God goes forth to war.*
265. *Bread of the world in mercy broken.*
276. *O most merciful!*
533. *I praised the earth, in beauty seen.*

HEERMANN, Johann H. (Raudten, 1585–1647, Lissa, Posen), son of a furrier, was educated at Wohlau, Fraustadt, and the gymnasia at Breslau and Briez. In 1611 he became diaconus of Köben, and in the same year pastor. In 1638 he retired to Lissa. Heermann was a distinguished scholar and in 1608 received the poet's laurel-crown at Briez. Among his works were *Flores* (1609); *Devoti Musica Cordis* (1630–44); *Exercitium Pietatis* (1644), &c.

99. *Ah, holy Jesus, how hast thou offended.*

HEINLEIN (HAINLAIN), Paul (Nuremburg, 1626–86, Nuremburg), learned to play keyboard and all wind instruments from a town musician, then went for further study to Italy. In 1649, when he returned, he was appointed musician to the town council. In 1655 he was organist at St. Egidius, in 1656 Kapellmeister at the Frauen-Kirche, in 1658 organist at St. Sebaldus. His compositions consisted of a large number of sacred songs by contemporary poets and some church music.

506. JESU, JESU DU MEIN HIRT.

HELDER, Bartholomaeus (Gotha, 1585–1635), studied theology and became a schoolmaster at Friemar, and was afterwards pastor of Remstedt in 1620. He wrote *Cymbalum Genethliacum* (1614), *Cymbalum Davidicum* (1620), and also a number of sacred and secular songs.

322 (ii). HELDER (WOHLAUF THUT NICHT VERZAGEN).

HELMORE, Thomas (Kidderminster, 1811–90, London), was educated at Magdalen Hall, Oxford; became curate of St. Michael's and priest-vicar of the Cathedral, Lichfield, 1840; Vice-Principal and Precentor of St. Mark's College, Chelsea, 1842; Master of the Choristers of the Chapel Royal, 1846; and a priest-in-ordinary there, 1847. He was one of the pioneers of the revival of the use of the Gregorian Tones in Anglican services. He translated Fétis's *Treatise on Choir and Chorus Singing*; composed music for some of Neale's translations of *Hymns of the Eastern Church*; and published as author or editor—*The Psalter Noted*; *The Canticles Noted*; *A Manual of Plain Song*; *A Brief Directory of Plain Song*; *The Hymnal Noted*; *Carols for Christmas*; *Carols for Easter*; *St. Mark's College Chaunt Book*; *The Canticles Accented*; *A Catechism of Music*, &c.

66. VENI IMMANUEL.

HERBERT, George (Montgomery, 1593–1633, Bemerton), belonged to a famous English family, and was the younger brother of the soldier-philosopher Lord Herbert of Cherbury. Educated at Westminster and at

Trinity College, Cambridge, he numbered among his friends Wotton, Donne, and Bacon. He was Fellow of Trinity, 1615, Public Orator, 1619, and as a young courtier he enjoyed the favour of James I, but in the following reign took Holy Orders and on 26 April 1630 became rector of Bemerton in Wiltshire, where he spent the remaining three years of his life. His principal work is *The Temple*, a book of poems wrought with infinite care, the history of his own spiritual conflicts. His *Life*, written by his friend Izaak Walton, made him at once popular; and to-day he stands second only to Henry Vaughan as a religious poet.

401. *Enrich, Lord, heart, mouth, hands in me.*
474. *Come, my way, my truth, my life.*
553. *King of glory, King of peace.*
556. *Let all the world in every corner sing.*
650. *Sweet day, so cool, so calm, so bright.*
652. *Teach me, my God and King.*
653. *The God of love my shepherd is.*

HERBERT, MARY, COUNTESS OF PEMBROKE (Ticknell, Worcestershire, 1561–1621, Crosby Hall), sister of Sir Philip Sidney, was carefully educated in Latin, Greek, and Hebrew. In 1577 she married Henry Herbert, 2nd earl of Pembroke. Her brother's *Arcadia* was written at her suggestion, and, after Philip's death, she issued editions, both of this and of his poems, revised and corrected by herself. She also collaborated with him in *The Psalmes of David, Translated into Divers and Sundry Kinds of Verse, &c.*, circulated in manuscript and first printed in 1823; in this work she seems to have been responsible for all but the first 43 psalms. She herself wrote *A Discourse on Life and Death*, and a translation of R. Garnier's tragedy *Antonie*. Her great fame, however, rested on her generous patronage of poets and men of letters, from whom she received countless tributes in prose and verse, culminating in Ben Jonson's renowned epitaph:

Underneath this sable hearse
Lies the subject of all verse,
Sidney's sister, Pembroke's mother.
Death! ere thou hast slain another,
Learn'd and fair and good as she,
Time shall throw a dart at thee.

605. *O Lord, in me there lieth nought.*

HERBERT, PETRUS (d. 1571, Eibenschütz). The place and date of Herbert's birth have not been ascertained. He lived at Fulnek in Moravia, and belonged to the Unity of what were known as the Bohemian Brethren, from which afterwards sprang the Moravian Church. By the Unity Herbert was entrusted with missions to Calvin, the Duke of Württemberg, the Emperor Maximilian, and other important persons. He helped to compile the Brethren's enlarged hymn-book or *Kirchengesang* (1566), and contributed to it about 90 hymns, some of which are translations from the Czech.

48. *Now God be with us, for the night is falling.*

HERBST, MARTIN (Rothenbach, 1654–81, Eisleben), attended St. Lorenz School at Nürnberg, studied philosophy and theology at Altdorf, and at Jena. In 1680 he became rector of the Gymnasium at Eisleben, and also pastor of the Church of St. Andreas there, but the plague carried him off in the following year. Zahn attributes four chorales to him, printed with the initials M.H.

97. HEINLEIN (AUS DER TIEFE).

HERRICK, ROBERT, M.A. (London, 1591–1674, Dean Prior), apprenticed for ten years to his uncle, Sir William Herrick, then went to St. John's College, Cambridge, but graduated from Trinity Hall, 1617. He did not take Orders till he was nearly 40, was Incumbent of Dean Prior, Devonshire, 1629, but was ejected in 1647. He then lived in Westminster until 1662, when he was restored. *Hesperides* with *Noble Numbers* were first issued in 1648. A contemporary of George Herbert, whom he outlived 40 years, 'At last he has come to take his place among the greatest of English lyric poets', says Dr. Moorman, 'and, among all these singers of a day when England was a nest of singing-birds, Herrick reigns as king'.

35. *When virgin morn doth call thee to arise.*
348. *In this world, the Isle of Dreams.*
402. *Here a little child I stand.*

HERMANN (HEERMANN), NICOLAUS (? *c.* 1485–1561 ?), was cantor at Joachimsthal in Bohemia towards the middle of the 16th century. He was also a clever versifier.

159. HERMANN (ERSCHIENEN IST DER HERRLICH TAG).
481 (ii). NICOLAUS (LOBT GOTT).

HEY, JOHANN WILHELM (Leina, 1789–1854, Ichtershausen), studied theology at the universities of Jena and Göttingen. In 1818 he became pastor at Töttelstadt, and in 1827 court preacher at Gotha; from 1832 he was superintendent of Ichtershausen. Hey's best-known work was his two collections of poems for children *Fabeln für Kinder* (1833, 1837), which contained more serious poems and hymns in an appendix to each volume, and have appeared in several English translations.

462. *Can you count the stars that brightly.*

HEYWOOD, THOMAS (*c.* 1575–*c.* 1641), was probably born in Lincolnshire, and was described some twenty years after his death as a Fellow of Peterhouse, Cambridge. A member of the theatrical company of the third Earl of Southampton, and later of the fourth Earl of Worcester, and various other similar companies, he said that he had a finger in 220 plays. He arranged the Lord Mayor's pageants until 1640, and produced a vast quantity of many forms of literature, with remarkable industry. Much of his work is now lost, but even so the list of his publications of all kinds is a formidable one.

534. *I sought thee round about, O thou my God.*

HINKSON, KATHARINE TYNAN (Dublin, 1859–1931, London), daughter of Andrew C. Tynan of Clasdalkin, Co. Dublin, was educated at the Dominican Convent of St. Catherine of Siena, Drogheda, and privately. Her first verses appeared in Irish periodicals, and her first volume of poems in 1885. She contributed much to various journals, and published further volumes of poems. She went to London after her marriage in 1893, and there continued journalistic work and published also volumes of prose and verse up to the time of her death.

196. *I would choose to be a doorkeeper.*

HINTZE, JAKOB (Bernau, Brandenburg, 1622–1702, Berlin), became in 1666 court-musician to the Elector of Brandenburg at Berlin. After Crüger's death, he undertook to edit the twelfth and succeeding editions of the *Praxis Pietatis Melica*; and added a collection of new melodies as an appendix.

558. SALZBURG.

HOATSON, FLORENCE (Leyton, London, 1881–   ), daughter of the Rev. John Hoatson, a Congregational minister, was educated in Christchurch, New Zealand, and Melbourne, Australia. She has been engaged in kindergarten teaching for many years, and in 1917–20 was lecturer and demonstrator to the National Sunday School Union in Cardiff. Among her publications are *The Little White Gate* and *Lavender's Blue*, volumes of poems for children; and *The Palace of Gifts*, a book of stories for young children. She also contributed many hymns to Carey Bonner's *Child Songs*.

359. *God whose name is Love.*

HOLDROYD, ISAAC (*fl. c.* 1725), published *The Spiritual Man's Companion or the Pious Christian's Recreation, containing an historical account of music, &c.*, which ran through several editions in the second quarter of the 18th century; *Chants and Anthems* (1733), and some other works. Beyond these publications little is known of his life.

395 (Part IV). ST. NICHOLAS.

HOLLAND, HENRY SCOTT, D.D., D.Litt. (Underdown, Ledbury, 1847–1918, Oxford), was educated at Eton and Balliol College, Oxford. He became senior Student and tutor of Christ Church. He was select preacher at Oxford, 1879–80, and again, 1894–6; canon of St. Paul's, 1884 to 1910; Romanes Lecturer, Oxford, 1908; Regius Professor of Divinity, Oxford, 1910–18. He was one of the founders and most ardent supporters of the Christian Social Union, and from 1896, when it was founded, to the end of his life, he edited *The Commonwealth*. A lover of music, he did much to raise the musical quality of the services in St. Paul's. He was part-editor of the *New Cathedral Psalter*. Among his published works were: *Creed and Character*; *Logic and Life*; *Christ or Ecclesiastes*; *On Behalf of Belief*; *God's City*; *Vital Values*; *A Bundle of Memories*; and with W. S. Rockstro (q.v.) *A Memoir of Jenny Lind*. He wrote only one hymn:

552. *Judge eternal, throned in splendour.*

HOLMES, JOHN, organist of Winchester Cathedral in the latter part of the 16th century, and organist of Salisbury Cathedral from 1602 to 1610. He contributed to the *Triumphes of Oriana*.

App. 3 (iii). AMEN.

HOLMES, OLIVER WENDELL, M.D., LL.D., D.C.L. (Cambridge, Massachusetts, 1809–94, Boston), son of Abiel Holmes, D.D., of the First Congregational Church, Cambridge, Mass., was educated at Phillips Academy, New Hampshire, and at Harvard, where he graduated in Arts and Medicine; he studied in Europe also. In 1838 he was appointed Professor of Anatomy and Physiology in Dartmouth College, and in 1847 accepted the Chair of Anatomy at Harvard, where he continued to teach with high distinction till 1882. A constant contributor to periodical literature, he was the chief founder of the *Atlantic Monthly*, and it was largely his contributions that won it international fame. Essayist, novelist, poet, wit, humorist, humanist, and the raciest of talkers, he became one of the best-known and best-loved men on both sides of the ocean. *The Autocrat of the Breakfast-Table*; *The Professor at the Breakfast-Table*; *The Poet at the Breakfast-Table*; and *Over the Teacups* contain his most characteristic writings.

564. *Lord of all being, throned afar.*
620. *Our Father, while our hearts unlearn.*

HOLST, GUSTAV (THEODORE) (Cheltenham, 1874–1934), of English blood on his mother's side, was of Swedish extraction on his father's; his great-grandfather came to England about 1808. He was originally intended for a career as a pianist, but symptoms of neuritis led to a change of intention, and at the age of 17 he became organist at Wyck Rissington, Gloucestershire. Educated subsequently at the Royal College of Music, London, he served for five years as trombonist in the Scottish Orchestra, and later in the Carl Rosa Opera Company. In 1903 he became a music master in London and Reading, and in 1919 a teacher of composition in the Royal College of Music; he is a great teacher as well as composer. In 1918 he went, under the education scheme of the Y.M.C.A., to Salonika, Constantinople, and Asia Minor, as musical organizer in army camps. He visited America in 1923, and was Cramb Lecturer in the University of Glasgow, 1925. His works include *The Planets*, a suite for full orchestra; *The Hymn of Jesus* (2 choruses and semi-chorus); *Ode to Death*, to Walt Whitman's words; an *Ave Maria* for female chorus; a *Hymn to the Unknown*; five operas; *A Somerset Rhapsody*, &c.

75. CRANHAM.
86. HILL CREST.
293 (i) VALIANT HEARTS.
319 (i). THAXTED.
325. STEPNEY.
348. BROOKEND.
397. PRINCE RUPERT.
496. SHEEN.
498. CHILSWELL.
*502. THEODORIC.
534. MONK STREET.

HORNE, CHARLES SILVESTER, M.A. (Cuckfield, Sussex, 1865–1914, Toronto), son of a Congregational minister, was educated at Newport Grammar School, the University of Glasgow, and Mansfield College, Oxford, where he was one of the small band of students with whom the College was opened in 1886. His reputation as a preacher led to his being called, nearly two years before his theological course was finished, to the pulpit of Allen Street Church, Kensington. Ordained in 1889, he remained there until, in 1903, he accepted an invitation to take charge of the congregation at Whitefield's Chapel, Tottenham Court Road. There he spent eleven most fruitful years. He was chairman of the Congregational Union in 1909; entered Parliament as M.P. for Ipswich in 1910; was elected President of the National Brotherhood Council in 1913; and delivered the Yale Lectures on Preaching in 1914. Soon afterwards, as a vessel on which he had sailed from Niagara was entering Toronto harbour, he fell dead on the deck at his wife's feet.

495. *For the might of thine arm we bless thee, our God, our father's God.*

HORSLEY, William, Mus.Bac. (London, 1774–1858, London), was in youth articled to a pianist and composer from whom he received little instruction and much ill-usage. In 1794 he became organist of Ely Chapel, Holborn; in 1802, organist of the Asylum for Female Orphans, in succession to W. H. Callcott, whose daughter he married; in 1812, organist of Belgrave Chapel; and in 1838, organist of the Charterhouse. He was an intimate friend of Mendelssohn. He published five collections of glees; many songs, sonatas, &c.; two collections of psalm- and hymn-tunes; and some works on theory. He was one of the founders of the Philharmonic Society.

131. HORSLEY. 694. BELGRAVE.

HOSMER, Frederick Lucian, D.D. (Framingham, Massachusetts, 1840–1929, Berkeley), was descended from James Hosmer of Hawkhurst, Kent, one of the first settlers at Concord in 1635. Educated at Harvard, he entered the Unitarian ministry in 1872, and held charges at Northboro, Mass.; Quincy, Illinois; Cleveland, Ohio; St. Louis; and Berkeley, California, where he later lived in retirement. He was lecturer on hymnody at Harvard in 1908. He published *The Way of Life*; *Prayers and Responsive Services for Sunday Schools*; along with W. C. Gannett (q.v.) and J. Vilas Blake, *Unity Hymns and Carols*; and also with W. C. Gannett, *The Thought of God in Hymns and Poems*, containing 56 hymns by himself.

192. *O light from age to age the same.*
322. *O beautiful, my country!*
347. *Father, to thee we look in all our sorrow.*
575. *Made lowly wise, we pray no more.*
589. *Not always on the mount may we.*
614. *O thou in all thy might so far.*
680. *Thy Kingdom come! on bended knee.*

HOW, William Walsham, D.D. (Shrewsbury, 1823–97, Dhulough Lodge, Leenane, Co. Mayo, Ireland), son of William Wybergh How, solicitor, was educated at Shrewsbury School and Wadham College, Oxford, and was ordained in 1846. After curacies at Kidderminster and Holy Cross, Shrewsbury, he became rector of Whittington, 1851; rural dean of Oswestry, 1853; hon. canon of St. Asaph, 1860; rector of St. Andrew Undershaft, and Bishop Suffragan, titularly of Bedford, but really of East London, 1879; and Bishop of Wakefield, 1888. He was totally without ambition in the worldly sense, declined the offer of the see of Manchester without even mentioning it to his wife, and, later, refused also one of the most distinguished posts in the Anglican Church, the bishopric of Durham. In 1854 he collaborated with the Rev. Thomas Baker Morrell in editing a collection of *Psalms and Hymns*; and in 1871 was joint-editor of the S.P.C.K. *Church Hymns*, while in 1886 a collected edition appeared of his own *Poems and Hymns*.

7. *Summer suns are glowing.*
15. *The year is swiftly waning.*
202. *For all the saints who from their labours rest.*
332. *We give thee but thine own.*
642. *Soldiers of the cross, arise!*

HOWARD, SAMUEL, Mus.Doc. (London, 1710–81, London), was a chorister of the Chapel Royal under Croft; became organist of St. Clement Danes and of St. Bride's, Fleet Street. He wrote for the theatre and gardens as well as the Church, and composed many songs popular in their day.

253. ISLEWORTH. 699. ST. BRIDE.

HOWE, JULIA WARD, *née* WARD (New York, 1819–1910, Middletown, R.I.), American poetess and philanthropist, married in 1848 Samuel Gridley Howe, who in his young manhood took part in the Greek War of Independence, and wrote *Historical Sketches of the Greek Revolution*, and who afterwards devoted his life in America to philanthropic causes. Mrs. Howe was passionately interested all her life in social reform, and an eager advocate of women's suffrage and international peace. She was an influential figure on public platforms and often preached in Unitarian and other pulpits. She published three volumes of verse: *Passion Flowers* (1854), *Words for the Hour* (1856), and *Later Lyrics* (1866); and also books on *Sex in Education*; *Modern Society*; and *Margaret Fuller*.

578. *Mine eyes have seen the glory of the coming of the Lord.*

HOWELLS, HERBERT (Lydney, Gloucester, 1892–), became a pupil of Herbert Brewer and was articled in 1909. In 1911 he withdrew from Gloucester Cathedral to devote himself to composition and won an open scholarship at the Royal College of Music, where he studied under Stanford. In 1917 the Carnegie Trust accepted his *Piano Quartet in A minor*. This was the first work under their auspices. His *Phantasy String Quartet* received the Cobbett Prize. He was sub-organist at Salisbury Cathedral for a short time but his health broke down. In 1920 he was appointed teacher of Composition at the Royal College of Music. Other publications are *A Sonata in E minor* (*Violin and Piano*); a *Piano Concerto* (1921); and many songs, &c.

582. SEVERN.

HUGHES, HUMPHREY VAUGHAN, M.A. [Dom Anselm Hughes, O.S.B.] (London, 1889–), was educated at Westminster, Keble College, Oxford, and Ely Theological College. Since 1922 he has lived as an Anglican Benedictine, and is honorary secretary of the Plainsong and Medieval Music Society. Among his publications are *Early English Harmony* (1913); *Latin Hymnody* (1922); *Worcester Medieval Harmony* (1928); and *The House of my Pilgrimage* (1929).

*132. BRESLAU.

HUGHES, THOMAS, M.A., Q.C. (Uffington, Faringdon, Berkshire, 1823-96, Brighton), the son of a country squire, was educated at

Rugby under Dr. Arnold, and at Oriel College, Oxford. He went to the Bar in 1848, and joined the Christian Socialist group of Maurice and Kingsley. He became a Q.C. in 1869, and a County Court Judge in 1882. For some years he sat in Parliament as a Liberal, first for Lambeth, then for Frome. In 1870 he went to the United States on a lecturing tour, and ten years later was chiefly instrumental in founding a colony, settled mainly by Englishmen, at Rugby, Morgan County, Tennessee. His famous *Tom Brown's Schooldays* (1856) was first published anonymously.

597. *O God of truth, whose living word.*

HUPTON, Job (Burton-on-Trent (near), 1762–1849, Claxton, Norfolk), began life as a blacksmith, but later became a preacher of Lady Huntingdon's connexion for several years. In 1794 he became pastor of the Baptist church at Claxton, where he remained. He contributed much to the *Gospel Magazine*, and his addresses, &c., were issued in the *Truth as it is in Jesus* (1843).

477. *Come, ye people, raise the anthem.*

HUTCHESON, Charles (Glasgow, 1792–1860, Glasgow), was a Glasgow merchant, and a member of St. George's parish church there. He was an amateur composer, and one of the founders of the Glasgow Dilettanti Society. He published *Christian Vespers* (Glasgow, 1832), containing hymn-tunes harmonized in three and four parts, with an introductory essay on church music.

438. STRACATHRO.

INGELOW, Jean (Boston, Lincolnshire, 1820–97, Kensington), was the daughter of a Boston banker; her mother was of Aberdeenshire stock. She lived in the fen country or at Ipswich till about 1863, when she settled in London. Her first venture in verse was *A Rhyming Chronicle of Incidents and Feelings* (1850), published anonymously; but it was not till the first series of her *Poems* was issued in 1860 that her powers attracted notice. Her most ambitious poem, *A Story of Doom*, recounts in blank verse the Biblical account of Noah. She wrote successful novels and fairy stories also.

447. *And didst thou love the race that loved not thee?*

INGEMANN, Bernhardt Severin (Thorkildstrup, Denmark, 1789–1862, Sorö), son of a Lutheran pastor, studied for the law, but finally devoted himself to literature and became Lector of Danish Language and Literature at the Academy of Sorö, Zealand. Youthful experience of the defence of Copenhagen against the British, and the influence of Walter Scott's books, led him to write a series of patriotic, historical novels, such as *Valdemar the Great and his Men* (1824), *Queen Margaret* (1836), &c.; and these and his stories and hymns for children made him, with Hans Andersen, one of the two most popular authors in Denmark. In 1825 he published *High-Mass Hymns*, and in 1851 his collected works appeared in 34 volumes.

678. *Through the night of doubt and sorrow.*

IRELAND, John, Mus.Doc. (Bowden, Cheshire, 1879–   ), son of Alexander Ireland, a well-known author and editor of the *Manchester*

Examiner, was educated at Leeds Grammar School and the Royal College of Music. One of the most distinguished of contemporary English composers, he is pre-eminent as a writer of songs and pianoforte music, but has also produced important work in the larger forms. Among his publications are orchestral works such as the *Forgotten Rite*, and *Mai Dun*; a *Pianoforte Concerto*; sonatas for pianoforte, and for violin, &c.; many pianoforte solos, such as *London Pieces*, &c.; and a large number of exquisite songs.

127 (i). LOVE UNKNOWN. 164. CHELSEA.

ISAAK, HEINRICH (*c.* 1460–*c.* 1527), may have been a Netherlander, but more probably was born in Germany. He went to Italy, became organist and chapelmaster of the Church of San Giovanni, Florence; was organist of the Medici Chapel, 1477–93, and music-master to the children of Lorenzo the Magnificent. After the death of his patron in 1492 he appears to have remained for some years in Italy, where he enjoyed a great reputation. He was in Vienna in 1496, and from 1496 to 1515 was chapel-master to the Emperor Maximilian I at Innsbruck. On his retirement with an annual pension of 150 florins, he returned to Italy, but failed to secure a renewal of favour. The last trace history gives of him is at San Lorenzo Maggiore in Rome, 'old, and sick, and without means'. He composed 23 masses, motets, chorales, and songs.

57. INNSBRUCK.

JACKSON, THOMAS (? 1715–81, Newark), was organist of St. Mary's, Newark-on-Trent, and master of the song-school there. He composed *Twelve Psalm Tunes and Eighteen Double and Single Chants . . . composed for four voices* (1780).

445. JACKSON.

JACKSON, WILLIAM (Exeter, 1730–1803, Exeter), studied in Exeter with Sylvester, organist of Exeter Cathedral, and became for some time a teacher of music in that city. In 1777 he was appointed organist and choirmaster of the Cathedral. He was a versatile man, being a writer and painter, as well as an accomplished musician; and he published a large quantity of music, operas, odes, songs, part-songs, anthems, services, and hymns; and some volumes of essays and letters.

338. EXETER.

JENKINS, DAVID, Mus.Bac. (Trecastell, Brecon, 1848-1915, Aberystwyth), was at first self-taught, but later studied under Dr. Joseph Parry, and graduated at Cambridge, 1878. Appointed in 1899 Lecturer in Music (Professor a few years afterwards) and head of the new Department of Music in the University College of Wales, Aberystwyth, he held that post till his death. For many years he acted as precentor to the Presbyterian Church at Aberystwyth, and was a prominent figure at the National and other Eisteddfodau, first as a competitor, and later as adjudicator and composer. Among his published compositions were: cantatas (*A Psalm of Life*, *Llyn y Morwynion*); oratorios (*David and Saul*, *Dewi Sant*, *Job*); an opera (*The Enchanted Isle*), songs, part-songs, anthems, and hymn-tunes (*Gemau Mawl*).

453. LLANLLYFNI.

JOHN DAMASCENE, St., (8th century), Greek theologian and hymn-writer of the Eastern Church, was born at Damascus, and educated by a learned Italian monk named Cosmas. He retired to the Monastery of St. Sabas near Jerusalem, was ordained priest late in life, and died at a very advanced age. His theological works include treatises in defence of the orthodox faith, and orations in favour of image-worship, which had been condemned by the Emperor Leo the Isaurian. His fame as a hymn-writer mainly rests on his 'canons'. The canon, in Greek hymnology, was a series of odes, usually eight, sometimes nine, threaded on an acrostic. John wrote a number of these and arranged them to music, the best known being the Easter canon or 'Golden Canon'.

144. *Come, ye faithful, raise the strain.*
146. *The day of resurrection.*
168. *Thou hallowed chosen dawn of praise.*

JOHNSON, Samuel, M.A. (Salem, Massachusetts, 1822–82, North Andover, Mass.), studied at Harvard and Cambridge Divinity School. He collaborated with Samuel Longfellow (q.v.) in producing *A Book of Hymns* (1846) and *Hymns of the Spirit* (1864). In 1853 he formed a Free Church at Lynn, Mass.; there he remained till 1870. His chief work was one embodying great research, on *Oriental Religions, and their Relation to Universal Religion.* Besides many essays on religious, moral, political, and aesthetic subjects, he published a treatise on *The Worship of Jesus, in its Past and Present Aspects* (1868).

468. *City of God, how broad and far.*
559. *Life of ages, richly poured.*

JOHNSTON, Julia Harriette (Salineville, Ohio, 1852–?), was educated at Gettysburg and Peoria, Illinois, High School. She was extensively interested in missionary and Sunday-school work, and a frequent contributor to periodicals concerned with those subjects. Among her publications were *The School of the Master*; *Bright Threads*; *Life of Adoniram Judson*, &c.

386 (ii). *Here we come with gladness.*

JONES, Joseph David (Brynerugog, Montgomery, 1827–70, Ruthin), was a teacher of singing at Ruthin and in the British School there. He published several collections: *Alawon y Bryniau* (1866); *Casgliad o Donau ac Anthemau* (1873); *Cydymaith y Cerddor* (1863); *Caniadau Bethlehem* (1857), &c.; and, with E. Stephen, *Llyfr Tonau ac Emynau* (1870).

553. GWALCHMAI.

JONES, J. R. (1762–1822), was a Baptist minister, possibly a Campbellite, in the village of Llanfrothen, Merionethshire; Ramoth was the name of a little hill-side chapel near by.

464 (i). RAMOTH.

JONES, William (Lowick, Northamptonshire, 1726–1800, Hollingbourne), was educated at the Charterhouse and University College, Oxford. He became vicar of Bethersden, Kent, 1764; and, in succession, rector of Pluckley, Kent; rector of Paston, Northants; then perpetual curate of Nayland, Suffolk, from which he came to be known as Jones of

Nayland; and, two years before his death, rector of Hollingbourne, Kent. He published many theological, philosophical, and scientific works. A musician also of great ability, he published *A Treatise on the Art of Music* (1784); and *Ten Church Pieces for the Organ, with Four Anthems in Score* (1789). He established the *British Critic* in 1793.

250. ST. STEPHEN.

JOSEPH, St. (known as the Hymnographer), (Sicily, *c.* 800–83, ?), spent most of his life in the East. He embraced the monastic life at Thessalonica, and went thence to Constantinople, but during the iconoclastic persecution fled to Rome, was captured by pirates, and remained for many years a slave in Crete. Returning to Constantinople he established a monastery, and by the favour of the Empress Theodora was made keeper of the sacred vessels in the Great Church of that city. He was more than once banished owing to his defence of image-worship. A voluminous hymn-writer, he is reported to have composed as many as a thousand canons.

215. *Let us now our voices raise.*

JOSEPH, or Josephi, Georg (*c.* 1657), was a musician in the service of the Prince Bishop of Breslau. He edited the music of Scheffler's *Heilige Seelenlust, oder Geistliche Hirtenlieder der in ihren Jesum verliebten Psyche*, three books (Breslau, 1657). Of 123 tunes in these books, 107 are by Joseph; of 32 in a fourth book, subsequently published, 30 were his; and of 50 in a fifth book, 48 were by him—185 in all. Many of these were probably adaptations from secular melodies.

42 (ii). ANGELUS (DU MEINER SEELEN).

JOSEPH, Jane M. (London, 1894–1929, London), was educated at Norland Place School, St. Paul's Girls' School, Brook Green, and Girton College, Cambridge. She composed music from early girlhood, and at Girton conducted the choir. At Cambridge she took the Classical Tripos, and, on going down, studied composition under Gustav Holst. She conducted two choirs in Kensington, was musical director at Eothen Girls' School, Caterham, and much concerned in various musical festivals and competitions. Among her compositions are *Bergomask* for orchestra (performed at the Coliseum); *A Festival Venite* for chorus and orchestra (performed at Queen's Hall); *A Hymn for Whitsuntide* (many performances); many carols, part-songs, &c.; unaccompanied solo songs; and much piano and other music. A gifted composer, her early death cut off a career of great promise.

651. ESKDALE.

JULIAN, John, D.D., LL.D. (St. Agnes, 1839–1913, Topcliffe, Yorkshire), eldest son of Thomas Julian of St. Agnes, Cornwall, was educated privately. From 1876 to 1905 he was vicar of Wincobank, from 1905 onwards vicar of Topcliffe, and from 1901 canon of York. Publications: *Concerning Hymns*; *The Outgrowth of some Literary, Scientific, and other Hobbies*; he wrote and translated many hymns, but is chiefly known by his great work the *Dictionary of Hymnology*.

252. *Father of all, to thee.*

KEBLE, John, M.A. (Fairford, 1792–1866, Bournemouth), was first educated by his father, the vicar of Coln St. Aldwyn, entered Corpus Christi College, Oxford, at 14, and after a college career of great brilliance, won, at 19, a fellowship of Oriel. He spent 9 years at Oxford, as tutor and examiner, but left Oxford in 1823, and spent the next 13 years as a curate in Gloucestershire, in order to be with his father. In 1827, at the instance of friends to whom he had from time to time shown them, he published anonymously the poems of the *Christian Year, or, Thoughts in Verse for the Sundays and Holy Days throughout the Year.* The book at once stirred great interest. After he became vicar of Hursley, near Winchester, in 1833, the profits from the book enabled him to rebuild the parish church, and his friends filled all its windows with stained glass. In 1833 he was appointed Professor of Poetry at Oxford, and published his *Prelections on Poetry.* He became one of the triumvirate of leaders in the Oxford Movement with Newman and Pusey. Some of the more important of the *Tracts for the Times* were written by him. A second volume of poems, *Lyra Innocentium* (1846), and his *Psalter, or Psalms of David in English Verse* were less successful than the first. He wrote a *Life of Bishop Wilson,* author of the *Sacra Privata*; edited Hooker's *Works*; and his *Letters of Spiritual Counsel,* his *Miscellaneous Poems,* including 45 hymns contributed to *Lyra Apostolica,* and 12 volumes of parochial sermons, were issued posthumously.

31. *New every morning is the love.*
55. *Sun of my soul, thou Saviour dear.*
171. *Lord, in thy name thy servants plead.*
455. *Blest are the pure in heart.*
664. *There is a book who runs may read.*

KELLY, Thomas (Kellyville, Athy, Queen's County, Ireland, 1769–1854, Dublin), the son of an Irish judge, was educated at Trinity College, Dublin, and intended for the Bar. Coming, however, under strong evangelical influences, he resolved to devote his life to religious work, and was episcopally ordained in 1792. The Archbishop of Dublin (Dr. Fowler), disapproving of his 'methodistical' activities, inhibited him and Rowland Hill from preaching in his diocese. Thereupon Kelly seceded from the Church of Ireland, founded a new sect, now extinct, and, being a man of means, built places of worship at Athy, Portarlington, Wexford, and elsewhere. His *Hymns on Various Passages of Scripture* (1804) went through several editions, with increasing numbers of hymns included, until the 1853 edition contained 765. His musical knowledge and skill enabled him to publish in 1815 a companion volume containing tunes composed by himself, suited to every kind of metre in the hymnal; some of them are original and attractive. Nearly 140 of his hymns were till lately in common use.

132. *We sing the praise of him who died.*
175. *The head that once was crowned with thorns.*

KEN, Thomas (Little Berkhampstead, Herts., 1637–1711, Longleat, Wiltshire), belonged to a Somersetshire family. Educated at Winchester and New College, Oxford, he displayed among other gifts an early aptitude for music. He held several livings, among them that of Brighstone (Brixton), Isle of Wight, where the hymns by which he is best known were written. Returning to Winchester in 1666 as a Fellow of the College, he prepared his *Manual for Prayers* for the scholars there. Ken was noted throughout his life for strength of conviction and fidelity to conscience. Appointed in 1679 chaplain to the Princess Mary at The Hague, he incurred her husband's displeasure through his outspokenness, and returned to England. Holding a similar post at the Court of Charles II, his refusal to give the use of his house to Nell Gwyn, the King's mistress, is said to have moved that monarch to appoint him Bishop of Bath and Wells. In the following reign he was one of the seven bishops sent to the Tower for refusing to read the Declaration of Indulgence; while at the Revolution he was deprived of his see for failure to take the oath of allegiance to the new Sovereign. He was given a home by his friend Lord Weymouth at Longleat, where he spent the remainder of his days. His principal work was *Hymns and Poems for the Holy Days and Festivals of the Church.*

25. *Awake, my soul, and with the sun.*
45. *Glory to thee, my God, this night.*

KENNEDY, Geoffrey Anketell Studdert, M.C. (Quarry Hill, Leeds, 1883–1929, Liverpool), was educated privately, at Leeds Grammar School, and Trinity College, Dublin. After two years as a schoolmaster at West Kirby, he entered Ripon Clergy College, was ordained in 1908, and became curate first at Rugby, and, in 1912, of St. Mary's, Leeds. From 1914 onwards he was vicar of St. Paul's, Worcester. During the War he was, from 1915, chaplain to the forces, and won the M.C.; he became famous as 'Woodbine Willie'. After the War he was appointed chaplain to the King, and in 1922 became rector of St. Edmund, King and Martyr, Lombard Street. Most of his post-War activity, however, was in connexion with the Industrial Christian Fellowship, of which he was Messenger. From 1916 onwards he wrote much, his publications including *Rough Rhymes of a Padre*; *The Hardest Part*; *Lies*; *Food for the Fed-up*; *The Word and the Work*, &c.

450. *Awake, awake to love and work!*
469. *Close by the heedless worker's side.*
698. *When through the whirl of wheels, and engines humming.*

KETHE, William, is said to have been a native of Scotland, but neither the place nor the date of his birth is known. During 1555–8 he lived in exile in Frankfort and Geneva, and was afterwards employed as an envoy from Geneva to the other English-speaking congregations on the Continent. He was chaplain to the forces under the Earl of Warwick in 1563 and again in 1569, and for some time held the living of Childe Okeford in Dorsetshire. He died probably about the end of the century. Kethe is described as 'no unready rhymer', and was the author of some popular religious ballads. Twenty-five of his psalm versions are included in the *Anglo-Genevan Psalter* of 1561, and all of these were adopted in the *Scottish Psalter* of 1564–5. The only one transferred to the later *Scottish Psalter* of 1650 is the well-known version of Psalm 100, which was also included in *Day's Psalter* of 1561.

443. *All people that on earth do dwell.*

KING, Oliver A. (London, 1855–1923, London), was educated under Sir Joseph Barnby and W. H. Holmes, and at Leipzig; he was pianist to

Princess Louise, winner of the Philharmonic's Society's Prize for the best overture (1883), precentor of St. Marylebone Church 1884–6, and from 1893 Professor of Pianoforte at the Royal Academy of Music. Publications: a symphony, *Night*; *Among the Pines* (overture); concerto for pianoforte and orchestra; violin concerto; cantatas; organ suites, piano and violin solos, many songs and part-songs, and 50 anthems, church services, &c.

117. OLIVER.

KING, ROBERT, Mus.Bac. (*fl.* 1684–1711), graduated at St. Catharine's College, Cambridge, in 1696. He was a member of the band of William and Mary, and also of Queen Anne. At Christmas, 1689, a licence was granted him to establish a concert. Otherwise, apart from the fact that he was still living in 1711, nothing is known of him except from his works. Many of his songs appear in *Choice Ayres, Songs and Dialogues* (1684); *Comes Amoris* (1687–93); *The Banquet of Music* (1688–92); *The Gentleman's Journal* (1692–4); and *Thesaurus Musicus* (1695–6). A collection of 24 songs by him, engraved on copper, was published under the title, *Songs for One, Two, and Three Voices, composed to a Thorough Bass for ye Organ or Harpsichord.*

476. DAVID'S HARP.

KINGSLEY, CHARLES, M.A. (Holne Vicarage, Devonshire, 1819–75, Eversley, Hampshire), son of a country gentleman who became vicar of Clovelly, Devonshire, and rector of St. Luke's, Chelsea, was educated at Clifton; at Helston, under Derwent Coleridge; at King's College, London, and Magdalene College, Cambridge. Ordained in 1842, he became curate of Eversley, on the borders of Windsor Forest, and in 1844 rector. He was one of the founders of the Christian Socialist movement, and, after the publication of his novels *Yeast* and *Alton Locke*, was prohibited by the Bishop of London from preaching within his diocese, on the grounds of 'revolutionary ideas'. Kingsley, however, rebutted the charge, and in 1859 was appointed chaplain to the Queen; in 1860 Professor of Modern History at Cambridge; in 1869 a canon of Chester; and in 1873 a canon of Westminster. His publications were many and various, the two most famous being *Westward Ho!* and *The Water Babies*, and some of his lyrics have found a permanent place in anthologies.

285. *From thee all skill and science flow.*
310. *The day of the Lord is at hand, at hand.*

KIPLING, RUDYARD (Bombay, 1865–1936), son of J. Lockwood Kipling, C.I.E., was educated at the United Services College, Westward Ho, N. Devon, and from 1882 to 1889 was assistant editor of the *Civil and Military Gazette*, and the *Pioneer*, India, where his first stories were published and laid the foundation of his fame. In 1907 he was awarded the Nobel Prize for Literature, and has received honorary degrees from universities all over the world; in 1922–5 he was Rector of the University of St. Andrews. Among his publications are novels (*Kim*, *The Light that Failed*, &c.); collections of short stories (*Plain Tales from the Hills*, *Life's Handicap*, *Traffics and Discoveries*, *Actions and Reactions*, &c.); children's books (*The Jungle Books*, *Just-So Stories*, *Puck of Pook's Hill*, &c.); war books and histories (*The New Armies in Training*, *The Irish Guards in the*

Great War, &c.); several volumes of verse, collected in *Inclusive Verse*; and many other books.

317. *God of our fathers, known of old.*
488. *Land of our birth, we pledge to thee.*

KIRKPATRICK, William James (Duncannon, Pennsylvania, 1838–1921, Germantown, Philadelphia), was educated at the common schools, and studied music while learning his trade of carpenter at Philadelphia, where he was associated with the Methodist Episcopal Church. In 1858 he assisted A. S. Jenks in collecting camp-meeting songs for *Devotional Melodies*, and thereafter, in the intervals of his commercial engagements, poured out a stream of compilations, issuing some 47 volumes in conjunction with J. R. Sweney, and over 40 more after the latter's death. Many tunes of his own composition were included among these collections, which had an immense success.

353. CRADLE SONG.

KITSON, Charles Herbert, M.A., Mus.Doc., F.R.C.O., F.R.C.M. (Leyburn, Yorkshire, 1874–1944), son of James Kitson, was educated at Ripon School and Selwyn College, Cambridge, where he was organ scholar. In 1913 he became organist and choirmaster at Christ Church Cathedral, Dublin, till 1920, and Professor of Music in University College, Dublin, 1915–20. He held several posts as an Examiner and is now Examiner for degrees in Music in the Universities of Oxford, Wales, and London, and a professor at the Royal College of Music. Publications: *The Art of Counterpoint*; *Applied Strict Counterpoint*; *Studies in Fugue*; *The Evolution of Harmony*; *Rudiments of Music*; *Invertible Counterpoint*; *Elementary Contrapuntal Harmony*, &c.; and church music. He was co-editor of the *Irish Hymnal* (1919).

*294. FANAD HEAD.

KITTEL, Johann Christian (Erfurt, 1732–1809, Erfurt), was one of the last pupils of J. S. Bach and was first organist at Langensalza, 1751, but left in 1756 to be organist of the Predigerkirche, Erfurt. He endured great poverty in spite of the small pension allowed him by Prince Primas of Dalberg. His playing was celebrated but his works were unimportant. The best are some *Grand Preludes for Organ* (in 2 books), *Six Sonatas*, and a *Fantasia for Clavier*, and *Der angehende praktische Organist* (an organ school) (1801–8).

238. QUEDLINBURG.

KNAPP, William (Wareham, 1698–1768, Poole), is said to have been of German extraction. He is referred to as 'a country psalm-singer', and is believed to have been organist both at Wareham and at Poole. In 1738 he published *A Sett of New Psalms and Anthems in four parts . . . and an Introduction to Psalmody after a plain and familiar manner*; and in 1753 *New Church Melody, a sett of Anthems, Psalms and Hymns, in four parts, with an Imploration wrote by Charles I. during his captivity in Carisbrooke Castle*. For 39 years he was parish clerk of St. James's, Poole.

631. WAREHAM.

KNECHT, Justin Heinrich (Biberach, Swabia, 1752–1817, Biberach), studied under Krämer, organist in his native town, and at the college of the convent of Esslingen, learning to play flute, oboe, horn, trumpet, and violin, as well as the organ. He was recalled to Biberach to undertake the Professorship of Belles Lettres, but in 1792 relinquished it to undertake the duty of director of music for the town. In 1807 he removed to Stuttgart, to conduct the court and theatre orchestra there; but after ten years he was glad to return to his old post at Biberach. As an organist he had no rival but Vogler, but his compositions are commonplace. He wrote many theoretic works and books on instruction, but his most valuable production was the *Würtemberg Choralbuch*, which he edited along with J. F. Christmann, and to which he contributed 97 tunes of his own composition.

357. VIENNA.

KNORR, Christian. See ROSENROTH.

KOCHER, Conrad, Ph.D. (Ditzingen, Württemberg, 1786–1872, Stuttgart), was intended for the teaching profession, and at 17 went as a tutor to St. Petersburg; but the impression made on him by hearing there the music of Haydn and Mozart determined him to devote himself to a musical career. After studying in the Russian capital, he returned to Germany and published compositions of such promise that means were found by the publisher Cotta to enable him to proceed to Italy. What he learned there, particularly of the work of Palestrina, made him an enthusiast for church choral music. On his return to Germany, he set himself to improve church music by popularizing choral singing. From 1827 to 1865 he was organist of the Stiftskirche, Stuttgart, and a school of sacred song (Gesangvereins Liederkranz) founded by him in that city started a movement which spread throughout Württemberg. In 1852 Tübingen University gave him his degree. He published a large collection of chorales under the title *Zionsharfe* (1854–5); an oratorio, *Der Tod Abels*; several operas, sonatas, &c.

83. DIX.

KÖNIG, Johann Balthasar (1691–1758), was director of the music in several churches in Frankfurt-am-Main. He is best known as editor of the most comprehensive chorale-book of the 18th century, *Harmonischer Lieder Schatz, oder Allgemeines evangelisches Choralbuch* (Frankfurt, 1738). This collection contains 1,940 tunes, including those to the French Protestant psalms. In these, however, the original variety of rhythm is destroyed, and the reduction of the tunes to uniformity of pattern seriously reduces the value of the work. It also contains several tunes of König's own composition.

212. AUCTOR OMNIUM BONORUM. 455. FRANCONIA.

LACEY, Thomas Alexander, M.A., D.D., F.S.A. (Nottingham, 1853–1931), was educated at Balliol College, Oxford, and ordained in 1876. He was assistant master at Wakefield Grammar School and Denstone College, became vicar of Madingley, Cambridge, in 1894, and Warden and Chaplain of the London Diocesan Penitentiary, Highgate, from 1903 to 1919. In 1918 he became a canon of Worcester, Proctor in Convocation, diocese of Worcester, from 1922 to 1929, select preacher at Oxford, 1916–18, &c. His publications include *De Hierarchia Anglicana* (1895); *The Mysteries of Grace* (1908); *Catholicity* (1914); *Oxford Sermons* (1918); *Essays in Positive Theology* (1931). He was one of the editorial committee of the *English Hymnal* (1906).

66. *O come, O come, Emmanuel!*
148. *A messenger within the grave.*
246. *O faith of England, taught of old.*

LA FEILLÉE, François de (*fl. c.* 1750), was a priest attached to the choir of Chartres Cathedral. He published an abridgement of the Roman Antiphonary, and a manual of plainsong, *Méthode pour apprendre les régles du plain-chant et de la psalmodie* (1745). This famous work passed through many augmented editions; that revised by F. D. Aynés in 1808 contains material not found in either previous or subsequent issues.

48 (ii). CHRISTE SANCTORUM. 200. REGNATOR ORBIS.
688. ANNUE CHRISTE.

LAMPE, Johann Friedrich (Saxony, 1703–51, Edinburgh), came to England, in 1724, as a bassoon player at the opera. He wrote much music for the theatre, and many songs, and edited several miscellaneous collections of songs. After coming under the influence of Charles Wesley, he wrote many tunes for the Methodist hymns, and was partly responsible for the new, florid style which became popular. In 1746 he composed the music for Charles Wesley's *Hymns on the Great Festivals*, and probably edited the Dublin publication of 1749, since he was there during 1748–9. In 1750 he went to the Theatre Royal, Edinburgh, but died there the following year.

524. KENT.

LANIER, Sidney (Macon, Georgia, 1842–81, Lynn, N.C.), was educated at Oglethorpe College, graduating in 1860. An early volunteer in the Confederate army, he devoted his life, after the war, to letters and the flute. His publications included *Tiger-Lilies* (a novel), 1867; *Florida: its Scenery, Climate, and History, &c.* (1875); *Poems* (1877); *The Science of English Poetry*, and many articles and essays on music, poetry, history, &c., posthumously collected into volume form.

126. *Into the woods my master went.*

LARCOM, Lucy (Beverly, Mass., 1826–93, Beverly), worked in the cotton-mills at Lawrence till she was about 21, after which time she became a school teacher, and later, having had three years' training at Monticello Seminary, Alton, spent some years in Boston in the higher branches of her profession. She began writing while still in the mills, among her publications being *Poems* (1869); *Childhood Songs* (1875); *Poetical Works* (1885); *At the Beautiful Gate* (1892); *A New England Girlhood* (autobiography); and other works, including some in collaboration with J. G. Whittier.

531. *I learned it in the meadow path.*

LAWES, Henry (Dinton, Wiltshire, 1596–1662, London), was a pupil of John Coperario, famous as a composer for the lute and the viol. He became an epistler of the Chapel Royal, then one of the gentlemen, and later, clerk of the cheque there. He made the music for Milton's *Comus* when it was first represented, at Ludlow Castle, in 1634. Milton was thenceforward his friend, and addressed a sonnet to him beginning, 'Harry, whose tuneful and well-measured song'. He composed the Christmas songs in Herrick's *Hesperides*. Along with his brother William, he published a collection of *Choice Psalms* in 1648, just at the end of the Civil War. During the Protectorate he lost all his appointments, but was reinstated in them at the Restoration. Lawes excelled as a song-writer, and published several volumes of *Ayres and Dialogues for one, two, and three voices*. He is buried in the cloisters of Westminster Abbey.

22. FARLEY CASTLE. 227. FALKLAND.
290. BATTLE. 589. WHITEHALL.

LEATHAM, Edith Rutter (Meadowfield House, Durham, 1870–), daughter of William Rutter, architect, was educated privately, and, in 1898, married G. H. Leatham. Her first contributions, published in the *Spectator*, met with considerable success; she became a frequent contributor to various periodicals, and series of booklets, &c., and many of her poems have been set to music as solo songs. Among her publications in volume form are *Lyrics and Poems* (1913); *Silver Tongues* (1916); and *Music of the Day* (1933).

404. *Thank you for the world so sweet.*

LEECH-WILKINSON, Arthur, M.A., B.M., B.Ch. ['John Law'] (Taunton, 1899–), was educated at Liverpool College, 1908–17, and Trinity College, Oxford, 1919–22, being organist of the former from 1914, and of the latter during the whole of his residence. He is now senior resident medical and surgical officer of Park Hospital, Davyhulme.

491 (ii). MONTESANO.

LEESON, Jane Eliza (London, 1807–82, London), was for many years a well-known figure in the Catholic Apostolic Church, to the hymn-book of which she contributed nine hymns and translations. Some of her hymns were improvised as 'prophetical utterances'. Late in life, Miss Leeson entered the Roman communion. She published several books of hymns specially for children: *Infant Hymnings*; *Hymns and Scenes of Childhood*; *The Child's Book of Ballads*; *Songs of Christian Chivalry*; *Paraphrases and Hymns for Congregational Singing*, mostly re-written from the Scottish *Psalms and Paraphrases*.

366. *Loving Shepherd of thy sheep.*
370. *Saviour, teach me, day by day.*

LEIGHTON, Sir William (died before 1617), was one of the band of Gentleman Pensioners of Elizabeth and James I. In 1614 he published *The Teares or Lamentacions of a Sorrowful Soule*, &c., this consisted of 54 metrical psalms and hymns; but several other celebrated composers contributed some of the music, e.g. John Bull, William Byrd, John Dowland, Orlando Gibbons, &c. He also wrote a poem in praise of James I called *Vertue Triumphant*, 1603.

245. LEIGHTON.

LEISENTRITT, JOHANN (Olmütz, *c.* 1527–86, Bautzen), studied for many years in Krakau (Cracow) with his friend Antonius Brus, who later became archbishop of Prague. He rose in position in the church until in 1561 he was appointed Administrator ecclesiasticus and, in that capacity, enjoyed the powers of a bishop. Publications: *Geistlichen Lieder und Psalmen* (2 parts in 1567); *Gesangbuch*; and his *Catholisch Pfarbuch* (Cologne, 1577).

144. AVE VIRGO VIRGINUM.

LEONI (real name MYER LYONS), died Kingston, 1797, a noted vocalist and uncle to John Braham, was first a chorister at the Great Synagogue, Aldgate, London, then appeared at Covent Garden in 1775, and was subsequently appointed 'hazzan' at the Jewish Synagogue, Kingston, Jamaica. He composed several pieces for the theatre and for use in the Jewish ritual.

398. LEONI.

LEY, HENRY GEORGE, D.Mus. (Chagford, Devon, 1887–), was trained as a chorister at St. George's Chapel, Windsor, as a music scholar at Uppingham, at the Royal College of Music, and as an organ scholar at Keble College, Oxford. He was precentor of Radley College; organist of Christ Church, Oxford; Choragus of the University, Oxford, and Professor of the Organ at the Royal College of Music, London. He is now organist of Eton College. He is one of the best of modern organists, and has published much organ music, songs, part-songs, &c.

*96. ST. JAMES. *154. VULPIUS (GELOBT SEI GOTT).
*230, 611. LONDONDERRY. *391. HEILIGER GEIST.

LITTLEDALE, RICHARD FREDERICK, LL.D., D.C.L. (Dublin, 1833–90, London), was educated at Trinity College, Dublin, where he received the LL.D. degree in 1862, and in the same year received the Oxford D.C.L. *comitatis causâ*. He served as curate at Thorpe Hamlet, Norfolk, and St. Mary's, Soho; but chronic ill health obliged him to devote himself mainly to literary work. His *Plain Reasons against joining the Church of Rome* had a great circulation. He was one of the most learned of liturgiologists and a notable translator of hymns—from Greek, Latin, Syriac, German, Italian, Danish, and Swedish. He was joint-editor of the *Priest's Prayer Book* (1864) and the *People's Hymnal* (1867). He contributed to the Rev. Orby Shipley's *Lyrae*, and published in 1863 *Carols for Christmas and Other Seasons*.

177. *Come down, O Love divine.*

LLOYD, JOHN AMBROSE (Mold, Flintshire, 1815–74, Liverpool), though in the main self-taught, became one of the best-known and most influential musicians of his time. He founded the Welsh Choral Union of Liverpool, and often acted as adjudicator at the National Eisteddfodau. He composed many hymn-tunes and published two collections of them—the first, *Casgliad o Donau*, in 1843; the second, *Aberth Moliant*, in 1873. His cantata, *The Prayer of Habakkuk*, was the first work of its kind published in Wales. His part-song, *Blodeuyn Olaf*, is regarded as a Welsh classic.

531. CROMER.

LLOYD, WILLIAM (Rhos Goch, Llaniestyn, Carnarvon, 1786–1852, Rhos Goch), was self-educated. Travelling often in England, being probably a cattle-dealing farmer, he took the opportunity to hear English congregations sing, and profited by all he heard. He had a fine voice, knowledge of music, and ability to sing. Many people resorted to his house for teaching, and he travelled through the parishes and districts of Lleyn to hold singing meetings and to conduct music classes.

629. MEIRIONYDD.

LOCKHART, CHARLES (London, 1745–1815, London), was blind from infancy. He became, however, a notable musician, excelling especially in the training of children's choirs. He was organist in succession of the Lock Hospital, where he was associated with Martin Madan; St. Katherine Cree; St. Mary's, Lambeth; Orange Street Chapel; then of the Lock Hospital again. His earliest tunes were published on separate sheets. He issued also *A Set of Hymn-Tunes and Anthems for Three Voices* (1810); an *Epithalamium, or Nuptial Ode* (1770); and many songs.

458. CARLISLE.

LONGFELLOW, SAMUEL, M.A. (Portland, Maine, 1819–92, Portland), was a younger brother of Henry Wadsworth Longfellow. He was educated at Harvard for the Unitarian ministry, and served congregations at Fall River, Mass.; Brooklyn; and Germantown, Pennsylvania. He resigned this last charge to write his brother's *Life* (1886), and spent the remaining years of his life quietly at Cambridge, Mass. With Samuel Johnson (q.v.) he published *A Book of Hymns* (1846), and with Col. T. W. Higginson edited *Thalatta: a Book for the Seaside* (1853), which included some original material. He published *Vespers* and *Hymns and Tunes* in 1859, and, with Samuel Johnson, *Hymns of the Spirit* (1864), as a substitute for the former *Book of Hymns*. A volume of *Sermons and Essays* and *Hymns and Verses* were published posthumously.

8. *The summer days are come again.*
16. *'Tis winter now; the fallen snow.*
134. *When my love to God grows weak.*
520. *Holy Spirit, truth divine.*
532. *I look to thee in every need.*
602. *O life that makest all things new.*

LOWELL, JAMES RUSSELL (Cambridge, Mass., 1819–91, Elmwood), took his degree at Harvard in 1838, and was called to the Bar two years later. He succeeded Longfellow as Professor of Modern Languages and Literature in Harvard, in 1855. From 1857 to 1862 he edited the *Atlantic Monthly*, and the *North American Review* for the nine years following. In 1877 he was appointed American minister to Spain, and in 1881 was transferred to London, where he was ambassador till 1885. His publications included a large variety of subjects; in early life he was conspicuous as an anti-slavery writer both in prose and verse; his best-known works are his various volumes of poetry; *My Study Windows*; *Among my Books*; and the *Biglow Papers*.

306. *Men, whose boast it is that ye.*
309. *Once to every man and nation.*

LÖWENSTERN, MATTHÄUS APELLES VON (Neustadt, 1594–1648, Breslau), was the son of a saddler. His musical proficiency and his business ability were alike recognized by the various princes under whom he successively served, by the Duke of Münsterberg, under whom he became Stattsrath (privy councillor) at Oels, and by the Emperor Ferdinand II and his son Ferdinand III, who ennobled him. Löwenstern wrote about 30 hymns, accompanied with melodies by himself, mostly in the various classical lyric metres.

236. ALCAIC ODE.
349 (i). CHRISTE DU BEISTAND.
670. LÖWENSTERN (HEUT' IST O MENSCH).
349. *Lord of our life, and God of our salvation.*

LOWRY, SOMERSET CORRY (Dublin, 1855–1932), was educated at Repton and Trinity Hall, Cambridge; ordained 1879, and, after two curacies, was vicar of North Holmwood; St. Augustine's, Bournemouth; Wonston; and St. Bartholomew's, Southsea. He then retired and lived at Bournemouth. He published several devotional books, about 60 hymns in various books and periodicals, and a collection of *Hymns and Spiritual Songs.*

339. *Son of God, Eternal Saviour.*

LUTHER, MARTIN (Eisleben, 1483–1546, Eisleben), by his personality and influence the greatest force in the Reformation of the 16th century, was the son of a miner at Eisleben. His education, attended with considerable hardship, was mainly at Magdeburg, Eisenach, and the University of Erfurt, where he took his Master's degree in 1505. He entered the Augustinian Convent at Erfurt, where he spent three years, being ordained priest in 1507. A visit to Rome in 1511 opened his eyes to the corruptions of the Church, and his opposition to these reached a climax when the Dominican friar Tetzel appeared at Wittenberg selling indulgences. Luther's theses denouncing these and denying the Pope's right to forgive sins were nailed to the church door at Wittenberg. Luther was summoned to Rome to answer for his theses, but his University and the Elector of Saxony refused to let him go. His treatise, *The Babylonian Captivity of the Church*, provoked a papal bull directed against him, which he publicly burned at Wittenberg. His books were condemned and he was summoned in 1521 before the Diet at Worms, where he insisted on appearing, and refused to retract his doctrines. On his way home he was captured by the friendly Elector who feared for his life, and lodged him for a year in the Wartburg, where he translated the Scriptures and wrote various works. He returned to Wittenberg in 1522, his presence being necessary to settle disputes and disorders. In 1525 he married Katharina von Bora, a former nun, with whom he lived happily; but the latter part of his public life was less tranquil, being occupied in controversies with Erasmus, Henry VIII, the Swiss reformers, and with the troubles of the Peasants' War. Luther was a firm believer in the power of song. He wrote 37 hymns, and arranged many melodies for congregational use, from various sources. He was himself a musician, and the composition of some of the chorales is attributed to him by tradition; there is, however, no definite proof of this. The importance he attached to music is shown by his own words: 'I am strongly persuaded', he wrote, 'that after theology, there is no art that can be placed on a level with music; for besides theology, music is the only art capable of affording peace and joy of the heart, like that induced by the study of the science of divinity. A proof of this is that the devil, the originator of sorrowful anxieties and restless troubles, flees before the sound of music almost as much as before the Word of God.'

436. EIN' FESTE BURG.
436. *A safe stronghold our God is still.*

LYNCH, Thomas Toke (Dunmow, Essex, 1818–71, London), began his career as usher in a school, but later took successive charge of congregations in Highgate Independent Church, in Mortimer Street, and in Grafton Street, Fitzroy Square. In 1855 he published *The Rivulet: Hymns for Heart and Voice*, a volume which roused a storm of controversy in the Nonconformist churches (see p. 2). Mornington Church was built for him, and there he remained till his death. For 25 of his hymns he composed tunes, which were posthumously published.

297. *Dismiss me not thy service, Lord.*
506. *Gracious Spirit, dwell with me.*
699. *Where is thy God, my soul?*

LYRA DAVIDICA, a little book published anonymously in 1708, contained for the most part translations from Latin and 'the High German', with some original pieces. The intention of the compiler was to commend a freer type of tune than the solid psalm-tunes then almost exclusively in use. It marks the introduction of the florid tunes which, in the period then opening, acquired a great but transient popularity.

145. *Jesus Christ is risen to-day.*
145. EASTER HYMN. 172. LYRA.

LYTE, Henry Francis, M.A. (Ednam, near Kelso, 1793–1847, Nice), son of Captain Thomas Lyte, was educated at Portora, the Royal School of Enniskillen, and at Trinity College, Dublin, where he thrice won the prize for an English poem. He first intended to follow the medical profession, but took Orders and became curate of Taghmon, near Wexford, in 1815. Two years later he removed to Marazion, Cornwall, and in 1823 was appointed perpetual curate of Lower Brixham, Devon, a fishing village newly constituted a parish. Here his health finally broke down, and, continental travel failing to restore it, he died at Nice. He published *Tales on the Lord's Prayer in Verse* (1826); *Poems, chiefly Religious* (1833); *The Spirit of the Psalms* (1834); and an edition, with a memoir, of the *Poems of Henry Vaughan.*

104. *Long did I toil, and knew no earthly rest.*
170. *God of mercy, God of grace.*
437. *Abide with me; fast falls the eventide.*
623. *Praise, my soul, the King of heaven.*

MACDONALD, George, LL.D. (Huntly, Aberdeenshire, 1824–1905, Sagamore, Ashtead, Surrey), the son of a farmer, was educated at King's College, Aberdeen, and Highbury (Congregational) College, London. The only charge he served as a minister was at Arundel, Sussex; his spiritual and intellectual independence displeased his congregation, and he resigned, and turned to literature as a career. He still preached, but as a layman, and a friendship with F. D. Maurice led to his becoming a member of the Church of England. A long succession of novels, mystical and historical romances, literary and religious essays, and poetry, won him wide popularity; the novels that portray Scots life and character—such as *David Elginbrod*, *Robert Falconer*, and *Alec Forbes of Howglen*—have abiding value. His poems, appearing in various volumes—*Within and Without*; *The Disciple, and Other Poems*; *Exotics*; *A Threefold Cord*, &c.—were published in collected form in 1896. For some time he was editor of *Good Words for the Young*, and wrote several stories for children—*At the Back of the North Wind*; *The Princess and the Goblin*, &c. Most of his hymns were contributed to *Hymns and Sacred Songs for Sunday Schools and School Worship*, edited by his brother and the Rev. G. B. Bubier, and published in Manchester in 1855.

668. *They all were looking for a king.*

MACNUTT, FREDERICK BRODIE, M.A. (London, 1873–1949), was educated at St. Paul's School and Trinity College, Cambridge, and Ridley Hall, Cambridge. He became vicar of St. John's, Cheltenham, in 1904, and of St. Matthew's, Surbiton, from 1907 to 1918. From 1909 to 1918 he was canon residentiary of Southwark Cathedral, and from 1915 to 1918 chaplain with the British forces in Flanders and France. Since 1918 he has been vicar of St. Martin's, Leicester; since 1920 archdeacon of Leicester; since 1927 provost of Leicester Cathedral; and chaplain to the King since 1931. His publications include *The Inevitable Christ* (1911); *The Reproach of War* (1914); *Classics of the Inner Life* (1924); *From Chaos to God* (1929), &c.

156. *Let all the multitudes of light.*

MADAN, MARTIN (Hertingfordbury, 1726–90, Epsom), son of a Colonel Madan, and cousin, through his mother, of the poet Cowper, was educated at Westminster School and Christ Church, Oxford, and called to the Bar in 1748. Later, however, he took Orders, and became chaplain to the Lock Hospital, where, owing to the popularity of his preaching, a new chapel had to be opened for him. In 1780 he published *Thelyphthora*, in which he advocated polygamy, according to Old Testament principles, and the resulting scandal led him to resign his post and retire into private life at Epsom. His fame now rests on his miscellany, *A Collection of Psalms and Hymn-Tunes, never published before* (1760), which was reissued with an appendix in 1763, and appeared also in subsequent editions.

74. *Hark! the herald angels sing.*

MAGDALEN CHAPEL HYMNS. At the Magdalen Hospital, London, as at several of the other great charitable institutions founded in the 18th century, the choral singing of the inmates was made a special feature, and was one of the causes of the reform in psalmody at that period. For the present Hospital five sets of *Psalms and Hymns* were published, afterwards collected under the title *A Companion to the Magdalen Chapel.*

19. LYNE. 122. PLAISTOW.

MANT, RICHARD, D.D. (Southampton, 1776–1848, Ballymoney, Co. Antrim), was educated at Winchester and Trinity College, Oxford.

He became a Fellow of Oriel. In 1810 he was appointed vicar of Coggeshall, Essex; in 1811 Bampton Lecturer; in 1815 rector of St. Botolph's, Bishopsgate, London, and in 1818 rector also of East Horsley, Surrey, these two livings being held simultaneously. In 1820 he was appointed Bishop of Killaloe and Kilfenoragh; in 1823 was translated to the see of Down and Connor; and in 1833 the see of Dromore was united with the latter diocese under him. He wrote the *History of the Church in Ireland* (1840), and many other works. Most of his hymns appeared in *Scripture Narratives* (1831); and in *Ancient Hymns from the Roman Breviary, with Original Hymns* (1837).

203. *For thy dear saint, O Lord.*
460. *Bright the vision that delighted.*

MARCHANT, Stanley Robert, Mus.Doc., F.R.A.M., F.R.C.O. (London, 1883–1949), was educated at the Royal Academy of Music, where he was Goss Scholar. From 1916 to 1927 he was sub-organist at St. Paul's Cathedral, and became organist there in 1927. He has published church music—anthems, services, &c.—organ music, and many songs, part-songs, &c.

*682. EPSOM.

MARCKANT, John (16th century), incumbent of Clacton Magna (1559) and Shopland (1563–8). Little is known of him, save as the author of a few hymns and other poems. He contributed four psalms (118, 131, 132, 135) to Sternhold and Hopkins's version of the Psalter. In this also appears the under-noted hymn known as 'The Lamentation'.

116. *O Lord, turn not away thy face.*

MARRIOTT, John, M.A. (Cottesbach, near Lutterworth, 1780–1825, Broadclyst, near Exeter), was educated at Rugby and Christ Church, Oxford. Ordained in 1804, he spent four years at Dalkeith Palace as tutor to Lord George Scott, elder brother of the 5th Duke of Buccleuch. He was also domestic chaplain to the 4th Duke, who, on the death of Lord George in 1808, presented him to the living of Church Lawford, Warwickshire. Ill health, however, made residence there impossible; and he had to live in Devonshire, where he served several curacies. He would not permit publication of his hymns during his lifetime.

303. *Thou whose almighty Word.*

MARTINEAU, James, D.C.L. (Norwich, 1805–1900, London), was educated at Norwich Grammar School, Bristol, and Derby, and as a student of Divinity in Manchester College, York. After ministry in Dublin and Liverpool, he became, in 1840, Professor of Mental and Moral Philosophy and Political Economy in Manchester New College, and, after the college's removal to London, became its Principal from 1869 to 1885, when he retired. One of the greatest theologians of the 19th century, he published *A Study of Spinoza* (1882); *Types of Ethical Theory* (1885–6); and other books. He also edited three hymn-books: *A Collection of Hymns for Christian Worship* (Dublin, 1831); *Hymns for the Christian Church and Home* (London, 1840); and *Hymns of Praise and Prayer* (London, 1873).

124. *A voice upon the midnight air.*

MASEFIELD, JOHN, LL.D. (Liverpool, 1875–), Poet Laureate, spent his youth in various occupations, both in England and America and at sea. These early experiences make themselves felt throughout his work as poet and as novelist. His publications include *Salt-Water Ballads* (1902); *Captain Margaret* (1908); *Multitude and Solitude* (1909); *The Tragedy of Nan* (1909); *The Everlasting Mercy* (1911); *The Daffodil Fields* (1913); *Reynard the Fox* (1919); *Sard Harker* (1924); *Odtaa* (1926); *The Coming of Christ* (1928); *The Hawbucks* (1929); *Minnie Maylow's Story* (1931); and many other plays, poems, and novels, as well as editions of voyages, &c.

86. *By weary stages.*
165. *Sing, men and angels, sing.*
593. *O Christ who holds the open gate.*

MASSEY, GERALD (Gamble Wharf, Tring, 1828–1907, South Norwood), was self-educated, and published his first volume at the age of 20, *Poems and Chansons* (1848). He joined the Chartists, and shortly afterwards allied himself with the Christian Socialist movement. Later he was much engaged in journalism and popular lecturing, both in England and America. George Eliot's *Felix Holt* is said to be founded on Massey's career. In later years he was much occupied with spiritualism. He was a prolific author, his most important books being *Voices of Freedom and Lyrics of Love* (1850); *The Ballad of Babe Christabel and other Poems* (1854); *Poetical Works* (1857); *My Lyrical Life* (1899); many other volumes of poetry, and works on Shakespeare's Sonnets, Egyptian civilization, spiritualism, &c.

313. *Through all the long dark night of years.*

MASSIE, RICHARD (Chester, 1800–87, Pulford Hall), came of an ancient Cheshire family, and was son of the Rev. R. Massie of Coddington, sometime rector of St. Bride's, Chester, and of Eccleston. A man of wealth and leisure, with two estates—Pulford Hall, Coddington, Cheshire, and another near Wrexham, Denbighshire—he devoted himself to literature. He published a translation of *Martin Luther's Spiritual Songs* (1854); *Lyra Domestica* (2 series), a translation of Spitta's *Psalter und Harfe*; and contributed many similar translations to various collections.

27. *Come, thou bright and morning star.*

MATHAMS, WALTER JOHN (London, 1851–1931), spent his early life at sea. He then received training for the Baptist ministry at Regent's Park College, London, held charges in Preston, Falkirk, and Birmingham, and was chaplain to the Forces in Egypt for three years, before, in 1905, he was admitted to the ministry of the Church of Scotland. He served as ordained assistant in Stronsay, Orkney; then, from 1909 to 1919, was in charge of Mallaig mission church. In the latter year he resigned. He published many books: *At Jesus' Feet*, hymns and poems; *Fireside Parables*; *Rough Sermons*; *Jack Ahoy*; *Comrades All*; *Maxim Shots for Soldiers*; *A Bowl of Amber*; *The Day of the Golden Chance*; *Maxims for Boys*, &c.

363. *Jesus, friend of little children.*

MATHER, WILLIAM (Sheffield?, 1756–1808, Sheffield), was organist of St. Paul's and St. James's, Sheffield. He was the compiler of *Sacred Music consisting of Twenty-six Psalm and Hymn Tunes* (1805).

118. ATTERCLIFFE.

MATHESON, GEORGE, D.D., LL.D., F.R.S.E. (Glasgow, 1842–1906, North Berwick), was the son of a Glasgow merchant. From infancy he suffered from defective vision, but had a distinguished scholastic career at Glasgow Academy and University. Licensed as a preacher in 1866, he became assistant to Dr. J. R. Macduff in Sandyford Church, Glasgow, and in 1868 minister of Innellan, Argyllshire. In 1886 he was translated to St. Bernard's parish church, Edinburgh, where he remained for 13 years. In 1874 he published *Aids to the Study of German Theology*, and this was followed by many works such as: *The Growth of the Spirit of Christianity*; *Natural Elements of Revealed Theology* (Baird Lectures); *Landmarks of New Testament Morality*; then by several essays in apologetic—*Can the Old Faith live with the New?*; *The Spiritual Development of St. Paul*; *The Distinctive Messages of the Old Religions*; and finally by books of spiritual meditation and devotion—*My Aspirations*; *Moments on the Mount*; *Voices of the Spirit*; *Times of Retirement*; *Rests by the River*; *Searchings in Silence*; *Studies in the Portrait of Christ*, &c., and one volume of verse, *Sacred Songs*.

497. *Gather us in, thou love that fillest all.*
576. *Make me a captive, Lord.*

MATHEWS, BASIL JOSEPH, M.A. (Oxford, 1879-1951), was educated at Oxford High School and University. After five years as private secretary to Principal Fairbairn of Mansfield College, he was for some years on the staff of the *Christian World*, then became editorial secretary of the London Missionary Society. He was chairman and secretary of the Literature Committee of the Ministry of Information in the closing years of the War; he then became director of the Press Bureau of the Conference of British Missionary Societies, and editor of its magazine, *Outward Bound*. He is now International Literature Secretary (Boys' Work) of the World's Committee of Y.M.C.A.s, Geneva, editor of a new magazine, *The World's Youth*; and author of *A Life of Jesus*.

299. *Far round the world thy children sing their song.*

MAUDE, MARY FAWLER, *née* HOOPER (London, 1819–1913, Overton, Flintshire), while yet in her teens, wrote three text-books, based on the writings of Eastern travellers, on *Scripture Manners and Customs*, *Scripture Topography*, and *Scripture Natural History*. These, published by the S.P.C.K., were widely used for many years. In 1841 she married the Rev. Joseph Maude, vicar of St. Thomas's, Newport, Isle of Wight.

258. *Thine for ever! God of love.*

MENDELSSOHN-BARTHOLDY, (JAKOB LUDWIG) FELIX (Hamburg, 1809–47, Leipzig), was the son of a Jewish banker, and grandson of the famous Jewish philosopher, Moses Mendelssohn. The family settled in his childhood in Berlin, and were baptized into the Lutheran Church, adding Bartholdy to the name on that occasion. Felix showed extraordinary musical gifts. At the age of 10 he made his first appearance as a pianist, and while yet a boy composed profusely. In his youth he discovered Bach, and while a student at the University got together a choir of 16 voices, and practised *The Passion according to St. Matthew*. In 1829 it was performed for the first time since Bach's death, Mendelssohn conducting. Bach's influence on him was profound. His overture to *A Midsummer-Night's Dream* (1826) had already given him high rank as a composer. In 1829 he visited Great Britain for the first time. His visit to Scotland inspired the overture *Fingal's Cave*. In 1833 he accepted the directorship of concerts at Düsseldorf, where he invented the new form of composition for the pianoforte now familiar in the *Lieder ohne Worte*. From 1835 to 1843 he was director of the Gewandhaus concerts at Leipzig. Reluctantly, in the latter year, at the urgent request of the King of Prussia, he left Leipzig for Berlin, to be the royal Kapellmeister, and director of the musical division of the newly founded Academy of Arts; but in 1845 he was glad to return to Leipzig, to resume the directorship of the Gewandhaus concerts, and to found the Conservatorium and give his direction to it. His industry was boundless, and in 1847, after he had made his last visit to London to conduct his *Elijah*, the shock of the news of a beloved sister's death broke his overstrained constitution. As a pianist and organist he was in the first rank. He left great masses of compositions—two oratorios, *St. Paul* and *Elijah*; symphonies, overtures, string quartets, concertos and other pieces for the pianoforte, organ sonatas, much vocal music, secular and sacred.

74. MENDELSSOHN.
*90. WIE SCHÖN LEUCHTET DER MORGENSTERN.
*132. BRESLAU.

MENZIES, George Kenneth, M.A., C.B.E. (London, 1869–), was educated at St. Andrews University and Balliol College, Oxford. In 1893 he became assistant Professor of Greek in St. Andrews University, in 1896 private secretary to Sir William Dunn, Bt., M.P., in 1904 secretary in the Academic Department of the University of London, in 1908 assistant secretary to the Royal Society of Arts, and since 1917 has been the secretary of that society. He has for many years been a frequent contributor to various well-known periodicals.

325. *What heroes thou hast bred.*

MERRILL, William Pierson, D.D. (Orange, New Jersey, 1867–), studied at Rutgers College and at Union Theological Seminary, New York. From both these foundations he received later the D.D. degree. Ordained to the Presbyterian ministry in 1890, he held charges at Philadelphia; Sixth Church, Chicago; and since 1911, the Brick Church, New York. A preacher of note, he has published several books that have wide acceptance: *Faith Building*; *Faith and Sight*; *Footings for Faith*; *Christian Internationalism*; *The Common Creed of Christians*; *The Freedom of the Preacher*; *Liberal Christianity*.

635. *Rise up, O men of God!*

MEYER, Johann David, whose name is also spelt variously Meier, Mayer, and Mejer, was, in 1691, 'Ratsherr' at Ulm. He published, at Ulm, in 1692 a collection entitled *Geistliche Seelen-Freud: oder Davidische Hauss-Capell*, &c., containing 111 melodies, of which 54 were his own composition.

289, 583. MEYER (ES IST KEIN TAG).

MILFORD, Robin (Oxford, 1903–), was educated at West Downs, Winchester, Rugby, and the Royal College of Music. Many of his works have had several public performances: *A Prophet in the Land*, for chorus, soli, and orchestra, being first produced at the Three Choirs Festival at Gloucester, 1931; the *Double Fugue* at a Bach Choir concert in 1927; while the *Suite for Oboe and Strings*, and *Rain, Wind, and Sunshine*, a children's cantata, have each been frequently heard. Among his other publications are a *Suite for Chamber Orchestra*; *The Darkling Thrush* for solo violin and small orchestra; *The Pilgrim's Progress*, for soli, chorus, and orchestra; *Go, little book*, a suite for flute and strings, &c.; and many songs, and piano and organ music.

504. PRAYERS. *517. DUNFERMLINE. 520. HARTS.

MILGROVE, Benjamin (Bath? 1731–1810, Bath?), was precentor and then organist of the Countess of Huntingdon's Chapel in Bath. He published *Sixteen Hymns as they are sung at the Right Honourable the Countess of Huntingdon's Chapel in Bath. Set to Music* (*c.* 1769), and two or three further collections of the same kind.

161. HARWICH. 203. MOUNT EPHRAIM.

MILLER, Edward, Mus.Doc. (Norwich, 1731–1807, Doncaster), was apprenticed to his father's trade of pavior, but ran away to follow his bent towards the study of music. He became a pupil of Dr. Burney, and for a time played the German flute in Handel's orchestra. For over fifty years (1756–1807) he was organist of Doncaster Parish Church. He wrote on antiquarian subjects, and published a *History of Doncaster*. Dissatisfaction with the existing state of church music led him to publish an edition of the *Psalms of David*, with tunes, in 1790; *Psalms and Hymns set to New Music* (1801); *Sacred Music . . . an Appendix to Dr. Watts' Psalms and Hymns* (1802).

133. ROCKINGHAM.

MILMAN, Henry Hart, D.D. (London, 1791–1868, Sunninghill, Ascot), was son of Sir Francis Milman, Bt., physician to the King. He was educated at Greenwich, Eton, and Brasenose College, Oxford, where he had a career of extraordinary brilliance; he won the Newdigate Prize with his *Belvidere Apollo*, 'best of Oxford prize poems', and became a Fellow of his college. Ordained in 1816, he received in 1818 the living of St. Mary's, Reading; in 1821–31 was Professor of Poetry at Oxford; in 1827 was Bampton Lecturer; in 1835 received a canonry of Westminster, with the rectorship of St. Margaret's; and in 1849 accepted the Deanery of St. Paul's. He wrote several dramas, of which *Fazio* met with success, and translations of Horace, and Greek plays; but his work as an historian was the most important, beginning with his *History of the Jews* (1830), which aroused much opposition, and had to be withdrawn and reissued in a revised edition, and continuing with the *History of Christianity from the Birth of Christ to the Abolition of Paganism in the Roman Empire*, followed by his *History of Latin Christianity to the Pontificate of Nicholas V* (1856). His *Poetical Works* were collected in 3 volumes. His *Annals of St. Paul's Cathedral* appeared after his death. His 13 hymns appeared in *Hymns Adapted to the Weekly Church Service of the Year*, and in *Hymns for the Use of St. Margaret's, Westminster* (1837).

114. *O help us, Lord! Each hour of need.*
137. *Ride on! ride on in majesty!*

MILTON, JOHN (*c.* 1563–1646/7, London), the father of the poet and the son of Richard Milton, a well-to-do yeoman of Stanton St. John, near Oxford, is said to have been educated at Christ Church, Oxford. In 1595 he apprenticed himself to James Colbron, a member of the Scriveners' Company, and in 1599 or 1600 was admitted to the Freedom of the Company. He amassed a fair fortune and retired to Horton, Bucks.; in 1634 was elected to the Mastership of the Scriveners' Company, and in 1643 returned to London and lived with his son the poet. Milton's musical abilities are alluded to by his son in his poem *Ad Patrem*. The following works were printed while he yet lived: *Fair Oriana in the Morn* from *The Triumphes of Oriana*; *Thou God of Might*; *O Lord, behold*; and *O had I wings* (1614).

*628. YORK.

MILTON, JOHN (London, 1608–74, London), the poet, was educated at St. Paul's School, and went to Christ's College, Cambridge, which he left for a time owing to disagreement with his tutor, but returned and took his B.A. in 1628 and M.A. in 1632. Milton's literary life falls into three well-marked periods, the first including his earlier and shorter poems, the second almost entirely occupied with controversial and political writings, and the third containing his poems on a grander scale. Much of his best work was produced at a comparatively early age. Thus his paraphrase of Psalm 136 (our 12) was written before he was 16 years of age; while the *Ode on the morning of Christ's Nativity* was composed in 1629, *L'Allegro* and *Il Penseroso* about 1630, *Comus* in 1634, and *Lycidas* in 1637. Shortly after an Italian tour in 1638–9, Milton's energies were diverted into the controversies leading to the Civil War and the establishment of the Commonwealth. For many years his chief writings were of a polemical character, the most famous being *Areopagitica*. He was appointed Secretary for foreign tongues to the Council of State, a post which he continued to fill, notwithstanding his blindness (which became total in 1652), until the eve of the Restoration. This period saw also his *Defences* against Salmasius and Morus. On the re-establishment of the monarchy, for some years he lived in close retirement. The publication in 1667 of *Paradise Lost* (written in 1665 but projected many years earlier) brought him favour and the admiration of even his political enemies. In 1671 followed *Paradise Regained* and *Samson Agonistes*.

12. *Let us, with a gladsome mind.*
525. *How lovely are thy dwellings fair!*
634. *Ring out, ye crystal spheres!*
658. *The Lord will come and not be slow.*

MONK, WILLIAM HENRY, Mus.Doc. (Brompton, 1823–89, Stoke Newington), organist of St. Matthias, Stoke Newington, and at the same time director of the choir and organist of King's College, London, and from 1874 professor of vocal music there. In 1876 he was appointed a professor in the National Training School for Music and at Bedford College. He published many anthems, &c., and edited *Hymns of the Church* and *The Scottish Hymnal*; but his chief title to fame is his identification with *Hymns Ancient and Modern*, of which he was the first musical editor.

Thomas Hardy noted as a lad the mutilation of the old psalm-tunes, and recorded his disapproval in later years:

Stripped of some of your old vesture
By Monk or another. Now you wore no frill,
And at first you startled me. But I know you still,
Though I missed the minim's waver
And the dotted quaver.

61. MERTON. *87. CRÜGER. 147. VICTORY.
437. EVENTIDE. *570. RAVENSHAW. 641 (ii). ST. ETHELWALD.

MONSELL, JOHN SAMUEL BEWLEY, LL.D. (St. Columb's, Derry, 1811–75, Guildford), was the son of an archdeacon of Londonderry and brother of the first Lord Emly. He was educated at Trinity College, Dublin, and ordained in 1834. He became chaplain to Bishop Mant; Chancellor of the diocese of Connor; rector of Ramoan; then, proceeding to England, was vicar of Egham, Surrey; and rector of St. Nicholas, Guildford. Here he died of injuries caused by an accident (not the fall of a stone) in his church while he was watching rebuilding operations. He published 11 volumes of poetry, including nearly 300 hymns, of which more than 70 have been in use: *Hymns and Miscellaneous Poems*; *Parish Musings*; *Spiritual Songs for the Sundays and Holy Days throughout the Year*; *Hymns of Love and Praise for the Church's Year*; *The Passing Bell*; *Litany Hymns*; *The Parish Hymnal after the Order of the Book of Common Prayer*; *Watches by the Cross*; *Simon the Cyrenian*; *Nursery Carols*, &c.

93. *O worship the Lord in the beauty of holiness.*
272. *I hunger and I thirst.*
491. *Fight the good fight with all thy might.*

MONTGOMERY, JAMES (Irvine, Ayrshire, 1771–1854, Sheffield), the son of an Ulster Scot who became a Moravian minister, was educated at Fulneck for the ministry, but, failing to satisfy the Moravian Brethren by his progress, found himself, after various adventures, in Sheffield as assistant to a bookseller and printer, named Gales, on the staff of the *Sheffield Register*. Two years later, in 1796, Gales, owing to his 'liberal' articles in the paper, was forced to leave the country, and Montgomery became editor of the sheet, renamed the *Sheffield Iris*, retaining the position for 31 years. He twice suffered fines and imprisonment in York Castle—for printing a song on the fall of the Bastille, and an article on a political riot in Sheffield—but so established his position that in 1833 he received a royal pension.

He published *The West Indies, a Poem in honour of the Abolition of the Slave-Trade* (1807); *The World Before the Flood* (1813); *Songs of Zion* (1822); *The Pelican Island* (1828); *The Poet's Portfolio* (1835); *Original Hymns* (1853). Most of his 400 hymns were written early in life.

71. *Angels from the realms of glory.*
87. *Hail to the Lord's Anointed!*
195. *'For ever with the Lord!'*
259. *According to thy gracious word.*
298. *Pour out thy Spirit from on high.*
301. *Lift up your heads, ye gates of brass.*
630. *Prayer is the soul's sincere desire.*
644. *Songs of praise the angels sang.*

MOORE, Thomas (Dublin, 1779–1852, Sloperton, Devizes), son of a grocer and wine-merchant, was educated at Trinity College, Dublin, and studied law at the Middle Temple, London. In 1804 he went to Bermuda as registrar to the Admiralty Court, but soon returned to England after appointing a deputy, whose later misconduct involved Moore in financial ruin, and compelled him to spend three years in exile on the Continent. His first volume of poetry was *Poems by the late Thomas Little* (1801), his second *Odes and Epistles* (1806); these and his social graces made him a favourite in London, but later he retired to a cottage in Derbyshire, whence he issued *National Airs*; *Sacred Songs and Trios*; *Irish Melodies*; and the immensely successful *Lalla Rookh*. The last years of his life he spent near Devizes, and there prepared his collected *Poetical Works*. He was a great friend of Lord Byron, and, after the latter's death, edited his *Life and Letters*.

20. *Thou art, O God, the life and light.*
679. *Thy heaven, on which 'tis bliss to look.*

MORE, Henry, D.D. (Grantham, 1614–87?), was educated at Eton and Christ's College, Cambridge. He graduated in 1635, became a Fellow in 1639, declined several offers of high preferment and spent his life in the study of philosophy and in private tutoring. He published in 1640 *Psychozoia, or the first part of the song of the Soul.* In 1710 his memoirs were published. A leader, in an intolerant age, of the elect band of broad-minded scholars called the Cambridge Platonists, his works greatly influenced John Wesley and Coleridge.

80. *The holy son of God most high.*

MORICE, Francis David, M.A. (1848–1926, Woking), was educated at Uppingham, Winchester, and New College, Oxford, where he was a scholar and won many academic distinctions; he was ordained and became a Fellow of Queen's College, Oxford, in 1871; an assistant master at Rugby in 1874, a house-master from 1884 onwards; and he remained at Rugby until 1894. He was not professionally a musician, but wrote a few hymn-tunes, of which one appears in the *Rugby School Hymn Book* (1897). He published *Stories in Attic Greek*; *Pindar for English Readers*, &c.

676. ASCENDIT.

MORISON, John, D.D. (Cairnie, Aberdeenshire, 1750–98, Canisbay), studied at King's College, Aberdeen, where he graduated, and after holding several teaching appointments in Caithness, repaired to Edinburgh for further study, especially in Greek. In 1779 Morison was presented to the parish of Canisbay, Caithness, and was ordained nine months later, in September 1780. At the Assembly of the following year he was appointed a member of the Committee for revising the collection of *Translations and Paraphrases* to which he had himself contributed. A number of poetical pieces by him appeared in the *Edinburgh Weekly Magazine*, over the signature of 'Musaeus'; he wrote also the account of the parish of Canisbay for Sir John Sinclair's *Statistical Account*, and collected the topographical history of Caithness for Chalmers's *Caledonia*.

96. *The race that long in darkness pined.*

MORRIS, REGINALD OWEN (York, 1886–1948), was educated at Harrow and New College, Oxford, and at the Royal College of Music, where he is now on the teaching staff. He held a post in America, 1929–31. Publications: *Contrapuntal Technique in the 16th Century* (1922); a *Fantasy for String Quartet* published by the Carnegie Trust; some *Motets for String Quartet*; two symphonies; concertos for violin and for two violins; *Corinna's Maying* for chorus and orchestra; and much other music, songs, part-songs, &c.

92. HERMITAGE. 501 (i). CONSTANTIA.

MOULTRIE, GERARD (Rugby, 1829–85, Southleigh), was educated at Rugby and Exeter College, Oxford, and became assistant master and chaplain of Shrewsbury School. He was vicar of Southleigh in 1869, and four years later Warden of St. James's College, Southleigh. His publications included *Hymns and Lyrics for the Seasons and Saints' Days of the Church* (1867); *The Espousals of St. Dorothea and Other Verses* (1870); *Cantica Sanctorum* (1880), &c.

136. *Come, faithful people, come away.*

MUIRHEAD, LIONEL BRULTON CAMPBELL LOCKHART (1845–1925), the eldest son of James Patrick Muirhead of Hasely Court, Oxon., D.L., was educated at Radley, Eton, and Balliol College, Oxford. He was the friend to whom Robert Bridges dedicated the Fourth Book of his *Shorter Poems.*

248. *The Church of God a kingdom is.*

MÜLLER, JOHANN MICHAEL (Schmalkalden, 1683– ?), was music-director, organist, and preceptor of the Gymnasium at Hanau from 1718 to 1736. He published *Zions Harpffen-Lieder, &c.* (1718), and *Neu aufgesetztes, vollständiges . . . Psalm- und Choral-Buch, &c.* (1718), and a supplement to the latter in 1739.

642. MÜLLER.

MULLINAR, MICHAEL (Bangor, North Wales, 1896–   ), was a pupil of Dr. Roland Rogers, organist of Bangor Cathedral, and from 1915 to 1917 was deputy organist at the Cathedral. From 1923 to 1925 he studied at the Royal College of Music, and, later, was a pupil, for composition, of Dr. R. Vaughan Williams. Since 1922 he has been accompanist to the City of Birmingham Municipal Orchestra. His compositions include several songs and part-songs, pianoforte music, and incidental music to a children's play, *The Princess and the Swineherd* (1930).

497. BILLESLEY.

MYERS, ERNEST JAMES (Keswick, 1844–1921, Etchingham, Sussex), was educated at Cheltenham and Balliol College, Oxford, where he gained the Gaisford Prize for Greek verse in 1865. In 1868 he became a Fellow of Wadham College, where he was a lecturer for three years. He was called to the Bar, but never practised. During his residence in London from 1871 to 1891 he wrote much, and was also secretary to the London Society for the Extension of University Teaching for five years, was on the Council of the Hellenic Society from 1879, and later did much work for the Charity Organization Society. In 1891 he left London and lived in the country until his death. Among his publications were translations of the classics; *Poems* (1877); *The Defence of Rome* (1880); *The Judgement of Prometheus* (1886); *Gathered Poems* (1904), &c.

591. *Now in life's breezy morning.*

MYERS, Frederic William Henry (Keswick, 1843–1901, Rome), brother of the above, was educated at Cheltenham and Trinity College, Cambridge, was a classical lecturer from 1865 to 1869, and from 1872 onwards was on the permanent staff of school inspectors in the Educational department. He published many volumes of poems between 1867 and 1882, including *St. Paul*, from which our hymn is taken; in 1883 a volume of *Essays Classical and Modern*; and monographs on Wordsworth and Shelley. He was one of the founders of the Society for Psychical Research, and co-author of *Phantasms of the Living*, one of the earliest serious books on the subject of spiritualism. His great work, *Human Personality and its Survival*, was first published in 1903, after his death.

511. *Hark what a sound, and too divine for hearing.*

NAYLOR, Edward Woodall, Mus.Doc. (Scarborough, 1867–1934), son of Dr. John Naylor, organist of York Minster, was trained as a chorister under his father, and was an organ scholar of Emmanuel College, Cambridge. After periods of service in St. Michael's, Chester Square, and St. Mary's, Kilburn, London, he became, in 1897, organist of Emmanuel College, Cambridge, of which he is now also a lecturer and hon. Fellow. He is also Lecturer in Musical History in the University. His first appearance as a composer was in 1892, in the old St. James's Hall, London, with *Merlin and the Gleam*. He has since published *The Angelus*, an opera performed at Covent Garden in 1909; *Arthur the King*; *Pax Dei*, a requiem; anthems, &c.; also books on historical music, *Shakespeare and Music*; *An Elizabethan Virginal Book*; *Shakespeare Music, &c.*; papers on H. Schütz and J. Handl, &c.

641 (i). FROM STRENGTH TO STRENGTH.

NEALE, John Mason, D.D. (London, 1818–66, East Grinstead), was educated at Sherborne Grammar School and Trinity College, Cambridge. He became a Fellow of Downing College, and gained the Seatonian prize for a sacred poem 11 times. In 1843 he was presented to the small living of Crawley, Sussex, but was never instituted to the charge, owing to an attack of lung trouble which compelled him to go to Madeira. There, fortunately, a remarkable library enabled him to read enormously and to store up materials for his subsequent books. In 1846 Earl de la Warr presented him to the wardenship of Sackville College, East Grinstead, a refuge for indigent old men. There, at a salary of £27 a year, the most learned hymnologist and liturgiologist of his time remained for the rest of his too short life (see 295 and cf. 199). He was also offered the Provostship of St. Ninian's Cathedral, Perth, but the climate was too cold to permit him to reside there. For 14 years Neale was inhibited by his bishop. He occupied himself in literary pursuits, producing *A Commentary on the Psalms, from Primitive and Mediaeval Writers* (with R. F. Littledale, q.v.); *The History of the Holy Eastern Church*; *The Patriarchate of Alexandria*; *Essays on Liturgiology and Church History*; but his chief title to remembrance and gratitude rests on his translations. He brought to light Greek and Latin hymns, many of which had long been buried in monasteries and cathedral libraries on the Continent and in Asia Minor. An excellent classical scholar and a master of medieval Latin, he published, from the Latin—*Mediaeval Hymns and Sequences*; *The Hymnal Noted* (94 hymns out of 105 translated from Latin are his); *Hymns, chiefly Mediaeval, on the Joys and Glories of Paradise*; and from the Greek—*Hymns of the Eastern Church*, in which he broke entirely new ground.

51. *O Trinity of blessèd light.*
70. *A great and mighty wonder.*
135. *All glory, laud, and honour.*
143. *Ye sons and daughters of the King.*
144. *Come, ye faithful, raise the strain.*
146. *The day of resurrection!*
168. *Thou hallowed chosen dawn of praise.*
180. *Come, thou holy Paraclete.*
190. *Blessèd city, heavenly Salem.*
198. *Jerusalem the golden.*
199. *Light's abode, celestial Salem.*
200. *O what their joy and their glory must be.*
215. *Let us now our voices raise.*
239. *Around the throne of God a band.*
295. *They whose course on earth is o'er.*
459. *Brief life is here our portion.*
490. *Fierce was the wild billow.*
548. *Jesu! the very thought is sweet!*
599. *O happy band of pilgrims.*

NEANDER, Joachim (Bremen, 1650–80, Bremen), whose real name was Neumann, was educated at the Pädagogium and the Gymnasium Illustre in his native city. He associated himself with the Pietists, and became a friend of Spener, the leader of that School. His zeal, when appointed in 1674 to the head mastership of the Reformed Grammar School at Düsseldorf, induced him to go beyond his official duty and he was suspended from office and obliged to leave the town. For some months he lived in a cave near Mettman on the Rhine, which is still called Neander's cave. In 1679 he returned to Bremen as second preacher in St. Martin's. Again his preaching aroused opposition. But his ministry was brief; for he was seized with consumption and died the following year. A man of scholarship and accomplishment in poetry, letters, and music, as well as theology, he wrote some 60 hymns and composed tunes for them. They were collected and published in 1680 under the title *A und Ω, Joachimi Neander Glaub- und Liebesübung*.

442. *All my hope on God is founded.*
626. *Praise to the Lord, the Almighty, the King of creation.*
442. MEINE HOFFNUNG. 477. NEANDER.

NEUMARK, Georg (Langensalza, Thuringia, 1621–81, Weimar), son of a clothier, was educated at the Gymnasia of Schleusingen and Gotha; but, being robbed of all his money on his way to the University of Königsberg, was compelled to endure many adventures and privations in various towns, before he was able to save enough to matriculate there in 1643. He studied law and poetry, and, after completing his course, again earned a precarious livelihood in Warsaw, Thorn and Danzig, and Hamburg. In the latter city, where he arrived in 1651, he found employment through the Swedish ambassador, Baron von Rosenkranz, and later returned to Thuringia as court poet, librarian, and registrar to Duke Wilhelm II of Saxe-Weimar, and finally became custodian of the ducal archives. In

1656 he was made secretary of the Fruit-Bearing Society, the chief German literary union of the 17th century. He became blind in 1681, shortly before his death.

606. NEUMARK.

NEWBOLT, Sir HENRY JOHN, C.H., M.A., LL.D., D.Litt., &c. (Bilston, 1862–1938), was educated at Clifton College and Corpus Christi College, Oxford, where he was a scholar, and, later, an honorary Fellow. From 1887 to 1899 he practised as a barrister, and was editor of the *Monthly Review* for the four succeeding years. He has since then held various administrative posts, among them that of Controller of Wireless and Cables during the War, and President of the English Association in 1927–8, while he was Official Naval Historian in 1923. His publications include *Admirals All* (1897); *Songs of the Sea* (1904); *The Old Country* (1906); *Poems New and Old* (1912); *Tales of the Great War* (1916); *A New Study of English Poetry* (1917); *A Naval History of the War* (1920); *Studies Green and Gray* (1926), &c.

323. *O Lord almighty, thou whose hands.*

NEWELL, EBENEZER JOSIAH, M.A. (Southwark, 1853–1916, Neen Sollars), was educated at Worcester College, Oxford, where he graduated in 1876. He was ordained in 1890, and was Head Master of Neath School, and curate there till 1891, after which he held the curacy of Newton-Nottage until 1900. From 1900 till his death he was rector of Neen Sollars, Salop. Among his publications were *The Sorrow of Simona, &c.* (1882); *A Popular History of the Ancient British Church* (1887); *A History of the Welsh Church* (1895); and *Diocesan History, Llandaff* (1902).

225. *We praise thy name, all-holy Lord.*

NEWMAN, JOHN HENRY, Cardinal, D.D. (London, 1801–90, Edgbaston), son of a banker, after a distinguished career at Trinity College, Oxford, became a Fellow of Oriel, and Vice-President of St. Alban's Hall. From 1828 to 1843 he was vicar of St. Mary the Virgin, the University Church, and with Pusey, Keble, and Hurrell Froude, a leader of the Oxford Movement, and the chief writer in the *Tracts for the Times*. In 1843 he resigned his living, and, after three years of hesitation at Littlemore, entered the Roman Communion, 1845. For many years, however, he was distrusted by the authorities of the Roman Church, and lived in seclusion at the Oratory of St. Philip Neri, Edgbaston, Birmingham. At length, in 1879, his great gifts and sincerity were recognized by his elevation to the Cardinalate. He wrote many works, the best known to-day being the *Dream of Gerontius*, and his *Apologia pro Vita Sua*, though even this is now little read.

554. *Lead, kindly Light, amid the encircling gloom.*
625. *Praise to the Holiest in the height.*

NEWTON, JOHN (London, 1725–1807, London), son of a shipmaster, served first at sea with his father, was impressed on board a man-of-war, became a midshipman, was degraded for attempted desertion, and for some years was engaged in the slave-trade (see 2). In 1754 he became tide-surveyor at Liverpool, and in 1764 took orders and accepted the curacy of Olney. In 1779 he became rector of St. Mary Woolnoth, London, where he remained till his death. His most important writings were his *Autobiography*, and the *Olney Hymns* (1779), in which he collaborated with Cowper, 280 being from his own pen.

2. *Kindly spring again is here.*
473. *Come, my soul, thy suit prepare.*
500. *Glorious things of thee are spoken.*
527. *How sweet the name of Jesus sounds.*

NICHOLSON, Sydney Hugo, M.V.O., M.A., Mus.Doc. (London, 1875–1947), son of Sir Charles Nicholson, Bt., D.C.L., LL.D., was educated at Rugby, New College, Oxford, and the Royal College of Music, where he studied under Sir Walter Parratt and Sir Charles Stanford. His principal posts have been as organist of Carlisle Cathedral, Manchester Cathedral (1908–18), Westminster Abbey (1918–27), and, since 1928, Director of the School of English Church Music, and Warden of the College of St. Nicolas, Chislehurst, Kent. He has been much concerned in various organizing and executive work in connexion with church music in England, and is musical editor of later editions of *Hymns Ancient and Modern*. He has published cantatas, much church music, songs, &c.

315 (ii). MUSIC-MAKERS. *458. CARLISLE. *566. VATER UNSER.

NICOLAI, Philip, D.D. (Mengeringhausen, Waldeck, 1556–1608, Hamburg), was the son of a Lutheran pastor who dropped his patronymic of Rafflenböl in favour of an adaptation of his father's Christian name Nicolaus. He studied at the Universities of Erfurt and Wittenberg. Ordained at 20 to a pastorate in his native town, he passed in 1583 to Herdecke in the Ruhr, but in 1586 he resigned office. He was a fervid Lutheran, and a keen and even acrimonious controversialist, alike with Romanists and with leaders of the Reformed Church. For a time he ministered to a secret Lutheran congregation 'under the cross' in the Catholic stronghold of Cologne; then held pastorates at Niederwildungen and Altwildungen; was court preacher to the Dowager Countess of Waldeck and tutor to her son; and after five years of pastorate at Unna, Westphalia, was from 1601 till his death chief pastor of St. Katherine, Hamburg. During his Unna ministry a severe visitation of the plague moved him to write and publish his *Freuden-Spiegel des ewigen Lebens* (Frankfurt, 1599).

90. *How brightly gleams the morning star!*
687. *Wake, O wake, for night is flying!*
90. WIE SCHÖN LEUCHTET DER MORGENSTERN.
687. WACHET AUF.

NIGIDIUS, Petrus, was a professor at the Pädagogium in Marburg who in 1551 published the collection *Geminae undeviginti*. Little else is known about him.

48. (i). DIE NACHT IST KOMMEN.

NOEL, Caroline Maria (London, 1817–77, London), daughter of the Rev. and Hon. Gerard Thomas Noel, wrote her first hymns between her 17th and 20th years. For the succeeding 20 years she produced nothing, but in her 40th year, under the stress of sickness, again began to write. She published two volumes, *The Name of Jesus, and Other Verses for the Sick and Lonely* (1861); and *The Name of Jesus, and Other Poems* (1878).

392. *At the name of Jesus.*

OAKELEY, Frederick, D.D. (Shrewsbury, 1802–80, London), son of Sir Charles Oakeley, Bt., formerly Governor of Madras, was educated privately and at Oxford, where he became a Fellow of Balliol. In 1839 he entered upon the incumbency of Margaret Chapel, London (later, All Saints, Margaret Street), but, being interested in the Tractarian Movement, and having published pamphlets of a controversial nature, was suspended from clerical duty. Thereupon he resigned his prebendal stall at Lichfield and all appointments in the Church of England, joined Newman at Littlemore, and in the same year (1845) was received into the Church of Rome. He afterwards worked for many years in Westminster, and was made a D.D. He published a preface on antiphonal chanting to Redhead's *Laudes Diurnae*; *Lyra Liturgica* (1865).

78. *O come, all ye faithful.*

OAKLEY, Charles Edward, M.A., B.C.L. (1832–65, Rhyl, North Wales), was educated at Oxford, where he was examiner in the School of Jurisprudence, 1859–60, and for degrees in Civil Law, 1859–60; and Select Preacher, 1860 and 1862. In 1856 he became rector of Wickwar, and in 1863 rector of St. Paul's, Covent Garden.

64. *Hills of the North, rejoice.*

OLIVERS, Thomas (Tregynon, Montgomeryshire, 1725–99, London), was early left an orphan; he grew up uncared for, and had little education. Apprenticed to a shoemaker, for a time he led a restless life, roaming about and earning a living precariously as a cobbler. He chanced to hear Whitefield preach in Bristol. This changed his life; he became one of Wesley's itinerant preachers, and for 22 years travelled far and wide in this work, through England, Scotland, and Ireland. In 1775 Wesley appointed him supervisor of the Methodist press, but removed him from that post in 1789. He spent the rest of his life in retirement in London.

398. *The God of Abraham praise.*

O'SHAUGHNESSY, Arthur William Edgar (London, 1844–81, London), was educated privately and in 1861 became a junior assistant in the British Museum Library, and in 1863 was promoted to the zoological department, where he became an expert on herpetology. He published *An Epic of Women and other Poems* (1870); *Lays of France* (1872); *Music and Moonlight* (1874); and, in conjunction with his wife, *Toyland* (1875). Shortly before his death he had also been appointed English correspondent to *Le Livre*.

315. *With wonderful deathless ditties.*

OSLER, Edward, M.R.C.S., F.L.S. (Falmouth, 1798–1863, Truro), was educated for the medical profession by Dr. Carvasso and at Guy's Hospital, and was House Surgeon at Swan's Infirmary, 1819–36. He went to London and associated himself with the Society for Promoting Christian Knowledge, in London and Bath. In 1841 he became editor of the

Royal Cornwall Gazette and resided at Truro. Publications: *Burrowing and Boring Marine Animals*; *Church and Bible*; *The Voyage, A Poem written at Sea*; *The Life of Lord Exmouth, &c.*; he was associated with W. Hall in producing *Psalms and Hymns adapted to the Services of the Church of England* (1835–6), contributing 15 versions of the Psalms and 50 Hymns.

624 (Part II). *Worship, honour, glory, blessing.*

OSWALD, HEINRICH SIEGMUND (Nimmersatt, near Liegnitz, Silesia, 1751–1834, Breslau), received his education at Schmiedeberg, Silesia, then, in 1765–6, entered the office of his brother Ferdinand, who held a public appointment. Seven years later he became secretary to the Landgrave von Prittwitz at Glatz, but illness lost him this position, and he returned to Schmiedeberg and entered the service of a merchant who sent him on business to Hamburg. Later, he tried business for himself at Breslau, but was not successful, and he took work again as a merchant's clerk. His circumstances subsequently improved; in 1790 King Friedrich Wilhelm II of Prussia appointed him a court councillor at Potsdam, and in the following year he was made a privy councillor. On the king's death he received a pension, and he devoted his last years to the composition of poetical, musical, and religious works.

115. *O let him whose sorrow.*

OWEN, FRANCES MARY, *née* SYNGE (Glanmore Castle, Co. Wicklow, 1842–83, Cheltenham), was educated privately, and in 1870 married the Rev. James Albert Owen, assistant master at Cheltenham College. There she devoted much of her time to philanthropic work in the town, especially the education of working men and the care of friendless girls. Her publications include *John Keats: A Study*; *Soldier and Patriot: A Life of George Washington*; *A Lost Piece of Silver*; *Edith Vernon's Life Work, &c.*; *Across the Hills* and *Essays and Poems* were published posthumously.

103. *Lighten the darkness of our life's long night.*

OWEN, MORFYDD (Treforest, 1892–1918, Gower), was educated at Pontypridd County School and at University College, Cardiff, where she gained her bachelorship of music in 1912. In this latter year she entered the Royal Academy of Music, where she obtained many prizes and was later elected an associated professor. She married Ernest Jones, M.D., the well-known authority on psycho-analysis. From early childhood she showed a gift for composition, and was trained both as a pianist and a singer, making several public appearances in the latter capacity, and also acting as adjudicator at Eisteddfod meetings. Her early death was a great loss to Welsh music. She was a prolific composer, having to her credit over 80 songs, much piano music, choral music, and orchestral and chamber music. A memorial edition of her works, consisting of two volumes of songs, a volume of piano music, and the score of a *Nocturne* for full orchestra has been issued by the Oxford University Press.

25 (Part II). RICHARD.

OWEN, WILLIAM [called PRYSGOL] (1814–93), was a Welsh musician long resident at Caeathraw, Carnarvon. Many of his anthems and hymn-tunes are to be found in his publication *Y Perl Cerddorol* (1886).

274 (i). BRYN CALFARIA.

'OXENHAM, John' (pseudonym of William Arthur Dunkerley), (1852-1941), was educated at Old Trafford School and Victoria University, Manchester. He was for some years engaged in business, which necessitated extensive travel in Europe, America, and Canada. Later he began to write as a distraction, but finding the occupation congenial and profitable, devoted himself entirely to authorship. His first book was *God's Prisoner* (1898), since when he has published a very large number of novels and volumes of verse, among the latter being *Selected Poems* (1925).

537. *In Christ there is no East or West.*

PALESTRINA, Giovanni Pierluigi Sante da (Palestrina, 1525–94, Rome), son of a wealthy peasant, Pierluigi Sante, received his training in Rome, where he came under the influence of the Netherlander, Orlandus Lassus. For some years he was chapel-master in Palestrina, and later master of the boys in the Julian chapel, and in 1555 became one of the pontifical singers in the Sistine chapel. Dismissed from his post on his marriage, he became chapel-master first of St. John Lateran, and then of the Liberian Chapel of Santa Maria Maggiore. Church music at this time had fallen into a degraded state, and the Council of Trent had in 1552 ordered its reform. Palestrina, whose *Improperia* (1560) had become famous, was asked to write a mass which should be a model of what church music ought to be. He produced three famous services, of which the *Missa Papae Marcelli* has been ever since regarded as one of the most sublime creations of all music. Soon afterwards Palestrina was appointed composer to the Pontifical chapel, and in 1571 chapel-master of St. Peter's. He wrote an immense quantity of music: 93 masses, 179 motets, as well as hymns, prayers, madrigals, &c.

147. VICTORY. 280 (ii). TANTUM ERGO (NO. 2).

PALGRAVE, Francis Turner, M.A. (Great Yarmouth, 1824–97, London), son of Sir Francis Palgrave, was educated at Charterhouse School and Balliol College, Oxford, and became a Fellow of Exeter College, Oxford, in 1847. After a short period as Gladstone's secretary, he entered the education department, was vice-principal of Kneller Hall from 1850 to 1855, again held various posts in the education department from 1855 to 1884, and in 1885 became Professor of Poetry at Oxford. He was art critic to the *Saturday Review*, and published several volumes of essays and poems; but he is now chiefly remembered by his anthology, *The Golden Treasury of Songs and Lyrics* (1864), which has since passed through a long series of editions.

120. *Thou say'st, 'Take up thy cross'.*
374. *Thou who once on mother's knee.*
615. *O thou not made with hands.*

PALMER, Clement Charlton, D.Mus. (Oxon.), F.R.C.O. (Barton-under-Needwood, Staffs., 1871–1944), son of Clement Palmer, J.P., was educated at Repton. In 1887 he became organist and choirmaster of St. Leonard's, Wichnor, from 1890 to 1897 he was organist of Lichfield Cathedral, and is now organist and master of the choristers, Canterbury Cathedral. Compositions: many pieces for the organ, a *Morning, Communion and Evening Service in E flat*; *Evening Service in F minor*; *Evening service in B flat*; *Morning and Evening Service in F* (*men's voices*); and *Casabianca, Ballad for Chorus and Orchestra*.

*12. MONKLAND.

PALMER, RAY, D.D. (Little Compton, Rhode Island, 1808–87, Newark, New Jersey), was the son of a judge. He spent his early life in Boston, and was for a time a draper's assistant. Thereafter he studied at Phillips' Academy, Andover, and at Yale, where he graduated in 1830. He became Minister of the Central Congregational Church, Bath, Maine, where the best of his hymns were written; then of the First Congregational Church, Albany, New York; then Corresponding Secretary of the American Congregational Union, with his head-quarters in New York. In 1879 he retired to Newark. He published *Hymns and Sacred Pieces* (1865); and *Hymns of my Holy Hours* (1867). His complete *Poetical Works* were published in 1876.

549. *Jesus, thou joy of loving hearts.*
550. *Jesus, these eyes have never seen.*
563. *Lord, my weak thought in vain would climb.*
580. *My faith looks up to thee.*

PARRY, Sir CHARLES HUBERT HASTINGS, Bt., D.Mus. (Bournemouth, 1848–1918, Rustington, Littlehampton), was the son of Thomas Gambier Parry, of Highnam Court, Gloucestershire, the decorative artist. He was educated at Twyford, near Winchester, Eton, and Exeter College, Oxford. While still at Eton he took the Oxford B.Mus. degree. His father being opposed to his devoting himself to music, he entered Lloyd's, and continued there for three years; but the work was uncongenial and unsuccessful, and he renounced it to embark on a musical career. In 1883 he became Professor of Composition and Lecturer in Musical History in the R.C.M., and also Choragus at Oxford; in 1894, Director of the R.C.M.; in 1898, Professor of Music, Oxford. He was knighted in the same year, and made a baronet in 1905. His interests were endless; he was squire, magistrate, author, amateur scientist, teacher, administrator, composer, organist, pianist, diarist, playgoer and critic, motorist, yachtsman, and expert in many games. He was a masterly writer on musical subjects; a born teacher, infectious in his enthusiasm; a stimulating lecturer, and perhaps in his time the leading intellectual force in music in this country. His books on *The Art of Music*; *The Eighteenth Century* in *The Oxford History of Music*; *Style in Musical Art*; *Bach*; and *College Addresses*, are of the highest quality. Of music he produced a vast amount: his choral works in particular exhibit exceptional mastery. Sir Henry Hadow says, 'There was no side of musical life in England which was not the better and nobler because he had lived'.

307. INTERCESSOR. 446. JERUSALEM. 481 (i). REPTON.

PARRY, JOSEPH, Mus.Doc. (Merthyr Tydvil, 1841–1903, Penarth), showed marked musical gifts in childhood, but had to begin work at a puddling-furnace when only ten years old. In 1854 he emigrated to America with his family. On a return visit he won Eisteddfod prizes. A harmonized hymn-tune submitted by him at Swansea Eisteddfod in 1865, and awarded a prize, so impressed Brinley Richards, one of the adjudicators, that he secured the raising of a fund to enable Parry to come back from the United States and enter the R.A.M. He took his Mus.Bac. degree at Cambridge in 1871, and his doctorate seven years later. In 1874 he became Professor of Music in University College, Aberystwyth, and in 1888 Lecturer in Music, University College of South Wales, Cardiff. In 1896 the Eisteddfod awarded him £600 for his services to Welsh music, upon which he exercised a great influence during thirty years. He wrote oratorios, cantatas, operas, choral works of all kinds, and some instrumental music, as well as anthems and many scores of hymn-tunes.

312. MERTHYR TYDVIL (DIES IRAE). 441. ST. JOSEPH.
479. DINBYCH. 542. ABERYSTWYTH.

PARSONS, WILLIAM, is known to us only as the composer of musical settings for four voices, which appeared in John Day's *Psalter* in 1563.

*329. OLD 124TH.

PATRICK, ST. (*c.* 372–466, Saulpatrick), the apostle and patron saint of Ireland, is said to have come of clerical descent, his father having been a deacon and his grandfather a presbyter. At the age of 16 he was carried off to Ireland, where he was sold as a slave and employed in feeding cattle. During his captivity he became a fervid Christian. The ship in which he ultimately escaped carried him to France, where he spent some years. But he returned, as Ireland's second bishop, to spend his life in heroic efforts to win its people to Christianity. The story of his life is involved in a mass of doubtful legendary matter, but there is no doubt about his apostolic zeal and the remarkable success of his labours. By the time of his death Ireland had been to a great extent Christianized and a powerful Church was organized and in operation. Before long the Irish Church was sending missionaries abroad, and Ireland won fame throughout western Europe as 'the Island of Saints and Scholars'.

528. *I bind unto myself to-day.*

PAULUS DIACONUS (Triuli in Italy, *c.* 730–*c.* 799, Monte Cassino), studied at Pavia, and was some time tutor to Adelperga, daughter of Desiderius, the last of the Lombard Kings, and subsequently went to live at the Court of her husband Archisius of Benevento. He became a monk at Monte Cassino. He was the author of several works, including *De Gestibus Langobardorum*.

231. *Let thine example, holy John, remind us.*

PEARSALL, ROBERT LUCAS DE (Clifton, 1795–1856, Wartensee, Constance), descended from an ancient Gloucestershire family, was educated for the Bar, to which he was called in 1821. After practising for four years, he forsook law for music, which he studied at Mainz and elsewhere on the Continent. Most of his life thereafter was spent in Germany, first at Carlsruhe (1830), and from 1837 at the Castle of the Wartensee on the Lake of Constance. An enthusiastic archaeologist, he turned Roman Catholic and called himself *de* Pearsall. He composed madrigals and part-songs of first-rate excellence, and wrote the words of many of his own madrigals. The *St. Gall Gesangbuch* of 1863 was partly edited by him.

198 (ii). PEARSALL.

PEERS, EDGAR ALLISON, M.A. (Leighton Buzzard, Bedfordshire, 1890–), was educated at Dartford Grammar School, abroad, and at Christ's

College, Cambridge, where he was a scholar. He has been a visiting professor and lecturer at many universities in Europe and America. He was the founder of the Modern Humanities Research Association, and is now Gilmour Professor of Spanish in the University of Liverpool. He has published many works on Spanish literature, history, and topography, such as *Rivas and Romanticism in Spain* (1923); *Spanish Mysticism* (1924); *Royal Seville* (1926); *Studies of the Spanish Mystics* (1927–30); *Spain, a Companion to Spanish Travel* (1930), &c., as well as on other subjects such as *Elizabethan drama and its Mad Folk* (1914); *Selected Poems of Alfred de Vigny* (1918), &c.

600. *O heavenly Beauty, lovelier far.*

PENSTONE, Maria Matilda (London, 1859–1910, Highgate), was trained at the Home and Colonial Training College, and in 1880 was appointed Head Mistress of St. Jude's Girls' National School, Southwark. After two years there she became a member of the staff at the Training College, and, later, was in charge of the department for training secondary school teachers, first at Mecklenburg Square, and afterwards at Highbury. She was also Head Mistress of the high school for girls which was attached to the Training College at Highbury. She was widely concerned in educational matters, and was a member of the Council of the Teachers' Guild and of the Board of the National Froebel Union. For the last seven years of her life she resigned her teaching posts, and devoted her time to educational propaganda. Among her publications are volumes on *Town Study* and *Nature Study*, &c. It was the work of such women that freed children's hymnals from matter like:

Youth! on length of days presuming,
Who the paths of pleasure tread,
View the leaves, so lately blooming,
Numbered now among the dead!

378. *When lamps are lighted in the town.*

PERRONET, Edward (1726–92, Canterbury), belonged to a family of French refugees from Chateau d'Oex in Switzerland. His father, Vincent Perronet, vicar of Shoreham, was greatly esteemed by the Wesleys. Edward was on intimate terms with both John and Charles Welsey. He was John's companion on his visit to the north in 1749, and became one of his itinerant preachers. In *The Mitre*, a religious satire published in 1757, he attacked the abuses of the Church in a way which aroused Wesley's anger, and the book was suppressed. He also differed from Wesley in urging separation from the Church of England, and the grant of licence to itinerant preachers to administer the Sacraments. By 1771 he had ceased co-operation with the Wesleys, and had joined the Countess of Huntingdon's Connexion. She in turn disagreed with him owing to his violent language about the Church of England, and he ended his days as pastor of a small Independent Church at Canterbury. His hymns were published at various dates in a series of small volumes.

440. *All hail the power of Jesus' name.*

PESTEL, Thomas (? 1585–1659?), was educated at Queens' College, Cambridge, where he took his M.A. degree in 1609. He was at one time chaplain to the Earl of Essex, and rector of Packington, Leicestershire, until 1646, when he was sequestrated from it by the Westminster Assembly. He published *Sermons and Devotions, Old and New* (1659).

72. *Behold the great Creator makes.*

PETER (PETRAEUS), CHRISTOPH (Weida, Vogtlande, 1626–69, Guben), became 'Kantor' in Guben in 1650 and in 1656 had the freedom of that city conferred upon him. Publications: *Andachts-Zymbeln* (275 songs with 211 tunes set to 4 or 5 voices, 30 of which appeared then for the first time and were of his own composition); *Geistliche Arien* (1667); and 40 tunes in J. Franck's *Geistlichen Sion* (1674).

636 (i). CHRISTOPHER (IHR GESTIRN').

PIAE CANTIONES (1582), a valuable collection of medieval sacred and secular song, gathered and edited by Theodoricus (Didrik) Petri, son of a landed proprietor in Borgå, Finland, whose father had migrated thither from Denmark. Didrik was a student at the University of Rostock when he made the compilation. The collection was published at Greifswald, then, as Finland also was, part of the Swedish kingdom. Most of the contents were doubtless of Swedo-Finnish origin, but some are from German and possibly other sources. Until late in the 19th century some of them continued to be sung and danced by school children at Björneborgs in Finland. Petri became secretary to King Sigismund in 1591, but of his later history little is known except that his last years were spent in Poland.

4. TEMPUS ADEST FLORIDUM.
272. O MENTES PERFIDAS.
385. OMEGA AND ALPHA (PUER NOBIS NASCITUR).
387. DIVINUM MYSTERIUM.
502. THEODORIC.
4. *Spring has now unwrapped the flowers.*

PIERPOINT, FOLLIOTT SANDFORD, M.A. (Bath, 1835-1917, Newport), was educated at the Grammar School, Bath, and Queens' College, Cambridge, where he graduated in 1857. For a time he was classical master at the Somersetshire College. Thereafter he lived at various places, principally at Babbicombe, on a small patrimony, and occasionally doing a little classical teaching. He contributed to *Lyra Eucharistica*, was the author of the Hymns for the Canonical Hours in the *Hymnal Noted*, and published collections of his poems—*The Chalice of Nature and Other Poems; Songs of Love;* and *Lyra Jesu*.

494. *For the beauty of the earth.*

PIGGOTT, WILLIAM CHARTER (Huddersfield, 1872–1943), was educated at Huddersfield College and Headingley College for the Wesleyan ministry. He entered the Congregational ministry in 1902. After serving charges at Greville Place, London, and Bunyan Meeting, Bedford, he succeeded the Rev. C. Silvester Horne at Whitefield's, Tottenham Court Road, London. He is now minister at Streatham.

289. *For those we love within the veil.*
342. *Lord of life, who once wast cradled.*
346. *Lord, from whose hand we take our charge.*
516. *Heavenly Father, may thy blessing.*
538. *In our work and in our play.*

PLAYFORD, JOHN (Norwich, 1623–93, London), was the founder and head of the music publishing firm of that name. He came to London *c.* 1648, and there established himself. In 1651 he issued *The English Dancing Master* and *A Musical Banquet*; *Catch that Catch Can* (1652); *Select Musical Ayres and Dialogues* (1652); *Musick's Recreation on the Viole, lyra way* (1652); *Breefe Introduction to the Skill of Musick* to which is added the *Art of Descant* by Dr. Thomas Campian; *Psalms and Hymns in Solemn Musick of foure parts on the Common Tunes to the Psalms in metre* (1671); *A Paraphrase upon the Psalms of David by George Sandys, set to new tunes for private devotion. Revised and corrected by John Playford* (1676), and *The Whole Book of Psalms*, &c. (1677).

116. ST. MARY. 323. WORCESTER. 503. LONDON NEW.

PLUMPTRE, EDWARD HAYES, D.D. (London, 1821–91, Wells), was educated at King's College, London, and University College, Oxford. He became a Fellow of Brasenose. Ordained in 1846, he was successively Chaplain of King's College, London; assistant preacher, Lincoln's Inn; Dean of Queen's College, Oxford; Prebendary of St. Paul's, and Professor of New Testament Exegesis, King's College, London; rector of Pluckley, Kent; vicar of Bickley, Kent; and in 1881, Dean of Wells. He was select preacher repeatedly at Oxford; Boyle Lecturer in 1866; and a member of the Old Testament Company of Revisers of the Bible. He wrote many excellent works—the standard *Life of Bishop Ken*, translations of Dante, Aeschylus, and Sophocles, *Biblical Studies*, and several volumes of poems.

287. *Thine arm, O Lord, in days of old.*
606. *O Lord of hosts, all heaven possessing.*

PLYMOUTH COLLECTION. This was a book entitled *The Plymouth Collection of Hymns and Tunes*, published in New York, U.S.A., in 1855. It was edited by Henry Ward Beecher (1813–87) the renowned preacher, whose church at Brooklyn was the most fashionable and popular in America, and who was the brother of Harriet Beecher Stowe, authoress of *Uncle Tom's Cabin*. The music was edited by John Zundel and the Rev. Charles Beecher. Many of the tunes are headed 'Western Melody', and the internal evidence suggests that these were founded on popular traditional melodies.

306. IVES. 516 (i). PLEADING SAVIOUR. 604 (ii). ADVENT.

POPE, ALEXANDER (London, 1688–1744, Twickenham), son of a linen draper, showed extraordinary precocity both as scholar and poet, but, by the age of 12, had ruined his health by too great assiduity of study; the subsequent weakness of physique and constitution had much to do with the perpetual quarrels, intrigues, and treacheries which marred his literary career. Apart from these the events of his life are virtually his consecutive publications beginning with *Pastorals* (1709), and continuing with the *Essay on Criticism* (1711); *The Rape of the Lock* (1712); *Windsor Forest* (1713); translations of Homer from 1715 to 1720, and 1725 to 1726; *The Dunciad* (1712 and 1729); *Essay on Man* and *Moral Essays*, &c. His *Works* were issued in 1735, but this was not a definitive edition.

693. *What conscience dictates to be done.*

POPE, ROBERT MARTIN, M.A. (London, 1865-1944), son of the Rev. H. J. Pope, D.D., was educated at Manchester Grammar School, Victoria

University, Manchester, and St. John's College, Cambridge, where he took his degree in 1887, and in 1888 became a Wesleyan minister. He has contributed various articles on Latin hymnody and also translations to periodicals, and published (with R. F. Davis) *The Hymns of Prudentius* (1905); *The Poetry of the Upward Way* (1906); *An Introduction to Early Church History* (1918); *Early Christianity and the Modern Church* (1924), &c.

37. *Ye clouds and darkness, hosts of night.*

POPPLE, Herbert (Berkhamsted, 1891–), was educated at Berkhamsted School, Lichfield Theological College, and University College, Durham. After active service in the War, he was ordained in 1923, was curate of St. Mary's, Blyth, from 1923 to 1930, and, since 1930, of St. Peter's, Streatham. Among his publications are two masses, and a nativity play, *The Prince of Peace*.

331. ST. AIDAN.

POTT, Francis, M.A. (Southwark, 1832–1909, Speldhurst), was educated at Brasenose College, Oxford. He was rector of Northill, Bedfordshire, from 1866 to 1891, when he retired owing to increasing deafness, and went to live at Speldhurst, near Tunbridge Wells. He was a member of the original Committee that produced *Hymns Ancient and Modern*. In 1861 he published *Hymns fitted to the Order of Common Prayer*, and his keen interest in the reform of chanting led him to publish *The Free Rhythm Psalter* (1898).

147. *The strife is o'er, the battle done.*

PRAETORIUS, Michael (Kreuzberg, Thuringia, 1571–1621, Wolfenbüttel). Praetorius was the assumed surname of more than one family of musicians in Germany whose real patronymic was Schultz. At an early age he attended the University of Frankfurt-on-the-Oder, and began his career as Kapellmeister at Lüneburg; in 1604 he entered the service of the Duke of Brunswick, and was soon after appointed prior of the Ringelheim Monastery, but without compulsion to reside there (Gozlar). His compositions are many in number, but his fame rests mainly on his great work *Syntagma musicum*, vol. i, 1614; vol. ii, 1619; vol. iii, 1619; but of vol. iv (on counterpoint) no printed issue is known.

33. Part II (ii). SPLENDOUR (PUER NOBIS NASCITUR).
*70. ES IST EIN' ROS' ENTSPRUNGEN.
146. GÖRLITZ (ACH GOTT VOM HIMMELREICHE).

PRICHARD, Rowland Hugh (Graienyn, near Bala, 1811–87, Holywell), spent most of his life at Bala, but in 1880 moved to Holywell Mill and was given a position as a loom-tender's assistant in the works of the Welsh Flannel Manufacturing Company. He possessed a good voice and acted as a precentor. Many good tunes composed by him appeared in Welsh periodicals of the period. *Hyfrydol* was a composition of his youth, while he was still under twenty. In 1844 he published *Cyfaill y Cantorion* (The Singer's Friend), mostly made up of his own original tunes. He subsequently brought out a booklet for the use of children.

260. HYFRYDOL.

PRID, W. (16th century), published *The Glasse of vaine-glorie: Faithfully translated (out of S. Augustine his booke, intituled Speculum peccatoris) into English by W. P., Doctor of the Lawes. Printed at London by John Windet dwelling at the signe of the white Beare, nigh Baynard's Castle* (*1585*).

393. *City of Peace, our mother dear.*

PROCTER, ADELAIDE ANNE (London, 1825–64, London), was the eldest daughter of Bryan Waller Procter (Barry Cornwall), a barrister and commissioner in lunacy, a poet and dramatist, and an intimate friend of Charles Lamb, Leigh Hunt, and Dickens. Her first poems were sent to Dickens as editor of *Household Words*, under the name of 'Mary Berwick'. He had continued publishing her contributions for nearly two years before he discovered through her mother that she was the daughter of his old friends. Two series of her poems were issued under the title *Legends and Lyrics, a Book of Verse*, in 1858 and 1862. In 1851 she became a Papist. Some of her songs became phenomenally popular, such as *Cleansing Fires*, *The Requital*, and *The Lost Chord.*

582. *My God, I thank thee who hast made.*

PRUDENTIUS, AURELIUS CLEMENS (348–*c.* 413), one of the best and most prolific of early Latin Christian poets, was born in the north of Spain. We know little of his life beyond what he tells us himself in an introduction to his works. From this it appears that he received a legal training, held a judicial post in two successive cities, and was afterwards promoted to an office of some dignity at the Imperial Court. In his 57th year he entered a monastery, and began to exercise the talent on which his fame now rests. The poetry of Prudentius belongs to the transition period when classical models had ceased to be followed, and rhyming verse had not begun. Centos from his works are freely used in the ancient Breviaries and Hymnaries. His best works are *Liber Cathemerinon*, or Hymns for twelve hours of the day, and *Liber Peristephanon*, hymns of the saints who had won the martyr's crown.

37. *Ye clouds and darkness, hosts of night.*
84. *Bethlehem, of noblest cities.*
387. *Of the Father's heart begotten.*

PRYNNE, GEORGE RUNDLE, M.A. (West Looe, Cornwall, 1818–1903, Plymouth), was educated at St. Catharine's College, Cambridge. Incumbent of the new parish of St. Peter's, Plymouth, of which he was vicar from 1848 until his death, he was deeply influenced by the Oxford Movement and for many years he had to encounter much unpopularity. He published *A Eucharistic Manual*; a volume of sermons; in 1857, *A Hymnal suited for the Services of the Church, together with a Selection of Introits* (177 hymns increased in the 1866 edition to 433); also, in 1881, *The Soldier's Dying Vision, and Other Poems*. He was a member of the Revision Committee of *Hymns Ancient and Modern* (1875).

543. *Jesus, meek and gentle.*

PRYS, EDMUND (Maen Twrog, Merionethshire, 1541?–1624, Maen Twrog), after studying at St. John's College, Cambridge, became rector of Festiniog, with the chapelry of Maen Twrog, in 1596; the rectory of Llaneddwyn was added in 1580, with the chapelry of Llanddwywe. In 1597 he became Archdeacon of Merioneth, and chaplain to Sir Henry Sidney, Lord President of Wales, and in 1602 received the second canonry of St. Asaph. He was an accomplished composer in Welsh metres, but did not adopt them when he translated the Psalms into Welsh, his aim being to foster congregational singing. This translation, *Llyfr y Psalmau wedi eu cyfieithu, a'u cyfansoddi ar fesur cerdd, yn Gymraeg*, was appended to a new issue of the *Book of Common Prayer* in Welsh, in 1621.

116. ST. MARY.

PSALMODIA EVANGELICA, a Complete Set of Psalm and Hymn Tunes for Public Worship, edited by Thomas Williams, a musician of the 18th century about whom nothing is known, was published in 1789.

23. BROMSGROVE. 337 (ii), 545. TRURO.

PSALTERS, EARLY METRICAL.

I. The French-Genevan Psalter, 1539–62.

The Metrical Psalter which was adopted in the Protestant Churches of France had its beginning in a small book printed at Strasbourg in 1539 under the title—*Aulcuns pseaulmes et cantiques mys en chant*. This contained metrical versions of seventeen psalms, five of which were by John Calvin, then living at Strassburg, and the remainder were attributed to the poet, Clément Marot. Calvin returned to Geneva in 1541, and he appears to have introduced this book in the worship of the church there. Early in 1542 Marot published in Paris an edition of 30 psalms versified by himself. This publication roused the ire of the Sorbonne, and Marot was obliged to fly for his life. He came to Geneva and found that his psalms were being sung there, but in a text differing to some extent from that in the edition published by himself.

Instigated by Calvin, Marot continued his work of versification, and several editions of the psalter appeared, the number of psalms being gradually increased. In 1543 there was published an edition in which the versions by Calvin were dropped, being replaced by others, by Marot, a number of new versions by the latter were added, and the author's correct text substituted for that which was in the Strassburg publication. In the end of 1543 Marot left Geneva for Turin, where he died in 1544.

Calvin then endeavoured to find some one to continue Marot's work and complete the psalter, but he did not succeed in this till the arrival in Geneva in 1548 of Theodore Beza. Calvin urged Beza to undertake the work, and in 1551 there appeared the first instalment of his labours, consisting of 34 psalms. Further additions were made in succeeding years and at last, in 1562, the complete Metrical Psalter was issued, containing 49 psalms by Marot, and 101 by Beza.

From 1542 to 1557 the arranging of the music for the psalms was in the hands of Louis Bourgeois (q.v.), but it is practically impossible to determine which of the melodies were composed by him, and which were adapted by him from existing sources.

Bourgeois left Geneva in 1557, at which date 62 psalms remained either untranslated or unprovided with tunes. It has not been established with any certainty who then undertook the work of providing tunes, but it seems beyond doubt that all the finest melodies in the completed Psalter are among those supplied by Bourgeois. As already stated, the complete psalter appeared in 1562. Of the 62 psalms above referred to only 40 are provided with tunes which had not already appeared, the remaining 22 repeat tunes already set to other psalms. In the complete book the number of separate tunes is 125.

26. MINISTRES DE L'ÉTERNEL.
50. NUNC DIMITTIS.
56 (i). LES COMMANDEMENS DE DIEU.
121. MON DIEU, PRÊTE-MOI L'OREILLE.
191. OLD 117TH.
208. PSALM 93.
210 (ii). PSALM 146.
244. AU FORT DE MA DÉTRESSE.
246. PSALM 68.
265. RENDEZ À DIEU.
291. PSALM 42.
324. DONNE SECOURS.
329. OLD 124TH.
347. L'OMNIPOTENT.
443. OLD HUNDREDTH.
473. LOUEZ DIEU.
512. OLD 107TH.
661 (i). PSALM 138.
696. O SEIGNEUR.
727. ST. MICHAEL (OLD 134TH).

II. The Anglo-Genevan Psalters.

During the persecution of the Protestants in England under Queen Mary a congregation of English exiles was formed at Frankfort. Division arose in that congregation and a considerable number betook themselves to Geneva, where they formed a congregation under the ministry of John Knox. In their order of public worship they followed the example of Calvin. In 1556 there was printed at Geneva *The forme of prayers and ministration of the Sacrament, &c. used in the Englishe Congregation at Geneva; and approved by the famous and godly learned man, John Calvyn.* The second section of the book consists of 51 metrical psalms, each provided with a tune. The psalms are those previously published in England (without tunes) by Thomas Sternhold and John Hopkins (see Introduction), with 7 by William Whittingham. Two of the tunes, the 128th and the 130th, are taken from the French Psalter, but nothing has been discovered as to the origin of the others. A second edition of this work, containing 62 psalms, and with some changes in the tunes, appeared in 1558. A much enlarged edition was issued in 1561 containing 87 psalms. The additional psalms are by William Kethe, and many of his versions are founded on these in the French book, then approaching completion. A considerable number of the tunes in this edition are also taken from the French; indeed, in many cases Kethe seems to have written his versions specially to suit these tunes. Unfortunately the attempt was not always a success, for even when the French and English versions have the same number of syllables in the line, the scansion and accents are quite at variance.

These Anglo-Genevan Psalters were the immediate precursors of the complete metrical psalters adopted in England and Scotland, and they contain the nucleus of the later books, as regards both words and music.

655. OLD 44TH.

III. The English Psalter.

The earliest edition of the Metrical Psalms with tunes, issued for use in England, is dated 1560. The only copy now existing is in the library of Christ Church, Oxford. It is an exact reproduction of the Anglo-

Genevan Psalter of 1558, with the addition of 3 psalms, 2 of these having tunes afterwards dropped. In 1561 another edition appeared. This contained all the psalms in that of the previous year, and has in addition 18 psalms mainly by Sternhold or Hopkins. A few new tunes appeared; but many of those in the earlier book are excluded, the psalms to which they were set being referred to the tunes of others. This book is entirely independent of the Anglo-Genevan edition of 1561, and it marks the beginning of the divergence between the English and Scottish Psalters. The complete English Psalter was issued in 1562, printed by John Day, the versions still required being supplied by Hopkins and other English writers, with 9 by Kethe (q.v.) from the Anglo-Genevan of 1561. This complete psalter contained only 46 tunes, which were known as the *Proper* or *Church* tunes. These tunes continue to appear in nearly all later books, and down to the present time they are still distinguished by the adjective 'Old' prefixed to the number of the Psalm to which they were originally attached. The psalters by Damon (q.v.) (1579 and 1591) and by Allison (1599) consist practically of these proper tunes in varying arrangements (DAY).

An important psalter was issued in 1592 by Thomas Este, the well-known music printer and publisher. In his 'Epistle Dedicatorie' Este says: 'In this booke the Church Tunes are carefully corrected, and other short tunes added, which are song in London, and other places of this Realme.' The tunes are harmonized in four parts, the harmony being by eminent musicians of the time whose names appear at the head of each tune. For the first time the four parts are printed at the same opening, the Cantus and Tenor (i.e. the Melody) on the left-hand page and the Altus and Bassus on the right.

The Church tunes are attached to their proper psalms and the remaining psalms are set to the short, or four line, tunes above referred to. Editions of this psalter with some slight changes were published in 1594, 1604, and 1611 (ESTE).

Another psalter, arranged on the same plan as that of Este, was edited by Thomas Ravenscroft, and printed in 1621 and 1633. This has the proper tunes as in the former books, and a large number of tunes under special names, many of which are still in use. In his Index Ravenscroft classes six of these as 'Scottish Tunes'. All of these are found among the 'Common Tunes' added to the Scottish Psalter in 1615. As in Este's psalter, the tunes are harmonized by various musicians whose names are given. In very many instances the arrangement is by Ravenscroft himself (RAVENSCROFT).

IV. THE SCOTTISH PSALTER.

In Scotland at the Reformation the church service was modelled on that used in Geneva under Calvin, and his example was followed in the provision of a metrical psalter. In the *First Book of Discipline*, 1560, the 'Order of Geneva' is mentioned as being 'in use in our Churches'. In compiling their psalter the Scottish Reformers adopted in its entirety the Anglo-Genevan edition of 1561, containing 87 psalms, and a considerable number of the French tunes. In 1562 the General Assembly lent to the printer Lekprevick £200 to help him in printing the psalter, and in 1564 the complete book was issued as part of the *Book of Common Order*. The psalter consisted of 87 versions referred to above, 42 from the English Psalter of 1562, and 21 by two Scottish writers, Robert Pont and John Craig. The great majority of the tunes in the Anglo-Genevan Psalters were retained, several were taken from the English of 1562 and a few more from the French. Altogether the psalms are provided with 105 different tunes; the Scottish Psalter being thus much richer in this respect than the corresponding English book. In subsequent years slight changes were made, and one or two additional tunes introduced; and in 1615 an entirely new feature appeared, namely, a number of those called *Common Tunes*, that is, tunes which were not attached to any particular psalm. In the edition printed by Andro Hart in 1615 these were in a group by themselves entitled 'The XII. Common Tunes, to the which all Psalmes of eight syllables in the first line, and sixe in the next may bee sung'. These tunes bear the following names: Olde Common, Kinges, Dukes, English, French, London, The Stilt (= York), Dumfermling, Dundie, Abbey, Glasgow, and Martyrs. Other Common Tunes appeared in later editions, and that of 1635 contains 31. In all the earlier editions the melody only of the tunes is given, but in 1635 there was issued what is perhaps the most important musical edition of the Scottish Psalter. In this the tunes, both proper and common, are all given in harmony, the work of Edward Millar, who in a lengthy preface explains his reasons for undertaking this task.

In 1643, in pursuance of the design to establish uniformity in government and worship between the churches of England and Scotland, the House of Commons, with the advice of the Westminster Assembly, resolved that one version of the psalms should be adopted and authorized for use throughout the kingdom. The version decided upon was that by Francis Rous, Provost of Eton. This version was subjected to much revision by Rous himself and by a Committee of the Assembly, and finally was sent to Scotland for the consideration of the General Assembly. The Assembly appointed a committee by whom it was again very carefully revised, and in 1650 this version, as still in use, was approved and authorized by the General Assembly. Unfortunately for the cause of church music in Scotland no tunes were provided for the psalms; and as a consequence it is probable that music in the churches was for long confined to a limited number of the common tunes, known by heart to the precentors and the people.

112. CAITHNESS.	191. OLD 117TH.	269. PSALM 80.
492. ABBEY.	503. LONDON NEW.	512. OLD 107TH.
517. DUNFERMLINE.	523. GLENLUCE.	530. CULROSS.
547 (ii). WINDSOR.	557. DUNDEE (OR FRENCH).	597. MARTYRS.
628. YORK.	630. WIGTOWN.	665. ELGIN.
686. MELROSE.		

PUSEY, PHILIP, D.C.L. (Pusey, Berkshire, 1799–1855, Christ Church, Oxford), was a grandson of the first Viscount Folkestone. His father gave up the family name of Bouverie for that of Pusey on inheriting the estate of the latter name. His elder brother was the famous Dr. Edward Bouverie Pusey, the Tractarian leader. Philip was educated at Eton and Christ Church, Oxford. On leaving the University he settled on his estate, and devoted himself to agriculture and the public service. On agriculture he wrote largely; and was one of the founders of the Royal Agricultural Society. Entering Parliament, he sat for Rye, Chippenham, Cashel, and Berkshire. He was a connoisseur of art, a collector of prints and etchings, a copious contributor to the reviews, and one of the founders of the London Library. Among his interests was hymnology; he wished to supplant Sternhold and Hopkins's version of the Psalms by Milman's hymns. In this his famous brother opposed him.

349. *Lord of our life, and God of our salvation.*

QUARLES, FRANCIS (Romford, Essex, 1592–1644, London), was educated at Christ's College, Cambridge, and studied for the law at Lincoln's Inn. On the Princess Elizabeth's marriage to the Elector Palatinate he went abroad as her cupbearer, but seems to have returned to England about 1620. He became private secretary to Archbishop Ussher, certainly before 1629, and about three years later retired to Essex. In 1639 he became chronologer to the City of London, and thenceforward gave a large part of his time to writing devotional handbooks. He published *The Feast of Wormes* (1620), a paraphrase of the book of Jonah; *Argalus and Parthenia* (1629), a poetic romance; *Emblems* (1635), his most famous work; and many other books of prose and verse.

670. *Thou art my life; if thou but turn away.*

QUARLES, JOHN (Essex, 1624–65, London), was the son of the foregoing Francis Quarles. He was educated at Exeter College, Oxford. An ardent royalist, he took part in the defence of Oxford against the Parliamentary forces, and is said to have held a captain's commission subsequently in King Charles's service. On the downfall of the King he retired to London, and betook himself to literature for a livelihood. He died of the plague. He published Jeremiah's Lamentations paraphrased, with *Divine Meditations* (1648); and *Divine Meditations upon Several Subjects, whereunto is annexed God's Love to Man's Unworthiness, with Several Divine Ejaculations* (1655), and other works.

104. *Long did I toil, and knew no earthly rest.*

RAMSAY, ROBERT, Mus.Bac. (*c.* 1600–*c.* 1650), was organist of Trinity College, Cambridge, 1623–44, and Magister Choristarum, 1637–44. He composed a Morning and an Evening Service in F, two anthems, &c.

App. 3 (iv). AMEN.

RANDALL, JOHN, Mus.Doc. (1715–99), was in youth a chorister of the Chapel Royal. At the age of 17 he sang the part of Esther in Handel's oratorio of that name. He became organist of King's College, Cambridge, in 1743; Professor of Music, Cambridge University, 1755; and, later, organist also of Trinity College: all three posts he held simultaneously. In 1794 he published *A Collection of Psalm Tunes, some of which are new, and others by permission of the authors, with six Chants and Te Deums, calculated for the use of Congregations in general.* Six original tunes of his own appeared in this book. He is best known by his two double chants. He was a friend of the poet Gray, one of whose Odes he set to music.

555 (i). LEWES. 653. UNIVERSITY (?).

RANKIN, JEREMIAH EAMES, D.D., LL.D. (Thornton, New Hampshire, 1828–1904, Cleveland, Ohio), was educated at Middelburg College, Vermont, and at Andover Theological Seminary. He was minister of Congregational churches at New York; St. Albans; Charlestown; Washington, and for several years was President of Howard University, Washington.

He edited the *Gospel Temperance Hymnal*, and later, *Gospel Bells*; and published *German-English Lyrics, Sacred and Secular* (1897). He was a frequent contributor to the periodical press.

334. *God be with you till we meet again.*

RAVENSCROFT, THOMAS, Mus.Bac. (*c.* 1582–1635), was a chorister of St. Paul's Cathedral, and became a Mus.Bac. of Cambridge when only 14 years of age. He edited much music, but is best known by his *Whole Booke of Psalmes* (1621). This book contains all the Psalms and Hymns in the Old Version, commonly known as 'Sternhold and Hopkins'. Ravenscroft adopted virtually all the *proper* tunes which had appeared in previous psalters, and to those psalms that had no such tunes associated with them he set a number of four-line tunes of more recent origin. There is no evidence that any of these melodies were his own: the title states that the tunes are 'composed into 4 parts by Sundry Authors'; which means that the musicians whose names were attached to the tunes were merely the harmonizers. Among these were such men, however, as Thomas and John Tomkins, and John Milton, the father of the poet. A large number of the settings are by Ravenscroft himself. This book became a principal source-book for all subsequent compilers of psalmody. Ravenscroft published also in his *Pammelia* the earliest collection of rounds and canons issued in Britain. The practice of naming tunes after places, though it did not originate with him, seems to have been established in England by him. A reprint of his Psalter, with an introduction by W. H. Havergal, was published in 1845.

*45. TALLIS' CANON.
*62. BRISTOL.
*82 (i). WINCHESTER OLD.
171. LINCOLN.
*188. ST. FLAVIAN.
211. OLD 104TH.
301. ST. DAVID.
*323. WORCESTER.
*443. OLD HUNDREDTH.
525. DURHAM.
557. DUNDEE (OR FRENCH).
577. NORWICH.
*628. YORK.

REDHEAD, RICHARD (Harrow, 1820–1901, Hellingley, Sussex), became a chorister of Magdalen College, Oxford. He was organist of Margaret Chapel (subsequently All Saints' Church), Margaret Street, Cavendish Square, London, 1839–64; then, till 1894, of St. Mary Magdalene, Paddington. Belonging to the second generation of the Oxford Movement, Frederick Oakeley (q.v.) found in him an ardent musical coadjutor. They edited together the first Gregorian Psalter, with the title *Laudes Diurnae*. Among his many other compositions for the Church were: *Church Music* (chants, sanctuses, responses); *Hymns for Holy Seasons*; *the Celebrant's Office Book*; *The Parish Tune Book*; *The Book of Common Prayer, with Ritual Songs*; *Ancient Hymn Melodies and Other Church Tunes*; *The Cathedral and Church Choir Book*.

460. LAUS DEO (REDHEAD NO. 46).
636 (ii). REDHEAD NO. 76.

REES, JOHN THOMAS, Mus.Bac. (Ystradgynlais, 1858-1949), received the barest elements of education, and began to work underground in the mines when only 9 years old. At that work he continued till he was 21. In music he was self-taught, until he was enabled to study under

Dr. Joseph Parry at the University College of Wales. After taking the Mus.Bac. degree of Toronto University, he definitely entered the musical profession, and has continued in it ever since. He is a Lecturer in the School of Music, University College, Aberystwyth, and is much called upon to lead festivals and to adjudicate at Eisteddfodau.

*241. BRYNHYFRID.

REESE, LIZETTE WOODWORTH (Baltimore, 1856-1935), has been chiefly engaged in the teaching of English in her native city, and has held important professional appointments in that capacity. As a poet she holds an esteemed position in America, but is little known in England. Among her volumes of poetry are *A Branch of May* (1887); *A Handful of Lavender* (1891); *A Quiet Road* (1896); *A Wayside Lute* (1909), &c. In 1927 a volume of *Selected Poems* was issued, the English edition of which contained an introduction by Walter de la Mare.

499. *Glad that I live am I.*

REGNART, JAKOB (*c.* 1540–1600, Prague), was early received as an Alumnus of the Imperial Chapel at Vienna and Prague, and in 1564 was tenor singer in the chapel, and as a member of the chapel went with the Emperor to the Augsburg Diet of 1566. In 1580 he declined the post of Kapellmeister at Dresden. In 1582 he left the Imperial Service for that of Archduke Ferdinand at Innsbruck, and remained there till 1595 as Kapellmeister, and then returned to Prague, where he died. Publications: *Sacrae cantiones* (1602) (posthumously published by his wife), a book of Masses (29) dedicated to the Emperor Rudolf II; *Sacrae cantiones* (35) (1577); *Canzone italiane* (2 books, 1574–81); and *Threni Amorum* (1595).

109. REGNART (AUF MEINEN LIEBEN GOTT).

REIMANN, JOHANN BALTHASAR (Breslau, 1702–49, Hirschberg), was at first Kantor in Neustadt, then in 1726 sub-organist at the Maria Magdalenen Kirche, Breslau, and in 1729 organist at Hirschberg in Schleswig. Publications: *Sammlung alter und neuer Melodien evangelischer Lieder gestochen und herausgegeben von L. H. Laue, Organist*, a collection of 362 chorales.

532, 663. O JESU.

REINAGLE, ALEXANDER ROBERT (Brighton, 1799–1877, Kidlington, Oxford), son of Joseph Reinagle, who was of Austrian extraction. The father was long well known in Scotland as a distinguished violoncellist, and for a time he was leader of the orchestra in the Edinburgh Theatre. Alexander became organist of St. Peter's-in-the-East, Oxford, from 1822 to 1853. He published two books of hymn-tunes, chants, &c.; also songs without words, music for violin, 'cello, organ, &c.

527 (ii). ST. PETER.

RHODES, SARAH BETTS (Sheffield, *c.* 1830–*c.* 1890, Worksop), gained most of her education, after her marriage, from her husband Jehoiada Alsop Rhodes, a master silversmith. She was a passable sculptress, as well as a hymn-writer of merit. On her husband's death she became the Head of a Girls' High School at Worksop.

358. *God who made the earth.*

RICHARD of Chichester, St. (Droitwich, 1197–1253, Dover), studied at Oxford, Paris, and Bologna, and became chancellor of Oxford University. Later he became chancellor of Canterbury, and, after some residence abroad, was elected bishop of Chichester, much to the anger of Henry III, who for some time refused to acknowledge his position. Richard was a stern disciplinarian and a firm upholder of the privileges of the Church. He was canonized in 1262.

399. *Day by day.*

RINKART, Martin (Eilenburg, 1586–1649, Eilenburg), the son of a cooper, was educated at Eilenburg and at Leipzig, where he graduated. After holding various appointments in other towns, he became in 1617 Archidiaconus at Eilenburg, where he spent the rest of his life. Rinkart was poet, dramatist, and musician.

350. *Now thank we all our God.*

RIPPON, John, D.D. (Tiverton, 1751–1836, London), was one of the most distinguished and influential Nonconformist ministers of his time. At the age of 22 he became minister of the Baptist congregation in Carter's Lane, Tooley Street (afterwards in New Park Street), London, and so continued till his death. In 1787 he published *A Selection of Hymns from the best authors, intended as an Appendix to Dr. Watts's Psalms and Hymns*; and, in 1791, *A Selection of Psalms and Hymn Tunes from the Best Authors*, adapted to Watts's collection and his own. *The Comprehensive Edition*, known as *The Comprehensive Rippon*, containing 1,174 hymns in 100 metres, appeared in 1844 after his death. It was the standard book of Baptist hymnody.

456. TIVERTON.

ROBERTS, Katharine Emily (Leicester, 1877–   ), daughter of the Rev. L. Clayton, was educated privately at Peterborough, and studied singing in London and Paris with a view to a professional career. In 1913 she married Robert E. Roberts (q.v.), and is now organizing secretary to the Rutland Rural Community Council. She has written the book of three historical pageants; several plays, two of which were produced in 1921 and 1922 respectively; and published, in collaboration with her husband, a history of *Peterborough* (1920); *Carol Stories* (1923), &c.

251. *O Lord, thy people gathered here.*

ROBERTS, Richard Ellis, B.A. (London, 1879–   ), was educated at Merchant Taylors' School and St. John's College, Oxford, where he graduated in 1901. He was on the staff of the *Pall Mall Gazette*, 1903–5, and has been a regular contributor to various well-known periodicals. In 1930 he became literary editor of the *New Statesman*, and acts in the same capacity now for *Time and Tide*. Among his publications are *Poems*; *A Roman Pilgrimage*; *The Other End*; *Life as Material*; *Reading for Pleasure*, &c.

231. *Let thine example, holy John, remind us.*

ROBERTS, Robert Edwin, M.A. (Llangerniew, 1878-1940), son of David Roberts, Llangerniew, Denbighshire, was educated at Ellesmere College, Shropshire (open scholarship), Hatfield College, Durham, and was Thorpe scholar at Durham University. From 1900 to 1902 he was assistant master at the Choir School, Westminster Abbey. From 1906 to

1910 he was minor canon of Peterborough Cathedral, precentor from 1908 to 1910, and vicar of St. Marks from 1910 to 1917. During 1915 and 1916 he was chaplain to the forces in France, and from 1917 to 1923 was vicar of Knighton, Leicester, in 1922 precentor of Leicester, and in 1929 rural dean and proctor in convocation. Publications: *Peterborough* (English Town Series) with Mrs. Roberts (1920); *Christian Auto-Suggestion* (1923); *The Transition Tune Book* (1924); *Faith and Life* (1926); *The Hope of the World* (1928), and *Hymns for Home Missions* (1929).

251. PHILIPPINE.

ROBINSON, Agnes Mary Frances [Mme Duclaux] (Leamington, 1857-1944), was educated in Brussels, Italy, and University College, London. She married first Professor James Darmesteter, F.S.A., and in 1901 Professor Émile Duclaux, director of the Pasteur Institute, Paris. She has written a large number of books in verse and prose, both in French and English, among them being *A Handful of Honeysuckles* (1878); *Arden, A Novel* (1883); *An Italian Garden* (1886); *The End of the Middle Ages* (1888); *Marguerites du Temps Passé* (1892); *The Return to Nature* (1904); *Twentieth Century French Writers* (1920); *La Pensée de Robert Browning* (1922); *A Portrait of Pascal* (1927), &c.

616. *O thou that movest all; O Power.*

ROBINSON, Richard Hayes (? 1842–92, Bournemouth), was educated at King's College, London. He was incumbent of the Octagon Chapel, Bath, and of St. Germain's, Blackheath, then a proprietary chapel. He was taken ill in the train on the day of his second wedding, and died the next day. He published *Sermons on Faith and Duty* and *The Creed and the Age.*

47. *Holy Father, cheer our way.*

ROCKSTRO, William Smith (Smyth) originally Rackstraw (North Cheam, Surrey, 1823–95, London), was a pupil of J. Purkis, and later of Sterndale Bennett and the Leipzig Conservatorium. He appeared at times as a pianist, was accompanist at the Exeter Hall Concerts, and was a high authority on ancient ecclesiastical music. Publications: *The Good Shepherd* (Gloucester Festival, 1886); *O too cruel fair*, madrigal, 5 voices; *Queen and Huntress*; *A Jewel for my Lady's Ear*; and other songs; *A History of Music for Young Students* (1879); *Practical Harmony* (1881); *The Rules of Counterpoint* (1882); *Life of George Frederick Handel* (1883); *A Memoir of Jenny Lind* (1891), with Henry Scott Holland (q.v.), &c.

*217 (i). OMNI DIE.

RÖNTGEN, Julius (Leipzig, 1855–1933, Amsterdam), son of Engelbert Röntgen, was a pupil of Franz Lachner, Hauptmann, Richter, and Reinecke; Conductor of the Society for the Advancement of Musical Art in succession to Verhulst, in 1886, having previously spent eight years as Professor in the Conservatoire at Amsterdam, of which he became Director in 1918. He was a friend of Grieg and of Brahms. Publications: *Brahms im Briefwechsel mit Th. W. Engelmann* (1918); *Fantasie für Klavier und Violine*; *Sonatas for Violin and Piano; Nordische Ballade*; *Holländisches Volksleben*; many short works; and two operas, *Agnete* (1914) and *Der Lachende Cavalier.*

*352. A LITTLE CHILD.

ROGERS, Benjamin, Mus.Doc. (Windsor, 1614–98, Salisbury), was the son of one of the singing-men in St. George's Chapel, Windsor. He became organist of Christ Church Cathedral, Dublin, but his stay there was cut short by the Irish Rebellion. For a time he taught at Windsor; in 1660 became organist of Eton College; in 1662, lay clerk at St. George's, Windsor; in 1664, organist of Magdalen College, Oxford. In 1685 he was removed from his post in Magdalen College because of irregularities, neglect of duty, and 'troublesome behaviour in chapel', and, pensioned by the College, lived the rest of his life in retirement on the outskirts of Oxford. He had a considerable reputation in his day, and many of his anthems and his *Service in D* are still in constant use.

607 (i). HYMNUS EUCHARISTICUS.

ROMANIS, William, M.A. (? 1824–99, Twyford), was educated at Emmanuel College, Cambridge, where he took his degree in 1846 and was ordained in 1847. He was a classical master at Cheltenham College from 1846 to 1856, and, after holding some curacies, became vicar of Wigston Magna in 1863, and of Twyford in 1888, retiring in 1895. He published *Sermons Preached at St. Mary's, Reading* (1862), and *Hymns written for Wigston Magna Church School* (1878).

52. *Round me falls the night.*
234. *Lord, who shall sit beside thee.*

ROOPER, Jasper Bonfoy (Penkridge, Staffs., 1898–), was educated at Bilton Grange, Lancing College, and at first studied electrical engineering; later, after four years training at the Royal College of Music, where he held the 'George Carter' scholarship for two years, he was appointed assistant music master at Lancing College in 1927. His publications include several songs and part-songs such as *Tryst Noel*; *Three Hindoo Songs*; *Balulalow*; *Prelude on Two Christmas Carols* for the organ, &c.

568. RISBY.

ROOTHAM, Cyril Bradley, M.A., Mus.Doc. (Bristol, 1875–1938), was educated at Bristol Grammar School, Clifton College, St. John's College, Cambridge, where he graduated in 1897, and at the Royal College of Music. In 1898 he succeeded Walford Davies as organist of Christ Church, Hampstead, and later became organist of St. Asaph Cathedral. In 1901 he returned to St. John's College as organist and musical director, became conductor of the University Musical Society in 1912, University Lecturer in 1913, and fellow of St. John's in 1914. His publications include many choral works such as *Andromeda*; *Milton's Ode on the Morning of Christ's Nativity* (which received a Carnegie Trust award); *Brown Earth*, &c.; an opera, *The Two Sisters*; three string quartets and other chamber music; songs, part-songs, &c.; and a manual on *Voice-training for Choirs and Schools*.

*301. ST. DAVID.

ROSENROTH, Christian Knorr, Baron von (Altrauden, Silesia, 1636–89, Sulzbach, near Arnberg, Bavaria), studied at Stettin, Leipzig, and Wittenberg, and became a pastor in Silesia. Before settling there, he had travelled in France, England, and Holland, and devoted himself to the study of oriental languages, chemistry, and cabbalistic science. He was an ardent seeker, for a time, after the philosophers' stone. His learning led to his being taken into the service of the Palsgrave Christian August of Sulzbach, and that prince in 1668 made him his prime minister. He was created a baron by the Emperor Leopold I. He wrote 70 hymns, in which he showed himself a mystic of the school of Scheffler (q.v.).

27. *Come, thou bright and morning star.*

ROSS, Sir RONALD, K.C.B., K.C.M.G., &c. (Almora, India, 1857–1932, Putney), was educated in the Isle of Wight and at St. Bartholomew's Hospital, London, entering the Indian Medical Service in 1881. His epoch-making discovery of the life-history of the parasite of malaria in mosquitoes, finally established in 1899, has overshadowed his literary gifts. He was awarded the Nobel Prize for Medicine in 1902, established the Ross Institute and Hospital for Tropical Diseases on Putney Heath, and received many honours and degrees both English and foreign. He was of a remarkable versatility being a musician and mathematician as well as poet and scientist. Among his publications were *Philosophies*; *Psychologies*; and *Poems* (1928); *The Prevention of Malaria*; *Memoirs* (1923); *In Exile* (1931); *Lyra Modulata* (1931); and many other scientific and literary productions.

452. *Before thy feet I fall.*

ROSSETTI, CHRISTINA GEORGINA (London, 1830–94, London), was the daughter of Gabriele Rossetti, an Italian refugee and Professor of Italian at King's College, London, and the sister of Dante Gabriel and William Michael Rossetti. She sat as model to several of the Pre-Raphaelite group of artists; hers is the face of the Virgin in her brother Gabriel's 'Ecce Ancilla Domini'. For some time she helped her mother with a small day-school in North London. But none of the external circumstances of her life were important; all the 'real' events, apart, perhaps, from her broken engagement, were spiritual and emotional, and these, for those who can read, are all in her poetry. She published in prose, *Time Flies, a Reading Diary* (1885); *Called to be Saints* (1881); *Seek and Find* (1879); *The Face of the Deep, a Devotional Commentary on the Apocalypse* (1892); and volumes of poems—*Goblin Market, and Other Poems* (1862); *The Prince's Progress, and Other Poems* (1866); *Poems* (1875); *A Pageant, and Other Poems* (1881); and *Verses* reprinted from her devotional books (1893).

5. *Spring bursts to-day.*
75. *In the bleak midwinter.*
92. *Love came down at Christmas.*
209. *What are these that glow from afar.*
240. *Service and strength, God's angels and archangels.*
372. *The shepherds had an angel.*
386 (III). *Who has seen the wind?*

RUSSELL, FREDERICK GEORGE, Mus.Bac. (Hoxton, 1867–1929, Stoke Newington), was educated at Haberdashers' Aske's School and at London University, where he took his B.A. and Mus.Bac. degrees. He was for 30 years organist and choirmaster of St. Edmund the King and Martyr, Lombard Street, and until his retirement, a few years before his death, a master and director of music at Haberdashers'. He was a great admirer of the Rev. G. A. Studdert Kennedy, and an enthusiast for the Industrial Christian Fellowship. He set several of Studdert Kennedy's poems to music, the best known being *Roses in December*, and wrote many school songs, hymn-tunes, church music, and pianoforte pieces.

698. LOMBARD STREET.

RUSSELL, George William [Æ.] (Lurgan, Co. Armagh, 1867–1935), was educated at Rathmines School, and for a time was in an accountant's office. In 1897 he joined the Irish Agricultural Organization Society, and from 1904 to 1923 edited the *Irish Homestead*; in the latter year he became editor of the *Irish Statesman*, in which post he continued until 1930. Among his publications are *Homeward: Songs by the Way* (1894); *The Earth Breath* (1897); *The Mask of Apollo* (1904); *Collected Poems* (1913); *The Interpreters* (1920); *Vale and Other Poems* (1931), &c.

122. *When the unquiet hours depart.*

RUSSELL, Studley Leslie Lane (Staines, Middlesex, 1901–), was educated at Clifton College, Christ Church, Oxford, where he held an organ scholarship, and at the Royal College of Music, where he studied composition, the viola and the piano, and won the Octavia travelling scholarship for composition, and thereafter continued his studies in Vienna. He is now director of music at Sutton Valence School, Kent.

115 (i). SUTTON VALENCE. 340. CHARING. 697. STANSTEAD.

ST. GALL GESANGBUCH.—The Benedictine monastery of St. Gall, founded in 614 by an Irish monk of that name, became one of the most famous centres of Church song in the Middle Ages. The monks cherished and cultivated the traditions of the Roman liturgic chant, and the type of hymn called Sequence had its origin, as we know it, among them. (See Notker.) From the 12th century the monastery declined, and in 1790 it was suppressed. Its celebrated library is intact, containing 1,158 *incunabula*, and 1,725 manuscript of great value. The old hymn-book of St. Gall, revised with R. L. de Pearsall (q.v.) as part-editor, was published in 1863 under the title *Katholisches Gesangbuch*.

13. ST. GALL.

SANDYS, William (London, 1792–1874, London), eldest son of Hannibal Sandys, was educated at Westminster School from 1800 to 1808, and in 1814 was admitted solicitor. From 1861 to 1873 he was the head of the firm Sandys & Knott, of Gray's Inn Square, but retired in 1873. He was an enthusiastic musical amateur from youth, and studied the violoncello under Robert Lindley. It is said that he possessed singular ability for mental arithmetic. Publications: *A History of Freemasonry* (1829); *Macaronic Poetry* (1831); *A Selection of Christmas Carols with tunes* (1833); *Specimens of Cornish Dialect*, and *Festive Songs* (both in 1848). Further, he published a Tract upon *Christmastide: its History, Festivities and Carols* (1852); and was mainly responsible for the earlier part of Sandys and Forster's *History of the Violin* (1864). His great service in the preservation of carols is described in the *Oxford Book of Carols*.

652. SANDYS.

SANTEÜIL, Jean-Baptiste (Paris, 1630–97, Dijon), was one of the regular canons of St. Victor, Paris, and wrote Latin poetry under the name of Santolius Victorinus. He was the author of many hymns in the

Cluniac Breviary (1686), the Paris Breviaries of 1680 and 1736, and his own *Hymni Sacri et Novi* appeared in 1689.

211. *Disposer supreme, and judge of the earth.*

SCHEFFLER, Johann, M.D., 'Angelus Silesius' (Breslau, Silesia, 1624–77, Breslau), was the son of Lutheran parents. He studied medicine at the Universities of Breslau, Strasburg, Leyden, and Padua, where he graduated M.D. He early evinced an interest in metaphysical and theological subjects, and fell under the influence of the writings of Jacob Böhme, and of such mystics as Tauler and Ruysbroeck. On returning to Silesia he was made private physician to the Duke of Württemberg-Oels. His controversy with the clergy of the Lutheran Church at Oels drove him into the Roman Church, into which he was received in 1653. He was then made imperial court physician to the Emperor Ferdinand III, but soon relinquished his profession, took orders, and in 1671 entered the Jesuit monastery of St. Matthias in Breslau. He adopted the name of Angelus, after Johannes ab Angelis, a Spanish mystic of the 16th century, usually adding to it Silesius, to indicate his country. His hymns were for the most part included in his *Heilige Seelenlust, oder Geistliche Hirten-Lieder* (Sacred Joy of the Soul, or Spiritual Pastorals), 1657, hymns addressed by 'Psyche, the soul, to her beloved Jesus'. The music of the book was edited by Georg Joseph (q.v.).

1. CULBACH. 559. KEINE SCHÖNHEIT HAT DIE WELT.
608. *O love who formest me to wear.*

SCHEIDT, Samuel (Halle, 1587–1654, Halle), son of Conrad Scheidt, overseer of salt works at Halle, owed his training to the famous Peter Sweelinck of Amsterdam, whose pupil he became *c.* 1605. In 1608/9 he became organist in the Moritzkirche in Halle, and in 1620, or possibly earlier, he had received the appointment of organist and kapellmeister to Christian Wilhelm Markgraf of Brandenburg, and a little later he became Protestant administrator of the Archbishopric of Magdeburg, in which capacity he officiated, however, in the Hofkirche at Halle. The Thirty Years War and the misfortunes of his patron would not appear to have made any difference to Scheidt's official position at Halle. Publications: *Cantiones sacrae octo vocum* (1620); his great work in 3 parts, *Tabulatura nova* (1624–53); and many pieces for the organ, and voice.

600. O JESULEIN SÜSS.

SCHEIN, Johann Hermann (Grünhayn, near Zwickau, Saxony, 1586–1630, Leipzig), was the son of a Lutheran pastor. For four years he was a chorister in the chapel of the Elector of Saxony, at Dresden; then he studied theology and philosophy at Leipzig. After some years of private tutoring he was appointed music director at the court of Duke Johann Ernst of Saxe-Weimar, in 1613. Two years later he was called back to Leipzig, to the office of cantor in St. Thomas's Church and School. One of the most distinguished musicians of his time, he devoted his life to the elevation and improvement of church music. He added largely to the literature of the chorale, and wrote much unaccompanied choral music on the Italian model; he composed many hymn-tunes, and some hymns also; but he is best known by the great hymn-book he edited for the Lutheran Church, *Cantional, oder Gesangbuch Augsburgischer Confession* (Leipzig,

1627). He published also *Musica Divina*, a collection of motets for 8, 16, and 24 voices.

48 (i). DIE NACHT IST KOMMEN.
168 (i). SCHEIN (MACH'S MIT MIR GOTT).

SCHENCK, HEINRICH THEOBALD (Heidelbach, near Alsfeld, Hesse, 1656–1727, Giessen), studied at the Paedagogium, and the University, Giessen. In 1676 he returned to his school as a teacher of the classics. In 1689 he was ordained as town preacher and definitor of the Stadtskirche in the same town. He is not known to have written any other hymn than the one by which he is represented here.

210. *Who are these, like stars appearing?*

SCHLEGEL, JOHANN ADOLF, D.D. (Meissen, Saxony, 1721–93, Hanover), son of Dr. Friederich Schlegel, Apellationsrath at Meissen, was educated at the school of Pforta and at the University of Leipzig. From 1746 onwards he was engaged in literary work, and held various posts, until, in 1754, he became chief pastor at the Holy Trinity Church at Zerbst, and Professor of Theology and Metaphysics in the Gymnasium there. In 1759 he went to Hanover as pastor of the Markt Kirche, and, later, held various administrative posts. His degree of D.D. he received from the University of Göttingen, on the occasion of its jubilee festival. He was a copious writer, among his chief works being three collections of hymns, *Sammlung geistlicher Gesänge* (1766, &c.).

90. *How brightly beams the morning star!*

SCHOP, JOHANN (Hamburg, ? –1664, Hamburg), described as 'an intelligent performer on the violin, lute, trumpet, and zinke', entered the Court orchestra at Wolfenbüttel in 1615. In 1644 he became music director at Hamburg, and 'Ratsmusikant' in 1654. He acquired great fame as a violinist. Besides much instrumental music, he wrote many hymn-tunes for the hymns of his fellow-townsman and friend Johann Rist, and others, and these came into general use in the collections of the day.

101. WERDE MUNTER.

SCHULZ, JOHANN ABRAHAM PETER (Lüneburg, 1747–1800, Schwedt), was the son of a baker, and was intended for the Church, but early set his heart on a musical career, and at 15 years of age left home, without money and against his family's wishes, to beg Kirnberger to accept him as a pupil. Against all likelihood he succeeded. Later, five years of travel in France, Italy, and Germany, with the Polish Princess Sapieta, formed his taste and genius. On his return he assisted Kirnberger and Sulzer with the musical articles for their *General Theory of the Fine Arts*, and edited Kirnberger's *Treatise on Pure Composition*. In 1776 he became director of the French Theatre in Berlin; in 1780 director of music in the household of Prince Henry of Prussia at Reinsberg; and in 1787 went in the same capacity to the Danish Court at Copenhagen. He exercised a great influence over Danish music, but returned to Germany in 1796. He published several collections of German songs, sacred and secular, operas, oratorios, and instrumental music.

14. WIR PFLÜGEN.

SCHUMANN'S GESANGBUCH. This was a collection published by V. Schumann in 1539 under the title *Geistliche Lieder auffs neu gebessert und gemehrt zu Witteberg, &c.* There are two prefaces by Martin Luther, and 112 *Lieder.*

80 (i) VOM HIMMEL HOCH. 566. VATER UNSER.

SCOTT, J. S. (Leicester, 1881–), was educated at Stoneygate, Leicester, Oakham School, and Emmanuel College, Cambridge, where he took the Classical Tripos in 1903. He studied the organ with Dr. E. W. Naylor and Dr. W. B. Brierley, and composition with Sir Ivor Atkins; he was assistant master at Giggleswick (1904–9); music master at The Leas, Hoylake (1909–10); and since 1910 has been an Inspector for the Board of Education. He has published solo songs, and some of his hymn-tunes appear in *A Missionary Hymn Book.*

471. SALONICA.

SCOTTISH PARAPHRASES (1781).—It is a mistake to suppose that hymns were not introduced into public worship in Scotland until the 19th century. The first complete Scottish Psalter was published in 1564: in an edition published by Thomas Bassandyne in 1575 there was an appendix containing five *Spiritual Songs*; and these were in use until the old Scottish Psalter gave place to Rous's version in 1650. Unfortunately, however, the latter contained no supplement of hymns. The General Assembly which authorized it recognized the need for some supplement, since a recommendation was made by it to Zachary Boyd 'to translate the other Scripturall Songs in meeter' with a view to their adoption. Boyd's *Songs of the Old and New Testament in Meeter* were published in Glasgow in 1646, but there is no evidence of their having been in any way brought before the Assembly. It was not until 1741 that an effort was made to supply the lack. An overture to the Assembly in that year led to the appointment in 1742 of a committee of 19 ministers and 3 elders 'to make a Collection of Translations into English Verse or Metre of Passages of the Holy Scripture, or receive in performances of that kind from any who shall transmit them'. In 1745 the Committee, enlarged, were ready with 45 versions of several portions of Scripture. These were printed and transmitted by the Assembly to Presbyteries for their opinions and observations. Apparently a majority were unfavourable; for delaying tactics proved so successful that the whole matter lay in abeyance for 20 years. The Synod of Glasgow and Ayr revived it in 1775. In that year a Committee was again appointed, and in 1781 their work was completed. A proof of the collection they had made was handed to every member of Assembly in that year. The Assembly, after appointing certain of its members to revise it, authorized the sending of copies to Presbyteries for their opinions, and allowed the use of it meantime in congregations where the minister might find it for edification. Thus, the *Translations and Paraphrases, in Verse, of Several Passages of Sacred Scripture*, with the five hymns appended to them, passed into Scottish use. There is no evidence that the opinions of Presbyteries were ever received or considered, or that a more formal authorization was ever given by the Assembly; but with tacit consent the custom arose of printing the *Paraphrases* along with the metrical version of the Psalms, and for nearly two centuries they have had an established place in Scottish Presbyterian worship.

96. *The race that long in darkness pined.*

SCUDDER, Eliza (Boston, U.S.A., 1821–96, Salem, Mass.), contributed hymns to various collections, and herself published *Hymns and Sonnets, by E. S.* (1880), which was reprinted in 1896 with a note by 'H. E. S.', i.e. her relative, Horace Elisha Scudder, a voluminous author.

673. *Thou long disowned, reviled, oppressed.*

SEARS, Edmund Hamilton, D.D. (Sandisfield, Berkshire, W., Massachusetts, 1810–76, Weston, Mass.), was educated at Union College, Schenectady, New York, and the Theological School, Cambridge. He ministered to Unitarian congregations at the First Church, Wayland, Mass.; Lancaster, Mass.; then returned to Wayland owing to failure of health, and devoted himself to literature. His later years were spent at Weston. He edited the *Monthly Religious Magazine*, and published among other books, *Regeneration* (1854); *Pictures of the Olden Time* (1857); *Athanasia, or Foregleams of Immortality* (1872); *The Fourth Gospel, the Heart of Christ*; *Sermons and Songs of the Christian Life* (1875).

76. *It came upon the midnight clear.*

SELNECKER, Nicolaus (Hersbrück, 1532–92, Leipzig), became organist in the chapel at Nürnberg when only 12 years old; he held successively the positions of lecturer at the University of Wittenberg, Court preacher at Dresden, Professor of Theology at Jena, and pastor of St. Thomas's Church at Leipzig. His frequent movements from one part to another were largely due to the atmosphere of acute theological controversy in which he lived. He helped to develop the famous Motett Choir of St. Thomas's Church, Leipzig, later conducted by J. S. Bach. He wrote much Latin verse, and many German hymns, and published *Christliche Psalmen* (1587).

435. SELNECKER (NUN LASST UNS GOTT DEM HERREN).

SEVEN SOBS OF A SORROWFUL SOUL FOR SINNE, comprehending those seven Psalmes of the Princelie Prophet David commonlie called Pænitentiall, framed into a form of familiar praiers and reduced into meeter by William Hunnis one of the Gentlemen of hir Majesties honourable Chapell, and maister to the children of the same. Whereunto are also annexed his Handful of Honisuckles; the Poor Widow's Mite; a Dialogue between Christ and a sinner; divers godlie and pithie ditties with a Christian Confession of and to the Trinitie, newly printed and augmented, 1583. This curious book gives the first instance of the use of 'Amen' at the end of hymns, and also of the use of the chorus or refrain (cf. p. 375). Hunnys's poem, 'The Widow's Mite', e.g., consists of seven meditations, and the direction is given to sing the following four lines at the close of each of the seven:

So shall my soul rejoice, rejoice,
  And still for mercy cry,
Peccavi, peccavi,
  Miserere mei.

A few tunes are printed in the book, to which the poems are set, and these are Hunnys's compositions.

108. HUNNYS. 519. MISERERE MEI.

SHAKESPEARE, WILLIAM (Stratford-on-Avon, 1564–1616, Stratford-on-Avon), was son of a tradesman, and probably educated at Stratford Grammar School. At 18 he married Anne Hathaway, and five years later went to London. He seems to have appeared, in small parts, on the stage of the Globe Theatre. In 1593 he published *Venus* and *Adonis*, in 1594 *The Rape of Lucrece*. He became proprietor of the Globe, and part-proprietor of the Blackfriars Theatre. The plays were written in the 20 years between about 1590 and 1611, though the exact dates and order of their composition is uncertain. In about 1612 he retired to Stratford-on-Avon, where he had bought a small property, and there apparently lived in retreat until his death. Apart from the immortal plays and poems, this is virtually all—and even some of these facts are disputed—that is known about England's, and possibly the world's greatest poet and dramatist.

622. *Poor soul, the centre of my sinful earth.*

SHARPE, EVELYN (Battersea, 1884–   ), the daughter of an architect, was educated privately, and in 1919 married Lewis John Saville. Her publications include solo songs and part-songs which have had many successful performances, not only on the concert platform, but also as test-pieces at several musical festivals both in this country and in the Dominions.

358. PLATT'S LANE.
367. BULSTRODE.

SHAW, GEOFFREY TURTON, B.A., Mus.Doc. (Clapham, 1879–1943), was educated at St. Paul's Cathedral Choir School, Derby School, and Caius College, Cambridge, where he was organ scholar. From 1902 till 1910 he was music master of Gresham's School, Holt. Since then he has been one of His Majesty's Inspectors of Music in Schools, and is now the Senior Inspector. He was master of music at St. Mary's, Primrose Hill, in succession to his brother, Martin (q.v.). At musical festivals throughout the country he is well known as an adjudicator. He has done much to raise the standard of church music and to foster popular interest in good music, and has been a moving spirit in many popular organizations, such as the League of Arts, and in training colleges, &c. He has edited collections of music, both sacred and secular, and has published *Pan's Festival* for female chorus and orchestra, numerous songs, part-songs, hymn-tunes, and other music.

18. HICKLING BROAD.
*25 (Part I). MORNING HYMN.
85 (ii). LIME STREET.
93 (ii). DYMCHURCH.
*100. ABRIDGE.
*116. ST. MARY.
*133. ROCKINGHAM.
*137. WINCHESTER NEW.
*175. ST. MAGNUS (NOTTINGHAM).
322 (i). FREEDOM.
326. LANGHAM.
*350. NUN DANKET.
*385. OMEGA AND ALPHA (PUER NOBIS NASCITUR).
386 (iii). FAIRLIGHT.
402. PADDOCKS.
*449. MARTYRDOM.
*467. ROBYN.
*494. ENGLAND'S LANE.
499. WATER-END.
*545. TRURO.
*558. SALZBURG.
586 (i). ROTHWELL.
588. GLYNTHORPE.
624. PRAISE.
*631. WAREHAM.
634. RING OUT.
649. GILLAM.
*657. CROFT'S 136TH.
*664. TALLIS' ORDINAL.
*677. WILTSHIRE.
*699. ST. BRIDE.

SHAW, MARTIN (FALLAS), Mus.Doc. (London, 1875–), son of James Shaw, composer of church music and organist of Hampstead Parish Church and elder brother of Geoffrey Shaw, studied at the Royal College of Music. At the end of his time as a student he 'embarked upon a long period of starving along'. He conducted for Ellen Terry, and toured Europe as conductor to Isadora Duncan. In later years he has held posts as organist and director of music at St. Mary's, Primrose Hill, St. Martin's-in-the-Fields, London, and master of music at the Guildhouse, London. With Gordon Craig he founded the Purcell Operatic Society in 1899, was a co-founder of the League of Arts in 1918, and has done much other organizing and executive work in connexion with the popularizing of good music, the encouragement of community singing, and generally freeing music, especially church music, from the Scylla and Charybdis of sentimentality and 'preciousness'. His principal published works include settings for soli, chorus, and orchestra of Laurence Binyon's *Sursum Corda* (Hereford, 1933), Eleanor Farjeon's *The Ithacans* (Queen's Hall, 1933), John Masefield's *The Seaport and her Sailors* (Queen's Hall, 1932); an opera *The Thorn of Avalon* (Crystal Palace, 1931); a ballad-opera *Mr. Pepys* (Everyman Theatre, 1925); and *Water Folk*, for voice, string quartet, and pianoforte (Worcester, 1932). He has also written much music for the theatre, light operas and incidental music, and many songs, part-songs, piano music, church music, works for chorus and orchestra, &c.; he has also published an autobiographical volume *Up to Now*; and was musical editor of the *English Carol Book*, and, with R. Vaughan Williams, of the *Oxford Book of Carols* and *Songs of Praise*.

5. SPRING.
*31. MELCOMBE.
64. LITTLE CORNARD.
*73. YORKSHIRE (or STOCKPORT).
*78. ADESTE FIDELES.
104. OXENBRIDGE.
*106. SOUTHWELL.
*151. ST. FULBERT.
*160. SAVANNAH (or HERRNHUT).
165. LEMON'S FARM.
187 (ii). BROMLEY COMMON.
196. DOORKEEPER.
*275. FARRANT.
300. PURPOSE.
304. PIONEERS.
327. ALL WATERS.
328 (i). DOWNSHIRE HILL.
335. ROYDEN.
345. WORKING.
356. GENTLE JESUS.
363. WESTRIDGE.
365. CAMBER.
372. BERWICK STREET.
386 (i). GREETING.
386 (ii). OPPIDANS MEWS.
386 (iii). BIRTHDAY.
386 (iv). CHILDREN ALL.
386 (v). MANOR STREET.
386 (vi). GOOD-BYE.
396 (i, ii, iv). MADDERMARKET.
396 (iii). ALDEBY.
433. GOD IS SPIRIT.
434. ALL CREATURES.
447. MUNDAYS.
*468. RICHMOND.
472. CHEERFUL.
486. GUN HILL.
*503. LONDON NEW.
518. OAKRIDGE LYNCH.
543. BELSIZE.
546. SWANWICK.
556. HIGH ROAD.
578. BATTLE SONG.
*597. MARTYRS.
*598. ST. ANNE.
616. HENHAM.
617. PIMLICO ROAD.
644. RILEY.
*647. SANTWAT.
*653. UNIVERSITY.
678. MARCHING.
*701. DARWALL'S 148TH.
*702. ST. MICHAEL (OLD 134TH).

SHEELES, JOHN (early 18th century), is known only by his two publications, *The Skylark, A Collection of all the Divine Odes and Hymns taken out of the 'Spectators', set to music by Mr. Sheeles* (*c.* 1720); *Suites of Lessons for the Harpsicord or Spinnett* (*c.* 1730). The latter work he dedicated to Dr. William Stukeley, Archdruid.

659. LONDON (or ADDISON'S).

SHELLEY, PERCY BYSSHE (Field Place, Warnham, 1792–1822, Gulf of Spezia), son of Sir Timothy Shelley, Bt., was educated privately, at Sion House Academy, Brentford; Eton; and, for a year, at University College, Oxford. His rather self-consciously unorthodox principles were the cause of the complications and scandals of his career, which need not be detailed here. His brilliant poetic genius was shown early in *Queen Mab*, written when he was 19, and increased in power in his later productions, such as *The Revolt of Islam*, *The Witch of Atlas*, *Adonais*, *The Cenci*, *Prometheus Unbound*, &c., and in his numerous shorter poems. He spent some time in Italy with Leigh Hunt, Byron, and others, and was at the height of his powers when he was drowned by the capsizing of his boat in a storm in the Gulf of Spezia. His ashes were buried near Keats's grave in Rome.

311. *The world's great age begins anew.*

SHRUBSOLE, WILLIAM (Canterbury, 1760–1806, London), was the son of a farrier at Canterbury, and was for seven years a chorister in the Cathedral there. In 1782 he was appointed organist of Bangor Cathedral, but his unconcealed sympathy with dissenters and his frequenting of 'conventicles' led to his being virtually dismissed from his office. Returning to London he became a teacher of music, and from 1784 till his death was organist of Spa Fields Chapel, of Lady Huntingdon's Connexion.

440. MILES LANE.

SHUTTLEWORTH, HENRY CARY, M.A. (Egloshayle, Cornwall, 1850–1900, London), was educated at Forest School, Walthamstow, and St. Mary Hall and Christ Church, Oxford. Ordained in 1873, he was curate of St. Barnabas, Oxford; minor canon of St. Paul's Cathedral, 1876–84; rector of St. Nicholas Cole Abbey, London, from 1883. He was also Professor of Pastoral and Liturgical Theology, and lecturer in other subjects, in King's College, London. He was a prominent member of the Christian Social movement. His published works include *The Place of Music in Public Worship*; *Hymns for Private use*. In an appendix to *Church Hymns*, compiled for use in St. Nicholas' Church, several hymns of his own appeared.

338. *Father of men, in whom are one.*

SIDNEY, Sir PHILIP (Penshurst, 1554–86, Arnhem), son of Sir Henry Sidney, was educated at Shrewsbury and Christ Church, Oxford. From 1572 to 1576 he travelled, and resided, abroad, but in the latter year returned to England, and, after travel with his father in Ireland, was sent on diplomatic missions to the Elector Palatine and Rudolf II. In 1581 he was M.P. for Kent, was knighted and appointed master of the horse in 1583, joint master of ordnance in 1585, and much engaged during these years in matters of State and politics. Made governor of Flushing, he assisted Prince Maurice in the surprise of Axel, and joined in the attack on Zutphen, where he received the wound in the thigh which caused his death some four weeks later. He wrote *Arcadia*; *Apologie for Poetrie*; *Astrophel and Stella*, and various other poems. None of these, however, was published in his lifetime.

605. *O Lord, in me there lieth nought.*

SIMPSON, JANE CROSS, *née* BELL (Glasgow, 1811–86, Glasgow), was a daughter of James Bell, advocate. In 1837 she married her cousin, J. B. Simpson, of Glasgow. While her brother was editor of the *Edinburgh Literary Journal*, she contributed to it over the pen-name 'Gertrude', and later she wrote for the *Scottish Christian Herald*. Her published works were: *The Piety of Daily Life* (1836); *April Hours* (1838); *Woman's History* (1848); *Linda, or, Beauty and Genius* (1859); *Picture Poems* (1879); *Linda, and Other Poems* (1879).

629. *Pray when the morn is breaking.*

SLATER, GORDON ARCHBOLD, Mus.Doc., F.R.C.O. (Harrogate, 1896–), son of William Henry Slater, of Harrogate, was educated privately and studied under Dr. E. C. Bairstow of York Minster, 1914 to 1916. He served in H.M. Forces from 1916 to 1919, and from 1919 until 1927 occupied several important musical posts, becoming organist and master of the choir in Leicester Cathedral in 1927. He was the founder, and conductor from 1927, of the Leicester Bach Choir. Publications: solo songs; choral songs; piano pieces, and much church and organ music.

361. BILSDALE. 527 (i). ST. BOTOLPH.
579. FOUNTAINS ABBEY.

SMART, Sir GEORGE THOMAS (London, 1776–1867, London), was a chorister in the Chapel Royal under Ayrton, and studied the organ under Dupuis, and composition under Arnold. He became organist of St. James's Chapel, Hampstead Road, London, and in 1811 was knighted at Dublin. From 1813 to 1844 he was conductor of the concerts of the Philharmonic Society, and in 1822 also became one of the organists of the Chapel Royal. He was closely connected with Weber, who died at his house in 1826. He became Composer to the Chapel Royal in 1838. All the principal festivals of his time were conducted by him, and he arranged and conducted the music at the Coronations of William IV and Queen Victoria. Publications: *A Collection of glees and canons* (1863); *Collection of Sacred Music* (2 vols.); *Three Sonatinas for Pianoforte*, &c. He also edited Gibbons's *First Set of Madrigals*, for the Musical Antiquarian Society (1841).

677. WILTSHIRE.

SMART, HENRY (THOMAS) (London, 1813–79, London), nephew of Sir George Smart, and son of a well-known violinist, studied law for four years, but abandoned it for music. He excelled as an organist, both as executant, composer, and designer. He held appointments at the parish church, Blackburn; St. Giles's, Cripplegate; St. Philip's, Regent Street; St. Luke's, Old Street; and St. Pancras, London. His sight, always defective, failed completely in 1865, but an excellent memory and skill in extempore playing enabled him to continue his duties. He wrote cantatas: *The Bride of Dunkerron*; *King René's Daughter*; *The Fishermaidens;* an oratorio *Jacob*; much church music, anthems, services, &c., and organ music; and edited the music of the *Presbyterian Hymnal* (1876).

170 (i). HEATHLANDS. 173 (ii). REX GLORIAE.

SMITH, ELEANOR (Atlanta, Illinois, 1858–), was educated at Cook Co. Normal School, at the Hershey School of Music, and also studied music in Berlin. She was chiefly engaged in the teaching of music, and from 1901 was head of the Department of Music, School of Education, in the University of Chicago. She has published much educational music, songs, part-songs, and various collections and compilations, &c.

362. *In another land and time.*

SMITH, ISAAC (London, *c.* 1725–*c.* 1800, London), was for a time clerk (precentor) to the Alie Street Meeting House in Goodman's Fields, London. He is said to have been the first dissenting clerk to receive for his services the munificent salary of £20 a year. Later he engaged in business which is believed to have been that of a linen-draper in Cheapside. About 1770 he published *A Collection of Psalm Tunes in Three Parts: to which are added 2 Anthems and 2 Canons.*

100. ABRIDGE. 635. FALCON STREET (SILVER STREET).

SMITH, JOSEPH (Halesowen, 1800–73, Halesowen), spent most of his life in his native town. He was not a professional musician, but was interested in music and had an excellent alto voice. He composed a number of hymn-tunes and similar pieces, chiefly for Sunday School festivals.

366. INNOCENTS.

SMITH, ROBERT ARCHIBALD (Reading, 1780–1829, Edinburgh), was son of a Paisley weaver who had gone to Reading for employment. He showed musical talent early, and could play the violin at 10, and, later, became a skilful violoncellist also. His father tried to make him a weaver, but he was allowed to give that trade up, and in 1803 he began teaching music. In 1807 he was appointed precentor (he had a fine tenor voice) and session-clerk of the Abbey Church, Paisley. In 1820 he began to publish his great work, *The Scottish Minstrel* (6 vols., 1820–4). In 1823 he went to Edinburgh to be leader of psalmody under Dr. Andrew Thomson, of St. George's, Edinburgh. He published *The Irish Minstrel* (1825); *Flowers of Scottish Song*; *Sacred Harmony, for the Use of St. George's Church, Edinburgh*; *Sacred Music* (1825); *Edinburgh Sacred Harmony for the Use of Churches and Families* (1829); *The Sacred Harmony of the Church of Scotland* (1828).

10. SELMA. 449. MARTYRDOM.

SMITH, WALTER CHALMERS, D.D., LL.D. (Aberdeen, 1824–1908, Kinbuck, Perthshire), was educated at the Grammar School and University, Aberdeen, and at New College, Edinburgh. Ordained in 1850 to the charge of a congregation in Chadwell Street, Islington, London, he afterwards became minister of Orwell Free Church, Milnathort; the Free Tron Church, Glasgow; and the Free High Church, Edinburgh (1876–94). He was Moderator of the Assembly of the Free Church of Scotland in its Jubilee year (1893), and in the following year he withdrew into retirement.

His published works were: *The Bishop's Walk* (1860); *Olrig Grange* (1872); *Borland Hall* (1874); *Hilda among the Broken Gods* (1878); *Raban, or Life Splinters* (1881); *North Country Folk* (1883); *Kildrostan* (1884); *Hymns of Christ and the Christian Life* (1876); *Thoughts and Fancies for Sunday Evenings* (1887); *A Heretic, and Other Poems* (1891); *Poetical Works* (1902).

535. *Immortal, invisible, God only wise.*

SMYTTAN, George Hunt, B.A. (*c.* 1822–70, Frankfort-am-Main), was son of Dr. Smyttan of the Bombay Medical Board. Educated at Corpus Christi College, Cambridge, he graduated in 1845, and was ordained in 1848. In 1850 he became rector of Hawksworth, Nottingham, but resigned in 1859. He died suddenly abroad and friendless. He published *Thoughts in Verse for the Afflicted* (1849); *Mission Songs and Ballads* (1860); *Florum Sacra* (n.d.).

97. *Forty days and forty nights.*

SOHR (Sohren?), Peter (Elbing?–*c.* 1693, Elbing). From 1674 he was Kantor in Elbing at the Church of H. Leichnam till 1675 when he became Kantor in Dirschau, but later he returned to his first post in Elbing. In his printed works he signs himself as 'bestalter Schul—und Rechenmeister der Christ. Gemeine zum H. Leichnam' in Elbing 1668–76. In 1668 he edited Johann Krüger's (Crüger's) *Praxis Pietatis Melica*, enlarging and adding thereto compositions of his own, and in 1683 he brought out a song book of his own, *Musikalischer Vorschmack der jauchtzenden Seelen im ewigen Leben*, in which were 238 tunes of his own composing.

168 (ii). DIES IST DER TAG. | 466. GUTE BAÜME BRINGEN.

SOLESMES is a village near Le Mans which acquired fame through the foundation there, in 1833, of a Benedictine monastery which became a centre for the study and execution of the old liturgical music. For the propagation of this the monks established a printing-press with special type, and their work came to be recognized as authoritative. Their official title was the Order of the Congregation of France. The passing of the French Law of Associations, however, drove them from that country. In 1901 they settled at Quarr House, near Ryde, in the Isle of Wight, where they continue to study and foster the development of plainsong.

273. ADORO TE.

SOMERVELL, Sir Arthur, M.A., F.R.C.M., Mus.Doc. (Windermere, 1863–1937), was educated at Uppingham and King's College, Cambridge, studied at the Berlin Hochschule and at the Royal College of Music, and also privately with Sir Hubert Parry. In 1901 he was made H.M. Inspector of Music for England, Wales, and Scotland, to the Board of Education. Publications: *Mass in C minor* (1891); *Helen of Kirkconnell* (1893); *The Forsaken Merman* (Leeds Festival, 1895); *A Song of Praise* (1891); *Ode to the Sea* (cantata); *Seven Last Words from the Cross; Song Cycle* from Tennyson's *Maud*; *Quintet for Clarinet and Strings*; and many other pieces.

314. KENDAL. 332. WINDERMERE.
394. BLENCATHRA. 399. STONETHWAITE.

SPENSER, Edmund (East Smithfield, London, *c.* 1552–99, Westminster), son of John Spenser, a cloth-maker from Lancashire, was educated at

Merchant Taylors' School and Pembroke Hall, Cambridge, making an especial study of Greek, Latin, Italian, and French. In 1578 he obtained a place in Leicester's household, where he became intimate with Sir Philip Sidney and other literary figures. In 1580 he was posted as secretary to Lord Grey de Wilton, lord-deputy of Ireland, where Spenser remained, occupied in administrative and literary work, till within a month before his death. Among his publications are *The Shepheard's Calendar*; *Astrophel*; *Epithalamion*; *View of the Present State of Ireland*; and *The Faerie Queene*.

22. *Most glorious Lord of life, that on this day.*

SPRING-RICE, Sir CECIL ARTHUR, G.C.M.G., K.C.M.G., G.C.V.O., LL.D. (London, 1859–1918, Ottawa), son of the Hon. C. Spring-Rice, was educated at Eton and Balliol College, Oxford, and became a clerk in the War Office and the Foreign Office, and private secretary to Earl Granville. After various secretaryships at Brussels, Washington, and elsewhere, he became Chargé d'affaires at Teheran in 1900, and British Commissioner of Public Debt in Cairo in 1901. In 1903 he was first secretary of the embassy at Petrograd; in 1906 Minister and Consul-General for Persia; in 1908 Minister to Sweden; and in 1912 British Ambassador to the United States. His *Poems* were posthumously published in 1920.

319. *I vow to thee, my country.*

STAINER, Sir JOHN, M.A., D.Mus. (London, 1840–1901, Verona), was a chorister of St. Paul's, 1847–56. During this time an anthem and several chants of his composition were sung in the services, and latterly he often acted as organist. He became organist of St. Benet and St. Peter's, Paul's Wharf, at 14, and two years later was appointed by Sir F. Gore Ouseley first organist of St. Michael's, Tenbury. In 1859 he matriculated at Christ Church, Oxford, and was appointed organist of Magdalen College, and then of the University. In 1872 he succeeded Sir John Goss at St. Paul's Cathedral. Other appointments held by him were those of Professor of the Organ, and then Principal, of the National Training School for Music; organist to the Royal Choral Society; Government Inspector of Music in Training Schools; Professor of Music in the University of Oxford. He was knighted in 1888. He wrote a book on the *Music of the Bible*; *A Treatise on Harmony*, and other theoretical works; an oratorio, *Gideon*; several cantatas, of which the *Crucifixion* is widely known; many service anthems, hymn-tunes, and other church music, and his editorial work was extensive.

373. IN MEMORIAM.

STANFORD, Sir CHARLES VILLIERS, Mus.Doc. (Dublin, 1852–1924, London), early revealed musical gifts of a remarkable order, and at ten years of age heard one of his own compositions played in Dublin Theatre Royal. At Cambridge—Queen's and Trinity Colleges—he had a classical education and graduated with honours. He succeeded Dr. J. L. Hopkins as organist of Trinity College; became leader of the University Musical Society, into which he infused new life; conductor of the London Bach Choir, 1885; of Leeds Festival, 1901; Professor of Music, Cambridge, 1887, and of composition at the Royal College of Music in the same year. He was a Mus.Doc. of Cambridge and Oxford, and was knighted in 1901. One of the most distinguished figures in the world of music in his time, he appeared as conductor in Berlin, Paris, Amsterdam, Brussels, and America. He did much to help in the revival of interest in folk-music; he was a most gifted teacher, and largely responsible for the revival of English music during this century. He was a prolific composer, producing 7 operas, 7 symphonies, cantatas (*Phaudrig Crohoore* and *Revenge*); 4 *Irish Rhapsodies*; a *Stabat Mater*; *Songs of the Sea*; *Songs of the Fleet*; and much other work in almost all forms.

56 (ii). JOLDWYNDS.

STANLEY, ARTHUR PENRHYN, D.D. (Alderley, Cheshire, 1815–81, Westminster), was a nephew of the first Lord Stanley of Alderley. His father was rector of Alderley till, in 1837, he was appointed bishop of Norwich. Arthur was educated first by his father, then at Rugby under Dr. Arnold; and at Balliol, where he had an exceptionally brilliant career, gaining the Newdigate Prize for English verse, the Ireland Scholarship in Greek, first class classical honours, and the prizes for the Latin, English, and theological essays. He was elected a Fellow of University College, and was a tutor for twelve years. In 1845–6 he was select preacher; in 1850–2 secretary to the Oxford University Commission; in 1851 was given a canonry at Canterbury; in 1855 was appointed Regius Professor of Ecclesiastical History at Oxford and canon of Christ Church; and in 1863 became dean of Westminster. His marriage in 1863 to Lady Augusta Bruce, sister of the Earl of Elgin and an intimate friend of Queen Victoria, brought him into close relation with the Court. In 1872 he took part in the Old Catholic Congress at Cologne, and in the same year was again select preacher at Oxford. In 1875 he was elected Lord Rector of St. Andrews University. He published *Historical Memorials of Canterbury*, and *of Westminster*; *Sinai and Palestine*; *The Life of Arnold of Rugby*; and a *History of the Jewish Church*.

95. *The Lord is come, on Syrian soil.*
149. *All the toil and sorrow done.*
235. *O Master, it is good to be.*

STANLEY, SAMUEL (Birmingham, 1767–1822, Birmingham), at the age of 20 became leader of the singing at Carr's Lane Meeting House, Birmingham, and soon made its music famous. He continued with the congregation when it moved in 1818 to a larger chapel in Steelhouse Lane, and served it altogether for 33 years. His position in it was not then regarded as inconsistent with his keeping for a time the Crown Tavern in the town. As violoncellist he was long a member of the orchestra of the Birmingham Theatre and the Festival Choral Society. He published *Twenty-four Tunes in Four Parts*; *Nineteen Psalms, Hymns and Charity Hymn-Tunes*; *Sacred Music, comprising two new Psalm and Hymn Tunes*; and *Psalm and Hymn Tunes*, in three books.

333 (Part I). CALVARY. 513. WARWICK. 551. SIMEON.

STATHAM, HEATHCOTE DICKEN, Mus.Doc., F.R.C.O. (1889–), was educated at St. Michael's College, Tenbury, Gresham's School, Holt, Caius College, Cambridge, and the Royal College of Music. In 1913 he became organist of Calcutta Cathedral, in 1920 of St. Michael's

College, Tenbury, and in 1926 of the parish church, Southampton; he was also conductor of the Southampton Philharmonic in 1927, and of the Norwich Philharmonic in 1928. He is now organist and choirmaster at Norwich Cathedral. His publications include songs, part-songs, an operetta, and organ music; he has also edited the church music of Dr. John Blow.

328 (ii). TENBURY.

STEGGALL, CHARLES, Mus.Doc. (London, 1826–1905, London), was educated at the Royal Academy of Music. As organist he served Christ Church, Maida Hill; Christ Church, Lancaster Gate; and Lincoln's Inn Chapel. For half a century he was chief Professor of the Organ at the Royal Academy of Music. He was one of the founders of the Royal College of Organists. The 'Bach crusade' in this country found one of its most powerful supporters in him; he was honorary secretary of the Bach Society. He was one of the early enthusiasts for plainsong, and for the English 'Elizabethan school'. He composed anthems and Church music, and had a lifelong interest in hymnology. He succeeded W. H. Monk as musical editor of *Hymns Ancient and Modern.*

197 (ii). CHRISTCHURCH.

STEINER, JOHANN LUDWIG (Zürich, 1688–1761, Zürich), was towards 1705 'Stadttrompeter'. He did very much to improve the art of song in Switzerland and composed many songs which achieved wide popularity. His principal works were: *Neues Gesangbuch auserlesner geistreicher Lieder, &c.* (1723); *Musicalisch-italiänischer Arien-Krantz* (1724); *Kurz leicht gründliches Notenbüchlein, &c.* (1728) (a self-tutor for rapidly becoming a good singer or musician); *Gottgeheiligte Fest- und Zeitgedanken nach Ordnung der Festtage, &c.* (1739); *Generalbass zu den Psalmen Davids* (1734), &c.

487. GOTT WILL'S MACHEN.

STEPHENS, JAMES (1882-1950), was self-educated during a youth of hardship spent in many parts of Ireland. He was for a time in a solicitor's office in Dublin, until the success of his first book of poems *Insurrections* enabled him to devote himself seriously to literature. In 1912 *The Crock of Gold* confirmed a growing reputation, and since then he has published much both in prose and verse, including *Here are Ladies*; *The Demi-Gods*; *In the Land of Youth* (1924); *Collected Poems*; *Etched in Moonlight*; *Poems* (1931), &c.

305. *Little things that run and quail.*

STERLING, JOHN (Kames Castle, Bute, 1806–44, Ventnor, Isle of Wight), son of Edward Sterling, was educated at Trinity College and Trinity Hall, Cambridge. With F. D. Maurice he ran the *Athenaeum* in 1828; in 1831 was manager of a sugar estate in St. Vincent; and, after study in Germany, became, in 1834, curate at Hurstmonceaux for two years. He contributed many articles and reviews to periodicals, was intimate with most of the eminent literary figures of his day, but his fame chiefly depends on Carlyle's biography of him, in 1851. His *Essays and Tales* were posthumously published in 1848.

612. *O source divine, and life of all.*

STEWART, Charles Hylton, M.A., Mus.Bac. (Chester, 1884–1932, Windsor), son of the Rev. C. Hylton Stewart, vicar of New Brighton and canon of Chester, was educated at Magdalen College School, Oxford, and Peterhouse, Cambridge (organ scholar). He served as assistant organist, King's College, Cambridge; organist and choirmaster, Sedbergh School, St. Martin's, Scarborough, Blackburn parish church, Rochester Cathedral, 1916–30, Chester Cathedral, 1930–2, organist of St. George's Chapel, Windsor, 1932, where he died a month after coming into residence. He composed an evening service in A minor, and other church music.

*105. CHESHIRE. 594. ROCHESTER.

STÖRL Johann Georg Christian (Kirchberg a.d. Jaxt, 1675–1719, Stuttgart), was a chorister at the Stuttgart Royal Chapel (Hofkapelle), and was sent to Pachelbel in Nürnberg by Duke Eberhard Ludwig in 1697 and became organist and head organist there. In 1701 he went to Vienna to complete his studies under Fischer, and went thence to Italy. On his return he became Kapellmeister. Publications: *Die in Christo Jesu, &c.* (2 V., 2 Fl., Soprano solo with Cembalum) (1710); *Würtemberg Gesangbuch*, or *Neu bezogenes Davidisches Harpfen und Psalter-Spiel* (1710, with later editions in 1721 and 1744); *Airs allemands transposés pour l'usage de son Altesse Sérénissime M. le Prince Héréditaire de Wirtemberg* (1714), &c.

255 (ii). BREMEN.

STONE, Samuel John, M.A. (Whitmore, Staffordshire, 1839–1900, Charterhouse), was educated at Charterhouse and Pembroke College, Oxford. He was curate, first of Windsor, then of St. Paul's, Haggerston, London. He succeeded his father as vicar in 1874. In 1890 he accepted the rectorship of All-Hallows-on-the-Wall, London. He published *Lyra Fidelium* (1866); *The Knight of Intercession, and Other Poems* (1872); *Sonnets of the Christian Year* (1875); *Hymns* (original and translated) (1886); *Order of the Consecutive Church Service for Children, with Original Hymns* (1883); and his *Collected Poems and Hymns* were edited, with a Memoir, by F. G. Ellerton, after his death. He was a member of the committee of *Hymns Ancient and Modern* in the later stages of that work.

249. *The Church's one foundation.*

STRUTHER, Jan (Joyce Placzek, née Anstruther) (London, 1901–), is a pseudonym formed from the authoress's maiden name. She was educated privately in London, and has for some time been a frequent contributor of both verse and prose to several well-known periodicals. Her publications in volume form are *Betsinda Dances, and other poems* (1931); and *Sycamore Square, and other verses* (1932).

63. *High o'er the lonely hills.*
162. *Round the earth a message runs.*
163. *Sing, all ye Christian people.*
219. *When Stephen, full of power and grace.*
223. *When Mary brought her treasure.*
233. *Unto Mary, demon-haunted.*
236. *O saint of summer, what can we sing for you.*
282. *God, whose eternal mind.*
354. *Daisies are our silver.*
377. *When a knight won his spurs, in the stories of old.*
565. *Lord of all hopefulness, Lord of all joy.*
692. *We thank you, Lord of Heaven.*

STUBBS, Simon (late 16th and early 17th centuries), was a composer of church music. He contributed several settings to *Ravenscroft's Whole Book of Psalms* (1621) and two anthems to Thomas Myriell's collection *Tristitiae remedium* (1616); and also composed *The Lord is my Shepherd* (anthem) and an evening service.

*628. YORK.

SULLIVAN, Sir Arthur Seymour, Mus.Doc. (London, 1842–1900, London), was the son of a musician and became a child of the Chapel Royal in 1854; his first song was published in 1855. After studying at the Royal Academy of Music and Leipzig Conservatorium, he was organist of St. Michael's, Chester Square, and St. Peter's, Onslow Gardens; musical director, Royal Aquarium, Principal of the National Training School for Music, and Professor of Composition, 1876; conductor of Glasgow Choral Union, 1875–7; of Covent Garden Promenade Concerts, 1878–9; of Leeds Festival from 1880 onwards; and of the Philharmonic Society, 1885–7. He received the Legion of Honour in 1878, and in 1883 was knighted. He wrote oratorios, *The Light of the World*, *The Prodigal Son*, &c.; a *Festival Te Deum*, to celebrate the recovery of the Prince of Wales in 1872; music for *The Tempest* and *The Merchant of Venice*; many songs, much choral and instrumental music, and church music. But it is by his attractive music for the Savoy Operas, in which he was associated with Sir W. S. Gilbert, that he won international fame. His hymn-tunes were mostly written between 1867 and 1874, and were contributed principally to the *Hymnary* and *Church Hymns*. Of the latter he was musical editor.

76. NOEL.

SUMSION, Herbert Whitton, Mus.Bac., F.R.C.O. (Gloucester, 1899–), was organist and choirmaster at Christ Church, Lancaster Gate, an assistant master at Bishop's Stortford College, an instructor in music at Morley College, and teacher of theory in the Curtis Institute, Philadelphia, from 1926 to 1928, in which latter year he was also conductor of the Three Choirs Festival, and became organist of Gloucester Cathedral, a position he still holds.

*210 (i). ALL SAINTS.

SUPPLEMENT TO THE NEW VERSION. This was a supplementary volume to Tate and Brady's *New Version of the Psalms* (1696), and first appeared in 1700 (see pp. xv, 56). The most important edition, musically, was that of 1708, the sixth issue, in which William Croft almost certainly edited the music, and is believed to have composed some of the tunes.

189 (ii), 237. ALFRETON. 317. FOLKINGHAM. 598. ST. ANNE.

SWINBURNE, Algernon Charles (London, 1837–1909, Putney), was educated at Eton, and Balliol College, Oxford, showing especial proficiency in French and Italian at both school and university. His career was wholly literary, though he professed, especially in early life, nihilistic and revolutionary principles both in politics and poetry. The most famous of his publications were *Poems and Ballads* (1866), which was received with a storm of criticism and withdrawn, for the time, from circulation; *Atalanta in Calydon* (1865); *Songs before Sunrise* (1871); plays such as *Bothwell* (1874); prose studies such as *Essays and Studies* (1875); *A Study of Shakespeare* (1880); *A Study of Victor Hugo* (1886), &c.

81. *Thou whose birth on earth.*

SYMONDS, John Addington (Bristol, 1840–93, Rome), was educated at Harrow and Balliol College, Oxford, where he achieved brilliant distinction, and became a Fellow of Magdalen. Overwork brought on a tendency to consumption; and he embraced literature as his career. For a time he lived at Clifton, with intervals abroad, but finally he built a house at Davos Platz, in the Swiss highlands. His chief works were: his great *Renaissance in Italy* (6 vols.); *Introduction to the Study of Dante*; *Studies of the Greek Poets*; *Shakespeare's Predecessors in the English Drama*; *Sketches in Italy and Greece*; *Our Life in the Swiss Highlands*; translations of the Autobiographies of Benvenuto Cellini and Count Carlo Gozzi, and of the sonnets of Michelangelo and Campanella.

312. *These things shall be! A loftier race.*
681. *To God, the everlasting, who abides.*

SYNESIUS (Cyrene, *c.* 375–430?) came of an illustrious family. After studying at Alexandria under the renowned Hypatia, he devoted himself to philosophy and the life of a country gentleman. When his country was attacked by Libyan nomads he raised a corps of volunteers for the defence of Cyrene. Though he became a Christian in 401, and was consecrated bishop of Ptolemais in response to the will of the people, he had none of the narrow ecclesiastic in his composition. He was no ascetic, adhered to the married state, and loved sport and open-air life. He wrote a number of odes. A good sketch of his character is to be found in Charles Kingsley's *Hypatia*.

106. *Lord Jesus, think on me.*

TALLIS, or Tallys, Thomas (*c.* 1510–85, Greenwich), was 'the father of English cathedral music'. Beginning, probably, as a chorister of a metropolitan choir, he became organist of Waltham Abbey. On the dissolution of the monasteries he was dismissed with 20*s.* for wages, and 20*s.* as reward. Soon afterwards he became a gentleman of the Chapel Royal. In 1575–6 he and William Byrd (q.v.) obtained letters patent, according them the exclusive right to print music and ruled music-paper for 21 years. The first work printed under the patent was their own *Cantiones quae ab argumento Sacrae vocantur, quinque et sex partium*, containing 34 motets, 16 by Tallis, and 18 by Byrd. This is a fine example of early English musical typography, but it proved a failure financially, and Queen Elizabeth granted the two musicians compensation in various tithes and lands to the value of £30 a year. Tallis conformed to the changes in the forms of worship from Henry VIII to Elizabeth, though most of his work was composed during the earlier stages of the Reformation. He was buried in the chancel of Greenwich parish church. It is only of late years that Tallis has been appreciated at his true value as a composer. With technical skill as great as that of any of the Netherlanders, as is shown by his forty-part motet 'Spem in alium non habui', he possessed also, in the highest degree, gifts of melody and emotional power, which place him, with Byrd and Palestrina, among the greatest composers of his kind.

45. TALLIS' CANON.
178. VENI CREATOR (TALLIS).
483. FIFTH MODE MELODY.
625. FIRST MODE MELODY.
664. TALLIS' ORDINAL.
675. THIRD MODE MELODY.
App. 3 (v). AMEN.

TANS'UR, William (Dunchurch, Warwickshire, 1706–83, St. Neots), was the son of a labourer, whose name is spelt Tanzer in the parish register. In his youth he became a teacher of psalmody, and in pursuance of this profession appears to have moved about a great deal from town to town; he is found for a time in Barnes, Ewell, Cambridge, Stamford, Boston, Leicester, and other parts of England. Latterly he settled in St. Neots as a bookseller and teacher of music. His classes did much to improve psalm-singing in the Church of England. An eccentric man, skilled in the art of self-advertisement, he described his first book, *A Compleat Melody, or, The Harmony of Sion* (1734), as 'the most curiosest Book that ever was published'. Some of the tunes in it, such as 'Bangor' and 'Colchester', are believed to have been composed by him. He published also *Heaven on Earth, or, The Beauty of Holiness* (1738); *Sacred Mirth, or, The Pious Soul's Daily Delight* (1739); *The Universal Harmony, containing the Whole Book of Psalms* (1743); *The Psalm-Singer's Jewel, or Useful Companion to the Book of Psalms* (1760); *Melodia Sacra, or, The Devout Psalmist's Musical Companion* (1771); *A New Musical Grammar, or, The Harmonical Spectator* (1746); *The Elements of Musick Displayed* (1772); *Poetical Meditations* (1740).

259. BANGOR.

TATE, Nahum (Dublin, 1652–1715, London), son of an Irish clergyman, was educated at Trinity College, Dublin. Though his poetical talent did not rise above mediocrity he was, through Court influence, appointed in 1690 Poet Laureate in succession to Shadwell. He also became historiographer-royal in 1702. Tate wrote largely for the stage, besides translating and adapting other men's works. Among his efforts in this field were versions of Shakespeare's *King Lear* and *Richard II*. He also wrote, apparently with Dryden's approval and help, a continuation of that poet's *Absalom and Achitophel*. Along with Nicholas Brady, Tate produced in 1696 the *New Version* (metrical) of the Psalms, which partly supplanted the older version of Sternhold and Hopkins. See Introduction.

82. *While shepherds watched their flocks by night.*
449. *As pants the hart for cooling streams.*
677. *Through all the changing scenes of life.*

TENNYSON, Alfred, Lord (Somersby, Lincolnshire, 1809–92, Aldworth), was the third son of the Rev. George Clayton Tennyson, LL.D., rector of Somersby. He was educated at Louth Grammar School, privately, and at Trinity College, Cambridge. *Poems by Two Brothers* (1827), in which his brother Charles made a first venture with him, showed a promise which *Poems, chiefly Lyrical*, in 1830, confirmed; but it was the *Poems by Alfred Tennyson*, in 1842, which placed him definitely in the first rank of poets. When he succeeded Wordsworth as Poet Laureate in 1850, that pre-eminence was everywhere regarded as his by native and indisputable right. His successive homes were at Twickenham and Farringford, Freshwater, Isle of Wight; and from 1869 onwards he spent the summer and early autumn at a second home he acquired at Aldworth, Haslemere, Surrey. A peerage was conferred on him in 1884, with the title of Baron Tennyson of Aldworth and Farringford. On his death he was buried in Westminster Abbey.

633. *Ring out, wild bells, to the wild sky.*
648. *Strong Son of God, immortal Love.*
649. *Sunset and evening star.*

TENNYSON, FREDERICK (Louth, 1807–98, Kensington), elder brother of Alfred Tennyson, was educated at Eton and Trinity College, Cambridge, where he gained the Browne medal for Greek verse. He spent most of his life abroad, first in Florence, later in Jersey. He contributed to the volume *Poems by Two Brothers*, and published several volumes of verse, such as *Days and Hours* (1854); *The Isles of Greece* (1890), &c.

328. *The night is ended and the morning nears.*

TERSTEEGEN, GERHARD (Mörs, Westphalia, 1697–1769, Mühlheim), was the son of a tradesman, and apprenticed at 15 to an elder brother, a shopkeeper at Mühlheim. From the age of 16 he retired to a lonely cottage where he devoted himself to prayer and good works, and later to the writing of devotional books. For some years he supported a meagre existence by weaving silk ribbons, but in time the concourse of persons who sought his spiritual guidance became so great, that he was compelled to give all his time to an informal ministry. He also became involved in a vast correspondence, and the preparation of various editions of his hymns and tracts, which included *Geistliches Blumen-Gärtlein* (1729) and a selection of his sermons *Geistliche Brosamen von des Herrn Tisch gefallen*.

191. *Lo, God is here, let us adore.*
671. *Thou hidden Love of God, whose height.*

TESCHNER, MELCHIOR (*c.* 1615), was Lutheran cantor at Fraustadt, in Silesia, at the beginning of the 17th century, and subsequently was pastor of Oberprietschen, near Fraustadt. The chorale tune which made him famous was composed in 1613 for an acrostic hymn written during a time of pestilence by Valerius Herberger, a famous preacher, then pastor at Fraustadt.

135. ST. THEODULPH (VALET WILL ICH DIR GEBEN).

THATCHER, REGINALD SPARSHOTT, O.B.E., M.C., M.A., D.Mus., F.R.C.O. (Salisbury, 1888–), was educated privately, at the Royal College of Music, and Worcester College, Oxford, being organ scholar at both. He became an assistant music-master at Clifton College in 1911; director of music at the Royal Naval College, Osborne, in 1914; director of music at Charterhouse School in 1919; and is now director of music at Harrow. In 1928 he was also president of the Music-Masters Association.

465. LONG MYND.

THEOCTISTUS (? –*c.* 890, Constantinople?) was a monk of the famous monastery in Constantinople known as the Studion, having been founded by the consul Studios in *c.* 462 and dedicated to St. John the Baptist. It became the pattern for many other eastern monasteries, such as those on Mt. Athos, and from about 800 was renowned as a centre of calligraphy and religious poetry.

101. *Jesus, name all names above.*

THEODULPH OF ORLEANS, ST. (*c.* 821), is said to have been born in Italy, where he became abbot of a monastery in Florence. Brought to France by Charlemagne he was appointed soon afterwards to the bishopric of Orleans; but he fell into disfavour with the Emperor Louis (the Pious) on suspicion of conspiracy against him, and was imprisoned in a monastery at Angers. While in confinement there, he is said to have composed the original of the under-noted hymn.

135. *All glory, laud, and honour.*

THOMAS À KEMPIS (Kempen, 1379/80–1425, Zwolle) was the son of a peasant whose family name was Hammerken. After six years in the poor-scholars' house attached to the Brethren of the Common Life at Deventer, he was received, at 18, in the brotherhood, and a year later entered the new monastery at Mount St. Agnes, near Zwolle. He took the vows in 1407, became priest in 1413, and sub-prior in 1425. He wrote a chronicle of his monastery, several biographies, tracts, and hymns, and, though the attribution is not certain, is usually credited with the renowned *Imitation of Christ.*

199. *Light's abode, celestial Salem.*

THOMAS, JOHN, M.A. (Blaenarch, Cardiganshire, 1839–1922, Llanwrtyd Wells, Breconshire), was a self-taught amateur musician and student of Welsh literature, who became a popular adjudicator and conductor of Welsh religious singing festivals. He composed many part-songs and anthems, of which the best known were *Bendigedig fyddo Arglwydd Dduw Israel, Jerusalem*, and *Dattod mae Rhwymau.* Shortly before his death he received the honorary M.A. degree from the University of Wales.

222. BLAENCEFN.

THOMPSON, FRANCIS (Preston, 1859–1907, London), was the son of a doctor. He was educated at Ushaw College, near Durham, and Owens College, where he studied medicine. He left Manchester, however, for London and there earned a precarious living in various menial employments. Some verses published in a magazine brought him friends, who, finding him on the streets in extremely broken health, sent him, after treatment, to Storrington, in Sussex, to recuperate. Here he found his true powers as a poet. The rest of his life was spent in a continuous struggle with ill health, and in various literary activities such as reviewing and journalism, but, above all, in the writing of poetry. He published several volumes: *Poems*; *Sister Songs*; *New Poems*; and one thin book of prose, *Health and Holiness.* Probably his best-known poems are the *Hound of Heaven*, and the undermentioned verses, which were found among his papers after his death.

617. *O world invisible, we view thee.*

THRING, GODFREY, B.A. (Alford, Somerset, 1823–1903, Ploncks Hill, Shamleigh Green, Guildford), was a son of the rector of Alford and brother of Lord Thring and of Edward Thring, the distinguished educationist and Head Master of Uppingham. Educated at Shrewsbury and Balliol College, Oxford, he became curate of Stratfield-Turgis; then of Strathfieldsaye; and in 1858 succeeded his father as rector of Alford-with-Hornblotton. He was rural dean in 1867–76, and in the latter year became prebendary of East Harptree in Wells Cathedral. He resigned his living in 1893. In 1866 he published *Hymns Congregational and Others*; *Hymns and Verses* in 1866; *Hymns and Sacred Lyrics* in 1874; and *A Church of England Hymn Book adapted to the daily services of the Church throughout the Year* (1880). This book set a higher literary standard than any other hymn-book of its time. An improved edition of it appeared in 1882 under the title *The Church of England Hymn Book.*

388. *From the eastern mountains.*
489. *Fierce raged the tempest o'er the deep.*

TOMKINS, THOMAS (St. David's, 1573–1656, Martin Hussingtree), was the second son of the Rev. Thomas Tomkins, father of a notable family of musicians. The son became a chorister in Gloucester Cathedral, and organist there about the year 1596, and in 1607 took the B.Mus. degree at Oxford. He studied under Byrd and became a gentleman of the Chapel Royal in 1621, and later in the same year organist. Although Tomkins lived till the middle of the 17th century he remained chiefly a composer in the polyphonic style. Publications: *Songs of 3, 4, 5, and 6 parts*, 1622; and *Musica Deo Sacra et Ecclesiae Anglicanae*, or *Musick dedicated to the Honor and Service of God* issued in 10 parts in 1664.

*323. WORCESTER.

TOPLADY, AUGUSTUS MONTAGUE (Farnham, 1740–78, London), son of a Major who was killed in the siege of Cartagena, was educated at Westminster School and at Trinity College, Dublin. Ordained to the ministry of the Church of England in 1762, he was some time afterwards appointed vicar of Broadhembury, Devon. In 1775 he was preacher in a chapel of French Calvinists in Leicester Fields, London. He was a powerful and popular preacher. He wrote a series of vituperative tracts in a long and bitter controversy with John Wesley, but is now remembered only for one hymn.

636. *Rock of ages, cleft for me.*

TRAHERNE, THOMAS (Hereford, 1637–74, Teddington), son of a shoemaker, was educated at Brasenose College, Oxford, graduating in arts and divinity. In 1657 he became rector of Credenhill, near Hereford, and, some ten years later, chaplain to Sir Orlando Bridgman, with whom he remained until his death. Of his works only *Roman Forgeries* (1673) was published during his lifetime, *Christian Ethics* appearing in 1675, and *A serious and patheticall Contemplation of the Mercies of God* in 1700. The most important of his writings remained in manuscript until the present century, his *Poems* being published in 1903, and *Centuries of Meditations* in 1908.

651. *Sweet Infancy!*

TRENCH, RICHARD CHENEVIX, D.D. (Dublin, 1807–86, London), was, on his mother's side, partly French. He was educated at Twyford School, Harrow, and Trinity College, Cambridge, took Orders in 1832, and became curate of Hadleigh, Norfolk, in 1835. He made an especial study of Spanish literature, and travelled much abroad in early manhood. He was Hulsean lecturer in 1845–6; Professor of Divinity in King's College, London, 1846–58; became dean of Westminster in 1856, and was consecrated archbishop of Dublin in 1864, resigning in 1884. He was a prolific author of works on history, literature, divinity, and philology, which last he did much to popularize by his *Study of Words* (1845); he also has the credit of having suggested the monumental *Oxford English Dictionary*. Among his other publications one of the most important was *Sacred Latin Poetry* (1849).

505. *Good cheer!*

TREVELYAN, ROBERT CALVERLEY (London, 1872–), son of Sir G. O. Trevelyan, Bt., was educated at Harrow and Trinity College, Cambridge. He has published many volumes of poetry, among which are *Mallow and Asphodel* (1898); *The Bride of Dionysus* (1912); *The Death of Man* (1919); *The Deluge* (1926); *Three Plays* (1931), &c.; verse translations of *The Oresteia of Aeschylus*; *Theocritus*; *Translations from Lucretius*, &c.; and a prose essay *Thamyris, or the Future of Poetry* (1925).

352. *A little child on the earth has been born.*

TURLE, JAMES (Taunton, Somerset, 1802–82, Westminster), was for some years a chorister in Wells Cathedral. Coming to London at 11, he was articled as pupil to J. J. Goss, an uncle of Sir John, but gained most of his training by his own exertions. After serving Christ Church, Blackfriars, and St. James's, Bermondsey, as organist, he became in 1831 organist of Westminster Abbey, and there spent the next 51 years of his life. He acted as organist at some of the great musical festivals, notably that at Norwich in 1839, when Spohr directed the production of his own oratorio *Calvary*, and the Handel Festival in Westminster Abbey in 1834. Beyond some anthems, chants, and hymn-tunes, he composed little, but he edited *The People's Music Book* (1844), *Psalms and Hymns*, for the S.P.C.K., 1862. His hymn-tunes were collected and published in 1885.

581. WESTMINSTER.

TWELLS, HENRY, M.A. (Ashted, Birmingham, 1823–1900, Bournemouth), was educated at King Edward's School, Birmingham, and at Peterhouse, Cambridge. He was sub-vicar of Stratford-on-Avon, where he was chiefly instrumental in building the new church of St. James's; master of St. Andrew's House School, Wells; Head Master of Godolphin School, Hammersmith. In 1870 he became rector of Baldock, Hertfordshire; in 1871, rector of Waltham-on-the-Wolds, Melton Mowbray; was select preacher at Cambridge, 1873–4, and was made hon. canon of Peterborough in 1884. He acted as Warden of the Society of Mission Clergy in the diocese of Peterborough. Owing to failing health he retired to Bournemouth in 1890, but built there and partly endowed with his own means the new church of St. Augustine, and, his health improving, served it as priest-in-charge until his death. He took an active part in the preparation of *Hymns Ancient and Modern*, and was on the Committee for the *Appendix* of 1889.

42. *At even when the sun was set.*

VAN DAMME, PIERRE JEAN (St. Laurent, Belgium, 1832–98, Ghent), was educated at the University of Louvain, where he studied theology. He was for some time Professor of Rhetoric at the Little Seminary of St. Nicolas, and in 1869 became a professor in the Ghent Seminary. In 1871 he was appointed honorary canon of St. Bavon Cathedral at Ghent, and in 1880 titular canon, synodic examiner, and member of the bishop's council. He founded the *Revue-Musica-Sacra de Belgique* and of the École de Musique religieuse at Malines, was an acknowledged expert in plainsong accompaniment. Among his publications were a *Te Deum*; many hymns and canticles, &c.

7. GHENT (ADORO TE, NO. 2).

VAN DYKE, HENRY, D.D., LL.D., D.C.L. (Germantown, Pennsylvania, 1852-1933, Princeton, New Jersey), was educated at the Brooklyn Polytechnic Institute, Princeton College and Theological Seminary, and Berlin University, and possessed degrees from various universities. From 1878 he was pastor of the United Congregational Church, Newport; from 1882 of the Brick Presbyterian Church in New York City, and in 1902 moderator of the Presbyterian Church in the United States. From 1899 to 1923 he was a professor at Princeton University, and held various lectureships at different times. He was, during the War, United States Minister to the Netherlands, and from 1917 lieutenant-commander in charge of the chaplains of the United States Navy. His publications include *The Poetry of Tennyson*; *The Builders and other Poems*; *The Poetry of the Psalms*; *The Spirit of America*; *Companionable Books*; *Half-Told Tales*; *The Man behind the Book*, &c.

18. *By the breadth of the blue that shines in silence o'er me.*

VAUGHAN, HENRY (Skethiog, Wales, 1621–95, Skethiog), belonged to an old family of South Wales, the land of the ancient Silures (hence his self-conferred name 'The Silurist', by which he is still known). Along with his twin brother Thomas, the alchemist and Rosicrucian, he was educated at Jesus College, Oxford. Both brothers were staunch royalists, and suffered imprisonment and loss of property on account of their loyalty. At the age of 24 Henry published a volume of poems, including a translation from the tenth satire of Juvenal. He afterwards became a physician, and practised for some time in Wales, ultimately retiring to his native Skethiog. Various poems, prose translations, and other works appeared from time to time, some of which were published by his brother without his own consent. Vaughan's poems were practically forgotten for two centuries, till Henry Francis Lyte edited them in 1847. They were known, however, to Wordsworth, whose *Intimations of Immortality* owes something to Vaughan's *Retreat*. Apart from this his best-known poems are *The World* and *Beyond the Veil*. He belonged to the 'Metaphysical' school of which Donne is the chief representative.

294. *They are all gone into the world of light.*
585. *My soul, there is a country.*
686. *Up to those bright and gladsome hills.*

VAUGHAN WILLIAMS, RALPH, Mus.Doc. (Down Ampney, near Cirencester, 1872–   ), was educated at Charterhouse School, Trinity College, Cambridge, where he graduated in Arts and Music, and at the Royal College of Music under Stanford, Parry, and Charles Wood; also at Paris and Berlin. He was organist of South Lambeth Church, 1896–9; Extension Lecturer for Oxford University; Professor of Composition, Royal College of Music, London. He joined the R.A.M.C. as a private at the outbreak of the European War in 1914, and later held a commission in the artillery. He has done work of great value in collecting and editing for publication folk-songs and carols, chiefly in East Anglia and Herefordshire;

and folk-song music and old English music from the Tudor period to Purcell has deeply influenced his own composition. His gift of melodic invention is marked, his style is severe and noble, and his music as a whole is of great originality and beauty. His works include the operas *Hugh the Drover* and *Sir John in Love*; *Job*, a masque; *Sancta Civitas*; *Towards the Unknown Region*; *Willow Wood*; *A Sea Symphony*; *A London Symphony*; *A Pastoral Symphony*; *In the Fen Country*; *The Wasps*; *Mystical Songs*; *On Wenlock Edge*; *Mass in G minor*; *Concerto accademico*; *The Lark Ascending*; *The Shepherds of the Delectable Mountains*; rhapsodies on folk melodies, chamber music, many songs, &c. He was musical editor of the *English Hymnal*, and, with Martin Shaw, of *Songs of Praise* and *The Oxford Book of Carols*.

53. MAGDA.	58. OAKLEY.	*65. HELMSLEY.
*87. CRÜGER.	126. MANTEGNA.	177. DOWN AMPNEY.
202. SINE NOMINE.	213. CUMNOR.	302. MARATHON.
316. GUILDFORD.	319 (ii). ABINGER.	334. RANDOLPH.
390. SALVE FESTA DIES.	392. KING'S WESTON.	432. FAMOUS MEN.
*437. EVENTIDE.	489. WHITE GATES.	

VETTER, DANIEL (d. 1730?), was organist of St. Nicholas Church, Leipzig. He is believed to have composed four of the melodies, though he lays claim only to one, in his *Musicalische Kirch- und Hauss-Ergötzlichkeit* (1713). No other source of them is known.

679. DAS WALT' GOTT VATER.

VINER, WILLIAM LETTON (Bath, 1790–1867, Westfield, Massachusetts), studied under Charles Wesley, was for 18 years organist of St. Michael's, Bath, and for 21 of St. Mary's, Penzance; then, in 1859, he went to the United States. He composed organ music, church music, and songs, and edited *One Hundred Psalm and Hymn Tunes in Score* (1838); *A Useful Selection from the most approved Psalms* (1846); and *The Chanter's Companion* (1857).

333 (Part II). DISMISSAL.

VULPIUS, MELCHIOR (Wasungen, Canton of Henneberg, Thuringia, *c.* 1560–1616, Weimar), became cantor at Weimar about 1600. He composed a number of tunes which were published in two important collections which he edited and issued in 1604 and 1609—*Ein schön geistlich Gesangbuch, &c., durch M. V. Cantorem zu Weymar*. Others were published after his death, in the *Cantional* of Gotha.

80 (ii). JENA (DAS NEUGEBORNE KINDELEIN).
154. VULPIUS (GELOBT SEI GOTT).
215. WEIMAR.
475. MELCHIOR (LOBT GOTT).
563. DER TAG BRICHT AN.
585. CHRISTUS DER IST MEIN LEBEN.

WAGNER, WILHELM RICHARD (Leipzig, 1813–83, Venice), was educated at the Kreuzschule, Dresden, the Nikolai Gymnasium, Leipzig, and Leipzig University. In music he was chiefly self-educated, but studied for a time with Gottlieb Müller and Theodor Weinlig. In 1833 he became chorus-master at the Würzburg Theatre, and, after two similar posts and a visit to Paris in 1839, he was appointed conductor in Dresden from 1843 to 1849. In the latter year he was compelled to leave Germany owing to suspicion of revolutionary sympathies, and until 1861 led a chequered career, often in straitened circumstances, in Weimar, Paris, London, and Zürich. In 1861 he was allowed to return to Germany, and the practical sympathy and assistance of Ludwig of Bavaria in 1864 relieved him of some of his financial anxieties. He settled for some years at Triebschen, Lucerne, where he completed *Der Ring des Nibelungen* and *Die Meistersinger*. In 1872 the corner-stone of the Bayreuth theatre was laid; it was completed in 1876, and became the spiritual home and object of pilgrimage of all true 'Wagnerians'. He wrote many prose works, and much orchestral music—overtures, the *Siegfried Idyll*, &c.; but his fame rests on his music-dramas, which, in addition to those already mentioned, include *Der Fliegende Holländer*; *Tannhäuser*; *Tristan und Isolde*; *Lohengrin*; and *Parsifal*.

271. MEISTERSINGER CHORALE (DA ZU DIR DER HEILAND KAM).

WAINWRIGHT, JOHN (Stockport, 1723?–68, Stockport), settled in Manchester in 1746, and was 'singing man' of the Collegiate Church, now the Cathedral there. In 1750 he appears to have been organist of Stockport parish church, his famous tune to Byrom's Christmas carol having been first sung there on Christmas Day of that year. He composed anthems and hymn-tunes, and in 1766 published a *Collection of Psalm Tunes, Anthems, Hymns and Chants, for 1, 2, 3, and 4 voices*.

73. YORKSHIRE (OT STOCKPORT).

WAINWRIGHT, RICHARD (Manchester, 1758–1825, Liverpool), younger son of John, was organist of the Collegiate Church and of St. Ann's, Manchester. In 1782 he succeeded his elder brother Robert in St. Peter's, Liverpool. For a time he officiated in St. James's, Toxteth Park, Liverpool, but afterwards returned to St. Peter's. He wrote the well-known glee, *Life's a Bumper*, and published a *Collection of Hymns* composed for the children of the Liverpool Blue-Coat Hospital.

355. WAINWRIGHT. 673. MANCHESTER.

WALTHER, JOHANN (Gotha, near Cola, Thuringia, 1496–1570, Torgau), was in 1524 bass singer in the choir at Torgau, when Luther, knowing his merit, summoned him to Wittenberg to assist in the preparation of the music for the services of the Lutheran Church there. The Elector Johann of Saxony made him his choir-master in 1526 at Dresden, and took into his pay the choir of 18 men-singers and 12 boys which it was his duty to direct. Four years later, on the disbandment of the Electoral Orchestra, it was reconstituted under his leadership by the town of Torgau, and in 1534 he was appointed singing-master also to the school there. In 1548 he accompanied the Elector Moritz to Dresden as his Kapellmeister. Pensioned in 1554, he retired to Torgau. He wrote a number of hymns, a few of which have been translated, but he was more notable as a composer and adaptor. He published *Deutsche Messe und Ordnung Gottes-Dienst*; *Geystliche Gesangk Buchleyn* (Wittenberg); *Wittenbergisch deudsch geistlich Gesangbuchlein*.

295. NUN KOMM, DER HEIDEN HEILAND.

WARDLAW, Ralph, D.D. (Dalkeith, 1779–1853, Glasgow), was the son of a merchant who became a magistrate of Glasgow. He studied Arts in Glasgow University, then entered the Theological Hall of the Secession Church, but left it for Congregationalism. His only church was Albion Chapel, Glasgow, which he founded and built up. In 1811 he was appointed Professor of Divinity in the Congregational Theological Hall, Glasgow, an office he held for 40 years. Offers of the Principalship of Hoxton Academy, of Spring Hill College, and of Lancashire Independent College, failed to draw him from Glasgow. He published a number of theological, expository, and polemical works. To displace the badly edited hymn-book then in use in 'the Tabernacles in Scotland', he published in 1803 *A Selection of Hymns for Public Worship*. Though this was an advance upon its predecessor, it also was ill-arranged and presented many hymns in a badly 'tinkered' form. It contained 11 hymns of his own, and had considerable popularity.

465. *Christ, of all my hopes the ground.*

WARRACK, Guy (Edinburgh, 1900–), was educated at Winchester and Magdalen College, Oxford. In 1922 he studied at the Royal College of Music, winning the Foli Prize and the Tagore Medal, and in 1925 joined the teaching staff there. He has also held many posts as conductor. His compositions are mostly for orchestra, including *Variations for Orchestra*, a symphony in C minor, &c.

*29. ANGEL'S SONG. 219. WELLINGTON SQUARE.

WARRELL, Arthur Sydney, M.A., F.R.C.O. (Farmborough, Somerset, 1883–1939), studied under Dr. Hubert W. Hunt, organist of Bristol Cathedral, and was assistant organist there from 1902 to 1911. He is now organist of Clifton parish church, lecturer in music in the Department of Education, Bristol University, conductor of the University Choir, Orchestral Society, and Madrigal Singers, and also conductor of the Bristol Royal Orpheus Glee Society. Among his publications are many choral works of which the most important are *A Lyke Wake Dirge* for double choir (performed by the Cambridge University Choral Society in 1932) and *The Winging Souls*.

689. FARMBOROUGH.

WASHBOURNE, Thomas, M.A., D.D. (Wichenford, Gloucestershire, 1606–87, Gloucester), came of an ancient Gloucestershire family, and entered Balliol College, Oxford, in 1622. He became rector of Loddington, Northamptonshire, in 1639, of Dumbleton, Gloucestershire, in 1640, prebendary of Gloucester Cathedral in 1643, and from 1660 onwards was vicar of St. Mary's, Gloucester. He published *Divine Poems* (1654), and two sermons.

107. *Lord, thou hast told us that there be.*

WATTS, Isaac (Southampton, 1674–1748, Stoke Newington), was the son of an Independent who kept a boarding-house at Southampton, and who suffered imprisonment for his convictions. Isaac was offered an education at one of the universities with a view to ordination in the

Church of England, but refused, and entered an Independent Academy. For six years he was tutor in the family of Sir John Hartopp, and in 1702 he became pastor of the distinguished Independent congregation in Mark Lane, London. Not long afterwards his health began to fail, and Mr. Samuel Price was appointed his assistant and afterwards his co-pastor. From 1712 till his death, 36 years afterwards, he lived the quiet life of a semi-invalid as the guest of Sir Thomas Abney and afterwards of his widow, devoting his time to the production of theological and lyrical works. His *Logic* was for long a text-book at Oxford. In 1728 he received the degree of D.D. from Edinburgh. Watts wrote about 600 hymns and versions, an extraordinary number of which are still in common use. Judged by his best hymns, he takes rank with the greatest of English hymn-writers. (See p. xvi.)

23. *This is the day the Lord hath made.*
133. *When I survey the wondrous cross.*
201. *There is a land of pure delight.*
204. *Give me the wings of faith to rise.*
207. *How bright these glorious spirits shine!*
245. *Christ hath a garden walled around.*
382. *Hush! my dear, lie still and slumber.*
408. *From all that dwell below the skies.*
451. *Awake, our souls! away, our fears!*
472. *Come, let us join our cheerful songs.*
512. *Hast thou not known, hast thou not heard.*
545. *Jesus shall reign where'er the sun.*
584. *My Lord, my Life, my Love.*
598. *O God, our help in ages past.*

WEALE, WILLIAM, Mus.Bac. (*c.* 1690–1727), was organist of St. Paul's, Bedford, from about 1715. In 1719 he received his degree from Cambridge University. Beyond this nothing is known of him.

114. BEDFORD.

WEBB, GEORGE JAMES (Rushmore Lodge, near Salisbury, Wilts., 1803–87, Orange, New Jersey), was intended for the ministry, but chose music as his profession. He became organist of a church in Falmouth, but in 1830 emigrated to the United States. There he quickly took a leading position as music teacher, and for 40 years was organist of the Old South Church in Boston. Along with Lowell Mason, he acted as Professor in the Boston Academy of Music for many years. In 1870 he left Boston for Orange, New Jersey, and six years later removed to New York, but he settled again in Orange in 1885. He published a work on *Vocal Technics*, was part author of another on *Voice Culture*, and, with Lowell Mason and others, edited about a score of volumes of sacred and secular music.

646 (ii). MORNING LIGHT.

WEBBE, SAMUEL, sen. (England, 1740–1816, London), was the son of a Government official in Minorca, but was not born there, as is usually stated. He was apprenticed to a cabinet-maker, but after serving his articles abandoned that trade for music. He became organist of the chapel of the Sardinian Embassy in London, and was secretary to the Catch

Club and librarian of the Glee Club. He composed a very large quantity of glees, catches, madrigals, &c., and much religious music—masses, motets, hymn-tunes, &c.—some of which is contained in his and his son's *Collection of Motetts or Antiphons* (1792).

31. MELCOMBE.	199. TANTUM ERGO (WEBBE).
143 (ii). O FILII ET FILIAE (2).	257. BENEVENTO.
180 (ii). VENI SANCTE SPIRITUS.	342. ST. THOMAS.

WEBBE, Samuel, jun. (London, 1770–1843, Hammersmith), son of the preceding, studied under his father and Clementi. He became organist successively of the Unitarian Church, Paradise Street, Liverpool; the Spanish Ambassador's Chapel, London; St. Nicholas Church, and St. Patrick's Roman Catholic Chapel, Liverpool. He was a composer of glees of considerable merit, songs, motets, madrigals, &c. He published a *Collection of Psalm Tunes, interspersed with Airs adapted as such, for four voices*, in 1808; *Convito Armonico* (4 vols.), a collection of madrigals, glees, canons, catches, &c.; *Harmony epitomized, or Elements of Thoroughbass*, &c.

*468. RICHMOND.

WEIMAR, Georg Peter (Stotternheim, Saxe-Weimar, 1734–1800, Erfurt), was devoted to music in his earliest youth. In 1752 he entered the Gymnasium at Erfurt. For a time he was cantor at Zerbst; in 1763 became cantor of the Kaufmannskirche, Erfurt, and in 1774 music director at the Gymnasium there. He composed songs, motets, cantatas. His *Choral-Melodienbuch* was published after his death, in 1803. It included five melodies of his own.

521. ERFURT (ALLGÜTIGER, MEIN LEBELANG).

WEISSE (or Weiss), Michael (Neisse, Silesia, *c.* 1480–1534, Landskron, Bohemia), became a priest, and for a time was a monk at Breslau. Luther's writings moved him deeply, and with two other monks he left the convent and took refuge in the Bohemian Brethren's house at Leutomischl, Bohemia. He joined the Brethren in 1531, and became their preacher at Landskron, and at Fulnek, Moravia. He was a man of great influence among them, a member of their council, and editor of their first hymn-book in German, *Ein New Gesengbuchlen* (1531). This book contained 155 hymns, most, if not all, of which were either translations by him from Bohemian into German or originals by himself.

153. *Christ the Lord is risen again.*

510. FREUEN WIR UNS.	570. RAVENSHAW.

WESLEY, Charles (Epworth, 1707–88, London), brother of the great John Wesley, was the youngest son of Samuel and Susannah Wesley. He was educated at Westminster School and at Christ Church, Oxford, where he graduated in 1729 and became a college tutor. In the same year he became one of the band known as the 'Oxford Methodists'. In 1735, having been ordained, he went with his brother John to Georgia as secretary to General Oglethorpe, but returned after a few months' stay. Not long afterwards he came, as did John, under the influence of Peter Böhler and other Moravians. His work after 1738 was mainly identified with that of his brother. In 1756 he gave up itinerating and settled in Bristol, and in 1771 removed to London. Charles was even less of a separatist than John, and disapproved of the latter's ordination, declaring that he had lived and would die in the communion of the Church of England. He wrote more than 6,500 hymns. (See p. 50 and Index.)

26. *Christ, whose glory fills the skies.*
29. *Forth in thy name, O Lord, I go.*
65. *Lo! he comes with clouds descending.*
74. *Hark! the herald angels sing.*
88. *Hark, how all the welkin rings.*
113. *O for a heart to praise my God.*
118. *Shepherd divine, our wants relieve.*
160. *Love's redeeming work is done.*
172. *Hail the day that sees him rise.*
256. *O thou who camest from above.*
263. *Author of life divine.*
356. *Gentle Jesus, meek and mild.*
476. *Come, O thou Traveller unknown.*
517. *Help us to help each other, Lord.*
541. *Jesus, Lord, we look to thee.*
542. *Jesu, lover of my soul.*
557. *Let saints on earth in concert sing.*
573. *Love divine, all loves excelling.*
595. *O for a thousand tongues to sing.*
632. *Rejoice! the Lord is King.*
641. *Soldiers of Christ, arise.*

WESLEY, Charles (Bristol, 1757–1834, London), was a son of the Rev. Charles Wesley, the hymn-writer. Like his brother Samuel he showed a precocious musical talent; before he was three years old, he was able to play a tune on the harpsichord 'readily and in just time', and 'always put a true bass to it', although he had to be strapped into the chair while doing it. His father was unwilling that he should follow his natural bent and become a musician, and refused an opportunity of having him trained as one of the Children of the Chapel Royal. Partly, perhaps, because he missed that early training, his early promise never came to the expected brilliant fulfilment. He proved a good practical organist in several London churches, and finally in Marylebone parish church. His compositions made no great mark in their time, and they are now for the most part forgotten.

224. EPWORTH.

WESLEY, John (Epworth, 1703–91, London), founder of Methodism, was a son of the Rev. Samuel Wesley, rector of Epworth in Lincolnshire. Educated at Charterhouse and Christ Church, Oxford, he became in 1726 Fellow of Lincoln and Greek Lecturer, and later acted for a time as curate to his father. In 1735 he undertook a mission to Georgia under the Society for the Propagation of the Gospel. There he published the first hymn-book issued in America. Conscious, however, of failure in his mission, he returned to England in 1738. In May of that year he experienced a great spiritual change and devoted himself to the work of itinerant evangelism. His activity is recorded in his famous *Journal*. Riding up and down the country on horseback he is said to have covered 250,000 miles, to have preached some 40,000 sermons, and to have sometimes addressed as many as 30,000 people at one time. He translated large portions of the classics, wrote many grammars, dictionaries, and histories, edited the works of Bunyan, Baxter, and other religious writers, and brought out a 'Christian Library' of 50 volumes for the use of his itinerant preachers. If he did little in the way of original hymn composition, his fine taste is shown in his translations from the German (see 26).

191. *Lo, God is here! Let us adore.*
263. *Author of life divine.*
479. *Commit thou all thy griefs.*
671. *Thou hidden Love of God, whose height.*

WESLEY, SAMUEL SEBASTIAN, Mus.Doc. (London, 1810–76, Gloucester), was a son of Samuel Wesley the musician (1766–1837). He was one of the Children of the Chapel Royal, and became an organist at 16. He served five parish churches, including that of Leeds, and four cathedrals—Hereford, Exeter, Winchester, and Gloucester. While at Gloucester he conducted the Three Choirs Festival. In 1844 he was a candidate for the Professorship of Music in Edinburgh University, but Sir Henry Bishop was preferred to him. He was of a rather eccentric disposition, with an ineradicable passion for fishing, about which many stories are told. His notorious quarrels with cathedral authorities, however, mostly arose from a very justifiable desire for much-needed reform in church music, which was, at that date, in a very poor state. He was a fine organist, and the greatest English composer of the first half of the 19th century. He published a large amount of church music—services, anthems, &c.—and in 1872 issued *The European Psalmist*, a collection of 733 hymn-tunes, of which 130 were his own. In 1873 he received belated recognition of his great services to music by a Civil List Pension of £100.

249 (ii). AURELIA. 464 (ii). HAREWOOD.

WHATELY, RICHARD, D.D. (London, 1787–1863, Dublin), was so delicate as a child that he was not expected to live. His precocity in calculation and reasoning was extraordinary. He had a brilliant career at Oxford, and became Fellow of Oriel at a time when Copleston, Thomas Arnold, and Keble were already, and Newman and Pusey were about to be, Fellows there. In 1822, after six years as a College tutor, he accepted the living of Halesworth, Suffolk; in 1825 returned to Oxford as Principal of St. Alban's Hall; in 1829 became Professor of Political Economy; and in 1831 was appointed archbishop of Dublin. He was the chairman of a Royal Commission on the Condition of the Irish Poor. In 1832 he founded a Chair of Political Economy in Trinity College, Dublin. Among his writings were *The Elements of Logic*; *The Elements of Rhetoric*; *Historic Doubts relative to Napoleon Bonaparte*; *Peculiarities of the Christian Religion*; *Difficulties of the Writings of the Apostle Paul*; *Thoughts on the Sabbath*; *Christian Evidences*; *The Kingdom of Christ Delineated.*

46 (2). *God, that madest earth and heaven.*

WHITE, HENRY KIRKE (Nottingham, 1785-1806, Cambridge), the son of a butcher, was first put to a stocking-frame to learn the hosiery business, and later articled to an attorney, but the bent of his mind was always towards languages and literature. At about the age of 17 he felt a call to the ministry, and, with the help of friends, including Charles Simeon and Henry Martyn, entered St. John's College, Cambridge. Here he showed brilliant promise; but his health broke down, and he died before his gifts had time to mature. He published, at 17, *Clifton Grove and other Poems*, and his *Remains* were published, with a memoir, by Southey.

619. *Oft in danger, oft in woe.*

WHITEFIELD, George (Gloucester, 1714–70, Newburyport, Massachusetts), was educated at St. Mary le Crypt school and Pembroke College, Oxford, where he graduated in 1736, and was ordained deacon in the same year. In 1737 he began preaching, for the 'Society of Methodists', which he had joined in 1735. Thereafter he divided his time between England and America, which he first visited in 1738, becoming incumbent of Savannah. His travels extended over most of England, Scotland, Ireland, and the American colonies. He was closely associated with Lady Huntingdon's Connexion, many of whose chapels he opened. In 1756 he opened his famous chapel in Tottenham Court Road, which was rebuilt in 1899. In 1769 he made his final voyage to America, where he died the next year. His followers and those of Wesley were, to a certain extent, rivals, and his emendations of the Wesleys' hymns did not meet with the authors' approval. His publications included tracts, sermons, autobiographical works, collected in 1756 as *The Two First Parts of his Life with his Journals revised, corrected and abridged*, and other pieces. Browning's lines remind one of his fame:

> To Hephzibah tune, without further apology,
> The last five verses of the third section
> Of the seventeenth hymn of Whitefield's Collection,
> To conclude with the doxology.

74. *Hark! the herald angels sing.*

WHITING, William (Kensington, 1825–78, Winchester), educated at Clapham and Winchester, for 20 years master of the Winchester Choristers' School, he wrote *Rural Thoughts and other Poems* (1851).

336. *Eternal Father, strong to save.*

WHITLOCK, Percy William, A.R.C.M. (Chatham, Kent, 1903-46). was educated at the Choir School and King's School, Rochester, and was assistant organist at Rochester Cathedral from 1920 to 1930; he also studied at the Guildhall School of Music, and from 1919 to 1923 held the Kent scholarship at the Royal College of Music. He is now organist at St. Stephen's, Bournemouth, and the Bournemouth Municipal Pavilion. His publications include anthems, services, and organ music.

*460. LAUS DEO (REDHEAD NO. 46).

WHITMAN, Walt (Long Island, New York, 1819–92, Camden, New Jersey), was the son of a farmer and carpenter, and spent his early youth in Brooklyn, as errand-boy in a printing office, and as a school teacher. From 1836 onwards he was engaged in journalism, editing papers in Huntingdon, Brooklyn, and New Orleans, and writing also, besides articles for magazines, several novels. In 1862 he went to Washington, where he remained as a volunteer nurse during the war, and as a clerk in Government departments afterwards. In 1873 he was partly crippled by a paralytic stroke, and retired to Camden. He was, in his own words, the poet of democracy 'carried far beyond politics into the region of taste, the standards of manners and beauty, and even into philosophy and theology'. He published *Leaves of Grass* (1855, frequent later augmented editions); *Drum Taps* (1866); *Democratic Vistas* (1871), &c. A complete edition of his prose and verse was issued in 1889.

304. *All the past we leave behind.*

WHITTIER, John Greenleaf (Haverhill, Massachusetts, 1807–92, Hampton Falls, New Hampshire), began life as a farm boy and a slipper-maker. A copy of Burns's poems led him to experiment in verse himself. His sister sent some of his verses to a newspaper edited by William Lloyd Garrison, who sought out young Whittier. The friendship thus begun led the lad to enter the journalistic profession. He became, like Garrison, an ardent abolitionist, and used his pen powerfully in the anti-slavery crusade. In 1828 he became editor of the *American Manufacturer*; in 1830, of the *New England Review*; in 1836, of the *Pennsylvania Freeman*; he was also for some time corresponding editor of the *National Era*. He was a member of the Society of Friends, and to the last wore the distinctive garb of the Quakers and used their mode of speech. He made his home, in 1840, at Amesbury, Mass., but his last years were spent at Oak Knoll, Danvers.

189. *All things are thine; no gift have we.*
307. *O brother man, fold to thy heart thy brother.*
327. *Sound over all waters, reach out from all lands.*
331. *Thine are all the gifts, O God.*
438. *All as God wills, who wisely heeds.*
481. *Dear Lord and Father of mankind.*
530. *I know not what the future hath.*
536. *Immortal love for ever full.*
603. *O Lord and Master of us all.*
610. *O sometimes gleams upon our sight.*
697. *When on my day of life the night is falling.*

WILKES, John Bernard (1785–1869), was organist at Monkland, near Leominster, the parish of Sir H. W. Baker, about 1860, at the time when *Hymns Ancient and Modern* was about to make its first appearance, and was thus associated with the first edition of that famous book. Later, he became organist of St. David's, Merthyr Tydvil, and then of Llandaff Cathedral. In 1865 he retired to London.

12. MONKLAND.

WILKINS, Matthew (Great Milton, Oxford, 1704–72, Great Milton), was by calling a butcher, but he was also an organist, teacher of music, and composer. He published *A Book of Psalmody, containing some easy instructions for young beginners, to which is added a select number of psalm tunes, hymns and anthems* (*c.* 1725).

185. STROUDWATER.

WILLIAMS, Aaron (London, 1731–76, London), was a music engraver and publisher of psalmody, a music teacher also, and he acted as clerk to the Scots Church, London Wall. He compiled and published *The Universal Psalmodist, containing* (1) *a Complete Introduction to Psalmody* ... (2) *a choice and valuable Collection of Tunes* (4th ed., 1770); *New Universal Psalmodist* (1770); *Harmonia Coelestis, or, the Harmony of Heaven imitated, a Collection of scarce and much-esteemed anthems* (6th ed., 1775); *Psalmody in Miniature* (1778); *Royal Harmony, or the Beauties of Church Music* (1780).

68. ST. THOMAS.

WILLIAMS, Edith Mary (Holloway, London, 1889–), was educated privately; she is the sister of Charles Williams, the poet and novelist. Up to the present her writing has been only occasional, and she has not published anything in volume form.

546. *Jesus, so lowly.*

WILLIAMS, Isaac, B.D. (Cwmcynfelin, Cardiganshire, 1802–65, Stinchcombe), was the son of a Chancery barrister at Lincoln's Inn. He was educated at Harrow and Trinity College, Oxford. The Oriel College circle influenced him deeply; Keble he called 'his spiritual father'. Ordained, he became curate at Windrush; Fellow and tutor of Trinity; Newman's curate at St. Mary's; and curate to Thomas Keble at Bisley. His candidature for the Oxford Chair of Poetry in succession to Keble was bitterly opposed because of his association with the Tractarian Movement and his authorship of Tract LXXX, *On reserve in Communicating Religious Knowledge*. His disappointment led to his retirement to Stinchcombe in 1848, where he lived until his death. In addition to sermons, he published *The Cathedral*; *Thoughts on Past Years*; *Hymns Translated from the Parisian Breviary*; *Hymns on the Catechism*; *The Baptistery*; *The Altar*; *Ancient Hymns for Children.*

100. *Be thou my guardian and my guide.*

WILLIAMS, Peter (Laugharne, Carmarthenshire, 1722–96, Carmarthen), one of the most prominent figures in the Methodist Revival in Wales, was educated at Carmarthen Grammar School, and while there was converted under the preaching of George Whitefield. Ordained by the Bishop of St. David's, he held several curacies, but the fervency of his preaching was not acceptable, and he was eventually compelled to leave the Established Church and throw in his lot with the Revivalists. He travelled much and suffered great persecution. He was an eloquent preacher, and did great service by his *Expository Bible*. His connexion with hymnody is slight, the first stanza only of the under-noted hymn being doubtfully attributed to his translation of one of Williams of Pantycelyn's hymns.

508. *Guide me, O thou great Redeemer.*

WILLIAMS, Robert (Mynydd Ithel, Llanfechell, Anglesey, *c.* 1781–1821, Mynydd Ithel), was a basket-maker; he was born blind, but became a skilled craftsman and an able musician.

149. LLANFAIR.

WILLIAMS, William (Cefn-y-coed, 1717–91), Pantycelyn, near Llandovery), the chief hymn-writer of Wales and one of her greatest poets, was the son of a well-to-do farmer. He received a good education, and was sent to Llwynllwyd Academy (later, the Presbyterian College), Carmarthen, to be trained for the medical profession. But in 1738 he decided to enter the ministry, and was ordained and licensed to the curacy of Llanwrtyd, Breconshire. There he spent about three years. Being refused priest's orders, however, because of his evangelical views, he withdrew from the Established Church and threw himself into the evangelistic work led by the Rev. David Rowlands and Howel Harris. He composed over 800 hymns in Welsh and over 100 in English, and in addition wrote two long poems, *Theomemphus*, and *Golwg ar Deyrnas Crist* (A View of the Kingdom of Christ), several prose treatises, and many elegies.

508. *Guide me, O thou great Redeemer.*

WILLIS, LOVE MARIA *née* WHITCOMB (Hancock, New Hampshire, 1824–?), was married to Frederick L. H. Willis, M.D., in 1858, and resided mainly in Rochester, New York, and at Glenora, on Seneca Lake.

487. *Father, hear the prayer we offer.*

WILSON, DAVID FREDERICK RUDDELL, M.A. (Tyholland, 1871–), was ordained in 1895 in the Church of Ireland, served as curate, St. Anne's, Belfast, 1898–9; was Succentor and Master of the Choir School, St. Patrick's Cathedral, Dublin, 1899–1916; rector of Drumcondra, 1914, and of Donnybrook, 1917; and is canon and precentor of St. Patrick's. He is an authority on church music, and was general editor of the *Irish Hymnal* and of the *Irish Chant-book*.

*541. PEACEFIELD. 601. DRUMCONDRA.

WILSON, STEUART (Clifton, Bristol, 1889–), son of the theologian, Dr. J. M. Wilson, was educated at Winchester College and King's College, Cambridge. Since the end of the War, during which he was on active service, he has become well known as a singer both on the concert platform and at the principal choral festivals in the United Kingdom, and in America and Australia. He has edited collections of songs, and, with A. H. Fox-Strangways, has published translations into English of the songs of Schubert, Schumann, and Brahms.

344. *Lord, who didst send, by two and two before thee.*
627. *Praise we the Lord, who made all beauty.*

WINKWORTH, CATHERINE (London, 1829–78, Monnetier, Savoy), was a daughter of Henry Winkworth of Alderley Edge, Cheshire, and spent most of her life in the neighbourhood of Manchester. She was the best of our translators from the German. Her *Lyra Germanica* (two series, 1855 and 1858) ranks with the devotional classics of the 19th century. She published also *The Chorale Book for England* (translations with music, 1863) and *Christian Singers of Germany* (1869).

153. *Christ the Lord is risen again!*
267. *Deck thyself, my soul, with gladness.*
350. *Now thank we all our God.*
478. *Cometh sunshine after rain.*
544. *Jesus, priceless treasure.*
608. *O Love who formest me to wear.*
626. *Praise to the Lord, the Almighty, the King of creation.*

WISE, MICHAEL (Wiltshire, probably Salisbury, 1648–87, Salisbury), in 1663 became a lay clerk and alto singer in St. George's Chapel, Windsor; in 1668, organist of Salisbury Cathedral; in 1675/6 a gentleman of the Chapel Royal and counter-tenor singer there; was given the right to play the organ in any church visited by Charles II during his royal progresses; and in 1686/7 was appointed almoner and master of the choristers in St. Paul's Cathedral. He was a troublesome man, of hasty and uncertain temper, which got him into frequent trouble, and finally brought about his death by a quarrel with a night-watchman. He wrote much church music, which ranks with the finest of its kind.

622. CONGLETON.

WITHER (or WYTHER), GEORGE (Hampshire, 1588–1667, London), was educated at the Grammar School of Colemore (Colemere) under John Greaves, and entered at Magdalen College, Oxford, in 1604, but left without taking his degree. He then went to Lincoln's Inn. He wrote over a hundred books and pamphlets, but his *Abuses Stript and Whipt* (1613) caused James I to have him imprisoned in the Marshalsea. Whilst in prison he composed *A Satyre to the King* (1615) and signed it '*his Majesty's most loyall Subject and yet Prisoner in the Marshalsey*'. He was released. In 1639 he served Charles I as a captain of horse against the Covenanters. In 1641–2 he sold his hereditary estates and raised a troop of horse for the Parliament, and was made a J.P. by the Long Parliament. At the Restoration he was committed to Newgate because of his *Vox Vulgi*, and for his *Prisoner's Plea humbly offered* he was put in the Tower. Among his other publications were *Juvenilia* (1622 and 1633) and *Hymnes and Songs of the Church* (1623). (See p. xv.)

43. *Behold the sun, that seemed but now.*
176. *To God, with heart and cheerful voice.*
657. *The Lord of Heaven confess.*

WOLDER, DAVID (sixteenth century), is known as the compiler and publisher, with Theodosius Wolder, of the *Neu Catechismus Gesangbüchlein Darinne Mart. Lutheri und anderer Christen geistliche gesenge Durch Davidem Wolderum nach Ordnung der heupstücke des Catechismi sein abgetheilet, und mit ihren Melodeyen und Summarien gedruckt. Anno Christi* 1598. This work has a dedication to King Christian IV of Denmark, and contains 250 numbered songs and 178 tunes which appear for the first time.

660. WOLDER (AUS MEINES HERZENS GRUNDE).

WOOD, CHARLES, M.A., Mus.Doc., LL.D. (Armagh, 1866–1926, Cambridge), studied at Armagh, the Royal College of Music, London, and Cambridge, where he became a Fellow of Gonville and Caius College. He became Professor of Harmony at the Royal College of Music in 1888; assistant to Villiers Stanford as conductor of the Cambridge University Musical Society, 1888–94; University Lecturer in Harmony and Counterpoint, 1897; Professor of Music, 1924. He published *Patrick Sarsfield* (symphonic variations); choral works, *Ode to the West Wind*; *Milton's Odc on Time*; *Dirge for Two Veterans*; *Swinburne's Ode on Music*; *Song of the Tempest*; *Ballad of Dundee*; many part-songs, solo songs, chamber music, and church music.

288. CAMBRIDGE.

WOOD, THOMAS, M.A., D.Mus. (Chorley, Lancs., 1892-1950), was educated at Exeter College, Oxford. During the War he was engaged in Admiralty service; from 1919 to 1924 was director of music at Tonbridge School; was lecturer and precentor at Exeter College, Oxford, from 1924 to 1928; and during 1930–2 travelled in Australia and the East. His publications include orchestral works; *Forty Singing Seamen*; *The Ballad of Hampstead Heath*; *Master Mariners*; *A Seaman's Overture*; much vocal music, songs, piano and organ music; a book on *Music and Boyhood*, and the *Oxford Song Book* (vol. ii).

344. SCHOOL HOUSE. 511. ST. OSYTH.

WOODFORD, James Russell, D.D. (Henley-on-Thames, 1820–85, Ely), was educated at the Merchant Taylors' School, London, and Pembroke College, Cambridge. He became incumbent of St. Saviour's, Coalpit Heath, and of St. Mark's, Easton, Bristol; rector of Kempsford, Gloucestershire; vicar of Leeds; honorary chaplain to the Queen; several times select preacher at Oxford; and in 1873 bishop of Ely. His published works included sermons, *Lectures on the Creed*; *Hymns arranged for the Sundays and Holy Days of the Church of England* (1852 and 1855). He was joint-editor of the *Parish Hymn Book* (1863 and 1875), and his original hymns and translations from the Latin appeared in these books.

279. *Thee we adore, O hidden Saviour, thee.*

WOOLDRIDGE, Harry Ellis (Winchester, 1845–1917, London), was from 1895 Professor of Fine Art at Oxford University, and was an antiquarian musical expert who specialized in old polyphonic music. He published the *English Metrical Psalter* (1890), edited an abridged edition of *Chappell's Music of the Olden Time* (1893), and wrote volumes 1 and 2 of the *Oxford History of Music*. He was editor also of examples of English harmony prior to 1500; of three volumes of *Purcell's Church Music*; and, with Robert Bridges, of the *Yattendon Hymnal* (1899). Robert Bridges dedicated the First Book of his *Shorter Poems* to Wooldridge, and wrote the notice of him in the *Dictionary of National Biography*.

*245. LEIGHTON.

WORDSWORTH, Christopher, D.D. (Lambeth, 1807–85, Harewood), was a nephew of the poet Wordsworth, and youngest son of Christopher Wordsworth, in 1807 rector of Lambeth, and afterwards Master of Trinity College, Cambridge. Educated at Winchester and Trinity College, he had an extraordinarily brilliant career, graduating as Senior Classic and Senior Optime in the Mathematical Tripos. He became Fellow and Classical Lecturer in his College, and in 1836 Public Orator of the University. At Harrow, as head master, he began in 1836 a great moral reform. In 1844 he was given a canonry at Westminster; in 1848–9 was Hulsean Lecturer at Cambridge; in 1850 began a nineteen-years' ministry in the quiet country parish of Stanford-in-the-Vale-cum-Goosey, Berkshire, where he proved a model parish priest; and in 1868 was appointed bishop of Lincoln. He was unceasingly diligent as a writer, publishing sermons, addresses, a *Commentary* on the whole Bible—an enormous undertaking for one man; books on *Athens and Attica*, *Pompeian Inscriptions*, &c.; and in 1862, *The Holy Year*, hymns for every season and for every phase of each season in the Christian Year.

150. *Alleluya, alleluya!*
173. *See the Conqueror mounts in triumph.*
206. *Hark the sound of holy voices.*
507. *Gracious Spirit, Holy Ghost.*

WORDSWORTH, William (Cockermouth, 1770–1850, Grasmere), was educated at Hawkshead and St. John's College, Cambridge. In early life he was deeply stirred by the French Revolution; this and an intense love of external nature were the first motive powers of his poetry. In 1798 he published, with Coleridge, *Lyrical Ballads*; and in 1799 settled at Grasmere, and lived for the remainder of his life there and at Rydal Mount. From 1813 to 1842 he was stamp distributor for Westmorland, and in 1843 succeeded Southey in the post of Poet Laureate. His longest poems are *The Excursion* and *The Prelude*, both, in a sense, autobiographical; but his shorter poems, and especially the sonnets, have always been the more popular part of his superb poetry.

40. *Blest are the moments, doubly blest.*
647. *Stern daughter of the voice of God.*

WOTTON, Sir Henry (Boughton Hall, Kent, 1568–1639, Eton), was educated at Winchester, New College and Queen's College, Oxford, where he graduated in 1588. After some continental travel he entered the Middle Temple in 1595, became agent to the Earl of Essex for the collection of foreign intelligence, and settled in Venice, where he was ambassador at the court from 1604 to 1624, with two intervals (1612–16, and 1619–21) during which he was engaged in diplomatic missions to other countries, and in parliamentary work in England. From 1624 till his death he was provost of Eton. In his lifetime he published *The Elements of Architecture* (1624) and *Ad Regem e Scotia reducem, &c.* (1633); the collected *Reliquiae Cottonianae* were published posthumously in 1651.

524. *How happy is he born and taught.*

WREFORD, John Reynell, D.D. (Barnstaple, 1800-81, London), was educated at Manchester College, York, for the Unitarian ministry. He became colleague-minister of the New Meeting, Birmingham, in 1826, but was compelled to resign in 1831 because of failure of voice. He then withdrew from the ministry and opened a school at Edgbaston. The later years of his life were spent in retirement at Bristol. He wrote *A Sketch of the History of Presbyterian Nonconformity in Birmingham* (the Unitarian form), and several volumes of devotional verse. In 1837 he contributed 55 hymns to the Rev. J. R. Beard's *Collection of Hymns for Public and Private Worship*, which was designed 'as a protest against hymn-tinkering, and as a novel effort to reconstruct Unitarian Hymnody out of materials exclusively Unitarian'. It rejected all Trinitarian and evangelical hymns, and thus sacrificed all the great hymns of the Church, Beard refusing to adapt them to Unitarian use. Even among Unitarians the book had no success.

134. *When my love to God grows weak.*
320. *Lord, while for all mankind we pray.*

WRIGHT, Thomas (Stockton-on-Tees, 1763–1829, near Barnard Castle), was first taught to play the organ by his father but at 11 years of age went to John Garth, whom he succeeded at Sedgefield in 1784/5. He was organist of Stockton Church in succession to his father, 1797–1817, when he resigned his post; but after a short interval he returned, as a teacher, to Stockton. Publications: *Rusticity* (an operetta, 1800); *Fifth ode of the first book of Horace* (1796); *Concerto for harpsichord or pianoforte, 2 violins, 2 oboes, 2 horns, a tenor and bass* (1795); and anthems, songs and psalm-tunes.

113. STOCKTON.

THE YIGDAL is a hymn used at the opening of the morning service and at the close of the evening service in the Jewish ritual. It was written by Daniel ben Judah Dayyan in 1404, and is founded on the 13 creeds of Moses ben Maimon. It is sung to a very large number of traditional tunes, derived from various countries.

398. *The God of Abraham praise.*

SUPPLEMENTARY INDEX

The references are to the numbers of hymns, except in the case of roman numerals, and where otherwise stated.

METRICAL INDEX OF TUNES

METRICAL INDEX OF TUNES

D. C. M.
Double Common Measure.
8 6 8 6. D.

L. M.
Long Measure.
8 8. 8 8.

D. L. M.
Double Long Measure.
8 8 8 8. D.

2. 8 8 8. 8 8.
(SPONDAIC-IAMBIC)

3 8. 6 5 6. 3.

4 4. 11. 4 4. 11.

4 7. 4 6. 4 7. 6 4 8.

4. 8 4. 4 8.

4 8. 8 4.

4. 10.

4 10. 10 10 4.

ALPHABETICAL INDEX OF TUNES

INDEX OF ORIGINAL FIRST LINES OF TRANSLATIONS

GREEK

LATIN

INDEX OF ORIGINAL FIRST LINES OF TRANSLATIONS

INDEX OF FIRST LINES

INDEX OF FIRST LINES

INDEX OF FIRST LINES

INDEX OF FIRST LINES

PRINTED PHOTOGRAPHICALLY IN GREAT BRITAIN
BY JARROLD AND SONS LIMITED, NORWICH